The Social History of
Crime and Punishment
in America

The Social History of Crime and Punishment in America

AN ENCYCLOPEDIA

2

Wilbur R. Miller ■ EDITOR

State University of New York at Stony Brook

$SAGE reference

Los Angeles | London | New Delhi
Singapore | Washington DC

SAGE

Los Angeles | London | New Delhi
Singapore | Washington DC

FOR INFORMATION:

SAGE Publications, Inc.
2455 Teller Road
Thousand Oaks, California 91320
E-mail: order@sagepub.com

SAGE Publications India Pvt. Ltd.
B 1/I 1 Mohan Cooperative Industrial Area
Mathura Road, New Delhi 110 044
India

SAGE Publications Ltd.
1 Oliver's Yard
55 City Road
London EC1Y 1SP
United Kingdom

SAGE Publications Asia-Pacific Pte. Ltd.
3 Church Street
#10-04 Samsung Hub
Singapore 049483

Vice President and Publisher: Rolf A. Janke
Senior Editor: Jim Brace-Thompson
Project Editor: Tracy Buyan
Cover Designer: Bryan Fishman
Editorial Assistant: Michele Thompson
Reference Systems Manager: Leticia Gutierrez
Reference Systems Coordinators: Laura Notton, Anna Villasenor
Marketing Manager: Kristi Ward

Golson Media
President and Editor: J. Geoffrey Golson
Director, Author Management: Susan Moskowitz
Production Director: Mary Jo Scibetta
Layout Editors: Kenneth Heller, Stephanie Larson, Oona Patrick, Lois Rainwater
Copy Editors: Mary Le Rouge, Holli Fort
Proofreader: Barbara Paris
Indexer: J S Editorial

Copyright © 2012 by SAGE Publications, Inc.

All rights reserved. No part of this book may be reproduced or utilized in any form or by any means, electronic or mechanical, including photocopying, recording, or by any information storage and retrieval system, without permission in writing from the publisher.

Library of Congress Cataloging-in-Publication Data

The social history of crime and punishment in America : an encyclopedia /
Wilbur R. Miller, general editor.
    v. cm.
  Includes bibliographical references and index.
  ISBN 978-1-4129-8876-6 (cloth)
    1. Crime--United States--History--Encyclopedias. 2. Punishment--United
States--History--Encyclopedias. I. Miller, Wilbur R., 1944-
  HV6779.S63 2012
  364.97303--dc23
                                    2012012418

SFI Certified Sourcing
www.sfiprogram.org
SFI-00453

12 13 14 15 16 10 9 8 7 6 5 4 3 2 1

Contents

Volume 2

List of Articles   *vii*

Articles

D (*cont.*)	*463*	H	*727*
E	*515*	I	*811*
F	*573*	J	*869*
G	*661*	K	*937*

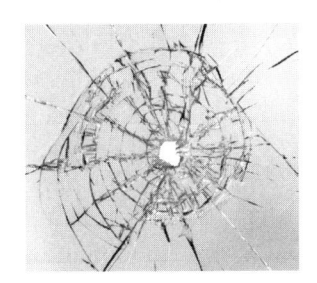

List of Articles

A

Ableman v. Booth
Abortion
Abrams v. United States
Adair v. United States
Adams, John (Administration of)
Adams, John Quincy (Administration of)
Adultery
Adversarial Justice
African Americans
Alabama
Alaska
Alcatraz Island Prison
Alien and Sedition Acts of 1798
American Bar Association
American Civil Liberties Union
American Law Institute
American Revolution and Criminal Justice
An American Tragedy
Anarchists
Anti-Federalist Papers
Antitrust Law
Appeals
Appellate Courts
Arizona
Arkansas
Arpaio, Joseph M.
Arraignment
Arthur, Chester (Administration of)
Articles of Confederation

Atlanta, Georgia
Attica
Auburn State Prison
Augustus, John
Autobiographies, Criminals'
Automobile and the Police
Aviation and Transportation Security Act of 2001

B

Bail and Bond
Bail Reform Act
Bailey, F. Lee
Bakker, Jim
Ballistics
Baltimore, Maryland
Barron v. Mayor of Baltimore
Beaumont, Gustave de
Bedford Hills Correctional Facility
Berkowitz, David
Bertillon System
Bible
Bigamy/Polygamy
Bill of Rights
Billy the Kid
Birmingham, Alabama
Black Panthers
Blackstone, William
Blood Sports
Blue Laws. *See* State Blue Laws
Bodie of Liberties

Bodine, Polly
Boles, Charles
Bonnie and Clyde
Book of the General Lawes & Libertyes
Booth, John Wilkes
Bootlegging
Borden, Lizzie
Border Patrol
Boston, Massachusetts
Bounty Hunters
Bowers v. Hardwick
Brandenburg v. Ohio
Brennan, William J., Jr.
Brocius, William
Brockway, Zebulon
Brown v. Board of Education
Brown v. Mississippi
Buchanan, James (Administration of)
Buck v. Bell
Bundy, Ted
Buntline, Ned
Bureau of Alcohol, Tobacco, Firearms and Explosives
Buren, Martin Van (Administration of)
Burger, Warren
Burglary, Contemporary
Burglary, History of
Burglary, Sociology of
Bush, George H. W. (Administration of)
Bush, George W. (Administration of)
Byrnes, Thomas

C

California
Camden, New Jersey
Caminetti v. United States
Capital Punishment
Capone, Al
Carter, Jimmy (Administration of)
Chain Gangs and Prison Labor
Chandler v. Florida
Chapman, Mark David
Chicago, Illinois
Chicago Seven/Democratic National Convention of 1968
Child Abuse, Contemporary
Child Abuse, History of
Child Abuse, Sociology of
Child Murderers, History of
Children, Abandoned
Children's Rights
Chillicothe Correctional Institution
Chinese Americans
Chinese Exclusion Act of 1882
Chisholm v. Georgia
Christie, Agatha
Cincinnati, Ohio
Citizen Participation on Juries
Civil Disobedience
Civil Rights Act of 1866
Civil Rights Act of 1875
Civil Rights Laws
Clayton Anti-Trust Act of 1914
Clemency
Cleveland, Grover (Administration of)
Cleveland, Ohio
Clinton, William (Administration of)
Clinton Correctional Facility
Code of Silence
Codification of Laws
Cohens v. Virginia
Coker v. Georgia
Colonial Charters and Grants
Colonial Courts
Colorado
Common Law Origins of Criminal Law
Community Policing and Relations
Community Service
Compton, California
Computer Crime
Comstock Law
Confession
Confidence Games and Frauds
Connecticut
Constitution of the United States of America
Convention on the Rights of the Child
Convict Lease System
Coolidge, Calvin (Administration of)
Corporal Punishment
Corrections
Corruption, Contemporary
Corruption, History of
Corruption, Sociology of
Counterfeiting
Court of Common Pleas
Court of Oyer and Terminer
Court of Quarter Sessions
Courts
Courts of Indian Offenses
Coverture, Doctrine of

Crabtree v. State
Crime and Arrest Statistics Analysis
Crime in America, Causes
Crime in America, Distribution
Crime in America, Types
Crime Prevention
Crime Rates
Crime Scene Investigation
Criminalization and Decriminalization
Criminology
Critical Legal Studies Movement
Cruel and Unusual Punishment
Cruelty to Animals
Cummings, Homer
Cunningham, Emma
Customs Service as Police
Czolgosz, Leon

D
Dahmer, Jeffrey
Darrow, Clarence
Davis v. State
Dayton, Ohio
Death Row
Declaration of Independence
Defendant's Rights
Delaware
Democratic National Convention of 1968. See Chicago Seven/Democratic National Convention of 1968
Dennis v. United States
Deportation
DeSalvo, Albert
Detection and Detectives
Deterrence, Theory of
Detroit, Michigan
Devery, William
Dewey, Thomas E.
Dillard v. the State of Georgia
Dillinger, John
Dime Novels, Pulps, Thrillers
Discretionary Decision Making
District Attorney
Domestic Violence, Contemporary
Domestic Violence, History of
Domestic Violence, Sociology of
Douglas, William O.
Dred Scott v. Sandford
Drinking and Crime
Drug Abuse and Addiction, Contemporary
Drug Abuse and Addiction, History of
Drug Abuse and Addiction, Sociology of
Drug Enforcement Administration
Due Process
Duren v. Missouri
Dyer Act

E
Earp, Wyatt
Eastern State Penitentiary
Eddy, Thomas
Eisenhower, Dwight D. (Administration of)
Eisenstadt v. Baird
Electric Chair, History of
Electronic Surveillance
Elkins Act of 1903
Elmira Prison
Embezzlement
Emergency Quota Act of 1921
Enforcement Acts of 1870–1871
English Charter of Liberties of 1100
Enron
Entrapment
Environmental Crimes
Equality, Concept of
Espionage
Espionage Act of 1917
Estes v. Texas
Ethics in Government Act of 1978
Everleigh Sisters
Executions

F
Famous Trials
Fear of Crime
Federal Bureau of Investigation
Federal Common Law of Crime
Federal Policing
Federal Prisons
Federal Rules of Criminal Procedure
Federalist Papers
Felonies
Ferguson, Colin
Fillmore, Millard (Administration of)
Film, Crime in
Film, Police in
Film, Punishment in
Fingerprinting
Fish and Game Laws
Fletcher v. Peck

Florida
Floyd, Charles Arthur
Ford, Gerald (Administration of)
Forensic Science
Fornication Laws
Fraud
Freedom of Information Act of 1966
Frontier Crime
Frontiero v. Richardson
Fugitive Slave Act of 1793
Fugitive Slave Act of 1850
Furman v. Georgia

G
Gacy, John Wayne
Gambling
Gangs, Contemporary
Gangs, History of
Gangs, Sociology of
Gardner, Erle Stanley
Garfield, James (Administration of)
Gates v. Collier
Gender and Criminal Law
Genovese, Vito
Georgia
German Americans
Gibbons v. Ogden
Gideon v. Wainwright
Giuliani, Rudolph
Glidewell v. State
Gotti, John
Grafton, Sue
Grant, Ulysses S. (Administration of)
Great Depression
Green, Anna K.
Gregg v. Georgia
Griffin v. California
Griswold v. Connecticut
Grutter v. Bollinger
Guiteau, Charles
Gun Control
Guns and Violent Crime

H
Habeas Corpus, Writ of
Habeas Corpus Act of 1679
Habeas Corpus Act of 1863
Hamilton, Alexander
Hammett, Dashiell
Hanging

Harding, Warren G. (Administration of)
Harris, Eric. *See* Klebold, Dylan and Eric Harris
Harrison, Benjamin (Administration of)
Harrison Act of 1914
Hauptmann, Bruno
Hawai'i
Hayes, Rutherford B. (Administration of)
Hays, Jacob
Hereditary Crime
Hillerman, Tony
Hispanic Americans
History of Crime and Punishment in America: Colonial
History of Crime and Punishment in America: 1783–1850
History of Crime and Punishment in America: 1850–1900
History of Crime and Punishment in America: 1900–1950
History of Crime and Punishment in America: 1950–1970
History of Crime and Punishment in America: 1970–Present
Holden v. Hardy
Holmes, Oliver Wendell, Jr.
Holt v. Sarver
Homeland Security
Homestead Act of 1862
Hoover, Herbert (Administration of)
Hoover, J. Edgar
Hurtado v. California

I
Idaho
Identity Theft
Illinois
Immigration Crimes
Incapacitation, Theory of
Incest
Indecent Exposure
Independent Treasury Act
Indian Civil Rights Act
Indian Removal Act
Indiana
Infanticide
Insanity Defense
Internal Revenue Service
Internal Security Act of 1950
International Association of Chiefs of Police
Internment

Interrogation Practices
Interstate Commerce Act of 1887
Intolerable Acts of 1774
Iowa
Irish Americans
Italian Americans

J

Jackson, Andrew (Administration of)
Jackson, Mississippi
James, Jesse
Japanese Americans
Jefferson, Thomas
Jefferson, Thomas (Administration of)
Jewish Americans
Johnson, Andrew (Administration of)
Johnson, Lyndon B. (Administration of)
Johnson v. Avery
Judges and Magistrates
Judiciary Act of 1789
Juries
Jurisdiction
Justice, Department of
Juvenile Corrections, Contemporary
Juvenile Corrections, History of
Juvenile Corrections, Sociology of
Juvenile Courts, Contemporary
Juvenile Courts, History of
Juvenile Delinquency, History of
Juvenile Delinquency, Sociology of
Juvenile Justice, History of
Juvenile Offenders, Prevention and Education
Juvenile Offenders in Adult Courts

K

Kaczynski, Ted
Kansas
Kansas City, Missouri
Katz v. United States
Katzenbach v. McClung
Kennedy, John F. (Administration of)
Kennedy, Robert F.
Kent State Massacre
Kentucky
Kevorkian, Jack
Kidnapping
King, Martin Luther, Jr.
King, Rodney
Klebold, Dylan, and Eric Harris
Knapp Commission

Korematsu v. United States
Ku Klux Klan
Kunstler, William

L

La Guardia, Fiorello
Landrum-Griffin Act of 1859
Larceny
Las Vegas, Nevada
Law Enforcement Assistance Act
Law Enforcement Assistance Administration
Lawrence v. Texas
Laws and Liberties of Massachusetts
Lawyers Guild
Leavenworth Federal Penitentiary
Legal Counsel
Leopold and Loeb
Libertarianism
Lincoln, Abraham (Administration of)
Lindbergh Law
Lindsey, Ben
Literature and Theater, Crime in
Literature and Theater, Police in
Literature and Theater, Punishment in
Livestock and Cattle Crimes
Livingston, Edward
Lochner v. New York
Los Angeles, California
Louisiana
Loving v. Virginia
Luciano, "Lucky"
Lynchings

M

Macdonald, Ross
Madison, James (Administration of)
Madoff, Bernard
Magna Carta
Maine
Malcolm X
Mandatory Minimum Sentencing
Mann Act
Manson, Charles
Mapp v. Ohio
Marbury v. Madison
Marshall, John
Martin v. Hunter's Lessee
Maryland
Maryland Toleration Act of 1649
Massachusetts

Matteawan State Hospital
Mayflower Compact
McCarthy, Joseph
McCleskey v. Kemp
McCulloch v. Maryland
McKinley, William (Administration of)
McNabb v. United States
McVeigh, Timothy
Memoirs, Police and Prosecutors
Memphis, Tennessee
Menendez, Lyle and Erik
Miami, Florida
Michigan
Military Courts
Military Police
Minnesota
Minor v. Happersett
Miranda v. Arizona
Miranda Warnings. *See Miranda v. Arizona*
Mississippi
Mississippi v. Johnson
Missouri
M'Naghten Test
Mollen Commission
Monroe, James (Administration of)
Montana
Moonshine
Morality
MOVE
Mudgett, Herman
Mug Shots
Muhammad, John Allen
Muller v. Oregon
Munn v. Illinois
Murder, Contemporary
Murder, History of
Murder, Sociology of
Murders, Unsolved
Music and Crime

N

Narcotics Laws
National Association for the Advancement of Colored People
National Commission on Law Observance and Enforcement
National Congress on Penitentiary and Reformatory Discipline
National Organization for Women
National Police Gazette

National Prison Association
National Security Act of 1947
Native American Tribal Police
Native Americans
Nebraska
Nelson, "Baby Face"
Ness, Eliot
Neutrality Enforcement in 1793–1794
Nevada
New Hampshire
New Jersey
New Mexico
New Orleans, Louisiana
"New Punitiveness"
New York
New York City
Newark, New Jersey
News Media, Crime in
News Media, Police in
News Media, Punishment in
Nitti, Frank
Nixon, Richard (Administration of)
North Carolina
North Dakota
Northwest Ordinance of 1787

O

Oakland, California
Obama, Barack (Administration of)
Obscenity
Obscenity Laws
Ohio
Oklahoma
Oklahoma City Bombing
Olmstead v. United States
Omnibus Crime Control and Safe Streets Act of 1968
Oregon
Organized Crime, Contemporary
Organized Crime, History of
Organized Crime, Sociology of
Oswald, Lee Harvey

P

Padilla v. Kentucky
Paine, Thomas
Paretsky, Sara
Parker, Isaac
Parker, William
Parole

Peltier, Leonard
Pendleton Act of 1883
Penitentiaries
Penitentiary Study Commission
Penn, William
Pennsylvania
Pennsylvania System of Reform
People v. Pinnell
People v. Superior Court of Santa Clara County
Percival, Robert V.
Peterson, Scott
Petty Courts
Philadelphia, Pennsylvania
Pickpockets
Pierce, Franklin (Administration of)
Pittsburgh, Pennsylvania
Plea
Plessy v. Ferguson
Poe, Edgar Allen
Police, Contemporary
Police, History of
Police, Sociology of
Police, Women as
Police Abuse
Political Crimes, Contemporary
Political Crimes, History of
Political Crimes, Sociology of
Political Dissidents
Political Policing
Polk, James K. (Administration of)
Pornography
Posses
Presidential Proclamations
President's Commission on Law Enforcement and the Administration of Justice
Prison Privatization
Prison Riots
Prisoner's Rights
Private Detectives
Private Police
Private Security Services
Probation
Proclamation for Suppressing Rebellion and Sedition of 1775
Procunier v. Martinez
Professionalization of Police
Prohibition
Prostitution, Contemporary
Prostitution, History of
Prostitution, Sociology of

Punishment of Crimes Act, 1790
Punishment Within Prison
Pure Food and Drug Act of 1906
Puritans

Q
Quakers

R
Race, Class, and Criminal Law
Race-Based Crimes
Racism
Rader, Dennis
Ragen, Joseph
Ramirez, Richard
Rape, Contemporary
Rape, History of
Rape, Sociology of
Ray, James Earl
Reagan, Ronald (Administration of)
Reform, Police and Enforcement
Reform Movements in Justice
Rehabilitation
Religion and Crime, Contemporary
Religion and Crime, History of
Religion and Crime, Sociology of
Reports on Prison Conditions
Retributivism
Reynolds v. United States
Rhode Island
Ricci v. DeStefano
Riots
Robbery, Contemporary
Robbery, History of
Robbery, Sociology of
Roberts v. Louisiana
Rockefeller, Nelson
Roe v. Wade
Romer v. Evans
Roosevelt, Franklin D. (Administration of)
Roosevelt, Theodore (Administration of)
Roth v. United States
Rothstein, Arnold
Ruby Ridge Standoff
Rule of Law
Rural Police

S
Sacco and Vanzetti
Salem Witch Trials

San Francisco, California
San Quentin State Prison
Santobello v. New York
Schenck v. United States
School Shootings
Schultz, "Dutch"
Scopes Monkey Trial
Scottsboro Boys Cases
Secret Service
Securities and Exchange Commission
Sedition Act of 1918
Segregation Laws
Selective Service Act of 1967
Sentencing
Sentencing: Indeterminate Versus Fixed
Serial and Mass Killers
Sex Offender Laws
Sex Offenders
Sexual Harassment
Shaming and Shunning
Sheppard, Sam
Sheppard v. Maxwell
Sheriffs
Sherman Anti-Trust Act of 1890
Simpson, O. J.
Sin
Sing Sing Correctional Facility
Sirhan Sirhan
Slave Patrols
Slavery
Slavery, Law of
Smith, Susan
Smith Act
Smuggling
Snyder, Ruth
Sodomy
South Carolina
South Dakota
Spillane, Mickey
St. Louis, Missouri
Stamp Act of 1765
Standard Oil Co. of New Jersey v. United States
State Blue Laws
State Police
State Slave Codes
State v. Heitman
Steenburgh, Sam
Strauder v. West Virginia
Strikes

Students for a Democratic Society and the Weathermen
Supermax Prisons
Supreme Court, U.S.
Suspect's Rights
Sutherland, Edwin

T
Taft, William Howard (Administration of)
Tax Crimes
Taylor, Zachary (Administration of)
Taylor v. State
Tea Act of 1773
Technology, Police
Television, Crime in
Television, Police in
Television, Punishment in
Tennessee
Terrorism
Terry v. Ohio
Texas
Texas Rangers
Texas v. White
Thaw, Harry K.
Theories of Crime
Thoreau, Henry David
Three Strikes Law
To Kill a Mockingbird
Tocqueville, Alexis de
Torrio, John
Torture
Townshend Acts of 1767
Traffic Crimes
Training Police
Trials
Truman, Harry S. (Administration of)
Twining v. New Jersey
Tyler, John (Administration of)

U
Uniform Crime Reporting Program
United States Attorneys
United States v. Ballard
United States v. E. C. Knight Company
United States v. Hudson and Goodwin
United States v. Nixon
United States v. One Book Called Ulysses
Urbanization
USA PATRIOT Act of 2001
Utah

V

Vagrancy
Vermont
Vice Commission
Vice Reformers
Victim Rights and Restitution
Victimless Crime
Victorian Compromise
Vigilantism
Violence Against Women Act of 1994
Violent Crimes
Virginia
Vollmer, August
Volstead Act

W

Waco Siege
Walling, George
Walnut Street Jail
Wambaugh, Joseph
Warren, Earl
Washington
Washington, D.C.
Washington, George (Administration of)
Watergate
Weathermen, The. *See* Students for a Democratic Society and the Weathermen
Webb v. United States
Weeks v. United States
West Virginia
White-Collar Crime, Contemporary
White-Collar Crime, History of
White-Collar Crime, Sociology of
Whitney v. California
Wickersham, George
Wickersham Commission
Wilson, James Q.
Wilson, O. W.
Wilson, Woodrow (Administration of)
Wisconsin
Witness Testimony
Wolf v. Colorado
Women Criminals, Contemporary
Women Criminals, History of
Women Criminals, Sociology of
Women in Prison
Wuornos, Aileen
Wyoming

X

Xenophobia

Y

Yates, Andrea
Yates v. United States

Z

Zeisel, Hans
Zodiac Killer

Dillard v. the State of Georgia

Dillard v. the State of Georgia was an 1870 case tried before the Supreme Court of Georgia. It contemplated obscene language as defined by section 4306 of the Revised Code of Georgia. The decision of the court, and hence the interpretation of obscenity pursuant to the statute, pivoted on the intent of an offender in speaking certain words. The court held that a man uses obscene or vulgar language if, without provocation, and intending to propose sexual intercourse, he asks a female in his presence to "go to bed with him." The court's decision underscores a speaker's purpose or objective when issuing certain words to bring about certain results. It also implicates cultural notions of male chivalry and female virtue pertaining to language and obscenity. The justice of the peace of Oglethorpe County charged James T. Dillard with using obscene and vulgar language in the presence of Mary S. Sanders, William H. Sanders's wife. Apparently without provocation on the part of Mrs. Sanders, Dillard asked Mrs. Sanders to go to bed with him. Mrs. Sanders summoned her husband, in whose presence Dillard called Mrs. Sanders a "God-damned liar." At trial, Dillard waived indictment by a grand jury. His attorney argued that Dillard's words did not constitute obscene or vulgar language under section 4306. The justice of the peace disagreed, finding Dillard guilty and imposing a fine of $100 plus costs, or three months in jail if Dillard did not pay the fines and costs.

Dillard's case reached the Supreme Court of Georgia on a claim of error in a motion in arrest of judgment. The Supreme Court upheld all lower court findings on the grounds that the legislature, in enacting section 4306, probably contemplated both words and their corresponding mental state as requisites for the crime. The court suggested that words are contingent and relational because their meaning is dependent upon context and circumstance. Therefore, few if any words are unconditionally and universally banned; the prosecution of particular words makes sense only in light of the vulgarity or obscenity of the ideas that they convey. In the case at hand, Dillard's words were prosecutable because they signified a state of mind deemed indecent according to the standards of society in which the words were uttered. Concurring with the decision, Justice C. J. Brown approved of the principles of decorum underlying the statute but expressed reservations about prosecuting an individual for language that is obscene or vulgar if that individual takes no definite, physical steps toward carrying out the intent conveyed in such language. The concurrence recalls the long-standing principle in Anglo-American law that thoughts alone are not punishable. The question is whether the spoken word by itself constitutes an act and therefore satisfies the element of *actus reus*, or whether some physical act besides verbal articulation is necessary to prosecute an individual for a crime.

The *Dillard* case stands for the idea that the meaning of language—and, in particular, language deemed obscene—depends upon community consensus and prevailing moral standards. The majority and concurring opinions in *Dillard* refer to ideals about womanhood and gentlemanliness as criteria by which to review obscenity. Phrases such as "decent ideas," "public morals," "protecting females from insult," "female whose modesty has been unlawfully shocked," "virtuous woman," "moral decency," and "good breeding" signify cultural touchstones. The tendency of an utterance to become generally accepted or generally rejected determines its legal status as vulgar, obscene, or permissible. The judges in *Dillard* deemed that Dillard's words were not generally socially acceptable; therefore, his words were obscene.

Allen Mendenhall
Auburn University

See Also: Obscenity; Obscenity Laws; Sexual Harassment.

Further Readings
Dillard v. the State of Georgia, 41 Ga. 278 (1870).
Friedman, Lawrence Meir. *Crime and Punishment in American History*. New York: Basic Books, 1993.

Dillinger, John

American outlaw John Dillinger (1903–34) was a controversial bank robber and desperado during the 1930s Depression. His uncanny ability to escape the clutches of the law—while apparently demonstrating coolness under fire, ingenuity, defiance, and an unfailing sense of humor—won him many admirers, especially among those who had become economic victims of untrustworthy banks. On the other hand, most law enforcement officials regarded Dillinger as a bloodthirsty criminal with no redeeming qualities. Dillinger's sudden death and alleged betrayal by a mysterious woman have only enhanced his legendary mystique.

Dillinger was born June 22, 1903, in Indianapolis, Indiana, into a respectable, but not wealthy, family. His father worked as a grocer and his mother died when he was 3. Dillinger dropped out of school after the eighth grade and held a series of unskilled jobs before enlisting in the navy at the age of 20. However, military discipline did not suit Dillinger well; after several instances of desertion and disobeying orders, he was dishonorably discharged and returned home to Indiana. There, he married a local farm girl, Beryl Hovious, in 1924 but also befriended Edward Singleton, an older man with a criminal record. Dillinger and Singleton were arrested for forcibly robbing a grocery store. Pleading guilty to the crime, Dillinger received a harsh 10–20-year sentence and served nearly nine years in Indiana state prison before he was paroled in 1933.

If Dillinger was not a hardened criminal before entering prison, he emerged as one afterward by most accounts. His wife had divorced him in 1929, and an ex-convict was unlikely to find steady employment in the midst of the Great Depression. Like other 1930s outlaws already at large—such as Clyde Barrow, Bonnie Parker, Charles "Pretty Boy" Floyd, and the Barker gang—Dillinger and his criminal accomplices embarked on a series of bank robberies throughout the Midwest, frequently moving from one heist to another in stolen cars, and often seizing weapons and ammunition from police stations.

Although Dillinger's crime rampage in 1933–34 lasted only 14 months, it captured the imagination of an economically depressed populace. Many of Dillinger's criminal exploits seemed almost too bold and daring to be true. For instance, after he was captured in Arizona and transferred to prison in Indiana, he somehow escaped five weeks later, perhaps by using a fake gun. In the following month, while vacationing in a northern Wisconsin tourist lodge, Dillinger and his gang escaped unharmed despite being surprised by more than a dozen agents of the Federal Bureau of Investigation (FBI). Two months later, when Attorney General Homer Cummings announced a $10,000 reward for Dillinger's capture, many newspapers labeled him "Public Enemy Number One." The national hunt for Dillinger ended on July 22, 1934, when he was shot and killed by FBI agents as he was leaving a Chicago movie theater in the company of a woman who supposedly had betrayed him to federal authorities.

Nevertheless, Dillinger's demise at age 31—like the untimely death of several other youthful folk heroes—has seemed to confirm his reputation as a cunning and charming Robin Hood–like rogue who stole from rich banks but not from poor people. Stories continued to circulate of how Dillinger had written a letter to Henry Ford, thanking the automaker for producing such fast getaway vehicles, or how he had brazenly returned to his family's farm in Indiana to enjoy a Sunday dinner of fried chicken even while being hunted by the FBI.

In subsequent years, several forms of popular culture have further enhanced Dillinger's reputation. Ballads and popular songs have praised the outlaw's courage and cleverness. Lawrence Tierney, Nick Adams, Warren Oates, Robert Conrad, Martin Sheen, and Johnny Depp have all portrayed Dillinger sympathetically in Hollywood feature films. A street gang in Washington, D.C., called itself the Young Dillingers. A math-rock band from New Jersey became known as the Dillinger Escape Plan. Delmar Arnaud, a singer of West Coast Gangsta Rap, adopted Daz Dillinger as his stage name.

Finally, several long-standing legends claim that Dillinger had the last laugh on his pursuers by planning for another man, closely resembling the fugitive, to be killed in his place in Chicago by the FBI. According to this theory, the real Dillinger escaped to Hollywood, California, and did not disclose his fake death until he wrote a letter to an Indianapolis newspaper 25 years later.

James I. Deutsch
Smithsonian Institution

See Also: Bonnie and Clyde; Cummings, Homer; Federal Bureau of Investigation; Floyd, Charles Arthur; Great Depression; Hoover, J. Edgar; Nelson, "Baby Face."

Further Readings

Girardin, G. Russell, and William J. Helmer. *Dillinger: The Untold Story*. Bloomington: Indiana University Press, 2005.

Gorn, Elliott J. *Dillinger's Wild Ride: The Year That Made America's Public Enemy Number One*. New York: Oxford University Press, 2009.

Dime Novels, Pulps, Thrillers

Accounts of crime, whether fiction or nonfiction, have long been popular with a wide range of readers. Although all levels of literature have centered on crime, the terms *dime novels*, *pulps*, and *thrillers* tend to refer to rapidly written works that use sensational language, themes, and style. First appearing in the mid-19th century, dime novels became immensely popular. Although read by all types, dime novels, pulps, and thrillers often were considered to be "low-brow" and of less literary merit than other genres.

The terms *dime novels*, *pulps*, and *thrillers* were used originally to refer to different types of publications. Over time, however, the terms have come to be used interchangeably and now refer to any publication that features fast-paced action and racy subject matter. Originally ignored by more mainstream press, academia, and bookstores, some dime novels, pulps, and thrillers are now regarded as having literary merit. These works continue to be a source of profit and inspiration to publishers, film and television producers, and retail outlets.

Origins

As literacy rates in the United States increased during the 19th century, a market developed for reading material that was entertaining and inexpensive. *Dime novels* emerged as a generic term for several distinct but related forms, including story papers, thick-book reprints, five-and ten-cent weekly libraries, dime novels, and early pulp magazines. Although the last true dime novels were published during the 1920s and pulp magazines ceased publication during the 1950s, descendants of the forms exist today, including comic books, mass-market paperback novels, and television programs and films based upon popular genres first developed decades ago.

In 1860, the publishing house Beadle & Adams inaugurated Beadle's Dime Novel Series with Ann S. Stephen's *Maleaska, the Indian Wife of the White Hunter*. This book, a reprint of an earlier serial that appeared in the *Ladies' Companion*, is generally regarded as the first dime novel. The Beadle & Adams dime novels varied

A Beadle's Pocket Library issue featuring a story about "Calamity Jane, The Heroine of Whoop-Up," which appeared in February 1885. Weekly dime "libraries" in the 1880s were large tabloids in format, as big as 8.5 by 12 inches.

in size, although many measured approximately six and one-half by four and one-quarter inches, and most were limited to 100 pages in length. After 28 books were published with a plain salmon wrapper, Beadle & Adams added an illustration to the covers, all of which sold for 10 cents. The series was immediately popular and ran to 321 issues, many of which were reprinted through the 1920s.

Many of the Beadle & Adams books focused on themes from the frontier and the American west, and initially, reprints of serials and other novels were used exclusively. Beadle & Adams' success led to many competitors, including Bunce's Ten Cent Novels, Brady's Mercury Stories, and Champion Novels. Although all books of this genre were referred to as dime novels, actual prices ranged from 10 to 15 cents.

Although there was a certain look to the genre, the formats of dime novels varied over time and from publisher to publisher. In the interest of cutting costs, some publishers produced dime novels as short as 32 pages in length, although readers at first resisted these. Beginning in the 1880s, weekly dime "libraries" became increasingly popular. These publications were essentially tabloids in form and varied in size from seven by 10 inches to eight and one-half by 12 inches.

Dime novels tended to feature a single story, unlike story papers and other similar genres. Fierce competition between various publishers generated colorful covers, which attracted readers' attention and increased sales. In addition to Beadle & Adams, major publishers of dime novels included Street & Smith and Frank Tousey. Even after competition forced the price of many of these publications to five cents, the general public continued to refer to them as dime novels.

Other publications emerged as the market for dime novels began to decline. These included "thick books," which often reprinted multiple stories from dime novels, with the material slightly rewritten to tie the material together into a cohesive whole. Thick books were published by Street & Smith, J. S. Ogilvie, and Arthur Westbrook. Running roughly 150 to 200 pages, thick books were four and three-quarters inches by seven inches and often featured color covers and higher-grade printing stock. In 1896, Frank Munsey converted his juvenile magazine, *The Argosy*, into a fiction magazine for adults. *The Argosy* became the first pulp magazine.

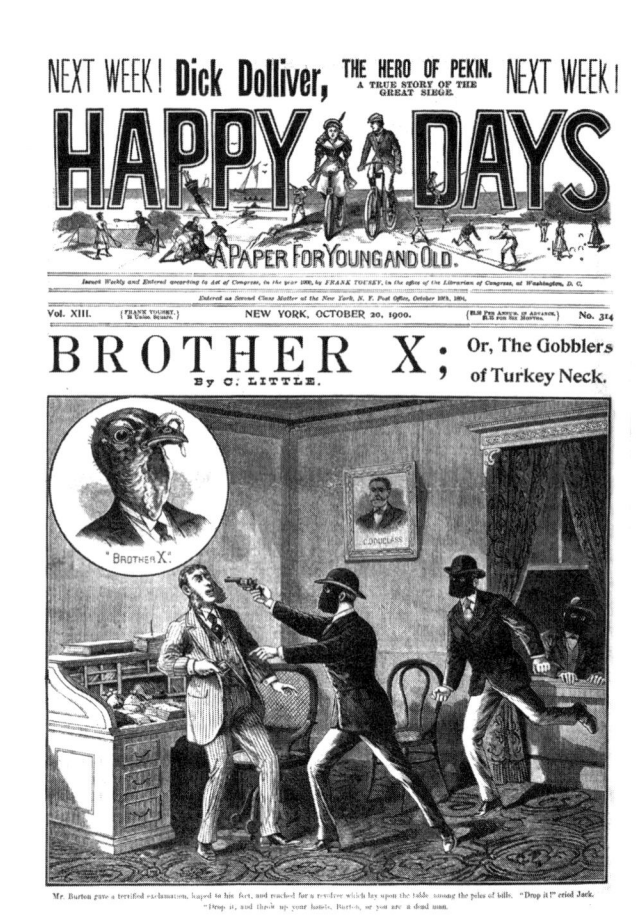

This black and white weekly from October 20, 1900, which was called Happy Days, A Paper For Young and Old, *would have had to compete with more elaborate color publications that had already begun to change the market.*

The term *pulp magazines*, also known as *pulps*, derives from the cheap wood pulp paper on which the publications were printed. Unlike magazines printed on more expensive paper (known as glossies or slicks), pulps featured lurid and exploitative stories and sensational cover art. The pulps took advantage of new high-speed presses, low payments to authors, and inexpensive paper to reduce the price of the magazine to ten cents per issue, as opposed to glossies, which generally sold for 25 cents. This cost differential greatly increased sales, although profit margins for publishers remained slim. Most pulp magazines measured 10 inches high by seven inches wide and were a half-inch thick with 128 pages.

Major pulp publishers included A. A. Wyn's Magazine Publishers, Clayton Publications, and Culture Publications.

At the height of their popularity during the 1920s and 1930s, many pulp magazines sold up to a million copies per issue. Popular titles included *Adventure, Amazing Stories, Black Mask, Dime Detective, Flying Aces, Horror Stories, Marvel Tales, Oriental Stories, Planet Stories, Spicy Detective, Startling Stories, Thrilling Wonder Stories, Unknown,* and *Weird Tales.* Pulp magazines remained popular from 1896 through the 1950s, when paperback books reduced their popularity.

"Paperback" books, sometimes known as softbacks or soft covers, refers to books with covers made of paperboard and held together by glue rather than stitches. Although paperbacks were first tried in Germany in 1931 by Albatross Books, the form was first financially successful in the United Kingdom beginning in 1935. The Penguin Books imprint of British publisher Allen Lane used many innovations introduced by Albatross, including color-themed covers indicating different genres and a conspicuous logo. In the United States, Robert de Graaf entered into a partnership with Simon & Schuster to create Pocket Books in 1939. Early paperback publishers used reprint rights from publishers and huge print runs (often 20,000 or more) to reduce unit prices. Paperbacks were sold in locations where books had not been stocked before, such as drug stores and supermarkets, overcoming initial bookseller reluctance to stock the new format. In addition to Penguin and Pocket Books, prominent paperback publishers included Ace Books, Ballantine Books, and Popular Library.

Many of the early leading paperback publishers—including Ace, Avon, and Dell—were started by pulp magazine publishers. Although initially publishing only reprints, paperback publishers also began to issue original material. Thrillers and other crime-related material were immensely popular with paperback readers. Comic books and graphic novels also have used some of the themes developed in earlier decades by dime novels and pulps. Because comic books appeal to children, critics have objected since the 1950s to the use of this form for certain adult themes, such as sex or violence. Despite this, comic books and graphic novels remain popular avenues to explore crime and detective fiction.

Themes and Subject Matter

Edgar Allen Poe's *The Murders in the Rue Morgue,* published in 1841, has been hailed as the first detective story. Since that time, a variety of writers have explored this genre, and slick magazines often featured the works of well-known crime and detective authors such as Arthur Conan Doyle and Edgar Wallace. Crime and detective themes became popular in dime novels almost from the beginning. Although the majority of early stories stood alone, publishers soon found that featuring a recurring series hero or theme would increase sales and help sales grow. Old Sleuth, who began appearing in *The Fireside Companion* story paper in 1872, was the first character who began the trend toward detective and crime fiction. While the term *sleuth* had earlier been used to refer to bloodhounds, Old Sleuth initiated the usage of the term to indicate a detective. Wildly popular, Old Sleuth inspired a host of competitors, all using the word *Old* in their names, including Old Broadbrim, Old Cap Collier, Old Ferret, Old King Brady, Old Lightning, and many others. Perhaps the most popular dime novel detective, Nick Carter, made his first appearance in *The New York Weekly* in 1886.

Nick Carter was a transformational character, who appeared in all formats of popular fiction, including dime novels, pulp magazines, and paperbacks, as well as being featured in films and radio and television programming. First created by Ormond G. Smith, the scion of the Street & Smith publishing empire, the Nick Carter stories never were credited to an author, since Carter himself ostensibly wrote the tales. While never especially well-written, the Nick Carter stories demonstrated the value of a well-known brand, as readers sought out any publication featuring his name. As a result, other popular characters with a crime theme emerged in pulp magazines, including Walter B. Gibson's The Shadow, Seabury Quinn's Jules de Grandin, and Rex Stout's Nero Wolfe.

Pulp authors enjoyed less status and received lower payments for their work than authors who published in the slicks, such as Agatha Christie, Ellery Queen, and other major mystery authors.

A 1910 issue of Old Sleuth Weekly *featuring the story "Old Sleuth to The Rescue." The character of Old Sleuth began appearing in* The Fireside Companion *story paper in 1872 and first popularized the use of the term* sleuth *to mean a detective.*

Nonetheless, pulp authors enjoyed a cult-like following among loyal readers. Certain authors who began working for the pulps later were recognized as masters of the crime genre, including Dashiell Hammet, Erle Stanley Gardner, James M. Cain, and Raymond Chandler.

Mainstream book publishers and slick magazines from the 1920s through the 1950s most commonly were part of the subgenre known as the "whodunit," short for "Who done it?" While whodunits and puzzle problem plots were not unknown in dime novels, pulps, and thrillers, these publications more commonly focused upon private eyes, police procedurals, supernatural tales, horror stories, and hard-boiled detectives. Mickey Spillane's Mike Hammer, who first appeared in 1947 in *I, the Jury*, was immediately successful, with the first novel selling over six million copies. Although tame by contemporary standards, Spillane's books featured more sex and violence than was common at the time. Thrillers were popular with commuters who read them on the train or bus and as weekend and vacation reading. Although often savaged by critics, the genre was popular with the public and often saw crossover success in films and comic books. Such works dealt with sexual themes, including extramarital intercourse, homosexuality, and loneliness, that were eschewed in more mainstream novels.

Up through the 1960s such forms were considered to be of lesser quality than other forms, and works of crime fiction that originated as dime novels, pulps, and thrillers were largely ignored except by devoted fans. As more readers and critics became familiar with crime fiction that had long been dismissed as pulp fiction, certain authors, especially Chandler, Hammett, and Cain, began to be viewed in a more favorable manner. Today, many who began as the writers of dime novels, pulps, or thrillers have received respect and acclaim from the academy, with university seminars and symposiums devoted to their work. As sexual mores evolved, dime novels, pulps, and thrillers were reexamined and reevaluated by a new generation.

Lasting Influence

Dime novels, pulps, and thrillers have had lasting influence. The works of many modern and contemporary authors such as Ross Macdonald, Robert B. Parker, Marcia Muller, Sara Paretsky, and Sue Grafton show the influence of dime novels, pulps, and thrillers from the first half of the 20th century. As women's liberation and the civil rights movement have become more accepted, many authors have re-examined genres such as police procedurals and hard-boiled private eyes so that they reflect more contemporary perspectives. Many feel that the themes originally developed in dime novels, pulps, and thrillers provide an ideal form in which to examine many problems and issues facing the contemporary United States.

Dime novels, pulps, and thrillers explore themes that have a dual allure to readers that are both lasting and persistent. On the one hand, the world is often portrayed as a dangerous and uncertain place where bad things happen to ordinary citizens. On the other hand, avenging forces exist that punish criminals and protect the innocent. While simplistic, occasionally vulgar, and often violent, the themes developed in dime novels, pulps, and thrillers have a durable appeal that continues to entice and enthrall readers. As the lines between books and other written works, films, and television have blurred, these themes can also be explored more readily.

Stephen T. Schroth
Jason A. Helfer
Diana L. Beck
Knox College

See Also: Buntline, Ned; Christie, Agatha; Gardner, Erle Stanley; Grafton, Sue; Hammett, Dashiell; Literature and Theater, Crime in; Literature and Theater, Police in; *National Police Gazette*; Paretsky, Sara; Poe, Edgar Allen; Spillane, Mickey.

Further Readings
Cox, J. R. *The Dime Novel Companion: A Sourcebook*. Westport, CT: Greenwood Press, 2000.
Hoppenstand, G. *The Dime Novel Detective*. Madison, WI: Popular Press, 1982.
Hoppenstand, G. and R. B. Browne, eds. *The Defective Detective in the Pulps*. Madison, WI: Popular Press, 1983.

Discretionary Decision Making

Modern criminal justice has evolved into a complex and loosely coordinated set of systems characterized by formality in rules and bureaucratization in organization. From a system composed of amateurs and extremely local and community-focused prior to the 18th century, criminal justice systems transformed into ones with significant growth in size, professionalism, and specialization. The codification and expansion of substantive and procedural criminal laws in the last two-plus centuries has increased pressures to use limited resources efficiently, to be selective in enforcement, and to be responsive to sovereigns on the part of criminal justice institutions and actors.

Today, law enforcement, adjudication, and correctional reform involve a significant number of actors making decisions about individuals and individual cases at multiple stages of each system. Coupled with the differences in the substance and operation of multiple systems, the potential and realization of significant gaps and inconsistencies between justice ideals and real practices make most criminal justice decisions potentially consequential and problematic. The ability to make decisions translates into considerable levels of power and resistance held by criminal justice actors, which also highlight the need to examine the policy, implementation, practice, and evaluation realities in modern criminal justice systems.

The exercise of power and authority by police officers, judges, prison wardens, and parole boards is highly diffused and hidden, making any examination and accounting of discretionary decisions be invariably politicized and open to varying interpretations. The growth of discretionary decision making paralleled the growth of criminal justice and societal changes in terms of increased heterogeneity, urbanization, and industrialization.

Diversity, anonymity, and standardized and bureaucratic provision of criminal justice services required formalization and the ability to process greater volumes of cases. The desire and ability to regulate the enforcers in their decision making was and continues to be limited (only the courts were able to exert any meaningful check on discretionary decisions but had few resources to independently and thoroughly monitor these decisions).

Only the due process and civil rights revolution supported by an activist higher court resulted in greater attention being given to discretionary decision making, but this was short-lived and superseded by rising crime rates and the reemergence of the crime control model. For these reasons, discretionary decision making was given greater attention in the 20th century, especially the second half of this century. Presently, most observers recognize that discretion is inevitable and the focus is on how to control such choices so as to minimize any negative externalities resulting from the making of such decisions.

Background

Discretionary decisions involve judgments and choices in relation to arrest, sentencing, rehabilitation, parole, and countless other decisions made by criminal justice actors. While noncriminal justice actors are influential, their decision making is more limited, sporadic, and specific to particular ends and, hence, the exercise of their discretion has not received extended scrutiny (examples would be the discretion of jurors and community correctional actors). However, the development and evolution of juvenile justice systems accompanied by the growth of community corrections presents a whole gamut of discretionary decisions being given a greater degree of emphasis in the last four decades.

The sources of discretion are varied and involve a mix of formal and informal factors. The allocation of power and the degree of discretion granted for any particular decision reflects value choices made in the larger society. Formal discretion reflects authoritative and legitimacy concerns with the distribution of power. Legitimate use of power and immunity from decisions was justified on the basis of critical functions provided by particular actors, including being fair, objective, and unbiased in enforcement of laws and dispensing justice.

Following Weberian analysis, the historical growth of criminal justice systems with a specialized set of personnel signified formalized discretionary powers and followed a division of labor across and within governments. Early modern societies placed greater emphasis on checking discretion through the organization of legal and executive governments than on balancing abuses of discretionary power across each branch as well as levels of government (as in the federal system). Discretion has been permitted to allow trained and experienced criminal justice professionals to make efficient and effective choices to fulfill the public interest and to provide flexibility to these professionals in achieving individualized justice.

The Eighteenth and Nineteenth Centuries

Providing individualized treatment of cases was stressed in most political revolutions, most notably the American Revolution. The humanness of the system was thought to be achievable through discretionary decisions that tempered the power of the state, provided and protected freedoms of citizens, and made punishments proportional and fair. Proposed penal reforms in the late 18th and early 19th centuries emphasized the necessity to reform offenders through isolation from society, religious training, and hard labor while making punishments more lenient overall. Many observers have noted opposite effects from the broad and unchecked discretion resulting during the 19th century, including Jacksonian democracy emphasizing local governance. Instead, this period saw increased discipline and punishment within prisons and development of formal police forces, who=ich served the functions of controlling surplus populations and dangerous classes produced by the spread of capitalism, urbanization, and industrialization.

With the development of legal systems and the growth of prisons (specifically, the distinctly American invention of the penitentiary), organizational and local political forces became increasingly important in discretionary decision making. Largely left unregulated, corruption and mismanagement by the police departments and prisons was rampant in the 19th century, partially because of the need to respond to urban riots and a significant increase in disorderly activities. Police were given deference and latitude to exercise their discretion without specific procedures to be followed, and these discretionary decisions were hidden from the public.

Further, many have pointed to the critical role police and corrections played in the labor markets as broadening the discretion by police to control the lower classes in the 19th century. Many of these decisions derived from vague and overbroad ordinances and laws offering extensive discretion in enforcement and interpretation. Criminal justice institutions provided vital welfare functions to poorer and marginalized populations as Western societies modernized. These discretionary decisions, then, were more directly connected to urban social problems and criminal justice systems served broader (manifest) functions than crime control and order maintenance.

The Twentieth Century

Even in the 20th century to the present, discretionary decision making is useful for a wide range of latent reasons, including increasing managerial efficiency, serving as politically expedient, allowing criminal justice actors to do publicly unmentionable activities without concern for legal scrutiny, permitting these institutions and actors to protect themselves from criticism, and providing a sense of accomplishment in being able to make choices and discretions based on their professionalism. The classist and racist nature of discretionary decisions dictated unduly by extralegal factors would only be acknowledged toward the later decades of the 20th century when legal discrimination ended.

The trust placed in these decision makers has been historically based on the separation of powers between the three branches of government, whereby the judicial and executive branches make various enforcement, administrative, and judicial decisions and the legislative branch is limited to decisions regarding criminal laws and penal codes. The classical approach championed by Cesare Becarria targeted the significant, arbitrary, and discriminatory nature of discretionary decision making by judges and magistrates. While this discretion was proposed to be shifted to legislators, the judicial branch and, later on, the executive branch still retained considerable discretion with regard to sentencing and related decisions. Further, the growth of formal police forces and prosecutorial offices in the late 19th century resulted in most discretionary decision making powers being shifted to these actors. Most prominently, discretionary decision making was reflected in the growth of plea bargaining and the strong incentives for police and prosecutors to cooperate with each other to meet the shared goals of maintaining social order, effectively responding to crime, and providing justice.

The Progressive Era was singly the most important period of time with regard to the increase in discretionary decision making in criminal justice. Replacing formalization with professionalism and accompanied by federalization and national attention to crime, police, legal, and correctional discretionary decisions were given the stamp of approval as being legitimate and necessary if placed in the hands of trusted professionals. Ironically, efforts to depoliticize criminal justice were undermined when professionalism created a permanent set of criminal justice institutions seeking to preserve their discretionary powers with control of this discretion regulated internally by these same organizations. In fact, a new professional and managerial criminal justice class was created and expanded considerably throughout the 20th century.

In the last century, the extent and character of formal discretion and discretionary decision making were rediscovered. Efforts to control discretion gained prominence with the work of the 1957 American Bar Association (ABA) Survey and the Presidential Crime Commission (1967) pointing to the lack of professionalism in the exercise of discretion and the considerable abuse, brutality, and use of extralegal factors in "formal" systems of criminal justice.

Various policies and proposals gained prominence to control discretion, including police use-of-force guidelines, mandatory minimum sentencing policies, and abolishing plea bargaining. Largely, these efforts were resisted by criminal justice actors for reasons that they were leading to excessive formality and rigidity, shifting discretion to other actors, and misplaced as the criminal justice systems were adequately and appropriating managing crime and risks posed by serious criminals. Ultimately, formalization of discretion and its control directly challenged the professionalism of criminal justice professionals and their discretionary decision making powers are not easily usurped or minimized.

Other Recent Developments

The exercise of informal discretion is more pervasive and historically has been considered contrary to principles of justice and governance in modern societies. Biased decision making and the abuse of discretionary powers were considered unfair and undemocratic. Nevertheless, extralegal factors continue to be prevalent in modern societies. Given the impossibility of full enforcement of laws and societal pressures for selective enforcement, the use of extralegal factors and nonlegal and nonprofessional norms to guide discretion is deeply ingrained in the history of criminal justice in modern societies. Colonial and premodern criminal justice systems relied exclusively on informal discretion exercised by public officials and religious and community leaders, with minimal monitoring and accounting for abuses of these discretionary powers. Dictated by community norms, discretion was exercised with the intent to solidify boundaries and provide lessons to all members of the community.

From the 1920s (and especially during the civil rights era) onward the links between the exercise of discretion and racial discrimination on the part of the police were increasingly brought to question, and pressures to control discretion gained substantial momentum in the 1960s. Courts were willing to put pressure on the police exercise of discretion but unwilling to push for the control of discretion by legal actors (the visibility of police and the closeness with fellow court actors may explain why this was the case).

Most of the focus from the politically liberal side was on eliminating the use of extralegal factors in the exercise of discretion by the police and courts, while conservatives viewed discretion as allowing for leniency (mainly due to technicalities and excessive focus on suspect and prisoner rights, which are also extralegal factors but of a different kind) in responding to crimes and criminals. Discretion was seen as hiding patterns of social bias on the one hand and hampering effectiveness on the other hand. In the neoliberal and neoclassical contexts of the last four decades, the prospects for controlling discretionary decision making are poor at best.

Discretionary decision making as a problem was short-lived, as alternatives were impractical and nonexistent. Additionally, criminal justice systems actors were resistant to control and elimination of discretionary decision making. The wars on drugs and crime contributed heavily to making discretion a nonissue by enhancing formal discretion (increased discretionary decision making powers to the executive branch) and informal discretion (use whatever means necessary to win these wars). In current policy environments, decision making is dictated mostly by internal organizational norms and external political considerations.

Conclusion

Discretion is vital to criminal justice actors as a filtering device in classifying (and prioritizing) cases and criminals. Decision making dictated by professionals with vested interests in continuing to retain discretionary choices makes it likely that discretionary decision making will be widespread in criminal justice in the long-term future. At the heart of discretion are deference to experts and trusted authorities and dependency on these same professionals. Criminal justice personnel expect such respect and understand the significant discretionary powers in their hands.

Sanjay Marwah
Guilford College

See Also: Clemency; Judges and Magistrates; Justice, Department of; Race, Class, and Criminal Law; Sentencing: Indeterminate Versus Fixed.

Further Readings
Gelsthorpe, Loraine and Nicola Padfield, eds. *Exercising Discretion: Decision-Making in the Criminal Justice System and Beyond*. Portland, ME: Willan Publishing, 2003.
Walker, Samuel. *Taming the System: The Control of Discretion in Criminal Justice 1950–1990*. Oxford: Oxford University Press, 1993.

District Attorney

District attorneys are generally elected officials whose roles in the justice system include prosecuting violations of state and local laws on behalf of the state, ensuring a fair and equitable process, protecting victims' rights and safety, and working to ensure public safety. The district attorney of the 21st century has tremendous discretionary power over life and liberty, responsible for making decisions about whether or not to pursue criminal charges, which criminal charges to file in court, negotiating pleas, conducting trials, making sentencing recommendations, and in some states, handling appeals of criminal convictions. These responsibilities are quite unlike those of the first prosecutors in colonial America, who were relatively minor actors in local justice systems.

District attorneys, referred to more generally as prosecutors, have many different titles, including prosecuting attorney, county attorney, commonwealth attorney, state attorney, and in three states attorney general. Alaska, Delaware, and Rhode Island have elected statewide attorneys general who then appoint deputy attorneys general to handle prosecution at the county level. In Connecticut and New Jersey, the governor appoints a statewide prosecutor who then appoints prosecutors to handle prosecution at the county level. In the remaining 45 states, prosecutors are elected by individual counties or by judicial districts. Traditionally, district attorneys are thought of in terms of the criminal matters that they prosecute. However, 54 percent of prosecutors also represent the government in civil matters. All district attorneys have jurisdiction over the prosecution of felony offenses; not all, however, handle misdemeanor offenses. Similarly, all district attorneys have jurisdiction over adult criminal matters, but not all handle juvenile cases.

Origins of the District Attorney

The origins of today's modern district attorney are not well known, and in fact, there are many opinions about how the position of district attorney emerged. The first prosecutor-like figure appeared in the mid-1600s and evolved significantly in prominence through the 1700s. The original thirteen colonies had differing arrangements for addressing prosecution. Early prosecutorial functions were conducted on a colony-wide level. From these colony-level prosecutors emerged the local prosecution function and, ultimately, the modern-day district attorney. The first prosecutor-like officer in the courts appeared in Virginia in 1643 and was known as the king's attorney. The role of this officer was largely advisory and only used when the matter before the court directly involved royal interests. The king's attorney generally did not focus on domestic crimes, and as such, crime victims in the colonies had no formal advocate in the courts. Nearly a decade later, colony-wide attorneys general began to emerge with a focus on domestic criminal matters. These early attorneys general had the responsibility of representing colonial interests; however, here too the roles varied from more advisory-type roles to investigative roles. Zealous advocacy in court on the part of the colonies by attorneys general was limited.

Soon thereafter, the first true "local" prosecutors were created, which were ultimately the precursors to the modern-day district attorney. Recognizing a need to provide deputy attorneys to handle criminal matters in outlying counties of the colonies, colonial governments and/or the attorney general began appointing deputy attorneys general. Because of the importance of the deputy attorneys general in meeting local county needs in courts, the appointment of the deputies increasingly occurred at the county level. In 1711, in Virginia, local men were nominated by the colonists to serve as their county-level deputy attorney general. In 1732, counties in Virginia began paying salaries to the deputy attorneys general, thereby creating the first locally appointed and locally paid prosecutor.

Around the same time, in the former Dutch colonies of New York and New Jersey, another form of local prosecution was emerging—the "schout." Like the attorneys general and deputy attorneys general in many of the colonies, the schout had responsibility for handling domestic criminal matters but, unlike the attorneys general and deputy attorneys general in other colonies,

New York District Attorney Thomas Gagan photographed in late 1914 or early 1915 while he was serving as the prosecutor in a murder trial in Rockland County, New York.

had two distinguishing characteristics. First, the schout's role in some areas included an investigatory function, which meant that the schout acted essentially as a quasi-sheriff and prosecutor. Second, a schout was essentially a private prosecutor, retained and paid for by crime victims. In return, the schout would file charges that victims wanted pursued and advocate on their behalf in court.

In 1704, Connecticut became the first colony to pass a law creating a formal system of public prosecution, abandoning private prosecution. By the mid-1700s, prosecutors were operating at the county level and in courts of original jurisdiction in most of the colonies. It wasn't until the mid-1800s that the system of publicly elected prosecutors began to emerge. Between 1820 and the American Civil War, there was increased concern with the ability to hold prosecutors accountable for their work and methods for reviewing prosecutorial actions. In response, states began providing for publicly elected prosecutors. Thus, by the end of the 1800s, the system of public prosecution in America was fully realized, although the role of the prosecutor would continue to undergo significant expansion into the following century.

Case Screening and Plea Bargaining

Between the American Civil War and the early 1970s, prosecutorial power and discretion increased significantly, placing today's district attorney among the most powerful actors in the modern-day criminal justice system. Rapidly growing cities and changing demographics of the populace brought about by mass immigration during the Industrial Revolution virtually eliminated informal solutions to criminal activity and deviant behavior. Professional police agencies were developed and flourished; correctional facilities and departments emerged and grew; and the need for a more professional prosecution function to meet these new demands on the justice system increased. Up to this point, victims and the public often served as the source of criminal complaints to local prosecutors. Now police responded to the victims, conducted the investigations, and brought the matters to the prosecutors' offices. Prosecutors' offices began to grow in size with the volume of cases, as did the need for mechanisms to manage the increasing caseload and still provide for due process. These mechanisms—case screening and plea bargaining—also became among the most controversial forms of prosecutorial power.

Case screening is the function that gives prosecutors unparalleled power over life and liberty. As prosecutorial caseloads began to increase substantially, there was a pressing need to create a mechanism to control which cases would be pursued and which would not. Standards began to emerge related to evidentiary sufficiency (whether or not the evidence is sufficient enough to convict beyond a reasonable doubt) trial sufficiency (i.e., the likelihood that a case could be won at trial), and whether or not prosecution of the case was in the best interest of the state. These standards were, and still are, used to evaluate the strength of a case and to make determinations about whether formal charges will be filed in court and, if charges are to be filed, what the appropriate charges should be. Although the new case screening processes were thought to encroach upon the traditional case-initiation role of the police, who up to this point made decisions about charges, the processes were upheld in case law and further solidified in the 1967 President's Commission on Law Enforcement and Administration of Justice.

The other controversial practice, plea bargaining, is perhaps the most studied and highly criticized practice of the traditional prosecutor and remains a point of contention in modern-day prosecution. The practice allows the prosecutor to further control caseload by offering and accepting pleas in exchange for concessions in the defendant's sanction. In the plea bargaining process, prosecutors can negotiate the number and type of charges and the types of sanctions that the defendant may face. This practice, which generally did not exist prior to the Civil War, became the most frequent type of case disposition by the end of the 19th century. It is this singular practice that significantly altered the justice system—moving it from a jury-based system with its power rooted in the judiciary to a plea-based system in which the power lies with the local prosecutor.

It is also during this period (from the mid-1800s through the 1970s) that the day-to-day activities of the district attorneys' offices were solidified. In addition to reviewing cases brought to the attention of the office by law enforcement and making decisions about what, if any charges to file, attorneys became engaged in all facets of case processing—making appearances in all hearings, convening grand juries in states that provide for such a practice, interviewing victims and witnesses, participating in jury selection for trial, and making recommendations for sanctions. In addition, in some states, prosecutors began to handle criminal appeals of misdemeanor offenses. Apart from the actual processing of cases, prosecutors began acting in an advisory capacity to law enforcement—conducting training on the law and legal process and providing input on the investigations. At each decision point in the adjudicative process, the prosecutors' influence has increasingly greater power because of the discretion afforded to them. Finally, the autonomy of the district attorneys' offices was solidified, allowing them discretion with regard to the internal policies and practices that would be used in their jurisdiction with regard to how their offices would be structured, how cases would be assigned and handled, and even the authority line attorneys would have with regard to specific case decisions. As a result, there is variation across states, and even within states, as to how district attorneys' offices operate.

By the 1970s, a new evolution of the prosecutorial role began—the movement toward community-based prosecution. If the other significant developmental periods in prosecution are marked by increasing power and representation of the state, the movement toward community-based prosecution has expanded the district attorneys' domain into the larger social goals of crime control and problem-solving. A slight shift in focus includes the invocation of the interests of the communities that district attorneys serve, in addition to representing the interests of the state.

A number of changes in the legislative and social climate can be related to the newest focus for prosecutors. On the heels of the civil rights movement and antigovernment sentiment in the late 1960s came significant reform in the justice system, including recognition that the community was as much a patron of the system as were the state and crime victims. The upsurge of drugs and new laws increasing the penalties for drug use brought an unprecedented volume of cases into the criminal justice system, creating significant backlogs, and reform began to find alternative ways of handling certain crimes. Closures of mental health institutions and decreasing services for at-risk populations brought new types of offenders, with new problems under the purview of the justice system. The district attorney, as the gatekeeper to the justice system, was poised to configure modern prosecution with modernist ideologies in a way that would have a more meaningful impact on public safety and address the underlying problems associated with certain types of criminal offending, particularly low-level, nuisance-type crimes.

Proactive Approach to Crime

Alternatives to traditional prosecution strategies emerged that embodied the elements of the traditional prosecution period (efficient and equitable case processing) and sanction setting with the more modern strategies focused on problem solving to prevent and reduce crime, strategic investment to build capacity for responding to crime, and a leadership role in restoring the social institutions that provide both formal and informal crime control. The practices that emerged included mediation, arbitration, and victim restoration, which were intended to find lower-cost alternatives to traditional case processing for low-level offenses and focused on dispute resolution in lieu of criminal charges. Coordination with law enforcement and other justice system sectors also became prevalent to address specific forms of crimes that victimize whole communities. At the same time, this coordination produced an increased volume of cases that required swift and certain sanctioning, and the practice of vertical prosecution became widespread. Vertical prosecution is the practice of assigning the same prosecutor to a case from the initial charging decision through its final disposition. With vertical prosecution comes a connection between the line attorney, the victim, and the community that harkens back to the relationships of the early prosecutor to crime victims.

A natural progression, then, was increased interaction with community members to address crime and disorder. In this model, district attorneys' offices take a proactive approach to crime with an emphasis on identifying the problems associated with criminal offending, particularly in low-level offenses, as well as quality-of-life issues and forming and solidifying partnerships with law enforcement and other allied professionals such as schools, mental health agencies, treatment programs, and businesses to bolster their institutional capacity for both informal and formal problem solving. While traditional case processing activities still occur, line attorneys are often assigned to geographic areas within the jurisdiction to handle the cases that come from these communities.

These new roles of the modern district attorney are not without controversy. With prosecutorial approaches influenced by the community, concerns arise that access to justice varies, with some populations having greater access than others. Similar concerns are raised that question the appropriateness of the new problem-solving and institution-building roles as overstepping the legal authority of the prosecutor's office or encroaching upon the traditional investigative and case initiation roles of law enforcement. In addition, even though the intent behind the movement toward community prosecution was to help quell the crush of low-level offenses entering the system, there are unanswered questions about whether the focus on these offenses diverts limited prosecutorial resources from more serious crimes. Finally, the emphasis on nontraditional approaches to these crimes and less reliance on formal adjudication is viewed by some as "soft on crime."

M. Elaine Nugent-Borakove
Justice Management Institute

See Also: Plea; President's Commission on Law Enforcement and the Administration of Justice; Trials; Wickersham Commission.

Further Readings
DeFrances, Carol J. "Prosecutors in State Courts, 2001." http://www.bjs.ojp.usdoj.gov/content/pub/pdg/psc01.pdf (Accessed January 2011).
Jacoby, Joan. *The American Prosecutor: A Search for Identity*. Lexington, MA: Lexington Press Books, 1980.
Nugent-Borakove, M. Elaine and Gerard Rainville. "The Evolution of the Local Prosecutor From Case Processor to Community Problem-Solver." In *Visions for Change: Crime and Justice in the Twenty-First Century*, 5th ed., Rosyln Muraskin and Albert R. Roberts, eds. Upper Saddle River, NJ: Pearson Prentice Hall, 2009.

Tumin, Zachary. "Summary of the Proceedings: Findings and Discoveries of the Harvard University Executive Session for State and Local Prosecutors at the John F. Kennedy School of Government (1986–90)." Working Paper #90-02-05.

Domestic Violence, Contemporary

Domestic violence refers to the abuses such as name-calling, beating, stalking, rape, and even murder that occur between married or unmarried couples who currently live or previously have lived together. The Bureau of Justice Statistics gathers information on intimate partner violence, but the bureau acknowledges the difficulties in tracking such information. The bureau finds that women from nonwhite groups, particularly African American women, experience higher rates of domestic violence than women from white groups. Also, intimate partner violence occurs within ethnic groups more frequently than across ethnic groups.

Earlier initiatives surrounding domestic violence resulted in bringing the once-private issue into public awareness, educating people about the signs and dangers of it, and creating and enforcing legislation designed to protect victims and punish abusers. In addition to seeing a continuation of the previous efforts, the first decade of the 2000s saw some shifting in the news coverage of domestic violence, emerging technologies changing both public education and domestic violence crimes, growing money issues impacting domestic violence programs in various states, continuing initiatives from previous decades and the developing of new ones, and increasing understanding of domestic violence in various situations.

Media Coverage
Early news coverage regarding domestic violence crimes blamed the victims and sidestepped blaming the abusers. This approach has shifted slightly in recent years, particularly among celebrity news coverage. Actors such as Mel Gibson and Charlie Sheen drew media attention after being accused

The early 2000s brought many attempts to raise awareness of domestic violence and improve services for victims of abuse. The 2000 Violence Against Women Act mandated funding for programs run through the U.S. Department of Justice and the Department of Health and Human Services, and President Barack Obama also signed a Family Violence Prevention and Services Act in late 2010. The domestic violence awareness march shown here included members of the military in Columbia, South Carolina, in 2009.

of domestic violence, though coverage of Gibson did more to highlight Gibson's mean personality than to reinforce the seriousness of his crimes. Pop singer Rihanna received coverage for reports of domestic abuse from her then boyfriend, Chris Brown. While Rihanna received some media sympathy but no blame for what happened, the media also avoided calling for Brown's punishment.

Other celebrities took advocacy positions on the issue. Some celebrities shared their stories of domestic violence on the consciousness-raising Website endabuse.org. Still other celebrities participated in specific initiatives. For example, *Law & Order: SVU* star Mariska Hargitay participated in a 2010 documentary titled *Telling Amy's Story*, a public television program that attempted to raise awareness about domestic violence and its effects.

Other documentaries served as focal points for multimedia initiatives. Olivia Klaus's *Sin by Silence* (2008) follows the stories of several incarcerated women who murdered their abusers and chronicles their involvement with Convicted Women Against Abuse (CWAA). The documentary became a focal point for a national consciousness-raising tour, which included multimedia offerings that employed various social networking connections such as Facebook, Twitter, Flickr, MySpace, and a dedicated Website. CWAA founder Brenda Clubine also maintains a blog (brendaclubine.com), where she writes about her experiences and advocacy efforts.

Domestic Violence and the Internet

The proliferation of the Internet and the ease of setting up Websites has allowed domestic violence organizations to provide information to sufferers, survivors, and volunteers. Several organizations online include the National Coalition Against Domestic Violence (ncadv.org), the National Domestic Violence Hotline (thehotline.org), the Family Violence Prevention Fund (endabuse.org), and the U.S. Department of Justice's Office on Violence Against Women (www.ovw.usdoj.gov).

While new technologies offer opportunities to educate the public, they also offer opportunities to further oppress the victims of domestic violence. In the early 1990s, stalking first became recognized as part of domestic violence activities, and with the proliferation of new and easy-to-use technologies in the 2000s, instances of it have increased dramatically. Small cameras can track activities within the home, while global positioning devices allow stalkers to track their victims wherever they go. Disposable cell phones have allowed harassing phone calls to go untraced. Other devices can follow victims' activities online, recording Websites they visit, instant messages and e-mail they send and receive, and even every keystroke they make. In recognition of this online stalking, many domestic violence Websites feature an "escape key," which users can click to be redirected to a "safe" site such as weather.com or google.com.

Challenges and Outlook

With the recession hitting U.S. federal and state budgets, and with government deficits increasing, domestic violence programs have faced reduced or cut funding. In summer 2009, California Governor Arnold Schwarzenegger eliminated the entire $20.4 million budget for the state's domestic violence programs, including its 94 women's shelters. Six shelters closed within six weeks of the cuts, and many others were forced to cut back on staff, services, and operating hours. In October 2009, the California legislature approved $16.3 million for the programs, which the governor then approved. Three of the shelters managed to reopen. Similar budget reductions occurred in New York and Rhode Island.

Legislation has furthered efforts begun in the previous decades. First approved in 2000 and renewed in 2005, the Violence Against Women Act mandated funding for programs run through the U.S. Department of Justice and the Department of Health and Human Services. Other legislation continued efforts to recognize the impact of domestic violence on children, such as the Keeping Children and Families Safe Act of 2003. In late 2010, President Barack Obama signed the Family Violence Prevention and Services Act, which further recognized that domestic violence affected not just spouses but other household members, particularly children.

Other newer developments have included the recognition of the situational differences in domestic violence. For example, social expectations stipulate that women become the victims and that men become the abusers, but sometimes the roles get reversed. According to the Federal Bureau of Investigation, on average, about one man is murdered by a domestic partner each day, and this type of murder accounts for about 5 percent of murders of men each year. For women, the rates still hovered around 34 percent of male abusers killing their victims in 2009–10, though overall the rates decreased slightly. Starting in the 1990s and growing in the 2000s, the situations surrounding male abuse victims became a focus of research and advocacy. Another focus addressed those without convenient access to services, such as women living in rural communities.

Heather McIntosh
Boston College

See Also: Child Abuse, Sociology of; Children's Rights; Domestic Violence, History of; Domestic Violence, Sociology of; Obama, Barack (Administration of); Violence Against Women Act of 1994.

Further Readings

Buzawa, Eve S. and Carl G. Buzawa, eds. *Domestic Violence: The Criminal Justice Response*, 3rd. ed. Thousand Oaks, CA: Sage, 2003.

Catalano, Shannan. "Intimate Partner Violence in the U.S." Bureau of Justice Statistics. http://bjs.ojp.usdoj.gov/content/intimate/ipv.cfm (Accessed September 2011).

Cook, Philip W. *Abused Men: The Hidden Side of Domestic Violence*, 2nd ed. Westport, CT: Praeger, 2009.

DeKeseredy, Walter S. and Martin D. Schwartz. *Dangerous Exits: Escaping Abusive Relationships in Rural America*. New Brunswick, NJ: Rutgers University Press, 2009.

Jackson, Nicky Ali, ed. *Encyclopedia of Domestic Violence*. New York: Routledge, 2007.

Southworth, Cindy, Shawndell Dawson, Cynthia Fraser, and Sarah Tucker. "A High-Tech Twist on Abuse: Technology, Intimate Partner Stalking, and Advocacy." National Network to End Domestic Violence. http://www.nnedv.org/resources/safetynetdocs/94-a-high-tech-twist-on-abuse.html (Accessed September 2011).

Domestic Violence, History of

Domestic violence refers to abusive activities that occur between married or unmarried couples who currently live or previously have lived together. Harmful activities include verbal abuse such as name-calling, emotional manipulation such as withholding affection or victim blaming, physical abuse such as hitting or beating, and sexual abuse such as rape. Other activities include forms of stalking, such as monitoring all the victim's movements and communications, and forms of public humiliation, such as through defamatory Websites. The victim endures both physical and psychological traumas as a result of the violence. While some victims escape and survive, other victims die at the hands of their abusers.

Abusers in these relationships typically are male, and the victims are typically female. This construction follows the gendered expectations in both historical and contemporary societies that women hold less power and fewer rights in social and cultural positions. Early practices and later laws reinforced these gendered assumptions, even though domestic violence occurs among homosexual couples and occurs between a female abuser and a male victim. Early laws in the United States followed British and European models, though the laws changed slowly from the country's founding until the 1960s and 1970s, when social movements, particularly feminist movements, called attention to the need for domestic violence awareness and prevention, for survivor support and empowerment, and for proper legislation and enforcement within both communities and police and legal systems.

Early History

Early British and European ideas about domestic violence came from the Romans and later the Catholic Church. During Roman times, the Laws of Chastisement permitted husbands to beat their wives with an implement no larger in circumference than the base of the husband's thumb; this was known as the "rule of thumb." Husbands held complete control over their wives' lives and fates, and husbands even could divorce or murder them. Within the Catholic Church, wives were expected to submit and devote themselves fully to their husbands, and in the 15th century, Friar Cherbubino of Siena's *Rules of Marriage* condoned wife beating as part of a husband's role as a judge to his wife's soul. Overall, these matters remained private and were not considered part of public discourse. Following British common law, early U.S. laws first allowed wife beating with an implement that followed the rule of thumb. Later, Puritans prohibited family violence and some states made it illegal, but enforcement of the laws remained lax.

Legislation throughout the early and mid-1800s started with reinforcing the husband's right to beat his wife and eventually moved toward criminalizing the act of wife beating. An 1824 case in Mississippi upheld that a husband could beat his wife only in cases of emergency. In 1857, a Massachusetts court acknowledged marital rape. In 1871, Alabama became the first state to withdraw a husband's right to beat his wife, while in 1882, Maryland became the first state to make it a crime. Other states followed suit in the late 1800s, but the punishments for these crimes were weak or remained unenforced

Women faced difficulties in getting divorces during the 1800s, and getting them on grounds of domestic violence proved even more challenging. Cruel treatment became grounds for divorce in the early 1800s in some states. Alcoholism became recognized as grounds for divorce as early as the 1830s, and most divorces were granted on these grounds. Not until 1895 did abuse become grounds for divorce.

This 1782 drawing pokes fun at British Judge Francis Buller for his support of the common law that allowed wife beating with an implement no thicker than a thumb. He is shown carrying bundles of sticks while another man prepares to strike a woman.

In the early 1900s, the first family court appeared in Buffalo, New York. The civil court was intended to handle domestic issues, including domestic violence, through intervention and reconciliation instead of through criminal punishment. This separation moved domestic violence out of the criminal court, suggesting its lesser importance to other crimes. Because of the family court system and other influences, domestic violence cases remained personal issues, not social ones, with explanations pointing to individual or pathological causes and with solutions to crises occurring through mediation, not arrest or imprisonment.

Women's Movements

The various civil rights movements of the 1960s brought about radical upheavals in U.S. society, and laws and criminal justice activities relating to domestic violence issues began to change. A key change occurred with the fundamental idea of domestic violence: Instead of domestic violence remaining a private issue, efforts were made to make it a public one, following the new "personal is political" thinking supported by some aspects of the feminist movements. In the 1960s, courts continued to send domestic violence cases to the family (civil) courts, but social organizations began to address the needs of victims. As part of cooperation with Al-Anon programs, for example, Rainbow Retreat in Phoenix, Arizona, and Haven House in Pasadena, California, offered shelter to women abused by alcoholic husbands.

The feminist movement pushed the outreach to abused women forward. Abused women's stories brought into the public eye created a fuller picture of the realities of domestic violence, its manifestations, and its effects. Shelters for battered women began to open across the country, including one of the first in Maine in 1967, and some received Title XX funding to expand staff and services, which included hotlines and counseling. Educational programs, however, received no funding support at the time. Women attempting to escape abusive husbands still faced multiple challenges, such as ensuring personal safety, securing employment, and getting welfare. Many cities denied welfare assistance to these women because of their husbands' incomes.

Grassroots efforts grew in the 1970s. One of the first groups was Women's Advocates, which formed in 1971 in Minneapolis/St. Paul, Minnesota; in 1974, the organization purchased a house for a women's shelter. Other groups formed to engage women's empowerment, such as the Women in Transition group of Philadelphia and Transition House in Boston. On the legal side, states upheld laws that allowed victims to bring criminal charges against their abusers, but policing programs such as ones in California and Ohio still attempted to avoid making arrests in domestic violence calls. Police reluctance to make these arrests resulted in several lawsuits filed against departments in Los Angeles and Oakland, California; New York City; New Haven, Connecticut; Chicago; and Atlanta. Legislation shifted to allow police officers to make arrests without warrants in these cases, such as in Washington, D.C., though critics claimed that police still avoided it whenever possible. Officers found reasons to avoid the situations, such as citing the couple's refusal to cooperate or the couple's conflicting versions of events.

Other efforts recognized the unfairness that women suffering from domestic abuse experienced through the press, the public, and the legal system, with women being blamed for the abuse and with their being compared to a stereotyped helpless victim. In reality, though, battered women sometimes killed their abusers. A 1976 case centered on Francine Hughes, who had suffered abuse at the hands of her husband since the early 1960s and who had murdered him. Instead of a jail sentence, she pleaded temporary insanity and was acquitted. Another case in Washington State, *State v. Wanrow*, recognized that imminent danger and other factors were different for women than for men and thus allowed women to be judged differently than by male standards. Along with "battered spouse" and "battered woman" becoming part of the International Classification of Diseases, these rulings opened the door for battered woman syndrome to become a viable defense. While the court cases, classification, and research raised awareness of the battered woman's experiences, the courts still sentenced women who murdered their abusers to long sentences and repeatedly denied them parole. Brenda Clubine was sentenced to 17 years to life for murdering her abuser in 1983, and in 1989, from prison, she founded an organization called Convicted Women Against Abuse in an attempt to raise awareness about these issues.

Contemporary Domestic Violence Issues

In addition to the multiple organizations founded and shelters opened during the 1970s, state and federal governments began making attempts to recognize domestic violence, to pass legislation, and to fund other initiatives. The first Take Back the Night rally happened in 1977. The National Coalition Against Domestic Violence started in 1978. The Domestic Violence Act of 1978 passed in the Senate but failed in the House of Representatives.

Women's monetary and legal struggles persisted into the 1980s. After Ronald Reagan's election to office, in 1981 the Office on Domestic Violence was dismantled, and its remaining funding dwindled so that no other federal programs received financial support. Funding for state-level initiatives continued through Title XX grants, and the Ford Foundation began offering grants to organizations such as the Women of Color Task Force of the National Coalition. In 1980, a proposed Domestic Violence and Services Act failed to pass in the Senate. In 1984, Lenore Walker wrote the first book-length treatment on *The Battered Woman Syndrome*. Later in the decade, the syndrome became a key component in courts in terms of training officials and prosecuting cases.

The awareness and outreach efforts also continued, addressing key issues to create a fuller picture of domestic violence across different legal and social organizations. One study revealed that mediation techniques favored by policy proved ineffective. Other initiatives recognized the place of domestic violence within the military, among both women serving and military wives. In 1981, Domestic Violence Awareness Week was recognized for the first time. The number of shelters also grew significantly, and some shelters even turned away victims because of insufficient capacity.

Significant advances on multiple fronts occurred in the 1990s. In legal changes, in 1992, California passed the first state law that established stalking as a crime. After several attempts dating back to the 1970s, Congress passed the Violence Against Women Act in 1994. The act offered funding for domestic violence services and training for police and court officials. Further, the act granted victims the right to sue in civil courts for gender-based crimes. The medical implications also received some attention. In 1992, U.S. Surgeon General Antonia Novello established abuse from husbands as the key cause of injuries in women ages 15–44. Further, the American Medical Association acknowledged the risks of domestic violence through suggesting guidelines for screening women for its signs. Domestic Violence Awareness Week expanded to become Domestic Violence Awareness Month in October 1997 and later recognitions of the month include the Silent Witness Project, Take Back the Night rallies, and the Clothes Line Project.

Increasing Awareness

The 1990s also saw grassroots organizational efforts attempt to assist members of different groups to find help for domestic violence. The

Gay Men's Domestic Violence Project (GMDVP) started in 1994 in response to other programs denying services to gay men. The project grew to include a telephone hotline, legal help, and counseling services, as well as rent assistance programs and initiatives to rewrite the laws to include all gender identities and sexual orientations. Other groups addressed different ethnic groups and their specific needs, such as Asian Task Force Against Domestic Violence, founded in 1992, and Alianza, National Latino Alliance for the Elimination of Domestic Violence, founded in 1997. The Arab American Chaldean Council also offers the Safe at Home Project, in conjunction with HAVEN. The organizations developed following initiatives that recognized the different experiences with domestic violence among immigrants and other groups in the 1980s.

Celebrity news coverage of domestic violence cases began grabbing headlines in the 1980s. A key case from the 1980s occurred between boxer Mike Tyson and actress Robin Givens, who accused Tyson of abuse in 1988 and was granted a divorce in 1989. An even more sensational case occurred in the early 1990s, when O. J. (Orenthal James) Simpson was accused of murdering his ex-wife Nicole Brown Simpson and her friend Ron Lyle Goldman. The news media covered the police chase of Simpson's white Chevrolet Blazer down California highways, and it covered the trial in which Simpson was acquitted. In 1997, Simpson lost a civil trial that found him liable and was ordered to pay $33 million in damages to the families. Both cases pushed awareness of domestic violence issues into the new century.

Heather McIntosh
Boston College

See Also: 1777 to 1800 Primary Documents; Domestic Violence, Contemporary; Domestic Violence, Sociology of; Simpson, O. J.

Further Readings
Buzawa, Eve S. and Carl G. Buzawa, eds. *Domestic Violence: The Criminal Justice Response*, 3rd. ed. Thousand Oaks, CA: Sage, 2003.
Dobash, R. Emerson and Russell P. Dobash. *Women, Violence, and Social Change*. New York: Routledge, 1992.
Jackson, Nicky Ali, ed. *Encyclopedia of Domestic Violence*. New York: Routledge, 2007.
Lemon, Nancy. *Domestic Violence Law: A Comprehensive Overview of Cases and Sources*. San Francisco, CA: Austin & Winfield, 1996.
McCue, Margi Laird. *Domestic Violence: A Reference Handbook*. Santa Barbara, CA: ABC-CLIO, 1995.
Peterson del Mar, David. *What Trouble I Have Seen: A History of Violence Against Wives*. Cambridge, MA: Harvard University Press, 1996.

Domestic Violence, Sociology of

The historical context of domestic violence can be understood when one examines how society has named this event. In colonial America, domestic violence was referred to as "wife disciplining" or as chastisement. As social and legal ideas of family and women's rights progressed, these events came to be known by terms such as *wife beating*, *wife abuse*, *family violence*, *domestic violence*, and *intimate partner violence*. Each name was led by theoretical explanations and resulted in changing social and legal philosophies and responses.

Historical and Social Context
Within colonial America, Puritans were the only group to prohibit wife beating. Puritan law required a practice known as "holy watching" as a form of social control. This practice required that neighbors watched each other in order to keep wives free from bodily harm. However, Puritan law's approach to wife beating did not dominate as the typical justice response to the problem. Even where wife beating was illegal, courts rarely heard these cases. In Plymouth colony, for example, between 1633 and 1802, only 12 cases were brought before the court.

The early American legal and social context of domestic violence is reflected in English common law. As early as the 1780s in England, Judge Sir Francis Fuller ruled that a husband could physically discipline his wife with a weapon, as long as the weapon was no thicker than his thumb. While written reference to this English ruling is hard to find, this "rule of thumb" was officially adopted by U.S. courts in *Bradley v. State* in 1824. Since all actions of the wife and child were the ultimate responsibility of the husband, it was at this time that the court officially ruled that wife chastisement or disciplining was a continued expectation. Furthermore, in 1879, the North Carolina court ruled in *State v. Oliver* that husbands cannot be held criminally responsible for violence against their wives as long as the violence was not cruel in nature and did not cause irreversible damage.

These court rulings fell in line with social beliefs that the wife's place was in the home and that wives were required be obedient to their husbands. Even as late as 1962, in *Joyner v. Joyner*, the court ruled that a husband had a right to use force in order to keep his wife in line. Notions that the man is the king of his castle pushed the justice system's response to this form of violence into the 1970s. Until then, problems of wife beating were believed to be few and far between. In most cases, the incidents were viewed as being provoked by the incorrigible wife or as committed by the mentally unstable husband. In these instances, police often dismissed calls for help as the man's right to discipline a nagging wife. If police did make an arrest or mandate a husband to court, then prosecutors and judges often dismissed these cases. When cases did make it through the entire judicial process, sentencing often involved mandated treatment for the husband and sometimes the wife. Jail or prison time was a rare event, as was probation (a sentence in which the offender is supervised in the community by a probation officer but does not serve time within a jail or prison).

Early identification of this form of abuse did not acknowledge the victim who was not married to her abuser. Terms such as *wife battering* and *abuse, family violence*, and *domestic violence* depicted a family environment in which the couple was married. It was not until the civil unrest of the 1970s that these definitions began to change. With the onset of the women's rights movement, domestic violence movement, and anti-rape movement, women began to influence social and legal change toward this problem.

The Scope of Domestic Violence

A sociological examination of domestic violence must begin with defining violence. Sociologists (and psychologists) have identified domestic violence to include physical violence, sexual violence, stalking, economic abuse, and psychological abuse. The distinction between violence and abuse has been debated. At what point does the violence become abusive? Physical violence includes any nonsexual person-on-person or object-on-person violence, whereas sexual violence is any unwanted sexual contact or threat of sexual contact. Researchers have found that 4.8 million females fall victim to physical or sexual domestic violence every year. Males represent 2.9 million physical domestic violence victims annually. Physical violence has always been the quintessential example of domestic violence. However, it was not until the 1970s that sexual violence was learned to be a common occurrence within relationships plagued by domestic violence. It was also in the 1970s that the concept of marital rape, in which the law criminalized the rape of a woman by her husband, was recognized by the courts.

Stalking involves two or more unwanted occasions of visual, audio, or physical proximity or communication toward one individual by a current or former intimate partner. Initially, the crime of stalking was thought to be committed by a stranger and usually only famous victims ever became the subject of news reports. However, later research found that 59 percent of women and 30 percent of men are stalked by intimate partners. Additionally, contrary to popular belief, half of all victims are stalked while still in a relationship with their stalkers. Economic abuse is much more difficult to study and involves limiting a victim's access to money, whether it is by depriving the victim of the right to work or of the right to keep what he or she earns. This form of abuse works to keep the victim trapped in the abusive relationship.

The psychological abuse experienced by victims within domestic violence has more often been examined within the field of psychology. Within this form of abuse, victims experience an array of emotional assaults that work to make the victim feel fearful, incompetent, blameworthy, isolated, and even mentally unstable. Many sociologists and psychologists have determined that since domestic violence involves so many debilitating forms of abuse, the most accurate explanation of domestic violence is power and control. It is argued that abusers feel a sense of entitlement that

U.S. Air Force personnel act out a role-playing scenario of a law enforcement confrontation with an angry spouse during a crisis intervention and domestic violence response training exercise in 2009 at Peterson Air Force Base family housing in Colorado Springs, Colorado. While there are 4.8 million female victims of physical or sexual domestic violence every year in the United States, researchers have found that there are also about 2.9 million male physical domestic violence victims as well.

justifies their need to assert their power over their victims by controlling the victim's body and mind. While this is currently the most widely accepted explanation of domestic violence, many theories have been developed over the decades.

The Etiology of Domestic Violence

Domestic violence was not identified as a social problem until the 1970s. *Family abuse* was the term for this violence in the 1960s. This was followed in the 1970s by terms such as *wife abuse* and *wife battering*, and in the 1980s by *domestic violence*. Common to all of these names, however, were their theoretical explanations.

Social constructions guide our theoretical explanations of and responses to domestic violence. To be sure, early ideas of domestic violence focused on the victims (usually women) as the primary cause of the violence. Since men had a legal responsibility for the actions of the women under their care, they also had a legal right to physically chastise them. As a result, any violence placed on the woman was deemed to be her fault. Only when a man took the violence too far (often a subjective ruling) was he identified as a criminal. Social scientists, also holding these constructs, developed their theoretical explanations of them. As a result, psychological explanations dominated most early examinations of domestic violence.

Early examinations into the causes of domestic violence took on a clinical analysis and attempted to create batterer typologies. Many of these typologies examined the mental condition of the victim, which was thought to push the batterer toward the violence. Other explanations examined the codependency of the offender on the victim. These typologies shared a common ground in placing much of the blame and control in the hands of the victim. However, many categories within these typologies identified the batterer as mentally unstable.

Later psychological examinations, however, focused on the harms of the abuse to the victims and identified conditions of trauma, including post-traumatic stress disorder, the cycle of violence, and battered woman syndrome. Studies on the psychological damage of domestic violence became so widely accepted that many courts today allow battered woman syndrome as a criminal defense in cases where victims kill their abusers.

Sociologists, however, have a different focus. They tend to reject the abuser or victim as mentally ill and instead examine the family/relationship dynamics of domestic violence or the structural conditions that lead to such widely found patterns within this crime. Early sociological focus was placed on the family and the roles that the members played (or failed to play). Most famous was Richard Gelles and his exchange/social control theory. Gelles argued in the 1980s that the role of the family was reproduction and socialization of its members into society. Members within the family unit understand the roles they play and operate on a reward/punishment system. If there are ample controls within the family, then violence is not an option as a punishment. As a result, if a member, for example the wife, does not fulfill her role within the family unit and there are not enough controls within the family to prevent violence, then the husband will engage in abuse.

At the same time, other sociologists examined the family or intimate relationship as a violent subgroup. Straus argued that most domestic violence situations involve "mutual combat," in which there is ongoing conflict and both partners engage in violence at various times during the relationship. Murray Straus developed the Conflict Tactics Scale (CTS) in order to measure this behavior and determined that women were just as violent as men. Further, this finding was adopted within police practices along with an increase in the arrest of women during domestic violence incidents in the 1980s and 1990s. The problem that was later identified was that, among other things, self-defense was identified as combative, that is, victims were identified as abusive. In reaction to this, feminist scholars brought forth their own set of theories.

The most widely accepted feminist theoretical explanation is the power and control model discussed above. This model has been utilized in many criminal justice laws and policies that mandate arrest or incarceration or within treatment programs that operate on the notion that the male must change his definition of the power structure within the relationship. Intersectionality is another feminist theory used to explain domestic violence. This theory emphasizes that in addition to the sexual politics and inequalities, we must examine additional marginalities of race, class, age, and sexual orientation. People may experience more than one minority status (e.g., poor, black women). This necessarily affects their lives in a society with interconnecting systems of power and oppression.

The common denominator within feminist theories is patriarchy as the center of women's oppression. However, other sociologists argue that male entitlement cannot explain same-sex intimate partner violence or female-on-male violence. As a result, sociologists focus on these inequalities minus the patriarchy variable. Structural inequalities based on racism and classism are often examined. Another theoretical focus is on a subculture of violence. Many of these studies examine poor urban environments as the nexus for the subculture of violence in which violent norms are transmitted. Recently, however, studies of domestic violence in rural areas have called into question subcultural violence explanations. Yet other sociologists have examined the intergenerational transmission of violence theory (or cycle of violence). This theory explains that domestic violence is the product of children learning violence as a result of observing or experiencing violence in their families.

The numerous explanations have forced the continued evolution of our understanding of domestic violence. As a result, we now accept that though females are far more likely to be victims of domestic violence, males are also victims that we have yet to examine. We have branched out explanations to cohabitating and even dating couples. We understand that dating violence is commonplace, and even commonplace among teens. Further, the newest term, *intimate partner violence*, which was officially used in 2000, now incorporates the need to acknowledge and study same-sex intimate partner violence.

Evolving Debates and Solutions

Evolving debates continue to examine whether arrest should be mandated in domestic violence cases. The debate itself reveals continued social beliefs that domestic violence may in fact be a private affair. Advocates continue to fight for equal protection for victims. As the emphasis remains on arrest, we have seen an increase in arrests of women in domestic violence cases. Many argue that women are just as violent as men, and so arrest is justified. However, there has been evidence contrary to this assumption for the past two decades. Furthermore, the increase in dual arrests since the implementation of mandatory arrest policies points to other factors.

Dual arrest refers to the arrest of both the victim and the offender. Many claim that the increased arrest of both parties may be a result of a backlash effect of the major social redefinitions of intimate partner violence. The redefinition is in fact a redefinition of the institution of the family and the place of women in society. Many claim that as society equalizes gender structures, backlash tends to occur in an effort to maintain the status quo.

Other redefinitions of domestic violence have also extended to what is an acceptable union. Historically, domestic violence was socially defined to be an act committed by a husband against his wife. As social change progressed, the term *domestic violence* was replaced in the social but not so much the legal context by the term *intimate partner violence*. This renaming was required as it incorporates violence against intimates who are not married or cohabitating or who may no longer be intimate. Dating violence was recognized as a social problem in the 1990s, especially among teenagers.

The term *intimate partner violence* also incorporates female-on-male violence and same-sex partner violence. The latter two unions have often been rejected as possibilities. First, women have often been viewed to be nonviolent while males are defined as aggressors and protectors but never as victims. Second, same-sex partners have often been denied any kind of legal protection.

Another focus of the courts has been on the defense of domestic violence victims who kill their abusers. Sociologists and psychologists have examined the causes and effects of domestic violence since the 1970s. One finding has been that many victims experienced increasing violence that results in social and mental instability. When women kill their abusers, it has been argued that they have experienced post-traumatic stress disorder (PTSD). This is also known as shell shock among soldiers. PTSD is the psychological distress that follows traumatic events and can result in destructive—both internal and external—actions. Researchers claimed that battered women who kill experience PTSD that can be identified as battered woman syndrome. *State v. Ciskie* (1988) and *State v. Baker* (1980) were the first cases to uphold the use of battered woman syndrome evidence via expert testimony.

The use of battered woman syndrome within the court is a big step forward in recognizing the enormity of domestic violence as a social problem. However, battered woman syndrome brings the victim full circle to the mentally unstable individual as was defined prior to the social movement of the 1970s. As society progresses in efforts to eliminate violence against women, changing social definitions bring changing legal responses. While the country has made progress toward equal protection under the law, many argue that we have taken two steps forward and one step back.

Venessa Garcia
Kean University

See Also: Courts; Domestic Violence, Contemporary; Domestic Violence, History of; Gender and Criminal Law; Insanity Defense; Violence Against Women Act of 1994.

Further Readings
Buzawa, Eve S. and Carl G. Buzawa. *Domestic Violence: The Criminal Justice Response*, 3rd ed. Thousand Oaks, CA: Sage, 2003.
Garcia, Venessa and Patrick McManimon. *Gendered Justice: Intimate Partner Violence and the Criminal Justice System*. Lanham, MD: Rowman & Littlefield, 2011.
Klein, Andrew R. *The Criminal Justice Response to Domestic Violence*. Belmont, CA: Thomson/Wadsworth, 2004.
Mills, C. Wright. *The Sociological Imagination*. New York: Oxford University Press, [1959] 1979.
Sherman, Lawrence W. and Richard A. Berk. "The Specific Deterrent Effects of Arrest for Domestic Assault." *American Sociological Review*, v.49/2 (1984).

Douglas, William O.

William O. Douglas (1898–1980) was one of the most famous justices of the U.S. Supreme Court who was known for his dissents and his liberal and libertarian perspectives. He was also the longest-sitting justice on the U.S. Supreme Court, serving for over 36 years.

Formative Years

Douglas was born in Minnesota on October 16, 1898. His father was a minister. His family resided in several different places before settling in Washington. Douglas's family was not wealthy, and he had to work at odd jobs. He won a scholarship that allowed him to attend college. While working picking cherries among the very poor, he was inspired to be a lawyer. During his work in the field, Douglas observed the harsh life of the Chicanos, migrant laborers, and those who fought to help them, such as the Industrial Workers of the World (IWWs), who were shot at by the police. Douglas graduated with a bachelor's degree in English and taught for a few years. He then attended Columbia Law School, graduating in 1925, and started working for a prestigious New York law firm. He later started teaching at Columbia Law School. He quit Columbia Law School in protest over an appointment by the university president and started teaching at Yale Law School.

While teaching at Yale Law School, he specialized in business law. At Yale, Douglas developed his pragmatic approach to the practice of law, placing him in the legal realism school of legal philosophy. He taught his law school courses from a practical perspective that won him much praise. He carried this approach with him through his life and onto the U.S. Supreme Court. In 1934, Douglas was asked to prepare a report on the Securities and Exchange Commission. His eight-volume work was highly praised for his revelations of deceit, manipulations, and illegal conduct. In 1936, Douglas was appointed as a commissioner of the Securities and Exchange Commission. As a commissioner, Douglas continued his attacks on corruption and started hearings to make the stock exchange a public institution. Douglas was appointed chairman of the Securities and Exchange Commission in 1937.

William O. Douglas on the day he was nominated to the Supreme Court by President Franklin D. Roosevelt in March 1939. He was 40 years old and was the chairman of the Securities and Exchange Commission at the time.

Appointment to the Court

In 1939, the famous Justice Louis Brandeis resigned from the U.S. Supreme Court. Douglas's friend, President Franklin D. Roosevelt, appointed Douglas to succeed him. Douglas's opinions on the bench gained him lasting fame. In his first major opinion, *Skinner v. Oklahoma*, Douglas displayed his support for individual rights over government power that would become his trademark. Douglas wrote that the government had no right to force sterilization onto people who had been convicted of three felonies for "moral turpitude." He was a staunch supporter of the First Amendment. He wrote the court's opinion in the decision of *Terminielllo v. Chicago* (1949), which reversed the criminal conviction for breaching the peace of a Catholic priest who had made anti-Semitic remarks.

In the decision of *Dennis v. United States* (1952), Douglas began to show his deep suspicion of government when he dissented on First

Amendment grounds from the affirmation of the criminal conviction of a Communist Party member. Douglas held the opinion that judges should not be neutral and that their primary purpose was to protect the individual person from the government. This principle was showcased in the famous opinion in *Griswold v. Connecticut* (1965), when Douglas wrote the court's opinion finding a constitutional right to privacy. As a member of the Warren Court through the 1950s and the 1960s, Douglas was a principal supporter of liberal changes brought to the nation by Chief Justice Earl Warren. For Douglas, the concept of equal protection meant that all people are equal, regardless of wealth, race, office, status, nationality, religion, age, or sex.

Environmentalism and Individualism

Douglas was widely known and respected for his love for and protection of the environment. He engaged in numerous activities to protect the environment in addition to legal decisions protecting it. He was a member of the Board of Directors of the Sierra Club. He was one of the initial supporters of the now-famous, and universally recognized as prophetic, environmental book *Silent Spring* by Rachel Carson. However, Douglas earned lasting fame (and ridicule in the minds of some people) that trees have standing to sue and protect themselves. In his famous dissent in the decision of *Sierra Club v. Morton* (1972), Douglas argued that inanimate objects should have standing to protect themselves on the basis that other inanimate objects, such as ships and corporations, have been granted such legal standing.

Douglas was a rugged individualist who frequently hiked and camped in wildernesses across the world. He had four wives. He was frequently criticized for his lifestyle and his judicial opinions. Douglas wrote numerous dissenting opinions and did not mind being the lone dissenter. In fact, Justice Potter Stewart is credited with once saying "Bill Douglas seems positively embarrassed if anyone agrees with him." Douglas, like Chief Justice Earl Warren, repeatedly incurred the ire of conservative politicians. He was frequently criticized for his opinions. Several attempts were made to impeach him, one on a stay of execution in the Rosenberg espionage case and another on his involvement with a private foundation and his liberal opinions, but they were unsuccessful.

In 1975, Douglas retired from the U.S. Supreme Court and was replaced by Justice John Paul Stevens. William O. Douglas, like Chief Justice Earl Warren, was a groundbreaking judge who stepped forward to do justice when so many others lacked such courage. He was not widely respected as a legal scholar or author, but he was unmatched in his recognition of individual rights and human dignity and for being willing to take the side of justice against the government.

Wm. C. Plouffe, Jr.
Independent Scholar

See Also: *Dennis v. United States*; Equality, Concept of; *Griswold v. Connecticut*; Warren, Earl.

Further Readings
Douglas, William O. *The Court Years, 1939 to 1975: The Autobiography of William O. Douglas*. New York: Random House, 1980.
Douglas, William O. *Go East, Young Man: The Early Years: The Autobiography of William O. Douglas*. New York: Random House, 1974.
Douglas, William O. *Points of Rebellion*. New York: Random House, 1970.
Murphy, Bruce Allen. *Wild Bill: The Legend and Life of William O. Douglas*. New York: Random House, 2003.
Schwartz, Bernard, ed. *The Warren Court*. New York: Oxford University Press, 1996.

Dred Scott v. Sandford

Dred Scott v. Sandford was a landmark U.S. Supreme Court case holding that Congress did not have the power to create citizenship for slaves, that freed slaves were not citizens as contemplated by the U.S. or Missouri constitutions, that the Missouri Compromise was unconstitutional, and that the right of property in slaves was affirmed in the U.S. Constitution. One of many catalysts for the Civil War, the court's decision, authored by Chief Justice Roger B. Taney, a slave-owning Marylander, denied people of African descent the right to citizenship and constitutional protection. The case is perhaps the most important Supreme Court decision on the issue of slavery.

Background

John Emerson purchased Dred Scott, a slave, around 1830. Emerson was an army surgeon who transferred Scott to Illinois, a free state, and then to the Wisconsin Territory, where Scott married Harriet Robinson, another slave. The army transferred Emerson to St. Louis, Missouri, and Emerson left the Scotts in the service of clients in the Wisconsin Territory. Because slavery was forbidden in the Wisconsin Territory, Emerson technically violated the law when he hired out the Scotts in that region.

Emerson moved to Louisiana, where he met and married Irene Sanford; he then summoned the Scotts, who boated down the Mississippi River to reunite with their master and his wife. John Emerson returned to St. Louis in 1838, bringing the Scotts with him. He died in 1843. Irene Emerson's brother, John F. A. Sanford, a former Missourian residing in New York, carried out the terms of John Emerson's will, including the distribution of Emerson's property. The Scotts were among that property.

The case began in 1846 in Missouri state trial court, where Scott sued to purchase his and his family's freedom on the grounds that Scott became a free man during his travels in the Wisconsin Territory. Scott sought freedom under the "once free, always free" principle that Missouri courts previously and regularly had recognized. This principle maintained that slaves taken into free territory would become and remain free, even if they later returned to slave states. Despite this long-standing principle in Missouri, the judge dismissed Scott's suit on a technicality.

Scott was granted a new trial in 1847. His claim made its way to the Missouri Supreme Court, which, in 1848, held that Scott was a slave and therefore could not prevail in the matter. The Scotts then sued John F. A. Sanford in 1853, filing in federal court based on diversity jurisdiction, which was established because the Scotts resided in Missouri while Sanford resided in New York. The Scotts couched their claim in terms of trespass *vi et armis*, alleging that Sanford assaulted Scott and his family. Historians have debated the truth of this allegation.

A wood engraving of Dred Scott that appeared in Century Magazine *in 1887. Scott sought freedom under the principle that maintained that slaves taken into free territory would become and remain free, even if they later returned to slave states.*

A Pivotal Supreme Court Decision

In 1854, the First Circuit Court of Missouri ruled against the Scotts, who appealed to the U.S. Supreme Court. Montgomery Blair, who would later serve in the cabinet of Abraham Lincoln, was one of Scott's lawyers at the Supreme Court level. The case was argued before the court on February 11–14 and December 15–18, 1856. In a notorious misspelling, the U.S. Supreme Court referred to "Sandford" rather than "Sanford" in the case name.

Writing for the majority, Chief Justice Taney dismissed the Scotts' claim for lack of jurisdiction, reasoning that Scott was a slave of African descent and therefore was neither a citizen of Missouri nor of the United States within the meaning of Article III of the Constitution. Federal courts therefore could not hear the Scotts' claim. Accordingly, Taney excluded slaves or any individuals of African descent from being citizens of the United States or citizens of the several states, establishing that such individuals fell outside the protection of the Constitution. Taney also held that Congress's power to declare certain states free or slave extended only to territories belonging to the United States in 1787. The constructive effect of this holding was that the Missouri Compromise—Congress's attempt to regulate the admission of new slave states—was unconstitutional.

Justice Taney was joined by six justices in the majority opinion: Justice James M. Wayne, Justice John Catron, Justice Peter V. Daniel, Justice Samuel Nelson, Justice Robert C. Grier, and Justice John A. Campbell. Only two justices dissented: Justice Benjamin R. Curtis and Justice John McLean, both northerners. Long after the decision, historians discovered that President James Buchanan had corresponded with Justices John Catron and Robert Grier about the case while the matter was still pending. Buchanan's correspondence could have influenced Justice Grier to join the southern majority.

The court's decision further divided a country that was already split over the matter of slavery. It led to speculation about whether newly admitted states or territories would become slave or free areas. The case remains one of the most cited and criticized matters in Supreme Court history.

Allen Mendenhall
Auburn University

See Also: Fugitive Slave Act of 1850; Racism; Slavery; Slavery, Law of; Supreme Court, U.S.

Further Readings
Ehrlich, Walter. *They Have No Rights: Dred Scott's Struggle for Freedom*. Westport, CT: Greenwood Press, 1979.
Ewing, Elbert William Robinson. *Legal and Historical Status of the Dred Scott Decision*. Washington, DC: Cobden Publishing, 1909.
Fehrenbacher, Don E. *The Dred Scott Case*. New York: Oxford University Press, 1978.
Graber, Mark A. *Dred Scott and the Problem of Constitutional Evil*. Cambridge: Cambridge University Press, 2006.
Hopkins, Vincent C. *Dred Scott's Case*. New York: Fordham University Press, 1951.
Konig, David Thomas, Paul Finkelman, and Christopher Alan Bracey, eds. *The Dred Scott Case: Historical and Contemporary Perspectives on Race and Law*. Athens: Ohio University Press, 2010.
Kutler, Stanley I. *The Dred Scott Decision: Law or Politics?* Boston: Houghton Mifflin, 1967.

Drinking and Crime

The existence of a relationship between alcohol consumption (drinking) and criminal behavior has been acknowledged for decades by the public at large and by policy makers and researchers in particular. The precise nature of this relationship, however, has not been identified. As many researchers point out, the relationship between alcohol consumption and crime can only be fully understood when placed in social, cultural, and historical contexts.

Because drinking and crime are two complex social phenomena, one must look at the fluctuations in both behaviors across time and observe the social responses that accompanied these changes, while considering that the interaction of both behaviors within the social nexus is influenced by a multitude of factors. The complexity of this relationship is apparent in the piecemeal approach undertaken by scholarly literature in this field and reflected in the variety of methodologies employed. Some have examined the intersection of alcohol and crime in offenses that are alcohol specific, such as drunk and disorderly conduct, drunk driving, and underage drinking, while others have looked at a continuum of offenses that involve alcohol to a greater or lesser degree (i.e., non-alcohol-specific offenses). This latter category includes studies at the aggregate level, which contrast variations in crime rates to variations in rates of alcohol availability and alcohol consumption in various populations, and individual-level studies, which focus on criminal events in which either the perpetrator or the victim is intoxicated. Other research perspectives include attempts at explaining the relationship between alcoholism and criminality, and the relationship between alcohol consumption and aggressive behavior. Understanding the drinking-crime relationship is of great interest to the criminal justice community, for it allows for the identification and implementation of specific intervention and prevention efforts. While decades of research on this issue confirm that alcohol correlates to criminal behavior, the issue of whether drinking causes crime is still pending.

Historical Survey

Historical research shows that, up until the mid-19th century, alcohol consumption was a social fact of life in America, although drunkenness was never well accepted. Beer and hard cider were common beverages in colonial America, and as distilled spirits became widely available in the 1700s, drinking patterns shifted to more potent beverages. Through the 17th and 18th centuries, people drank alcohol regularly, and in large quantities. Records indicate that the nation's alcohol consumption peaked around 1830. By contemporary standards, alcohol consumption was quite high in this period, with an annual average per capita alcohol consumption at about five drinks a day, which is nearly four times what it is today.

Drinking declined in the mid-1800s, a likely result of the temperance movement—a social reform to reduce alcohol consumption—in particular, that of distilled spirits. Adherents to the temperance movement viewed alcohol as the cause of serious personal and social problems. Among the early leaders of this movement was physician and signer of the Declaration of Independence Benjamin Rush. In his 1784 pamphlet "An Inquiry Into the Effects of Ardent Spirits on the Human Mind and Body," Rush decried the use of hard liquor, warning of the mental (e.g., madness, moral degeneration), physical (e.g., jaundice, epilepsy), and social (e.g., poverty and crime) dangers of excessive alcohol consumption. Rush is credited as the first to introduce the concept of alcoholism and the view of alcohol addiction as a disease. While he did not condemn drinking per se, Rush advocated abstinence from alcohol for those with a drinking problem.

While social drinking remained prevalent at the dawn of the 19th century, the seeds of the temperance movement were planted, and Rush's ideas infused into political and religious groups that saw alcohol as a social evil, contributing to poverty, social disorganization, civil disobedience, and other public order crimes and concerns. Supported by the upper classes, ministers, and business elites, the temperance movement expanded rapidly in the early 1830s. For instance, the American Society for the Promotion of Temperance (later renamed the American Temperance Union) boasted within only a couple of years after its establishment hundreds of chapters across the nation and hundreds of thousands of members who had renounced the consumption of distilled beverages. The Temperance "crusade" was on the march. By the 1850s, legislation forbidding the sale of distilled spirits had been introduced in 12 of the 30 U.S. states, and in two Canadian provinces. At the same time, the trend in annual per capita alcohol consumption was drastically declining.

The temperance movement reached its peak during the Progressive Era (late 1800s to early 1900s). In 1874, both the National Prohibition Party and the Woman's Christian Temperance Union (WCTU) were formed and pushed a morally conservative agenda that shaped public perception of drinking and social perceptions of the effects of drinking on behavior. Alcohol became vilified and was viewed as a threat to both the public and political orders. The WCTU soon became a political player and paved the way for national prohibition through protest marches, organized letter-writing campaigns, and fundraising. Soon, the belief that alcohol played a causal role in the commission of crimes became widespread. Between 1907 and 1919, 34 states enacted legislation enforcing statewide prohibition. The temperance view was officially imposed on America by the National Prohibition Act (Volstead Act of 1919), which set up the enforcement procedures of the Eighteenth Amendment to the U.S. Constitution prohibiting the manufacture, sale, transportation, or importation of intoxicating liquors.

Prohibition took effect on January 16, 1920, and did show some positive outcomes in its early years, with a significant reduction in alcohol-related health problems and alcohol-related crimes. But Prohibition did not result in an alcohol-free society. Clandestine alcohol production provided the country with liquor, and people continued to purchase and consume alcohol illegally. Enforcement of Prohibition proved to be an issue, and criminal activity—organized crime, and violent crime in particular—associated with illegal drinking expanded to unprecedented proportions. The Twenty-First Amendment repealing the Volstead Act was signed in 1933, marking the end of the "Noble Experiment" and returning regulatory control over alcohol to the states. The effects of Prohibition on alcohol consumption persisted long after its repeal, and per capita consumption rates did not return to pre-Prohibition rates until the early 1940s.

Modern scientific interests in the explanation of the drinking-crime relationship can be traced to the late 1800s in the works of Italian criminologist Cesare Lombroso. Lombroso believed that alcohol was a contributing factor to criminality, reporting that increases in crime and alcohol consumption fluctuated at comparable rates.

American social science literature remained silent on this issue until the middle of the 20th century. In 1950, Robert Seliger expressed concerns that alcohol abuse and crime posed a threat to the social health of the nation, and pointed to a correlation between alcoholism and aggressive and violent criminal behavior, as evidenced by official police and prison statistics. Seliger warned of an occurrence of such acts at increasing rates. The alcohol-crime link was further supported in the scientific community by a seminal study of criminal homicides by Marvin Wolfgang, who pointed to the possible link between alcohol and violent crimes based on the results of his research, where homicides were frequently associated with the consumption of alcohol by one of the protagonists. By the 1970s, several studies were undertaken to better understand the relationship

This illustration shows a group of women staging a protest in a barroom against the sale of alcoholic beverages in 1874, the year of the founding of both the National Prohibition Party and the Woman's Christian Temperance Union (WCTU). Through protests such as these, letter-writing campaigns, marches, and fund-raising, the WCTU helped pave the way for national prohibition. These groups also shaped public perception of drinking as a threat to social order.

between alcohol consumption and various criminal behaviors in an attempt to explain the potential causality of this relationship. The debate then fundamentally shifted from the view of alcohol as a public order crime to alcohol as a factor contributing to criminal behavior.

Alcohol-Specific Crimes

There are crimes in which the consumption of alcohol itself is the primary object of the offense, such as public intoxication, drunk driving, and underage drinking, by contrast to crimes in which alcohol plays a secondary or indirect role.

Public drunkenness is a public order crime covered by various legal definitions, depending on the jurisdiction, such as disorderly conduct, breach of peace, drunk in a public place, and inability to care for one's own personal safety. While extending to all age categories, drunkenness as a crime tends to be associated primarily with juveniles and college students, particularly as it relates to binge drinking. Indeed, underage drinking is considered one of the biggest public health concerns of our times. Data from the 2008 National Survey of Drug Use and Health indicates that 10.1 million youth aged 12–20 reported having consumed alcohol in the 30 days preceding the survey, which corresponds to 26 percent of youths in this age group. The National Institute on Alcohol Abuse and Alcoholism reports that about 5,000 youth under age 21 die each year from incidents involving underage drinking, such as vehicle crashes, homicides, suicide, and other incidents.

Impaired driving is also a national concern, particularly as many drunk-driving fatalities involve young drivers. Currently, 44 of the 50 U.S. states prohibit possessing and/or consuming an open container of alcohol (including beer, wine, and distilled spirits) in public. Open container laws also extend to the passenger compartments of noncommercial motor vehicles and were designed to reduce impaired driving by limiting access to alcoholic beverages inside a motor vehicle. Additionally, many states have adopted zero-tolerance laws for underage impaired driving in recent years. Official statistics attest to the national effort being made to fight drunk driving. According to the National Highway Traffic Safety Administration, the rate of alcohol-impaired driving fatalities decreased 38 percent nationwide over the past two decades (from 6.3 per 100,000 in 1991 to 3.9 per 100,000 in 2008). The reduction was even more pronounced for underage drivers, with a 55 percent decrease in drunk-driving fatalities (from 3.8 to 1.7 per 100,000 between 1991 and 2008). Despite all efforts being made, alcohol-impaired driving still accounts for 32 percent of all traffic fatalities.

Non-Alcohol-Specific Crimes

Alcohol consumption is also associated with a wide array of offenses in a less direct fashion. Interestingly, this perspective has received the most attention in academic literature. Various methodologies have been employed in this endeavor, ranging from aggregate-level studies to individual-level approaches.

Studies of population constitute the primary approach to explore the alcohol-crime link at the aggregate level and come from diverse perspectives, including economics, criminal justice, and public health. Such studies correlate trends in alcohol consumption of particular populations with trends in crime rates, and trends in alcohol availability with rates of crime across populations. The underlying interest of such studies resides in the theory that alcohol regulation can become a crime control strategy, since access to alcohol can be manipulated by public policy.

There seems to be a general consensus in literature regarding a positive correlation between per capita alcohol consumption and crime rates, particularly for violent and property crimes. Regarding the relationship between crime and alcohol availability, literature reports decreases in rates of violence (e.g., child abuse, spousal abuse, physical assault, and trouble with the police) with increases in state alcohol taxes. A major limitation of population studies, however, concerns the probable spuriousness of the alcohol-crime relationship. Indeed, while the two measures correlate at the aggregate level, researchers suggest that there may be other factors explaining this association at the individual level.

Studies of criminal events constitute another approach to studying the drinking-crime relationship, specifically examining whether individuals have been consuming alcohol prior to perpetrating subsequent criminal acts or prior to being victimized. Such studies typically use official statistics and police reports, as well as victimization surveys and studies of correctional populations. They focus on a variety of crimes, most of which represent interpersonal violence offenses (e.g., homicide, assault, rape, family violence). The Bureau of Justice Statistics reports, for instance, that about 3 million violent crimes occur each year in which victims perceived the offender as intoxicated at the time of the offense. In cases of homicide, studies have consistently reported frequent intoxication of both perpetrator and victim. In cases of intimate partner violence (e.g., spousal abuse), studies reveal that a great majority of victims reported that alcohol had been a factor.

Overall, among the studies that have addressed the issue of alcohol intoxication in violent crimes, results show that the offender was intoxicated at the time of offense in the majority of the situations. A more in-depth review of the literature, however, reveals a wider range of results, which is likely to be related to the wide range of methodologies used in the studies. The validity of results of criminal event studies is of concern for several other reasons. First, some of those studies often ask whether the victim or the arresting officer perceived the offender as intoxicated. As such, the reliability of the measure may be questionable. Second, there may be a self-selection process in which intoxicated offenders are more likely to be arrested by the police than nonintoxicated offenders. In a similar fashion, intoxicated individuals constitute more suitable targets of interpersonal violence. Finally, report of the eventual intoxication of the offender by either the arresting officer or the victim may depend on the subsequent criminal proceeding of the case.

Alcoholism and Criminality

Another approach at the individual level consists of analyzing the incidence of drinking problems among criminal populations. More specifically, this entails looking at the relationship between alcohol and criminal careers. This issue is usually examined based on interviews and self-reports of various populations of interest, from the general population to samples of arrestees, incarcerated offenders, and probationers.

Results of research on chronic drinking indicate that individuals who drink more frequently are more likely to engage in violence. By contrast to matching samples of the general population, violent offenders seem more likely to be heavy drinkers. This trend can be found in groups of various offenders and is not necessarily limited to violent offenders. Overall, it appears that heavy drinking is intrinsic to the criminal lifestyle. Professional criminals, however, tend to avoid drinking before committing a crime, and some studies have reported that not all violent offenders drink in excess. Indeed, some studies have reported a low prevalence of alcoholism among murderers. Evidently, the diversity of criminal activities is reflected by a diversity in drinking patterns. For instance, while alcohol is used by some burglars as "Dutch courage" prior to committing a crime, other groups of criminals tend to ostracize those who drink on the job because they constitute a potential threat and may not be able to carry out their task carefully.

Several limitations are associated with research on alcoholism and crime. First, the very definition of alcoholism is a potential methodological hindrance when comparing different samples. Also, depending on the type of study, the instruments used to measure drinking habits and classify them may vary heavily. Second, different samples may produce varying results simply because of the nature of the population under study. Indeed, it has been reported that offenders may either exaggerate or minimize their drinking habits, depending on the type of crime committed, their history of alcohol abuse, and the subsequent disposition of the case. Third, correctional research has long shown that prison populations are not representative at all of the general population. Another bias resides in that studies of inmates have a tendency to overestimate the frequency of alcoholics in the criminal population. The necessity of having a control group for any meaningful comparison then becomes evident.

Drinking and Aggressive Behavior

There is a common belief that alcohol consumption is related to aggressive behavior. Early experimental research on the relationship between alcohol and aggression began in the early 1970s, and produced mixed results: Some studies suggested a causal role played by alcohol in aggression, while others reported an absence of relationship between the two variables. Later studies then considered additional factors that might have an effect on the relationship, such as the type of beverage and the dose level, as well as situational elements, including, among others, alcohol expectancies, the perception of a threat, and the intervention of a third party, as well as individual elements. Such studies typically give subjects specific doses of alcohol in various situations in a controlled environment, while monitoring subjects' aggressive behavior.

An overview of empirical research in this area indicates that, in general, lower doses of alcohol typically inhibit aggressive behavior, while higher doses lead to greater interpersonal aggressive behavior among subjects. Literature also reports heightened levels of aggressive behavior among alcohol-intoxicated individuals when placed in a threatening environment. Some psychological experiments looked at the possible placebo effect of alcohol by comparing behavioral responses of two groups of subjects who believed that they had consumed alcoholic drinks, while in reality only one group was given alcoholic drinks. Findings revealed increased aggression among both groups when placed in various situations, regardless of the actual consumption of alcohol by the subject. Such experiments led to further research focusing

A U.S. Department of Transportation poster touting increased enforcement of drunk driving laws in 1985. These increases, along with public awareness campaigns, may have helped decrease drunken driving rates. The rate of alcohol-impaired driving fatalities decreased from 6.3 per 100,000 in 1991 to 3.9 per 100,000 in 2008, a reduction of 38 percent. However, alcohol-impaired driving still accounts for 32 percent of all traffic fatalities in the United States.

on individual responses to alcohol and in particular, looking at possible pathological intoxication, which is characterized by excessive aggressive behavior in intoxicated subjects.

The overall conclusion that can be drawn from research on drinking and aggressive behavior is that there is no simple direct relationship between alcohol and aggression. Situational factors appear to play a significant role in alcohol-related aggression, as well as the subjects' expectations regarding both the consumption of alcohol and the outcome of a situation. Individual psychological factors seem to be also at play.

A Causal Relationship?
While it seems agreeable that an association exists between alcohol consumption and criminal behavior, the question that remains is whether this relationship is a causal one. In other words: Does drinking cause crime? While the presence or absence of a causal link both are valid assumptions, scholars tend to agree that conceptualizing the alcohol-crime relationship as causal is overly simplistic.

Indeed, considering a strictly causal relationship seems only appropriate for alcohol-specific offenses (e.g., public drunkenness, drunk driving), which are defined by law as when alcohol is used alongside an otherwise lawful behavior. A causal link can also be a valid explanation in other offenses that are either induced by alcohol (e.g., domestic violence) or inspired by alcohol (e.g., liquor store robbery). For most nonalcohol-specific offenses, however, alcohol consumption is indirectly associated with offending. As a matter of fact, researchers are very careful with the terminology they use to qualify the drinking–crime relationship, perhaps for the very reason that causation per se is rarely asserted in the social sciences. Rather, researchers usually point to alcohol as a determinant, correlate, or contributing factor to criminal behavior. In sum, alcohol consumption has a variable effect on criminal behavior. In such cases, several explanations have been advanced, including common-cause, interactive, conditional, conjunctive, and spurious relationships.

Common-cause explanations posit that alcohol consumption and crime are behaviors that result from common individual or circumstantial factors. Interactive, conditional, and conjunctive explanations all consider environmental factors that may affect the alcohol-crime relationship. Taking the example of a criminal encounter, the conditional effect of alcohol on violence can be understood as the likelihood of the argument ending violently being increased by the consumption of alcohol by one or both protagonists.

An interactive effect explanation would suggest that the probability of violence occurring is greater than the sum of the probabilities of either alcohol or argument occurring. Considering the relationship between criminality and alcoholism, one can ask whether criminal behavior is a condition of alcoholism itself or whether alcoholism increased the chances of criminal behavior because of the drinking. These questions still puzzle social scientists.

The spuriousness model, also referred to in literature as the coexistence model, assumes that drinking and crime are distinct activities that bear no relationship with each other, aside from the purely statistical association. An example of this spurious relationship can be found in surveys of correctional populations, which found disproportionate numbers of criminal offenders with drinking problems. A plausible explanation is that alcoholics are more likely to be arrested and incarcerated and not that they commit more crimes than nonalcoholics.

Conclusion
In conclusion, the relationship between drinking and crime is a complex one. A review of the literature by and large confirms its multifaceted aspect. Understanding this relationship requires an understanding of alcohol consumption and criminal behavior, which are in and of themselves complex social phenomena. Despite the extent of existing literature on this topic, much has still to be done, perhaps because of the lack of scientific rigor in much research. Also, many competing frameworks have been proposed, each uncovering one facet of the alcohol-crime relationship. Recent scholarship calls for a refocus on the issue, considering different types of offenses, types of individuals, as well as the conditions under which alcohol consumption was circumstantial to the commission of the offense. From a policy standpoint, however, the issue of causality is not so problematic. Indeed, scholars and policy makers

agree that what matters most is that an alcohol policy be effective in reducing crime, regardless of the causal mechanism.

Pierre M. Rivolta
Sam Houston State University

See Also: Bureau of Alcohol, Tobacco, Firearms and Explosives; Drug Abuse and Addiction, History of; Drug Abuse and Addiction, Sociology of; Prohibition.

Further Readings
Collins, James J., Jr. *Drinking and Crime: Perspectives on the Relationships Between Alcohol Consumption and Criminal Behavior.* New York: Guilford Press, 1981.
Dingwall, Gavin. *Alcohol and Crime.* Portland, OR: Willan Publishing, 2006.
Greenfeld, Lawrence A. *Alcohol and Crime: An Analysis of National Data on the Prevalence of Alcohol Involvement in Crime.* Washington, DC: Bureau of Justice Statistics, 1998.
Hore, Brian D. "Alcohol and Crime." *Alcohol and Alcoholism,* v.23/6 (1988).
Leigh, B. C. and R. Room. "Alcohol and Crime: Behavioral Aspects." In *Encyclopedia of Crime and Justice,* S. Kadish. New York: Free Press, 1983.
Lender, Mark E. and James K. Martin. *Drinking in America: A History.* New York: Free Press, 1987.
Pernanen, Kai. *Alcoholism in Human Violence.* New York: Guilford Press, 1991.
Rorabaugh, William J. *The Alcoholic Republic: An American Tradition.* New York: Oxford University Press, 1979.
Seliger, Robert V. "Alcohol and Crime." *Journal of Criminal Law and Criminology,* v.41/1 (1951).

Drug Abuse and Addiction, Contemporary

Drug abuse and addiction refer to an individual's continued use of a mind-altering substance, often illegal, despite negative consequences or an inability to stop using. While, clinically, the terms refer to varying degrees of severity, in the context of the criminal justice system, there is often no real distinction between abuse and addiction. The inclusion of the word *drug* in that same context generally implies either an illicit substance (such as marijuana, cocaine, or heroin) or the use of a prescription drug in a nonmedical way (such as OxyContin). While it is not a crime to be a drug addict, it is a crime to use, possess, manufacture, or distribute drugs.

Drug Use Statistics
Drug use declined in the 2000s, among both adults and adolescents, although arrests and convictions for drug-related crimes rose. In 2007, the Federal Bureau of Investigation's Uniform Crime Reports estimated that there were more than 1.8 million arrests for drug abuse violations in the United States, an increase of about 300,000 from 2000. More than 80 percent of these arrests were for drug possession, rather than drug sales. While the overall number of drug-related arrests increased during the 2000s, different drugs revealed different arrest patterns. The number of arrests for marijuana offenses increased by about 20 percent from 2000 to 2007, while the number of arrests for heroin and cocaine offenses increased by only about 2 percent over the same time period. Arrests related to synthetic drugs increased by almost 70 percent, although these arrests only accounted for about 5 percent of all drug-related arrests in 2007. Marijuana crimes accounted for almost half of all arrests in 2007.

Because of the continued increase in drug offenses, the 2000s also saw many states and counties change the way they processed drug-abusing offenders, with an increase in programs utilizing drug treatment. The most ambitious of these initiatives was the passage of Proposition 36 in California in 2000, which changed state law so that first- and second-time nonviolent, simple drug possession offenders would be sent to drug treatment instead of prison. At the close of the 2000s, there was also a considerable shift in federal drug policy; the Obama administration has taken a more public health approach to dealing with drug abuse and addiction in the United States than its immediate predecessor.

The most current survey of American adults, conducted in 2005, showed that overall rates of illicit drug use had not changed significantly during the first half of the decade. Marijuana was the most widely used illicit drug, a trend that has not changed since national surveys of drug use began in the 1970s. The same survey revealed that an estimated 6.9 million individuals (about 2.8 percent of the population age 12 and older) could be clinically diagnosed with illicit drug abuse or dependence, based on criteria in the *Diagnostic and Statistical Manual of Mental Disorders (DSM-IV)*. This was essentially the same number as the three previous years. The drugs with the highest levels of abuse and dependence were marijuana, cocaine, and pain relievers. Among high school students, overall drug use declined during the 2000s, although daily marijuana use remained constant (about 6 percent of the high school student population). Declines in past month illicit drug use among students were sharper from 2000 to 2005, and increased slightly between 2005 and 2010.

Sentencing Trends and Drug Treatment
During the 2000s, state and federal policies revealed a trend toward relaxing some of the most punitive policies that had been enacted since the 1980s, while integrating more substance abuse treatment into criminal case processing. For instance, the restructuring of New York State's Rockefeller Drug Laws, enacted in 1973, led to reducing the mandatory minimum sentence from 15 to 8 years for possession of four ounces of narcotics. The notorious 100:1 sentencing disparity in crack and cocaine possession sentences was also decreased at the federal level to the new ratio of 18:1. The restructuring of these and other laws was largely a response to the overcrowding of prisons and the public's sense that many of those incarcerated were nonviolent offenders in need of drug treatment.

As a result, there has been an immense increase in programs like drug courts, which incorporate drug treatment into criminal case processing. Because of the criminal justice system's expanded role in sending offenders to treatment (sometimes involuntarily), the criminal justice system has become the largest referral category for those currently in drug treatment. Prior to 2004, self-referrals made up the largest proportion of those in drug treatment.

In the near future, it appears that initiatives that incorporate drug treatment into criminal case processing will expand further and that federal drug policy will reflect a more public health approach to dealing with drug addiction. For instance, the Obama administration lifted the ban on federal funding for needle exchange programs. These programs, while overwhelmingly effective at reducing the transmission of human immunodeficiency virus (HIV) and other diseases, have been controversial because opponents argue that they encourage illicit drug use.

Changes are also on the horizon for how drug abuse and addiction are clinically conceptualized. The American Psychiatric Association's *DSM-IV*, published in 1994, currently refers to substance abuse and substance dependence as two separate ailments. The next revision, *DSM-5*, to be published in May 2013, combines substance dependence and substance abuse as one ailment and redefines it as "substance use disorder." The editors claim that the existing "dependence" label has been problematic and has resulted in many individuals being labeled "addicts" who have normal tolerance and withdrawal levels. The new edition will also include "Cannabis Withdrawal" as a diagnosable condition; the previous DSM editions did not include cannabis as a substance from which one could suffer withdrawal symptoms.

Jennifer Murphy
Michael Mazotti
Euijeung Kim
California State University, Sacramento

See Also: 1941 to 1960 Primary Documents; 1961 to 1980 Primary Documents; Crime Prevention; Drug Abuse and Addiction, History of; Drug Abuse and Addiction, Sociology of; Drug Enforcement Administration; Narcotics Laws; Obama, Barack (Administration of); Sentencing; Three Strikes Law.

Further Readings
American Psychiatric Association DSM-5 Development. "Substance-Related Disorders." http://www.dsm5.org/ProposedRevisions/Pages/Substance-RelatedDisorders.aspx (Accessed February 2010).
Bureau of Justice Statistics. "Drugs and Crime Facts." http://bjs.ojp.usdoj.gov/content/dcf/enforce.cfm#drugtype (Accessed February 2010).

Cohen, Peter J. *Drugs, Addiction, and the Law: Policy, Politics, and Public Health.* Durham, NC: Carolina Academic Press, 2004.

Monitoring the Future. "Marijuana Use Is Rising; Ecstasy Use Is Beginning to Rise; and Alcohol Use Is Declining Among U.S. Teens." http://www.monitoringthefuture.org/pressreleases/10drugpr.pdf (Accessed February 2010).

National Institute on Drug Abuse. "NIDA InfoFact: High School and Youth Trends." http://www.drugabuse.gov/infofacts/HSYouthtrends.html (Accessed February 2010).

Drug Abuse and Addiction, History of

Whereas many drugs' psychoactive qualities have been known for centuries, indeed for millennia, insofar as Western pharmacology and society are concerned, their use really began around 1800. The problematic use of these drugs began to peak in the late 1800s. Alcohol, of course, was noted and acknowledged as challenging, at least for some people, in ancient times, but in the Americas, especially in the British North American colonies, it was used prodigiously. Tradesmen and farmers drank beer at breakfast, at lunch, and during the day. Colonial leaders drank gallons of hard liquor and "punch" at political and social gatherings. Indeed, being a teetotaler was a deviant status. Problems with excessive alcohol use were recognized by founding father Dr. Benjamin Rush, who began a campaign for temperance. This simply meant, in the language of the late 1700s, to drink less often and to abstain from "spirituous (hard) liquor." In the next century, the definition of temperance came to mean abstaining from all alcohol use, and the temperance movement took on an evangelical Christian tone. Finally, in the late 1800s, temperance enthusiasts succeeded in proscribing alcohol in many states, and in the early 1900s, throughout the United States itself. The experiment of Prohibition proved to be disastrous insofar as promoting the interests of organized crime and concomitant disrespect for the law were concerned.

But the importance of alcohol for the discussion of drug abuse and addiction is as an exemplar of how not to control an addictive and highly problematic drug. Specifically, the use and growth of federal anti-alcohol enforcement informed federal control of opiates in the 1920s and in subsequent decades. Like Prohibition, federal law enforcement–oriented control of addictive drugs has proven to be counterproductive, driving normally conformist opiate users to the street to get stronger drugs (e.g., heroin) from expensive organized crime sources. Over time, this association with criminal elements led to the creation of a criminalized drug-based subculture. Variant drug-based subcultures evolved in a similar manner.

Brown's Iron Bitters, a patent medicine produced in the 1880s that claimed to "give new life to the nerves," contained cocaine. At the time, products like this were available over the counter at pharmacies and neighborhood general stores.

This model, rather than a more humane and possibly more effective medical model, is seen repeatedly in the history of drug regulation and enforcement in the United States since 1920. Current moral crusades to more tightly regulate opioid analgesics only repeat this lamentable narrative.

That being said, it must be admitted that in the late 1800s the United States was a "dope fiend's paradise." Morphine, in particular, was used by a wide variety of people. Housewives used morphine or liquid opium in patent medicines to deal with nerves, depression, or "female problems." Civil War veterans were acknowledged as a problematic at-risk subpopulation for "soldier's disease," that is, opiate addiction; opiates were used to deal with chronic stress, pain, and post-combat trauma reactions. Working-class men—for example, cowboys, longshoremen, and laborers—flocked to opium dens, where they could both relax and get relief from chronic pain. Doctors both prescribed and freely used morphine and cocaine themselves. Children were routinely given opioid-based nostrums to help with teething, diarrhea, and colic. Cannabis was available in a variety of forms but at the time was not extensively used recreationally.

Patent medicines, often containing large amounts of cocaine, opioids, and cannabis dissolved in a strong alcohol base, were available over the counter at pharmacies and neighborhood general stores. Mail order houses sold morphine, cocaine, and syringes—no prescription needed. Morphine was even used to treat alcoholics. That is, doctors deliberately tried to get alcoholics to transfer their addiction to the less damaging opioid. Under these conditions, drug addiction was common and was not necessarily socially or criminologically problematic. Drug addicts could work and participate fully in their families and communities while maintaining their drug habit.

Mobilization of Bias

The specter of intoxicated veterans and wives and mothers on drugs proved too much for moral crusaders. Linking opioids to "Chinese opium dens" in explicitly racist appeals, such reformers were able to mobilize bias against drugs and drug users. Cocaine use, which was a minor issue in the same period, was similarly vilified and connected to African American criminals. Cannabis, called "marijuana" in order to link it to unsavory Mexican laborers, was correspondingly stigmatized. This process also included presenting only a single policy option: total prohibition. Accordingly, myriad social problems were linked to drug use, including crime, rape, and recruitment into prostitution ("white slave trade"). Importantly, all drug use and "abuse" was seen as essentially equivalent. Therefore, there could be no legal or wholesome context for recreational drug use. All drug users ("fiends") and sellers ("pushers") were regarded as loathsome spreaders of the contagion of drug use to children at worst, and as parasites at best. Those who defended drug use or drug users or who questioned the prohibition approach were reviled, stigmatized, and marginalized. This process was begun with opium and repeated throughout the history of drug regulation in American history. It enjoys currency today.

Regulation

In 1875, laws banning opium dens and requiring prescriptions for opioid use were passed in various locales. Not surprisingly, these ordinances often directly impacted Chinese opium dens. In succeeding decades, federal laws followed, the most notable being the Harrison Narcotics Act of 1914. This created a tax structure on importers and distributors of narcotics. Doctors and pharmacists were forced to register and pay a small tax in order to prescribe and sell narcotics. Federal enforcement agencies interpreted the law to mean that medically maintaining addicts on drugs was illegal and began a full-scale persecution of doctors who utilized drugs as a treatment philosophy. In short, the Harrison Act and subsequent legislation and Supreme Court decisions drove previously respectable citizens into the streets and into the arms of organized crime. This enforcement approach became the foundation of American drug policy. It has proven counterproductive as it criminalized a large population who found that they had little choice but to commit crimes to get money in order pay inflated street prices for formerly cheap drugs. Heroin, formerly shunned by opioid addicts in favor of morphine, became the drug of choice due to its superior strength and availability. Organized crime members preferred to deal with heroin as it was much easier to smuggle than other opioids due to its compactness. Heroin proved to be much

Two Chinese men smoking in an opium den around 1909. Opium dens in Chinese American neighborhoods were targeted by often racist and xenophobic local laws in the late 19th century.

more addicting and much more problematic than the opioids like morphine and patent medicines that were used previously. But throughout the 1920s and 1930s, heroin use declined as federal drug seizures increased. Cocaine and cannabis were similarly stigmatized and criminalized and, likewise, fell into disuse for decades. The campaign against cannabis in the 1930s, led by federal bureaucrats and other moral crusaders, was a masterpiece of mobilization of bias and misinformation and made much use of media such as the propaganda movie *Reefer Madness*.

After World War II, heroin use increased, primarily in African American neighborhoods. Working-class whites in urban areas began to experiment with drugs while bohemian intellectuals (Beats) began to advocate the use of drugs such as cannabis and hallucinogens in order to expand consciousness. The influence of such figures as writers Jack Kerouac, Allen Ginsberg, and Aldous Huxley and academic Timothy Leary in popularizing recreational drug use can scarcely be overestimated. The attention paid to drugs by magazines, television, and cinema made drugs somewhat respectable and led to the hippie movement in the mid- and late 1960s, in which cannabis use might be said to have been a sacrament and LSD use could be seen as a form of seriously subcultural commitment. This social movement reached a climax in 1969 with the Woodstock and Altamont festivals and fell into dissolution over the following years. Many of the youth involved continued involvement with cannabis but moved from urban hippie concentrations to rural communes or communities. Others fell prey to the lure of the hard drug–based subcultures and lifestyles. Prescription drugs and illicitly manufactured amphetamines (e.g., "speed" and "meth") became more popular. Cannabis became normalized, and its use reached an all-time high in 1978. At that time, moral crusaders were able to derail attempts to decriminalize or legalize its use.

More problematic was the increase in the use of cocaine that occurred in the 1970s. Initially and erroneously thought to be as innocuous as the cannabis of the 1960s, cocaine proved to produce strong psychological dependency and was, perhaps, addictive. Its use became widespread in the late 1970s. Even more ominous was the proliferation of "crack," a chemically altered and inexpensive cocaine by-product. Its spread through American cities in the mid-1980s was marked by frank addiction, violence by gangs competing for control of its distribution, and neighborhood chaos. Penalties affixed to crack use, a drug assumed to be used primarily by African Americans, were so harsh and disproportionate compared to those levied on powdered cocaine users that many urban juries refused to convict. It was only in 2010 that the penalty structure was adjusted.

Abuse of pharmaceutical drugs, a growing problem since the 1950s, when the pre-benzodiazepine minor tranquillizers hit the market, became a matter of concern throughout the following decades. The problems with these early tranquilizers were somewhat exaggerated though they were overprescribed, as were the early benzodiazepines. In the 1990s, analgesic opioids such as oxycodone and hydrocodone became popular for recreational use. However, such casual use often led to addiction. Time-released oxycodone (OxyContin), particularly popular in rural areas, became known as "hillbilly heroin" and was linked to poor whites in media accounts. Housewives and "soccer moms" were also linked to this drug and a variety of benzodiazepine sedatives, most notoriously alprazolam, or Xanax. Recreational use of methamphetamine by rural folk became a media focus in the 1990s and into the next century.

Francis Frederick Hawley
Western Carolina University

See Also: 1921 to 1940 Primary Documents; 1941 to 1960 Primary Documents; 1961 to 1980 Primary Documents; Criminalization and Decriminalization; Drug Abuse and Addiction, Contemporary; Drug Abuse and Addiction, Sociology of; Drug Enforcement Administration; Narcotics Laws; Prohibition.

Further Readings
Brecher, E. *Licit and Illicit Drugs.* Boston: Little, Brown, 1972.
Inciardi, J. *The War on Drugs IV: The Continuing Sage of the Mysteries of Intoxication, Addiction, Crime and Public Policy,* 4th ed. Upper Saddle River, NJ: Pearson, 2008.
Musto, D. *The American Disease: Origins of Narcotics Control,* 3rd ed. New York: Oxford University Press, 1999.

Drug Abuse and Addiction, Sociology of

The sociology of drug abuse and addiction ranges among many different topics, including drug policy, drug treatment, the labeling of drug abuse and addiction, subcultures of drug use, theories of drug abuse, and trends in drug use. A sociological perspective of drug abuse and addiction emphasizes social and cultural processes around drugs. That is, how and what is labeled drug abuse and addiction is about much more than just the physiological or psychological properties of drugs or individuals. What is labeled a "drug," "abuse," or "addiction" in society reflects larger cultural values, is often the result of underlying conflicts in society between groups (i.e., social class, race, and ethnicity), and is political. Sociologists attempt to put the study of drugs into a social context. The sociology of drug abuse and addiction emerged out of several other sociological areas, namely, the sociology of deviance, criminology, and medical sociology. Each has made significant contributions to the understanding of sociological issues around drugs and addiction, although each focuses on a different area and/or uses a different theoretical perspective.

Drug Policy

Since what is considered today to be illicit drug use was mostly unregulated and legal through the early part of the 20th century, sociologists did not really study drug abuse and addiction until after Prohibition. Heroin and cocaine were not illegal until the passage of the Harrison Act in 1914; marijuana was legal until 1935. Many contemporary sociologists have studied the history of drug prohibition. They often use a constructionist perspective to understand the processes of how certain legal drugs became redefined as illegal and, as in the case of alcohol prohibition, back to legal. These sociologists attempt to understand who the major claims-makers were in each historical period, or those people who were able to construct and control the wider debate around drugs and drug use. Sociologists argue that drug policy is often the result of moral panics around drug use. In different historical moments, the public shows rising concern for particular substances, and more strict policies usually follow.

In the 1930s, marijuana was portrayed as violence-inducing, extremely dangerous, and would lead to a host of other criminal and social problems. As a result, it became criminalized in 1935. Similar drug scares occurred in the 1980s, around crack cocaine. Crack cocaine, which is pharmacologically identical to powder cocaine, became used more widely in the 1980s, especially in poor urban areas, because it was relatively inexpensive. Early researchers argued that crack cocaine was more addictive than powder cocaine and could cause users to become violent. As a result, legislation penalized the possession of crack cocaine much more heavily than powder cocaine. Further research showed that crack cocaine was not actually more addictive than powder cocaine and did not have different pharmacological results than powder cocaine (such as causing the user to become violent). Still, the disparity in sentencing between the two drugs remained until 2010, when Congress passed the Fair Sentencing Act, reducing (but not eliminating) the disparity between crack and powder cocaine. Sociologists viewed the labeling of crack cocaine as the most dangerous and addictive drug ever as a result of who typically used crack (poor people of color) compared to who typically used powder cocaine (wealthier white individuals).

Medicalization of Drug Addiction

Another contribution from sociologists regarding how drug addiction is defined is within the area of medicalization, that is, how something viewed as immoral (or criminal) becomes redefined as a medical problem. Alcoholism became accepted as a disease in the 1950s by the World Health Organization and the American Medical Association. Drug addiction slowly became accepted as a legitimate disease because of the medicalization of alcohol abuse. By the beginning of the 21st century, a majority of Americans agreed with the principle that addiction was a disease. However, while drug addiction has been medicalized in many ways (in definition and treatment), it is still also managed by the criminal justice system and also still retains a great deal of stigma, preventing complete medicalization. Sociologists examine this issue by showing how addiction still retains a great deal of stigma, how treatment for it is still largely punitive and has moral overtones. Twelve-step practices, founded in Alcoholics Anonymous, are the dominant framework for drug treatment, even in publicly funded treatment programs.

When studying the etiology of drug abuse and addiction, sociologists emphasize the social and environmental context rather than individual-level factors. For instance, while psychologists might focus on personal characteristics, such as self-esteem or mental health problems, as possible explanations for drug addiction, sociologists examine social factors, such as peer and family dynamics, poor structural conditions, or unemployment. The major sociological theories used to explain drug addiction are learning theory, control theory, strain theory, and conflict theory. These theories were originally formulated to explain criminal behavior and delinquency and were eventually extended to explaining drug abuse and addiction.

Social Learning Theory

Social learning theory posits that individuals learn how to become drug abusers, that is, they do not have an inherent quality that makes them drug abusers. They learn this deviant behavior either from their family members or their peers. The theory argues that individuals are socialized to be drug abusers due to those closest to them also being drug abusers. According to Ronald Akers, a contemporary theorist in the social learning tradition, individuals encounter a social reinforcement for drug use by their peers. That is, drug use is tolerated and encouraged, creating a positive reinforcement for the individual to also use drugs. Control theory argues that those who are not sufficiently "bonded" to society will engage in criminal behavior, such as using drugs. Those who have more attachment to society, either through positive social networks, activities, or religion, will be less likely to engage in antisocial behaviors.

Strain Theory

Strain theory, developed by sociologist Robert Merton, posits that some individuals feel more strain than others because they lack the appropriate resources to achieve goals. According to Merton, just about everyone in a society has similar goals, what that culture determines as success. Not everyone, however, has the means to achieve those goals. Those who lack the means will often resort to other methods (criminal) to achieve their goals. Merton argued that a drug user rejects both the socially approved goals and the "legitimate" ways of achieving them. These individuals become "retreatists" and become socially isolated. The drug use serves as an escape from the strain they feel, often because they initially lacked resources to achieve their goals. Research has not given much support to strain theory in explaining drug addiction, although it may be better at explaining initial drug experimentation.

Conflict Theory

Conflict theory emphasizes social and political inequality as a main contributor to drug addiction. Those who use conflict theory to study drug addiction tend to focus on poorer, inner-city communities with high rates of drug abuse. They argue that drug rates are higher in these areas because of the lack of economic opportunities in these areas and the resulting alienation that the residents feel. They also argue that the current war on drugs has been unsuccessful at alleviating these structural problems, and as a result, has not dramatically reduced the chronic drug abuse in these communities. Conflict theorists contend that only large-scale and dramatic shifts in our economic and social policy will reduce the inequality in these communities, and hence, drug addiction. While research has not found strong support for any one of these theories in explaining drug addiction, they are useful for emphasizing the social, economic, and political contexts around drug use, and their utility might lie in conjunction with other theories for a multidisciplinary perspective.

Arrest and Treatment

Arrest and incarceration rates for drug-related crime have skyrocketed since the 1980s because of the continuing escalation of the war on drugs. Most of these arrests have been for drug possession, not drug sales, which has led many local and state governments to adopt new approaches to drug-related crime, such as including drug treatment in criminal case processing. One such approach is drug courts, begun in Miami in 1989, where nonviolent offenders are given the opportunity to attend drug treatment and complete a 12-month program in exchange for a dismissed record. To be eligible for such programs, offenders must be evaluated as having a drug problem. In most drug courts, if the offender remains conviction-free for one year following graduation from the program, their record is expunged. However, if the individual fails to complete the program, he or she is sent to prison. Drug courts now operate in every state, as well as the District of Columbia and Puerto Rico, with many more added each year. Another change in policy is California's Proposition 36, passed by voters in 2000, which automatically diverts first- and second-time, low-level drug offenders into drug treatment. While the program has suffered from a lack of state funding, a 2007 report by researchers at the University of California, Los Angeles, found that the initiative saved California $2.50 for each $1 spent. Critics of the program highlight the fact that many of those eligible for the program never complete treatment and argue that it is basically a "get out of jail free" card. Supporters contend that addiction research shows that most people who eventually become drug-free require numerous treatment attempts. An expansion of the program was rejected by California voters in 2008.

Sociologists also study subcultures of drug users to understand the social organization of drug use and abuse. What they have found is that drug-using subcultures share similar sets of norms (i.e., language, behaviors, and knowledge) that exist because drug use is illegal. If drug use were legal (such as alcohol), norms would develop around the appropriate use of the drug and users would not necessarily be part of a separate subculture. Sociological research on the "careers" of drug users also shows that most people who consume drugs, even those who do so heavily for a period of time, eventually stop using on their own without formal treatment.

Jennifer Murphy
California State University, Sacramento

See Also: 1921 to 1940 Primary Documents; 1941 to 1960 Primary Documents; 1961 to 1980 Primary Documents; Criminalization and Decriminalization; Criminology; Drug Abuse and Addiction, Contemporary; Drug Abuse and Addiction, History of; Narcotics Laws; Prohibition; Sentencing.

Further Readings

Becker, Howard S. *Outsiders: Studies in the Sociology of Deviance*. New York: Free Press, 1963.
Faupel, Charles E., Alan M. Horowitz, and Greg S. Weaver. *The Sociology of American Drug Use*. New York: McGraw-Hill, 2004.
Goode, Erich. *Drugs in American Society*, 7th ed. New York: McGraw-Hill, 2007.
Mosher, Clayton J. and Scott Akins. *Drugs and Drug Policy: The Control of Consciousness Alteration*. Thousand Oaks, CA: Sage, 2007.

Drug Enforcement Administration

Established in 1973, the Drug Enforcement Administration (DEA) is a federal law enforcement agency of the U.S. government operating under the auspices of the Department of Justice. In order to safeguard American society, DEA agents work to bring drug kingpins and local suppliers to justice by enforcing controlled substance laws and regulations, conducting narcotics investigations, and tackling international drug trafficking and those organizations and members involved in the growing, production, and distribution of illegal drugs appearing in or destined for the United States. They are also tasked with advocating and implementing prevention initiatives aimed to reduce the demand and availability of controlled substances domestically and internationally.

Although the DEA shares jurisdiction concurrently with two other federal law enforcement agencies—the Federal Bureau of Investigation (FBI) and Immigration and Customs Enforcement (ICE)—it has sole authority over drug investigations conducted abroad. Appointed by the president and confirmed by the Senate, the administrator heads the DEA and reports to the attorney general through the deputy attorney general. Currently, this position is filled by Michele Leonhart, who assumed office on December 22, 2010, after serving as acting administrator since November 2007 following the resignation of Karen Tandy. Second in command is the assistant administrator and chief of operations, which is currently filled by Thomas Harrigan, who assumed office in 2008.

History

The federal policing of controlled substances—and thus the roots of the DEA—can be traced back to a series of laws, for example, the Harrison Narcotics Act of 1914 (opiates), the Eighteenth Amendment of the Constitution (alcohol), the Narcotics Drugs Import and Export Act of 1922, the Marijuana Tax Act of 1937, the Boggs Act of 1956 (heroin), and the Controlled Substance Act of 1970, to name a few. Consequently, a number of agencies with similar functions were formed—the Bureau of Narcotics and Dangerous

Agents with the DEA and Immigration and Customs Enforcement peer into a cross-border smuggling tunnel connecting a house in Nogales, Arizona, to another in Mexico in June 2007. Forty such tunnels were found from 2001 to 2007.

Drugs, the Office of Drug Abuse Law Enforcement, the Office of National Narcotics Intelligence, and other offices—which, in some cases, led to interagency rivalry and hampered federal law enforcement efforts. As such, on March 28, 1973, President Richard Nixon signed Reorganization Plan No. 2—an executive order to consolidate and establish a unified federal agency in order to more effectively enforce narcotics laws, investigate infractions, and prosecute violators, primarily in response to the growing drug problem plaguing the nation. Several months later, on July 1, 1973, the DEA officially commenced operations, powered by a budget of $73 million and

2,775 employees and headquartered in Washington, D.C., in order to stay in close proximity with the attorney general, an office the agency worked with closely. Then, in 1989, considerable expansion of the DEA spurred by increased federal anti-drug efforts (the "war on drugs" in the 1980s) necessitated relocation to larger headquarters in Arlington, Virginia, opposite the Pentagon.

The main objectives of the DEA are to identify, apprehend, and prosecute major violators of controlled-substance laws, which may also include drug gangs utilizing violence, fear, and intimidation as weapons to terrorize citizens and communities. To do so, investigations are conducted on both the interstate and international levels and in cooperation with a number of authorities—local, state, federal, and foreign—for the collection, analysis, and dissemination of drug intelligence and related information. Additionally, the agency has authority to confiscate any proceeds or assets discovered to be linked to, derived from, or intended to be used for drug trafficking.

Working in cooperation with authorities in a number of jurisdictions, including the United Nations and Interpol, the DEA is also responsible for the implementation, coordination, and cooperation of drug enforcement efforts and nonenforcement programs designed to reduce availability of illegal substances in the U.S. drug market, such as through crop eradication or substitution. Agents also work to raise awareness of the adverse affects of drugs through drug resistance education programs and provide police training programs in cooperation with domestic and foreign counterparts. In addition to illegal substances, the DEA enforces laws involving the regulation of those controlled substances legally produced, such as prescription and over-the-counter medication.

In addition to the two aforementioned chief administrators, other executive leadership offices include the chief inspector, chief counsel, chief financial officer, and two assistant administrators—one for operations and a second for human resources. These offices are supported with executive staff from equal opportunity and employee assistance, planning and policy, and public affairs offices. Further compartmentalized into six divisions, the human resources division includes two boards for career and professional conduct and a training office. The operations division, which includes two divisions for aviation and special operations, comprises five offices—operations management, diversion control, international programs, and financial and enforcement operations. The El Paso Intelligence Center and Organized Crime Drug Enforcement Task Force (OCDEFT) Fusion Center are housed in the intelligence division, which includes three offices for strategic, special, and investigative intelligence, and one for intelligence policy and management. Three offices for acquisition management, finance, and resource management make up the financial division. In the operational support division, there are offices for administration, information systems, forensic sciences, and investigative technology. The inspection division includes offices for inspection, professional responsibility, and security programs. The agency also operates a rigorous 16-week federal training academy at the same location as the FBI Academy—the U.S. Marine Corps base in Quantico, Virginia.

Evolution

In the 1970s and 1980s, international drug trafficking and the crack epidemic were the center of DEA operations. During this time, although heroin was starting to enter the United States from the Golden Triangle countries of southeast Asia, the Colombian Medellín cartel was growing rapidly, leading to a heavy flow of cocaine and marijuana to the United States. The violence associated with these drug activities made this a globally feared crime syndicate, which allowed members to easily infiltrate and insulate themselves into legitimate sectors of the U.S. economy. Consequently, the DEA in cooperation with other federal agencies conducted a number of high-profile operations such as Operation Grouper in 1981, which led to the arrest of 122 indicted subjects, the seizure of more than $1 billion in drugs, and the forfeiture of $12 million in assets such as vessels and airplanes. In the mid-1980s, crack cocaine, which fueled street crime and devastated communities, only added to the agency's agenda and thus prompted the passage of new laws and drug prevention programs to arm the DEA with additional fighting power and authority to tackle the nation's drug epidemic.

In the 1990s, the agency notoriously captured and prosecuted Manuel Noriega, the president of Panama, for his alleged role in smuggling cocaine into the U.S. drug market. During this decade, increased attention to the legalization of marijuana was a growing concern for the DEA, with proponents arguing the prescription of marijuana cigarettes for purposes of treating terminally ill patients and therapeutically benefiting those with painful conditions would be unlikely to add to the crime problem, which was an obvious concern to the agency.

Interestingly, although California voters passed Proposition 215 to allow physicians to prescribe marijuana for serious health conditions, federal law still holds marijuana to have no legitimate use, even medically, and thus still allows the DEA to prosecute those in possession of this drug. Today, the concern has shifted to various synthetic designer drugs, especially MDMA/ecstasy, given the growing availability and popularity among young people, as well as connections to terrorist financing.

Since 1986, DEA efforts have resulted in 623,454 arrests, with 30,567 in 2009. During that same time, agents have seized more than 1,484,222 kilograms of cocaine, 15,060 kilograms of heroin, 7,362,303 kilograms of marijuana, 26,026 kilograms of methamphetamine, and 149,583,030 dosage units of hallucinogens. Operating on $2.4 billion annually, these efforts were accomplished by nearly 11,000 DEA staff and 5,500 special agents working in more than 200 domestic field offices and 87 foreign offices in 63 countries worldwide.

Michael J. Puniskis
Middlesex University

See Also: 1961 to 1980 Primary Documents; Bureau of Alcohol, Tobacco, Firearms and Explosives; Drug Abuse and Addiction, Contemporary; Federal Bureau of Investigation; Federal Policing; Justice, Department of; Narcotics Laws; Nixon, Richard (Administration of); Secret Service; Smuggling.

Further Readings
U.S. Drug Enforcement Administration. http://www.justice.gov/dea/index.htm (Accessed January 2011).
U.S. Drug Enforcement Administration. *Tradition of Excellence: The History of the DEA 1973–1998.* Washington, DC: U.S. Department of Justice, 1999.

Due Process

Underlying and protecting the principle of fairness in crime and punishment is the constitutional protection of due process. Due process protects against arbitrary deprivation of life, liberty, or property. Therefore, due process requires that before the government deprives people of their life, liberty, or property, the applicable law is publicly accessible, the person is notified of the action and reasons for the action, he or she is allowed a trial in accordance with legal principles at which he or she can present evidence and witnesses in his or her defense, and he or she is not subjected to any punishment unless and until he or she is found guilty. Due process appears in two places in the U.S. Constitution, each having a different impact on crime and punishment. As it appears in the Fifth Amendment, due process protects against the arbitrary actions of the federal government. Due process in the Fourteenth Amendment is used to incorporate, or apply, the federal constitutional rights to the states.

Historical Perspective

The concept of due process, or not arbitrarily depriving people of life, liberty, or property, can be traced back to the Magna Carta. Chapter 39 of the Magna Carta requires a trial by peers according to the law before punishment can be taken against a person. These provisions were further clarified by Sir Edmund Coke in 1628 in the Petition of Right. Coke expanded and clarified the protections in the Magna Carta by protecting against deprivation of life, liberty, and property without either parliamentary action or due process of law. Therefore, in the English context, due process protected against arbitrary action by the Crown.

As the American constitution was being drafted, the framers included the concept of due process to protect against arbitrary action by all branches and actors of the federal government. Due process is part of the Fifth Amendment, which also protects against self-incrimination, double jeopardy, and taking of property without compensation. In the context of the Fifth Amendment, the federal government is prevented from prosecuting and punishing criminal activity without fair proceedings that are in accordance with established legal practice. The U.S. Supreme Court has consistently applied the Fifth Amendment due process guarantees to actions by the federal, not state, government.

With its inclusion in the Fourteenth Amendment, due process, and through its interpretation other rights, were applied to actions by the state governments. As worded, the Fourteenth Amendment specifically requires states to follow the principles of fairness and legal process in the deprivation of life, liberty, or property. Thus, while the Fifth Amendment protects against arbitrary federal action, the Fourteenth Amendment protects against arbitrary state action. Yet the power of the Fourteenth Amendment's due process clause has been in its interpretation. The U.S. Supreme Court has interpreted due process in the Fourteenth Amendment to extend the protections in the Bill of Rights to actions by state governments.

In the American context, due process has evolved from a protection against arbitrary action by the Crown to protections against arbitrary action by actors and institutions at all levels of government. The American interpretation of due process has also expanded to encompass more

This 1903 illustration titled "Due Process of Law" uses a figure representing justice riding a snail up a winding path to comment on the perceived slowness of the legal system caused by due process. The path is strewn with boulders labeled "certificate of reasonable doubt," "appeals," "change of venue," "injunctions," and "stays," and ends at the "Hall of Justice" at the top of the hill.

than a process for determining punishment. Due process in the American legal context has a procedural and substantive context. Grounded in the Magna Carta tradition, procedural due process recognizes that before a person can be deprived of life, liberty, or property, a person has the right to procedural safeguards such as notice of intent and a fair trial. The intent of the procedural due process is to ensure that government action does not infringe on rights enumerated in the Constitution. Substantive due process recognizes that not all rights are enumerated in the Constitution.

Lawrence v. Texas (2003) illustrates the difference between procedural and substantive due process as well as the evolution of due process within the American context. Lawrence was arrested and charged with violating the Texas anti-sodomy law. Procedurally, Lawrence was afforded due process. The law was publicly accessible, he was notified of the charges, he was convicted through a fair trial, and he was not punished until after conviction. However, the Supreme Court found a substantive due process violation of the right to privacy. Although there is no right to privacy enumerated in the Constitution, the Supreme Court found privacy to be fundamental to the concept of liberty and, therefore, protected against arbitrary government intrusion. In the American legal system, therefore, due process has evolved from the prevention against arbitrary arrest by the Crown to protection against laws that infringe on the privacy of individuals.

Principles

Due process is grounded in the principles of fairness, protection against arbitrary government action, and procedures based in law. Therefore, for someone to be tried and punished for a crime according to due process, several criteria must be met. First, there needs to be a law in effect at the time of the action prohibiting the alleged criminal action. People must have the ability to know in advance that their action would be considered criminal. This does not mean the person must know that the law exists, only that there is an enforceable law, passed and enacted according to established rules, which the person is expected to obey. The person must also be appropriately notified that he or she has violated the law and is being charged with a crime.

Once the person is charged with a crime, due process requires that he or she is tried in an impartial court of law. The trial must be fair such that the accused cannot be disadvantaged and neither side can prejudice the outcome. This principle of fairness extends through all aspects of the trial process, including assignment of counsel, discovery, jury selection, presentation of witnesses and evidence, jury instruction, and sentencing. The actions of those involved with the trial (judge, prosecutor, counsel) must also be grounded in fairness.

Due process requires that fairness and protection against arbitrary action apply to the punishment for crimes as well. Punishment cannot occur unless and until the person is convicted. Although pretrial detention may be warranted to ensure appearance at the trial, it cannot amount to punishment for the crime. When a person is sentenced to detention, any disciplinary actions during the detention must follow due process, including notification of the reason for disciplinary action and the ability to present a defense against the charges.

It is important to remember that due process protects against arbitrary deprivation of life, liberty, or property. Therefore, a violation of due process must be associated with an interest in life, liberty, or property. For example, substantive due process in *Lawrence v. Texas* was based on a violation of the right to privacy associated with liberty. If an interest in one of these three areas cannot be identified, due process requirements are not applicable.

Development of Substantive Due Process

Substantive due process evolved slowly through the Supreme Court's application of the Fourteenth Amendment. Through a series of economic cases, beginning with the *Slaughterhouse Cases* in 1873, the Supreme Court slowly developed substantive limits to state regulatory powers. The *Slaughterhouse Cases* considered whether a state could regulate business to the point where one company had a monopoly on an industry. Although the majority supported the state's actions, a dissent raised the point that this limited employment thus deprived citizens of employment opportunities, and the associated quality of life and property, without due process.

The Supreme Court first upheld substantive due process in 1897. In *Allgeyer v. Louisiana*, the court struck down a state regulation preventing the purchase of insurance from a company not licensed in Louisiana. The court found that the regulation violated a person's freedom of contract. Consistent with the dissent in the *Slaughterhouse Cases*, the court felt that freedom of liberty included the ability to choose whom to contract with and whom to work with. This was the first of a long line of cases in which the court struck down state legislation.

However, while substantive due process was used to support and expand free enterprise, too much liberty can sometimes be a bad thing. This was demonstrated in *Lochner v. New York* (1905). In this infamous case, the Supreme Court used substantive due process and liberty of contract to invalidate laws that limited employee work hours. When analyzing the statute in question, the court concluded that the goals of the statute could have been achieved through less restrictive means. In the years that followed, the court repeatedly struck down economic legislation. However, the court was willing to support regulation for groups that needed extra protection and thus upheld statutes that set maximum hours for women.

Economic times changed, Roosevelt introduced the New Deal programs, and the composition of the Supreme Court changed. In 1934's *Nebbia v. New York*, the court began moving away from the *Lochner* standards by assessing whether there was a relationship between the law and goals to be achieved. Three years later, the court expressly overturned *Lochner* by upholding minimum wage laws for women (*West Coast Hotel v. Parrish*). Over the years, the Supreme Court has continued to remove itself from the review of state economic legislation unless it impacts a "fundamental right" such as the right to privacy.

Fundamental rights are also key to the Supreme Court's treatment of noneconomic rights through substantive due process. As the court's review of state economic legislation has decreased, it has become increasingly willing to review noneconomic legislation. To pass the court's review, the state's legislation must have a compelling interest and means used must be necessary to achieve the goal. Rights that fall into this category frequently involve the right to privacy and include the areas of sex, marriage, and children. Because this standard is so strict, few state statutes have been upheld by the court.

American Crime and Punishment

In its application, the most basic role of due process is to ensure that the prosecution and punishment of crime is fair and not arbitrary. This begins with fair laws that are neither vague nor discriminatory. If someone is suspected of committing a crime, due process requires that he or she be treated in a fair and informed manner. The Miranda warnings are intended to ensure that suspects are informed of their rights and consequences of their actions during interrogation. Access to counsel is an important aspect of due process because it ensures that someone familiar with the legal system, and the legal procedures to ensure due process, is assisting the accused in making informed decisions and protecting the rights of the accused.

As the accused is brought to trial, due process requires fairness in relation to the jury. Selection cannot result in a jury biased as to the accused, the outcome of the trial, or the outcome of sentencing. During the trial, juries cannot hear or see information that would bias their opinion. For example, because the Miranda warnings provide an option of silence, the fact that the accused chose to remain silent cannot be used against him or her at trial. It would also be prejudicial to the jury to see the accused in a manner that presupposed his guilt without justifiable cause. Fairness must also prevail in instructions given to the jury, both for deliberation and sentencing, so they understand what they are to do in a way that does not prevent independent thought and allows them to consider all options. This is particularly the case where a sentence of death is involved.

If convicted, due process also applies to probation, detention, and parole, although there are limitations on the rights involved, and there must be a life or liberty interest. For example, a prisoner does not necessarily have a liberty interest in being transferred from one facility to another. Disciplinary actions, including revocation of probation or parole, are subject to notification of charges and the ability to present a defense. In these cases, the person must be informed of the reason for the disciplinary action, be allowed to present a defense, and be notified of the reason for the outcome of the hearing. However, the hearing is not a court of law, the person does not have a right to an attorney for the process, and the use of witnesses is subject to consideration of the situation of detention. Even if there is no life or liberty interest, actions must meet the minimum standard of not being arbitrary.

It is important to remember that there is a separation between due process protections at the federal and state levels. The rights enshrined in the Bill of Rights, including Fifth Amendment due process rights, are applicable to actions by the federal government. The Supreme Court has selectively incorporated rights to the states through the Fourteenth Amendment so not all rights are protected from state action. For example, double jeopardy has not been incorporated to the states. Furthermore, the Supreme Court has consistently respected the sovereignty of state laws and state courts. This is seen clearly in the cases of due process requirements for disciplinary actions while in detention, such as transfers or probation. There is no constitutionally protected right for prisoners to remain in a particular prison or to probation. Therefore, if the state has not enacted laws that create expectations of probation, and the associated liberty, due process does not apply.

When considering due process challenges, it is important to understand requirements that have been established by the Supreme Court. When convicting someone of a crime, the burden of proof lies with the prosecution. In addition, the prosecution must prove guilt beyond a reasonable doubt. Due process does not allow shifting the burden of proof to the defendant. Nor does due process allow conviction at a standard less than reasonable doubt. When due process is violated in this respect, it is usually in communication to the jury.

Defendants must meet certain criteria when presenting a due process challenge. Before raising a challenge on the evidence presented during a trial, consideration must be given to the ability of a reasonable fact finder to determine guilt beyond a reasonable doubt. If the instructions given to the jury are being challenged, it must be shown that the specific instruction being challenged violated due process. In other words, consideration must be given to the impact of the challenged instruction in the context of both the trial and the full instructions given to the jury. Due process challenges to state prison transfers and disciplinary actions must consider expectations created in state law for both process and liberty.

Kathleen Barrett
Georgia State University

See Also: Constitution of the United States of America; Defendant's Rights; Federal Rules of Criminal Procedure; *Lawrence v. Texas*; Magna Carta; *Miranda v. Arizona*; Prisoner's Rights; Punishment Within Prison; Supreme Court, U.S.

Further Readings
McGehee, Lucius Polk. *Due Process of Law Under the Federal Constitution*. Northport, NY: Edward Thompson, 1906.
Weinberg, Louise. "An Almost Archaeological Dig: Finding a Surprisingly Rich Early Understanding of Substantive Due Process." *Constitutional Commentary*, v.27/163 (2010).

Duren v. Missouri

The Sixth Amendment to the U.S. Constitution provides that "In all criminal prosecutions, the accused shall enjoy the right to a speedy and public trial, by an impartial jury of the State and district wherein the crime shall have been committed...." The Fourteenth Amendment guarantees due process to each citizen of the United States by ensuring that the Sixth Amendment will apply in all criminal prosecutions within each state of the union. In *Duren v. Missouri* (1979), the U.S. Supreme Court held that a Missouri law permitting a high percentage of women to be excluded from the venire (jury pool) resulted in their underrepresentation on juries. Women, unlike men, were able to receive an automatic exemption from jury service. While women represented 54 percent of the county population, they were 9.4 percent of the prospective jurors, and none of those on Duren's jury; as a result, neither the venire nor the jury represented a fair cross-section of the community, a key requirement of ensuring an impartial jury.

In 1975, Billy Duren was indicted for first-degree murder and first-degree robbery. In 1976, he was convicted by an all-male jury. In both a pretrial motion and in a post-conviction motion for a new trial, Duren "contended that his right to a trial by a jury chosen from a fair cross-section of his community were denied by provisions of a Missouri law granting women, who so request, an automatic exemption from jury service." His motions were denied. During the six months prior to his trial, 26 percent of the 11,197 persons summoned were women; and during the week his trial began, 15.5 percent of the venires were women, but from the 53 individuals on his jury panel (~9.4 percent women), none were selected for his jury.

In *Peters v. Kiff* (1972), the court upheld a petitioner's challenge to the exclusion of jurors to either a grand jury or a petit jury on the basis of race as a violation of his due process rights. He was also not required to show any actual harm or that the individuals who were excluded from a jury were the same race as the defendant; the mere exclusion was sufficient for due process denial.

In *Taylor v. Louisiana* (1975), Taylor was convicted of aggravated kidnapping by an all-male jury that was selected from a venire that did not contain any female members. The Supreme Court held that juries were to "be drawn from a source fairly representative of the community." The court was clear when it noted that the "... fair cross-section requirement as fundamental to the jury trial guaranteed by the Sixth Amendment, and are convinced that the requirement has solid foundation. The purpose of a jury is to guard against the exercise of arbitrary power—to make available the common sense judgment of the community...." This will not happen when *any* group is deliberately excluded from a jury. The requirement that a petit jury be selected from a representative cross-section of the community, which is fundamental to the jury trial guaranteed by the Sixth Amendment, is violated by the systematic exclusion of women from jury panels, which in the judicial district here involved amounted to 53 percent of the citizens eligible for jury service.

In deciding *Duren*, the court relied on *Taylor* and provided a three-prong test to be followed in order to establish "a prima facie violation of that (cross section) requirement." The defendant must show "(1) that the group alleged to be excluded is a 'distinctive' group in the community; (2) that the group's representation in the source from which juries are selected is not fair and reasonable in relation to the number of such persons in the community; and (3) that this underrepresentation results from systematic exclusion of the group in the jury selection process."

While of no legal significance regarding the holding of this case, Ruth Bader Ginsburg, Esq., was co-counsel with Lee M. Nation, Esq. on behalf of the petitioner and provided legal argument regarding a defendant's right to have a jury that represented a fair cross-section of the community. She went on to become an Associate Justice of the Supreme Court.

Keith Gregory Logan
Kutztown University

See Also: Citizen Participation on Juries; Juries; Race, Class, and Criminal Law; Racism.

Further Readings
Duren v. Missouri, 439 U.S. 357 (1979).
Peters v. Kiff, 407 U.S. 493 (1972).
Taylor v. Louisiana, 419 U.S. 522 (1975).

Dyer Act

The Dyer Act, also called the National Motor Vehicle Theft Act, was enacted on October 29, 1919, to impede the interstate trafficking of stolen vehicles by organized thieves. The act makes it a crime to transport stolen motor vehicles across state borders in interstate or foreign commerce.

Throughout the early part of the 20th century, development of automotive technology was rapid. The advent of the Ford Model T in 1908 revolutionized availability of the automobile to all Americans, as the Model T was the first car to be mass-produced. In 1909, a Model T could be purchased for $825, making it affordable enough for most middle-class Americans. Ford sold more than 10,000 cars in its first year of production. As the availability of cars increased dramatically over the next year, so did the complex but logical nature of a relationship between cars and crime.

New automobiles for sale in a showroom between 1921 and 1922. The increase in car ownership and related crime in the late 1910s led to the enactment of the Dyer Act in 1919. It requires three elements that must be established beyond a reasonable doubt for conviction: (1) that a vehicle is stolen, (2) that the defendant knows that the vehicle is stolen, and (3) that the defendant transports the vehicle in interstate or foreign commerce.

As more Americans were able to own and drive cars, they were being used more often to facilitate crime. Cars were used as getaway vehicles, for the transportation of illegal goods, and to aid in the ability of criminal offenders to elude police capture. However, cars were also a commodity worthy of crime themselves and were often stolen. The Dyer Act was passed in part to respond to this new crime issue facing the United States.

Response to Changing Times

The Dyer Act gave the Federal Bureau of Investigation (FBI) the authority to investigate auto thefts that crossed state lines. Prior to the passage of this act, law enforcement officials were not as easily able to thwart interstate auto theft rings or investigate these offenses because of jurisdictional issues. Auto theft was often a component of other organized criminal activity that crossed state lines. The Dyer Act gave law enforcement officials the ability to use federal information, resources, and personnel to track and investigate these offenses. The notorious Barker gang was well known for serious offenses throughout the midwestern United States, including auto theft, robbery, and murder. The willingness of offenders such as these to flee jurisdictions warranted involvement and concern from federal law enforcement.

Three elements must be established beyond a reasonable doubt for conviction under the Dyer Act: (1) that a vehicle is stolen; (2) that the defendant knows that the vehicle is stolen; and (3) that the defendant transports the vehicle in interstate or foreign commerce. Any person who aids or abets the commission of this crime is also guilty and equally culpable as a principal who actually commits the crime. Anyone who receives, possesses, conceals, stores, barters, sells, or disposes of any motor vehicle, vessel, or aircraft that has crossed a state or national boundary after being stolen will be punished under the act. The punishment for conviction under the Dyer Act is an unspecified fine, imprisonment of no longer than 10 years, or both.

As with any legislation, there has been legal controversy surrounding the Dyer Act, particularly the meaning of the word *stolen*. Federal courts reviewing cases under the act have disagreed as to the meaning of this term: Some have limited it to the common law larceny definition, while others have begun to expand the definition to other crimes of theft, including embezzlement. Courts attempting to expand the application of the Dyer Act have argued that *stolen* refers to any and all unlawful misappropriations; therefore, the Dyer Act is applicable to these circumstances as well.

Nicole Hendrix
Radford University

See Also: Automobile and the Police; Crime in America, Types; Federal Bureau of Investigation; Felonies; Gangs, History of; History of Crime and Punishment in America: 1900–1950; History of Crime and Punishment in America: 1950–1970; Larceny; Organized Crime, History of; Robbery, History of.

Further Readings
Davilman v. United States, 190 F.2d 284 6th Circuit (1950).
Eckermann, Erik. *World History of the Automobile.* Warrendale, PA: SAE Press, 2001.
Friedman, Lawrence. *Crime and Punishment in American History.* New York: HarperCollins, 1993.
Friedman, Lawrence. *A History of American Law.* New York: Simon & Schuster, 2005.
United States v. Adcock, 49 F. Supp. 351 W.E. Ky. (1943).

Earp, Wyatt

Wyatt Earp (1848–1929) is popularly known as a lawman, though in his varied career he was a land speculator, teamster, farmer, gambler, bar owner, gunman, and possibly a bouncer in a brothel. His fame as a law officer in the West stems from his stint as town marshal of Tombstone, Arizona, and most specifically, his role as participant in the iconic gunfight at O. K. Corral. This brief gunfight, which took less than a minute from beginning to end, gave Earp a perhaps undeserved notoriety and a place in the pantheon of the Wild West.

Born in Iowa, Earp drifted into minor lawlessness, such as horse-stealing and financial irregularity, after the tragic death of his first wife. He was also involved in pimping and protecting a brothel in Peoria, Illinois. He then became a low-ranking lawman (and card dealer) in a series of cow towns (like Lamar, Missouri) and boom towns—places like Wichita and Dodge City, Kansas, ultimately ending up in the silver boom town of Tombstone, Arizona, in 1879. Interspersed with lawman duties, he worked as a teamster and buffalo hunter and gambled in Texas, where he met "Doc" Holliday, a notorious gunman and gambler who would become his friend.

Earp worked in law enforcement in Tombstone with his brothers Morgan and Virgil. The latter was the federal marshal for the area. He also bought an interest in a saloon and a silver mine. Shortly thereafter, he came into conflict with a group of ranchers who were allied with Democratic and ex-Confederate ranching interests, called the Cowboys. The Republican Earps began to brawl with the McLaury brothers, "Curley Bill" Brocius, the Clantons, and the Democratic Sheriff John Behan of Tombstone. Additionally, Earp took up residence with Behan's mistress, a fact that pulled the two men even further apart. Election irregularities and political shenanigans further alienated the two lawmen.

The conflict flared into open warfare on the morning of October 26, 1881, when Earp and his brothers Virgil and Morgan, together with "Doc" Holliday, shot it out with the Clantons and the McLaurys. Frank and Tom McLaury were killed, as was Billy Clanton. Ike Clanton and a retainer ran from the scene, and Vigil and Morgan Earp were wounded. While this event electrified the frontier, local citizens were not so sanguine, and a trial was convened. Johnny Behan testified against the Earps and Holliday, and although they were found innocent and freed, their reputations were damaged. After the trial, Virgil Earp was wounded in an ambush and Morgan Earp was killed. Consequently, Wyatt Earp and some companions were on the hunt for Clanton and his gang. A shoot-out accorded in Tucson, and Wyatt killed Frank Stillwell. Later, the Earps formed a posse and killed "Curley Bill" Brocius and Indian Charlie Cruz, cowboys who were supposedly involved in Morgan's death.

When warrants were issued for the Earps and pursued by Sheriff Behan, they left the Arizona Territory forever. Their properties and assets were seized for back taxes and they moved on to places all over the West. Wyatt apparently married Josie, the woman whose affections he alienated from Johnny Behan in 1883, and they roamed the West together until his death. Earp spent the next few years working in saloons and as an investor in the northwest. He moved to San Diego, California, in 1885, and became a real estate speculator and gambling hall impresario. In 1893, the Earps moved to San Francisco and then on to Alaska in 1897. He later moved back to California, where he became a Hollywood film consultant and performed certain off-the-books activities for the Los Angeles Police Department. During the latter part of his life, he was the subject of numerous newspaper stories, some laudatory and others scandalous. His reputation was by no means secure.

Earp died in Los Angeles in 1929 after a failed attempt to revive his fortunes mining in California. He was discovered there by Stuart Lake, who wrote a highly flattering and exaggerated account of the lawman's life and exploits. This account was to have a huge influence on cinematic and televised portrayals of Earp and other western lawmen.

Earp lives on in legend in such films as *My Darling Clementine* (1946), *Gunfight at O. K. Corral* (1957), *Wyatt Earp* (1994), and *Tombstone* (1993), to name just a few. *Tombstone* comes the closest to catching the spirit of the times, preserves the richness of the frontier argot, and accurately portrays the moral ambiguity of Earp and his milieu. It also points out that Earp was a flawed hero and thug, who consorted with gamblers, prostitutes, and amoral gunslingers. It basically ignores the political dimension of the struggle to bring a certain brand of law and order to the post-bellum West.

Francis Frederick Hawley
Western Carolina University

See Also: Arizona; Brocius, William; Film, Crime in; Frontier Crime; Gun Control; History of Crime and Punishment in America: 1850–1900; Kansas; Sheriffs.

Further Readings
Bartholomew, Ed. *Wyatt Earp, the Man and the Myth*. Toyahvale, TX: Frontier Book Co., 1964.
Brown, Richard M. *Strain of Violence: Historical Studies of American Violence and Vigilantism*. New York: Oxford University Press, 1975.
Roberts, Gary. *Doc Holliday: The Life and Legend*. Hoboken, NJ: Wiley, 2007.
Trachtman, Paul. *The Gunfighters*. London: Caxton Publishing, 1974.

Eastern State Penitentiary

Philadelphia's infamous Eastern State Penitentiary (1829–1971) was the most famous example of a prison administered according to the Pennsylvania System of Separate Confinement, which argued that inmates should be totally segregated from one another while incarcerated. Eastern State Penitentiary's roots stretch back to an organization called the Philadelphia Society for Alleviating the Miseries of Public Prisons (PSAMPP), which was formed in 1787 by a group of prominent citizens including Benjamin Franklin, Dr. Benjamin Rush, and William White (Philadelphia's Anglican bishop).

Initially, the PSAMPP focused its efforts on reforming conditions at Philadelphia's Walnut Street Jail, which was overcrowded and filthy. The PSAMPP's efforts led to the addition of a "penitentiary house" to the Walnut Street Jail; prisoners incarcerated in the penitentiary house were physically separated from one another, received some religious instruction, and were expected to learn and practice a trade during their sentence. The goal of this program, which formed the basis of what later came to be called the Pennsylvania System, was reforming inmates, making the Walnut Street Jail the world's first penitentiary.

Pennsylvania System
Unfortunately, the Walnut Street Jail's penitentiary house quickly became overcrowded, making strict practice of the Pennsylvania System impossible. The PSAMPP advocated the construction

of replacement penitentiaries, specifically built to practice the Pennsylvania System. The first of these, Western State Penitentiary, opened near Pittsburgh in 1826, but the building did not allow for the full implementation of the Pennsylvania System because the cells were not large enough for inmates to practice their newly acquired trades.

By contrast, Eastern State Penitentiary, which was built 1821–36, was specifically designed to implement all aspects of the Pennsylvania System. Designed by Philadelphia architect John Haviland, Eastern State Penitentiary was the largest and most expensive public works project of its time because of the need to guarantee that all inmates were totally separated from one another and had enough space in their cells to practice their trades.

The building was constructed on a radial plan, with all seven of the original cellblocks meeting at a central location like the spokes of a wheel. Surrounding the cellblocks was a massive wall designed to resemble a castle. Each cell opened to a small, walled exercise yard where prisoners were allowed one hour of recreation per day (weather permitting). Because inmates were expected to spend most of their time in their cells, each cell had indoor plumbing and running water at a time when President Andrew Jackson was still using an outhouse.

Eastern State's administration could be surprisingly relaxed and shockingly brutal. On the one hand, inmates were allowed to keep pets in their exercise yards and could decorate their cells and exercise yards. At the same time, punishments for breaking the penitentiary's rules included straitjackets and the shower bath, whereby prisoners were chained to a wall or strapped to a chair and deluged with gallons of chilled water. One particularly fearful punishment called the "iron gag" was a bit placed in the mouth and was attached to the convict's hands, which were bound behind him; as the inmate lowered his hands from fatigue, the bit was pulled tight and slowly choked the inmate. Use of this device led to at least one inmate's death (Matthias Maccumsey) and triggered an investigation that revealed mismanagement, embezzlement, and perverse sexual encounters between inmates and staff.

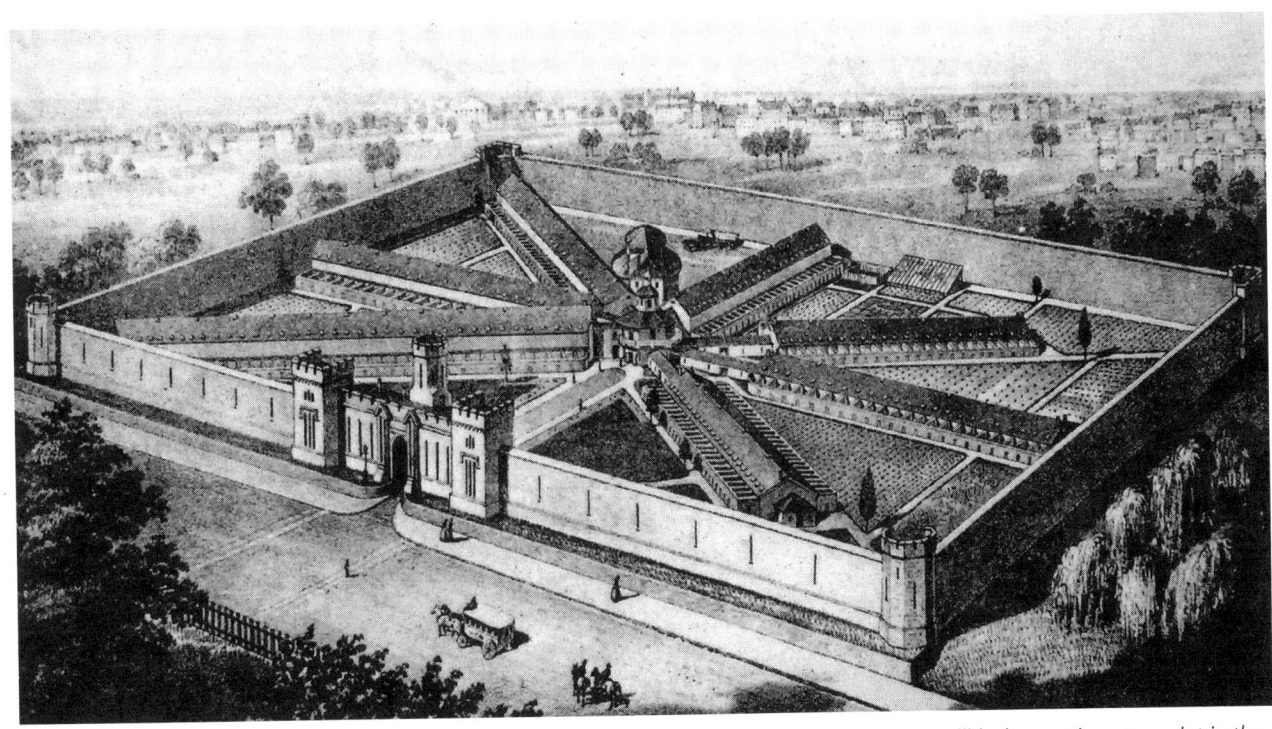

This 1855 lithograph shows the Eastern State Penitentiary's radial design, with its seven separate cellblocks meeting at a point in the middle. Each cell had a private walled exercise area behind it where the prisoners could go outside alone for an hour per day. For the majority of the time, they were meant to stay inside their cells working at solitary trades, but overcrowding soon made this impossible.

Overcrowding and Other Difficulties

Because it was so complex, Eastern State's administrators were never able to fully implement the Pennsylvania System. From the day the penitentiary opened, inmates were recruited to work around the prison site as a cost-cutting measure, frustrating attempts to keep them separated. After the Civil War, the penitentiary's inmate population quickly swelled beyond the number of available cells, making it impossible to adequately separate inmates. Despite the construction of multiple additional cellblocks, by the early 20th century, the Pennsylvania System at Eastern State was more often honored in the breach than the practice. Furthermore, Western State Penitentiary had abandoned the Pennsylvania System in 1869, and by the 1870s, the penitentiary model had been eclipsed by the reformatory model developed by Zebulon Brockway at the Elmira Reformatory. Though Eastern State's administrators clung to the Pennsylvania System into the 20th century, the penitentiary officially abandoned it in 1913.

Though no longer the cutting-edge penal institution it had once been, Eastern State Penitentiary's administrators continued working with local and national leaders in penology to reform inmates. During the 1910s and early 1920s, penitentiary administrators implemented many of the reforms initiated by famed penal reformer Thomas Mott Osborne at Eastern State's onetime rival, New York's Sing Sing; unfortunately, these reforms were short-lived due to a series of well-publicized scandals involving drugs, alcohol, and a prison-wide counterfeiting operation. These scandals led to a period of military-style discipline at Eastern State and a de-emphasis on inmate reform. However, following a series of prison riots throughout the United States, in the early 1950s, Eastern State once again became a cutting-edge laboratory for inmate reform.

Rechristened "State Correctional Institution—Philadelphia" (SCI-PHA), Eastern State's administrators divided the institution into a correctional facility and a diagnostic center where newly arrived convicts were offered psychological and medical treatment. Moreover, some of the more horrific aspects of discipline at Eastern State, like the group of underground cells known as "Klondike," were removed. During its final years, Eastern State Penitentiary returned to the spirit of inmate reform that had characterized its founding more than a century before.

Closure of the Facility

Unfortunately, the changes at Eastern State only made clear that the penitentiary's aging physical plant was simply not up to the challenge of functioning as a modern, maximum-security state prison. Proposals for closing Eastern State had appeared as early as the turn of the 20th century, and in 1929, the state opened the new Eastern State Penitentiary (SCI—Graterford). It was only the Depression, which drastically increased Pennsylvania's inmate population, that kept Eastern State Penitentiary open.

As Pennsylvania's inmate population declined in the 1950s and 1960s, many observers began calling for Eastern State's closure, especially following a riot at the penitentiary in 1961. In 1970, the state closed Eastern State Penitentiary, though

A cell at the now closed Eastern State Penitentiary as it looked in the early 2000s. The massive building complex still stands, though the last prisoners left in 1971.

the city of Philadelphia used the building to house inmates following a riot at the city jail the following year. However, this respite was only temporary, and by 1971, the penitentiary closed its doors for the last time as a correctional facility, leaving behind an imposing monument to American correctional history.

Paul Kahan
Montgomery County Community College

See Also: Auburn State Prison; Brockway, Zebulon; Corrections; Penitentiaries; Pennsylvania; Pennsylvania System of Reform; Sing Sing Correctional Facility.

Further Readings
Johnston, Norman. *Eastern State Penitentiary: Crucible of Good Intentions*. Philadelphia: Philadelphia Museum of Art, 1994.
Kahan, Paul. *Eastern State Penitentiary: A History*. Charleston, SC: History Press, 2008.
Rothman, David J. *The Discovery of the Asylum: Social Order and Disorder in the New Republic*. Boston: Little, Brown, 1971.

Eddy, Thomas

Thomas Eddy (1758–1827) was born in Philadelphia to Irish Quakers who had immigrated five years earlier. His father was in shipping before moving into hardware in 1766. A few years after Eddy's father died in 1766, the family relocated to Bucks County, Pennsylvania. At age 13, Eddy became a tanner's apprentice in Burlington, New Jersey. At age fifteen, he left the apprenticeship for New York with plans of being a merchant, despite having a lack of capital or experience. He dealt in goods shipped by his brother Charles from Ireland and England. He also made a significant sum of money from the British in 1781 by remitting money from the New York headquarters to troops imprisoned in Lancaster, Pennsylvania, after the fall of Yorktown.

In the general economic downturn after the end of the American Revolution, in 1784, Eddy and his brothers Charles and George went bankrupt in Philadelphia. Eddy returned to New York, where he was an underwriter and then broker and speculator in public funds. He became the director of the Mutual Insurance Company, and in 1803, he was one of the founders of the New York Savings Bank. He also was among the founders of the New York Bible Society.

Eddy was a principal advocate of the Erie Canal, second only to DeWitt Clinton in working for the project. One of his enterprises was the Western Inland Lock Navigation Company, which sought to make the Mohawk River navigable to Lake Ontario. When the Western Inland Lock Navigation Company became financially unstable, Eddy shifted his attention to the building of a canal. He and Federalist State Senator Jonas Platt proposed a commission to explore canals to Lake Ontario and Lake Erie and reported in favor of the Erie Canal.

Penal Reform
Eddy advocated moral uplift of blacks and the poor and other unfortunates. By 1793, his charitable impulse led him to an interest in penal reform. He wanted an end to branding, solitary confinement, whipping posts, and pillories. Eddy served on the prison reform commission and helped Senators Philip Schuyler and Ambrose Spencer draft the penitentiary reform bill that became law in 1796. Eddy's penal legislation authorized two state penitentiaries, one in Albany and the other in New York City. The Albany plan was abandoned, apparently because there was expectation of insufficient demand upstate.

Eddy oversaw construction of the old Newgate prison in Greenwich Village. Eddy relied on knowledge of Philadelphia's Walnut Street Jail in designing Newgate, but he differed in creating a prison with no accommodation for vagrants, debtors, or suspects. Newgate was for felons only. He also included a large room for public religious services, which Walnut Street did not have because there was no expectation when it was constructed that prisoners would be interested in religious exercises.

Eddy served as penitentiary director for four years, from 1797 to 1801, during which time he reformed the institution by emphasizing cleanliness and discipline. Deterrence to Eddy was merely temporary. Restitution was also good, but the long-term goal was eliminating the habits and urges, the patterns of guilt. Punishment had as its end reform. He was unsentimental and stern but humanitarian. His underlying assumption was that the felons were wicked and depraved, always plotting to cause a disturbance or to escape. But he did not believe that all prisoners were alike, so he treated each as an individual. For rehabilitation, he divided them into three categories: hardened criminals, depraved but not totally lost offenders, and young first timers.

His rehabilitation included religious worship and night school (open to the well-behaved and costing additional labor as tuition.) Prisoners had to work together in the shops, which promoted discipline and a sense of community and turned a small profit. There was no corporal punishment under the law, and guards were not allowed to strike prisoners. Discipline was through solitary confinement, which Eddy earlier sought to ban, with reduced rations. Well-behaved prisoners earned visits with wives and family members each quarter. Among Eddy's innovations was the individual cell for each convict rather than the community cell then in use. He also rejected the idea that prisoners should be kept in solitary confinement at night, not being enthusiastic about solitary confinement even in daytime.

In 1803, Eddy was on the outs with the new Jeffersonian prison inspectors, being a good Federalist, and the final straw—implementation of a contract shoemaking enterprise in the prison— caused him to resign in 1804. After leaving the prison, Eddy continued to criticize the increasing mismanagement, harsh discipline, and financial deficits of the new administration. He still insisted in 1818 that prisoners should work together during the day and sleep in individual cells at night, as they had during his tenure.

Eddy was also instrumental in getting the legislature to build mental institutions. In 1793, he became one of the governors of the New York state mental hospital, and he got the legislature to be more liberal in financial support for mental institutions. In 1798, the Quakers assigned John Murray and Eddy to visit New York state Native American tribes, and Eddy worked to make conditions for them better. In 1815, he cofounded Bloomingdale, an insane asylum. Eddy also published *State Prison of New York* in 1801.

John H. Barnhill
Independent Scholar

See Also: Corrections; History of Crime and Punishment in America: 1783–1850; New York; Penitentiaries; Punishment Within Prison; Rehabilitation.

Further Readings
Graber, Jennifer. "'When Friends Had the Management It Was Entirely Different': Quakers and Calvinists in the Making of New York Prison Discipline." *Quaker History*, v.97/2 (Fall 2008).
Knapp, Samuel Lorenzo. *The Life of Thomas Eddy: Comprising an Extensive Correspondence With Many of the Most Distinguished Philosophers and Philanthropists of This and Other Countries*. New York: Conner & Cooke, 1834.
Lewis, David W. *From Newgate to Dannemora: The Rise of the Penitentiary in New York, 1796–1848*. Ithaca, NY: Cornell University Press, 1965.

Eisenhower, Dwight D. (Administration of)

Thirty-fourth President (1953–61) Dwight Eisenhower was a war hero, a grandfatherly figure, and a natural leader for a decade of rest and recovery from two turbulent decades of depression and war. His administration was one of unparalleled prosperity and peace. Crime was defined broadly, although traditional crime rates were at record lows. Order was the word of the day.

The Cold War and Organized Crime

With political and social conservatism came paranoia and suspicion during the cold war. Joe McCarthy was allowed free rein during the early Eisenhower years in a paranoid pursuit of communists. Eisenhower initiated an anti-crime effort targeting dissident groups. The Supreme Court in the 1950s was limiting government power to intervene overtly against dissident groups. The Counter Intelligence Program (COINTELPRO) was a Federal Bureau of Investigation (FBI) effort to infiltrate and disrupt anti-American organizations and cause defections. It had antecedents in the World War I targeting of dissents and J. Edgar Hoover's ongoing anticommunist crusade through

Fidel Castro (bearded) at a meeting of the United Nations General Assembly in 1960. Dwight Eisenhower was responsible for authorizing an effort to kill Castro, which at one time involved 400 full-time members of the Central Intelligence Agency.

the 1940s. Under Eisenhower, the first to be targeted under COINTELPRO was the Communist Party USA but under Kennedy, COINTELPRO spread to include the socialists, Ku Klux Klan, Black Muslims, Black Panthers, and new left groups. Eisenhower received information about political and social contacts by such individuals as Bernard Baruch, Eleanor Roosevelt, and William O. Douglas. Eventually, Congress and the courts agreed that COINTELPRO violated legal restrictions on the FBI as well as individual constitutional rights to free speech and association.

Another issue was corruption and dictatorial management in organized labor. The Kefauver Committee hearings into organized crime had made Estes Kefauver a presidential contender in 1952, but organized crime was not a priority with FBI head J. Edgar Hoover. In 1957, the McClellan Committee investigated links between organized labor and organized crime. The AFL-CIO expelled three major abusers—laundry, bakery and confectionary, and teamsters—but the president was not satisfied. The Landrum-Griffin Act (Labor-Management Reporting and Disclosure Act) of 1959 required honest and democratic internal union arrangements. The act established federal penalties for misuse of union funds, violence against union members seeking to exercise legal rights, other specified crimes, and, in support of Taft-Hartley, bans on secondary boycotts and greater power for states to define their own labor relations in the right-to-work effort. But the Eisenhower administration was weak on organized crime.

Eisenhower made a gesture toward fighting the Mafia when he established an organized crime unit in the Criminal Division of the Department of Justice in 1954. But anticrime efforts were secondary when it came to dealing with Fidel Castro, the strongly anti-American Cuban dictator and potentially an ally of America's enemy the Soviet Union. Eisenhower authorized Operation Mongoose, an effort to kill Castro, an effort involving 400 full-time Central Intelligence Agency (CIA) agents.

When developing a paramilitary force in Cuba proved unfeasible, the next option was to hire the Mafia to assassinate Castro. The Mafia was willing because Castro had destroyed the lucrative casino and brothel business it enjoyed under Fulgencio Batista. The CIA liked the plan because they had plausible deniability. The CIA and FBI arranged immunity for Mafia figures in return for Mafia efforts to kill Castro. The Mafia, benefiting from the immunity, hustled the CIA, talking a good game but not actually doing much against Castro. When Eisenhower left Mongoose to Kennedy, Kennedy renamed it Operation Freedom, and the effort began to include poisoned diving suits and exploding cigars, as well as the more traditional snipers and assassins.

Juvenile Delinquency

In 1960, Eisenhower referred to a worldwide problem, one that most industrialized countries, including the harshly repressive Soviet Union, shared but could not control. The problem was juvenile delinquency, and Eisenhower wanted a program that would address the causes without mentioning juvenile delinquency, but instead talking about positives such as healthy development of intellect, morality, and physical condition. For Eisenhower, the beginning was the child's home environment. Historically, the solution to juvenile crime was jail, but in the 19th century, particularly late in the century and into the early 20th, juvenile delinquency became another target of the reformers who thought by intervention to turn poor juveniles away from the criminal path. In the late 1940s and 1950s, the problem spread into the middle class, and public opinion was excited by the popular press, national magazines, and Hollywood. Latchkey kids and unsupervised teens meant a doubling of the juvenile justice workload between 1948 and 1956, with 1954 the peak year. In 1955, Eisenhower asked Congress for federal aid to states for antidelinquency programs. Congress rejected Ike's calls in 1955 and again in 1956 and 1960. Aid to the states began under Kennedy.

Causes of juvenile delinquency included gangs, parental failure, rock and roll, bad neighborhoods, and, according to the federal government, the international trade in drugs. The war on drugs dates at least to 1914's Harrison Narcotics Tax Act that regulated distribution of heroin and other opiates and the 1937 Marihuana Act that broadened the scope of the 1914 legislation. In 1954, Eisenhower established the U.S. Interdepartmental Committee on Narcotics, a coordinating body for executive actions against drugs. The largely symbolic measure was lauded by the *New York Times* as a new war on narcotic addiction. Not until 1971 would the term *war on drugs* come into use, and Richard Nixon was first to use it.

Immigration and Civil Rights

Eisenhower was the last president to enforce the effort to block illegal immigrants. In 1954, he instituted Operation Wetback, a repatriation effort of the Immigration and Naturalization Service (INS) that saw 750 federal agents in cooperation with local and state authorities remove 1.3 million Mexican nationals in a single year with no protest from government-funded Hispanic advocacy groups. The border patrol as well as state and local police in the southwest swept Mexican American neighborhoods, made random stops and ID checks of "Mexican-looking" people, and deported both illegal aliens and, sometimes, legal citizen children. Eisenhower was the last president to authorize the execution of a soldier, signing a death warrant in 1958 for an execution carried out under Kennedy in 1961.

One law-and-order issue that Eisenhower largely sidestepped was civil rights. The Eisenhower administration accepted *Brown v. Topeka* and promised to support federal laws against poll taxes and lynching. Integration of the government and armed forces would continue. But Eisenhower needed southern votes for his foreign policy and let civil rights groups fight their battles without the federal government. The exception, intervention in the Little Rock desegregation crisis in 1957, was a matter of countering the flouting of federal authority rather than upholding a court decision. In a sense, it was a matter of law and order. Eisenhower presided over a nation enjoying prosperity and peace and relatively low crime rates. Anticrime efforts were relatively moderate, and there was no campaign for harsher punishments or more prisons.

John H. Barnhill
Independent Scholar

See Also: 1941 to 1960 Primary Documents; Civil Rights Laws; Federal Bureau of Investigation; Italian Americans; Juvenile Delinquency, History of; Juvenile Delinquency, Sociology of; Landrum-Griffin Act of 1859; Organized Crime, History of; Political Crimes, History of.

Further Readings
DeFrank, Thomas M. "Servicemen on Death Row." *Daily News Washington Bureau* (June 24, 2001).
Eisenhower, Dwight David. "Papers of Dwight David Eisenhower." http://www.eisenhowermemorial.org/presidential-papers/first-term/documents/1887.cfm (Accessed June 2011).
Holt, Marilyn Irvin. "Children as Topic No. 1: White House Conferences Focused on Youths and Societal Changes in Postwar America." *Prologue Magazine*, v.42/2 (2010).
Tracy, Kathleen. "The Political Landscape of 1960." http://www.netplaces.com/jacqueline-kennedy-onassis/political-ambitions/the-political-landscape-of-1960.htm (Accessed June 2011).

Eisenstadt v. Baird

This Supreme Court case, argued in November 1971 and decided in March 1972, declared unconstitutional a Massachusetts statute that imposed a five-year jail term for distributing contraceptives unless by a licensed physician or pharmacist, or distributing contraceptives to unmarried persons. The decision removed the institutionalization of punitive premarital sex standards, allowing unmarried, consenting adults to engage in sexual conduct for reasons other than procreation. With *Griswold v. Connecticut* before it and *Roe v. Wade* after it, the court accepted a zone of privacy recognized in the Fourteenth Amendment's due process clause. The court decided the crux of the case, however, on the Fourteenth Amendment's equal protection clause.

Students at Boston University invited William Baird, Jr., a birth control activist, former medical student, and former employee of a pharmaceutical company, to deliver a lecture on contraception and overpopulation. He preceded the hour-long lecture on April 6, 1967, with a statement that he meant to test the Massachusetts law on contraceptives by distributing products. He urged his audience of nearly 2,000 students and faculty to petition the state legislature to repeal the law and to come forward at the end of the lecture to take contraceptive supplies from his display. When Baird handed a single woman Emko contraceptive foam, officials arrested him on two counts: displaying contraceptives and distributing contraceptives without a license. Although the woman's marital status was not an issue at the arrest, it became important in the court's deliberations.

Joseph Nolan argued for appellant Thomas Eisenstadt, sheriff of Suffolk County. Because Baird did not have a medical license, he could not appreciate the dangers of contraceptives. Privacy was not an issue because Baird had openly displayed contraceptives. The state, in Nolan's view, had a compelling interest to deter fornication among unmarried couples. Joseph Tydings argued for Baird, supported by amicus briefs from the Planned Parenthood Federation of America, Inc., Planned Parenthood League of Massachusetts, the American Civil Liberties Union, and Human Rights for Women, Inc. Tydings contended that Massachusetts had no compelling basis for this law, and that legislation already existed to regulate dangerous and unsafe products.

In a 6–1 decision, the court found no rational reason for the state to restrict contraceptives to married women. Justice William Brennan, writing for the majority, argued that because the statute treated differently married and unmarried persons who were "similarly situated," it violated the Fourteenth Amendment's equal protection clause: "the rights must be the same for the unmarried and the married alike."

The court also expanded the Ninth Amendment's right of privacy enunciated in *Griswold*:

> It is true that in *Griswold* the right of privacy in question inhered in the marital relationship. Yet the marital couple is not an independent entity ..., but an association of two individuals each with a separate intellectual and emotional make-up. If the right of privacy means anything, it is the right of the *individual*, married or single, to be free from unwarranted governmental intrusion into matters so fundamentally affecting a person as the decision whether to bear or beget a child.

The court extended the zone of privacy not only to contraception but also to adults' right to engage in sex as they saw fit, including sodomy. While the decision implied heterosexual couples, the court broadened this right to all consenting adults with *Lawrence v. Texas* (2003).

Justice William Douglas concurred but wrote an opinion invoking First Amendment rights to free speech. The state could not restrict an individual's right to deliver an educational lecture on birth control: "The teachings of Baird and those of Galileo might be of a different order; but the suppression of either is equally repugnant." Chief Justice Warren Burger cast the lone dissent. President Richard Nixon appointed Justices William Rehnquist and Lewis Powell, Jr., too late for them to participate in the deliberations. This case fits within the larger historical context of expanding individual rights, especially for teenagers. The Twenty-Sixth Amendment, in 1971, lowered the voting age from 21 to 18. In 1972, Title IX prohibited discrimination in schools receiving federal funds, including prejudice against pregnant students. *Carey v. Population Services International*

(1977) explicitly ruled that the right to privacy with regard to procreation extended to minors under the age of 16. In 1978, congressional actions led to teen rights to use family planning clinics confidentially and without parental consent.

Simone M. Caron
Wake Forest University

See Also: 1851 to 1900 Primary Documents; *Griswold v. Connecticut*; Morality; *Roe v. Wade*.

Further Readings
Goldstein, Leslie Friedman. *The Constitutional Rights of Women*, Rev. ed. Madison: University of Wisconsin Press, 1989.
Gordon, Linda. *Woman's Body, Woman's Right: A Social History of Birth Control in America*. New York: Viking, 1976.
Johnson, John W. Griswold v. Connecticut: *Birth Control and the Constitutional Right of Privacy*. Lawrence: University Press of Kansas, 2005.

Electric Chair, History of

The use of electricity for execution dates back to the 18th century. Benjamin Franklin and other scientific minds of the time fired jolts of electricity into animals in order to kill them. This practice originated with Luigi Galvani, an Italian inventor who attempted to shock animals and persons back to life after they had died. The process was far more useful in killing than in saving lives—no records indicate that a test subject was ever brought back to life. Franklin and others postulated that electrical currents, shot into the vital areas of an animal, would kill it instantaneously and result in a painless and humane death. Franklin used electrocution regularly in order to slaughter his own chickens or cows, as he thought that the animals suffered far less with that method than with traditional methods. While experiments of this nature continued to be performed during the 19th century, the focus of electrical research was redirected. The harnessing of electrical power for lighting was far more important for inventors such as Thomas Edison and George Westinghouse because of the potential for commercial gain. However, from the 1850s forward, a group of activists centered in the northeast began to press for increased humanity in execution. Hanging came to be seen as "old world" and "barbaric" and completely unacceptable in a civilized, modern nation.

As early as 1878, the Ohio state penitentiary system had modified Thomas Edison's Inductrium device to punish prisoners. The device was originally intended to deliver a small shock of electricity to a person, as this was thought to improve circulation and general health. The penitentiary altered the device to produce a much larger jolt and attached electrodes from the Inductrium directly to the skin of an unruly prisoner to administer a painful shock.

Throughout 1879, the *New York Times* ran a series of articles detailing the possibilities for more humane execution methods. Electrocution was brought up a number of times in the article as something that needed to be examined further, but after the articles stopped running, the small public debate about electrocution ended. In 1882, three individuals were accidentally electrocuted. The news of these electrocutions coincided with a resuscitation of the debate over the humanity of hanging. A growing number of death penalty detractors called for the abolition of the practice altogether, but an even larger number saw execution as a necessary part of law and order. A large percentage of these were, however, moved to step away from hanging, as the idea of execution as a public spectacle had become distasteful.

Westinghouse's Dynamo
In the early 1880s, George Westinghouse devoted time to the creation of a more powerful electric generator capable of delivering far greater voltage than Edison's device. The Dynamo was the result. A prototype unit caused the accidental death of a worker when he inadvertently grasped both poles at once. In the autopsy, physicians could find no discernible cause of death, save for a large coagulation of blood in his lungs. On closer inspection, a faint line was observed under the epidermis on his chest where the electrical current had been delivered. Alfred Porter Southwick, a dentist from Buffalo, New York, was convinced that electrocution was just the thing for humane executions and resumed experimenting with animal

This electric chair in the execution chamber at the Louisiana State Penitentiary is a replica of one known as "Gruesome Gertie," which was used for 87 executions from 1957 to 1991. The electric chair was still in widespread use until the 1980s, when lethal injection increasingly replaced it as a method of execution. Through 2003, 4,432 people in the United States had been executed in electric chairs.

electrocutions. He decided, after a number of trial runs on stray dogs, that a current delivered to the brain would kill quickly and painlessly.

Southwick took the helm of a New York committee to explore execution and decide upon the most humane method. An encyclopedic manual was drawn up, which alphabetically listed and discussed historical execution and torture tactics. Two possible candidates were named: poison by injection, or electrocution. At the behest of New York physicians, poison was eliminated because they feared it would lead the public to refuse to use hypodermic syringes. When Southwick wrote to Edison asking his opinion on the matter, Edison initially remained silent and only said that he was opposed to the death penalty. Weeks later, when asked again, Edison had reconsidered. He thought that electrocution was the most humane method of ending a life. Further, he thought that George Westinghouse's relatively new "alternating current" electricity was the best suited sort of electric current for the job, because of the high voltages that it made possible. The Gerry Report, named for Chairman Elbridge Gerry, was compiled and presented January 17, 1888. The final report stated that of all methods of execution, electrical current was the most humane because the shock traveled faster than nerves could receive information, and so death was instantaneous and completely painless. The idea was to deliver a shock to the brain of the condemned by way of wire connected to one of Westinghouse's Dynamo machines. The committee further estimated that executions that used this method would be inexpensive—the entire chair should cost less than $500, they estimated.

First Execution by Electric Chair

A bill was proposed in New York the same year and passed quickly. On January 1, 1889, New York was the first state to abolish hanging and institute electrocution as the only acceptable method of execution. William Kemmler, convicted of the murder of Tillie Ziegler, was to be the first man executed by electric chair. He was actually scheduled to be second, but due to a last-minute pardon, the line was cut shorter. The execution took place at Auburn Prison in New York the week of August 4, 1890. The execution was a failure. Kemmler was attached to the chair by 11 leather straps and had a skullcap placed on his head. The skullcap held a sea sponge into which was injected a soda solution intended to speed to current. A similar fixture was placed on the small of his back, and the shock of 1,000 volts was delivered. Kemmler was shocked for a short time and then pronounced dead. When the skullcap was removed, he was still breathing, and so he was shocked again for far longer with 2,000 volts, at which time his skin was charred and reportedly caught fire.

All sides of the equation placed the blame elsewhere—doctors blamed the attendants, attendants blamed the equipment. George Westinghouse denounced the execution and noted that there would have been more success with an ax. Thomas Edison, however, stuck by his statement that electrocution was perfectly valid; he just thought there were some mistakes made that caused the botched execution. He cited his own animal experiments as proof of instantaneous death. Refinements to the chair continued, and in 1897, Edwin F. Davis was awarded a patent for the "electrocution chair," which, along with one designed by Charles Adams, represents the final form of the electric chair.

The botched execution did not stop the acceptance of electrical execution. After New York's 1888 adoption, Ohio adopted it in 1896, Massachusetts in 1898, and New Jersey in 1906. Acceptance of the chair moved beyond government and into the medical profession. By 1910, the *Journal of the American Medical Association* and other esteemed publications either encouraged or at least acknowledged the chair as humane. The public was also fascinated by the chair. Edison's film company produced two movies, first in 1901, *The Execution of Czolgosz*. The film was a short reenactment of the electrical execution of William McKinley's assassin. In 1903, Edison produced a film wherein a rogue elephant that escaped from a circus tent and trampled onlookers was electrocuted. By the middle of the 20th century, at the greatest extent of the electric chair's use, it had been adopted by 25 states.

Conclusion

Throughout the 1950s and 1960s, detractors of capital punishment pressured governments to rethink execution. A series of court cases and decisions slowed the rate of executions over this time, and in the late 1960s, capital punishment by any means had essentially stopped. In 1972, the National Association for the Advancement of Colored People (NAACP) reported on the tremendous racial disparity in executions, especially in the south. The report stated that between 1908 and 1930, 148 people were electrocuted in Virginia. Of these, only 18 were not black. Capital punishment in the United States resumed in the early-to-mid 1970s, but the electric chair fell out of favor. The method that replaced it, and is still the most widely practiced in the nation, is lethal injection. By 2003, 4,432 persons had been executed in the electric chair in the United States.

Robert W. Watkins
Florida State University

See Also: Auburn State Prison; Capital Punishment; Czolgosz, Leon; Death Row; Executions; Hanging; Sing Sing Correctional Facility.

Further Readings
Banner, S. *The Death Penalty: An American History*. Cambridge, MA: Harvard University Press, 2002.
Essig, Mark. *Edison and the Electric Chair*. New York: Walker & Company, 2003.
Moran, Richard. *Executioner's Current*. New York: Alfred A. Knopf, 2002.

Electronic Surveillance

Electronic surveillance has been an important part in the debate between civil liberties and national security. Soon after the invention of the telegraph, the government began intercepting communications. Enterprising individuals intercepted communications for profit. State legislatures responded by prohibiting electronic surveillance. Soon after, the government learned that electronic surveillance provided intelligence and evidence against criminal conspiracies. As electronic surveillance increased, supporters and opponents of it lobbied for legislation. Though legislation followed to restrict surveillance, the debate now focuses on the proof necessary to permit judicially authorized wiretaps.

Wiretapping

Electronic communication began with the invention of the telegraph in the first half of the 19th century. Its first governmental use was to send news of Henry Clay's presidential nomination from Baltimore to Washington, D.C. By the outbreak of the Civil War in 1861, the telegraph was an important communication device. Both sides employed it for war communications. Sending news of troop movements and strategy across telegraph wires permitted commanders to remain safe from the battlefield while directing their troops. It also gave the opposition the opportunity to gather intelligence about enemy plans. Specialists attached unauthorized cables to opposition cables. These unauthorized cables, wiretaps, permitted outsiders to listen to communications intended for others.

Following the Civil War, telegraph use expanded. Commercial enterprises used telegraphs to transmit stock and commodity prices. People in London could buy cotton from New Orleans through telegraph communications. The telegraph also featured prominently among the gambling community. Betting halls could place a person at the horse track and have the results telegraphed to the betting hall. Those seeking to ensure victory tapped the telegraph lines. These incidents led to laws prohibiting wiretapping. Technology evolved, first to the telephone, then radio. State governments passed laws prohibiting intercepting these communications, but law enforcement ignored them. They learned that wiretapping phone lines provided strong evidence against criminal conspiracies, especially against those involved in illegal alcohol distribution. In *Olmstead v. United States*

An unidentified man examining telegraph lines in an 1862–63 photograph attributed to the Civil War–era U.S. Military Railway Department. Surveillance of telegraph communications during that war marked the beginning of widespread use of wiretapping.

(1928), Roy Olmstead challenged the government's wiretapping. The Supreme Court upheld the search because the government did not enter Olmstead's property. Justice Louis Brandeis dissented, arguing that Olmstead's privacy rights were violated, creating a battle between privacy and law enforcement interests.

Following *Olmstead* and the disclosure of wiretapping during World War I, Attorney General William Mitchell banned governmental wiretapping. Congress passed the Federal Communications Act, barring wiretap evidence in federal courts. Law enforcement's demand for wiretapping soon overtook the prohibition and used the information obtained from wiretaps for leads. By the end of the 1930s, the Supreme Court effectively ended the practice. However, with the outbreak of World War II, President Franklin Roosevelt needed information about German and Japanese activities. He ordered J. Edgar Hoover, the director of the Federal Bureau of Investigation (FBI), to oversee these efforts. In doing so, Roosevelt set the precedent for separating criminal justice and national security surveillance.

Cold War Fears

Following World War II, electronic surveillance expanded greatly with the advent of the cold war. The threat of communist expansion served to justify extensive electronic surveillance. Hoover directed surveillance of political opponents, arguing that opposition was fueled by communist infiltration. Targets included organized crime, the Hollywood filmmaking establishment, the civil rights movement, and other government agencies. The Supreme Court tacitly approved by excluding national security surveillance from judicial review. As national security surveillance increased, law enforcement pushed for electronic surveillance in criminal cases. Congress relented and, in 1968, established procedures for judicially authorized electronic surveillance. The law limited electronic surveillance to specific criminal offenses and required a judicial probable cause determination and procedures designed to minimize interception of innocent conversations.

Ten years later, Congress regulated national security surveillance. The Foreign Intelligence Surveillance Act (FISA) established criteria for national security surveillance. Although similar to the requirements for criminal cases, significant differences existed. Congress created the secret Foreign Intelligence Surveillance Court to review surveillance applications. Probable cause standards were relaxed by only requiring evidence that the subject of the surveillance was connected to a foreign power. The dual systems created difficulties for national security–related criminal cases. FISA surveillance often uncovered evidence of crimes. Courts uniformly admitted evidence obtained via FISA, but expressed concerns about potential abuse. To avoid judicial exclusion of FISA evidence in criminal cases, the Justice Department erected a "wall" preventing FISA-obtained evidence from entering criminal investigations.

Surveillance and Terrorism

Within 10 years, the "wall" contributed to the United States not detecting Al Qaeda's plot to crash commercial airliners into the World Trade Center and the Pentagon. Analysts later concluded that separating intelligence from law enforcement contributed to the surprise attack. To rectify the problem, Congress passed legislation permitting sharing between law enforcement and intelligence. Despite the legislation, President George W. Bush created the Terrorist Surveillance Program, a top secret policy whereby the National Security Agency, the agency assigned to handle national security electronic surveillance, intercepted communications entering or leaving the United States from nations hosting suspected terrorists. The program's disclosure renewed debate about government electronic surveillance, which culminated in amendments to FISA, permitting more surveillance without immediate judicial approval.

The history of electronic surveillance in the United States is that of attempts to balance the need for law enforcement and national security with the desire for privacy and protection from government eavesdropping. For the most part, this debate has been resolved through judicial supervision. However, on multiple occasions, presidents have assumed the power to covertly conduct electronic surveillance outside established judicial procedures, sparking renewed debate.

Scott Ingram
High Point University

See Also: Bush, George W. (Administration of); Defendant's Rights; Espionage; Federal Bureau of Investigation; Homeland Security; Hoover, J. Edgar; *Katz v. United States*; *Olmstead v. United States*; Omnibus Crime Control and Safe Streets Act of 1968; Prohibition; Supreme Court, U.S.; Terrorism.

Further Readings

Cinquegrana, Americo R. "The Walls (And Wires) Have Ears: The Background and First Ten Years of the Foreign Intelligence Surveillance Act of 1978." *University of Pennsylvania Law Review*, v.137 (1988).

Howe, Daniel Walker. *What God Hath Wrought: The Transformation of America, 1815–1848*. New York: Oxford University Press, 2007.

Lichtblau, Eric. *Bush's Law: The Remaking of American Justice*. New York: Pantheon Books, 2008.

McGee, Jim and Brian Duffy. *Main Justice: The Men and Women Who Enforce the Nation's Criminal Laws and Guard Its Liberties*. New York: Simon & Schuster, 1996.

Olmstead v. United States, 277 U.S. 438 (1928).

Powers, Richard Gid. *Secrecy and Power: The Life of J. Edgar Hoover*. New York: Free Press, 1987.

Elkins Act of 1903

The Elkins Act of 1903 expanded the Interstate Commerce Act of 1887 by addressing the issue of how to regulate the practice of rebates used by the railroads in the United States. The legislation signed into law by President Theodore Roosevelt ended the practice of special rates and rebates that hindered commerce and also placed the railroad industry under further regulatory surveillance by the Interstate Commerce Commission. The initial legislation sponsored by Stephen B. Elkins, Republican senator from West Virginia, also became known as the Elkins Anti-Rebating Act of February 19, 1903. A major influence behind this bill was the Pennsylvania Railroad and its president, Alexander Cassatt, who long opposed the increasingly expensive practice of special rates and rebates and recognized the weakness of the current law under the Interstate Commerce Act of 1887. Another influence was state legislation written by James A. Logan, the solicitor general of Pennsylvania in 1902. Many people claim responsibility for the text of the Elkins bill, but ultimately it was a compromise version of the bills that passed the Congress.

The first version of the Elkins bill was proposed as Senate Bill 521 in 1902, sponsored by Elkins, and was largely based upon Logan's ideas. Elkins proposed that the Interstate Commerce Commission set the rates, created legalized pooling with a review process, made it punishable by fine for both the corporations and individuals to give or accept rebates, abolished imprisonment as a punishment, and gave circuit courts the right to review cases at the commission's request. This version of the bill did not have the support of the members of the commission because the commission already proved powerless. Alternately, the Corliss Nelson bill, proposed as Senate Bill 3575, received the support of the commission members. The bill written by Michigan Republican Senator John Corliss and Minnesota Republican Senator Knute Nelson offered the same strict opposition to rebating practices, with additional provisions that the commission could set rates for two years if a complaint is filed against a railroad, followed by judicial review by the circuit courts. The main difference between the two bills was whether to legalize pooling.

Legislators opted to propose a compromise bill named the Elkins bill (Senate Bill 7038). The final version came to a Senate vote in February 1903 and passed unanimously, followed by a vote of 250–6 in the House. In its final version, the Elkins bill made both individuals and corporations liable for any violations of the law. The penalty for illegal activity was reduced to fines not to exceed $20,000 and no prison time. The Interstate Commerce Commission and state attorneys general could request that a circuit court try a case and enforce rates if they deemed the grounds existed for intervention. Railroads could establish joint rates and file them with the commission for violation tracking. Anyone who violated the rates, either giver or receiver, was liable under this new law.

President Theodore Roosevelt signed the Elkins Act into law on February 19, 1903, and thus updated the Interstate Commerce Commission Act of 1887, making it more effective in enforcing rates with the railroads. The act did not fix all of the problems between merchants and the railroads, but it did accomplish what the railroads sought—an end to rate fixing and pooling. It further federalized the railroads and attempted to strengthen the weak Interstate Commerce Commission. Railroads often kept information from the commission's investigators and thus stalled investigations by withholding evidence. Large railroads could then keep their costs down while maintaining control of the major commercial and passenger routes in the country. Smaller railroads could not compete, nor could small businessmen and farmers. The law improved their situation and gave them a course of action to make business practices more fair.

The law remained in effect until further amendments under the Hepburn Act of 1906 strengthened the commission and its powers while addressing the weaknesses that remained in the Elkins Act. This legislation also had the unforeseen impact of leading to a devaluation of railroad securities, contributing to a depression in 1907. The Elkins Act increased the influence of the Interstate Commerce Commission and helped further regulate the American railroad industry.

Theresa S. Hefner-Babb
Lamar University

See Also: Antitrust Law; Interstate Commerce Act of 1887; Roosevelt, Theodore (Administration of).

Further Readings
Chapter 708 Stat. 847. "An Act to Further Regulate Commerce With Foreign Nations and Among the States." Washington, DC: Government Printing Office, 1904.
Kolko, Gabriel. *Railroads and Regulation: 1877–1916*. Princeton, NJ: Princeton University Press, 1965.
Ripley, William Z. *Railroads: Rates and Regulation*. New York: Arno Press, 1973.

Elmira Prison

The history of Elmira as a prison has two discrete periods. The second period is well known to criminologists; the first period, almost not at all. But it was in Elmira's period of infamy as a prison camp for Confederate prisoners of war that the adjacent community discovered the profitability of prison as industry. The primary attraction of its location was that it was near an important railroad junction and that the prisoners could not be freed by a sudden Confederate lunge into Maryland, where most prisoners had previously been housed. Prisoners were confined at Elmira from mid-1864 though mid-1865. Food and adequate clothing were apparently deliberately withheld as abundant provisions existed in the area and in the north during the latter part of the war. Accordingly, Elmira had the highest death rate of any Union prisoner of war camp; 25 percent of those

A memorial for the nearly 3,000 Confederate prisoners who are buried at Elmira, New York. They died because of harsh conditions in the original prison camp, which was demolished.

held there died. Families of prisoners flocked to the area during and after the war, and prison guards' free spending and camp provisioning helped the local economy.

The Reformatory Period
When the war ended, the community was highly enthusiastic about a new "reformatory prison" that was planned for the area. At the National Prison Association Meeting in Cincinnati, Ohio, in 1870, the concept of *reform* was advocated as a primary goal of imprisonment, and the focus of that meeting was on creating a prison at Elmira with this in mind. Reformers planned to use vocational education, parole, and a sentence of indefinite duration (indeterminate) to give

inmates the skills they needed to successfully return to society. Zebulon Brockway, a noted reform advocate and warden, planned to employ ideas first used by Sir Walter Crofton in Ireland. This "marks system" was based on accumulation of positive points and could be called a merit-based system. It was confidently believed that in the process of accretion of points, inmates would learn that work was rewarding in itself and that virtue was its own reward. This was very much in tune with late-Victorian ideology about work and morality.

Accordingly, Brockway initiated a system in which inmates progressed through three stages. Brockway was successful in excluding from the program all but first-time youthful offenders; it was thought that these neophytes to the system would be more amenable to reform than would be recidivists. After an interview with Brockway, inmates were assigned to the second grade. Inmates who responded well to classes and vocational efforts after six months would earn a specified number of marks and be promoted to the first grade. Inmates in the first grade could earn a parole hearing after a year of full marks. Those who transgressed or otherwise did not get with the program were demoted to the third grade. Third grade involved quasi-solitary confinement and was manifestly unpleasant. Only through earning positive marks for a month could inmates hope to be restored to second grade, whereupon they would have to work their way into the first grade all over again.

Brockway was an energetic self-aggrandizer and tireless self-promoter. In his many speeches and publications, he promulgated four rules for sound correctional practice. His first maxim was that custody should be so secure as to defeat any attempt at escape. His hope was that inmates would stop thinking about escape and focus on getting with the correctional program. His second rule was to exclude outsiders (like family and ministers) as he felt they were a distraction and, moreover, that they seemed to imply that the institution itself was insufficient to accomplish the goal of correction. Third, he believed that the state had given him a grant of discretion and that he should have great latitude in matters administrative and disciplinary. Finally, in keeping with Victorian positivism, he believed in keeping prisoners fully occupied; thus, they were kept hopping from dawn to dusk.

Though Brockway claimed an 80 percent success rate for Elmira's parolees, few contemporary criminologists give that figure much credence. Most modern criminal justice academics posit that the prison was a failure because of its status as a total institution. Institutions of this type have conflicting goals and simply do not perform as one would hope or expect. Another problem was the constant attention paid to forcing Victorian middle-class Protestant standards of behavior, ambition, and demeanor on a captive population that was non-Protestant, non–Anglo Saxon, and poor. Exhortations to work hard for the sake of work itself were not bound to have much salience once the inmate returned to his native milieu—the streets, his subculture, and his family. Also, the pseudo-scientific approach itself was counterproductive and brutal. Prisoners were often beaten by guards and sometimes were slapped in the face by Brockway himself. Guards did not accept the goal of treatment and subverted it by unreasonable custody demands and excessive punishments. Finally, the inmate subculture proved to be an insurmountable obstacle. Brockway was eventually moved aside in 1900 but continued to defend his practices and system for another two decades. His biggest defense was that the inadequacies of the system were the result of prisoners being released prematurely.

Conclusion

The Elmira system emerged as the primary exemplar of the reformatory system—the system that, for good or ill, constituted the rationale for modern corrections throughout the nation and the world. The word *reformatory* itself has come to mean a prison for juveniles, or at least for first-time offenders. This reflects society's superficial disposition to accept vocational training and education as goals. But even Elmira abandoned those goals by the 1930s; even when the goals were in place, the resources devoted to their realization were pitiful and demonstrated a lack of societal commitment to attaining them. But probably the most destructive factor was the problematic linkage between street culture and institutional inmate culture: a vicious and caustic nexus noted especially in today's ineffective prisons.

Elmira State Correctional Facility stills exists today as a maximum-security facility for male inmates and holds about 1,800 inmates.

Francis Frederick Hawley
Western Carolina University

See Also: Brockway, Zebulon; Corrections; National Congress on Penitentiary and Reformatory Discipline; Penitentiaries; Prisoner's Rights; Rehabilitation.

Further Readings
Gray, M. *The Business of Captivity: Elmira and Its Civil War Prison.* Kent, OH: Kent State University Press, 2001.
Pisciotta, A. W. *Benevolent Repression: Social Control and the American Reformatory-Prison Movement,* New York: New York University Press, 1994.
Putney, S. and G. Putney. "Origins of the Reformatory." *Journal of Criminal Law, Criminology, and Police Science,* v.53/4 (December 1962).

Embezzlement

Embezzlement is a form of white-collar crime that involves the misappropriation of assets by an individual or group of individuals to whom those assets have been entrusted. Embezzlement typically involves the abuse of power that results from one's position within an occupational structure. Many examples of embezzlement involve bank employees who were responsible for handling transactions, issuing loans, and other bank functions, and who were entrusted to do so with little supervision or oversight. Nonetheless, by definition, embezzlement involves some degree of motivation on the part of the offender, and the primary motivation appears to be material self-interest or greed.

From a legal standpoint, embezzlement is the fraudulent conversion of another's property by a person who is in lawful possession of the property. Through the early 20th century, U.S. law enforcement rarely concerned itself with the investigation of embezzlement or with other forms of white-collar crime. Though laws prohibiting embezzlement were enacted by this time and were enforced in some cases, the general public did not consider white-collar crime to be a serious problem. The change in attitudes regarding the importance of these crimes appears to have occurred in 1939, when Edwin H. Sutherland coined the term *white-collar crime* and urged a shift of attention away from more traditional forms of street crime, such as homicide and burglary, in his presidential address to the American Sociological Society. At this time, people began to recognize the magnitude of costs imposed upon society as a result of white-collar crime.

Incidents of embezzlement are rare compared to other forms of crime. This remains true, even when comparing it to other forms of white-collar crime. For example, in 2009, official data from the Federal Bureau of Investigation (FBI) indicates that there were 210,255 arrests for fraud and 85,844 arrests for forgery and counterfeiting, while there were only 17,920 arrests for embezzlement. Though the numbers vary slightly from year to year, this trend has remained consistent throughout modern U.S. history. The fact that the crime of embezzlement requires some degree of opportunity to commit may contribute to this observed infrequency.

Although rare, embezzlement schemes often span several years and result in the theft of large sums of money. In most cases, embezzlers go to great lengths to evade detection and mask their schemes by maintaining an upstanding image in the community. Often, the embezzled funds are utilized to bolster their status. Many members of the community, including some of the victims, tend to be sympathetic to the embezzler, believing that the acts were not committed with malicious intent.

Nevertheless, two unique features distinguish embezzlement from other forms of crime and highlight the seriousness of these embezzlement offenses. First, the duration and complexity of embezzlement schemes suggest that criminal intent is well established. That is, in most cases, the embezzler knew that his/her actions were illegal and continued to commit them regardless. Mens rea is present. Second, embezzlement often involves the theft of millions of dollars. This both deprives individual clients of their property and devastates the employing institution.

Many institutions victimized by embezzlers file for bankruptcy or are forced to close because of the losses incurred.

The Evolution of Embezzlement Law

Historical accounts of embezzlement date back at least to the time of the ancient Greeks, when Andocides (ca. 400 B.C.E.) detailed the fraudulent acts of Agyrrhius, who was reportedly imprisoned for several years after embezzling public money in the region of Attica. Despite this long and well-documented history, embezzlement was not a primary concern in the development of Western law through the late Middle Ages and into the early modern period. While English common law, which serves as the basis of modern law in U.S. society, dealt with the closely related crime of larceny, it did not contain explicit provisions for how to deal with the crime of embezzlement.

Perhaps the earliest legal case related to embezzlement was *Rex v. Bazeley*, which occurred in 1799 in England. In this instance, Joseph Bazeley, a bank clerk, received a deposit from George Cock, a servant of William Gilbert who was a customer at the bank. After recording the deposit, Bazeley pocketed the money, for which he was later charged with larceny. However, because Bazeley was in lawful possession of the money at the time, he was not convicted. This prompted Parliament to pass legislature that held employees liable for embezzlement, a misdemeanor at the time. The key elements introduced by this case were the conversion of property rights and the notion that embezzlement involves a violation of trust by persons in legal possession of the property of others—elements that are included in modern U.S. laws regarding embezzlement.

Though no uniform definition exists, embezzlement is considered a statutory offense within the context of U.S. society, and punishments range from misdemeanor to felony depending on the value of the embezzled property. Despite variations in the definition of embezzlement from state to state, five principal elements distinguish this form of crime from others and are incorporated into most contemporary statutory laws: (1) the act is fraudulent, (2) the act involves conversion of property rights or ownership, (3) the act involves property that is subject to law, (4) the specified property is owned by a person or entity other than the accused, and (5) the accused individual is in lawful possession of the property at the time of conversion due to his/her position of trust.

The requirement of fraud suggests that the act was committed purposefully, with the intent to deceive another. Deceit entails a certain degree of trust between individuals and often involves concealment or misrepresentation of information by one party to the other. As it pertains to embezzlement, the fraud requirement means that the conversion of property rights did not result from a mistake. That is, the embezzler intended to take ownership of another's property without legal claim.

Because the crime of embezzlement pertains specifically to situations in which an individual or group is entrusted to handle the assets of another, the conversion requirement is related to the issue of ownership. In this instance, conversion suggests that the true owner's property rights have been significantly impinged upon. More specifically, this means the true owner is unable to use his/her property as a result of embezzlement.

The property requirement relates to the types of property that are subject to embezzlement. Under most statutory laws, various forms of personal property and decision making are subject to embezzlement. However, real property and land holdings are typically excluded. In general, statutes follow the law of larceny when determining the types of property subject to embezzlement. Additionally, an individual accused of embezzlement must be in lawful possession of the property at the time of conversion. This again relates to the position of trust held by the embezzler. As opposed to larceny, which involves the trespassory taking of another's property, the perpetrator is in lawful possession of the property, which has been entrusted to him or her, at the time when the fraudulent conversion of ownership occurs.

Famous Embezzlers in Modern U.S. Society

In the past century, the social history of the United States has been marked by a number of high-profile embezzlement cases. These cases share many similarities. Namely, they typically involve fraudulent schemes that last several years, deprive

Wachovia bank tellers with a delivery of brand new bills and silver dollars ordered to meet demand over the holidays in December 1962. Embezzlement requires opportunity and is relatively rare; in 2009, there were 17,920 embezzlement arrests.

others of substantial sums of money, and are conducted by individuals who are generally trusted by other members of the communities in which they live. Despite the similarities between their offenses, there is great variation in the individual characteristics of the offenders. High-profile embezzlers vary in terms of age, race, and gender, as well as other characteristics.

Gilbert H. Beesemyer was the secretary and general manager of Guaranty Building and Loan Association in Hollywood, California. In 1930, Guaranty maintained a clientele of nearly 24,000 depositors, including several actors and others involved in the movie industry. It was discovered in 1930 that Beesemyer had embezzled nearly $8 million. He accomplished this by overdrafting client accounts. These acts came shortly after the onset of the Great Depression and had a devastating impact on the victims. Many were institutionalized in mental health facilities; others committed suicide, apparently from the stress of the times and the burden of these unexpected financial losses.

Beesemyer confessed to being a "dirty crook" during his trial, and indicated that he had intended to pay the money back at a later date to those he had defrauded. Because he was a trusted member of the community, several people, some of whom had suffered losses as a result of Beesemyer's embezzlement scheme, came to his defense during the trial and believed that he deserved a second chance. Nonetheless, Beesemyer was found guilty and was sent to San Quentin Prison to serve a 44-year term. He was paroled after serving 10 years.

Minnie Mangum was a trusted employee of the Commonwealth Building and Loan Association in Norfolk, Virginia, for more than 30 years. In 1955, it was discovered that Mangum had embezzled close to $3 million from the bank. Her scheme lasted for 22 years and initially involved small sums of money, which she skimmed from the bank's reserve accounts. Because she was responsible for nearly all aspects of the bank's operation, including hiring, Mangum surrounded herself with inexperienced bookkeepers who could not detect her fraudulent acts. Eventually, she resorted to stealing larger amounts, taking cash directly from the bank's drawers. Mangum reportedly embezzled $600,000 in 1955 alone.

In the fall of that same year, Mangum hired Esther Marie Cannon, who had previous accounting experience. Cannon began to question the bank's bookkeeping practices, which prompted Mangum to fire her. Shortly afterward, Cannon provided an anonymous tip to authorities and an investigation was quickly opened. The subsequent discovery of the extent of Mangum's theft shocked the Norfolk community, who viewed her as a kind and generous woman. Over the years, she had distributed most of the stolen funds to family and friends in the form of gifts and through the financing of businesses and other large purchases. At her 1956 trial, Mangum pleaded guilty to embezzling from her employer and was also found guilty by a jury of issuing false bank reports to state agencies. Mangum was sentenced to 20 years in the Goochland State Prison for Women. She was paroled after serving nine years.

Lloyd Benjamin Lewis was an operations officer at the Beverly Drive branch of Wells Fargo Bank in Los Angeles, California. In 1981, it was discovered that Lewis aided Harold Rossfields

Smith, a boxing promoter and head of Muhammad Ali Professional Sports, Inc. (MAPS), in the embezzlement of more than $21 million. By the time of discovery, Lewis had been an employee of Wells Fargo for 10 years and was also a board member of MAPS. The MAPS organization held several accounts with the bank, and Lewis's scheme involved routinely issuing false credits and debits to those accounts from 1978 to 1981.

Following one of these fraudulent transactions, the bank's computer system noted suspicious activity in the MAPS accounts, which led to an internal investigation. It was quickly revealed that Lewis had been taking advantage of the delay involved with updating accounts when transactions occurred across several of the bank's branches, which gave Lewis the opportunity to mask the embezzlement. The fraudulent acts appeared as corrected transaction errors. For his efforts in this scheme, Lewis received a reported $300,000, along with other gifts. At his trial, Lewis pleaded guilty to conspiracy and embezzlement. He also agreed to testify against others involved, which led to a reduced sentence of five years. In 1982, Smith was found guilty of embezzlement, along with various other offenses, and was sentenced to 10 years.

Ricardo S. Carrasco was an employee of the international private lending division of BankBoston in New York City. He had worked at BankBoston, initially in his native Uruguay, since 1977, and had relocated to the United States in 1988. In 1998, Carrasco went into hiding when it became clear to bank officials that he had issued approximately $73 million in fraudulent loans. His embezzlement scheme was simple: Carrasco disbursed the loans to Oldemar C. Barreiro Laborda, an Argentinean with a scattered criminal past, who had no intent of repaying the debt.

When Carrasco's fraudulent acts were discovered, BankBoston dismissed or reprimanded 20 employees for their negligence in the matter. While much of the theft was covered by the bank's insurance policies, neither the stolen money nor Carrasco were recovered. He abandoned much of his property and told family members of his intent to disappear. Carrasco is still considered a fugitive.

Melissa G. King was the benefit funds administrator for the Sandhogs Union Local 147 in New York City. In 2008, it was discovered that King had embezzled more than $40 million from the nearly 1,000 construction workers who were members of the union at the time. Her scheme lasted from 2002 to 2008. King's company, King Care LLC, was initially hired by the union to provide administrative services, for which the union paid $540,000 annually. However, King utilized this position of trust to transfer in excess of $40 million from the union's accounts to those held by King Care, from which she could directly withdraw funds.

King reportedly used the stolen money to fund her lavish lifestyle. This included the purchase of high-end commodities, from designer clothes and jewelry to luxury automobiles. Additionally, King used a substantial proportion of the money to advance her children and her career in the equestrian industry and to build an elite stable of horses. Though she gained much respect in the horse industry, several people noted the quickness of her ascent through the purchase of expensive horses, many of which cost several hundreds of thousands of dollars. King still awaits sentencing, which could involve up to 115 years in prison, and is also facing civil charges from the Sandhogs Union, which is attempting to recover the losses brought about by King's alleged embezzlement.

Travis F. Whalen
Virginia Polytechnic Institute and State University

See Also: Confidence Games and Frauds; Fraud; Larceny; White-Collar Crime, Contemporary; White-Collar Crime, History of; White-Collar Crime, Sociology of.

Further Readings
Cressey, Donald R. *Other People's Money: A Study in the Social Psychology of Embezzlement*. New York: Free Press, 1953.
Hirschi, Travis and Michael Gottfredson. "Causes of White-Collar Crime." *Criminology*, v.24/4 (1987).
McDougal, Jonathan G., ed. *Financial Crimes: Fraud, Theft and Embezzlement*. Hauppauge, NY: Nova Science Publishers, 2011.
Schoepfer, Andrea and Nicole Leeper Piquero. "Exploring White-Collar Crime and the American Dream: A Partial Test of Institutional Anomie Theory." *Journal of Criminal Justice*, v.34/3 (2006).

Emergency Quota Act of 1921

Also known at the Emergency Immigration Act of 1921, the Emergency Quota Act of 1921 proved to be a highly controversial piece of legislation, placing, for the first time, a direct quota on nationalities for immigration into America. Proponents of the measure cited anarchist and unlawful elements of the migrant population as well as adverse impacts of foreign labor influxes on American workers. Some even spoke of the "poisonous" influence of European and other migration that threatened American ideals. The act primarily targeted European immigrants, who had flooded into America following World War I and the subsequent economic depressions in Europe, severely curbing immigration from those countries. The term *emergency* was used since the legislation was meant to be a stopgap to reduce the problem of mass immigration while other options could be considered. However, in reality, the quota approach persisted and was tightened in the subsequent 1924 act. A key figure in the passing of the act and more generally within the immigration debates of the period was Congressman Albert Johnson.

Justification for a stringent check on immigration came from different quarters. Some have linked the demand for restrictions on immigration to racism and xenophobia, and it is possible to identify elements of these attitudes in the politics and interest groups of the day; Albert Johnson, for example, was associated with such circles. The way in which the quota operated, allowing more populous settled groups to continue immigration on a greater numerical level than less populous groups, served to exacerbate racial tensions; more established white western European settlers had prominence over southern European and other immigrants.

There were opponents to such radical checks on immigration, and one participant of the congressional debate on immigration restriction in April 1921 claimed that such efforts were a continuation of the "war against humanity." Others noted the foundation of immigration upon which America had been built. The act had been considered for some time prior to its enactment; however, it was not until 1921 that such a piece of legislation could be passed. The act stipulated that in a given year, immigration totaling a maximum of 3 percent of a given nationality's population size already settled in America would be permitted. This was based on data from the 1910 census. There were some exceptions to the quota; for example, government officials and their families were excluded.

Such a decision to restrict immigration must be considered in light of the isolationist mood within America during the period and the wider pressures of unchecked immigration after World War I as Europeans flocked to America in search of a better life. A central issue was the pressure placed on wages by large influxes of postwar immigrants, particularly those from Europe. In effect, this served to drive down wages for native-born Americans and served as a catalyst for extremism. Thus, such a reform of immigration policy is perhaps understandable, given the wider context, even though influxes of labor had been fueling the American economy. Additionally, the threat against law and order posed by alien groups was cited by some commentators of the period, some questioning the purpose of allowing the "criminal classes" from Europe to enter the country.

The Emergency Quota Act of 1921 became the basis of American immigration policy that lasted until the 1960s. The 3 percent quota stipulated in the 1921 act was subsequently reduced to 2 percent through the Quota Act of 1924. When viewed together, the two acts had a significant impact on immigration in America. Kristofer Allerfeldt has commented on the collective ramifications of the 1921 and 1924 acts, in stating that following these quotas

> Immigration as an issue lost much of its potency. The spectacle of massive trans-Atlantic liners daily depositing huge numbers of immigrants at Ellis Island was gone forever.

The acts served to greatly reduce immigration into America. They dictated that annual arrivals never reached more than 1 million until much later in the century, when the total population of America was much greater.

Tony Murphy
University of Westminster

See Also: Alien and Sedition Acts of 1798; Immigration Crimes; Racism; Xenophobia.

Further Readings

Allerfeldt, Kristofer. "'And We Got Here First': Albert Johnson, National Origins and Self-Interest in the Immigration Debate of the 1920s." *Journal of Contemporary History*, v.45/1 (2010).

Gjerde, Jon. *Major Problems in American Immigration and Ethnic History: Documents and Essays*. Boston: Houghton Mifflin, 1998.

U.S. Immigration Legislation Online. "Congressional Debate on Immigration Restriction." http://library.uwb.edu/guides/USimmigration/1921_emergency_quota_law.html (Accessed September 2011).

Enforcement Acts of 1870–1871

The Enforcement Acts of 1870–71 were passed to safeguard the voting rights of African American voters following the ratification of the Fourteenth and Fifteenth Amendments to the U.S. Constitution. These amendments served to recognize civil rights and voting rights for freedmen as part of the wider process of reconstruction following the Civil War. African American voters were often subject to intimidation and violence as part of the growing political violence in the postwar south. The legislation sought to stop the Ku Klux Klan and other white supremacists who perpetrated the intimidation. However, despite the intentions of the legislation, the first Enforcement Act in 1870 was inadequate, and victims often failed to testify because of the intimidation they faced. Subsequently, other Enforcement Acts were passed to prop up the original, the key aims of which were essentially the same as the first. In all, the acts outlawed a range of behaviors directed at intimidating voters and perverting the course of voting. Despite a high number of enforcement cases in the first few years, the legislation became ineffective by 1874, and the number of successful convictions plummeted. Ultimately the enforcement agenda was a failure.

The Fifteenth Amendment was ratified in 1870, and it formally recognized the right to vote for all Americans. However, this was in the context of the postwar Reconstruction, which had failed to heal the country's divisions, prejudice, and segregation. After passage of the Fifteenth Amendment, African American citizens had the right to vote but suffered intimidation and even violence on trying to exercise that right. The role of the Ku Klux Klan within this is well documented. The Enforcement Acts between 1870 and 1871 were a response to the problems African American voters faced. Initially, a prime motive was the destruction of the Ku Klux Klan; however, the legislation also served to stop election fraud.

Protecting the Right to Vote

The first act in 1870 addressed officials, discriminating against voters on the basis of race and color in the application of election law, outlawed the use of intimidation and violence against voters, and addressed the issue of depriving citizens of employment in order to control voting. The second act strengthened federal control of voting processes by the use of supervisors in cities where malpractice was suspected. Their role involved overseeing registration and voting procedures. The third act, commonly known as the Ku Klux Klan Act, made it an offense to seek to prevent persons, holding office, serving on juries, receiving equal protection of the laws, and voting.

Thus the acts came to define a series of new offenses, which included failure to register and receive lawful voters and failure to prepare accurate returns. The 1870 act also made it an offense to use violence or threats in order to prevent voters' exercising their right to vote; penalties for such tactics included a fine, a custodial sentence, or both; later legislation related to persons' grouping together for the same purpose and attracted a much greater level of fine and a possibility of up to 10 years in prison. Additionally, the legislation made provisions for the president to suspend habeas corpus and use military force in order to enforce voting rights.

However, African American electoral participation and African American civil rights more generally continued to be violated. Attorneys and other officials tasked with working on enforcement cases were themselves often subjected to intimidation and attacks from the Ku Klux Klan and other groups challenged by the acts. Despite

This illustration from a February 1872 issue of Harper's Weekly *depicts Ku Klux Klan harassment of an African American family at home. Two hooded Klansmen appear in the doorway aiming a rifle at the unsuspecting family, while another looks in through the window. Violence and voter intimidation by the early incarnation of the Ku Klux Klan in the late 1860s and early 1870s led to the signing of the Enforcement Acts of 1870–71, although their effectiveness was short-lived.*

a high number of Enforcement Act cases being brought before the courts and a high indictment to conviction rate in the first few years, enforcement cases yielded a much lower ratio for convictions after 1874. The government took a more moderate stance after this period, and a number of unfavorable court rulings made successful prosecutions almost impossible after 1874.

The fiscal and wider resource demands created by the number of enforcement cases became problematic, and decisions by the Supreme Court in 1876 were catastrophic, marking the failure of the enforcement agenda. Everette Swinney has noted that a combination of what can be termed "southern intransigence" and "northern apathy" meant that the enforcement program capitulated. White extremism and African American disenfranchisement continued.

Tony Murphy
University of Westminster

See Also: Habeas Corpus, Writ of; Ku Klux Klan; *Mississippi v. Johnson*; Race-Based Crimes; Racism.

Further Readings
Cresswell, Stephen. "Enforcing the Enforcement Acts: The Department of Justice in Northern Mississippi." *Journal of Southern History*, v.53/3 (August 1987).

Swinney, Everette. "Enforcing the Fifteenth Amendment, 1870–1877." *Journal of Southern History*, v.28/2 (May 1962).

English Charter of Liberties of 1100

The English Charter of Liberties, also known as the Coronation Charter, was promulgated at the ascension of Henry I to the throne of England. The charter was adopted by Henry I as a way to build support for his claim to the English throne among the nobility. The charter was essentially an oath given by Henry to enforce the laws of England as his father, William the Conqueror, had done. Subsequent charters stating English rights can be traced back to this proclamation as the first postconquest charter of liberties.

Henry I was the youngest son of William the Conqueror and was not expected to rule in either England or Normandy. Instead, his brother Robert inherited the dukedom of Normandy and his brother William Rufus was crowned William II of England. In August 1100, William was accidently killed while hunting. With his brother Robert away on crusade, Henry seized the crown of England and was coroneted in Westminster Abbey five days after William II's burial. The Coronation Charter was issued as a way for Henry to solidify the allegiance of the nobles by promising to enforce the laws of the realm, which his brother William II had eroded during his reign.

The charter gives the king's assurance that he will not tax or take land from the church or its leaders, a practice implemented by his brother William. In the mediaeval period, the lands of a nobleman reverted to the king upon his death for redistribution. It was practice for the king to simply grant the lands to the next male heir; however, there was a pernicious practice by William II to charge fees for heirs to regain their land. In the charter, Henry promised not to charge any fees to regrant the lands to heirs of barons or earls. He also promised to end the practices that had started under William II to charge nobles for approval of the marriages of their children. Indeed a key aspect of the charter is Henry's releasing all persons from debts owed to the Crown, except for lawful taxes. The key criminal elements of the charter were a full pardon to all persons who had committed murder before the coronation of the king. The granting of pardons, of varying degrees, was a common practice among English monarchs upon their coronation as a way to gain favor with the populace and as a sign of mercy. In addition, the crime of theft from the king was to be forgiven as long as the property was returned.

The Coronation Charter was printed the following year, which accounts for it sometimes being referred to as the Charter of 1101, and was distributed around the realm. Henry periodically republished the charter during his reign. Subsequent Norman and Plantagenet kings offered their own charters of rights culminating with Magna Carta, issued under the reign of King John.

John Felipe Acevedo
University of Chicago

See Also: Bodie of Liberties; Common Law Origins of Criminal Law; Magna Carta.

Further Readings
Green, Judith A. *The Government of England Under Henry I*. Cambridge: Cambridge University Press, 1986.
Green, Judith A. *Henry I: King of England and Duke of Normandy*. Cambridge: Cambridge University Press, 2006.
Medieval Source Book Online. "Charter of Liberties of Henry I." http://www.fordham.edu/halsall/source/hcoronation.html (Accessed September 2011).

Enron

Enron Corporation was an American corporation based in Houston, Texas, that was a leading energy, commodities, and services company. After its bankruptcy and collapse in 2001, Enron served as a synonym for corporate greed, corrupt accounting practices, and deceit. Enron's collapse was historic in its scope, as it had been considered an innovative "blue chip" corporation and remains one of the largest U.S. business entities to fail. The Enron scandal, the largest audit failure in U.S. history, also brought about the demise of Arthur Andersen LLP, then one of the "big five" global accounting firms. Enron's demise, which cost shareholders approximately $11 billion in equity, was the largest bankruptcy filing ever at the time, as Enron had assets of $63.4 billion. Enron's failure brought calls for increased federal regulation of corporations and accounting firms and resulted in legislation intended to better control corporate accountability.

Background
Enron was descended from the Northern Natural Gas Company, which was founded in Omaha, Nebraska, in 1932. Reorganized as part of the holding company InterNorth, Inc., in 1979, the organization specialized in natural gas pipelines, plastics, and exploration for and production of coal and petroleum. In 1985, InterNorth acquired Houston Natural Gas Company (HNGC), and HNGC's chief executive officer (CEO), Kenneth Lay, became InterNorth's CEO, changing the corporation's name to Enron later that year. Lay moved Enron's headquarters to Houston and began a program of rapid expansion for the corporation. To reduce debt, Lay sold off various Enron businesses, choosing to concentrate on natural gas pipelines and the operation of power plants. In 1990, Lay hired Jeffrey Skilling to serve as CEO of Enron Finance Corporation after serving briefly as a consultant. Skilling immediately hired Andrew Fastow to work with him, having been impressed with Fastow's knowledge of asset-backed securities acquired while working for Continental Illinois National Bank & Trust Company. Together, Lay, Skilling, and Fastow would make many of the decisions that would later lead to Enron's demise.

During the 1990s, the federal government and many states deregulated the natural gas and electricity markets, permitting Enron to grow rapidly. Lay encouraged the creation of energy markets, which allowed electricity to be sold at market prices, and in 1992 Congress passed laws that deregulated the sale of natural gas. These changes allowed Enron's revenues and profits to soar. Enron was able to sell energy at higher prices, and by 1992, it had become the largest seller of natural gas in North America. Deregulation caused increasing price volatility for energy, and many began demanding increased regulation to end this. Enron and other energy companies, however, lobbied against the proposed changes and were ultimately successful in retaining the free market approach. Between 1990 and 1998, the price of Enron's stock increased by over 300 percent, beating market indexes and proving a lucrative windfall for Enron executives, who were paid bonuses based upon the stock's performance.

Scandal and Downfall
Enron's growth during the 1990s was largely fueled by its rapidly increasing stock value. Enron had some businesses, such as its pipelines, which were highly profitable. The soaring value of its stock, however, was built upon financial statements that obfuscated the true condition of its operations and its financial condition. Reported income and cash flow were kept high, while asset values were inflated and liabilities were hidden. Together, this caused Enron to be highly touted by analysts, allowing the company to be regarded as a model corporation and winning accolades as highly innovative and a great place to work. Skilling was appointed CEO of Enron Capital & Trade Resources, the subsidiary responsible for energy trading. Under Skilling, Enron adopted market-to-market accounting, which permits a corporation to account for the fair market value of an asset based upon the current market price of an asset. Fastow, working under Lay and Skilling, devised a series of shell companies, known as special purpose entities, which did business only with Enron. Fastow used these shell companies to make it appear as though Enron had no debt, although in reality, the shell companies hid over $30 billion of liabilities. Fastow had a financial interest in several of the shell companies and is estimated to have made tens of millions of dollars in profits from their operation.

Skilling was named president of Enron in 1997, and was appointed CEO (succeeding Lay, who remained chairman) in 2001. Fastow had served as chief financial officer (CFO) since 1997. By 1998, Enron employed over 20,000, many of whom had invested in the corporation's employee stock ownership program. Annual revenues increased from approximately $13.3 billion in 1996 to over $100

A 2008 view of the former Enron headquarters building in Houston; construction began on the building in 1999 and was not complete at the time of the company's bankruptcy in 2001, the largest filing ever at that time.

billion in 2000, a 750 percent increase. Much of this increase was later discovered to stem from Enron's practice of using a "merchant model" for reporting revenue, which included costs of goods sold as well as services provided.

Arthur Andersen LLC, Enron's auditors, was also working for the firm as consultants, which was later decried as a conflict of interest. Andersen did not question Enron's special purpose entities, even after it became obvious that they would never turn a profit and should be written off as losses. Enron pressured Andersen not to do so, threatening to take its auditing business to Andersen's rivals. Although Enron's board of directors had an audit committee, this group seldom met and never questioned the financial statements the firm generated.

By early 2001, Enron's stock was trading at 55 times earnings. In August of that year, Skilling resigned as CEO of Enron, a position he had held for six months. In October, Enron announced adjustments to its earning statements from 1997 through 2000. Enron's stock plunged 50 percent in a week, and rumors of a cash shortage caused credit agencies to lower its credit rating. Although Enron explored a possible merger with Dynergy, Inc., this fell through because of concerns regarding Enron's books and financial condition. Another correction of Enron's earnings in years past was announced in November, its stock price plunged to 40 cents per share, and the company entered bankruptcy in December. Criminal charges were brought against Lay, Skilling, and Fastow, with Fastow entering a plea agreement with prosecutors in exchange for a six-year sentence, while Lay was convicted of securities and wire fraud, although he died before he could be sentenced. Skilling was also found guilty and sentenced to 24 years in prison, and over 20 other individuals pled guilty or were convicted of infractions related to Enron's collapse. Arthur Andersen LLP was also charged with obstruction of justice regarding the shredding of documents, found guilty, and forced to surrender its certified public accountant (CPA) license, causing the firm to go out of business and costing 85,000 employees their jobs. In response, the U.S. Congress passed the Sarbanes-Oxley Act, which created new reporting requirements for public corporations in an effort to protect investors.

Stephen T. Schroth
Christian D. Mahone
Knox College

See Also: 2001 to 2012 Primary Documents; Corruption, Contemporary; Embezzlement; Fraud; Securities and Exchange Commission; White-Collar Crime, Contemporary. White-Collar Crime, History of; White-Collar Crime, Sociology of.

Further Readings
Fox, L. *Enron: The Rise and Fall*. Hoboken, NJ: John Wiley & Sons, 2003.
McLean, B. and P. Elkind. *The Smartest Guys in the Room: The Amazing Rise and Scandalous Fall of Enron*. New York: Portfolio, 2003.

Salter, M. S. *Innovation Corrupted: The Origins and Legacy of Enron's Collapse*. Cambridge, MA: Harvard University Press, 2008.

Entrapment

Entrapment is considered an affirmative defense primarily in criminal cases when government officials induce an individual to commit a crime that she/he was not predisposed to commit, but for which he/she is consequently prosecuted. Entrapment law bars the government from invoking the criminal process to get a conviction because those who are entrapped are not criminally liable. The purpose of entrapment law is to prohibit government agents from coercing a person to commit a crime and then arresting that person for committing that crime.

The prosecution bears the burden of proof, namely, "proof beyond a reasonable doubt," that the defendant was not entrapped by government agents. That is, the person charged was not predisposed to commit the crime for which he/she is charged, but rather violated the law as the direct result of encouragement from government agents. However, if government officials simply present a person with the opportunity to commit a crime, which he/she then commits, the entrapment defense may not be used. Further, government agents do not need reasonable suspicion before choosing the person upon whom their efforts are targeted. The distinction between inducement and opportunity makes the entrapment defense difficult to prove. At the core of the entrapment defense is inducement and deception by government agents. However, prior involvement in a similar criminal act for which a person is charged, which resulted in a conviction, makes the success of an entrapment defense highly unlikely.

Entrapment History

Both civil and criminal cases have been addressed by U.S. courts as early as the 1800s. The first few cases to officially recognize the entrapment defense were *U.S. v. De Bare*, 1874 and *Woo Wai*, 1915. While few offenses are exempt from entrapment efforts by overzealous government agents. In the 1900s, Prohibition violators were often targeted. *Sorrells v. United States*, 1932 was the first entrapment case to be heard by the Supreme Court. Today, common crimes with an entrapment defense are vice crimes such as the sale of illegal drugs, prostitution, or gambling. More recently, Internet-based crimes of fraud, child abuse, child endangering, embezzlement, blackmail and forgery have become common types of crimes involving entrapment.

Entrapment Tests and Due Process

In the United States, it is through the evolution of both state and federal case law that the boundaries were developed that establish when a defendant may use the entrapment defense. These boundaries are grounded on a variety of circumstances. The three conditions exemplifying the circumstances that must exist for the entrapment defense are (1) the idea for committing the crime originated with government agents, (2) the government agents persuaded, induced, or coerced the person into committing the crime, and (3) the person was not predisposed or inclined to commit the crime.

The first two circumstances are referred to as the objective test. That is, the focus is on the aggressive actions of the government agents who convinced the otherwise law-abiding citizen to commit the crime. This test is a matter of procedural law because of the manner in which the defendant was coerced by government officials, affecting his/her legal responsibility or culpability. Although government agents are legally permitted to use deception, trickery, or other undercover techniques; on the state level, the boundaries are decided by a judge or a jury. The normative standard would be that of "fundamental fairness" of the government agents to carry out their duties. In this case, the predisposition of the defendant would not be considered.

The third criteria is the subjective test: predisposition or inclination to commit the crime; it considers the state of mind of the defendant. In these cases, the focus is on the individual's predisposition to commit the crime and thus the states have the latitude to decide whether the defendant was entrapped. This test is a matter of substantive law, where the lack of the defendant's predisposition to commit the crime does not make him/her culpable or criminally responsible. These decisions are most often made by a jury. Most states have chosen the subjective test with regard to the entrapment defense. If it is proven by the prosecution that the defendant was predisposed to commit the crime(s), it does not matter what government officials did to coerce the commission of the crime(s). Both objective and subjective tests for entrapment have at their core the issue of the defendant's legal responsibility and culpability.

Beyond the subjective and objective tests, the federal courts consider the "outrageous conduct defense," focusing on government's behavior. This defense is similar to the objective test and claims as a defense a violation of the due process clause of the Fifth Amendment), even if the defendant was predisposed to commit the crime. In this case, government agents may be prosecuted. This exemplifies the federal court's supervisory role over law enforcement, with a purpose much like that of the exclusionary rule. The exclusionary rule is a tool used by the courts to limit law enforcement from illegal search and seizure. This parallels the court's use of entrapment law to limit law enforcement methods to induce the commission of a crime. This defense is successful in sting operations, where contraband is bought from a government agent, or in reverse sting operations, where contraband is sold to a government agent. Anytime the behavior of government agents violates the standards of fundamental fairness and by the extent of their temptation puts in question the defendant's predisposition to commit the crime, the entrapment defense is appropriate.

As long as there is the possibility that government officials behave in such a way to mitigate the defendant's predisposition to commit a crime, the entrapment defense is a necessary part of a just legal system. The nature of case law is its flexibility to redefine law to coincide with society's current standards. Entrapment law is no exception. As with all case law, the issue is that of fundamental fairness. It is the nature of this defense that makes the roles of law enforcement, the prosecution, and the defense vital in the pursuit of justice, as it is rare that a defendant worthy of the entrapment defense is aware of the covert operations that affect the appropriateness of this defense.

Marilyn Simon
University of Cincinnati, Blue Ash

See Also: 1941 to 1960 Primary Documents; Ruby Ridge Standoff; *State v. Heitman*; Supreme Court, U.S.

Further Readings
Jacobson v. United States, 503 U.S. 540, 548 (1992).
Sherman v. United States, 356 U.S. 369, 372, 78 S. Ct, 819, 821, 2 L.Ed.2d 848 (1958).
Sorrells v. United States, 287 U.S. 435, 53 S. Ct. 210, 77 L.Ed. 413 (1932).
United States v. Russell, 411 U.S. 42,393 S. Ct. 1637, 36 L.Ed.2d 366 (1973). 507 F.2d 832 (1974).

Environmental Crimes

Few subspecialties of American law reveal this nation's swiftly evolving ethos as well as environmental law. Over the past four decades, this nascent subspecialty of law has progressed as surges in both the human population and technology have precipitated unprecedented environmental harms. From 1950 to 1970, the U.S. population jumped from 151 million to 203 million people, and per capita energy use sharply increased. With no comprehensive national environmental policy, environmental concerns captivated the American public's interest. Rachel Carson's *Silent Spring* raised America's consciousness in and around issues of pollution in 1962. Such awareness inaugurated the annual celebration of Earth Day in 1970. In 1971, biologist Barry Commoner published *The Closing Circle*, which imparted ecological values to Americans. Such work initiated new ethical and moral questions regarding the previous notions of smokestack emissions or sewage discharge as inconvenient externalities or technical problems.

Although the term *environmental crime* now permeates 21st-century vocabulary, this concept must not be taken for granted. The concept of "crime" itself has a history and a myriad of meanings. Environmental crime now emerges with the violation of an array of statutes and is enforced and penalized in a complex and contentious legal atmosphere.

Definitions and History
Ways of knowing environmental harms qua crime are ever changing. Under a legalist perspective, a

These workers equipped with full hazmat gear were dredging samples from the New Bedford, Massachusetts, harbor Superfund site in 1998 in order to measure the levels of contaminants, most notably PCB, that had collected for over 40 years at the site.

crime is a behavior that violates a law. But what sort of law must be violated? Some argue that the violation must be of criminal law. Those who study corporate, white-collar, or environmental crimes argue that violations of laws and codes of a noncriminal nature (e.g., administrative and regulatory law) commit environmental crime when such behaviors inflict significant harm to the environment. Anthropocentric, biocentric, and ecocentric values and interests suggest different priorities regarding criminalizing environmental harms. Environmental crime is more broadly defined by environmental justice, which advocates the fair treatment and meaningful involvement of all people with respect to law development and enforcement, while ecological justice emphasizes justice between human and nonhuman nature. Affluent oil, chemical, pharmaceutical, and automobile companies seek to influence the fashioning of environmental law or regulations to promote their interests. Public media and perception also help forge legal definitions of environmental crime. High-profile media coverage of hazardous waste dumping at sites such as the Love Canal, New York, and Times Beach, Missouri, played a considerable role in the criminalization of environmental harms. As environmental law is a relatively recent construction, it is constantly being reevaluated and modified by new legal precedence or the scientific identification of new harms.

Until 1970, environmental laws and regulations designed to protect the air, water, and land, and hence public health, were overseen by dispersed federal and state programs. The violation of such laws was not rigorously punished. Claims of environmental harm usually went to court as torts or civil law was applied. The resulting civil fines and penalties provided minimal deterrent effect to mitigate future environmental degradation. Many corporations regarded civil fines as a cost of doing business. With rampant pollution by 1970, including rivers that literally burned and flowed with human and industrial waste and towns built upon toxic waste sites, President Richard Nixon set up a cabinet-level Environmental Quality Council as well as a Citizens' Advisory Committee on Environmental Quality. They asserted the need for uniform and strong enforceability, which would be impossible unless the government could fuse the air and water programs as well as those for pesticides and radiation into one effective, working entity. In 1970, the Environmental Protection Agency (EPA) was established to enforce environmental protection standards. The EPA currently has a primary national role in environmental regulation and crime enforcement.

From 1969 to 1979, the establishment of the EPA, passage of 27 environmental laws, as well as hundreds of administrative regulations began a paradigm shift in American environmental law. The U.S. Department of Justice (DOJ) took the unprecedented action of criminal prosecution of environmental laws. In 1982, the DOJ created the Environmental Crimes Unit in its Land and Natural Resources Division and there was a subsequent robust increase in criminal prosecution of environmental laws. In 1981 the EPA formed the Office of Criminal Enforcement and hired its first criminal investigators in 1982. In 1988, Congress endowed the EPA with full authority to enforce environmental laws. The EPA now delegates certain statutory permitting and enforcement programs to individual states to administer and enforce. As a result of those delegations, as well as independent state environmental requirements, state agencies also play a critical role in environmental enforcement.

Today, the criminal enforcement program of the EPA successfully prosecutes hundreds of significant violations across all major environmental statutes, including data fraud cases (e.g., private laboratories submitting false environmental data to state and federal environmental agencies); indiscriminate hazardous waste dumping that results in serious injuries and death; oil spills that cause significant damage to waterways, wetlands and beaches; and illegal handling of hazardous substances such as pesticides and asbestos. Penalties can include multimillion-dollar fines and prison sentences.

Major U.S. Environmental Statutes and Regulations

After tumultuous decades of defining, quantifying, and punishing environmental harms, the EPA and federal and other agencies now monitor and enforce eight major environmental statutes: the Clean Air Act (CAA), Clean Water Act (CWA), Safe Drinking Water Act (SDWA), Toxic Substances Control Act (TSCA), Federal Insecticide, Fungicide, and Rodenticide Act (FIFRA), Resource Conservation and Recovery Act (RCRA), Environmental Response, Compensation, and Liability Act (CERCLA), and the Endangered Species Act (ESA).

Although in the 1880s New York City passed the nation's first air regulations of industrial smokestack emissions, the 1963 Clean Air Act (CAA) was the nation's inaugural air quality law. The original act set few enforceable standards. The act provided for federal abatement action in egregious air pollution problems, but by 1970, only one case was prosecuted as a criminal CAA violation. The 1990 Clean Air Act Amendments followed, creating permit requirements for air emissions and establishing clear enforcement standards for stationary and mobile hazardous air pollutants. The 1990 amendment also established that criminal violations can be prosecuted as felonies.

The Rivers and Harbors Act of 1899 is often considered the first environmental criminal statute because it rendered the discharge of refuse into navigable waters without a permit a misdemeanor. The 1948 Water Pollution Control Act was amended in 1972, and again in 1977, creating the Clean Water Act (CWA). The CWA bolstered the role of federal government by establishing the basic structure for regulating discharges of pollutants into the waters of the United States and creating quality standards for surface waters. The CWA made it unlawful to discharge any pollutant from a point source into navigable waters without a permit. Section 404 of the CWA established a permit program to regulate the discharge of dredged or fill material into waters of the United States, including wetlands. Regulated activities that require permitting include fill for development, water resource projects (such as dams and levees), infrastructure development (such as highways and airports), and mining projects. The 1987 Clean Water Act amendments included felony provisions.

The 1974 Safe Drinking Water Act (SDWA) established nationwide domestic water quality standards and oversees the states, localities, and water suppliers that implement those standards. The law was amended in 1986 and 1996 and requires many actions to protect drinking water and its sources. Under SDWA, states may play a pivotal role in enforcement. Compliance is encouraged, but formal enforcement actions including civil and criminal court cases are possible.

The 1947 Federal Insecticide, Fungicide, and Rodenticide Act (FIFRA) implemented federal regulation of pesticides via a registration process. Before the EPA may register a pesticide under FIFRA, the applicant must document that the pesticide will perform without unreasonable risks to people and environment. During the 1970s, public alarm about the safety of new organic compounds mounted when it became apparent that many of these substances had deleterious health effects. This concern yielded the 1976 Toxic Substances Control Act (TSCA). The 1976 TSCA regulates existing chemicals as well as the introduction of new compounds to market, and addresses the production, importation, use, and disposal of several classes of chemicals. While it requires full disclosure of available testing and safety data, it prescribes no specific protocol for methodically testing newly invented compounds.

Several agencies were created in the 1970s to regulate the energy industry, although few statutes are enforceable as environmental crime. The 1990 Oil Pollution Act (OPA) broadened the liability of responsible parties involved with oil spills. It streamlined and strengthened the EPA's ability to prevent and respond to catastrophic oil spills by establishing a trust fund financed by a tax on oil that is available to clean up spills. In April 2010, the oil rig Deepwater Horizon, under lease to British Petroleum (BP), exploded and released a tremendous amount of oil into the Gulf of Mexico. The DOJ announced civil suits against several corporations, but Attorney General Eric Holder indicated a criminal investigation was under way as well. Wary environmentalists noted that BP had previously been convicted of two felonies, but the financial sanctions were insufficient to modify corporate behavior.

Until 1976, the federal government regulated the disposal of neither solid nor hazardous waste. The 1976 Resource Conservation and Recovery Act (RCRA) addressed these issues by giving EPA the authority to control hazardous waste. The Federal Hazardous and Solid Waste Amendments (HSWA) are the 1984 amendments to RCRA that expanded the scope of criminal culpability for RCRA violations by adding false statements and recordkeeping violations to the list of RCRA felonies. The HSWA permits stricter criminal penalties to be administered to the guilty party who treated, disposed of, or stored waste in a manner that posed imminent danger to another. A convicted individual can be sentenced to up to 15 years in prison and given a $250,000 fine, while a company can be fined up to $1 million.

The 1980 Comprehensive Environmental Response, Compensation, and Liability Act (CERCLA), commonly referred to as the Superfund Act, sought to clean up hazardous waste sites. The act imposes liability on parties responsible for the presence of hazardous substances at a site and provides a federal "Superfund" for the cleanup of hazardous waste sites. Superfund also requires hazardous waste notification. If a manager of a waste treatment facility dumps hazardous waste onto the ground without a permit, the dumping constitutes illegal disposal of the waste in violation of RCRA. If the amount of waste is a reportable quantity, the release of the waste triggers a CERCLA duty to notify authorities. Failure to report the release is a felony under CERCLA. Thus, the illegal disposal charge (RCRA) dovetails with the failure-to-notify charge (CERCLA), and both violations could logically arise in a single prosecution.

The 1973 Endangered Species Act (ESA) sought to protect species from extinction. The ESA prohibits the "taking" (defined as the harassment, harming, pursuit, hunting, shooting, wounding, killing, trapping, capturing, or collection) and the interstate or international trade of listed plants and animals, except under federal permit. The ESA is administered by the U.S. Fish and Wildlife Service, which is responsible for terrestrial and freshwater organisms, and the Commerce Department's National Marine Fisheries Service (NMFS), which is responsible for marine wildlife.

Environmental Crime Enforcement

Law enforcement is integral to management of public lands such as the national forest, national wildlife refuge, and national park service lands, and locally owned natural areas such as parks. Agency-based law enforcement officers investigate and enforce applicable laws, regulations, rules, orders, and codes that are designed to protect public safety, prevent resource damage, preserve particular area use objectives (such as nonmotorized use), or protect wildlife populations. For example, the secretary of agriculture regulates the occupancy and use of developed recreation sites on national forest system lands. A violation of these regulations with actions such as unpermitted forest product removal or leaving a fire without completely extinguishing it can be penalized with up to $5,000 or six months incarceration or both.

Federal statutes that are enforced across all federally managed public lands include the 1979 Archaeological Resources Protection Act (ARPA), the 1964 Wilderness Act, and the Wild Free-Roaming Horse and Burro Act of 1971 (WHBA). The ARPA established civil and criminal penalties for the unauthorized excavation, removal, damage, or trafficking of archaeological resources. To preserve the untrammeled, primeval character of federally designated wilderness areas, the Wilderness Act prohibits uses of mechanical transport

After the BP Deepwater Horizon oil spill in the Gulf of Mexico that began in April 2010, birds and other animals had to be cleaned of oil by hand at four wildlife rehabilitation centers established for that purpose. This Northern Gannet was being washed at the Theodore, Alabama, Oiled Wildlife Rehabilitation Center on June 17, 2010. The U.S. government investigated and, in a report issued in September 2011, found that the companies Halliburton, BP, and Transocean were all at fault in the oil spill.

and prohibits road establishment or structure installation with some established exceptions. The WHBA establishes civil and criminal penalties any person who willfully removes or attempts to remove or maliciously causes the death or harassment of wild-free-roaming horses or burros.

Prior to the 1970s, tort law was the prevalent legal means whereby American society mobilized against escalating environmental degradation. Under tort law, the action brought to control pollution is a nuisance case in which a landowner sues for unreasonable interference with the use and enjoyment of their land. Historically in the United States, courts often awarded individuals money damages in these cases but were loath to grant injunctions. With the establishment of the EPA, the prevention and enforcement of environmental crime was institutionalized with established process. While compliance with environmental laws and regulations became the ultimate objective, enforcement was a vital part of motivating regulated entities to meet their environmental obligations. Most environmental laws such as the CWA depend upon honest self-reporting of permitted discharges, and EPA uses various methods to achieve compliance and to increase voluntary and self-directed actions. In 1995, the EPA began to provide incentives for regulated entities to come into compliance with the federal environmental laws and regulations. It encourages regulated entities to discover, promptly disclose, and correct noncompliance, making formal EPA investigations and enforcement actions unnecessary. With violations, however, federal and state enforcement entities can use a set of enforcement mechanisms (as established in the environmental statutes) at their discretion. Three such enforcement tools dominate: administrative enforcement actions, civil judicial enforcement cases, and criminal prosecutions.

The EPA's Office of Enforcement and Compliance Assurance (OECA) houses both EPA headquarters lawyers and headquarters enforcement personnel. It is broadly divided into two offices: an Office of Regulatory Enforcement, which has a lead role in developing enforcement cases; and an Office of Compliance, which is responsible for investigation and inspection targeting, compliance monitoring, and compliance assistance. In addition to the OECA, the DOJ plays a major role in environmental crime enforcement. Since 1977, the EPA uses the DOJ in all civil cases to file judicial actions on its behalf. The DOJ's role in environmental criminal cases is even more substantial. Environmental crimes cases begin with EPA criminal investigators, who develop evidence that provides the basis for a prosecution. Criminal cases are then initiated in federal court—either by indictment of the defendants or by information—and they are negotiated and (as needed) tried by assistant U.S. attorneys.

Administrative Enforcement Actions. Administrative enforcement actions are frequently used actions taken by the EPA or a state under its own authority, without involving a judicial court process. An administrative compliance order (referred to in some states as a cease and desist order or an abatement order) is a potent administrative enforcement device, and is typically enforceable in court with monetary penalties. If not complied with, these orders allow a government agency to require a regulated party to take specific steps to achieve compliance. The elements that the government is required to prove in civil enforcement actions vary among statutes, although most violations may be proven by showing the defendant's noncompliance.

Civil Judicial Enforcement. Civil judicial actions, used less frequently than administrative enforcement actions, are formal lawsuits, filed in court, against persons or entities that have failed to comply with statutory or regulatory requirements or with an administrative compliance order. Such actions have high public visibility and can be pursued against more serious infringements and violators who are perceived to be recalcitrant. They can also be employed where legal precedents are sought or where prompt judicial action is needed to stop an environmentally damaging activity.

Administrative enforcement and civil judicial violations generally result in a settlement, which is generally an agreed-upon resolution to an enforcement case, or in civil penalties, which are monetary assessments. Civil penalties act as an incentive for coming and staying in compliance with the environmental statutes. Civil violations may also result in injunctive relief, which consists of the tasks that a violator must carry out to come into compliance, or in Supplemental Environmental Projects (SEPs). As opposed to civil judicial actions, criminal actions are usually reserved for violations that gave rise to serious harm to public health or the environment, where the defendant has engaged in the false reporting of environmental data, or where the defendant's conduct reflects willfulness, bad faith, or recalcitrance. Criminal actions can result in a court conviction, with fines or imprisonment. In addition to fines, a judge may impose an order of restitution, where a defendant is ordered to pay those affected by the violation a monetary amount.

Criminal Prosecutions. Congress categorized criminal actions as misdemeanors in the major environmental laws when they were enacted during the 1970s. They resulted in relatively few prosecutions, as the laws were new and the legal norms they created were not sufficiently well established to justify criminal enforcement except in the most egregious cases. Federal prosecutors and investigators rarely prosecuted misdemeanors. Criminal actions surged when Congress amended the CAA, CWA, CERCLA, and RCRA during the 1980s and 1990s to include felony provisions. The number of environmental criminal cases increased even more dramatically after Congress passed the Pollution Prevention Act of 1990, which required the EPA to hire 200 criminal investigators.

Under most environmental legislation, to prove criminal intent, the government must prove that the defendant "knowingly" violated the law. The courts usually define that term as requiring the government to demonstrate (beyond a reasonable doubt) that the defendant was aware of its actions that violated the law. The government need not show that the defendant knew that these actions were unlawful. In contrast, criminal violation of some environmental laws impose strict liability, relieving the government of the burden of proving that the defendant acted with fault or with an intent to break the law. Environmental criminal enforcement actions are problematic in that environmental standards, unlike most traditional crimes, present questions of degree rather than of kind. Murder and burglary are simply unlawful. There is no threshold level below which such conduct is acceptable. In contrast, some pollution, in many circumstances, is acceptable. It is only pollution that exceeds certain proscribed levels that is unlawful.

Congress imposed few limits on which environmental regulations could be subject to criminal enforcement. This vagueness gave prosecutors broad discretion to determine what is criminal. While Congress may have intended to provide the government a range of enforcement options (administrative, civil, and criminal remedies), similar violations can be treated differently depending upon who investigates the matter and who decides how the violation should be addressed. With broad discretion comes the risk that criminal prosecution will occur in circumstances where criminal enforcement may not seem appropriate. Some safeguards ensure that prosecutors do not abuse their discretion. First, due process concerns preclude criminal prosecution when the meaning of the law is unclear in "void for vagueness" requirements. The "rule of lenity" reinforces the void for vagueness doctrine by requiring courts in criminal cases to resolve ambiguities about the meaning of the law in favor of the defendant.

In addition to these legal safeguards, the EPA requires its criminal investigators to focus on matters involving significant environmental harm and culpable conduct, with culpability defined to include repetitive violations, deliberate misconduct, and acts of concealment or falsification. Likewise, DOJ prosecutors must follow the DOJ's Principles of Federal Prosecution, which require prosecutors to consider the nature and seriousness of the offense, the deterrent value of the prosecution, and the availability of noncriminal alternatives to prosecution. No factor is more decisive than deception in making a criminal case out of what might otherwise be a civil matter. Fair and effective administration of the environmental laws, like other regulatory programs, cannot occur if the government does not have complete and accurate information.

Federal environmental statutes usually subject "any person" to criminal sanctions, a term that is often broadly defined to include individuals as well as corporations, partnerships, associations, states, and political subdivisions of states. With respect to corporate entities, the knowledge and actions of individuals who act on the corporation's behalf (aside from independent contractors) are imputed to the corporation through the doctrine of *respondeat superior*. The 1985 case *United States v. Mottolo* found that a corporate executive may be personally liable for relevant violations, and this Superfund criminal suit began a concentrated effort among EPA and DOJ enforcement to target white-collar (corporate) environmental crime.

Karie J. Wiltshire
U.S. Department of Agriculture Forest Service
M. Nathan Mason
University of Nevada School of Medicine

See Also: 1961 to 1980 Primary Documents; 1981 to 2000 Primary Documents; 2001 to 2012 Primary Documents; Fish and Game Laws; White-Collar Crime, Contemporary; White-Collar Crime, History of; White-Collar Crime, Sociology of.

Further Readings
Banks, D., C. Davies, J. Gosling, J. Newman. M. Rice, J. Wadley, and F. Walravens. *Environmental Crime: A Threat to Our Future*. London: Environmental Investigation Agency, 2008.
Brickey, Kathleen F. "Environmental Crime at the Crossroads: The Intersection of Environmental and Criminal Law Theory." *Tulane Law Review*, v.71 (1996).
Burns, R. G. and M. J. Lynch, *Environmental Crime: A Sourcebook*. New York: LFB Scholarly Publishing, 2004.
Drielak, S. C. *Environmental Crime*. Springfield, IL: Charles C. Thomas, 1998.
Environmental Protection Agency. "Compliance and Enforcement." http://www.epa.gov/oecaerth/index.html (Accessed February 2011).

Kubasek, N. K. and G. S. Silverman. *Environmental Law*, 7th ed. Upper Saddle River, NJ: Prentice Hall, 2011.

Mandiberg, S. F. "Locating the Environmental Harm in Environmental Crimes." *Utah Law Review*, v.4 (2009).

Uhlmann, David M. "Environmental Crime Comes of Age: The Evolution of Criminal Enforcement in the Environmental Regulatory Scheme." *Utah Law Review*, v.4 (2010).

Equality, Concept of

While equality before the law is often considered the bedrock of the United States' legal system, the concept is relatively new and was not guaranteed in the Constitution until the enactment of the Fourteenth Amendment. In fact, the famous statement "We hold this truth to be self-evident, that all men are created equal" appears in the Declaration of Independence and, it would seem, was purposely left out of the Constitution—due to tension around the issue of slavery. Even the phrasing in the Declaration of Independence explicitly excludes women, regardless of race, and implicitly excludes blacks and Native Americans.

From the country's founding until the civil rights revolution, people of color were excluded from even formal equality before the law through the triple mechanisms of exploitation (of black labor under slavery), expropriation (of Mexican and Native American lands), and exclusion (of Asian immigrants). During this period, the laws in the United States, including but not limited to criminal laws, mandated unequal treatment.

Nonetheless, equality before the law has unfurled from the time of the country's founding to the present—beginning, perhaps, with the enactment of the Thirteenth, Fourteenth, and Fifteen Amendments in the 1860s and continuing with civil rights laws enacted in the 1960s. As the United States approaches a policy, if not yet a practice, of equality before the law, activists and scholars have begun to articulate fear that equality, particularly defined as it is in current case law, will not succeed in engendering justice.

Unequal Before the Law

In slaveholding states, the code that simply bore the state name was in fact only applicable to whites; a separate code, the slave code, was applicable to blacks. The slave code governed, among other things, the punishment of slaves accused of "wrongs." According to both these legal codes and the courts' interpretations of them, slave owners were legally free to punish their slaves for any offense without intervention from the judiciary. This meant that punishment of blacks was generally inflicted on the body and that a conviction, or any legal process, was not necessary as a precursor to punishment. On the rare occasions when blacks were tried for their offenses, generally slaves whose alleged offenses bore upon the larger (white) community and free blacks, they were often subject to separate legal codes. These codes mandated different punishments for the same offenses and blacks were subject to some punishments that whites were not. In Virginia, it was typical for slaves who ran away to be sentenced to castration or hobbling, while no such crime existed for whites. Likewise, there was no crime for which whites could be sentenced to either of these punishments. Moreover, prescribed punishments for many crimes were lighter for whites than for blacks. Virginia decreed imprisonment for whites but death for blacks convicted of a variety of felonies, ranging from buying or receiving a stolen horse to rape. Blacks were tried in separate courts without juries, comprised of county justices and often slave-owning assessors.

While state laws mandating unequal treatment of slaves, free blacks, and whites proliferated, it was the infamous *Dred Scott* decision of 1857 that provided federal sanction for these laws. After failing to purchase the freedom of his family and himself, Scott sued his master, John Emerson, for his freedom in 1846, claiming that his and his wife Harriet's presence and residence in free territories and their daughter's birth on a steamboat between free and slave territories should be all that was required for emancipation. The Supreme Court found against Scott and argued, among other things, that black people were racially ineligible for citizenship. Chief Justice Roger Taney wrote the majority decision, declaring most infamously that "The negro has no rights which the white man is bound to respect." From the *Dred Scott* decision in 1857 until at least the enactments of the Thirteenth, Fourteenth, and Fifteenth Amendments, state and federal laws not only permitted but also required unequal treatment before the law, in criminal and other realms.

Eight years after the *Dred Scott* decision, in 1865, the Thirteenth Amendment was enacted, abolishing slavery except as punishment for a crime. In the same year, every former slave state enacted Black Codes, which controlled the labor, migration, and other activities of newly freed men and women, who were emancipated but not yet full citizens. Black Codes granted black people certain rights, such as legalized marriage (although not to whites), ownership of property, and limited access to the courts, but simultaneously denied them the rights to testify against whites, to serve on juries or in state militias, or to vote. And in response to planters' demands that freed people be required to work on the plantations, the Black Codes declared that those who failed to sign yearly labor contracts could be arrested and "hired out" to white landowners. Similar to the slave codes, Black Codes mandated that black people could be arrested for behaviors, such as failure to obtain work, for which white people were not subject to arrest and that black people were subject to punishments, most notably legally enforced work arrangements, to which whites were not. But Black Codes did not last long.

Toward Equality

A year after emancipation, the Civil Rights Act of 1866 was passed by Congress over Andrew Johnson's presidential veto; the act states that all persons born in the United States are citizens. Two years later, the Fourteenth Amendment was enacted, Section 1 of which requires due process and equal protection. Finally, in 1870, the Fifteenth Amendment was enacted, guaranteeing the right to vote to all adult men who are citizens of the United States "regardless of race, color, or previous condition of servitude." With the enactment of the Thirteenth, Fourteenth, and Fifteenth amendments, the promise—if not the practice—of equality before the law became enshrined in the United States' Constitution. Fortifying these federal changes, Republicans put the South under military rule, beginning the period of Reconstruction. Each former Confederate state held new

This illustration titled "The First Vote," which depicts African American men from various professions lined up to cast their first ballots in an election, was published on the cover of Harper's Weekly *on November 16, 1867.*

elections in which both freed men and poor white men, who were also previously excluded from the franchise, could vote. The freshly enfranchised black and poor white men elected new governments, each of which repealed their state's Black Codes by 1870.

While Black Codes were never reenacted, they were replaced with a complex jurisprudence called Jim Crow. These laws continued the practice of legally mandated unequal treatment before the law for black people, and in some states Mexican and Native Americans as well. Nonetheless, during the period from the late 19th century to the mid-20th century, states were shifting to a model wherein inequality in punishment was produced both legally and extra-legally.

Convict lease systems, which were in place from 1865 to 1927, were emblematic of this new method. In these systems, states "leased" prisoners to private individuals or companies, for whom prisoners labored in a variety of highly exploitative contexts, from plantations to mines. This system was even more profitable for plantation and mine owners and even more deadly for blacks than slavery. In 1850, Alabama's state prison held 167 white men, three white women, and four "free colored people." By 1888, 85 percent of prisoners in the state were black. While white prisoners were generally left in prisons and taught a trade or used on chain gangs to make and maintain roads, black prisoners were leased to mining companies. These convicts mined five tons of coal per day, making Alabama's leasing system the most profitable in the country. Nine percent, or nearly one in 10, of leased prisoners died each year.

This system relied on the pairing of the enactment of vacuous laws—such as those against dead falls, or selling goods after sunset—purportedly applicable to all, but only blacks were arrested for the new "crimes," paid a system of fees and fines, and fell into a (racially and gendered) selective process that determined to whom inmates were leased. The racialized practice of convict lease existed in the absence of explicitly racialized laws. The methods used to produce the convict lease system were, in fact, strikingly similar to those used to produce mass racialized incarceration during the last quarter of the 20th century. Thus, the period of convict lease represents a turning point in the concept and practice of equality in punishment.

The movement toward increased formal equality in punishment stagnated from the 1920s to the 1950s, but then picked up speed again during the civil rights era, when groups of committed black activists and their allies fought for inclusion into the United States' political and civil society. While claims for restorative and other forms of justice were present throughout the movement, it was claims to equality—defined as the right of nonwhite people to be treated like similarly situated white people—that were legitimated through the Civil Rights Act of 1964, the Voting Rights and Immigration Acts of 1965, and the Fair Housing Act of 1968. Concurrent with Congress's enactment of these landmark legislations, the Supreme Court, led by Earl Warren, issued a tripartite of momentous decisions that increased the rights of defendants and, thus, the practice of equality before the law in the realm of criminal punishment.

First, in *Mapp v. Ohio* in 1961, the court ruled that it was unconstitutional for prosecutors to use evidence seized in illegal searches. Two years later, in *Gideon v. Wainwright*, the court held that the Sixth Amendment requires that all indigent criminal defendants receive publicly funded counsel. Finally, and perhaps most famously, in *Miranda v. Arizona* in 1966, the court ruled that police were required to explain a number of inviolable rights to people being interrogated while in custody, including the right to an attorney.

However, while rights to equality before the law and to due process have increased, racial disparities in criminal punishments have not faltered. Moreover, while scholars have unearthed racial disparities in punishment outcomes at nearly every juncture of criminal processing— the decision to deny a defendant bail, the setting of bail type and amount, the decision to grant a nonfinancial pretrial release, and the decision to sentence an offender to incarceration—the court, in *McCleskey v. Kemp* in 1987, opined that statistical evidence of patterned racially based disparities in criminal processing was not sufficient as evidence of discrimination. In particular, the court wrote that the "racially disproportionate impact" in the Georgia death penalty indicated by a comprehensive scientific study was not enough to overturn the guilty verdict without showing a "racially discriminatory purpose."

Critiques of Equality

While contemporary sentencing policies are formally race and gender neutral, they nonetheless punish noncriminal behaviors and traits, like being in or on public housing or having a prior record, that correlate closely with race. Proponents of determinate sentencing rely on color-blind discourse when they argue that in a nondiscriminatory criminal legal system every defendant with the same legal characteristics receives the same criminal legal outcome. In contrast, critical race scholars and others argue that contemporary discourses about discrimination provide no language with which to critique the assessment of social acts as criminal. Since some people arrested for white-collar (white) crime are black and some people arrested for street (black) crime are white, these laws do not classify on the basis of race. Thus, even if sentencing policies could alleviate all racial disparities in punishment that occur when members of a group receive more or less beneficial criminal legal decisions because of their group membership, those disparities stemming from racialized notions of merit, criminality, and threat would still remain. As such, eliminating group membership–based distribution of criminal legal outcomes may alleviate the most egregious forms of discrimination, but it cannot eradicate racial stratification in criminal legal outcomes.

Similarly, determinate sentencing systems that increase formal equality may simultaneously disproportionately impact women in several ways. These policies make it difficult for judges and other criminal justice officials to consider socially relevant and highly gendered characteristics, such as child-care responsibilities. Additionally, mandatory terms and sentencing enhancements treat marginally and substantially involved offenders as legal equivalents, thus glossing over traditional questions of culpabability. Finally, these policies increase the weight given to the gendered behavior of prosecutorial assistance. Since women are generally less culpable, they often simply do not have "substantial" information to trade; as a result, prosecutors are more likely to help men avoid new mandatory terms and sentencing enhancements than they are women.

In regard to the racialized and gendered nature of putatively race- and gender-neutral sentencing policies, scholars argue that since the statutes and courts have defined equality as "treating likes alike" and require disadvantaged groups to prove that they are similarly situated. Similarly situated requirement laws that promote equality will not necessarily promote justice. In fact, the more manifest the results of historical and present discrimination are, the less likely this equality principle

Armed guards watch as prisoners in striped suits clear land at the McNeil Island Prison in Puget Sound around 1890, a time when convict leasing to mines and plantations was a common practice. The convict lease system, which was even more deadly to African Americans than slavery, lasted from 1865 until 1927. The mass racialized incarceration that resulted, and which continues today, can be seen as a turning point in the concept and practice of equality in punishment.

is to promote the undoing of systematic privilege and oppression. As such, sentencing policies that are formally race and gender neutral, but which are nonetheless race and gender salient, will not only fail to undermine the systems of privilege that leave criminal defendants dissimilarly situated but in fact disproportionately burden people of color and white women by ignoring the racialized and gender-specific situations of people in conflict with the law.

Traci Schlesinger
DePaul University

See Also: 1851 to 1900 Primary Documents; African Americans; Chain Gangs and Prison Labor; Civil Rights Laws; Convict Lease System; *Dred Scott v. Sandford*; Gender and Criminal Law; Morality; Race, Class, and Criminal Law; Racism; Segregation Laws; Sentencing; Slavery; Slavery, Law of.

Further Readings
Bloom, Barbara, Barbara Owen, and Stephanie Covington. "Women Offenders and the Gendered Effects of Public Policy." *Review of Policy Research*, v.21 (2004).
Curtin, Mary Ellen. *Black Prisoners and Their World, Alabama 1865–1900*. Charlottesville: University of Virginia Press, 2000.
Delgado, R. "Rodrigo's Eighth Chronicle: Black Crime, White Fears—On the Social Construction of Threat." *Virginia Law Review*, v.80 (1994).
Freeman, Alan. "Legitimizing Discrimination Through Anti-Discrimination Law: A Critical Review of Supreme Court Doctrine." *Minnesota Law Review*, v.62 (1977–78).
Gotanda, Neil. "A Critique of Our Constitution Is Colorblind." *Stanford Law Review*, v.44/1 (1991).
MacKinnon, Catharine. "Reflections on Sex Equality Under Law." *Yale Law Journal*, v.100 (1991).
Raeder, Myrna. "Gender Issues in the Federal Sentencing Guidelines and Mandatory Minimum Sentences." *Criminal Justice*, v.8 (1993).
Schlesinger, Traci. "The Failure of Race-Neutral Policies: How Mandatory Terms and Sentencing Enhancements Increased Racial Disparities in Prison Admission Rates." *Crime & Delinquency*, v.57/1 (2001).
Sellin, Thorsen. *Slavery and the Penal System*. New York: Elsevier, 1976.

Espionage

Espionage has been a part of the human condition since time immemorial. It is frequently referred to as the second-oldest profession, after prostitution. Being so closely linked with prostitution raises a number of interesting moral questions about espionage, but this article is not an ethical critique of espionage but, rather, a brief history and examination of the dark art of espionage and the social and political effects of espionage in the United States of America.

Espionage is a popular topic for action and thriller novels and movies in modern society. This popularity is aptly illustrated by the incredible success of the James Bond novels by Ian Fleming and the continuing series of movies focused on Bond. Although Bond is a fictional character, some authorities have suggested that he was based on real-life spy Sidney Riley. Regardless, modern fiction and cinema have created a common public understanding of a spy and espionage as engaging in all sorts of covert activities, including sabotage, kidnapping, assassination, and foiling the nefarious plans of various evil psychopathic geniuses from either ruling or destroying the world. Although related to such activities, espionage itself is in fact much more limited.

Espionage is primarily concerned with information. Specifically, espionage involves secretly obtaining secret information from an opposing person, entity, or nation. The information sought is usually secret in that the opposing party, entity, or nation does not want it revealed to the seeker, for whatever reason. The reason can involve any number of considerations, such as industrial secrets, political secrets, military secrets, or national security. Furthermore, the actual obtaining of the information must also be kept secret so that the person, party, or nation in the possession of the secret information does not discover that the seeker has obtained the information. The reason for this requirement is that if the person, entity, or nation in possession of the secret information discovers that it has been compromised, then that person, entity, or nation will take steps to counter the effect of the revelation and loss of secrecy of the information. For example, assume one nation were able to discover the defensive plans of another nation in the event of a military attack by the first nation. If the second nation discovered that the first nation had obtained the secret plans, then the second nation would change the plans, making the previously secret information of significantly less value. When such espionage operations themselves are meant to be kept secret, they are commonly referred to clandestine operations.

Counterespionage is simply those activities designed to detect, prevent, and defeat espionage. There are numerous ways that counterespionage is undertaken. One of the most obvious is physical security. Denying access to those facilities that are intended to be kept secret is a basic step in counterespionage. Access to information raises other questions. The basic step to protect the secrecy of information is to enact laws that prohibit the revelation of such information. This is usually accomplished by the classification of information according to the level of security needed to protect it. In the United States, the three basic levels of information classification are confidential, secret, and top secret. Of course, there are higher levels of security for the classification of highly secret information. Another method of counterespionage is the use of codes and encryption. Communications and electronic records can be encoded to prevent unauthorized access to them. Cryptography, which is the science of codes and encryption, is one the most important fields of counterespionage.

Classifications of Targets of Espionage
There are four major classifications of information that is usually sought and gathered through the use of espionage. These classifications are HUMINT, SIGINT, IMINT, and open source intelligence. Generally speaking, open source intelligence is not, strictly speaking, obtained by espionage. Open source intelligence is when one person, entity, or nation can deduce certain secret information about an opposing person, entity, or nation through the use of material, publications, broadcasts, and information that is publicly available. This publicly available material may include books, journals, and newspapers. Such information does not need to be gathered in a clandestine manner. However, the subsequent analysis of such publicly available information may lead to (hopefully) accurate conclusions about the opposing person, entity, or nation that would otherwise be secret. Of course, the conclusions gained through publicly available sources would not be revealed to the opposing person, entity, or nation.

HUMINT is an acronym for the phrase *human intelligence*. Human intelligence is the information that is directly gathered or collected by human beings. In the military, this is usually accomplished by special operations units, such as the Special Forces (Green Berets) or the long-range surveillance units. These units are sent behind enemy lines to secretly observe enemy military activities and report them to their military commanders to assist in the successful execution of military missions. In the nonmilitary context, human intelligence is usually gathered or collected by spies. A spy can be anyone. A spy can be a professionally trained intelligence operative who is directly employed by an intelligence agency. A spy can be a foreign national who is recruited by an intelligence case officer working directly for an intelligence agency. A spy can be a diplomat in a foreign nation who uses his position to gain the needed secret information. A spy can also be an average citizen who travels to or works in a foreign country and has access to the needed secret information. The methods used to gather or collect secret information are varied and can include theft, burglary, eavesdropping, blackmail, and even assassination.

SIGINT is an acronym for the phrase *signal intelligence*. Generally, signal intelligence is the information that is gathered or collected by intercepting the communications of an opposing person, entity, or nation. The communications are usually electronic, such as transmissions on telephone lines or radio signals. Usually, these secret communications are encoded or encrypted in an effort to keep them secret. Once the communication has been intercepted, it is usually sent to a specialized agency that will try to break the code or cipher, thereby being able to read and understand the secret communication. The encoding of communications is usually called cryptology, and the breaking of codes is usually called cryptanalysis. The methods of accomplishing such interception of electronic communications include the tapping of telephone lines, the installation of electronic eavesdropping devices, the tapping of transoceanic telephone cables by submarines, or the monitoring of radio communications by communication dishes. SIGINT also encompasses the identification of certain technology by detecting and identifying that technology's electronic signature. For example, a particular type of submarine might have a distinctive sound based upon the type of its engines. Using this type of SIGINT, the type of submarine can be identified.

IMINT is an acronym for the phrase *image intelligence*. Image intelligence is usually used to describe information gained through the use of photography. It is especially useful when trying to determine the nature and purpose of secret foreign military and intelligence installations and facilities. For example, a spy satellite, using highly advanced and specialized photographic technology, can take very detailed photographs of installations and facilities in foreign nations by merely orbiting many miles above it, without violating the geographical borders of that nation. Spy planes can accomplish the same type of mission by flying at extremely high altitudes but not going into space. IMINT can be gathered by human intelligence operatives but it is more commonly associated with the use of either spy planes or satellites.

What Is a Spy?

Modern literature and cinema have placed in the current culture the image of a spy as the strong, daring, bold, courageous, and colorful person who always gets the better of the evil villain. These spies of the imagination and fiction are not the people who, in real life, are spies. To be a spy, no doubt, requires intelligence, training, and courage. However, intelligence agencies generally do not want the type of person who will make a large splash as a spy. The essential nature of espionage operations is that they are clandestine and meant to be kept secret. People who are perceptive about other people, who are inquisitive, who are intelligent, who have a high degree of ingenuity, who work well under stress, and who can keep a secret make the best spies.

Every nation has laws prohibiting and criminalizing espionage. Espionage, in the context of national security and national survival, is rightfully considered to be a fundamental danger that must be prevented. Espionage is prohibited by U.S. law and is defined as a crime in Title 18 United States Code §§ 792–98. Punishments for espionage are usually quite severe, especially where the harm to the nation is significant.

General History of Espionage

Espionage existed and was practiced long before the founding of the United States. It has a long, dangerous, bloody, and oftentimes secret history. Many times, successful espionage operations are not revealed until decades or even centuries later, if at all.

As previously stated, espionage is one of the oldest professions. Not only has it been practiced for thousands of years, but it has been the subject of scholarly works. As long ago as the 5th century B.C.E., Sun Tzu, a famous Chinese philosopher and general, wrote *The Art of War*. In this rather amazing text, Sun Tzu devoted an entire chapter to explaining the different types of spies, how to employ them, and how to operate an intelligence operation.

However, spying in the ancient world was not limited to Asia. One of the first records of spying in the Western world is in the Bible. Moses sent spies to investigate the land of Canaan before he brought the Jewish people to settle there. Further, before the attack on Jericho, Joshua sent spies to discover the weaknesses of the city.

The ancient Greeks and Romans were also not strangers to the effective use of espionage. In 480 B.C.E., when the Greeks and the Persians were at war, the Greeks sent spies to determine the size of Xerxes's military force prior to battle. In turn, Xerxes also employed spies.

During the 15th and 16th centuries, the famous Italian political philosopher Machiavelli gained renown for his rather harsh philosophy of politics in *The Prince*. However, he also wrote on the employment of spies and the techniques of espionage in his work *The Art of War*, which coincided with his stark recognition of "realpolitik" in *The Prince*. During this time period, the Catholic Church was also known to employ spies in its fight against Protestantism and in support of its fight against heresy, showing that espionage was not beneath any entity, including the church.

During the 16th and the 17th centuries, Europe saw the rise of nationalism and religious wars. At this time true professionals in the art of intelligence and formal intelligence services began to appear. One of the most famous was Sir John Walsingham, who was the secretary of state for Queen Elizabeth I. After the time of Elizabeth I, during the 17th century, Oliver Cromwell, during the course of his rule, established one of the first formal intelligence agencies in the Western world.

Early American Espionage

Any history of espionage, no matter how extensive, will have numerous gaps. This is because the essential nature of espionage involves secrecy, and many espionage operations, especially the failures, will be kept secret, if for no other reason than to protect the reputation and funding of that agency. However, over time, some espionage operations, both successes and failures, can and do come to light.

Generally speaking, espionage operations in early America were informal operations. During the American Revolution, General George Washington extensively employed spies. The most famous American spy during the Revolutionary War was Nathan Hale, who is famed for his statement that he regretted that he only had one life to give for his country. After the loss of Hale, Washington organized an intelligence organization that gathered a significant amount of information on the British forces. Further, Washington engaged in counterespionage, which resulted in the capture of British spy Major John Andre. There is little doubt that without this information, it would have been much more difficult for the colonists to win the Revolutionary War. Although there are few records of these espionage activities, Washington's financial records show that he spent $17,000 on espionage during the Revolutionary War, which was a large sum in those times.

Espionage was practiced during the Civil War but was not very effective. According to a number of authorities, no major battle during the Civil War was won or lost because of espionage, although there were a number of famous spies for both sides, which included Belle Boyd and Pauline Cushman. However, there are several circumstances that warrant specific attention. Allen Pinkerton, who gained notoriety working for the railroads providing security, was competent at counterespionage and was instrumental in protecting President Abraham Lincoln during the early part of the Civil War but had little success at the gathering of information from the Confederate forces. Pinkerton resigned after General George McClellan was relieved by President Lincoln. The Union organized an intelligence unit after the departure of Pinkerton known as the Bureau of Military Information. Although this organization was successful at gathering intelligence, it was woefully inadequate at counterespionage. One of its agents became head of the agency to protect the president, which obviously failed when President Lincoln was subsequently assassinated. Balloons were also used to gather information about the opposing military forces. This activity foreshadowed the use of airplanes and satellites in the late 20th century to gather secret information.

Confederate Civil War spy Belle Boyd, shown here in a photograph taken sometime between 1855 and 1865, conveyed intelligence about Union movements to General Thomas "Stonewall" Jackson and others fighting in Virginia.

After the end of the Civil War, in the 1880s, the United States began to develop its own military intelligence services. The Military Information Division was created for the army and the Office of Intelligence was created for the navy. Also, during this time period, the United States began to assign military attachés to foreign embassies so that they could gather military information about foreign nations using their status as diplomats to facilitate their espionage activities.

Unfortunately, during the succeeding period up to World War I, intelligence services were not supported and they dwindled. With the entry of the United States into World War I, it might be assumed that intelligence would regain its prominence but such was not the case. As the United States had entered World War I late, it relied on the intelligence services of the French and British. There was no pressing need for the United States to increase its own intelligence capabilities. However, the United States did enact the Espionage Act of 1917, which increased the penalties for espionage and included the death penalty. There is one espionage event that occurred during World War I that had a significant effect on the United States. The British intelligence service had decoded a German telegram, which is now known as the Zimmerman Telegram. It revealed how the Germans were trying to get Mexico to enter the war on its side in the event that the United States entered the war on behalf of the Allies. The effect on America was profound. Approximately a month after the Zimmerman Telegram was made public, the United States declared war on Germany. Regardless of the lack of espionage activity by the United States during World War I, the United States did maintain its intelligence branches in both the army and the navy and created a particularly important entity, the Black Chamber.

The Black Chamber was a highly secret organization that operated under the aegis of the State Department and developed a significant expertise in cryptography. The Black Chamber continued to operate after World War I, until 1929, when Secretary of State Henry Stimson made the now infamous statement, "Gentlemen do not read other gentlemen's mail." Despite the obvious naïveté of Secretary Stimson, the military continued with the cryptography started by the Black Chamber. The groundwork that was laid by the Black Chamber and the subsequent work of the military resulted in the breaking of the Japanese naval and diplomatic codes, which proved invaluable during World War II.

World War II–Era Espionage

With the advent of World War II, the United States recognized the need for espionage services. During the war, the Office of Strategic Services (OSS) was formed to conduct espionage, sabotage, and guerrilla operations behind enemy lines. The OSS was very successful. Although it was disbanded at the end of World War II, its success was so great that the continuing need for the particular services offered by such an intelligence organization were recognized. The OSS is considered the forerunner of the U.S. Army Green Berets and the Central Intelligence Agency (CIA). The CIA, was formed by the National Security Act of 1947. The CIA was tasked with espionage and covert operations overseas. The CIA was forbidden to conduct intelligence operations within the United States. Domestic counterintelligence operations were left to the Federal Bureau of Investigation (FBI). The primary espionage role of the CIA is the gathering of HUMINT.

Prior to the outbreak of the Korean War in 1950, SIGINT was handled by specialized agencies in each branch of the military, which were coordinated under the Armed Forces Security Agency. SIGINT was less than adequate during the initial phase of the Korean War. In response, the National Security Agency (NSA) was formed on October 24, 1952, by presidential directive. The NSA is one of the most secretive intelligence organizations in the United States. Its basic mission was and continues to be the interception and analysis of foreign communications.

With the start of the cold war between the Soviet Union and the Western powers, espionage gained a much greater importance in national policy. One of the most important secrets was atomic weapons. Julius and Ethel Rosenberg were indicted in 1950 and were subsequently convicted of passing atomic secrets to the Soviet Union. The trial and the verdict were marred with controversy. Not until 1995, when secret material was released, was it accepted that Julius Rosenberg had been a Soviet spy, but serious doubt was cast upon whether Ethel Rosenberg was guilty.

The Rosenberg case was a watershed in political and espionage history, as it led to the McCarthy era. Also involved in passing of atomic weapons secrets to the Soviet Union was Klaus Fuchs.

The McCarthy era was a time during the 1950s when the nation was caught in a frenzy of witch hunts for Communist spies. The major progenitor of this era was Senator Joseph McCarthy from Wisconsin, who held numerous hearings investigating allegations of Communist espionage and sympathy among American citizens. The lives of thousands of American citizens were ruined by innuendo, investigations, employment black lists, and denouncements by friends and family. It was a dark time for America, and since that time, the use of the phrases *McCarthyism* and *witch hunts* has been synonymous in America with tyrannical government behavior.

However, through the 1950s, the espionage ability of the United States increased. The United States was starting to collect IMINT through the use of high-altitude spy planes, known as U-2s, taking pictures of installations and facilities in the Soviet Union. Unfortunately, in 1960, one of these planes was shot down by the Soviet Union and the pilot, Gary Francis Powers, was taken captive. He was convicted by the Soviet Union of espionage and was sentenced to prison, although he was later repatriated in a prisoner exchange. The U-2 incident was politically damaging to the United States and foreshadowed later foul-ups by the American intelligence community. In contrast, a success involving IMINT in the 1960s was the spy plane photographs of Soviet nuclear weapons in Cuba, which resulted in the Cuban Missile Crisis, in which the world came to the brink of worldwide nuclear war.

Modern-Era American Espionage

During the 1960s, American espionage activities generally did not generate high-level publicity, which suited the intelligence community. Unfortunately, complaints and leaks of information on the activities of the CIA and the FBI combined with the involvement of CIA personnel in the Watergate scandal led to the formation of the Church Committee in the U.S. Senate in 1975. The Church Committee was a disaster for the American intelligence community, although many people consider it to be a great success for protecting American citizens from the abuse of power by intelligence agencies. The Church Committee found that the FBI, the CIA, and the U.S. Army were engaging in illegal political surveillance of American citizens. One of the most infamous operations was COINTELPRO by the FBI. The Church Committee also found that the CIA was engaging in the attempted assassinations of foreign leaders and engaged in the subversion of foreign governments. Although much of the Church Committee report is still classified, what was revealed shocked the nation. As a result, extensive limitations and oversight were placed on the intelligence community. One of these limitations was the creation of the Foreign Intelligence Surveillance Act (FISA) of 1978 courts, which are secret courts that can approve or disapprove warrants for the surveillance of people. Because these courts operate in secret, they were subjected to a great deal of criticism, which increased after the terrorist attacks of September 11, 2001.

Unfortunately for the CIA, 1975 also saw another disaster for the intelligence community with the publication of the famous book *Inside the Company: A CIA Diary*, which was written by former CIA agent Philip Agee. Agee's book was an exposé of CIA operations and agents that did serious harm to CIA operations in the world. As a result, laws were enacted that limited the ability of former intelligence agents from publishing their activities or knowledge concerning intelligence operations.

In the following years, the CIA, the NSA, and the many other intelligence agencies saw the arrival and departure of various directors. These years were considered a time of rebuilding to recover from the Church Committee. Unfortunately, the subsequent years saw the exposure of a number of American spies who had severely compromised the United States. In the 1980s, Jonathan Pollard, an intelligence analyst, was arrest for spying for Israel. John Anthony Walker, a naval chief warrant officer who specialized in communications, spied for the Soviet Union from 1968 to 1985. It is estimated that he helped the Soviet Union decrypt more than 1 million secret communications. Aldrich Ames, a CIA counterintelligence officer, spied for the Soviet Union from 1985 until his arrest in 1994. It is believed that Ames was responsible for the disappearance of

A soldier with the U.S. military police in Germany training in advanced surveillance photography techniques in 2009. For use in criminal investigations, image intelligence (IMINT) may come from traditional photography such as this, but surveillance of secret foreign military and intelligence installations more often comes from spy satellites or planes today.

many American spies. Robert Hanssen, an FBI agent, was arrested in 2001 after it was discovered he had spied for the Soviet Union for 22 years from 1979 to 2001. But not all arrests of alleged spies were successful. The FBI arrested a nuclear weapons physicist, Wen Ho Lee, in 1999 on suspicion of spying for the People's Republic of China. Wen Ho Lee had been working at Los Alamos National Laboratory. The case fell apart and despite being indicted on numerous counts, he was only convicted of one minor charge. He was eventually awarded more than $1 million in damages from the government for the attempted prosecution.

Espionage in the Twenty-First Century
Prior to September 11, 2001, the intelligence community began to gain back some of the power and public respect that it had lost after the release of the Church Committee report. For example, in 1994, the FBI introduced the concept of Internet data mining with a program known as CARNIVORE. The project was strongly criticized, and the FBI responded by merely changing its name. Essentially, the same functions of Internet datamining are still being performed. Since that time, the government has been attempting to expand data mining on the Internet with programs such as Total Information Awareness (TIA).

A problem arose for the NSA in the early part of 2001 when the existence of a secret project known as Echelon was revealed. Echelon was reputed to be a highly advanced system to conduct surveillance of satellite communications and was supposedly started in the 1960s, though it had been upgraded since that time. European community nations complained that it was being used improperly by the United States to engage in industrial espionage on behalf of defense contractors and that it violated European Union privacy laws. Little is known about Echelon, and the complaints have reportedly not been addressed. This incident raised public awareness about the omnipresence of the NSA and the ability of the government to surreptitiously violate individual privacy at will.

With the terrorist attacks of September 11, 2001, which killed thousands and destroyed the World Trade Center, the intelligence community gained a new lease on life and an extraordinary increase in its powers. With the passage of the USA PATRIOT Act of 2001, the intelligence agencies were granted extensive powers. These powers included being able to access library and bookstore records to see which books were being read by people, and greatly expended search and surveillance authority, even bypassing the FISA courts in some cases. Although the act was subject to severe criticism by civil rights activists, the 9/11 attacks provided sufficient impetus to allow the passage and even renewal of the act. An additional result of the 9/11 terrorist attacks was the formation of the Department of Homeland Security, which concentrated all of the major security functions of the government under a single agency. Another result was the creation of the Office of the Director of National Intelligence to help coordinate all of the intelligence activities of the various intelligence agencies in the government. The reason for the creation of the Office of the Director of National Intelligence was that the 9/11 terrorist attacks arguably could have been prevented if the various intelligence agencies had shared information. However, the creation of this office has been viewed as a failure because it has not met its goal of agency coordination and cooperation. These new creations illustrated a fundamental change of the attitude of the American nation about civil rights and privacy.

In 2005, the NSA was caught illegally intercepting the communications of American citizens within the borders of the United States. Because of a courageous whistleblower, it was discovered that the major telecom corporations had been cooperating with the NSA in these illegal interceptions. A public uproar ensued, and a number of lawsuits were filed. As a result, bills were filed in Congress to grant the telecom corporations retroactive immunity from the lawsuits. These illegal violations of privacy by the NSA have brought the issue of espionage against a nation's own citizens to the attention of all.

Problems With Espionage

As has been so obviously illustrated by the brief history of espionage in America, there are many problems with espionage. First, it involves secrecy and deception. Second, it can be extremely dangerous. Spies who are caught will be prosecuted and may even face the death penalty. This leads to a third issue, which is legality. All nations have laws against espionage but almost all nations practice espionage against other nations. Perhaps it is just a calculated risk that the information gained will be worth the lives of the spies. Finally, there are the moral issues. But this article is not an analysis of the morality of espionage but merely a brief review of it and some of the issues and social and political effects surrounding espionage.

Conclusion

Espionage is a fact of life. Whether it should be done, the fact remains that it is practiced and it will continue to be practiced, despite the potential pitfalls and dangers. From a social and political perspective, at least in the last half of the 20th century and the beginning of the 21st century, espionage has had a significant impact on the United States. In the 1950s, the issue of potential espionage, no matter how farfetched, led to massive witch hunts, political paranoia, and the destruction of the lives of numerous American citizens. In the 1960s and the 1970s, the espionage failures and fiascos only aggravated the civil rights issues that were affecting American society. In the 1980s and the 1990s, the activities of the intelligence agencies in America were not as conspicuous in the American consciousness, except for the number of foreign spies caught and prosecuted. However, with the turn of the century, espionage has once again come to the forefront. It is especially relevant because espionage, especially against a nation's own population, can have a significant—and even devastating—effect on criminal prosecutions. Espionage and its associated covert operations are being touted as the solution to many of America's problems of national security, leading to a fundamental crisis in American political philosophy: Will America become a police state, where civil rights belong to a bygone era and citizens become informers on each other, and the police and intelligence agencies have almost complete access to the private lives of its citizens? Or will America return to the ideals fostered by the founding fathers and enshrined in the Bill of Rights?

Wm. C. Plouffe, Jr.
Independent Scholar

See Also: 1941 to 1960 Primary Documents; Bill of Rights; Declaration of Independence; Detection and Detectives; Electronic Surveillance; Espionage Act of 1917; McCarthy, Joseph; Political Policing; USA PATRIOT Act of 2001.

Further Readings
Agee, Philip. *Inside the Company: A CIA Diary*. New York: Penguin, 1975.
Aid, Matthew. *The Secret Sentry: The Untold History of the National Security Agency*. London: Bloomsbury, 2009.
Bamford, James. *The Shadow Factory*. New York: Doubleday, 2008.
Dulles, Allen. *The Craft of Intelligence*. New York: Lyons Press, 2006.
Knightly, Phillip. *The Second Oldest Profession: Spies and Spying in the Twentieth Century*. New York: Norton, 1987.
O'Toole, George. *Honorable Treachery: A History of U.S. Intelligence, Espionage, and Covert Action From the American Revolution to the CIA*. New York: Atlantic Monthly Press, 1991.
Ranelagh, John. *The Agency: The Rise and Decline of the CIA*. New York: Simon & Schuster, 1986.
Trento, Joseph. *The Secret History of the CIA*. Santa Ana, CA: Forum, 2001.
Wiener, Tim. *Legacy of Ashes: History of the CIA*. New York: Doubleday, 2007.

Espionage Act of 1917

The Espionage Act of 1917 was created to protect the United States from subversive activity but was used to suppress opposition to World War I and U.S. involvement in Russia following the war. Despite its suppression of dissent, the Espionage Act survived several constitutional challenges. After the war, it fell into disuse but it remains a tool for the United States as it seeks creative ways to fight the war on terror.

In 1914, Europe began fighting what would become World War I. Primarily, the war involved Great Britain, France, and Russia against Germany. Both sides sought the support of the United States and other neutral nations. For three years, the United States officially remained neutral and attempted to broker peace agreements. At the same time, the government adopted policies favoring the Allied powers of Great Britain, France, and Russia.

While the government opted for one side, the increasingly diverse citizenry of the United States never selected a side. This diversity created concern for President Woodrow Wilson and his administration. They feared that citizens of German descent would align themselves with Germany against the United States. They also feared that Germans would enter the United States and undermine its efforts to prepare for war. In 1916, explosions at munitions factories in Jersey City, New Jersey, and Seattle, Washington, cemented the idea that the United States required a law to prohibit subversive activity within its borders.

Resolute in its desire for a new law, the Wilson administration began drafting the proposed legislation. The Justice Department attorneys who drafted the statute were concerned with the potential for abuse that a law prohibiting subversive activity brought with it. Improper drafting or implementation would curtail freedom of discussion. Despite their concern, the drafters wrote the statute so that it covered an array of activity. They believed that carefully scrutinizing the facts in individual cases would prevent unjust application. Congress agreed and in 1917 passed the Espionage Act.

Provisions and Application of the Law
The act created four new crimes. The first two crimes prohibited the disclosure of national security information, making it an offense to communicate war information, plans, or operations to any foreign nation opposing the United States. The third new crime prohibited interference with

the war effort by persuading people not to enlist in the armed forces or making false statements about the United States. The final crime prohibited conspiracies to commit any of the previous three crimes.

The Espionage Act was one of three new statutes designed to protect the nation's internal security. The other two were the Trading with the Enemy Act and the Sedition Act. The latter was passed in order to strengthen provisions of the Espionage Act. A federal judge in Montana had interpreted the Espionage Act to restrict its application to instances in which a person spoke with the specific intent to undermine the government's war efforts. Believing this unduly restricted the government's ability to prosecute offenders, the Wilson administration drafted the Sedition Act. Over the next two years, the government initiated approximately 2,200 cases involving the three statutes.

With so many cases entering the system, it was inevitable that the law would be applied to cases involving minimal potential for actual harm. People throughout the nation were prosecuted for conversations in which they questioned administration policy or sympathized with Germany. While this went beyond the Department of Justice's intent, it had no control over the U.S. attorneys. Many U.S. attorneys prosecuted nearly every case brought to them that fell within the statute's technical language. Others prosecuted marginal cases to send a message to the larger population.

By 1919, several Espionage Act cases reached the U.S. Supreme Court. In each instance, the Supreme Court upheld the constitutionality of the act against First Amendment challenges. Through these cases, Justice Oliver Wendell Holmes announced the "clear and present danger" test and began refining it. Although not accepted by the court at first, the test eventually became the standard for judging whether a law violated the First Amendment.

Following the war, the Espionage Act fell into disuse. At the time, the United States lacked an organized intelligence community. Therefore, there was little basis for prosecuting Espionage Act cases when there was no formal war. Following World War II, the United States created a permanent intelligence community and, with it, a system for protecting national security information. The increased emphasis on national security information made the Espionage Act relevant again. Use of the statute, however, has been limited because of concerns that prosecutions may be nullified because the conduct to which the act applies remains vague.

Scott Ingram
High Point University

See Also: *Abrams v. United States*; Bill of Rights; Holmes, Oliver Wendell, Jr.; Political Dissidents; *Schenck v. United States*; Sedition Act of 1918; Supreme Court, U.S.; Wilson, Woodrow (Administration of).

Further Readings
Polenberg, Richard. *Fighting Faiths: The Abrams Case, the Supreme Court and Free Speech*. New York: Viking, 1987.
Schaffer, Ronald. *America in the Great War: The Rise of the War Welfare State*. New York: Oxford University Press, 1991.
Stone, Geoffrey R. *Perilous Times: Free Speech in Wartime From the Sedition Act of 1798 to the War on Terrorism*. New York: W. W. Norton, 2004.

Estes v. Texas

The First Amendment to the U.S. Constitution provides for freedom of the press. The Sixth Amendment guarantees a public trial by an impartial jury for the criminally accused. The U.S. Supreme Court extended freedom of the press to the criminal justice systems of the states through the due process clause of the Fourteenth Amendment in 1931. The court did the same with respect to public criminal trials in 1948 and trials by an impartial jury in 1966. In three cases decided in the early and mid-1940s, the justices considered how to resolve competing claims about the scope of these potentially conflicting liberties. In each instance, the freedom of the print media was vindicated despite anticipated violation of a criminal defendant's right to a fair trial attributable to judicially proscribed newspaper publication.

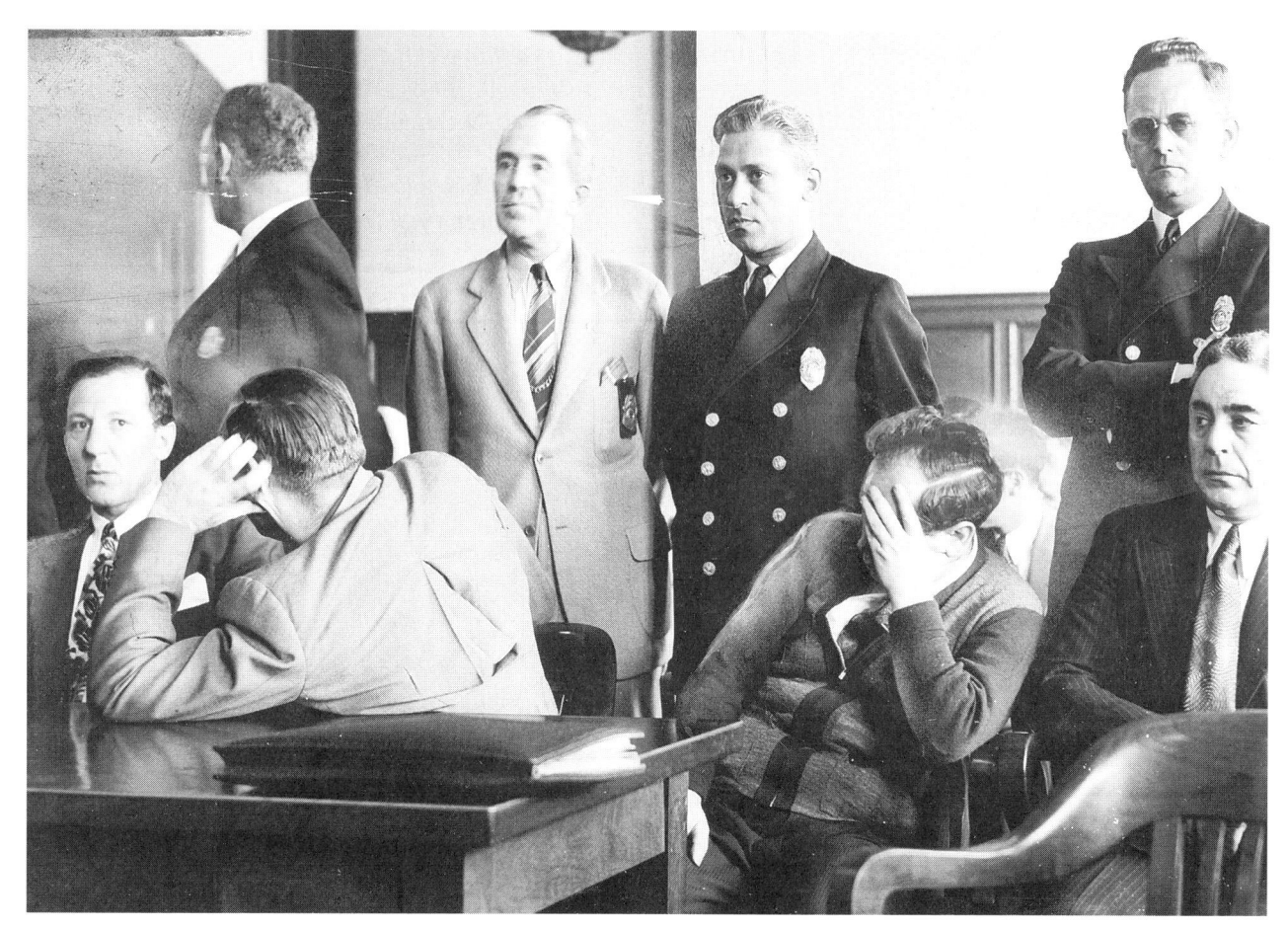

Defendants in an organized crime case shield their faces from a New York World-Telegram & Sun *newspaper photographer's camera that was present in a Brooklyn courtroom during jury selection in 1941. The presence or absence of cameras in the courtroom continues to cause controversy in state and federal courthouses nationwide nearly 50 years after the* Estes v. Texas *case.*

With the advent of electronic communication technology—radio in the 1930s and television in the 1940s—the likelihood of collision between these fundamental constitutional principles increased significantly. When confrontation occurred in the 1960s, the court's about-face was dramatic. In four consecutive cases—*Irvin v. Dowd* (1961), *Rideau v. Louisiana* (1963), *Estes v. Texas* (1965), and *Sheppard v. Maxwell* (1966)—the Fourteenth Amendment claims of the defendants prevailed over the freedom of the press.

Media Coverage and Jury Bias

Billie Sol Estes was charged in 1961 by the state of Texas and the U.S. Justice Department with committing multiple criminal counts of financial fraud and theft by swindle. Selling nonexistent anhydrous ammonia fertilizer tanks to farmers and purchasing nontransferable acreage allotments for planting cotton from farmers allegedly produced millions of dollars of illegal income. Estes's conviction in state court in October 1962 was reversed by a 5–4 vote of the U.S. Supreme Court on June 8, 1965.

Justice Tom Clark wrote for the majority that Estes had been deprived of his Fourteenth Amendment guarantee of due process of law. Unfettered access by broadcast journalists and television cameramen to the Tyler, Texas, courtroom during pretrial hearings in September and the less conspicuous presence of the press during the subsequent trial were decisive, despite a change of venue from Reeves County, where Estes resided, to Smith County, some 500 miles distant.

The two-day pretrial hearing was broadcast live by multiple television and radio stations. News photographers moved freely about a crowded courtroom as arguments by opposing counsel on a pair of defense motions ensued. The presiding judge rejected the motion to restrict television coverage, radio broadcasts, and news photography of the upcoming trial. The motion seeking a continuance to allow additional time for preparation for the trial was granted. During the nearly monthlong interval, because of renewed defense objections, the courtroom was altered to make the television cameras and operators less conspicuous. All live broadcasts of witness testimony were banned, and photographers were restricted to only those locations in the courtroom open to members of the public.

These differences between unrestricted press access to the pretrial hearing and the limitations in effect during the jury trial fragmented the justices' reasoning: (1) Clark acknowledged the differences but asserted that the guarantee of due process of law at trial must necessarily apply also to pretrial proceedings because those events may deeply affect opinion as to guilt or innocence in the community from which the trial jury was drawn; (2) Chief Justice Earl Warren, concurring, minimized the differences while finding the presence of electronic media personnel and equipment during the trial still to have been too intrusive to satisfy due process of law; and (3) Justice Potter Stewart, dissenting, drew a vivid contrast between the media presence during the hearing and the trial. But in sharp disagreement with Clark, he declared that the constitutional issue in this case pertained only to the trial. In contrast to Warren, Stewart concluded that the trial did not deprive the defendant of his liberty without due process of law.

At the time of Estes's trial, the appellate court of last resort in all states except Texas and Colorado had endorsed Canon 35 of the American Bar Association (ABA) Model Rules of Judicial Ethics that prohibited televised court trials. In Texas, the applicable rule, Judicial Canon 28, permitted the televising of trials at the discretion of the trial judge. The presence or absence of cameras in the courtroom continues to generate controversy in state and federal courthouses across the country nearly 50 years later.

Steven H. Hatting
University of St. Thomas

See Also: *Chandler v. Florida*; Fraud; News Media, Crime in; News Media, Punishment in; *Sheppard v. Maxwell*.

Further Readings
Duscha, Julius. *Taxpayers' Hayride: The Farm Problem From the New Deal to the Billie Sol Estes Case*. Boston: Little, Brown, 1964.
Estes, Pam. *Billie Sol: King of Texas Wheeler-Dealers*. Abilene, TX: Noble Craft Books, 1983.
Scherer, Mark R. and James W. Hewitt. *Rights in the Balance: Free Press, Fair Trial, and Nebraska Press Association v. Stuart*. Lubbock: Texas Tech University Press, 2008.

Ethics in Government Act of 1978

The Ethics in Government Act of 1978 established the Office of Government Ethics, allowing for the investigation of high-level government officials. The act was signed into law on October 26, 1978, by President Jimmy Carter. This act is also known as the Independent Counsel Act. The root of this legislation begins with the Watergate scandal during the presidency of Richard M. Nixon, which ultimately led to his resignation in August 1974. Until Watergate investigations fell under the responsibilities of the attorney general, however, the fact that the president appointed the position and Nixon actually fired the prosecutor investigating him led to a change in procedure. The American public needed reassurance that investigations would be carried out without interruption from government officials. After Nixon fired Archibald Cox and his presidency began to unravel, Congress decided to initiate hearings to seek a solution to prevent abuse by the executive branch in the future. After five years of hearings, the Ethics in Government Act became law in 1978, beginning a 20-year period of controversy related to the law.

The law authorized the attorney general to request a judicial panel composed of judges from the U.S. Court of Appeals to appoint a special prosecutor, later called an independent counsel, to investigate the government official in question. The counsel was called on to remain independent and impartial when investigating the person in question. Prosecutors were called on to investigate persons in the four presidential administrations during the law's existence. Lawrence Walsh led the investigation of the Iran-Contra affair during the administrations of Ronald Reagan and George H. W. Bush, investigating the illegal sale of arms to Iran and the money going to the Nicaraguan Contras. Walsh convicted two administration officials, Admiral John Poindexter and Lt. Colonel Oliver North, who later successfully appealed the decisions. The investigation ended, and President Bush pardoned the remaining suspected officials.

In 1992, Congress allowed the law to lapse because Republicans in Congress found the office to be expensive and it created an agency that fell outside of the system of checks and balances. The Supreme Court reviewed a number of cases challenging the law, but found it constitutional every time. In 1994, Congress passed a revised version of the Independent Counsel Law that was supported by President Bill Clinton and his attorney general, Janet Reno. At that point, Reno had already appointed Robert Fiske to investigate the Whitewater investment deal.

Pursuant to the new law, Fiske was replaced by Kenneth W. Starr, who expanded the investigation. Starr's investigation into the Whitewater land deal investments by the Clintons expanded over time to include a charge of perjury in *Clinton v. Jones*. Reno approved the additional investigation, which focused on whether Clinton lied in his deposition in the sexual harassment lawsuit filed against him by Paula Jones. The main emphasis of this case was a revelation of an affair with White House intern Monica Lewinsky that he denied in his deposition. Starr took this issue and published his findings in the Starr Report, which convinced Congress to pursue impeachment proceedings. The House voted to impeach Clinton, and the Senate later acquitted him in February 1999 by a party line vote, allowing him to complete his term of office.

Around the same time as Clinton's impeachment proceedings, Congress was considering the reauthorization of the Independent Counsel Act that would expire in June 1999. Consensus between both parties, the attorney general and the most recent counsel, was to let the law expire. Experiences with the Iran-Contra affair and the Whitewater investigation proved that the law did not work. Investigations in both cases were costly, exceeding $40 million each to conduct. Additionally, the goal of the law was that the appointed counsel would truly be independent of politics. The Starr investigations, report, and the subsequent partisan support of the investigation by the Republicans made it apparent that a counsel could not remain impartial. The outcomes of Iran-Contra and Whitewater did not reassure the public that it could trust executive branch officials to be honest, nor could it count on a nonpartisan investigation from an independent counsel. Congress has not found a solution to replace the role of the independent counsel because it was difficult to define the role to the satisfaction of both parties while making sure it met constitutional requirements.

After 20 years of investigations led by the independent counsel, the Justice Department resorted back to the process used during the Nixon administration, where counsels are appointed by the attorney general when needed. Given the partisan nature of investigating executive branch officials and the firing of investigator Cox during the Watergate investigations, Congress attempted to solve the problem by creating a position appointed by a panel of judges. However, this proved to be a more divisive solution, because the appointees to these positions failed to remain independent and nonpartisan. The current system of attorney general appointees for investigations is not the solution, so it remains a congressional challenge to find a replacement for this law that will be able to truly investigate executive branch members without bias.

Theresa S. Hefner-Babb
Lamar University

See Also: Clinton, William (Administration of); Nixon, Richard (Administration of); Political Crimes, Contemporary; Reagan, Ronald (Administration of); Watergate.

Further Readings
"An Act to Establish Certain Federal Agencies, Effect Certain Reorganizations of the Federal

Government, to Implement Certain Reforms in the Operation of the Federal Government and to Preserve and Promote the Integrity of Public Officials and Institutions, and for Other Purposes." 92 STAT. 1824 (October 26, 1978).

Harriger, Katy J. *Independent Justice: The Federal Special Prosecutor in American Politics*. Lawrence: University Press of Kansas, 1992.

Johnson, Charles A. *Independent Counsel: The Law and the Investigations*. Washington, DC: CQ Press, 2001.

Walsh, Lawrence E. *Firewall: The Iran-Contra Conspiracy and Cover-up*. New York: W. W. Norton, 1997.

Everleigh Sisters

The Everleigh sisters, Ada (February 15, 1864–January 5, 1960) and Minna (July 13, 1866–September 16, 1948), operated the Everleigh Club, a famous high-class brothel in Chicago, Illinois, from 1900 until 1911. The club was described by Chicago's Vice Commission as "the most famous and luxurious house of prostitution in the country." The sisters' notions of prostitution positioned harlots not as lost women devoid of virtue but as investments, deserving nutritious meals, thorough education, expert medical care, and competitive wages. The sisters' biographies, long-accepted as factual, were publicly debunked when Karen Abbott published *Sin in the Second City: Madams, Ministers, Playboys, and the Battle for America's Soul* in 2007.

Ada and Minna Everleigh were born in Virginia, to Montgomery Simms and his wife, who died shortly after their birth. The Simms family was wealthy but lost much of their wealth, including the family plantation, during the Civil War. The sisters left home hoping to become actresses. Stranded by a theater company in Omaha, Nebraska, the sisters changed their last name to "Everleigh," adapted from their grandmother's correspondence often signed "Everly Yours." They opened successful brothels in Omaha and then decided to relocate to a more affluent city. The sisters toured brothels in cities around the country and agreed that Chicago offered the most opportunity.

They bought a brothel south of the city's downtown on Dearborn Street from a retiring madam, fired all of the women, and redecorated with the most luxurious appointments they could acquire. Silk curtains, damask chairs, oriental rugs, mahogany tables, gold-leafed china, perfumed fountains, mirrored ceilings, fine art, and gold cuspidors graced the rooms. Gourmet meals and live musicians also added to the ostentatious atmosphere. When the Everleigh Club opened, admission was $10, dinner was $50, and private time with any working girl started at $50.

High standards governed employees of the Everleigh Club. The sisters demanded that their girls have pretty faces and figures, be in perfect health, be polite, and dress in lavish evening clothes. The sisters banned underage girls, pimps, white slavers, desperate parents looking to sell their children, knockout powders, thieving, and drug use from the house. They also regulated the clientele, which included wealthy businessmen, politicians, and celebrities, such as Marshall Field, Jr., Theodore Dreiser, Jack Johnson, John Rockefeller, Jr., John Barrymore, and Prince Henry of Prussia.

While the Everleigh sisters were working to improve their industry, reformers were working to eradicate the exploitation, crime, and disease that often accompanied prostitution. In 1901, Chicago hosted the National Purity Congress, which drew reformers from around the world to the city eager to purify a place so "great in sin." In 1904, reformer William Stead published *If Christ Came to Chicago*, which exposed much of the city's political corruption, underground economy, and vice establishments. The Chicago Vice Commission was appointed in 1910 to study the issue of prostitution and make recommendations for its continued legalization or prohibition. The commission determined that the tradition of segregation—containing prostitution to a designated area, or vice district—was ineffective, and that all vice districts needed to be permanently abolished. In 1911, Mayor Carter Harrison, Jr., ordered the Everleigh Club closed. Minna Everleigh responded, "If the Mayor says we must close, that settles it ... I'll close up shop and walk out with a smile on my face." The sisters determined that they had approximately $1 million in cash, $200,000 worth of diamonds, $150,000 in antique furnishings, and $25,000 in client IOUs to fund their departure from Chicago.

Ada and Minna Everleigh moved to New York's Upper West Side. They went by Ada and Minna Lester and denied any suggestion that they could be connected to their famous brothel from Chicago. When young writer Irving Wallace contacted the sisters about their history, Minna declared that she and Ada were socialites whose names had been co-opted by the famous Chicago madams. They explained their wealth with stories of rich ancestors and only privately entertained Chicago visitors. Minna died in 1948, at the age of 82, though publicly she maintained she was only 70. Ada followed in 1960, just weeks before her 96th birthday. The Everleigh sisters are buried together in Alexandria, Virginia.

Tiffany Middleton
Independent Scholar

See Also: Chicago, Illinois; Illinois; Prostitution, History of; Vice Commission; Vice Reformers.

Further Readings
Abbott, Karen. *Sin in the Second City: Madams, Ministers, Playboys, and the Battle for America's Soul.* New York: Random House, 2007.
Wendt, Lloyd and Herman Kogan. *Lords of the Levee.* Evanston, IL: Northwestern University Press, 2005.

William Henry Johnson, an African American private in the Civil War, was hanged in front of other Union soldiers near Petersburg, Virginia, on June 20, 1864. He had been accused of desertion and the attempted rape of a white woman.

Executions

Capital punishment came to the United States along with the first colonists. The first recorded execution in colonial America was of Captain George Kendall in the Jamestown colony of Virginia in 1608. His crime, as an alleged spy for Spain, was treason. Though treason remains a capital offense in most jurisdictions, people were executed for all manner of crimes, including stealing grapes, trading with the Indians, "buggery" (Joseph Ross, December 20, 1785, Westmoreland County, Connecticut), "witchcraft" ("Manuel," June 15, 1779), and "aiding a runaway slave" (Starling Carlton, 1859, South Carolina) in the early republic. Despite the irregularities of the application of the death penalty as to the rule of law, the practice itself remained relatively unchallenged through the 19th century. Instead, the history of execution describes the shift from public to private, from punishment to reform, and finally, from execution to mitigation.

Public Executions
At its outset, public execution emphasized the recuperative effect death might have, not on the criminal, but on the public that he or she had presumably wronged. Along with the public death of the criminal came a promise that civic order would be affirmed and restored. Though accepted as commonplace, the death penalty had early opponents, many of whom identified the

use of capital punishment with British rule. The text most responsible for generating arguments among Americans against the use of the death penalty was Cesare Beccaria's 1764 *Dei Delitti e delle Pene*. Translated as *An Essay on Crimes and Punishment*, it was published in London in 1767 and in the United States in 1777. In addition, many newspapers serialized Beccaria's essay. As historian Louis Masur explains, "The timing and content of the movement against the death penalty in the early Republic must be examined as a product of a social context shaped by the Revolution and an intellectual context governed by republican ideology and liberal theology." Thus, though execution was an accepted form of punishment and an ordinary fact of life, postrevolutionary America was ready to abandon executions in part as a way to distinguish republican values from those of European monarchies.

In addition to the death penalty's presence in political and legislative debates, it has been amply represented in the arts. According to historian Stuart Banner, public executions drew larger crowds than any other public gathering. Thus, it is not surprising that executions from the early colonial period generated all kinds of gallows literature—from sermons made on the occasion to conversion narratives and confessions. These were sold on execution day and were circulated broadly throughout the community. Some were more sensational than others, sometimes containing the last words and confession of the convict. Louis Masur points out, however, that many of these stories follow a formula of the cautionary tale, diminishing their value as historical documents.

Yet as attitudes toward capital punishment changed, so too did its literary treatment become more critical of the practice. Perhaps one of the most haunting depictions of a public execution is Herman Melville's poem about the hanging of the abolitionist John Brown. In its sparseness, his 1859 poem "The Portent" captures the eerie quality of a public execution once it has been shorn of the sensational glare created in much of the gallows literature that circulated in broadsides and the penny press. Melville marshals all of poetry's rhetorical power to condemn the act that foretold the war. The poem also emphasizes the absence of redemption, echoing a popular argument against the death penalty for vacating the promise of redemption. Melville further underscores the degenerative social effect of capital punishment as both the title and the poem's last lines indicate that this hanging—John Brown's shadow and then streaming beard—cast a shadow: the harbinger of war.

Private Executions

Although the last public execution to take place in the United States was that of Rainey Bethea in Owensboro, Kentucky, on August 14, 1936, the change from public to private had already begun in the 1800s. Social critics, politicians, and other architects of the new republic, including Alexander Hamilton and Thomas Jefferson, saw that watching another person die had toxic effects on the human psyche. Far from creating a sense of deterrence, many believed that witnessing the state-sanctioned death of another human being undermined the possibility of reform and encouraged the baser instincts. A just society rehabilitates its members rather than disposes of them. Efforts to reform the penal code and abolish the death penalty resulted in the development of the modern-day penitentiary. An emphasis on rehabilitation of the convict coincided with public recognition that the effect of shame—what we might think of as "the scarlet letter" approach—did not create positive change in criminal behavior. Since then, executions have taken place strictly within the privacy of the prison with the use of solitude as the preferred method of punishment. As executions moved from the public square to death row, from the gallows noose to lethal injection, the spirit behind capital punishment also changed.

More and more in the 19th century, as evidenced in John Greenleaf Whittier's 1843 poem "The Human Sacrifice," the public began to see capital punishment as a violation of not just republican values but of civilized principles more broadly. "The Human Sacrifice" portrays capital punishment as ghastly and barbaric. With no redeeming features, this waste of human life makes a mockery of law by ritualizing murder. Whittier joins a larger cadre of civil rights activists like William Lloyd Garrison, Wendell Phillips, and Theodore Parker, all of whom supported the abolition of both slavery and the death penalty. Today, the movement to end the death penalty still retains its roots in social justice in part because capital punishment has been inflicted on the socially marginal.

For instance, the largest single execution in U.S. history was the hanging of 38 Native Americans who had been convicted of murder in the 1862 Dakota War. They were executed at the same time in Mankato, Minnesota, on December 26, 1862. According to statistics assembled by Amnesty International, the focus on the disenfranchised has continued: "The death penalty is used disproportionately against the poor, minorities and members of racial, ethnic and religious communities."

A U.S. government report confirms that, since 1976, 77 percent of cases in which the death penalty was applied for murder involved a white victim. Long before these statistics were assembled, Richard Wright, in his 1940 novel *Native Son*, called attention to the racial dynamics of crime—and punishment—through his unforgettable character Bigger Thomas. Importantly, Bigger Thomas's story anticipates the broader arguments of the 20th and 21st century, especially as they have their roots in the fight to abolish slavery. Bigger's doom is a socially constructed one, as the novel makes plain. Bigger only did what he had been destined to do by a society that placed little or no value on him as a human being.

Contemporary Views

Members of the contemporary movement to abolish the death penalty, such as Angela Davis, focus on both the social murder of incarceration and the state-sanctioned killing performed at the time of execution. Likening the big business of slavery to the big business of incarceration, opponents of the death penalty refer to the criminal justice system as "the prison-industrial complex." The term is meant to emphasize the legacy of slavery as it has reconstituted itself in the economy of punishment. For a short time after the Supreme Court ruling in *Furman v. Georgia* (1972), the death penalty was abolished, in part in recognition of the fact that those who suffer the death penalty tend to be the real-life Bigger Thomases of their time: black and poor. Through a link to the Eighth and Fourteenth Amendments, the death penalty was ruled "cruel and unusual punishment."

This judicial abolition of the death penalty brought about a renewed focus on the procedures and methods of administering the death penalty. Training attention on the mechanisms of death allowed states to reinstate the death penalty by assuring "humane" practices in carrying out the sentence. In most states lethal injection, or more properly, lethal injections, is the preferred method. As of 2011, the controversy about execution in the United States has turned, once more, to the mechanism of death. Currently, most prisons use a set of three drugs, in combination, to deliver the lethal injection. The drug delivery method, as with the earlier debate over public versus private executions, focuses not on the moral right to take another life but rather on the moral imperative to make death the primary result by reducing the physical discomfort involved. According to state regulations, lethal injections commonly involve a sequence of three drugs that is set by state regulations: an anesthetic—sodium thiopental in every state but Oklahoma—intended to prevent pain, followed by a muscle relaxant and a drug that stops the heart.

In 2011, the drug company that makes sodium thiopental has stopped production in the United States, in part in protest of its use in the administration of the death penalty. A shortage resulted that has threatened to slow down scheduled executions. The company, Hospira, planned on resuming production at its factory in Italy, but this plan has reopened the debate regarding the death penalty, as Italy (and other European countries) have refused to allow the export of drugs for the purpose of the death penalty. The drug that could be used as an alternative—pentobarbital—is less preferable, in part because this drug is tainted by its history in veterinary medicine and physician-assisted suicide.

In any event, state procedures require a legal process be followed to change the protocol for lethal injection, thus a simple substitution cannot just be made. Officials at various penitentiaries have adopted an informal "supply and demand" system through which they circulate the remaining supply of sodium thiopental, but this practice—as with any possible substitutions for the drug—violates policies adopted to regulate state practices.

As a legal term, *execution* refers to the formal process by which a contract is made valid and put into binding effect. The death penalty, however, entails a multiplicity of possibilities, not all of which result in death—what law professor Stuart Banner terms its most "binding effect." Banner notes that there were "degrees of death" in operation under the death penalty. For instance, Banner reports one case in 1676 in which Elizabeth Rainer was taken to the gallows and had a noose put around her neck. For the crimes of fornication and infanticide, she was to stand on the gallows for a half hour to suffer a symbolic hanging for her actions and serve as a cautionary figure to the public. The notion that death need not be the only way to punish capital offenses has returned to the forefront of the debate.

Currently, efforts to abolish the death penalty have given way to more successful work in mitigation. Mitigation emphasizes not the innocence but the humanity of the person convicted. Mitigation has gained the upper hand in averting the death penalty in part because of the two-phase trial that was instituted for capital offenses. Attorneys whose focus is mitigation need not argue for the accused's innocence; rather, the focus is on the complex human story that brought him or her to the moment of the offense. Mitigators succeed in convincing juries to change the sentence from death to life in prison without parole (LWOP) in part because of DNA exonerations as well as other factors that can contribute to a wrongful execution. Thanks to organizations like the Innocence Project, at least 17 inmates have been released from death row. As a punishment, LWOP is the modern-day solution that had already gained favor with the death penalty's earliest opponents. Those reformers—from Thomas Jefferson to Benjamin Rush and beyond—saw life imprisonment as a "living death," capable of invoking greater horror in potential criminals than mere death, especially once executions were taken out of the public view.

Portrayals in Media

Not surprisingly, the death penalty has been central to several riveting literary treatments in the 20th century. *In Cold Blood* by Truman Capote (1968) described the killers Richard "Dick" Hickock and Perry Smith, their crimes, conviction, and ultimately, their execution. Norman Mailer's *The Executioner's Song* (1980) is the Pulitzer Prize–winning nonfiction treatment of Gary Gilmore's crimes, trial, and execution. This story has been revisited by Gilmore's younger brother Mikal in *Shot in the Heart*. Mikal Gilmore's book was later made into an HBO movie of the same title.

The subject has received prominent attention on the wide screen. In 1995, filmmaker Tim Robbins took the death penalty as his theme in *Dead Man Walking*. This full-length feature film focused on Sister Helen Prejean, achingly played by Susan Sarandon, and her relationship with death row inmate Mathew Poncelet, played by Sean Penn. The film garnered much praise. Sarandon won the Oscar for her performance; Penn and Robbins were both nominated.

More recently, and very powerfully, the full-length feature film *The Life of David Gale* (2003) directed by Alan Parker and starring Kevin Spacey takes on one of the most difficult facts abolitionists have to face. Unlike those who battled to abolish slavery and won in part through the focus on the good works of enslaved people, those who want to put an end to the death penalty must work through widespread public scorn for the men and women whose crimes have landed them on death row. As one of the characters in *The Life of David Gale* put it, there are no truly innocent people sentenced to death. The film explores that problem through its main character, a philosophy professor and abolitionist called David Gale.

Somewhat ironically, Gale finds himself facing the death penalty for murdering a colleague and close friend. As the plot unfolds, his conviction—and refusal to appeal—perplex a reporter who has been given the opportunity to interview Gale prior to his execution. She is convinced that he is innocent and yet is frustrated in her efforts to save his life. The film's conclusion, and without spoiling the dramatic twist that animates it, offers viewers an opportunity to rethink the death penalty from an entirely different vantage point.

Though the death penalty still exists in the United States, the number of people who are given the death penalty and the number of executions is on the wane. On December 2, 2010, Kenneth Lee Boyd became the 1,000th person to be executed in the United States since the death penalty was reauthorized in 1976.

Augusta Rohrbach
Washington State University

See Also: 1851 to 1900 Primary Documents; 1961 to 1980 Primary Documents; 1981 to 2000 Primary Documents; Capital Punishment; Cruel and Unusual Punishment; Death Row; Electric Chair, History of; Film, Punishment in; *Furman v. Georgia*; *Gregg v. Georgia*; Hanging; Literature and Theater, Punishment in; Lynchings.

Further Readings

Baird, R. M. and S. E. Rosenbaum, eds. *The Death Penalty: Debating the Moral, Legal, and Political Issues*. Amherst, NY: Prometheus Books, 2011.

Bienen, Leigh B. *Murder and Its Consequences: Essays on Capital Punishment in America*. Evanston, IL: Northwestern University Press, 2010.

Burnett, Cathleen. *Wrongful Death Sentences: Rethinking Justice in Capital Cases*. Boulder, CO: Lynne Rienner Publishers, 2010.

Culbert, Jennifer Louise. *Dead Certainty: The Death Penalty and the Problem of Judgment*. Stanford, CA: Stanford University Press, 2008.

Garland, David. *Peculiar Institution: America's Death Penalty in an Age of Abolition*. Cambridge, MA: Belknap Press of Harvard University Press, 2010.

Garland, David, Michael Meranze, and Randal McGowen, eds. *America's Death Penalty: Between Past and Present*. New York: New York University Press, 2011.

Jones, Paul C. *Against the Gallows: Antebellum American Writers and the Movement to Abolish Capital Punishment*. Iowa City: University of Iowa Press, 2011.

Wilson, R. Michael. *Legal Executions in the Western Territories, 1847–1911*. Jefferson, NC: McFarland & Co., 2010.

Famous Trials

In the United States, most legal cases are settled and never go to trial. This is true of both civil and criminal cases, in both state and federal judicial systems. Available data suggest that fewer than 20 percent of civil cases are decided by trial and that fewer than 4 percent of criminal cases are so decided. Jury trials are even rarer (most trials are judge-only bench trials). Most of the trials that do occur take place in the nation's local and state courts; only a fraction of all cases are filed in federal court, and the U.S. Supreme Court hears oral arguments in less than 100 cases each year. Despite the relative infrequency of the trial in contemporary courts, it plays an essential role in American society. Criminal trials exemplify the American spirit of independence from government interference: in order to convict a defendant, a prosecutor (representing the government) must prove each element of the crime beyond a reasonable doubt to a neutral fact finder (whether judge or jury). The jury trial in particular operates as an expression of democracy and as a check against despotic government.

While most trials occur with little or no fanfare, some trials become famous. People rely upon stories to make sense of the world. And, at root, trials are stories in which two protagonists struggle for control of the narrative. In trials, an audience (judge or jury) is built in, and dramatic tension is assured since in an adversarial system of justice one party must win and one must lose (like in a sporting event). Those who forgo the advantages associated with settling a case do so because they believe they have a winning story to tell. Trials also provide the public with morality-affirming rituals. Transgressing offenders, by violating the laws of the community, become enemies who, through trial and punishment, evoke solidarity and restore normative equilibrium.

Trials also become famous because they simultaneously reflect and shape culture. For example, in the landmark case *Brown v. Board of Education*, the Supreme Court considered the accumulated evidence on the relationship between race and education in the United States before unanimously holding that segregated schools violated the equal protection clause of the Fourteenth Amendment. That decision served as the foundation for American desegregation and fomented the civil rights movement. Because it both captured the zeitgeist of the country and influenced the social and legal events that followed, *Brown v. Board* has become a household name.

Not all trials have the impact of *Brown v. Board*. Many trials become famous simply because a noteworthy person has committed an offense or because the crime is especially disturbing. This occurs with some frequency. Gerald

The Nuremberg Trials were an international military tribunal for World War II European Axis criminals held at Nuremberg, Germany, from November 20, 1945, to October 1, 1946. The Office of the U.S. Chief of Counsel, led by Supreme Court justice Robert H. Jackson, worked alongside the British, French, and Soviets to indict 24 wartime leaders and six German organizations. They found 19 defendants guilty. From top right, defendants Hermann Goering, Rudolf Hess, Joachim von Ribbentrop, and Wilhelm Keitel appear in the front row.

Uelmen identified 37 different 20th-century trials that were touted as the "trial of the century." In 1999, NBC's *Today* show conducted a public survey of the "trial of the century" in which nearly 4,000 people responded.

The five most common selections were (1) O. J. Simpson (24 percent), (2) Nuremberg war crimes (21 percent), (3) Clinton impeachment (20 percent), (4) Scopes evolution (14 percent), and (5) Lindbergh kidnapping (7 percent).

Trials become famous in three different ways. Trials sometimes become famous because a celebrity or famous figure has become involved in a legal proceeding (either as a defendant or a victim) that, but for the involvement of the celebrity, would not be particularly newsworthy. Examples of this include the tabloid coverage of actor Hugh Grant's trial for lewd conduct with prostitute Divine Brown, actress Winona Ryder's trial for shoplifting, and actor Tom Sizemore's trial for engaging in domestic abuse against Heidi Fleiss. Other trials become famous because an offender's crime is especially egregious. Notorious serial killers sometimes become celebrities in this way. Political trials can be notorious, as well. Still other trials become famous because they establish a legal principle or rule. Members of the public may or may not know the precise legal issue that was disputed but may use the name of the trial as cultural shorthand to denote a principle (e.g., references to *Miranda* rights) or to reference a fault line in sociocultural values (e.g., *Roe v. Wade* with respect to legalized abortion). A single trial can include two or even three of these paths to fame.

Celebrity Trials

Trials sometimes become famous by virtue of their association with celebrity. Some trials become famous because celebrities or their relatives are victimized, such as when musician John Lennon was killed by Mark David Chapman in 1980; when actress Jennifer Hudson's mother, brother, and nephew were murdered in 2008; or when heiress Patty Hearst was kidnapped by the Symbionese Liberation Army (SLA) in 1974 (although Hearst is known not for her kidnapping but for joining the SLA and robbing a San Francisco bank). When the 20-month-old son of famous aviators Charles and Anne Morrow Lindbergh was kidnapped from his home and later found dead, German ex-convict Bruno Hauptmann (named the most hated man in the world) was tried in a "trial of the century," found guilty, and executed in New Jersey's electric chair in 1936.

Political assassinations belong to this category: While John Wilkes Booth never went to trial for the 1865 assassination of President Abraham Lincoln (Booth was shot), eight of his co-conspirators were tried and convicted. John Hinckley, Jr., attempted to assassinate President Ronald Reagan in March 1981 in an attempt to prove his love for actress Jodie Foster. Reagan survived the attempt, and in a high-profile trial, Hinckley was found not guilty by reason of insanity. In the wake of the decision, many jurisdictions amended their insanity statutes, and three states (Idaho, Montana, and Utah) abolished the insanity defense altogether.

Other trials become famous because of celebrity offenders. Often, these crimes are minor and would not attract media attention but for the involvement of the celebrity. Cases of public intoxication, driving under the influence (DUI), possession of drugs or firearms, and simple assault occur with regularity among actors, musicians, politicians, and athletes. These cases, however, are like catnip to media paparazzi and constitute an important part of tabloid entertainment news. Commentators have raised questions about the fairness of the justice system when it involves celebrities.

Occasionally, the charges against a celebrity are more serious, and these trials often draw significant media attention. America's homemaker Martha Stewart was convicted in 2004 of conspiracy, obstruction, and making a false statement in association with a stock sale; she served five months in a West Virginia federal correctional facility. Celebrities are sometimes charged with high-profile sex crimes: in 1977, director Roman Polanski was charged with six sex crimes and pled guilty to statutory rape, avoiding punishment by fleeing to France (Polanski later settled a civil suit with his victim); after boxer Mike Tyson's 1992 rape trial, he served three years in prison; basketball player Kobe Bryant was charged with sexual assault in 2003, and while the charges were dropped after preliminary hearings, Bryant settled in a civil suit for an undisclosed amount. In 2003, musician Michael Jackson was charged with seven counts of child molestation and two counts of intoxicating a minor (13-year-old Gavin Arvizo). In June 2005, Jackson was acquitted by a jury on all counts.

Sometimes celebrities are tried for homicide. In Hollywood's first great scandal, actor Roscoe "Fatty" Arbuckle was charged with manslaughter in 1921 in connection with the death of actress Virginia Rappe. Three trials followed (two mistrials of hung juries and an acquittal). In 2002, actor Robert Blake was charged with first-degree murder of his wife, Bonnie Lee Bakley. He was acquitted in 2005 but was found liable for $30 million in a wrongful death suit filed by Bakley's children. Songwriter and record producer Phil Spector was arrested in 2003 for the death of actress Lana Clarkson. After a mistrial in 2007, Spector was tried again, found guilty of second-degree murder in 2008, and sentenced to 19 years to life.

None of these trials, however, were as famous as the O. J. Simpson trial. In 1995, in the most publicized criminal trial in American history, football player and actor O. J. Simpson was tried for the 1994 stabbing murders of his ex-wife Nicole Brown Simpson and her friend Ronald Goldman. The televised trial lasted for nine months and made celebrities out of many of the lawyers and witnesses. Simpson's "dream team" of high-profile defense lawyers succeeded

Sharon Tate and four houseguests were murdered by Charles Manson and his "family." During the trial's opening statements, Manson appeared with a freshly cut bloody "X" on his forehead but his bizarre actions did not save him from a guilty sentence.

in raising reasonable doubt in the minds of the jury, and on October 3, 1995, he was found not guilty. Public reaction to the verdict revealed racial differences in the perception of the justice system. While whites overwhelmingly believed that Simpson was guilty, fewer blacks believed in his guilt, indicating distrust of the police and the courts. In 1997, a civil jury found Simpson liable for $33.5 million in compensatory and punitive damages for wrongful death.

Notorious Trials

Some trials become famous because they involve particularly disturbing crimes or because the offender or victim is especially attractive. They do not feature celebrities; rather, they make celebrities. Lorena Bobbitt, for example, became a household name throughout America in 1994 after a jury found her not guilty by reason of insanity for cutting off her husband's penis. Serial killers frequently achieve this celebrity of infamy. For example, after the 2003 publication of Erik Larson's *The Devil in the White City*, there has been renewed interest in the 19th-century trial of H. H. Holmes. Many contemporary serial murderers are also well known: Ted Bundy, Jeffrey Dahmer, John Wayne Gacy, Richard Speck, and Aileen Wuornos. Other killers become known by the names conferred by the press: "Son-of-Sam" David Berkowitz, "Boston Strangler" Albert DeSalvo, "Columbine Killers" Dylan Klebold and Eric Harris, "D.C. Snipers" John Allen Muhammad and Lee Boyd Malvo, and "BTK Killer" Dennis Rader. The 1970 trial of Charles Manson and three members of his "family" for the murder of seven victims in the Tate-LaBianca murders made *Helter Skelter* into a household phrase. Although not a serial killer in any traditional sense, Dr. Jack Kevorkian's 1999 trial for physician-assisted suicide reinforced his celebrity status in America.

Sometimes, controversy is sufficient to make a murder trial famous, such as the trial of Dr. Sam Sheppard (convicted for killing his wife in 1954 but acquitted on retrial in 1966), the televised 1993 trial of Lyle and Erik Menendez (convicted for killing their parents), or the 2004 trial of Scott Peterson (sentenced to death for the murder of his wife and her unborn child). In 1924, in another "trial of the century," Nathan Leopold and Richard Loeb faced the death penalty for the kidnapping and murder of 14-year-old Bobby Franks. Clarence Darrow's eloquent closing argument is considered to be one of the most masterful rejections of the death penalty in history.

The murder of attractive young girls (e.g., JonBenet Ramsey) sometimes draws national media attention to a trial, such as the 1996 trial of Richard Allen Davis for the murder of Polly Klaas. And when mothers kill their own children, the trials are often well publicized: Susan Smith was sentenced to life in prison in 1995 after drowning her two children in a car; Andrea Yates was found not guilty by reason of insanity in 2006 after drowning her five children in her bathtub.

Political Trials

Political trials can reveal the temper of the time. The 1770 trial of eight British redcoats for killing five civilian men during the Boston Massacre helped to precipitate the American Revolution and is still re-enacted each year. A trial was held in 1859 for revolutionary abolitionist John Brown and his failed raid on the Harpers Ferry Armory and Brown was executed for treason. It is generally agreed that Brown's raid played a major role in precipitating the Civil War, and he has been called the most controversial figure of the 19th century. The 1925 trial of biology teacher John Scopes involved Tennessee's Butler Act, which prohibited the teaching of evolution in school. Scopes was found guilty and fined $100. On appeal, the Tennessee Supreme Court upheld the sentence and the constitutionality of the act in 1927.

Political trials also punctuated the 20th century: The 1920 murder trial and 1927 executions of Italian immigrants Ferdinando Sacco and Bartolomeo Vanzetti can be traced to anti-Italian sentiments. The 1951 trial and 1953 executions of Julius and Ethel Rosenberg revealed as much about America's anti-Soviet hysteria as about the Rosenbergs' involvement in an espionage conspiracy. The mood of the country also explains the 1950 perjury conviction of Alger Hiss, whose testimony before the House Committee on Un-American Activities contradicted the assertion of Whittaker Chambers that he and Hiss had been involved in Soviet espionage. The 1913 murder trial of Leo Frank revealed a great deal about anti-Semitism in America, although not as much as his 1915 lynching death. The 1931–37 trials of the Scottsboro Boys, black teenagers charged with raping white women, reveal a great deal about the corrosive effect of racism on justice. In one early trial, the jury took just five minutes to decide on the death penalty and returned to the courtroom laughing. In 1967, Cecil Price was tried for his role in a Ku Klux Klan conspiracy to violate the civil rights of the three civil rights workers who were murdered in Mississippi in 1964. He was never charged with murder. His trial expressed the country's ambivalent attitude toward race and civil rights. Similarly, the 1969 trial of the Chicago Seven, arrested at a 1968 Democratic National Convention rally and charged with conspiracy to cross lines to incite a riot, reveals the antigovernment sentiment that boiled in the United States at that time. So, too, did the 1977 conviction of American Indian activist Leonard Peltier for the murder of two Federal Bureau of Investigation (FBI) agents on the Pine Ridge Indian Reservation. Numerous critics have suggested that political motives drove the prosecution against Peltier. The most famous political trial of the century was the impeachment of President Bill Clinton. Stemming from Independent Counsel Kenneth Starr's Whitewater investigation, Clinton was impeached by the U.S. House of Representatives in 1998 on charges of perjury and obstruction of justice. The Senate vote, however, fell short of the two-thirds majority required to convict.

Sometimes, trials become famous because of doubts about the propriety of conduct of government agents, such as in the 1993 Ruby Ridge trial of Kevin Harris and Randy Weaver or in the 1994 trial of the Branch Davidians involved in the standoff at Waco, Texas. Similarly, the 1991 videotaped beating of motorist Rodney King by four Los Angeles Police Department officers led to a high profile trial for excessive force. The jury's acquittal of all four officers precipitated a massive riot that led to 53 deaths, 7,000 arrests, and more than a billion dollars in property damage.

Sometimes, government actors are portrayed as "bad apples." For example, in 1970, Lieutenant William Calley was court-martialed for the murder of Vietnamese civilians during the 1968 My Lai massacre; between 2004 and 2006, 11 U.S. soldiers were convicted for their roles in the prisoner abuses at Abu Ghraib. Sometimes, criminals use their trials as a forum to attack the government that prosecutes them, as in the 1997 Oklahoma City bombing trial of Timothy McVeigh or the 2006 trial of 9/11 conspirator Zacarias Moussaoui.

Nonpolitical trials

Nonpolitical trials can reveal much about the temperament of a situation, as well. The moral panic of the Salem witch trials, for example, says a great deal about the isolationism and extremism that affected Massachusetts during 1692. Similarly, the mass hysteria associated with the 1987 McMartin Preschool trial, in which it was alleged that day care operators sexually abused children as part of their satanic rituals, led to the longest and most expensive trial in American history but produced no convictions.

The jury's acquittal of "Subway Vigilante" Bernhard Goetz for his 1984 shooting of four men who intended to mug him tells a great deal about the attitudes of crime-weary New Yorkers and serves as a lens through which that time and that place may be understood.

Principle-Establishing Trials

Some trials become famous neither because of celebrity involvement nor because they feature an egregious or controversial crime. They become famous because they establish a legal principle or rule that assumes cultural significance. *Roe v. Wade* and *Brown v. Board* are excellent examples of this phenomenon. A number of famous trials have shaped the course of criminal law in America; for example, two English trials: *M'Naghten* (establishing the most influential American standard for insanity), and *Regina v. Dudley and Stephens* (a lifeboat cannibalism case that outlined the limits of the necessity defense). A number of American cases have also been incredibly influential.

Ernesto Arturo Miranda's confession to kidnapping and rape changed the landscape of U.S. criminal procedure. The U.S. Supreme Court held that suspects in custody must be clearly informed of their right to remain silent and that anything they say can be used in court; they must also be informed of their right to have a lawyer present during interrogation. Many subsequent cases have refined the holding in *Miranda v. Arizona*, establishing exceptions and clarifying its application, but the case stands as a landmark in American criminal procedure.

When Charles Katz used a public telephone to make illegal gambling wagers, he did not realize the telephone had been bugged by the Federal Bureau of Investigation (FBI). When the U.S. Supreme Court heard his appeal in *Katz v. United States*, the court held that Katz had a legitimate expectation of privacy in the telephone booth and could rely upon the Fourth Amendment's protections against unreasonable searches and seizures. The *Katz* decision serves as the basis for most modern Fourth Amendment litigation and is central to the conception of a legal right to privacy.

In 1961, Clarence Earl Gideon was sentenced to five years in a Florida prison for breaking and entering the Bay Harbor Pool Room with intent to commit petty larceny. Gideon could not afford a lawyer, although he asked for one. Writing to the U.S Supreme Court on prison stationery, Gideon argued that he had been denied counsel in violation of the Sixth Amendment. In 1963, in *Gideon v. Wainwright*, the U.S. Supreme Court held that the right to counsel is fundamental and requires that indigent criminal defendants must be afforded counsel at trial. Gideon's conviction was overturned and he was granted a new trial: the jury acquitted him after one hour of deliberation.

The Supreme Court's decision in *In re Gault* extended the right to due process to juveniles accused of a crime, and in *In re Winship*, the court held that when a juvenile is charged with an act that would be a crime if committed by an adult, every element of the offense must be proved beyond a reasonable doubt, instead of the preponderance of evidence standard that had prevailed in juvenile courts. Today, *Winship* stands for a far more sweeping proposition: that in any criminal prosecution, every essential element must be proved beyond a reasonable doubt in order to secure a conviction.

Some principle-establishing trials involve the limits of cruel and unusual punishment. In *Harmelin v. Michigan*, the court revealed the legislatively deferential nature of its Eighth Amendment proportionality analysis, upholding a sentence of life imprisonment without parole for possession of 672 grams of cocaine. In *Gregg v. Georgia*, the court upheld the death penalty conviction of Troy Leon Gregg, who while hitchhiking had killed two men in 1973. The impact of the court's decision was profound. In 1972, in the case of *Furman v. Georgia*, the court had struck down the death penalty as unconstitutional because the death penalty was imposed in a wanton and capricious manner. With *Gregg*, the court indicated that states' death penalty statutes could survive judicial scrutiny if they simultaneously limited death penalty eligibility, narrowed the discretion of the sentencer, and allowed for individualized consideration of the defendant. Subsequent cases have narrowed the categories of offenders who are eligible for capital punishment (e.g., excluding the insane, the mentally retarded, and those who were juveniles at the time of their crimes) and the categories of death-eligible crimes (e.g., holding that capital punishment for the rape of an adult woman was unconstitutional, and later holding that capital punishment for the rape of a child was also unconstitutional).

James C. Oleson
University of Auckland

See Also: 1921 to 1940 Primary Documents; 1961 to 1980 Primary Documents; 1981 to 2000 Primary Documents; 2001 to 2012 Primary Documents; *Brown v. Board of Education*; *Buck v. Bell*; Bundy, Ted; Chapman, Mark David; Chicago Seven/Democratic National Convention 1968; Darrow, Clarence; DeSalvo, Albert; *Dred Scott v. Sandford*; *Furman v. Georgia*; Gacy, John Wayne; *Gideon v. Wainwright*; *Gregg v. Georgia*; Hauptmann, Bruno; *Katz v. United States*; Kevorkian, Jack; King, Rodney; Klebold, Dylan and Eric Harris; *Korematsu v. United States*; Kunstler, William; Leopold and Loeb; *Loving v. Virginia*; Manson, Charles; McVeigh, Timothy; Menendez, Lyle and Erik; *Miranda v. Arizona*; M'Naghten Test; Mudgett, Herman; Muhammad, John Allen; News Media, Crime in; News Media, Punishment in; Peterson, Scott; *Plessy v. Ferguson*; Rader, Dennis; *Roe v. Wade*; Sacco and Vanzetti; Salem Witch Trials; Scopes Monkey Trial; Scottsboro Boys Cases; Sheppard, Sam; Simpson, O. J.; Smith, Susan; Wuornos, Aileen; Yates, Andrea.

Further Readings
Boutrous, Theodore J., Jr., and Michael H. Dore. "Celebrity Justice: A New Double Standard." *Communications Lawyer*, v.22 (2004).
Chermak, S. and F. Y. Bailey. *Crimes and Trials of the Century.* Westport, CT: Greenwood Press, 2007.
Friedman, Lawrence M. *Crime and Punishment in American History.* New York: Basic Books, 1993.
Galanter, Marc. "The Vanishing Trial: An Examination of Trials and Related Matters in Federal and State Courts." *Journal of Empirical Legal Studies*, v.1 (2004).
Geis, G. and L. B. Bienen. *Crimes of the Century: From Leopold and Loeb to O. J. Simpson.* Lebanon, NH: Northeastern University Press, 2000.
Gibson, Dirk C. *Serial Murder and Media Circuses.* Westport, CT: Praeger, 2006.
Hariman, Robert, ed. *Popular Trials: Rhetoric, Mass Media, and the Law.* Tuscaloosa: University of Alabama Press, 1990.
Irons, Peter and Stephanie Guitton. *May It Please the Court.* New York: New Press, 1993.
Knappman, Edward W. *Great American Trials.* Detroit, MI: Visible Ink Press, 1994.
Levenson, Laurie L. "Cases of the Century." *Loyola of Los Angeles Law Review*, v.33 (2000).
Lewis, Anthony. *Gideon's Trumpet.* New York: Random House, 1964.
Linder, Douglas O. "Famous Trials." http://law2.umkc.edu/faculty/projects/ftrials/frtials.htm (Accessed April 2011).
Uelmen, Gerald F. "Who Is the Lawyer of the Century?" *Loyola of Los Angeles Law Review*, v.33 (2000).
Wilkes, Roger. *The Mammoth Book of Famous Trials: The 30 Greatest Trials of All Time, Including Charles Manson, Oscar Wilde, O. J. Simpson, and Al Capone.* New York: Carroll & Graf Publishers, 2006.

Fear of Crime

Fear of crime is an indirect form of victimization and a serious social problem that is related to, but distinct from, crime itself. It is an emotional response that may be a reaction to personal victimization, witnessing a crime, or being exposed to images of crime and victimization (e.g., through television). Fear of crime is a multidimensional concept that until fairly recently did not receive a great deal of attention from the research community. Recent theoretical advances into the causes of fear of crime suggest that fear can be triggered by perceptions of risk and vulnerability, both at the individual and contextual levels. From a policy perspective, it is important to foster a balance between objective and perceived risks of victimization, thereby encouraging appropriate crime prevention activities, without inciting fear.

Defining and Measuring Fear of Crime

Since it became an area of significant research interest among criminologists and victimologists in the mid- to late 1970s, those interested in studying fear of crime have struggled with how best to define, conceptualize, and measure the phenomenon. Early work into the study of fear of crime generally relied on indicators found in the general social survey (GSS) and what is today the

National Crime Victimization Survey (NCVS). For instance, the GSS measure of fear is based on the following survey question: "Is there any area right around here—that is, within a mile—where you would be afraid to walk alone at night?" This measure of fear and others like it have been criticized for failing to differentiate between perceptions of risk and fear of crime, two distinct but related concepts. Despite potential flaws, these measures of fear of crime were used by researchers for years and served as the basis for measuring fear of crime in several studies.

Today, most fear of crime research makes this distinction by measuring two distinct elements of fear of crime: one emotional and one cognitive. The emotional component of fear is characterized by a state of worry or anxiety. During a criminal event, this aspect of fear results in bodily changes (e.g., release of adrenaline, increased heart rate, and rapid breathing) and may trigger a primal fight-or-flight impulse in the interest of self-preservation. The cognitive aspect of fear is based on individual perceptions of risk (i.e., likelihood of victimization). Contemporary research into fear of crime has advanced a great deal in the past few decades, and today, fear of crime research is more consistent with a definition provided by K. F. Ferraro, one of the leading scholars to study the subject. Ferraro defines fear of crime as "…an emotional response of dread or anxiety to crime or symbols that a person associates with crime."

Some of the microenvironmental site features most likely to create fear of crime are illustrated by these stairs: low prospect (limited view ahead), high refuge (hiding places for offenders), and low escape (few avenues for escape from trouble).

Explaining Fear of Crime

Over time, as definitions and measures of fear of crime have developed, so have theoretical explanations for the phenomenon. The current state of the empirical literature highlights two pathways toward explaining fear of crime: one individually based and one contextually based. The former focuses on individual-level vulnerability based on indicators of actual victimization risk. An individual's perceptions of vulnerability may be either physical or social. For instance, one's age may be a reflection of physical vulnerability in that older persons may judge their ability to defend themselves from attack to be minimal. Further, the shadow of sexual assault hypothesis suggests that women generally report greater fear of victimization than men because of the pervasive threat that victimization can escalate into sexual assault. This possibility of escalation has the effect of driving up levels of fear for other types of crime among women, as well as increasing perceived risks of sexual assault.

With respect to social vulnerability, researchers hypothesize that certain groups (e.g., minorities and immigrants) may judge their ability to prevent or withstand criminal victimization to be reduced by the nature of their status in society. For example, immigrants may experience feelings of uncertainty about the law, language barriers to reporting, or confusion as to the best course of action if they witness or are victims of a crime, thereby increasing feelings of fear. Socially vulnerable populations may also believe that their risks of victimization are higher. The extant research on fear of crime supports the idea that these dimensions of physical and social vulnerability are strong correlates of fear of crime.

The second explanation for fear of crime focuses on the environmental context (e.g., streets, neighborhoods, and communities). Within this context, explanations of fear of crime have focused primarily on the concepts of disorder, social cohesiveness, and environmental site features. Signs of community disorder can be either physical (e.g., abandoned cars, litter, or graffiti) or social (e.g., presence of homeless people, prostitutes, or drug dealers) and signal to users that the environment may be conducive to crime and therefore unsafe. Social cohesiveness refers to the ability of community residents to regulate behaviors within their environment or community context. For instance, in a socially cohesive community, residents will challenge congregating youth and ask them to go home, while in a disorderly community, residents have withdrawn from the streets and such congregations go unchallenged.

Community disorder and social cohesiveness are key elements of broken windows theory. According to the theory, physical incivilities such as an untended broken window lead to more broken windows and other signs of physical disorder, which take hold and spiral out of control. Gradually, these cues of physical disorder signal would-be offenders that the area is a facilitating environment for crime, because no one is addressing these community problems. Community members begin to feel that the area is unsafe, and feelings of fear cause them to retreat into their homes. An unwillingness to intervene in neighborhood problems (i.e., lack of social cohesiveness) allows crime to flourish in the area. From this theoretical perspective, fear of crime is a key factor in explaining community crime.

The third explanation for fear of crime at the contextual level focuses on micro-environmental site features, namely, those that indicate to users the site's relative danger or safety. These site features include prospect, refuge, and escape. Prospect refers to the openness of the site; refuge represents potential hiding places within the site; and escape indicates that there are pathways or avenues to avoid danger should it present itself. The combination of site features most likely to elicit fear among site users, including fear of crime, would exist in an environment with low prospect, high refuge, and low escape. For example, a dark, narrow alley offering a limited view of what lies ahead, potential hiding places for likely offenders (e.g., behind dumpsters), and few avenues for escape if trouble is encountered would signal to potential travelers that the alley is unsafe and hence engender feelings of fear. Other important site features or environmental cues include darkness, shadow, curvature, length, mystery, and entrapment. Currently, researchers are expanding the scope of fear of crime research to examine whether explanations of fear are congruent for males and females (i.e., gendered approaches), age-graded and developmental explanations of fear, fear of crime across contexts (e.g., college campuses and secondary schools), and fear of cybercrimes.

Policy Implications

As M. Warr has pointed out, fear of crime can be beneficial to society, especially if a balance between objective and perceived risks of victimization can be struck. In this ideal scenario, individuals will exercise appropriate levels of cautionary behaviors to protect themselves from victimization without unduly constraining their daily routines. However, an imbalance is more likely. This relationship can be imbalanced in two ways. First, if individuals perceive their victimization risks to be higher than their objective risks, they will alter their daily routines, possibly to the point of unnecessarily constraining their behavior (e.g., staying home at night and avoiding certain places), and in a worst case scenario, living in fear. Conversely, when objective risks are higher than perceived risks, appropriate cautionary behaviors will not be taken, and individuals may be more vulnerable to victimization. From a policy perspective, encouraging this balance may be accomplished by educating the public regarding the objective risks of crime. The public tends to overestimate the prevalence and therefore the risks of rarer forms of crimes (e.g., homicide) and underestimates the prevalence and risks of more common crimes (e.g., theft). This may be because of media emphasis on these rarer, more serious forms of crime. Policy makers may well consider counterbalancing media influences with crime awareness and education programs.

Bradford W. Reyns
Weber State University

See Also: Crime Rates; Criminology; News Media, Crime in; Rape, Sociology of; Theories of Crime; Violent Crimes; Wilson, James Q.

Further Readings

Ferraro, K. F. *Fear of Crime: Interpreting Victimization Risk.* Albany: State University of New York Press, 1995.

Ferraro, K. F. "Women's Fear of Victimization: Shadow of Sexual Assault?" *Social Forces,* v.75 (1996).

Ferraro, K. F. and R. L. Lagrange. "The Measurement of Fear of Crime." *Sociological Inquiry,* v.57 (1987).

Fisher, B. S. and J. L. Nasar. "Fear of Crime in Relation to Three Exterior Site Features: Prospect, Refuge, and Escape." *Environment and Behavior,* v.24 (1992).

Schwartz, K., B. W. Reyns, B. Henson, and P. Wilcox. "Fear of In-School Victimization: Contextual, Gendered, and Developmental Considerations." *Youth Violence and Juvenile Justice,* v.9 (2011).

Warr, M. *Fear of Crime in the United States: Avenues for Research and Policy.* Rockville, MD: National Institute of Justice, 2000.

Wilcox Rountree, P. "A Reexamination of the Crime-Fear Linkage." *Journal of Research in Crime and Delinquency,* v.35 (1998).

Wilson, J. Q. and G. Kelling. "Broken Windows." *Atlantic Monthly,* v.21 (1982).

Federal Bureau of Investigation

The Federal Bureau of Investigation (originally the Bureau of Investigation) dates from President Theodore Roosevelt's request that Congress authorize a detective force for the Department of Justice. After failing to overcome fears that the detectives would be political spies, Roosevelt created the Bureau by executive order in 1908. The 20th century saw the explosion of American cities, factories, and transportation systems. As the disparity between the wealthy and the poor grew, robber barons and monopolies also expanded. The public began calling for a responsive federal government, particularly during the Progressive Era, and prior to Bonaparte's men, the federal government called on Secret Service agents to investigate federal matters. Since they reported to the head of the Secret Service, communications often lagged with the Department of Justice. In July 1908, Bonaparte appointed 34 agents within the Department of Justice, ordering them to report to Chief Examiner Stanley W. Finch. In 1909, Attorney General George Wickersham named the force the Bureau of Investigation.

Early History

In the early years, agents had little to investigate. The bureau's own history noted that it focused on banking, naturalization, antitrust, and land fraud. Yet as industry grew and laws like the Eighteenth Amendment passed, the bureau found itself with more work. In June 1910, the Mann Act (prohibiting the transportation of women over state lines for sex) passed, causing the first real growth in bureau activities. Within a decade, the bureau had more than 300 employees. The Mexican Revolution, the rise of drug trafficking, and U.S. entry into World War I also placed pressure on the bureau to increase its force and operations. During the war years, it enforced the Espionage, Sabotage, and Selective Service Acts. Immediately postwar the Bureau had a reduced workload because of the lack of federal crimes, but by 1921, Prohibition and the rise of gangsters gave rise to the agents.

Prohibition fell under the Department of the Treasury, but the bureau investigated gangsters and moonshiners as federal witnesses and for other crimes. This period also saw the rise of racism in the United States, as some perceived blacks as having gained too much standing. The bureau investigated elements of the Ku Klux Klan (KKK). In this postwar period, J. Edgar Hoover appointed as assistant director of the bureau, and he and Attorney General A. Mitchell Palmer led a series of raids to flush out anarchists, radicals, and socialists. The bureau, turning its focus toward political dissidents and so-called radicals, mirrored social fears about the threat of socialism and communism, as Russia pulled out of World War I because of its own Bolshevik Revolution. Of course, social anxieties grew as the public feared a secret police system, corrupt agents, and that vigilante campaigns would ensue.

Abuses of power did occur, but as the bureau's history attests, it attempted to learn from past mistakes to reform itself against public pressure and changing times.

The Hoover Era

In 1924, Hoover took over the bureau, which had about 441 special agents with a total of 650 employees. Within a decade, the bureau had 30 field offices throughout the country. Additionally, Hoover homogenized the organization with standardized performance reviews (removing the seniority system for promotion), mandated that incoming agents be between 25 and 35, and implemented a training program for incoming agents. Aside from training agents, Hoover began the process of collecting data and creating a database on known criminals. Fingerprint records were kept, and methods of tracking felons via identification tools had been in practice since the 19th century.

Franklin Roosevelt encouraged Congress to expand federal jurisdiction as crimes rose during the Great Depression, and in 1932, Hoover played on the public's thirst for sensationalized crime with the first "wanted" fugitive list. More so, Congress responded to crimes captured in the media. In 1932, responding to the kidnapping of the Lindbergh baby, it passed the federal kidnapping statute. In 1934, Congress expanded the bureau's jurisdiction with the rise of violent gangsters like John Dillinger. Also, the media frenzy surrounding Bonnie and Clyde (Bonnie Parker and Clyde Barrow) embarrassed the federal government because these criminals seemed to keep getting away. Agents now had the authority to carry weapons and make arrests, and the bureau was adjusting from an organization primarily focused on financial crimes to one focused on felonies of human violence.

During this expansion of powers and growth and adjustment to new crime trends and waves,

Early Federal Bureau of Investigation agents shooting at targets from a car in the 1930s. The bureau experienced significant growth and professionalization in the 1930s under the leadership of J. Edgar Hoover. By 1934, there were 30 field offices and Congress moved to expand the bureau's jurisdiction that same year in response to crime sprees by notorious criminals such as John Dillinger.

the bureau became the U.S. Bureau of Investigation in 1932, but a year later the Department of Justice experimented with a Division of Investigation and Bureau of Prohibition. Finally, in 1935, the bureau became the Federal Bureau of Investigation, and its training academy was born. A large factor behind the rapid growth of the FBI stemmed from Hoover's leadership and sensationalized journalistic and fictional accounts of crimes. Novelists like Theodore Dreiser sensationalized crimes by fictionalizing them in novels. The motion picture industry began honing in on the public's desire for crime dramas, and the FBI acted in response to changes in modern society.

Espionage

During World War II the FBI investigated Nazis, and indeed caught some spies. Even though the Soviet Union was America's ally, the United States continued its scrutiny of Communists. Further, the cold war, McCarthyism, another "red scare," and the rise of civil rights campaigns in the United States saw the FBI expand its control, surveillance, and covert operations. J. Edgar Hoover's book, *Masters of Deceit* (1958), highlighted postwar—and Hoover's—growing concerns about the threat of communist infiltration in the United States. Critics have questioned his leadership as using the FBI to illegally obtain files and evidence on political dissenters, politicians, and so-called radicals. Most notably, the FBI instituted its COINTELPRO program.

COINTELPRO began as a method of side-stepping U.S. Supreme Court decisions curtailing the FBI and the Justice Department from prosecuting individuals for political opinions. In this program—launched in 1956—FBI agents infiltrated groups like the Communist Party, the Black Panthers, and the Southern Christian Leadership Conference. COINTELPRO is said to have forged documents, started false rumors, and even committed murders. In 1975, the U.S. Senate Select Committee to Study Governmental Operations with Respect to Intelligence Activities deemed COINTELPRO illegal and unconstitutional. Yet during the program's tenure, it collected numerous files on politicians and activist groups throughout the country.

Alongside programs like COINTELPRO, Hoover's FBI targeted civil rights leaders. In 1956, T. R. M. Howard publically spoke out about the racial murders of George W. Lee, Lamar Smith, Martin Luther King, Jr., and Emmett Till (in Mississippi). Howard said the FBI failed to fully investigate the murders, and Hoover responded with public statements saying these proclamations were irresponsible. In turn, Hoover's FBI remained reluctant to engage in civil rights issues. Instead, the agency used a large percentage of its efforts to spy on communists and to obtain blackmail on prominent politicians. In 1959, only four agents investigated organized crime while 489 spied on communists.

Throughout the 1960s the FBI played a key role in helping blacks obtain the vote, serve on juries, and obtain a sense of equality because the expansion of federal authority began to usurp local ordinances. As the postwar years progressed, civil rights flourished, and the Vietnam War and protests began; at the same time, the FBI gained more power through federal legislation. Particularly after mob insiders began testifying about the national and organized nature of the Mafia, pressure mounted to quell the rise in organized and violent crimes. Also, critics argued that the laws needed to keep up with technology. The FBI later played a part in collecting the evidence for Watergate, and its focuses have expanded to cover most crimes on the federal level, greatly assisted by the Racketeer Influenced and Controlled Organizations Act (RICO) of 1970.

FBI Modernization

Hoover retained his tenure with the FBI until his death in 1972, at which time the FBI was forced to change its tactics and advance its probing for crimes. Most specifically, in 1972, a counterterrorism unit was launched in reaction to the bombings at the 1972 Summer Olympics in Munich, Germany. In 1984, Hostage Rescue Teams and the SWAT (Special Weapons and Tactics) team formed. Alongside the rising threat of terrorism—domestic and foreign—the FBI began reassigning agents from foreign to domestic duty in the 1980s. The expansion of counter–violent crime initiatives redirected much of the FBI's activities. Also, the ending of the cold war gave a temporary lapse in the threat of terrorism, and the FBI became more accessible to local police departments. FBI laboratories are also credited with developing DNA testing during this period.

Modern Federal Bureau of Investigation (FBI) analysts at work. The FBI addressed the growing threat of computer crime by creating a new Computer Investigations and Infrastructure Threat Assessment Center and the National Infrastructure Protection Center in 1998. The bureau's work on crimes related to identity theft and hacking has increased substantially since then.

The 1993 World Trade Center bombing provided a direct need for a resurgence of counterterrorism units, and the 1995 Oklahoma City bombing showed the threat of domestic terrorism. The 1990s saw the FBI greatly expand its counterterrorism initiatives, and in 1996, the agency came under scrutiny for the botched investigations of the Atlanta Olympic Games bombing. By 1998, the FBI launched the Computer Investigations and Infrastructure Threat Assessment Center (CITAC) and the National Infrastructure Protection Center (NIPC) to assess and quell computer threats. These programs began as a countermeasure to viruses, worms, and hackers. They have now increased to fight identity theft and the growing number of crimes connected with the Internet. These changes to the FBI internal structure continue to exist, as most recently the FBI (along with other federal agencies) found itself under scrutiny in the aftermath of the September 11, 2001, attacks. Since then, the FBI and the Central Intelligence Agency (CIA) have admitted partial blame for not pursuing terrorist evidence, and the agency has continued to adjust its internal structures and task forces to suit the needs of the modern era.

Annessa A. Babic
New York Institute of Technology

See Also: 1901 to 1920 Primary Documents; 1921 to 1940 Primary Documents; 1941 to 1960 Primary Documents; 1961 to 1980 Primary Documents; 1981 to 2000 Primary Documents; Bureau of Alcohol, Tobacco, Firearms and Explosives; Drug Enforcement Administration; Federal Policing; Homeland Security; Hoover, J. Edgar; Justice, Department of; Prohibition; Terrorism; Wickersham, George.

Further Readings
The FBI: A Centennial History. Washington, DC: U.S. Department of Justice, Federal Bureau of Investigation, 2006.
Greenberg, Ivan. *The Dangers of Dissent: The FBI and Civil Liberties Since 1965*. Lanham, MD: Lexington Books, 2010.

Kessler, Ronald. *The Bureau: The Secret History of the FBI*. New York: St. Martin's Paperbacks, 2002.

Newton, Michael. *The FBI and the KKK: A Critical History*. Jefferson, NC: McFarland and Co., 2005.

Potter, Claire Bond. *War on Crime: Gangsters, G-Men, and the Politics of Mass Culture*. New Brunswick, NJ: Rutgers University Press, 1998.

Powers, Richard Gid. *Secrecy and Power: The Life of J. Edgar Hoover*. New York: The Free Press, 1988.

Zegart, Amy. *Spying Blind: The CIA, the FBI, and the Origins of 9/11*. Princeton, NJ: Princeton University Press, 2007.

Federal Common Law of Crime

The federal common law of crime carries different meanings based on the time period in which one uses the term. Its initial meaning, covering the first two decades under the U.S. Constitution, refers to the ability of federal courts to decide cases involving common law crimes. Whether federal courts had this authority was a question left unanswered by the Constitution and the Judiciary Act of 1789. Later, during the 20th century, as the federal courts' caseload dramatically increased, the federal common law of crime became judicial interpretations of legislation. With the increase in federal cases, there was a corresponding increase in opinions for other judges to draw upon when making decisions. The collection became the common law of crime.

The Early Republic

When drafting the Constitution, the framers created a government whereby the three functions of government—legislative, executive, and judicial—would be divided among three branches. While providing details about the legislative and executive branches, the convention failed to provide much detail about the judicial branch, leaving the task to the first Congress. This occurred because the Constitution's drafters could not resolve disputes about the scope of federal judicial power. Some did not want any federal courts, fearing that a federal system would favor only those who could travel to the nation's capital. Others argued that federal courts were essential for enforcing federal law.

The first Congress dealt with the problem during its first session. While the House of Representatives crafted the Bill of Rights, the Senate wrote the Judiciary Act. The amendments addressed many concerns that emerged during debates on ratifying the Constitution. The Judiciary Act addressed most others and designed a hierarchical system of lower federal courts. In its next session, Congress passed legislation creating punishments for certain offenses. While doing this, however, they did not define the crimes nor state the extent of federal criminal jurisdiction.

The extent of federal criminal jurisdiction was important for enforcing the new government's laws. For example, some argued that if an importer assaulted a customs official attempting to collect import duties, there would be no recourse for the government unless Congress defined the act as a crime. However, with common law criminal jurisdiction, the importer could be prosecuted in federal courts. Those opposing this authority believed that state courts provided the appropriate forum for resolution. Supporters, known as Federalists, countered that state courts would favor local merchants against the federal officer.

During the George Washington and John Adams presidencies, the Federalist view prevailed. An initial test occurred in 1793 after President Washington declared neutrality in the war between Great Britain and France. Soon after the declaration, Gideon Henfield, an American citizen, arrived in Philadelphia as the prize-master aboard a French war ship. Henfield was arrested and indicted federally, although no federal statute prohibited his conduct. The government based its case on the theory that Henfield had disrupted the peace of the United States, a common law offense. While the jury acquitted Henfield, the government claimed victory because the court had not dismissed the indictment.

Despite the relative success of Henfield's case, support for common law criminal jurisdiction failed to materialize, even among Federalists. In 1798, as relations between France and the U.S. government deteriorated, the Adams administration feared France's influence on those who opposed Adams. To counter the opposition, the Adams administration sought to prosecute publishers who criticized the administration for libel. Rather than risk common law prosecutions, the administration persuaded Congress to pass the Sedition Act to provide a basis for the prosecutions.

The ensuing prosecutions benefited Adams's opponent, Thomas Jefferson. In 1801, when Jefferson assumed the presidency, he ended sedition prosecutions. However, prosecutions for common law libel continued, this time against Federalists. In one case against Connecticut newspaper editors, the U.S. Supreme Court settled the question of federal common law criminal jurisdiction. The court summarily dismissed the case, stating that no one seriously believed that the federal government possessed common law criminal jurisdiction. The decision was not without its detractors, however, because it left congressional statutes as the only authority for federal criminal prosecutions. At the time, Congress was unwilling to criminalize much behavior.

Modern Federal Common Law of Crime

Congressional reluctance to criminalize behavior eventually dissipated to the point where people argue Congress has now criminalized too much. The large number of federal criminal offenses has caused an increased number of criminal prosecutions. The large number of prosecutions has resulted in a large number of judicial opinions interpreting these statutes. Along with the increased number of federal offenses, Congress has drafted their statutes so that they apply to a wide range of conduct. Innovative prosecutors have taken statutes designed for one type of problem and have expanded their scope to address other conduct. As a result, the courts have had to define which conduct the statute covers and which it does not.

The combination of increasing cases and broadly worded statutes has led to a federal common law of crime. Judicial opinions have addressed both the meaning of words used in criminal statutes and limited the conduct to which they apply. These opinions serve as precedent for future cases, thereby limiting statutes and creating legal boundaries, much like legislation. Some scholars argue that the courts need to do more to limit the scope of criminal statutes. Others counter that it is not the judiciary's place to legislate. The three branches of government have yet to resolve this debate. Ultimately, the debate about the proper role of the federal judiciary as it relates to a federal common law of crime remains. Despite the Supreme Court's deciding that federal courts lack jurisdiction over common law offenses, practice, coupled with changes in the federal government's role, has led to the creation of a federal common law of crime.

Scott Ingram
High Point University

See Also: Adams, John (Administration of); Alien and Sedition Acts of 1798; Bill of Rights; Common Law Origins of Criminal Law; Constitution of the United States of America; Courts; Jefferson, Thomas (Administration of); Judiciary Act of 1789; Neutrality Enforcement in 1793–94; Supreme Court, U.S.; *United States v. Hudson and Goodwin*; Washington, George (Administration of).

Further Readings
Brickey, Kathleen F. "Criminal Mischief: The Federalization of American Criminal Law." *Hastings Law Journal*, v.46 (1995).
Marcus, Maeva and Natalie Wexler. "The Judiciary Act of 1789: Political Compromise or Constitutional Interpretation." In *Origins of the Federal Judiciary: Essays on the Judiciary Act of 1789*, Maeva Marcus, ed. New York: Oxford University Press, 1992.
Smith, James. *Freedom's Fetters: The Alien and Sedition Laws and American Civil Liberties*. Ithaca, NY: Cornell University Press, 1956.
Thomas, Charles M. *American Neutrality in 1793: A Study in Cabinet Government*. New York: Columbia University Press, 1931.

Federal Policing

The organization of law enforcement in the United States is based upon the concept of federalism, or the division of responsibilities between federal and state-based agencies, each with its own unique, clearly defined legal jurisdiction (the set of laws it is assigned the task of enforcing) and geographic jurisdiction (the physical boundaries of its authority). In practice, however, when there are criminal matters that involve multiple jurisdictional interests, the lines between federal agencies, or between federal and state agencies, can sometimes be blurred; this might occur, for example, when one federal agency temporary delegates certain authorities to another, or federal agents are deputized so that they are given the authority to enforce state laws.

American policing is highly decentralized, with thousands of independent, autonomous agencies of various sizes at the federal, state, county, and municipal level. As most of the activities defined as crimes exist within the penal codes of the states and the vast majority of police agencies operate at the local level, law enforcement is viewed as a primarily local phenomenon. The U.S. Constitution did not establish any federal-level policing agencies but does give the federal government the power to enforce certain criminal laws. Investigating any activities defined as crimes under federal law and enforcing such legislation, as well as responding to criminal activity that occurs on federal property, are wholly the responsibilities of the federal government, and since the 18th century, numerous law enforcement agencies have been created to direct these efforts.

Federal law enforcement is defined as any agency or organization employing sworn officers or agents with the authority granted by the United States Code (USC) to enforce a specified set of federal laws, make arrests, carry firearms, and conduct investigations of various levels of complexity. (This is to distinguish law enforcement entities from organizations at the federal level, such as the Central Intelligence Agency (CIA), whose agents collect information but do not have arrest powers; furthermore, some law enforcement agencies may employ intelligence officers who don't have inherent arrest powers.) Some federal agencies are primarily concerned with preventing criminal activity, securing particular locations, and interdicting illicit and/or dangerous materials and persons, whereas others have an investigative focus in addition to or instead of these tasks. Agents and officers may be uniformed or plainclothes (or, occasionally—if performing an investigative role—undercover) during the performance of their duties. There is no single agency with the responsibility of enforcing all federal law; rather, there are dozens of distinct federal law enforcement agencies (or law enforcement divisions within a larger agency that is not primarily concerned with law enforcement matters), employing more than 100,000 law enforcement agents or officers, operating under the auspices of numerous different cabinet departments. The largest agencies—employing the vast majority (approximately 75 percent) of nonmilitary federal law enforcement agents and officers—are found within the Department of Justice or the Department of Homeland Security, but many other agencies or divisions exist within the Department of the Interior (such as, for example, the Bureau of Indian Affairs Police—with the responsibility of law enforcement on reservations or in tribal communities that do not have their own police agencies—and the U.S. Park Police), the Depart-

A team from the U.S. Coast Guard Deployable Operations Group prepared to combat terrorism and other coastal threats in 2008. In wartime, the U.S. Coast Guard becomes a military organization under the Department of the Navy.

ment of State (including the Diplomatic Security Service, which protects the secretary of state and visiting foreign dignitaries), the Department of the Treasury (including the Criminal Investigation Division of the Internal Revenue Service, which investigates income tax fraud), the U.S. Postal Service (which includes the U.S. Postal Inspection Service, responsible for investigating the criminal misuse of the mail system and any attacks against its employees and facilities), and elsewhere.

U.S. Department of Justice
Established in 1870 and headed by the U.S. attorney general, the Department of Justice (DOJ) has the responsibility of enforcing the majority of existing federal laws, and within it are some of the largest and most prominent law enforcement agencies in the country.

The Federal Bureau of Investigation (FBI), which began operations in its earliest incarnation in 1908, has perhaps one of broadest legal jurisdictions of any federal law enforcement agency, in terms of the scope of its interests; among its responsibilities are the protection of the United States against terrorist attack and foreign espionage, the investigation of public corruption and civil rights violations at all levels of government, and the combating of white-collar and organized crime. The Drug Enforcement Administration (DEA), established in 1973 to spearhead President Richard Nixon's declared "war on drugs," enforces federal drug law, with a particular interest in combating trafficking activity and eradicating illicit drugs, whether they be cultivated or synthesized; as such, the agency operates offices in numerous countries around the world in order to collect intelligence on illicit drug exportation and to provide technical assistance in crop eradication and drug enforcement efforts. The U.S. Marshals Service is one of the oldest federal law enforcement agencies in existence, with its earliest incarnation—the position of U.S. marshal—established by the Judiciary Act of 1789. The activities of marshals ranged from enforcing the Fugitive Slave Law of 1850, chasing moonshiners in the late 19th century, fighting outlaws in the old west, to protecting African Americans trying to integrate southern schools during the civil rights era. Today, it has a close relationship with the federal court system, with the responsibility of protecting federal courthouses, judges, prosecutors, and jurors; escorting federal detainees to and from federal court; serving bench warrants issued in federal court; operating the Witness Security Program; and apprehending fugitives.

The Bureau of Alcohol, Tobacco, Firearms and Explosives (ATF) has a complex history that is characterized by numerous organizational changes. Its earliest incarnation was a laboratory that was established in 1986 within the Bureau of Internal Revenue for the purpose of detecting the adulteration of foodstuffs; it gained prominence in the 1920s because of its responsibilities enforcing the Volstead Act and the Eighteenth Amendment's prohibition of alcohol manufacture and sale. It was eventually assigned the task of federal firearms laws enforcement in the early 1940s and the responsibilities of bombing and arson investigations after the passage of federal laws regarding those offenses in 1970. The agency operated as a division of the Internal Revenue Service (and its precursor) for many years due to its responsibilities regarding the collection of tax revenue from alcohol and tobacco sales; it was established as a separate agency within the Department of the Treasury in 1972. It moved to the Department of Justice in 2003 as a result of the Homeland Security Act of 2002. Today, the ATF is concerned with the enforcement of federal laws relevant to firearms and explosives, including the regulation of firearms markets and the investigation of firearms trafficking and regulation of explosives sales and the investigation of bombings and arsons. The ATF also investigates persons involved in the trafficking of alcohol and tobacco products who employ schemes to avoid paying taxes on those items, although it no longer collects tax revenue itself (this task became the responsibility of the Alcohol and Tobacco Tax and Trade Bureau, established in 2003 for that purpose and administered within the Department of the Treasury).

Department of Homeland Security
Headed by the secretary of homeland security, the Department of Homeland Security (DHS) was created in direct response to the terrorist attacks of September 11, 2001. Established by the Homeland Security Act of 2002 and beginning operations in 2003, DHS consists primarily of pre-existing and reorganized agencies that were transferred there from elsewhere within the

federal government. All entities within the DHS share a general mission of preventing terrorist attack within the United States as well as minimizing damages from potential attacks and natural disasters. As such, not all agencies within the DHS are concerned with criminal law enforcement, but many of the agencies that do enforce laws are among the largest within the federal government.

Customs and Border Protection and Immigration and Customs Enforcement. U.S. Customs and Border Protection (CBP) and U.S. Immigration and Customs Enforcement (ICE) were created by essentially dismantling and reorganizing existing federal law enforcement agencies such as U.S. the Customs Service and the Immigration and Naturalization Service (which had been administered by the Department of the Treasury and the Department of Justice, respectively). Both agencies commenced operations in early 2003. Today, they are both concerned with enforcing laws relevant to customs and immigration. CBP officers are stationed at formal ports of entry (including locations along the borders with Canada and Mexico and international airports and seaports) into the United States as well as facilities that receive mail originating from outside the country. They have the goal of detecting and interdicting suspicious persons, plants, animals, illegal goods such as illicit drugs, and any other items that represent either an effort to violate customs or immigration laws or an attempt to undermine homeland security. The Border Patrol (which was established in 1924 and operated for many years within the Immigration and Naturalization Service prior to its dissolution) was placed under the operation of the CBP when the latter was established and has the same responsibilities but is a mobile uniformed unit that travels between ports of entry. ICE, meanwhile, is purely investigative in focus, with the task of uncovering smuggling and human trafficking operations, as well as identifying and apprehending individuals who have managed to enter the country illegally.

Secret Service. Prior to its move to the DHS, the U.S. Secret Service was administered within the Department of the Treasury because its sole responsibility at the time of its founding in 1865 was the investigation of counterfeiting. It is still involved in counterfeiting investigations and other crimes that threaten the nation's financial infrastructure (including credit card fraud, wire fraud, and identity theft) but is perhaps most prominent in the public imagination because of its role in protecting the president and vice president (a role it was formally assigned in 1902 following the assassination of President William McKinley), their immediate families, and visiting heads of state, as well as investigating any threats against those individuals.

Transportation Security Administration. The creation of the Transportation Security Administration (TSA) in 2001 was one of the most dramatic additions to the nation's landscape, as it symbolized the federal government's post–9/11 concerns regarding the vulnerability of U.S. transportation infrastructure (and air travel in particular) to terrorist attacks. Originally managed by the Department of Transportation, the TSA was transferred to the DHS in 2003. The TSA works in cooperation with state and local law enforcement to safeguard various facets of the transportation system, including highway, rail, and mass transit, but it is most widely recognized for its role in aviation security. Not all employees of the TSA are law enforcement agents per se, but within the TSA is the Federal Air Marshal Service (FAMS), which is considered to be the most prominent law enforcement division of the agency. The FAMS has existed since 1968 (created in response to a rash of "skyjackings" during that period) but was moved from the Department of Transportation to the DHS in 2003. Federal air marshals are entrusted with responsibility of detecting and deterring criminal activity on aircraft and terrorist behavior recognition in particular, and are trained in techniques to neutralize violent behavior in the close quarters of an airplane with minimum collateral damage to passengers and crew.

U.S. Coast Guard. The U.S. Coast Guard, which has been in existence since 1790, is one of the nation's uniformed services but has a unique dual status. It functions as a law enforcement agency within the DHS during peacetime and as a military organization during times of war, when it operates under the authority of the Department of the Navy. As a law enforcement agency, its responsibilities primarily involve enforcing federal law along coastal waterways and protecting maritime borders from criminal activity in general—with drug and illegal immigrant interdiction among its most important tasks—and terroristic threats in particular.

Federal-Level Police Forces

At the federal level, there are numerous agencies that exist primarily to provide physical security to specific federal properties. These policing agencies patrol their assigned locations and are expected to proactively deter, as well as retroactively respond to and investigate, any criminal activity that might occur therein. These agencies vary in size and often incorporate specialized units and response teams. Examples of such agencies include the Federal Protective Service (responsible for patrolling the thousands of federally owned and leased buildings throughout the country and protecting the federal employees working within), the U.S. Capitol Police, the U.S. Mint Police, the Bureau of Engraving and Printing Police, the Postal Police Force, the Veterans Affairs Police (with the task of patrolling facilities operated by the U.S. Department of Veterans Affairs and the Veterans Health Administration), the Uniformed Division of the U.S. Secret Service (which physically protects the White House, the vice president's residence, and embassies in Washington, D.C.), Amtrak Police, and the U.S. Supreme Court Police.

Most federal agencies typically have their own Office of Inspector General. These are designed to be autonomous units within their respective organizations that are analogous to a police department's internal affairs division, in that they have the responsibility of monitoring and auditing programs within that agency in order to combat waste, fraud, corruption, and abuse perpetrated by employees.

The Department of the Air Force, Department of the Army, Department of the Navy, and the Marine Corps are all responsible for policing themselves and their properties and investigating criminal activity (as well as breaches of military codes of conduct) among, and against, their personnel. These agencies include civilian as well as military police corps, as well as special offices of investigations.

Miriam D. Sealock
Towson University

See Also: Border Patrol; Bureau of Alcohol, Tobacco, Firearms and Explosives; Customs Service as Police; Drug Enforcement Administration; Federal Bureau of Investigation; Homeland Security; Immigration Crimes; Internal Revenue Service; Judiciary Act of 1789; Justice, Department of; Native American Tribal Police; Smuggling; Tax Crimes; Terrorism.

Further Readings

Gaines, Larry K. and Victor E. Kappeler. *Policing in America*. Waltham, MA: Anderson, 2011.
Jeffrey-Jones, Rhodri. *The FBI: A History*. New Haven, CT: Yale University Press, 2008.
Kurian, George T., Joseph P. Harahan, Morton Keller, Donald F. Kettl, and Graham T. T. Molitor, eds. *A Historical Guide to the U.S. Government*. New York: Oxford University Press, 1998.
Reaves, Brian A. *Federal Law Enforcement Officers, 2004*. Washington, DC: Bureau of Justice Statistics, 2006.
Transportation Security Administration. "Transportation Security Administration." http://www.tsa.gov (Accessed January 2011).
Travis, Lawrence F. and Robert H. Langworthy. *Policing in America: A Balance of Forces*. Upper Saddle River, NJ: Prentice Hall, 2007.
White, Jonathan R. *Terrorism and Homeland Security*. Belmont, CA: Thomson/Wadsworth, 2006.

Federal Prisons

Since the American colonies were first established by European imperialists, colonists have made use of incarceration or incapacitation as methods of punishment to deal with social deviants and criminal behavior. In the wake of the Revolutionary War, the method of incarceration focused primarily on using tight, stationary housing to lock away prisoners of war, those guilty of general deviance and criminal mischief, and eventually those convicted of federal crimes against the United States.

Beginning Federal Imprisonment

No federal offense could be possible without the existence of a unified government to identify such boundaries and definitions. Therefore, federal prisoners did not explicitly become such until

A 1936 view of snow-covered Mount Rainier from the ferry dock at the isolated McNeil Island Prison in Washington State. The facility began operating as a prison in 1875 but was not recognized formally as a federal penitentiary until 1909. When it finally closed in 2011, McNeil, then a state penitentiary, was the last island prison still in use in the United States.

1776 and the independence of the United States from England. During the 1770s, the Continental Congress began to realize that with the declaration came many who did not agree with the decision to cut ties with the English government. Among them were people with various amounts of political clout, such as governors. One in particular was William Franklin, once the governor of the New Jersey colony and son of Ben Franklin. With William Franklin loyally siding with the British, the Continental Congress had him arrested under the charge of treason and he was among the first of many (especially political officials) to be in federal custody during the war of independence.

Federal imprisonments for treason quickly became commonplace throughout the 1770s, as did military crimes and maritime cases, including crimes regarding sea vessels, such as their capture. Under the Constitution of 1787, these crimes necessitated more custodial facilities to aid in the federal trial processes in coordination with the newly established Bill of Rights. To remedy this, Congress recommended that the states pass laws authorizing that federal offenders be housed in the few state and county prisons and jails that already existed. One facility, the Walnut Street Jail in Philadelphia, was completely sequestered by Congress specifically for federal offenders, technically making it the first federal prison. Walnut Street Jail was eventually returned to state operation, became dilapidated, and was closed in 1835 because of overcrowding and a dearth of funds. Federal marshals and courts alike began utilizing New York's newly built Auburn penitentiary by 1819 and continued to use it for the remainder of the 19th century. During this time, prisoners were also sent to Sing Sing and Pennsylvania's Eastern State Penitentiary as they were constructed and the federal offender population grew.

There was also the need for a department to oversee the matters involving the processing, treatment, trial, and conviction of pressing matters. It was not until 1849, when the Department of the Interior was created, that federal imprisonment was actually under the jurisdiction of a distinct governmental entity. The secretary of the interior remained the position responsible for most issues regarding prison selection and construction. Finally, in 1870, the Department of Justice was created and headed by the already existing, yet underused, position of attorney general, who would thereafter be in charge of the control and distribution of all federal prisoners. With this position eventually came supporting "agents" and "examiners" whose job it was to inspect and report on matters involving federal prisoners and their housing arrangements.

In the following decade, the attorney general began receiving reports and complaints of physical beatings and whippings, particularly in the New York system, which included the Auburn, Albany, and Sing Sing penitentiaries. Similar issues of inmate abuse were found in California's penitentiary, San Quentin, as it received many federal prisoners during the gold rush era. As a result, the Department of Justice sought more humane facilities in other states; however, as the federal inmate population continued to grow, many of the state facilities had dwindling space to provide for federal need.

Meeting the Need for Federal Prisons

Much of the appeal for states to take federal prisoners outside of prison was grounded in the use of inmate labor. The practice of contracting out prisoners to profit on unpaid labor was common in the late 1800s. Aside from overcrowding, the states would not find much problem in taking in federal prisoners. This changed, however, in 1887 when Congress passed a law that barred all federal inmate labor from being contracted out for profit. This act was not popular among many prison administrators and state governments. Subsequently, fewer and fewer states were willing to accept federal prisoners. As federal offender populations continued to rise, so too did the cost of trips for U.S. marshals to transport prisoners. With the reality of the space problem coupled with horrific conditions of confinement provided by many state facilities that would still accept federal prisoners (much of the exposure of which can be attributed to the work of George Washington Cable for prison reform), the Department of Justice was forced to consider the notion of building federal prisons.

Even though the U.S. government owned five territorial facilities, they were infrequently used due to their remote and primitive location (Boise, Idaho; Deer Lodge, Montana; Salt Lake City, Utah; McNeil Island, Washington; and Laramie, Wyoming) as well as a severe lack of basic amenities and security. It was not until 1891 that Congress passed the Three Prisons Act that ordered the Department of Justice and the Department of the Interior to purchase three sites for the construction of federal prisons. As prescribed, one site was chosen in the north, east of the Rocky Mountains in Fort Leavenworth, Kansas. Originally used for prisoners during the westward expansion in the 1820s, Leavenworth was the first of the three prisons, annexed from the military and constructed virtually entirely by inmate labor. Though Leavenworth routinely took prisoners, it was not until two and a half decades later, in 1929, that the facility was finally completed. The second, southeastern site was purchased from the city of Atlanta, Georgia. Designed to have 1,200 cells in four wings, the Atlanta site began admitting prisoners in 1902. The third prison was to be west of the Rocky Mountains. To fulfill this need, the Department of Justice maintained McNeil Island, Washington, after the state declined the prison upon receiving statehood in 1899. McNeil Island was eventually recognized formally as a federal penitentiary in 1909.

Life in the U.S. penitentiaries was harsh, with intense institutional control and physical labor. Methods for controlling the inmates were often chosen by the acting warden. Systematic control in graduated processes of trust, escape, and problem prisoners often drove the different tactics, and the still frequent dependence on solitary confinement as a punishment mechanism. One consistent method of control in the late 1800s and early 1900s involved the use of mindless work to maintain security. A common practice was to have the inmate break rocks to a certain strict size. The inmate's performance quality would determine if he received lunch and dinner. If the quality was poor, then there would be no food for that inmate. Another common method was to have the prisoners build and maintain any portion of the prison's structure. From cleaning the premises to the construction of a new office or cell, inmate labor, while not used for profit and did not resort to abuse, yielded a cost-effective method for asserting authority over offenders while keeping up on maintenance of the prison.

Maintenance was particularly difficult for McNeil Island and later facilities like it, such as Alcatraz, because they lacked self-sustaining resources such as running water and plumbing, a steady connection to food and medical supplies, as well as communication lines to state and federal authorities in cases of emergencies. In the same capacity, natural elements such as storms and floods would often exile such facilities more so than their physical location already allowed.

First Rapid Expansion
Because of the Secretary of the Treasury's ability to account for the number and circulation of federal inmates beginning in 1846, by the time the Bureau of Prisons was established in 1930 (which was the bureaucracy responsible for overseeing all federally run custody settings), there was a reliable estimate as to the total population under federal supervision. With this estimation, it was possible for administrators to recognize patterns in the population and the potential impacts of laws such as the implementation of parole and probation. Perhaps more important to the Bureau of Prisons was the fact that the facility capacities and population growth could now be properly assessed. These estimates enabled the bureau to devise and integrate a new method of classification that would connect offender needs to the advantages of each of 11 institutions in the 1930s.

Along with the specific facets of each institution came the recognition of special programming that targeted education and vocational training. Vocational training was especially enticing to the bureau administrators because the training and programs were used to create certain products, such as furniture, that would be sold to the general society or to other organizations. While there was a ban on contracting out federal prison labor to outside entities, the selling of inmate products was and is still permitted with exceptions that may negatively impact certain industries. The utilization and selling of prisoner-made products became so enticing, in fact, that once a systematic approach was proposed by the bureau's director, James Bennett (in spite of much opposition by independent manufacturers), it was endorsed by Congress and signed into law by Franklin D. Roosevelt in 1934, creating the Federal Prison Industries, Incorporated.

As the population count continued to rise throughout the 1930s for a number of reasons, including longer sentencing practices, more institutions and responsibilities were added to the Bureau of Prisons' oversight. Much of the expansion was to accommodate the prisoner population as it doubled from just over 14,000 inmates in 1930 to over 24,000 inmates in 1940. However, the expansion of institutions was also used to combat the economic depression with jobs, as President Roosevelt authorized approximately $14 million to aid in the construction of a number of new facilities in 1938, going from 14 institutions in 1930 to 24 institutions in 1940. Many of these facilities were not solely for incarceration, as more were geared toward education, vocational training, and psycho-social treatment programs.

Treatment in Federal Prisons
Though treatment programs were emphasized throughout the 1940s and 1950s, the most notable change occurred in the 1960s. During this time, there was a new overarching belief that social science experts could identify criminality in individuals and subsequently develop methods to correct the behavior through specific treatment program options. Displaying many forms of creativity in programming, the movement gained much momentum as the Bureau of Prisons changed directors from the innovative, yet administratively focused mind of James Bennett as director, to the newly appointed, academically and theoretically based Myrl Alexander in 1961. Quickly, programs began by Bennett were further developed and expanded by Alexander and later by Norman Carlson, director of the Federal Bureau of Prisons in the early 21st century.

Several novel and extended initiatives were seen during the Alexander era that showcased the new priority in terms of federal corrections and

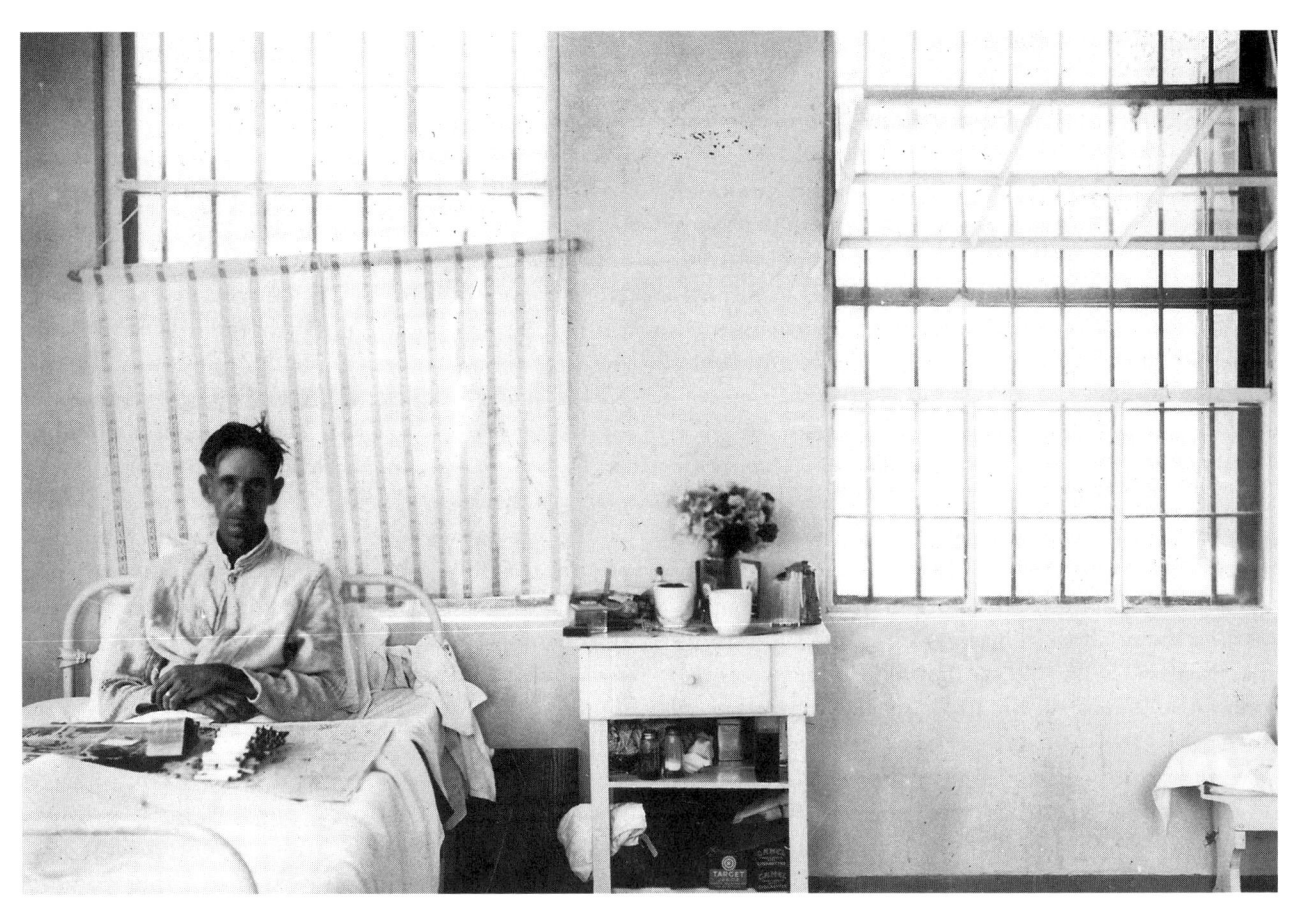

An inmate in a federal prison hospital ward in 1933. The prison system expanded over the decade of the 1930s, with the number of inmates nearly doubling from just over 14,000 to over 24,000 in 1940. By 1938, President Franklin D. Roosevelt had authorized about $14 million for construction of new federal facilities, which increased from 14 institutions in 1930 to 24 institutions in 1940.

programming. For instance, newly constructed institutions such as the facility in Butner, North Carolina, emphasized specially designed treatment for offenders with personality disorders and violent perpetrators. Another example of programmatic change was exemplified when wardens were hired who did not necessarily have the heavy background in administrative and managerial experience gained through years as a staff member, rather they were academics, scientists, and doctors. Still another was the implementation of halfway house programs, particularly for youth and other eligible offenders. However, the treatment movement as well as the continuing erection of new institutions became a political issue. Encompassing the backlash of an angry public highly sensitive to racial disparities with regard to mass imprisonment, coupled with the debate over whether treatment was effective and the prison riots beginning in the early 1970s, the philosophy began to shift yet again toward emphasizing safety and security over treatment and reentry.

Second Rapid Expansion

As trends that relied on treatment, also known as the "medical model," began to diminish during the early 1980s to switch toward a more "balanced model" incorporating equal portions of institutional control as well as programming, prison construction was forced to continue despite the efforts of the National Moratorium on Prison Construction, due to the prisoner intake surge of the time. From a 40-year trend of a steady population of approximately 24,000 inmates in 1980, the federal prison population spiked to over 65,000 by 1990, with 66 institutions. Much of the surge was a result of sentencing reform from indeterminate to fixed or determinate sentencing, the abolishment of parole, reducing good-time, the establishment of mandatory minimums, as well as the eventual incorporation of detaining illegal aliens for the Immigration and Naturalization Service.

Due to the increasing difficulties in prisoner volume, the sentencing, and diversified practices embodied, various political and criminal enforcement initiatives were also adding to the total population. Accompanied by the "tough on crime" approaches in law-making in the 1990s and other new enforcement tactics, the federal prison population saw yet another dramatic increase to over 145,000 in 2000. In contrast to the early years of the federal incarceration system where there was little effort put into planning for the future, under the direction of Kathleen Hawk Sawyer and eventually Harley Lappin, the Bureau of Prisons implemented the Forward Thinking Initiative, which was specifically designed to anticipate future systemic, managerial, and population needs. Throughout the 2000s, the bureau has been updating the now 115 institutions to incorporate more technological advancements to encompass the standards set by the Prison Rape Elimination Act and new trends in counterterrorism. These changes will not only aid in the managing of staff and inmates, but also provide a safer, more humane facility by relying on new, evidence-based techniques.

Christopher M. Campbell
Washington State University

See Also: 1941 to 1960 Primary Documents; 1961 to 1980 Primary Documents; 1981 to 2000 Primary Documents; 2001 to 2012 Primary Documents; Alcatraz Island Prison; Corrections; Leavenworth Federal Penitentiary; Penitentiaries; Sentencing: Mandatory Minimum Sentencing.

Further Readings
Bureau of Prisons. "Historical Overview." http://www.bop.gov (Accessed February 2011).
Carlson, N. A. "The Federal Prison System: Forty-Five Years of Change." *Federal Probation*, v.39/2 (1975).
Federal Bureau of Prisons. "Factories With Fences: The History of Federal Prison Industries." Washington, DC: Federal Prison Industries, 1996.
Keve, Paul W. *Prisons and the American Conscience: A History of U.S. Federal Corrections*. Carbondale: Southern Illinois University Press, 1991.

Federal Rules of Criminal Procedure

In 1946, the Federal Rules of Criminal Procedure were implemented to simplify and streamline the federal criminal justice process. At the time, these rules were praised by the legal community for both their simplicity and practicality. With only 60 (expanded to 61 in 2008) rules, the Federal Rules of Criminal Procedure provide a single set of procedures to be used in all aspects of the federal criminal justice process, from initiation of charges through appeal.

History

American legal procedure began with little legislative interference. However, as American democracy evolved in the 19th century, legislation was enacted that impacted or dictated both civil and criminal legal procedures. As a result, lawyers in the 20th century were faced with a complicated system of rules and procedures defined through multiple statutes and judicial interpretations. Variations across federal districts further complicated the criminal process.

The first effort to simplify the criminal process, in part as a response to a perceived increase in crime but lack of comprehensive statistics, was undertaken in 1925 by the American Law Institute to create a Code of Criminal Procedure. In response to this trend toward simplicity, Congress began investing the judiciary with the responsibility to determine procedures. The Criminal Appeals Rules Act of 1933 authorized the U.S. Supreme Court to determine the rules for the criminal appellate process. As a result, the Criminal Appeals Rules provided a single source of procedures for the criminal appellate process. In 1934, the Civil Rules Act was passed, which authorized the judiciary, as represented by the Judicial Conference of the United States, to simplify the civil law procedures. The result was the Federal Rules of Civil Procedure. Based on the success of these two efforts, Congress focused next on simplification of the criminal process.

Simplification

The first step was to bring the federal courts under a single administrative unit. The Federal

Administrative Office Act of 1939 united the federal courts under a single administrative unit and allowed self-regulation. The simplification of criminal procedures was addressed next with the Criminal Rules Act of 1940. With this act, the U.S. Supreme Court was authorized to establish a single set of procedures for the criminal legal process. The process involved creating an Advisory Committee to draft the procedures, review of the procedures by the legal community, approval of the procedures by the Supreme Court, and final approval and enactment by Congress.

The 18 members of the Advisory Committee included well-respected judges, lawyers, and academics who considered a broad range of laws, practices, and judicial interpretations to determine the best practices. Procedures used in U.S. criminal courts as well as criminal courts in other countries were studied. The myriad of laws and judicial decisions that were in existence at the federal, district, and state level were reviewed. The committee assessed the extensive research findings against its established standard of fairness and simplicity.

Drafting and Development
In developing the Federal Rules of Criminal Procedure, the Advisory Committee adhered to four objectives: simplify existing procedures by eliminating work and delay, improve the objective assessment of facts, realize democratic values, and improve uniformity across federal courts. As they drafted the rules, the Advisory Committee relied on seven existing legal sources: the Federal Rules of Civil Procedure, the Criminal Appeals Rules, state statutes, the U.S. Code, federal court decisions, common law, and the American Law Institute Code of Criminal Procedure. Yet, the Advisory Committee realized that these sources could not meet the standards of simplification or fairness in all situations and, therefore, created some new procedures.

The first draft of the Federal Rules of Criminal Procedure was completed in May 1943 and distributed throughout the legal community for comments. Responsibility for reviewing the draft rules was taken seriously by all within the legal community. In total, the Advisory Committee completed 10 drafts of the rules. The final draft was sent to the Supreme Court for its approval in August 1944. In December 1944, the chief justice of the Supreme Court forwarded the tules to the attorney general, who submitted them to Congress. The Federal Rules of Criminal Procedure were officially enacted in March 1945.

Although the Supreme Court ultimately approved the rules, it was neither unanimous or without changes. Each draft reflected changes made by the Supreme Court. Notably, the Supreme Court eliminated provisions for the alibi defense (which was added by amendment in 1974) and pretrial conferences (which was added by amendment in 1966). It also made findings of fact (i.e., the decision of the court based on the facts of the case) mandatory for cases tried without a jury, and limited the time available for the filing of a motion for a new trial when new evidence is discovered. Even with these changes, Justice Hugo Black refused to approve the rules, without providing a reason. Justice Felix Frankfurter also refused to approve the rules, citing three reasons. First, Justice Frankfurter felt that the Supreme Court's workload was too heavy to allow adequate review of the rules. Second, he felt that the judges of the Supreme Court were too far removed from the trial process to provide adequate and appropriate insight into the rules. Finally, Justice Frankfurter noted that since the rules may be challenged before the Supreme Court, it would not be appropriate for the court to approve the rules.

Results
The resulting Federal Rules of Criminal Procedure covered the criminal legal process from start to finish. They incorporate and supersede the Criminal Appeals Rules, although separate appellate rules were again introduced in 1967 (since that time, the full process requires a combination of the Federal Rules of Criminal Procedure and the Federal Rules of Appellate Procedure). The rules are applicable to criminal cases tried in any federal court as well as cases that are begun in state courts and transferred to federal courts. State courts, however, are not bound by the rules.

Because the rules combined federal statutes, common law, state law, and rules of courts, they introduced few procedures that were not in practice in a court. However, three changes were seen as immediately noteworthy. First, the rules simplified the procedure for change of venue to be more consistent with practices between states. Before this change, venue changes between divisions within federal districts required judicial proceedings, resulting in both costs and delays. Second, the rules regarding evidence reflected *Funk v. United States* (290 U.S. 371, 1933) because they would be governed by common law as interpreted at the time unless otherwise indicated by statute or rule. Finally, the rules simplified the process of filing for appeal by extending the time limits within which an appeal could be made and eliminating the intermediary step of having to put the disputed point of law on record through a bill of exception.

Even at their introduction, limitations were seen to the Federal Rules of Criminal Procedure. Although the simplicity of the rules allowed flexibility, they would not cover all cases, and constant interpretation and amendment would be required. In addition, statutes would still be required to respond to creative abuses in such areas as bail and jury selection. Finally, while these rules presented a uniform federal procedure, each state would still require their own criminal law procedures to accommodate differences in law, custom, and judicial interpretation.

Rules

Consistent with covering the criminal legal process from start to finish, the Federal Rules of Criminal Procedure are organized according to legal actions. The first section, applicability, explains the courts and proceedings covered by the rules and how the rules are to be interpreted. This section also defines key terms, such as *attorney* and *petty offense*, which are used in the rules. Preliminary proceedings are covered in the second section, including complaints, arrest warrants, and initial court appearance. The next step in the process, indictment, is covered in the third section. This section includes rules for the grand jury and the indictment. It also provides procedures for issuance of an arrest warrant or summons after an indictment has been issued and handling of situations where there are multiple offenders or multiple offenses. Arraignment and trial preparation are covered in the fourth section. This section also covers pleas, defenses, and discovery. Determination of venue is covered in the fifth section. The trial itself, including juries, witnesses, and verdicts, is the topic of the sixth section. Procedures that occur after conviction, such as sentencing and correcting errors, are covered in the seventh section. The eighth section covers special proceedings, including criminal contempt. This section originally covered the appeals process, but this was changed in 1968, reflecting the introduction of the Federal Rules of Appellate Procedure in 1967. The last section covers a broad range of topics, including calculation of time and dismissal.

Updates and Modifications

Since their enactment in 1945, the Federal Rules of Criminal Procedure continue to be updated yearly. Recent changes have involved incorporating the Crime Victim Rights Act of both 2007 and 2009. The Crime Victim Rights Act of 2009 was reflected in the 2010 amendments to the Federal Rules of Criminal Procedure, which eliminated automatic disclosure of a victim's telephone number and address and provided that a change of venue decision include consideration of the convenience of the victim. Incorporation of the Crime Victim Rights Act of 2007 necessitated the addition of a new Rule 60 (and moving the existing Rule 60 to Rule 61) to address victim's rights. Rule 60 covers notifying victims of hearings, allowing victims to attend proceedings, and allowing victims to be heard at plea, sentencing, and release hearings. This rule also provides that only victims or their lawful representatives may exercise these rights and, if multiple victims are involved, the court may proscribe a method that does not complicate or prolong legal proceedings. Furthermore, failure to accommodate the victim will not necessitate a new trial.

In 2002, the Federal Rules of Criminal Procedure were modified both stylistically and substantively. The rules were rearranged and reformatted to improve understanding and ensure that terminology was consistent. The substantive changes included requiring a judge to issue an arrest warrant for a defendant who fails to respond to a summons only at the government's request, allowing defendants to appear by video teleconferencing for initial appearance and arraignment, allowing the defendant to waive the right to appear at arraignment, requiring the defense to supply telephone numbers for alibi witnesses, bringing the discovery requirements for the defense in line with those for the government, and allowing filing by e-mail.

Notable additions to the Federal Rules of Criminal Procedure include the provision for foreign law added in 1966, procedures on the preliminary hearing added in 1972, procedures for the closing argument added in 1974, procedures to produce a witness statement added in 1979, the public authority defense added in 1988, procedures for criminal forfeiture added in 2000, procedures for a mistrial added in 1993, and the disclosure statement added in 2002.

One trend that has been noted in the amendments to the Federal Rules of Criminal Procedure is the erosion of secrecy surrounding grand jury proceedings. As originally drafted, the Federal Rules of Criminal Procedure afforded a high degree of secrecy to the grand jury proceedings. The original intent was that information from grand jury proceedings could only be disclosed to government lawyers or at the direction of the court. Exceptions to the prohibition on disclosure of grand jury information were introduced as early as 1983, but the rules maintained the practice of only disclosing to other government attorneys or with court approval. In 2002, the exceptions to disclosure were further expanded to include Indian tribes, government attorneys or banking regulators for use in civil suits, and armed forces personnel.

Kathleen Barrett
Georgia State University

See Also: 1961 to 1980 Primary Documents; Appeals; Common Law Origins of Criminal Law; Habeas Corpus, Writ of; Insanity Defense; Interrogation Practices; Judiciary Act of 1789; Juries; Legal Counsel; Plea; Probation; Sentencing; Supreme Court, U.S.; Trials; Victim Rights and Restitution.

Further Readings
Orfield, Lestor B. "The Federal Rules of Criminal Procedure." *California Law Review,* v.33 (1945).
U.S. Courts. "Federal Rules of Criminal Procedure." http://www.uscourts.gov/RulesAndPolicies/FederalRulemaking/Overview/CriminalRules.aspx (Accessed January 2011).

Federalist Papers

After the American Revolution, when the thirteen colonies revolted against the oppression of English rule, the founding fathers wrote the Constitution in an effort to create a more fair and equitable form of government than the monarchies then prevalent in Europe. However, when the founding fathers wrote the Constitution, there was not unanimous agreement among the states as to whether it should be ratified.

At that time, there were two main factions among the founding fathers: the Federalists and the Anti-Federalists. Essentially, the Federalists advocated a strong central government and were led by Alexander Hamilton. The Anti-Federalists favored a less centralized government and were led

A portrait of Alexander Hamilton, the leader of the Federalists. Hamilton is believed to have written the majority of the articles that make up The Federalist Papers.

by Thomas Jefferson. One of the other major differences between the Federalists and the Anti-Federalists was that the Anti-Federalists wanted a Bill of Rights added to the Constitution and the Federalists did not. The reason for this disagreement was that the Federalists thought that if a written document were created listing the rights of the people, then the government would likely recognize only those written rights, whereas the Anti-Federalists wanted a written list of rights, otherwise they thought that the government would not allow the people any rights. Given these differences, ratification of the Constitution was not certain.

A Colonial PR Team
Thus, the Federalists mounted a public relations campaign to help their cause for ratification of the Constitution by the various states. This campaign included, of course, advocacy within each state's legislature. Further, the articles were published to attempt to answer the objections to the Constitution raised by the Anti-Federalists. However, it also included a series of articles published in several newspapers—the *Independent Journal,* the *Daily Advertiser*, and the *New York Packet*—between October 1787 and August 1788. These articles presented a series of arguments about the potential benefits of the Constitution. Each article addressed certain issues concerning the Constitution. A total of 77 articles were published. In 1788, these articles were compiled and published under the tile *The Federalist*. When they were published, a few more articles were added, bringing the total number of articles to 85. *The Federalist* was widely published and read and was considered one of the most important expressions of the underlying political philosophy of the Federalists and the proposed Constitution. It was not until much later that this compilation of articles became more commonly known as *The Federalist Papers*.

The articles were published under the pseudonym Publius, which has been thought to be in honor of Roman Consul Publius Valerius. Some authorities consider the use of Publius as a pseudonym to reflect the idea that the author was a "friend of the people." Although secret at the time of their publication, it has been subsequently revealed that the authors were Alexander Hamilton, James Madison, and John Jay, all ardent Federalists. Most authorities have concluded that Hamilton wrote the majority of the articles, Madison wrote approximately a third of the articles, and Jay wrote only a few of them. However, there is some dispute as to which of the three authors wrote a few of the articles.

Some of the articles were considered to be more important and fundamental than the other articles. For example, in Number 84, Hamilton argues against the Anti-Federalist call for a Bill of Rights by arguing that the Constitution itself provides for sufficient protection for liberty. In Number 10, Madison discusses how a majority can be prevented from gaining power under the proposed Constitution. In Number 70, Hamilton argues for an executive function vested in a single man. In Number 78, Hamilton presents the principle of judicial review of both legislative enactments and executive actions. And in Numbers 39 and 51, Madison defines what "Federalism" under the proposed Constitution means and argues for the necessity of government.

In the context of crime and punishment, the most important articles were Numbers 78–83. These articles dealt with objections concerning the courts and trials under the Constitution. Article 78 is probably the most important of them and has been called the most cited article of the *Federalist Papers* by the U.S. Supreme Court. In this article, it is recognized that the judicial branch of government is the weakest of the three branches, although it recognized the power of judicial review. Article 79 highlighted that the power of federal judges could be controlled through the impeachment process. And Article 83 addressed the concern that jury trials in civil matters were not specifically addressed.

Conclusion
Although *The Federalist* was primarily published in New York, it was sent to and reprinted in other states during the ratification process of the Constitution. *The Federalist* has been considered to be the most important document to understanding the intent of the founding fathers concerning the writing of the Constitution and the meaning of the Constitution in its application. *The Federalist* has been quoted by the U.S. Supreme Court hundreds of times. It is interesting to note that the Federalists and the Anti-Federalists came to a compromise concerning their disagreement over

the inclusion of a Bill of Rights by later ratifying such a Bill of Rights but also including the Ninth Amendment to express the principle that the written Bill of Rights does not mean that the people do not have other rights.

Thus, historically, in the context of crime and punishment in the United States, it can be stated with little quibbling that the *Federalist Papers*, which arguably helped in the ratification of both the Constitution and the Bill of Rights, had a profound effect on crime and punishment, especially with the Fourth, Fifth, Sixth, and Eighth Amendments, which provide a series of constitutional protections for persons accused of crimes, which would likely not otherwise be present in the American criminal justice system.

Wm. C. Plouffe, Jr.
Independent Scholar

See Also: American Revolution and Criminal Justice; Anti-Federalist Papers; Bill of Rights; Constitution of the United States of America; Hamilton, Alexander; Jefferson, Thomas; Madison, James (Administration of).

Further Readings
Epstein, David F. *The Political Theory of the Federalist.* Chicago: University of Chicago Press, 1984.
Furtwangler, Albert, *The Authority of Publius: A Reading of the Federalist Papers.* Ithaca, NY: Cornell University Press, 1984.
Hamilton, Alexander, James Madison, and John Jay. In *The Federalist*, Jacob E. Cooke, ed. Middletown, CT: Wesleyan University Press, 1961.
Myerson, Michael. *Liberty's Blueprint: How Madison and Hamilton Wrote the Federalist Papers, Defined the Constitution, and Made Democracy Safe for the World.* New York: Basic Books, 2008.

Felonies

Originating from early English common law, a felony is a serious crime in the system of criminal law. Most individuals regard felonies as harmful and inherently dangerous acts with profound consequences to society. A person convicted of a felony is often referred to as a felon. In the United States, substantive criminal law, which defines crimes and sets forth penalties, describes a felony as a crime punishable by one year or more of incarceration in prison or in a penitentiary or by death. Examples of felonies include but are not limited to murder, rape, robbery, arson, aggravated assault, and burglary.

In contrast to felony crimes, misdemeanor crimes are considered to be less severe in nature and encompass many more illicit acts. Examples include disorderly conduct, public intoxication, vandalism, trespassing, and shoplifting or petty theft. Some misdemeanor crimes have been the subject of debate by members of society as to whether they should even be crimes at all (e.g., prostitution, marijuana use or possession of small quantities of the drug, underage drinking). Misdemeanors are punishable by fines and/or incarceration in a local jail for less than one year. Thus, the classification of a crime generally corresponds to the sanction imposed on that crime. The distinction between misdemeanors and felonies exists in U.S. courts as well as court systems abroad, although the distinction is absent in some legal systems abroad. In unusual cases, misdemeanors may be classified as felonies, especially for chronic offenders.

Early English Law
Historically, individuals in power would enforce their own ideals and impose punishment on those thought to be deserving of it. Justice was also administered in various ways, many of which would be considered cruel and unusual punishment by today's standards. Later in time, a unified system of law formed in England under the reign of King Henry II during the 12th century. The system aimed to be just by announcing law "common" to the land and developing a structured court system to hear disputes and resolve cases. The king's judges would make decisions and record them for other judges to follow in order to provide precedent and prevent arbitrary or unjust practices. English law eventually grew to include three core classes of crime: treason, felony, and misdemeanor. Treason was considered the most serious crime, followed by felony crime, then misdemeanor crime.

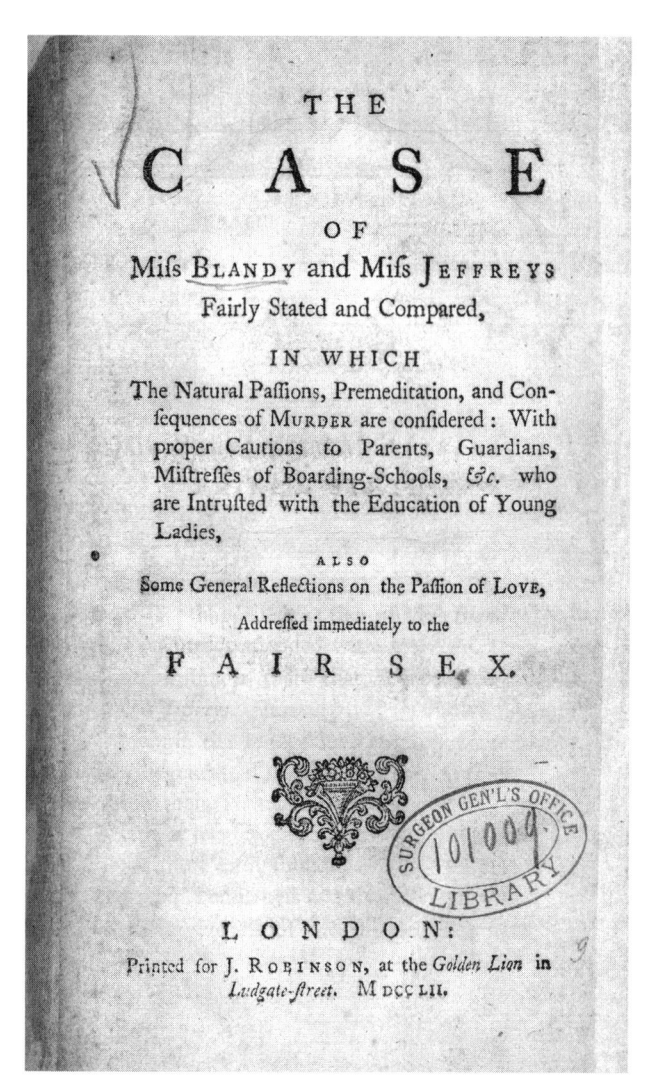

This pamphlet on the case of Mary Blandy, who was hanged in 1752 for poisoning her father with arsenic in Oxford, England, considers circumstances of the murder, such as "passion" and "premeditation," which are still used to help classify murders.

Treason involves a serious act of betrayal against one's nation or land. In 1351, the English parliament passed legislation against treason. Threatening or injuring the king or his court, having sexual relations with the queen or the unwed daughter of the king, attempting to overthrow the sovereign, waging war against the governance, and providing aid to an enemy are examples of acts that had been classified as high treason. Other acts of treason deemed less serious in nature were labeled as petty treason. This included the murder of individuals other than the king and his kin who were deemed to be superior in social standing. Someone found to commit an act of treason was known as a traitor. Traitors were punished by asset forfeiture (i.e., taking away the offender's land or property to give to the king) and were prohibited from inheriting any land or property from relatives. Relatives were also forbidden to take a traitor's land. As a crime, treason was considered so grave that traitors were punished by death. Male offenders were hanged while female offenders were burned at the stake. Beheadings were also used as a method of execution.

Like treason, felony crimes were considered to be severe offenses. A felon was subject to asset forfeiture and even the possibility of death. During this time, felony crimes included homicide, mayhem, arson, rape, robbery, burglary, and larceny. Misprision of a felony—when a person aware that a felony has taken place fails to report it to authorities—was also a crime. Those guilty of felony crimes were mandated to give up property and belongings to an overlord and could also face death. However, it was possible for an offender to avoid death as punishment for certain felonies if the offender pled "benefit of clergy." This request for mercy subjected the offender to a lesser form of punishment and was made available in the 14th century. In the case of mayhem (e.g., maiming, mutilating, or disfiguring an individual), however, offenders were inflicted with violent forms of punishment.

In contrast to felony crimes, misdemeanor crimes were minor offenses. Misdemeanor crimes consisted of any transgressions other than those that fell under the felony crime or treason classifications. These crimes did not place lawbreakers at risk of death.

Law in the United States

The English system of law implicitly served as a model for U.S. criminal law. In the late 17th and early 18th centuries, American colonies began to establish criminal law with the hope of setting social values and providing citizens with stability. Courts were given power to create law, define criminal offenses, establish classifications of crime, and set forth punishments for a given criminal offense. They followed much of what was rooted in the English tradition to structure and develop their own legal system. Shortly after, however, courts came under attack. The trouble resided in the fact that the U.S. Constitution gave Congress the power to make law, but granted the judiciary the power to interpret it. Thus, the courts did not dominate the entire system. This eventually gave way to the distribution of authority in the federal system where Congress was responsible for creating law and federal courts were responsible for construing it. In time, state legislatures were granted the capacity to set forth law, with each jurisdiction being responsible for defining crime and identifying appropriate punishment. Courts were tasked with their analysis.

Today, crimes are enumerated in the Constitution as well as in state statutes. In most jurisdictions, legislatures define crime and set forth the respective punishment for each offense; they also pass laws, amend laws, and repeal laws. The distinction between felony and misdemeanor classifications of crime originating in English common law has largely been retained in the contemporary legal system. These traditional concepts have been codified in the Model Penal Code, created by the American Law Institute in 1962, which provides a framework for criminal law and helps states discern the gravity of offenses. Where a crime falls is more often than not based upon punishment for that particular act. Crimes that fit the felony classification or are *mala in se* (i.e., inherently wrong) as defined by common law are punished by one year or more in prison or in a penitentiary or even by death. Crimes that fall into the misdemeanor classification or are *mala prohibitum* (i.e., wrong because they are prohibited by law) are punished by no more than one year of incarceration. States like New Jersey, New York, and Pennsylvania have adopted a vast majority of the provisions in the Model Penal Code for their own law.

Rather than stating whether a crime is a felony or misdemeanor in the actual definition of each crime, nearly all jurisdictions differentiate on the basis of such punishment. For instance, murder in the first degree is defined as the unlawful killing of one person by another that was premeditated and deliberate with malice aforethought. It is punishable by life imprisonment or the death penalty. Although not specifically stated, it is considered to be a felony given the level of punishment. However, there are a few offenses clearly classified in law such as "felony-murder" and "misdemeanor manslaughter." Nonetheless, the distinction plays an important role in shaping today's law across all jurisdictions. It also carries substantive and procedural implications.

Despite its following, the U.S. system of criminal law has slightly shifted away from some English common law crimes. For instance, treason was dropped as a unique category of crime and replaced by separate "high crimes" targeting those who undermine the government (e.g., attempting to overthrow a country, aiding an enemy, or committing perjury). Additionally, crimes relating to infidelity have been discarded. The punishments prescribed for crimes in contemporary law are thought to be less draconian when compared to earlier law. A wide range of sanctions also now exists outside the cruel and unusual punishment that was inflicted in earlier times (the death penalty may be viewed as an exception).

In addition to felony and misdemeanor crime classifications, infractions now exist. These trivial offenses typically violate city ordinances or administrative regulations. For instance, disturbing the peace, littering, jaywalking, and violating building codes are common infractions in the United States today. While some may be criminal, others are not. Infractions are often punished by a fine or warning rather than by incapacitation or incarceration.

Classifications of Felonies

The list of felonies in U.S. law is quite extensive and incorporates both violent and nonviolent crime typologies. Violent felony crime generally involves crime against a person or persons. For instance, criminal homicide (e.g., first-degree murder, second-degree murder, and manslaughter), kidnapping, rape/sexual assault, robbery, and aggravated assault (i.e., assault that causes serious bodily injury/harm; common law's equivalent of mayhem) are considered violent felony crimes. Nonviolent felony crime typically consists of crime against property: burglary, arson, destruction of property, grand theft including auto theft, embezzlement, counterfeiting, forgery, bribery, and some drug-related offenses (e.g., drug possession of a certain amount, drug manufacturing, and drug trafficking).

Felony crimes are now classified into various degrees and classes representing the seriousness of the offense as well as prescribed punishment, but these degrees and classes can vary from state to state. Common classifications in U.S. court systems include capital crime, first-degree felony, second-degree felony, and third-degree felony. Capital crime represents the most severe type of offense. It is this crime that can result in the death penalty. Following capital crime are first-, second-, and third-degree felonies. A first-degree felony involves a crime whereby a person commits a felony, although it is not as extreme as a capital felony offense. A second-degree felony is considered a lesser offense and includes an attempt to commit a serious felony or involves acts where one operates as a facilitator at the scene of the crime. A third-degree felony is a less severe but still serious offense that often encompasses behavior whereby a person functions as an accessory to the crime. This was taken from the common law of misprision. Some states classify a third-degree felony as a crime that occurs when one acts as an accessory to a crime before it happens, and a fourth-degree felony as a crime that occurs when one acts as an accessory to a crime after it happens.

In contrast to degrees of offenses, some jurisdictions classify felonies into classes determined by the gravity of the crime. Class A felonies are the most serious, followed by Class B, then Class C, Class D, and Class E. Class A felonies are punishable by death or lifelong incarceration and a substantial fine. Class B felonies are punishable by a shorter but still extensive sentence and a fine. Class C felonies are punishable by an even shorter sentence and a fine, and so forth. New York is an example of a state that uses such classes to represent the gravity of the offense, with Class A-I being the most serious and Class E being the least. These classes can also be represented by numbers. For example, Virginia places felonies into numerical classes. The more distant the number is from 1, the lesser the sanctions are. Interestingly, the Uniform Crime Reports (UCR) and the National Incident-Based Reporting System (NIBRS) collect data on crimes classified based on numbers and letters. The UCR breaks down crimes into Part I and Part II offenses while NIBRS breaks down crimes into Group A and Group B offenses. Part I and Group A crimes are considered the most serious offenses. Part II and Group B crimes are not deemed as severe in nature and are only recorded/reported when arrests are made.

Type of Crime and Degree or Class

When examining the type of offense and degree or class of crime, law can get rather complex. To clarify how these are used in our judicial system, the example of homicide is considered. Homicide is the killing of one human being by another. This term is broad in scope in that it includes murder, manslaughter, excusable homicide, and justifiable homicide. Murder is a narrow concept of homicide. It is viewed as the single most serious offense one can commit. Taken from common law, murder is defined as the unlawful killing of another human being with *malice aforethought* (i.e., a premeditated and deliberate act). This differs from other unlawful homicides like manslaughter, which holds an offender less culpable for his/her actions. A person who commits murder is dubbed a murderer. Murder is a capital crime or life felony deemed worthy of the highest and harshest sanction: life incarceration or death. Some states use also use long-term incarceration with the possibility of parole. The punishment often depends on the nature of the offense as well as jurisdictional practices.

Murder has been and still is divided into various degrees. Pennsylvania became the first state to pass legislation specifying the degrees of murder in 1794, and other states followed shortly thereafter. The degrees of murder have been infused into contemporary American law in an effort to restrict the death penalty to wicked and obscene cases of murder (i.e., murder in the first degree). First-degree murder involves premeditated and deliberate behavior with malice aforethought, or the malicious intent to kill. Premeditated behavior involves elements of planning, whether years or just seconds, while deliberate behavior involves the intention of causing harm upon someone. The most brutal and extreme cases of murder fall here, particularly those designed in advance that use torture or cruel methods. These are seen as aggravated forms of murder. Additionally, felony-murder may fall into this category, although it varies from state to state. This is when someone is killed during the commission of a felony crime. Although premeditation and deliberation for a murder may be lacking in this instance, the premeditation and deliberation of the felony (e.g., robbery or burglary) are transferred to the homicide. Fatality results from the act in which one is implicated can also result in this charge. Any participants in the felony can be charged for the murder. If police mistakenly shoot someone, those involved in the felonious act can be charged for that death. Some states like New York have also added special circumstances that permit one to be tried for first-degree murder. Taking the life of a police officer, killing a witness to a crime, or being involved in multiple murders can place one at risk of being tried for first-degree murder. Second-degree murder, in contrast, lacks premeditation but holds an element of malicious intent whereby the offender purposely set out to inflict serious injury, serious bodily harm, or death on another person. The act is spontaneous and is commonly committed under the influence of alcohol and/or drugs or even during a verbal altercation.

Manslaughter is a classification of homicide that lacks premeditation but encompasses reckless disregard for another's life. There are two common classifications of manslaughter: nonnegligent and negligent. The classifications for manslaughter vary greatly from state to state. Some states consider nonnegligent manslaughter to be a form of murder in the second degree while others categorize it as a third-degree offense. Similarly, some states consider negligent manslaughter to be a third-degree offense while others see it as a fourth-degree offense. Nonnegligent manslaughter, also known as voluntary manslaughter, is the intentional killing of another, often triggered by emotions or in the "heat of passion," under extenuating circumstances. Provocation (e.g., catching someone in an act of infidelity or being demeaned by another person), self-defense, and diminished capacity underlie this. For provocation, an individual does not have a cooling-off period in order for his/her crime to be classified as nonnegligent; if he/she did, it would be classified as a higher degree of murder. For self-defense, the actions must have been caused by the reasonable belief that lethal force was necessary. Diminished capacity refers to an abnormal state of mind but not insanity. In contrast, negligent or involuntary manslaughter is when negligence is involved whereby someone engages in an unlawful act with wanton disregard for the person's life. This "depraved heart" offense includes vehicular homicide as in the case of running a red light or operating a vehicle under the influence of alcohol and/or drugs, which results in another's death. Some states have upgraded the latter to third- or second-degree offenses (e.g., California, New York, and Wisconsin). Misdemeanor manslaughter also falls here, which is when the death of another results during the commission of a misdemeanor crime.

Forms of homicide considered noncriminal include excusable homicide and justifiable homicide. Excusable homicide is when an unintentional death occurs. In this case, a death may have resulted from an accident or legal activity surrounding the situation. Malice and unlawfulness are absent at the time of the incident. Justifiable homicide, in contrast, refers to an intentional death where one takes responsibility for the homicide but argues that the act took place to prevent a greater harm. This form of homicide limits criminal responsibility for committing a homicide. Police, corrections officers, or other authoritative personnel may commit a justifiable homicide in the course of their duties. In some cases, homicide resulting from self-defense is justifiable when lethal means are needed to prevent imminent harm.

Depending on the severity of the crime and whether the offender has committed the crime before, misdemeanors can be upgraded to felonies, and grades of the felony can change. The nature and circumstances of felonies are taken into consideration. For example, while driving under the influence is a misdemeanor for the first offense in many states, subsequent convictions place it as a felony. Further, sexual assault may be graded as a lesser degree of a felony, but subsequent charges can upgrade this to a first-degree offense with the possibility of life behind bars.

Extent of Felonies and Characteristics of Felons

The United States has one of the highest rates of felonies when compared to other Westernized countries. Criminologists use records of government agencies such as police departments, prisons, and courts in order to determine the extent of felonies and felony characteristics. The Federal Bureau of Investigation (FBI) collects the most important crime record data from local law enforcement agencies and publishes them yearly in the Uniform Crime Report (UCR). This includes data on the number of Part I or Index crimes, which are considered the most serious offenses (i.e., homicide and nonnegligent manslaughter, rape, aggravated assault, robbery, burglary, larceny/theft, arson, and auto theft) and data for Part II crimes, which are considered less serious crimes and misdemeanors; however, the most serious offense in an incident is recorded in the UCR, and Part II crime information is only included when an arrest is made. The published data includes figures by jurisdiction, city, county, metro area, and geographical division. In recent years, the FBI has also implemented the National Incident-Based Reporting System (NIBRS), which collects more detailed information on crimes (e.g., victim-offender relationship, types of offenses included in an incident, etc.) and attempts to address some shortcomings of the UCR.

According to the UCR, NIBRS, and even self-reports of criminal behavior, the vast majority of individuals who commit and have been convicted of felonies are males (about 80 percent). Males disproportionately commit violent crimes compared to females, while females are more commonly found to commit nonviolent crimes rather than violent crimes. The FBI has estimated that there are more than 1 million violent crimes and more than 9 million property crimes committed in the United States each year. Examining crime types, aggravated assault is the most common violent crime while larceny/theft is the most common property crime. State courts tend to sentence men to prison or jail at higher rates than women, and African Americans at a slightly higher rate than whites but without significant difference in sentence length. Examining macro-level aggregates, data have shown that large urban areas, which are more populated, have higher rates of felonies than rural areas. While some of these crimes are expressive (i.e., a reaction to stress, anger, or rage), a large portion consist of instrumental crimes (i.e., crimes designed to improve one's financial or social position). Southern and western states also have the highest rates of felonies. Additionally, states that support harsh punishment and use capital punishment for crimes have also been found to have higher rates of violent crime.

The availability of firearms correlates with felonious actions. These lethal weapons have been used in the majority of murders as well as other violent crimes like robberies, assaults, and rapes. Most are handguns, but other models have been used. People of all races/ethnicities are equally likely to use a gun, and the presence of one increases chances of serious injury/death. As a result, there is an ongoing debate about gun control in order to reduce the amount of serious crimes or felonies that exist. Some feel the high number of guns and their likelihood to cause injury is the reason the United States, compared to any other country, has such high violent crime rates. Yet others argue guns are needed for protection from crimes.

Crime scene tape at an arson site in Oregon in 2008. Nonviolent felony crime typically consists of crimes against property, such as burglary, arson, or destruction of property. There are an estimated 9 million such crimes per year in the United States.

Processing

Procedural law is important to examine in the processing of felony crimes, particularly with the courts. State and federal courts are responsible for reaching verdicts and imposing sentences on offenders. A state court of general jurisdiction is slightly above a state court with limited jurisdiction. State courts of general jurisdiction differ from those with limited jurisdiction in that they hear more serious cases. This includes superior, supreme, county, or circuit courts. They handle felony cases as well as civil cases that exceed a specified amount, and also hear appeals from the lower courts. Federal courts like U.S. district courts, on the other hand, handle cases involving the violation of federal law. In felony cases, each defendant has the right to a court-appointed attorney if he/she cannot afford a lawyer; this does not typically hold for other, less serious crimes. The felony also requires one to be present in court proceedings, which is not always the case for some misdemeanor crimes.

The process from arrest to sentencing can take as little as a few days or longer than one year; the more serious offenses take longer, but the majority of people go through the system within one year. State court systems process about 94 percent of felonies whereas federal court systems process about 6 percent of felony cases. State court systems convict more than 1 million individuals each year; about three-quarters of offenders are sentenced for a single felony while others are convicted of two or more. The majority of the felonies consisted of drug-related offenses, but more than 200,000 individuals were involved in violent crimes.

Most individuals who commit felonies are sentenced to prison or jail, yet about one-fourth are sentenced to probation without any form of incarceration. Violent offenders typically receive the longest sentences. The majority of offenders plead guilty, with the rest being found guilty by a jury or by a judge during trial. Those who go to trial and are found guilty receive longer sentences than those who plea-bargain. Capital or life sentences account for less than 1 percent of the felony sentences. Many felons also pay fines as a part of their sentence. When examining federal offenses, federal courts sentence about 70,000 felons every year. On average, federal courts impose longer sentences for felonies than state courts do.

Punishment

Since the law prescribes a range of possible punishments for a given crime, judges are able to use discretion to impose a particular punishment on an offender. Punishment for felonies, whether in state or federal court, takes a host of factors into account prior to prescribing punishment. These are referred to as mitigating and aggravating circumstances. These factors can make a less serious offense more severe or a more serious offense less severe. Mitigating circumstances tend to produce lighter punishment, while aggravating circumstances give way to harsher punishment. Having a prior criminal record, engaging in an offense with malice or reckless disregard for another life or safety, targeting a victim belonging to particular class (e.g., minors, minorities, or disabled or handicapped persons), and demonstrating a lack of remorse can yield harsh punishment. Conversely, acting out as a result of stress or adverse circumstances and having remorse may yield a lighter sentence.

Although felonies have traditionally been punishable by death, legislatures have regarded death sentences to be an excessively harsh and draconian measure. Consequently, they moved to limit capital punishment to the most violent and horrific cases of murder, which is often premeditated. The use of capital punishment has accordingly diminished and is no longer applied as commonly as it was in the past. In the current era, the death penalty is reserved for first-degree and felony murder in the United States, although some states have added additional offenses (e.g., attempted murder, espionage, terrorist-related activities, repeat sexual offenses against minors, previous conviction of other serious offenses) while others have abolished this form of punishment altogether.

Incarceration is commonly imposed for individuals found guilty of a felony crime. The length of a sentence may vary based on the crime itself as well as prior criminal history. Besides a period of incarceration, individuals convicted of felonies may face alternative forms of punishment. Intermediate sanctions are commonly imposed on felons. These involve a range of sanctions between prison and traditional probation, many of which

Capital or life sentences account for less than 1 percent of felony sentences, leaving released felons to live with the lasting consequences of their status as felons. Among the many ramifications of a felony conviction is the likelihood of being deported from the United States if one is not a legal citizen. Above, a Mexican citizen being deported by U.S. Customs and Border Protection.

take place in the community. They have grown to include intensive supervision probation (ISP), electronic monitoring, home confinement, and work release, to name a few. Lighter forms may involve day reporting centers, restitution, and community service. Individuals convicted of felonies may also receive court-mandated orders to partake in rehabilitative programs. Cognitive skills training in anger management and conflict resolution may be prescribed for violent offenders, and residential treatment for alcohol and substance abuse may be ordered for nonviolent offenders. Other forms of treatment also exist.

Collateral Consequences

After serving their sentences, felons encounter numerous social and legal consequences, known as the collateral consequences of crime. These are costs and deprivations that accompany formal punishment. They continue to impact offenders over time. Felons lose the right to vote and participate in democratic elections, referred to as felony disenfranchisement. Nearly 5 million individuals are barred from voting because of their criminal records. Felons also lose the right to serve on a jury, hold political office, obtain certain licenses, gain employment in certain professions (e.g., law and medicine, or governmental jobs), buy firearms and ammunition, and receive government assistance in housing and welfare. Additionally, felons are barred from obtaining visas and may face deportation if they are not legal citizens.

Along with the civil disabilities felons face, they also encounter a copious amount of challenges and life-altering consequences associated with their convictions. Incarceration often hampers relationships and may result in family dissolution as well as offer grounds for divorce. Thus, upon re-entry to society, felons may find themselves alone or with limited social support. They may also face social stigma associated with being a criminal. Felons can experience various obstacles that make it difficult to adjust to living on the outside. For instance, parole commonly requires felons who are released into the community to maintain steady employment and housing. However, this is of utmost difficulty for many felons given that employers as well as rental agencies are legally permitted to discriminate against individuals on the basis of felony convictions. Consequently, obtaining legitimate income and maintaining housing proves troublesome. Many felons are also at a disadvantage because they may not be able to obtain medical or other types of services that they had received while incarcerated. Such obstacles have been thought to contribute to the nation's high rates of recidivism.

However, some felons can have their status reverted through appealing their convictions, being granted clemency, or being given a presidential pardon. These techniques seek to restore some of the civil disabilities imposed on offenders. Some states have also allowed felons to obtain some of the rights after a long period of time has passed (e.g., 10 years). The Second Chances Act of 2009 is working toward providing relief and the ability to expunge records for certain nonviolent criminal offenses, but federal felons cannot have their records expunged: it is something that will stay with them for the rest of their lives.

Alison Marganski
Virginia Wesleyan College

See Also: Appeals; Capital Punishment; Codification of Laws; Common Law Origins of Criminal Law; Counterfeiting; Crime in America, Types; Crime Rates; Mandatory Minimum Sentencing; Sentencing.

Further Readings
Department of Justice. "Key Facts on Crime and Justice." http://www.justice.gov/archive/mps/strategic2001-2006/appd.htm (Accessed May 2011).
Federal Bureau of Investigation. "Crime in the United States." http://www2.fbi.gov/ucr/cius2009/index.html (Accessed May 2011).
Hall, Kermit. *The Oxford Companion to American Criminal Law*. New York: Oxford University Press, 2002.
Kirchmeier, Jeffrey. "Casting a Wider Net: Another Decade of Legislative Expansion of the Death Penalty in the United States." *Pepperdine Law Review*, v.34/1 (2006).
LaFave, Wayne and Austin Scott, Jr. *Criminal Law*, 2nd ed. Saint Paul, MN: West Publishing Co., 1986.
Manza, Jeff and Christopher Uggen. *Locked Out: Felon Disenfranchisement and American Democracy*. New York: Oxford University Press, 2006.
Myers, Martha. "Common Law in Action: The Prosecution of Felonies and Misdemeanors." *Sociological Inquiry*, v.52/1 (2007).
Rosenmerkel, Sean, Matthew Durose, and Donald Farole. *Felony Sentences in State Courts, 2006*. U.S. Department of Justice, Office of Justice Programs, Bureau of Justice Statistics. http://bjs.ojp.usdoj.gov/content/pub/pdf/fssc06st.pdf (Accessed May 2011).

Ferguson, Colin

Colin Ferguson (1958–) is a Jamaican immigrant who was convicted of murdering and critically wounding passengers onboard the Long Island Railroad in 1993. Ferguson's criminal trial and, in particular, his behavior and actions during the trial, attracted public and media attention and resulted in significant political and legal changes.

Colin Ferguson was born on January 14, 1958, in Kingston, Jamaica, to Von Herman Ferguson and Mary Ferguson. He attended Calabar High School, one of the most prestigious learning institutions in Jamaica, where he graduated at the top of his class. After the death of both of his parents, Ferguson obtained a visitor's visa and moved to the United States. Early experiences with racism, in conjunction with his inability to obtain high-skilled, high-paying employment, left Ferguson frustrated and angered. Ferguson was particularly troubled by the racism he perceived within American society, which he believed had prevented him from obtaining employment and limited his success. Prior to the Long Island Railroad murders, Ferguson was involved in a number of violent, criminal incidents, which included an arrest for harassing and threatening a woman on the subway. His behavior during these incidents suggested that Ferguson was becoming increasingly paranoid and obsessed with the idea of using violence and revolution to resolve racism.

On December 7, 1993, after nearly a week of planning, Ferguson opened fire onboard the Long Island Railroad commuter train. Ferguson murdered six and critically wounded 19 passengers before he was tackled and stopped by a group of fellow passengers. In January 1994, Ferguson was declared mentally stable to stand trial despite attempts by his defense attorney to prove that Ferguson suffered from and was driven by severe mental illness. Shortly before his trial, Ferguson fired his original defense attorney and sought the services of William Kunstler and Ron Kuby, who were known for taking on unpopular and difficult cases.

As a result of public outrage over the railroad murders, there was significant public and media attention devoted to the Colin Ferguson trial. This interest was heightened by the novel defense strategy used by Kunstler and Kuby to argue Ferguson's innocence. The defense argued that at the time of the murders Ferguson suffered from "black rage," a form of insanity, which resulted from years of racial prejudice. By adopting this strategy, the defense acknowledged that Ferguson was the shooter; however, they argued that he should not be held criminally responsible because of his mental instability.

The public's interest in the trial was increased by Ferguson's peculiar behavior. For example, throughout the trial, Ferguson maintained that he was not the shooter and rejected his attorney's "black rage" defense. Ferguson's unwillingness to accept his attorney's strategy ultimately led him to fire his attorneys and represent himself. By doing so, Ferguson became responsible for questioning the witnesses to the railroad murders and the police officers who had investigated the incident, arrested, and questioned him. Ferguson's use of third person during cross-examinations and his theory that a white man had stolen his gun and committed the murders were viewed by the public as proof of Ferguson's paranoia, guilt, and danger to society.

On February 17, 1995, Colin Ferguson was found guilty of six counts of murder and 19 counts of attempted murder, and was sentenced to 315 years in prison. The Long Island Railroad murders and the Colin Ferguson trial had a significant effect on American society and politics. Specifically, government officials in New York and gun control advocates used the incident to demand stricter gun control laws. New York Congresswoman Carolyn McCarthy, whose husband was murdered on the Long Island Railroad, is one of the most vocal opponents of New York's current gun control laws. The Colin Ferguson trial also led to a significant debate among psychologists and legal professionals over whether Ferguson's right to represent himself should have been questioned and revoked.

JoAnna Elmquist
Andrew Ninnemann
Butler Hospital and Brown University
Gregory L. Stuart
University of Tennessee, Knoxville

See Also: Gun Control; Kunstler, William; New York; Race-Based Crimes; Serial and Mass Killers.

Further Readings
Bardwell, Mark C. and Bruce A. Arrigo. *Criminal Competency on Trial: The Case of Colin Ferguson.* Durham, NC: Carolina Academic Press, 2002.
Ewing, Charles Patrick and Joseph T. McCann. *Minds on Trial: Great Cases in Law and Psychology.* New York: Oxford University Press, 2006.

Fillmore, Millard (Administration of)

Millard Fillmore (1800–74) was born in a log cabin at Moravia, Cayuga County, New York. He was apprenticed at age 14 to the cloth-making trade; however, he was able to gain enough education so that he could read for the law. He was admitted to the New York bar in 1823. He served in the New York militia during the Mexican–American War.

In 1828, Fillmore won election to the New York State Assembly as a member of the Anti-Masonic Party. While in the assembly, he promoted a bill

THE RIGHT MAN FOR THE RIGHT PLACE.

Millard Fillmore ran in the presidential election of 1856 as the American Party's candidate. While he won 21 percent of the popular vote, he garnered only eight electoral votes. This 1856 cartoon in support of Fillmore suggested that he was "the right man" to stand between the slave owners and the abolitionists. He is shown breaking up a fight between Republican John C. Fremont (left) and Democrat James Buchanan, who is being associated here with violence against antislavery settlers in Kansas and with slaveholders.

that would improve bankruptcy procedures and would also eliminate New York's debtors' prisons. In 1832, he won his first election to Congress as a member of the Whig Party, which opposed slavery. In 1844, Fillmore lost his bid to become governor of New York. Between 1848 and 1849, he served as New York state comptroller. While in office, he helped to revise New York's banking laws. The issue of slavery was an important factor in the Whig national convention in 1848. The presidential nominee Zachary Taylor was a slave owner, so Millard Fillmore was nominated as the vice presidential candidate from a non-slave state to balance the ticket. In fact, Taylor was opposed to the extension of slavery to the new western territory, while Fillmore supported allowing slavery in order to gain southern support.

Taylor and Fillmore won the election of 1848 and took office in 1849. As vice president, Fillmore was the presiding officer of the Senate, where he endured the debates on the Compromise of 1850. Close to the end of the debates, he intimated to President Taylor that he would cast the tie-breaking vote if necessary; however, President Taylor died suddenly on July 9, 1850, requiring Fillmore to assume the office.

Fugitive Slave Act

As president, Fillmore mollified southerners to prevent secession by supporting the Compromise of 1850. His support of the compromise created animosity for him among anti-slavery northerners. Ultimately, the compromise was sent to Fillmore as five separate bills drafted by Senator Stephen Douglas. The one that most afflicted Fillmore's future was the Fugitive Slave Act ("Bloodhound Law"), which he endorsed without trying to seem to be supporting the south.

The Fugitive Slave Act (1850) created special commissioners with concurrent jurisdiction with the federal courts and the territorial courts. Trial by jury was not allowed in cases before the commissioners, and accused fugitives did not have a right to testify. Federal officers who refused to help the commissioners or who allowed slaves to escape or individuals who aided escaping slaves were subject to serious penalties. Cash bounties were granted to those who brought in escaped slaves. Fees were paid to marshals for each slave captured that were twice the fees for those who were found not to be slaves. The decisions about individuals held as runaway slaves was purely ex parte, so free blacks could easily be enslaved on the testimony of a slave hunter.

The effect of the Fugitive Slave Act's abuses was to increase the number of abolitionists helping the Underground Railroad with fugitive slaves. Many northern states passed personal liberty laws that ordered state judges not to recognize claims arising from the federal act. In some states, the rights of habeas corpus and jury trials were given to alleged fugitives. In 1854, the Supreme Court of Wisconsin declared the Fugitive Slave Act unconstitutional.

In some states such as Pennsylvania, opposition to enforcement of the law turned violent. On September 11, 1851, in Christiana, a riot to defend a fugitive slave turned into the Battle of Christiana, in which the locals engaged in a gun battle with federal officers. A slaveholder was killed during the shooting. Fillmore's signature on the Fugitive Slave Act was unforgivable in the minds of some Whigs. They were able to deprive him of the 1852 Whig Party presidential nomination.

In 1856, the Whig Party disbanded because of strife among its members over the slavery issue, most notably over the Kansas-Nebraska Act of 1854. Many former Whigs joined the new Republican Party; however, Fillmore joined the American Party, which represented the anti-immigrant, anti-Catholic Know-Nothing movement. He ran in the election of 1856 as the American Party's candidate for president. He captured 21 percent of the popular vote, but just eight electoral votes.

Between 1861 and the 1870s, Fillmore commanded the Union Continental, a home guard unit from upstate New York, opposed President Abraham Lincoln and Reconstruction, and supported President Andrew Johnson. He died March 8, 1874, at Buffalo from the effects of a stroke.

Andrew J. Waskey
Dalton State College

See Also: Fugitive Slave Act of 1850; Lincoln, Abraham (Administration of); Slavery, Law of.

Further Readings
Finkelman, Paul, Jr., Arthur M. Schlesinger, Jr., and Sean Wilentz. *Millard Fillmore: The 13th President, 1850–1853*. New York: Henry Holt & Co., 2009.
Rayback, Robert J. *Millard Fillmore: Biography of a President*. Newtown, CT: American Political Biography Press, 1992.
Scarry, Robert J. *Millard Fillmore*. Jefferson, NC: McFarland & Co., 2010.

Film, Crime in

Films have been enjoyed by audiences for decades, and the portrayal of criminals and crime has played an important role in the film industry since its inception. Prison life, gangsters, homicide, and the police are all elements that have captivated audiences and contributed to the way in which people view both crime and the criminal justice system. Crime is either committed by individuals the audience supports during the movie, or it is committed by the villain that the audience hopes is brought to justice. Such films allow individuals to experience crime within the confines of a theater or their own homes. People enjoy being frightened, as long as there is a sense of security, which films provide. Films often sensationalize crimes and make them more elaborate than the typical crime. This may cause audiences to have

Part of a still from a famous scene in The Great Train Robbery *(1903) in which an actor shoots a gun at the camera. The moment was referenced in films throughout the 20th century.*

a skewed view of crime, but for the most part, it serves its ultimate goal of entertaining individuals and allowing them access to a different, albeit brief, situation.

What is interesting to note about crime in film is that crime films are not technically a subgenre of film. Instead, many movies that could be viewed as crime films are often classified as dramas, psychological thrillers, or comedies. This can be argued about other types of films, but crime in film has lasted as an ever-popular area and could arguably have its own subgenre within Hollywood. Another interesting point about crime in film is that crime has been portrayed in film essentially since films first became popular. For example, the 1903 silent film *The Great Train Robbery* depicted a robbery by Butch Cassidy and the Wild Bunch that had happened only a few years prior. The fact that crime films have lasted for so long indicates that individuals have always been preoccupied with crimes and criminals, and this trend shows no sign of stopping.

Dramatic Crime Films

In classic crime films, the criminals are depicted as the tough guys who grew up in hardened neighborhoods and turned to crime for a better life or because they lacked any other choice. The 1931 classic *The Public Enemy* tells the story of two friends who become involved in the gangster world at a young age, despite the main character's father being a police officer and his brother joining the armed services. Gangster movies date back to silent movies and have always been a favorite. Many well-respected actors made an enviable career starring in gangster movies, including James Cagney and Humphrey Bogart. The appeal is the characters' macho personality; typically, their crimes are less serious to be more palatable to audiences. Hollywood experienced a shift in character portrayal after the Motion Picture Production Code was enacted in 1930. Although not more thoroughly enforced until 1934, this code restricted the sexual innuendos so frequently included, as well as the drug use and levels of violence to which moviegoers had previously been exposed. Nonetheless, audiences found the movies of this time captivating and an escape from the routines of their daily lives.

Film noir is an entire subgenre of crime films that was extremely popular post–World War II and displayed a much darker side of Hollywood. *Film noir* is a French term that translates to "black film," but it largely represents American films. These films focused on crime, corruption, and overall deviant behavior and were indicative of the changes in American filmmaking. Often, audiences were left feeling uneasy or distressed about a film, or even a particular scene within the film. The crimes may confuse audiences who are trying to figure out the "whodunit" during the movie, and film noir does not always give audiences the orderly ending films typically provide.

Often, movies such as *The Godfather* (1972) and *Goodfellas* (1990) glamorize the life of a mobster, showing a life of luxury and extreme wealth, while still portraying the downfalls of those involved. Crime is portrayed as an exciting and fruitful endeavor, with the men and women wearing expensive clothes, drinking the best champagne, and smoking the best cigars. The crimes committed in films are also often elaborate and well planned. Movies such as *Die Hard* (1988) portray the criminals, in this instance Russian terrorists, as the bad guys. Others, such as *Ocean's 11* (2001), portray the criminals as the heroes of the film. The audience finds itself rooting for the "bad guys," because they are suave, smart, and committing crimes for a valid reason. Much of the movie focuses upon the planning of the crime more so than its execution, and it shows intelligent and systematic criminals.

True crime stories are presented to the American public through films as well. Often, these films are given a "Hollywood touch" in order to make the stories more appealing and sympathetic to audiences. The 1967 film *Bonnie and Clyde* depicted the true story of Clyde Barrow and Bonnie Parker and presented it in a more romantic way, highlighting the love between the two protagonists. Their death, in a shoot-out with the police, was also portrayed in a romantic way, when they embrace each other one last time before being shot multiple times and finally dying. Although they were bank robbers who were not afraid to kill, audiences were more moved by their deaths than by the crimes they committed. Part of the appeal of the characters in the movie was that the audience in the 1960s supported characters who went against the law and government, regardless of the crimes they committed. Although they were wanted criminals, the focus was more on the social statement of their actions as opposed to their misdeeds.

Another such movie is *Butch Cassidy and the Sundance Kid* (1969), which portrays the crime spree of two robbers in the late 19th century. Although both men commit murder, the audience grows a fondness for the two criminals, and the shootout scene at the end has people perhaps hoping for an alternate ending. Westerns are a great example of portrayals of crime in film, and they also encompass the role of the tough guy that is so prominent in classic films. They often portray robbers, thieves, or kidnappers, but in a time of the past that provides solid entertainment.

Other crimes that have been portrayed in film include terrorism and sex trafficking. These crimes are focused upon less than other types, but still exist. Terrorism is still a very relevant issue in America, and this fact is not lost on Hollywood producers. Portraying terrorism must be done carefully, because this is a crime that the whole nation experienced not too long ago, and the threat of it is still present. Other crimes may not be as topical or threatening and do not require the same amount of attention. As for sex trafficking, this is a crime that is committed on a global level and is not as menacing for some as other crimes. While that is not to say that these crimes are not atrocious, it simply means that because they are a global issue, they are not as threatening and focused upon.

Psychological Crime Thrillers

More recent films have focused upon American's fascination with serial killers or mass murderers. *The Silence of the Lambs* (1991) and *Se7en* (1995) both gave audiences a glimpse into the twisted and calculating minds of notorious killers who found pleasure in the crimes they committed and the hurt they inflicted. Other films, like *Henry: Portrait of a Serial Killer* (1986) and *Psycho* (1960), contain elements of true events and draw from true experiences to make the stories more terrifying and unsettling. They are highly dramatized as well, in order to attract audiences. Murder is not the only crime that is portrayed in movies, though. While it often makes for popular movies that thoroughly frighten audiences, films such as *American Gangster* (2007) and *Blow* (2001) focus upon serious drug dealers and the money and glamour associated with such life choices, until they are caught by the police and their world crashes around them. These are similar to the aforementioned gangster films, but there are slight variations among the films.

Movies such as *The Shawshank Redemption* (1994) and *Escape From Alcatraz* (1979) allow the public to view the life of criminals once they have been brought to justice and are serving their sentences in prison. What these movies do, however, is show the criminals as ordinary men who have met unfortunate circumstances. In *Escape From Alcatraz*, audiences pity the inmate who loses his painting privileges because the warden wants to make an example of him in front of the other inmates. He is a well-liked inmate and a model prisoner, and in this instance, the warden is portrayed as the evil individual who uses his authority to demoralize an inmate. *The Shawshank Redemption* tells the story of a man who is imprisoned for the murder of his wife and her lover, but his love for music and literature overshadows his role as a murderer.

His escape represents the second chance the audience hopes he will receive, although this penchant for second chances is not always experienced for criminals in the real world.

Comedic Crime and Heists

Crime comedies, such as *Fargo* (1996), add a touch of humor to a serious issue. The characters in the movie are completely ridiculous, with the main criminal inept and the main detective disturbingly pregnant. The entire scenario leaves audiences laughing and provides a different angle to a typically dark subject matter. *The Pink Panther* (1964) is another comedic display of a detective trying to solve the mystery of the theft of a rare and valuable diamond. Typically, the crime committed in these comedies is utterly outrageous, and all those involved are comical. Certainly, crime comedies will not succeed in all circumstances. Those who direct such films need to be aware of the attitude of the American public. Crimes such as rape will never be viewed as humorous. As a result, less serious crimes that typically do not harm individuals are something at which people can laugh and are more often the subject of crime comedies.

Heist movies are another popular subgenre of crime films, often filled with high-speed car chases and amazing stunts and special effects. *Reservoir Dogs* (1992), *The Italian Job* (1969, 2003), and *The Score* (2001) are such films that are typically full of intrigue and action, and while they do not always end in the success of the criminal, they still leave the audience satisfied with the journey. Such crimes are enjoyable for audiences to watch because they are not threatening and rarely occur. If cities like New York and Los Angeles had the number of high-speed chases and major bank or jewelry store break-ins as depicted in films, the police would have little to no time to focus on any other crimes that may be committed.

Women in Crime Films

Female criminals and their crimes have also been portrayed in various films. The "femme fatale" is an often-repeated character, in which the woman is mysterious, seductive, and typically leads the male character to his demise. The term translates to "deadly woman" in French, thus indicating the true nature of such a character. These characters were popular during success of film noir, and Phyllis Dietrichson in the 1944 film *Double Indemnity* is a perfect example of such a character. She seduces an insurance representative into helping her murder her husband in order to inherit the accidental death insurance policy. Women are typically secondary figures in the crimes committed throughout a movie, although films have focused on the crimes directly committed by women. One such film is *Monster* (2003), which tells the true story of female serial killer Aileen Wuornos. Female criminals are rarely the lead character in films compared to male criminals, and for some, their crimes may be more unsettling than their male counterparts. One film that portrayed females in a more lighthearted way was *Thelma and Louise* (1991). The audience follows the two women on their journey after shooting and killing a rapist and is with the characters until their demise at the end of the film.

A shootout between a man and a woman on a horse and two men on foot from a 1926 Western called The Highwaymen *featuring the actors Jack Hoxie and Helen Holmes.*

Conclusion

Hollywood and audiences alike shall see no shortage of crime films in the future. Whether they depict stories about real events, futuristic crimes, hardened gangsters, or incompetent robbers, the American public is fascinated with the life of crime and all it entails. While crimes typically are not realistically portrayed, audiences may enjoy watching events unfold that are unlikely to occur in real life. Crime in film provides an avenue of entertainment that is safe and nonthreatening. Furthermore, the crimes that are portrayed may be a reflection of the current state of the nation.

Hollywood is aware that changes in opinions and beliefs must be considered when making films. The film industry wants to make money and keep its customers satisfied. As a result, films that focus upon crime must not offend people or scare them to the point that they refuse to see any other crime films in the future. It is important to strike an appropriate balance between fictional and actual crimes in order to maintain the sense of security that is so important to the American public.

Jeanne Subjack
Sam Houston State University

See Also: 1921 to 1940 Primary Documents; Detection and Detectives; Film, Police in; Film, Punishment in; Literature and Theater, Crime in; Literature and Theater, Police in; News Media, Crime in; Television, Crime in; Television, Police in.

Further Readings
Allen, Jessica, Sonia Livingstone, and Robert Reiner. "The Changing Generic Location of Crime in Film: A Content Analysis of Film Synopses, 1945–1991." *Journal of Communication*, v.47/4 (2006).
Belton, John. *American Cinema, American Culture*, 2nd ed. New York: McGraw-Hill, 2005.
Blumer, Herbert and Phillip M. Blauser. *Movies, Delinquency, and Crime*. New York: Macmillan, 1933.
Decharne, Max. *Hardboiled Hollywood: The Origins of the Great Crime Films*. London: No Exit Press, 2005.
Leitch, Thomas. *Crime Films: Genres in American Cinema*. Cambridge: Cambridge University Press, 2002.
Rafter, Nicole Hahn. *Shots in the Mirror: Crime Films and Society*. New York: Oxford University Press, 2000.

Film, Police in

Police movies are a staple in comedy and action films throughout history. For the American male, little else beats heading to the theater for the newest film that examines the men and women in blue. Whether the movie deals with robotic supercops, old-school disciplinarians, or smart-mouthed newbies, if it involves police, it will always attract a following. Despite the fact that the genre is always able to attract an audience, there is quite a variety of police films. Representing the two ends of the spectrum, comedies and dramas explore different facets of the role of police in society along with what viewers want to see.

Comedies: *Police Academy* and *The Naked Gun*
The beginning of humorous police movies unquestionably starts with the *Keystone Kops* series that were produced between 1912 and 1917 as silent movies. These incompetent police officers—led by Fatty Arbuckle—aimed to have audiences laughing more than feeling protected. Funny police officers have never been more fully brought to screen than they were in the *Police Academy* series. Over the course of eight movies (the first in 1984), viewers follow a series of ragtag officers as they work honorably to protect the streets. The first movie focuses on a new mayor's policy that all willing recruits be accepted to the police force. As a result, a series of misfits comes into the academy unprepared and unable to conduct themselves like the rest of their classmates. In the second movie, the graduates are dropped into the worst precinct citywide and instructed to clean up conditions there. In this film, the inner battles over rank and control occur as a lieutenant goes out of his way to try to make the idea fail so he can become captain. The third movie in the franchise involves a competition between police academies when the governor announces budget cuts. Movie four introduced large audiences to the idea of citizens on patrol and the idea of average citizens partnering with police to help keep areas safe. Movies five, six, and seven all play on the traditional themes but become more focused: five and six both deal with jewel thieves, while seven sees the group head to Moscow to fight an international criminal. While the movies are intended to be more comedic than anything else,

they still present the world of policing on the silver screen. In particular, viewers are introduced to police training—from classroom settings to driving exams and apprenticeships.

Much like *Police Academy*, Leslie Nielsen developed a cult following of sorts with *The Naked Gun* series of police films beginning in 1988. Playing Frank Drebin, the rambling fool, in all three movies, Nielsen became forever remembered for his police behavior. In the original movie, Drebin and his colleagues work to uncover a plot to assassinate Queen Elizabeth II. Ultimately, it turns out that baseball player Reggie Jackson is triggered via remote control to be hypnotized and kill the queen. Thankfully, Drebin has become home plate umpire and is able to foil the plot. In all of the movies in the series, much like *Police Academy*, we are able to see how disruptive one individual can be to the overall efforts of police forces (even if in this case the disruptive individual ends up being the hero most of the time). Even though comedy is the main goal, the American public still receives truthful glimpses into the life of a police detective and the frustrations fellow officers can feel when standard protocols are not regularly followed.

Comedies: Other Interpretations
Three movies that offer different humorous interpretations of police work are *Turner & Hooch* (1989), *Kindergarten Cop* (1990), and *Paul Blart: Mall Cop* (2009). Released in the immediate aftermath of *K-9* (1989), *Turner & Hooch* focuses on the relationship between obsessive-compulsive detective Scott Turner and untrained, untamed Hooch—the dog of a murder victim. While the movie seemingly uses police work as nothing more than a necessary component of the plot, viewers are exposed to the frustrations of some police officers in towns with low crime levels. Turner is in the process of transferring to a more active police district with more opportunities to demonstrate his skills until he meets Hooch and has the opportunity to work the murder case of his owner. In *Kindergarten Cop*, undercover cop John Kimble takes over a kindergarten classroom in order to help track down a drug dealer before he is able to find his ex-wife and young son. This move highlighted the interaction between a tough-as-nails police officer who is suddenly pushed into a world dominated by small children. Again, police work is not necessarily the focus of the movie, but the dynamic of a serious police officer forced into a comical undercover assignment provides many snippets of the police frame of mind. In *Paul Blart: Mall Cop*, viewers are exposed to the nature of a different form of policing: mall security. The title character dreams of being a member of the New Jersey State Police but can never gain entrance because of his hypoglycemia. Stuck in his job at the local mall as a result, Blart does everything he can to protect and serve the customers. By the end of the movie, Blart has helped save lives and prevented major theft in the mall and is offered a job with the local police, which he promptly turns down to continue with the job he's grown to appreciate. Again, this movie is not based on the police, per se, but it does raise questions regarding different types of security forces in our country and how they interact.

Comedies: Partnerships
Other comedy police movies do hit at other interesting points of consideration related to the modern police force in America. The *Rush Hour* series, beginning in 1998, shows the importance of partnerships and how officers rely on each other. The movies demonstrate the potential difficulties when differing levels of law enforcement are asked to cooperate. In the first movie, the Chinese consulate decides the Federal Bureau of Investigation (FBI) is likely to be unsuccessful in helping them find a kidnapped diplomat's daughter so they hire a Hong Kong inspector and a street-smart, cocky Los Angeles police officer. The two struggle to get along and are ultimately successful. Their relationship shows the difficulties partners face in the high-stress world of policing.

An earlier film, *Beverly Hills Cop* (1984), follows a similar path as a young, reckless detective from Detroit comes to California to help find his best friend's murderer. While he is talented, the young detective has to overcome his own upbringing to show he can do the job. The movie really demonstrates the difficulties for police officers when there is a personal relationship to a victim and they want to help solve the crime. In this movie, the detective has to take personal vacation time to conduct an investigation because his superiors believe he is too closely related to the victim to be objective. *Lethal Weapon* (1987) follows much the same story line as a serious, middle-aged cop trying to make a career is partnered with a young, eager rookie partner out to rule the world.

As a final example, the movie *Blue Streak* (1999) involves a criminal going undercover as a police officer to locate stolen jewels that had been confiscated that he wants back. Comically, he attempts to act like a burglary detective while his unknowing partner continually applauds his unconventional methods. In the end, we see how professional police work (which the partner believes in) can be supplemented by street-smart individuals, even if they are not actually police.

Dramas: Corruption

As would be expected, while comedic movies tend to poke fun at police stereotypes and issues, dramatic movies instead exploit the potential for corruption or present action-packed scenarios and car chases that pit the stereotypical cops against the robbers. The 1930s police movies, particularly ones examining classic gangster portrayals and private detective films, present a unique debate when it comes to corruption. First, the movies can demonstrate police ineptitude, but more importantly, they show how the individual police officer oftentimes needs to break rules in order to protect society from the organization—which can be seen as corrupt or inept, depending on the particular film. This change in influence takes viewers from seeing corrupt cops to instead witnessing heroic individuals fighting against an overly bureaucratized system.

A teenage boy reads posters outside a theater advertising a double feature, including a Western with a law enforcement theme called Law for Tombstone, *in 1939. Films featuring the exploits of western sheriffs and both urban and rural police have been drawing large audiences since the days of the silent* Keystone Kops *films, which appeared between 1912 and 1917.*

Bad Lieutenant: Port of Call New Orleans (2009) follows a New Orleans police sergeant who sees his world spiral out of control in the Hurricane Katrina aftermath. After saving a prisoner, hurting his back, becoming a lieutenant, and becoming addicted to both painkillers and cocaine, he is asked to run the investigation into a family's murder. He begins dating a prostitute, losing money gambling, and stealing police property. To help get out of debt, he starts assisting drug dealers. By the end, the murder has gone unsolved and he has gone from bad to worse—showing everything potentially negative about police officers.

Likewise, *Brooklyn's Finest* (2010) shows how corruption can occur as three police officers—Tango, an undercover gang member; Sal, who is willing to do anything to get a bigger house for his family; and Eddie, who is about to retire from the force—work to do their jobs while not letting their personal lives suffer. *Training Day* (2001), on the other hand, does not directly deal with corruption but, instead, with questionable police tactics. The movie focuses on a Los Angeles Police Department detective who works narcotics and is well-known for his willingness to open fire, beat up suspects, and use any means necessary to rid the streets of drugs. As a rookie is introduced to his methods, viewers are left to wonder whether the ends justify the means. Even one of America's all-time favorite police movies—*Dirty Harry* (1971)—shows how very dirty rogues can also be the best police officers on the force.

Dramas: Heroism

The opposite of corruption appears in *Serpico*, a 1970s biopic of a New York detective whose anticorruption efforts led to the creation of the Knapp Commission. After learning early on that the plainclothes cops make more in graft than salary, he refuses to join in the corruption. As a result, he cannot find a partner and is routinely put in harm's way. He ends up shot by a drug dealer when his partner refuses to defend or support him. *Serpico* shows the battle police face when surrounded by corruption and graft. *L.A. Confidential* (1990) also shows the promise of police officers through the lens of 1930s Hollywood. This film is good, in particular, at showing the battle between good and evil that police face. In the film, officers are trying to do what they believe is right while still succumbing at times to the constant distractions around them.

In *Speed* (1994), a police officer on a bus rigged to explode if it drops below 50 miles per hour does everything in his power to get everyone off the bus safely. While more focused on action than police, there are glimpses of strategy and decision making throughout. Likewise, *Die Hard* (1988) puts a cop in the position to be a hero. A group of thieves, acting as terrorists, take over the office building where a cop is attending his wife's Christmas party. Their goal is to steal $600 million in bonds from vaults within the building. The movie focuses on the lone cop's efforts to take down all 12 terrorists on his own.

RoboCop (1987) presents a different type of hero cop. After being killed by a criminal, Alex Murphy returns as a crime-fighting robot owned by the company running Detroit at the time. The movie traces the steel-shelled RoboCop as he attempts to clean the city of crime while also seeking revenge on the man who killed him. While futuristic, the movie does raise many points related to police force and revenge. *The Border* (1982) focuses on border patrol agents and presents an agent who feels like he has no meaning in his job. That is, until he is given the opportunity to save a child sold on the black market, if he is willing to all but sell out in the process. Surrounded by corruption, the border agent works through what he really views his moral purpose to be. *Cop Land* (1997) does much the same when examining the life of a New Jersey sheriff who grew up dreaming of a job with the New York City Police Department. Once he learns how corrupt the police can be, however, he is faced with determining the best way to correct their misdoings.

Dramas: Realism

Bullitt (1968) is one of the more realistic police movies created as it traces a cop trying to get payback for a witness who was killed under his protection. The movie is packed full of car chases and demonstrates realistic criminal procedures throughout, and also ties in some of the political constraints that officers must worry about as they attempt to do their jobs.

Another film considered to be on point in how it represents police work is *The French Connection* (1971), which traces how officers work to foil the largest drug shipment ever attempted. It has been routinely heralded as the most realistic police movie to ever be made. The film *Heat* (1995) encapsulates a regular police film theme: a tortured cop and the criminal he never seems to be able to catch. Throughout the film, viewers feel sympathy for both parties as they continually attempt to stay one step in front of the other.

Conclusion

Overall, all of these movies come together in an attempt to entertain the viewing public through plot lines that focus on police officers and police work. Ultimately, none are spot-on in terms of their depictions. Numerous police documentaries have emerged over time, yet many are written with a particular purpose in mind. For example, the documentary *The Thin Blue Line* (1988), while well made, uses the screen to show how the police work together to frame someone as a cop killer to ease public sentiments. Just like any other element of bureaucracy, it is easier for the public to notice and fixate on the negatives with police officers. Movies that routinely praise their work are generally not made because excellence is expected. Instead, police movies typically involve corruption and ineptitude, and one can only hope that the general public is aware enough to remember that these films are created to entertain, not to inform.

William J. Miller
Southeast Missouri State University

See Also: Detection and Detectives; Film, Crime in; Film, Punishment in; Literature and Theater, Crime in; Literature and Theater, Police in; News Media, Crime in; News Media, Police in; Television, Crime in; Television, Police in.

Further Readings

Horzberg, Bob. *FBI and the Movies: A History of the Bureau on Screen and Behind the Scenes in Hollywood*. Jefferson, NC: McFarland & Co., 2006.

Leitch, Thomas M. *Crime Films*. New York: Cambridge University Press, 2002.

Lott, M. Ray. *Police on Screen: Hollywood Cops, Detectives, Marshals and Rangers*. Jefferson, NC: McFarland & Co., 2006.

Film, Punishment in

Cinematic images of the formal criminal law and punishment for its transgression provide insight into the web of cultural and social practices that shape and maintain boundaries between "criminals" and the rest of society. The prison movie is arguably quintessential and is certainly one of the most accessible modes through which we imagine, understand, and construct myths about the nature of discipline in contemporary society. Consequently, this article focuses on the canonical cinematic representation of discipline: American prison movies from the early 20th century to the mid-1950s, when cinema began to be displaced by television (which took over, until fairly recently, as the dominant form through which myths and assumptions about discipline have been circulated).

On one level, prison films reveal some of the brutalities of incarceration and elicit empathy for criminalized men and women. On another, they offer audiences a form of escapism by inviting identification with outlaws, titillation through contradictory modalities of repressed sexuality and nonnormative eroticism, a rare opportunity to enact a certain kind of surveillance, and a venue through which to problematize gender roles. On another level still, they are a conduit to explore long-standing philosophical questions about the human condition. Punishment, and confinement within prisons especially, works as a metaphor for social boundaries and the danger and possibilities that emerge when they are broken, irritated, or even dismantled.

Much scholarly attention to cinematic renderings of the disciplinary prison has engaged in content analysis and measured the veracity of the depictions of crime and "criminals." Fewer accounts grapple with the role of punishment and prison in films as a vehicle for interrogating broader social themes such as inclusion and exclusion, workers' rights, women's emancipation, slavery, and other modes of systemic racism. Both methods of inquiry can be explored through a discussion of the prison film's generic conventions, how these films have shifted over time, and the ways in which these conventions can be better understood when approached through the lens of social history.

Early Cinema and Pre-Code Movies

Many formative American prison films were short melodramatic films or documentaries that emerged during cinema's "silent" era (a misnomer, as sounds, whether music, live narration, or other effects, had, since the media's emergence, accompanied film screenings). As a new art form, cinema took up many of the questions raised in the novels, plays, and paintings of the time; however, by 1915, cinema had far surpassed these other art forms in accessibility, appeal, and popularity. Moreover, unlike these other artifacts, film was believed and was deployed as a newspaper with moving images. For instance, the films of Edwin Porter were marketed by the Edison Company as authentic live documentation of key moments in history. *The Execution of Czolgosz ith Panorama of Auburn Prison* (1901) is actual footage of the prison where the electric chair was invented and first used to kill a prisoner. However, the execution itself is a re-enactment. Theatricality aside, many of the prison films released in the early 20th century revealed anxieties over national identity; child labor and unions; attitudes about ethnicity, class, and gender; racial conflicts; and the spread of diseases. The prison institution was sometimes used as a narrative path to such questions.

Some denounced the exploitation of prisoners through work houses, as in *Convict's Parole* (1912, directed by Edwin Porter); others called for humane treatment of prisoners or suggested the transformative potential of treating prisoners with care and humane kindness, as in *Intolerance* (1916, D. W. Griffith). Usually, films told the story of someone erroneously or wrongfully charged and convicted, as in *Within the Law* (1923, Frank Lloyd). Indeed, characters' factual and moral innocence became a conduit to argue against the existence of capital punishment. *The People v. John Doe* (1916, Lois Weber), for instance, tells a story of corrupt police using police brutality to force a young, unemployed father to confess to a murder that he did not commit. The man is found guilty, but while he is on death row, a young lawyer who is convinced of his innocence collects new evidence. While John Doe is ultimately cleared of all charges, the film expresses a deep disquiet about state executions. In many of the prison movies of the era, when the protagonist has actually committed an offense, the criminal act was usually located within broader structures of inequality and poverty and often (in the fictional accounts, in any event) bookended by acts of bravery, extreme generosity, and kindness toward strangers, as in *The Ex Convict* (1905, Edwin Porter) and *Capital Punishment* (1925, James Hogan).

However, other iterations of the prison film that were released around the same time exhibited a contradictory mix of classical and positivist criminology's assumptions about criminal behavior and its punishment: On the one hand, crime was a result of rational choice by individuals who commit crime for hedonistic, thrill-seeking, or other self-interested motivations. Consequently, the purpose of punishment was to prevent further crime through deterrence. The documentary *Life in a Western Penitentiary* (1913) used gruesome images of prison life as a fear-generating tactic directed at younger male audiences. On the other hand, positivists believed that individuals could be born with criminal drives and thus crime was the result of biology (often race), atavisms, and physical or moral degeneration. Punishment, as a result, was best served when it was a means of treatment and reform. For instance, *Exposure of the Delaware Whipping Post* (1914) promoted the use of lashing as a stepping-stone to rehabilitation. In the 1920s, an era characterized by conservatism and repression, prison films tended toward the comedic shorts, such as Buster Keaton's *Convict 13* (1920, Buster Keaton and Edward Cline) and Laurel and Hardy's *Hoose-Gow* (1929, James Parrott).

The Production Code Era

Despite these earlier configurations, only in the 1930s did the prison movie—as a genre—develop and solidify its conventions, elements, and rules (with recurring symbols, stock characters, narrative structures, and similar settings) through "social problem" films. The release of *The Big House* (1930, George Hill), *Numbered Men* (1930, Mervyn LeRoy), and *I Am a Fugitive From a Chain Gang* (1932, Mervyn LeRoy) establish the genre's codes, conventions, and major themes. Produced at a time when Americans were still feeling the full effects of the Great Depression, these prison films reflect the political consciousness, the social purpose, and the overarching ethos of reform. During the 1930s, the incarceration rate in America was 137 per 100,000 (up from 79 before the economic crisis in 1929); of those people sentenced, there was (and continues to be) a gross overrepresentation of African American men (who often were targeted as vagrants during the Great Migration to the industrial cities of the north and the midwest).

Nevertheless, the gallery of characters in prison films tended to be white and to include the middle-class protagonist (a "born" but often unassuming hero); the hardened and often brutalizing lifer; the "square John" who does his time and minds his own business; the weakling, victimized by guards or fellow prisoners; the informer; the ineffectual but often well-meaning/tough-but-fair warden; the nasty guard who exacts arbitrary punishment; and the "kid" for whom the protagonist takes on a fatherly role. Key narrative moments include the development of friendship and loyalty between men and especially the (white) protagonist and his more weathered "buddy" (in more recent incarnations, usually an African American), the buildup of tension in a repressive space, and the prison riot or escape. Prison films also contain a number of formulaic scenes such as the "new fish's" introduction to the prison via guard or fellow prisoner, shivs passed under the dining hall table, cockroach races, and rumbles during recreation time. The overall aim is to engage the good/bad binary and emphasize the humanity of the prisoners juxtaposed against the inherent oppressive nature of institutionalized punishment rather than of the men behind bars or the (often justifiable or excusable) crimes they committed.

In social problem films, larger social conflicts are embedded and are interrogated through individual conflicts between characters, often who occupy different social locations based on class and sometimes race. Protagonists are often morally innocent, or at least ambiguously so, such as in *20,000 Years in Sing Sing* (1932, Michael Curtiz), in which a hardened criminal takes the rap for murder to protect his girlfriend and is ultimately sentenced to death. As a result, many prison films of the 1930s can be read as an explicit and implicit critique of institutionalized punishment. *I Am a Fugitive From a Chain Gang* (1932) is an insightful study that suggests the possibility of mutually constitutive relationship between popular images and public perceptions of acceptable modes of discipline. The story was based on actual facts; the film exposed the conditions on the chain gang, and is widely believed to have played an instrumental role in the mobilization and mass public upheaval and protest for their eradication in 1937.

The depiction of sympathetic outlaws was in direct contravention of the Motion Picture Producers and Distributors of America's (MPPDA) Production Code adopted in 1930. The code stipulated that all films receive a certificate of approval from its Studio Relations Office (SRO); it also included a proviso that "sympathy of the audience shall never be thrown to the side of crime, wrongdoing, evil, or sin." As a result, in to comply with code regulations, the protagonist of prison movies was meant to "get it" by the end of the film—whether by execution or by serving a life sentence to term. In practice, the narrative conventions developed through allusion, allegory, and double entendre or through characters whose motivations did not meet the code's standard of propriety but who were by any

This photoprint of a scene from a motion picture called The Lost New Year's Dinner, *copyrighted by the Edison Company around 1908, is part of an early prison-themed movie and shows a man and woman sharing a meal together inside a jail cell.*

account moral, or at the very least sympathetic, beings. Consequently, the depiction and critique of institutionalized punishment was in direct contravention of the code. In 1934, amendments were made to the Production Code's enforcement structure. According to a familiar narrative around Hollywood and censorship, a confluence of stakeholders in the industry—economic, political, and religious—pressured the code's drafters to vigilantly regulate the content of films in order to protect vulnerable groups (including women, children, and the destitute) from the harms of exposure to morally questionable images. Prison films released while the code was in full effect often included redemption stories—though, as is most evident with the distaff version of prison films, that redemption comes through the love of a "good man," not through institutionalized punishment.

Women in Prison Movies

With World War II mobilization, the United States mounted mass-scale propaganda campaigns that urged women to take paid employment in war industries and replace the thousands of men (and some women) who were leaving to fight. Some took industrial work, but those who were already earning wages in low-paid service sector jobs as waitresses and domestic workers could find higher-paid jobs (hitherto held by men), earn sufficient wages to be self-sufficient, and aspire to new modes of social, cultural, and physical mobility. At the same time, new configurations of the "dangerous" seductive woman—one who lured soldiers through sexual wiles into spilling military secrets—emerged in popular media. "Victory girls" and prostitutes became special targets of punishment, and some jurisdictions built special detention facilities for women who committed these "moral" offenses. These themes are foregrounded in films that take place in women's prisons.

Women in prison (WIP) films are most often subsumed within the more popular and more widely recognized prison film genre. While many of the conventions are reflected and reproduced in WIP movies, to reduce WIP films to a female version of prison films ignores the specificities of the WIP subgenre. By using women characters, WIP films can be read as critiquing certain hegemonic forms of masculinity and normative heterosexuality, as well as the total prison institution itself.

WIP films of the 1930s to the 1950s were primarily popular melodramas or "women's films" with a backlight of social protest about the conditions of women's prisons. They followed a (redomestication/redemption story—and by extension, the recuperation of the threat posed by independent women—about a young, attractive, often naïve woman who moves from being a criminal subject to a love interest and eventually becomes "big house angel" ready for marriage upon release. There are cause-and-effect connections ("good" girl is innocent); loose ends are tied ("good" girl is redeemed); and the main characters form a romantic heterosexual union. Despite variations in the cinematic vocabulary, the protagonist has usually been framed, often by her gangster or otherwise unsavory boyfriend, as in *Lady Gangster* (1943, Florian Roberts), or is wrongfully convicted, as in *Women Without Names* (1940, Robert Flory). Alternatively, a sympathetic working-class protagonist is sent to jail for a minor offense such as vagrancy, as in *Condemned Women*, (1938, Lew Landers). Upon arrival at the women's prison, she is confused, overwhelmed, and disembodied. She may discover that she's pregnant or unable to find a guardian for her child while she completes her sentence. She is often forced to hand her baby over to child and family authorities. In another cycle, she discovers corruption within the institution, as in *Caged* (1950, John Cromwell), is subjected to cruelty by a matron or another prisoner when she tries to speak up, and becomes increasingly hardened to her surroundings. More often than not, her bitterness subsides through the love or kindness of a good man, whether a chaplain or a minister who wants to save her soul, a doctor who teaches her life lessons, a reporter trying to expose corruption and cruelty within the prison, or a lawyer/district attorney convinced of her factual or moral innocence. Examples of this narrative can be found in *Ladies They Talk About* (1933, William Keighley and Howard Bretherton), *Acquitted* (1929, Frank Strayer), and *Girls of the Big House* (1945, George Archainbaud).

Post-1950s Prison Film

While our discussion ends in the mid-1950s, suffice it to say that by the 1960s, audiences were less inclined to expect that prison films would tell a story about tough though sympathetic individuals whose experiences in oppressive and hostile environments generate the conditions in which they redeem themselves for past wrongs.

The ethos of the sixties and seventies was one of uncertainty and of breakdown of discipline and social order on the one hand, and celebration of possibilities on the other. The general anxiety was in part due to dramatic changes and political upheaval from social movements (the new left, prisoners' rights, second-wave feminism, civil rights, gay and lesbian rights, environmentalism), the rise of postmodern and post-structural theories in the academy (and their challenge to entrenched understandings of authority and truth), the Vietnam War, the Watergate scandal, and a debilitating economic recession. Further, given the decreased popularity of cinema generally, filmmakers and production companies shifted toward narratives—of sexual exploitation such as *Caged Heat* (1974, Jonathan Demme) and escape and revenge movies such as *Escape From Alcatraz* (1979, Don Seigel)—and visual structures, especially television and direct to video programs that attracted a new audience base and ultimately raised questions of a different nature around the concept of crime and the function of punishment in contemporary society.

Suzanne Bouclin
University of Ottawa

See Also: Alcatraz Island Prison; Film, Crime in; Literature and Theater, Crime in; Literature and Theater, Punishment in; Punishment Within Prison; Television, Crime in; Television, Punishment in; Women in Prison.

Further Readings
Alber, Jan. "Bodies Behind Bars: The Disciplining of the Prisoner's Body in British and American Prison Movies." In *In the Grip of the Law: Trials, Prisons, and the Space Between*, M. Fludernik and G. Olson, eds. New York: P. Lang, 2004.
Bouclin, Suzanne. "'Women in Prison' Movies as Feminist Jurisprudence." *Canadian Journal of Women and the Law*, v.21/8 (2009).
Doherty, Thomas. "Criminal Codes: Gangsters Unbound, Felons in Custody." In *Pre-Code Hollywood: Sex, Immorality, and Insurrection in American Cinema 1930–1934*. New York: Columbia University Press, 1999.
Gonthier, David. *American Prison Film Since 1930: From* The Big House *to* The Shawshank Redemption. Lewiston, NY: Edwin Mellen Press, 2006.
Jarvis, Brian. *Cruel and Unusual: Punishment and U.S. Culture*. London: Pluto Press, 2004.
Mayne, Judith. "Caged and Framed: The Women in Prison Film." In *Framed: Lesbians, Feminists and Media Culture*. Minneapolis: University of Minnesota Press, 2000.
Rafter, Nicole. *Shots in the Mirror: Crime Films and Society*. New York: Oxford University Press, 2006.
Wlodarz, Joe. "Maximum Insecurity: Genre Trouble and Closet Erotics In and Out of HBO's *Oz*." *Camera Obscura*, v.58 (2005).

Fingerprinting

The practice of fingerprinting has been utilized for centuries as a source of identification that ranges in use from business transactions to the identification of human remains. Since as early as the 14th century, fingerprints have been used to identify individuals based on the accepted idea that no two are alike. In relatively recent years, fingerprinting has been one of the main sources used in the identification of criminals and the recording of criminal histories. The reason fingerprinting has become such a popular form of identification stems from the fact that fingerprints do not change over time, as physical characteristics do. Some scholars and practitioners say this practice has surpassed other human identification systems such as DNA. Fingerprinting has evolved over time to the practice it is today. Techniques will continue to change and grow to ensure the validity and reliability of fingerprinting and the use of this sound forensic tool by the police and court system.

Origin and History of Fingerprinting
Although the use of fingerprinting has become mainstream, the practice has not always been widely accepted. Before the use of fingerprinting for identification purposes arose, the Bertillon

FBI analysts individually examining fingerprint records stored in hundreds of numbered file cabinets in a federal armory during World War II. The FBI uses 10 points of comparison to make a positive identification of a fingerprint, but the traditional number of points used to determine whether the prints are indeed from the same person is generally 12, as established by Edmond Locard. The court system has not yet established a definitive number of points that must be used to determine identification of a fingerprint.

system was used. This system measured and recorded the dimensions of certain bony parts of the body. It was believed that this formula matched only one person and would not change over his/her lifetime. The use of the system was discontinued circa 1900 with the discovery of two individuals who had the same measurements. Will West was sentenced to the U.S. Penitentiary in Leavenworth, Kansas, where it was found that there already existed a prisoner, William West, with identical measurements. Therefore, the Bertillon system was suspended, and fingerprints were substituted for identification purposes.

The origins of fingerprinting are difficult to pinpoint directly; however, prehistoric pictures were discovered in Nova Scotia with detailed writings of ridge patterns of fingerprints. In ancient Babylon, fingerprints were discovered on clay tablets that were used for business transactions, showing that the ancient civilization viewed the prints as an identifying characteristic. Ancient Chinese artifacts show thumbprints on clay seals used for various business and personal purposes. In 14th-century Persia, various official government documents were found to have fingerprints and impressions. A government official of the time, who was also a doctor, noticed that no two fingerprints were alike. This was the first time it was recorded that individuals have distinctive and unique fingerprints.

From this discovery in the 14th century, the idea of unique fingerprints has been studied throughout history. Marcello Malpighi noted in his 1666 treatise that there appeared to be ridges, spirals, and loops in different configurations in fingerprints. He did not realize at the time that this could be a tool used for identification purposes but did discover a layer of skin that was 1.8 millimeters thick. This layer of skin was later named the Malpighi layer. John Evangelist Purkinji published his thesis, stating that there were nine different fingerprint patterns that existed. However, he too did not hypothesize that these patterns could be used for identification of individuals. Nevertheless, England started using fingerprints for identification in 1858 with the aid of Sir William Hershel. In India, Hershel used fingerprints on native contracts, requiring that the individual put his/her palm/handprints on the back of every contract. Based on their superstitious beliefs, this practice scared the natives, preventing them from going back on their word. This method was also used to prevent pension fraud by assembling files of pensioners' fingerprints. From his work with these impressions, Hershel noticed that the impression could be used to prove or disprove identities. There was no scientific backing for this practice at the time.

In 1880, Henry Faulds studied skin furrows (grooved or deep wrinkles) that were found on prehistoric pottery. From his study, he devised a method for classification for fingerprints and realized their identification power. His classification system was published in *Nautre* (Nature), where it explained how fingerprints could be used in identification and the use of printer's ink. He was credited with the first fingerprint identification of a greasy fingerprint left on an alcohol bottle.

Faulds passed his classification system on to Charles Darwin for continuation; Darwin in turn passed on the system to his cousin Sir Francis Galton for prolongation. Galton published his own book *Fingerprints* showing the first classification system where the main focus was on determining heredity and racial background. His book scientifically proves that both Herschel and Faulds were correct. Fingerprints do not change over time, and no two individuals have the same fingerprints, the odds of which he found was 1 in 64 billion. In his classification system, which is still used today, Galton described characteristics by which prints can be compared. These characteristics were called Galton ridges at the time and were described as line-like structures on the skin of the palm side of the finger past the last joint (now called minutia).

In the United States, Gilbert Thompson was the first individual to use his own fingerprints to prevent forgery during his geological survey of New Mexico. The first use of fingerprinting as an identification tool in criminal matters was by Juan Vucetich in 1892. Vucetich had been filing fingerprints following the teachings of Francis Galton. When a bloody fingerprint was found at a murder scene, Vucetich used the fingerprint to identify the killer. From there, Henry P. DeForrest pioneered the widespread use of fingerprinting as an identification resource in the United States.

In 1902, the first systematic use of fingerprints in the United States by the New York Civil Service Commission for testing was implemented. A year later, the New York state prison system began the first systematic use of fingerprints for criminals. A student of Bertillon, Edmond Locard, established the first rules for the minimum number of minutia (Galton ridges) necessary for identification: A minimum of 12 points must be established between the known and unknown prints in order to make an accurate identification. The use of fingerprints for identification purposes had already become mainstream in the United States, however, as evidenced by their inclusion in the identification of a murderer in the 1883 book *Life on the Mississippi* by Mark Twain (Samuel L. Clemens).

Collection and Comparison

Traditionally, fingerprints are detected using powder that sticks to the sweat, oils, and grease left after an individual touches an object. A technician, using a light hand, spins a fingerprinting brush that has been dipped in powder over the area in question. When a latent (unseen) print appears, the technician uses lifting tape to lift the print and place it on a print card for analysis. Collecting fingerprints has evolved over the years to involve chemical agents, such as ninhydrin and a cyanoacrylate mixture. Ninhydrin is a small particle reagent that reacts with the amino acids that are secreted from pores in the fingertips, turning the print a light purple/pink color. This chemical is mainly used on porous materials, such as paper or money. A cyanoacrylate mixture is used to fume an object for latent prints. Cyanoacrylate (superglue) is mixed with baking soda and sawdust to create a superglue mist that covers the object, gluing any prints that may be on said object and protecting them from disruption. From here, the technician can powder the print to lift and analyze.

The comparison of fingerprints is considered an art form mastered through practice and patience. To become a certified fingerprint technician, extensive training is required along with career-long maintenance training. To start a comparison between a known print and an unknown print (fingerprint lifted from an area of interest), an individual compares the cores. There are three main core patterns: arch, loop, and whorl. The arch pattern originates from one side of the print and moves laterally into a point. From here, the pattern falls back to the opposite side of the print, giving the pattern a parabolic shape. The arch pattern has two separate styles: plain or tented. The tented arch pattern differs from the plain arch by having an angle or upthrust within the arch. The loop pattern consists of the majority of ridges entering at one side of the print, recurving, and exiting on the same side as they entered. Two subgroups are associated with the loop pattern: ulnar and radial. The distinction between these subgroups can be made by determining the side in which the loop enters and exits the print (ulnar or radial side).

The last fingerprint pattern is the whorl pattern, consisting of four subpatterns: plain, accidental, double loop whorl, and central pocket loop whorl. The whorl pattern, or plain whorl, generally is described as looking like a bull's-eye starting in the middle of the print and making concentric circles that curve around themselves, moving outward. Whorl patterns generally contain two deltas (collections of ridges that form a triangular shape). The accidental whorl pattern contains two different types of patterns but excludes the plain arch pattern. The double loop whorl pattern is distinctive because it contains two loop formations and two deltas. The last subpattern, the central pocket loop whorl, must contain one recurring ridge within the pattern.

Once the fingerprint technician has determined the central core pattern, minutia points are determined to match the prints to one another. There exist a number of different minutia points, but the most widely used are as follows: delta, ending, island, bifurcation, enclosure, dot, bridge, double-bifurcation, trifurcation, spur, and crossover. As described above, a delta is a collection of ridges that form a triangular shape, as in the triangular shape of soil deposits when several rivers collide. An ending ridge steps abruptly and never picks up again. An island ridge has a starting and stopping point (most ridges do not have definitive beginnings and endings). A bifurcation involves a single ridge that divides into two ridges. An enclosure involves the splitting of a ridge into two ridges that eventually come back together. A dot is a short ridge that does not continue in any direction, with the appearance of a small dot. A bridge involves two ridges that are connected by another ridge, as in a bridge connecting two streets. A double bifurcation point involves a single ridge that divides into two ridges, then divides once again. In relation, a trifurcation point is where a double bifurcation divides a third time. A spur is a short ridge that extends off a longer ridge, as in a spur to a highway in relation to roads. A crossover point is where two ridges cross over one another.

Technicians use these minutia to compare known and unknown prints to one another to determine if they are from the same individual. Comparisons are made by picking a point on the known print to start from and finding the same point on the unknown or lifted print. From this point, another point is found on the known print and marked. The technician counts the ridges from the new point to the original point. He/she uses this number to determine if the second point of comparison exists on the unknown print as well. The technician continues to determine points of comparison and matches them to the unknown print to determine if the two prints are from the same individual. The traditional number of points used to determine whether the prints are indeed from the same person is generally 12, as established by Edmond Locard. However, the Federal Bureau of Investigation (FBI) uses 10 points of comparison to make a positive identification. There is no definitive number of points that must be used to determine identification of a fingerprint established by the court system as yet.

Flaws and Mistaken Identification

The admissibility of fingerprints as scientific/forensic evidence was debated within the court system for a number of years. However, in 1993, the Supreme Court case *Daubert v. Merrill Dow Pharmaceutical* determined the admissibility of scientific evidence in the court system by establishing five characteristics. The theory or technique must (1) have been or be able to be tested, (2) been subjected to peer review or publication, (3) have in existence standards controlling the use of the technique as well as maintenance, (4) have general acceptance in the scientific community, and (5) have a known potential rate of error.

Despite the best efforts of fingerprint technicians and the advancement of technology, mistakes can be made in fingerprint comparisons. Many factors can contribute to these errors, such as distortion, small segments, or the absence of a core. Sometimes when a print is lifted from an object, it is distorted because of the angle at which the print was positioned on the object. If distortion occurs, it is hard to accurately match minutia points because they may be missing or stretched. If only a small segment of the print exists or the core is missing, orientation of the print is almost impossible to determine.

Because of these distortions and errors, technicians and software used to compare fingerprints statewide and nationally can make mistaken identifications. There have been several cases involving the mistaken identification of individuals with the use of fingerprints. For instance, in 2004, Brandon Mayfield was originally identified as a participant in the Madrid bombings by a latent print found on the bomb. It was later discovered that a misidentification of fingerprints led to his detainment in relation to the bombings. In 1998, Stephan Cowans was convicted of the attempted murder of a police officer while fleeing a robbery in Massachusetts. He was acquitted six years later with DNA evidence that showed the fingerprint comparison to be flawed. In 1997, the fingerprint of Shirley McKie (an American citizen) was found at a murder scene in Scotland. Experts in the United States compared the prints found to McKie's and testified on her behalf, and she was cleared of suspicion.

Melissa J. Mauck
Sam Houston State University

See Also: 1921 to 1940 Primary Documents 1941 to 1960 Primary Documents; Bertillon System; Crime Scene Investigation; Federal Bureau of Investigation; Forensic Science; Technology, Police; Trials.

Further Readings
Clark, John D. "ACE-V: Is it Scientifically Reliable and Accurate?" http://www.latent-prints.com/ACE-V.htm (Accessed December 2010).
Cole, Simon A. *Suspect Identities: A History of Fingerprinting and Criminal Identification.* Cambridge, MA: Harvard University Press, 2001.
Maltoni, M. and P. Jain. *Handbook of Fingerprint Recognition.* New York: Springer, 2003.
National Library of Medicine. "Biographies: Juan Vucetich." http://www.nlm.nih.gov/visibleproofs/galleries/biographies/vucetich.html (Accessed December 2010).
Pankanti, Sharath, Salil Prabhakar, and Anil Jain. "On the Individuality of Fingerprints." *IEEE Transaction on Pattern Analysis and Machine Intelligence,* v.24/8 (2002).
Wayman, James L. "Daubert Hearing on Fingerprints." National Biometrics Test Center: San Jose State University. http://www.engr.sjsu.edu/biometrics/publications_daubert.html (Accessed December 2010).

Fish and Game Laws

The purpose of fish and game laws is to protect wildlife resources and habitats. Among the principal objectives of these laws are the protection and replenishment of endangered and threatened species, regulation of public harvest of fish and game species, conservation of migratory wildlife, protection of habitat and fisheries, and containment and eradication of invasive species. The earliest laws were often antipoaching initiatives at the local or state levels, designed to punish trespassers who took fish or game from private lands without permission or from public lands out of season or in excessive quantities. Formalized bodies of fish and game laws in the United States originated from justified public concern that wildlife resources and habitats faced increasing levels of strain from overuse. By the 19th century, in many areas of the United States, wildlife and wildlife habitats were threatened with eradication because of overuse occurring in part because of lack of governmental intervention such as the establishment of codified regulations. As the U.S. conservation movement became more prevalent, so did the number and scope of laws designed to safeguard American wildlife and many of its habitat areas.

National Regulation
While fish and game laws have existed in some form at the local and state levels almost since the nation's inception, substantive formal federal involvement with wildlife regulations can be traced to the 19th century. In 1869, Congress designated Alaska's Pribilof Islands as a national wildlife reservation with the objective of protecting fur seals. Two years later, congressional legislation created the U.S. Commission on Fish and Fisheries, the first federal agency responsible for wildlife resources. One of the principal purposes of the creation of Yellowstone National Park, the first national park in the United States, by act of Congress in 1872, was the protection of wildlife within its boundaries. Congress passed the U.S. Forest Reserves Act in 1891, granting the president executive authority to establish and maintain forest reserves on federal lands.

By the 20th century, the U.S. government had assumed an active role in the creation and maintenance of federally protected parks and wildlife refuges and in the creation of federal laws related to fish and game resources. The Lacey Act of 1900 was the first federal law designed to protect wildlife resources. It prohibited the interstate shipment of illegally obtained game and was expanded in 1935 to ban international trade in illegally taken wildlife. A spate of new federal legislation was implemented in the 1970s and 1980s, perhaps the best-known example of which is the Endangered Species Conservation Act, which banned commercial trade in all species threatened with extinction.

State Regulation
In the United States, most implementation and enforcement of fish and game laws occurs at the state level. Although significant coordination exists between federal and state efforts to protect and regulate wildlife, individual states assume most of the responsibility for preserving and regulating the use of fish and game within their jurisdiction. For example, the issuance of permits to hunt, trap, or fish recreationally and the limit concerning how many fish or game animals can be taken in a particular season is regulated primarily at the state level. Most wildlife officers who enforce fish and game laws are state officers who often work in conjunction with federal wildlife and environmental authorities as well as local law enforcement. Interjurisdictional cooperation in the establishment and enforcement of fish and game laws is customary practice and is necessary to, among other things, help address manpower shortages in fish and game law enforcement. For example, the U.S. Fish and Wildlife Service has only around 200 special agents and little more than 100 wildlife inspectors at its disposal nationally, making active cooperation with state and local authorities essential.

A U.S. Fish and Wildlife Service staffer holding a family of formerly endangered Aleutian cackling geese in Alaska in 2008. Successful conservation efforts led to the geese being taken off the endangered species list in 2001.

Advocacy groups have historically played an important role in helping to implement and monitor fish and game laws. From the founding of the Audubon Society in 1885 and the Sierra Club in 1892 up to the present day, many nongovernmental organizations (NGOs) and private citizens have worked, often in conjunction with government wildlife or environmental agencies, to implement and enforce laws related to fish and game conservation. A recent example of the latter was the 2007 creation of a new federal rule mandating that "circle hooks" be used in certain fishing tournaments in lieu of more traditional "J hooks." The National Marine Fisheries Service and the International Game Fish Association determined that circle hooks, in that they could be removed more easily and subsequently caused less physical trauma, significantly decreased fish mortality in catch-and-release settings and thus helped to ensure a stronger and healthier game fish population.

International Regulation

Fish and game laws and regulations can often have international scope. Many species of plants, animals, and fish, including threatened and endangered species, are traded internationally and are thus subject to import-export laws. Most countries protect indigenous flora and fauna through their own domestic laws, and most cooperate with and uphold the import-export laws of other nations as related to fish and game, meaning that if a species is banned from sale/export in one nation, most others will correspondingly ban its importation.

The United States has established numerous treaties that facilitate multilateral cooperation in laws related to wildlife conservation, examples of which include migratory bird treaties with several nations, including Canada, Mexico, and Japan, that are designed to protect species via cooperative enhancement of habitat, collaboration in research, and joint regulation of hunting. The United States and more than 160 other nations are signatories to the Convention on International Trade in Endangered Species of Wild Fauna and Flora, which supports sustainable trade in many nonthreatened species while safeguarding some 33,000 species of animals, plants, and fish that may be imperiled. The large volume of wildlife trade in the United States, approximately $2.8 billion in 2008, necessitates such formal governmental regulation.

Barry D. Mowell
Broward College

See Also: Blood Sports; Cruelty to Animals; Environmental Crimes; Livestock and Cattle Crimes; Rural Police; Smuggling.

Further Readings

Bean, Michael and Melanie Rowland. *The Evolution of National Wildlife Law*. Westport, CT: Praeger, 1997.

Chase, Harry. *Powers, Duties and Work of Game Wardens: A Handbook of Practical Information for Officers and Others Interested in the Enforcement of Fish and Game Laws*. Making of Modern Law Series. Farmington Hills, MI: Gale, 2010.

Freyfogle, Eric and Dale Goble. *Wildlife Law: A Primer*. Washington, DC: Island Press, 2009.

Reiger, John. *American Sportsmen and the Origins of Conservation*. Corvallis: Oregon State University Press, 2000.

Fletcher v. Peck

Fletcher v. Peck (1810) is a seminal Supreme Court decision written by Chief Justice John Marshall. Holding a state law unconstitutional, the decision reinforced the stability of legal contracts and expanded judicial review to include acts of state legislatures.

After the Treaty of Paris ended the American Revolution in 1793, the state of Georgia claimed 35 million acres of the Indian reserve to its west known as the Yazoo lands. Two years later, as the result of a bribery scheme involving nearly every state legislator, the state passed a grant for the sale of the territory for a bargain price of 1.4 cents per acre. The Yazoo lands, which would eventually become Alabama and Mississippi, were sold to four private land companies, bringing in a modest total of $500,000.

The subsequent public outrage resulted in the ouster of most incumbent legislators, and in 1796, the newly elected legislature hastily rescinded the law, voiding the property rights deriving from it. The repeal, however, was met with considerable opposition. The original purchasers refused to recognize the rescission and continued to sell the lands to third parties. As a result, the issue became more complicated as increasing numbers of Yazoo claimants lived outside Georgia and alleged to be innocent buyers unaware of the fraudulent 1795 grant.

The controversy over the Yazoo lands persisted for years, as every title was called into question. In an attempt to quiet the Yazoo claims, Georgia ceded the territory to the federal government in 1802. But after repeated petitions to Congress to enforce their rights failed, Yazoo claimants turned to the courts, making a case out of Robert Fletcher of New Hampshire and John Peck of Massachusetts, filing in federal court on diversity grounds in 1803.

A Case of Complicated Ownership

Fletcher purchased 15,000 acres of land for $3,000 from Peck, who bought the tract from another third-party buyer. In a collusive case, Fletcher brought suit against Peck for breach of warranty of title, arguing that Peck had no legal right to sell the land because the original title was annulled by the 1796 repeal. Fletcher also objected to the title granted by the state on the grounds that it was still subject to right of occupancy by the Indians. Both land speculators, Fletcher and Peck, brought the suit with the objective of invalidating the legislative rescission and quieting Indian title to the land. The case reached the Supreme Court in 1809.

Fletcher v. Peck put the Supreme Court in a difficult position. To bolster confidence in land purchased under state grants, the court needed to uphold the original fraudulent Georgia grant while voiding the uncorrupt repeal. Although the case centered on whether the contract between Fletcher and Peck could be nullified by an act of the Georgia legislature, the court considered generally whether vested property rights granted by an earlier law could constitutionally be invalidated by a subsequent law.

In a unanimous decision written by Chief Justice Marshall, with Justice William Johnson concurring, the court held that Peck's title was valid and that the Georgia state legislature's repeal of the land grant was unconstitutional. Marshall's opinion delineates two reasons for the decision: The Georgia rescission violated Article I, Section 10, Clause 1 of the Constitution (the contract clause) and undermined natural property rights.

Marshall held that the 1795 land sale was a binding contract and as such was protected under the contract clause, which prohibits states from passing ex post facto laws and laws impairing the obligation of contracts. Marshall explained that each third-party buyer of Yazoo land had a good title at law, even if the original grant had been fraudulently secured. Annulling contracts or grants made by previous legislative acts amounted to an unconstitutional ex post facto law, penalizing bona fide buyers for the wrongs committed by those from whom they were purchasing. Although the court acknowledged that a legislature may repeal any act of a former legislature, this did not apply where actions taken under the previous act were still valid.

Interested in safeguarding the stability of contractual obligations, Marshall also relied on natural law to justify his opinion. Connecting the natural law doctrine of vested rights to the rights protected by the contract clause, Marshall asserted that once absolute rights vested under a law contractual in nature, a repeal of that law cannot divest those rights. Marshall hoped to demonstrate that the Constitution's positive law was based on fundamental ideas of justice, the validity of which did not rely on explicit textual reference.

By ruling the 1796 Georgia repeal unconstitutional, *Fletcher* expanded judicial review to include acts of state legislatures, thereby reinforcing the Supreme Court's authority as the final interpreter of the Constitution. As a result, the contract clause became a chief means of bringing state legislation under the review of federal courts.

Matthew H. Birkhold
Princeton University, Columbia Law School

See Also: *Marbury v. Madison*; Marshall, John; *Martin v. Hunter's Lessee*; Supreme Court, U.S.

Further Readings

Haines, Charles Grove. *The Role of the Supreme Court in American Government and Politics, 1789–1835.* Berkeley: University of California Press, 1944.

Magrath, C. Peter. *Yazoo: Law and Politics in the New Republic: Case of* Fletcher v. Peck. Providence, RI: Brown University Press, 1966.

McBride, Alex. "*Fletcher v. Peck*." PBS. http://www.pbs.org/wnet/supremecourt/capitalism/landmark_fletcher.html (Accessed September 2010).

Florida

Florida became a U.S. possession in 1821 and formally a territory in March 1822; statehood followed in 1845. During the territorial era (1821–45), Florida was a sparsely settled frontier and a veritable rogues' paradise, which attracted escaped slaves and fugitive debtors, thieves, and other lawbreakers from neighboring states. As northeastern states retreated from the use of public punishments, Florida's territorial justice system retained fines, short confinement in county jail, whipping, and the pillory for white offenders, and cropping, branding, nailing to a post by the ears, and death for slave/free black offenders. In 1822, the legislative council mandated public hanging for those convicted of murder, rape, and arson, and this continued after 1845. Executions were to take place in the county of conviction and were performed by the local sheriff for a fee of $10.

Early Statehood

Statehood brought rapid economic and population growth, as the number of residents doubled between 1845 and 1860 to 140,000, 40 percent of whom were slaves. The convergence of the southern honor ethic, frontier conditions, continuing threats of Native American violence, slavery, ethnicity, ineffective law enforcement, and alcohol made antebellum Florida a dangerous place. Town marshals and constables were employed in emerging cities. A police department and a uniformed patrol were established in Tallahassee in 1841, but the main law enforcement officers in Florida were the county sheriffs. They were popularly elected (except during the Reconstruction period, when they were appointed) and their wide-ranging roles included tax collector, process server, court officer, prison-transport, and public auctioneer. Throughout the antebellum years, hard-pressed sheriffs struggled to apprehend lawbreakers and to keep hold of them because of the scarcity of secure jails.

Prior to 1861, indictments for crimes against people were far more frequent than those for crimes against property, but punishment for those convicted of property crimes was more severe than for those found guilty of violent crimes, excluding murder. There were also frequent prosecutions for crimes against public order and morals. However, more than half of all indictments never went to trial. Black offenders generally did not go to trial unless charged with the most serious offenses, but when they did, judges seem to have treated them fairly. Fines and corporal and capital punishments were the main forms of punishment in a criminal justice system more concerned with the resolution of disputes than the prevention of crime. James M. Denham suggests that the judicial system, particularly the courts, served as a unifying agent, albeit a not very effective one. Florida witnessed an explosion of violent outlaw gangs and extralegal activity in the 1850s against a background of national abolitionism and the intensification of sectional politics, and continued legislative and law enforcement ineptitude within the state. In response, Floridians formed secret regulator bands to lynch lawless gangs of thieves, particularly those involved in stealing slaves.

In January 1866, in the aftermath of Confederate defeat, state legislators passed Black Codes, harsh and discriminatory laws against the recently emancipated black population, which emphasized offenses such as rape, insurrection, and vagrancy, which were particularly associated with African Americans. Soon ruled unconstitutional, their main provisions and purpose—social, economic, and political control of freed people—appeared in other statutes. The Reconstruction years (1866–77) were a particularly violent period in Florida history but there were also significant changes to the criminal justice system. A new criminal code accompanied the 1868 constitution, the first state prison was established, and major cities adopted or expanded their uniformed police forces. Five black police officers were elected in the Jacksonville municipal elections in 1876.

The sparseness of the white population and state income partly explain why Florida failed to

Crew members from the Coast Guard cutter Thetis *in Miami standing guard over 62 bales of seized cocaine with an estimated wholesale street value of $48 million. The drugs were intercepted on December 17, 2010, by the U.S. Coast Guard. Miami and other parts of southern Florida have long been a hub for the cocaine trade and money laundering. In the 1980s, drug smuggling and related crime contributed to Florida's suffering from the highest crime rate in the United States.*

build a penitentiary before the Civil War, while the "problem" of rising numbers of black lawbreakers and precarious state finances explain its subsequent closure. In the last third of the 19th century, 90 percent of state convicts were black. Ad hoc convict leasing arrangements existed prior to 1879 but in that year, the legislature abolished the state prison and authorized the leasing to private contractors of all state convicts as a more profitable means of dealing with offenders. County prisoners were also leased out to private business operators who paid the state a set fee for convict labor.

Over the next 40 years, thousands of mostly male and black inmates, both state and county prisoners, labored in phosphate mines, naval stores, and lumber operations. From the 1890s, capricious enforcement of Jim Crow laws, vagrancy statutes, and the use of the criminal justice system to shore up white supremacy ensured a steady stream of convict laborers. Similarly, in turpentine camps deep in the pine forests, thousands of noncriminal black workers were kept in debt peonage and subjected to forced labor, and were beaten and sometimes killed.

Twentieth Century

State prisoners were gradually withdrawn from the convict lease beginning in 1914. Starting in 1919, Florida operated a dual system of punishment for noncapital state felons, whereby Grade 1 prisoners were sent to the State Convict Road Force (SCRF) or chain gangs, and Grade 2 prisoners were sent to the state prison farm, which began as a temporary stockade in November 1913 and was officially designated as the Florida State Prison in 1927. Inmates worked as agricultural laborers or in prison garment, shoe, and tag factories.

The murder of Martin Tabert, a northern white male short-term prisoner, by a convict guard in a Dixie County lessee camp in 1921, its exposure in 1923, and the resulting condemnation of Florida's penal practices, spurred key reforms, including the abolition of convict leasing, the abolition of corporal punishment of all prisoners, and the adoption of the electric chair rather than hanging as the preferred method of execution. Starting in the 1870s, executions were increasingly carried out within county jail yards, and the adoption of the electric chair, located at the state prison farm, completed an important shift to private execution. Yet the state led the nation in lynchings in the early 20th century. Sheriffs continued to perform legal executions until a state executioner was appointed in 1941.

Despite major enforcement problems during Prohibition and the fears over rising youth crime rates in the early years of the Great Depression, Florida's crime rates remained fairly stable in the first half of the 20th century. By 1955, there were five major prison facilities, including one for youth offenders, and the first women's prison was fully operational. Able-bodied inmates still performed road labor, although the chain gangs had been replaced by smaller close-custody permanent road prisons. Exponential state population growth beginning in the mid-1950s, rapid urbanization, civil rights protests and violent white backlash, and rising ethnic tensions, particularly in the southern counties, stretched law enforcement, the courts, and prisons. At the same time, the judicial revolutions of the 1960s owed much to key legal challenges that originated in Florida, including discriminatory treatment of female offenders by all-male juries in *Hoyt v. Florida* (1961) and the right to counsel in criminal cases for poor or indigent defendants in *Gideon v. Wainwright* (1963).

By the 1980s, Florida's crime rate was the highest in the nation, and by 1989, the state had the fourth-largest prison population and second highest number of people on death row. Acute prison overcrowding meant inmates often served less than 40 percent of their sentences prior to release. Drugs and the violence that accompanied the turf wars over their control and distribution generated intense fear of crime and criminals. For most of the decade, Miami was a leading center in the importation of drugs, particularly cocaine, and associated money laundering operations. The appearance of crack cocaine led to further financial and political pressures on police, courts, and prisons as they struggled to cope with rising numbers of offenders.

Crime rates began to stabilize in the 1990s. Nevertheless, Florida's prison population is now approaching a total of 101,000 persons, who are housed in 146 facilities that range from 62 major correctional institutions to 33 work-release centers and five road prisons. In mid-2011, there were seven privately operated prison facilities in the state. Florida remains an active execution state, with more than 390 persons waiting on death row.

Vivien Miller
University of Nottingham

See Also: Chain Gangs and Prison Labor; *Chandler v. Florida*; Convict Lease System; Drug Abuse and Addiction, Contemporary; *Gideon v. Wainwright*; Hispanic Americans; Miami, Florida; Sheriffs.

Further Readings
Crawford, George B. "Murder, Insanity, and the Efficacy of Woman's Role: The Gwendolyn Hoyt Case." *Florida Historical Quarterly*, v.89 (2010).
Denham, James M. *A Rogue's Paradise: Crime and Punishment in Antebellum Florida, 1821–1861*. Tuscaloosa: University of Alabama Press, 1997.
Lewis, Anthony. *Gideon's Trumpet*. New York: Random House, 1964.
Miller, Vivien M. L. *Crime, Sexual Violence, and Clemency: Florida's Pardon Board and Penal System in the Progressive Era*. Gainesville: University Press of Florida, 2000.
Rogers, William Warren and James M. Denham. *Florida Sheriffs: A History 1821–1945*. Tallahassee, FL: Sentry Press, 2001.
Shofner, Jerrell H. "Custom, Law, and History: The Enduring Influence of Florida's 'Black Code.'" *Florida Historical Quarterly*, v.55 (1977).
Vandiver, Margaret. *Lethal Punishment: Lynchings and Legal Executions in the South*. New Brunswick, NJ: Rutgers University Press, 2006.

Floyd, Charles Arthur

Charles Arthur Floyd (1904–34) was an American gunman, bank robber, and murderer. He used various aliases, including Jack Hamilton, Frank Mitchell, and George Sanders, but he is best known by his nickname "Pretty Boy" Floyd. In his day, many poor farmers in Oklahoma regarded him like Robin Hood. He made it to the top of the Federal Bureau of Investigation's (FBI's) Most Wanted list.

Charles Arthur Floyd was born February 3, 1904, near Adairsville in Bartow County, Georgia. In 1911, his family moved outside Hanson, Oklahoma. His father was a tenant farmer who moonlighted as a bootlegger. At 20 years of age, Floyd married 16-year-old Wilma "Ruby" Hargrove; they had a son, Jack Dempsey Floyd, born in 1922. In 1922, Charles Floyd was apprehended for a post office robbery, but there was insufficient evidence for conviction. Floyd had a reputation for getting drunk on Saturday nights on a local concoction known as Choctaw beer; for this he was nicknamed "Chock." His first known serious criminal offense occurred in 1925 when he purchased a pistol that he used on September 11, 1925, to commit a payroll robbery at a Kroger store-warehouse in St. Louis, Missouri. He was found and convicted for this robbery and on December 19, 1925, began serving his five-year sentence in the Missouri State Penitentiary in Jefferson County, Missouri. Floyd was paroled back to Oklahoma in 1929 and on his return learned that his father had been killed by Jim Mills. The Floyds and the Mills had carried on a blood feud for generations back in Kentucky. Mills was not convicted of the murder based on a claim of self-defense. Mills was never seen again. Floyd, immediately after the disappearance of Mills, fled to Kansas City, Missouri, and became a part of the Pendergast Machine, a crime organization led by Johnny Lazia. Floyd took refuge in a whorehouse run for Lazia by Ann Chambers. It was Chambers, upon seeing Floyd, who gave him the nickname "Pretty Boy."

In Kansas City, "Pretty Boy" Floyd began using his trademark submachine gun; there he also hooked back up with Red Lovett—they had served together in the Missouri State Penitentiary. The two recruited Jack Atkins and Tom Bradley and from late 1929 to early 1930 this gang robbed several small banks in Ohio. On March 11, 1930, the gang robbed a bank in Sylvania, Ohio, and sped out of town. They were pursued by a motorcycle officer, Harlan F. Manes, whom Bradley killed with a submachine gun fired out of the smashed rear window of the getaway car. However, the driver, Atkins, smashed into a telephone pole. Police arrived shortly and pried out Floyd, Atkins, and Bradley; Lovett had disappeared. Bradley was sent to the electric chair for killing Officer Manes; Atkins received a life sentence; and, Floyd was given a 15-year sentence for bank robbery. However, on May 25, 1930, while being escorted to the Ohio State Penitentiary, Floyd escaped.

He then robbed several banks in Michigan and returned to Kansas City, where, on March 23, 1931, he killed three plainclothes detectives and then on July 21, 1931, he killed Curtis Burks, a federal prohibition agent. On April 9, 1931, Floyd and accomplices drove into Bowling Green, Ohio, in a stolen car; local police approached the vehicle and Floyd killed Officer Ralph Castner. Floyd fled to Oklahoma. On April 7, 1932, Erv A. Kelly, a special state investigator, tried to arrest Floyd in Bixby, Oklahoma, but Floyd, wounded by Kelly, managed to put several bullets into Kelly, killing him. On June 17, 1933, Floyd, based on fingerprints, was involved in the murder of three policemen and an FBI agent in a botched attempt to free Frank Nash, who was also killed in this Kansas City Massacre outside Union Station. Floyd denied involvement in the incident. Floyd then joined up with John Dillinger and George "Baby Face" Nelson to rob the Merchants National Bank of South Bend, Indiana. After the FBI killed Dillinger, who had been listed as Public Enemy Number One, Floyd garnered the top spot on the FBI's Most Wanted list.

Charles Arthur Floyd died on October 22, 1934, in East Liverpool, Ohio. It was later related that Special Agent Melvin Purvis of the FBI had ordered Agent Herman Hollis to shoot Floyd. He was immortalized in the ballad "Pretty Boy Floyd" by Woody Guthrie and also mentioned in John Steinbeck's classic 1939 novel *The Grapes of Wrath*.

Victor B. Stolberg
Essex County College

See Also: Dillinger, John; Federal Bureau of Investigation; Great Depression; Kansas City, Missouri.

Further Readings

King, Jeffrey S. *The Life and Death of Pretty Boy Floyd.* Kent, OH: Kent State University Press, 1998.

Wallis, Michael. *Pretty Boy: The Life and Times of Charles Arthur Floyd.* New York: St. Martin's Press, 1992.

Ford, Gerald (Administration of)

Having spent his entire Washington career as a member of Congress building a reputation as a courteous and polite politician, Gerald Ford became president at a time when Americans were frustrated and distrustful of government. He sought to restore Americans' faith in their president and deal with a Congress skeptical of presidential power in the wake of Watergate, a scandal riddled with implications of government wrongdoing and presidential misconduct. On August 9, 1974, Gerald Ford became the first president to ascend to the position due to resignation. He was also the first candidate who was not previously vetted in a national election for president or even vice president. Only nine months earlier, on November 27, 1973, the Senate confirmed the nomination of Representative Ford (R-MI) to fill the vice presidency position vacated by Spiro Agnew's resignation. In his time as vice president, the investigation into the Watergate scandal implicated Richard Nixon, forcing him to resign or face certain impeachment.

President Ford effected two important acts of leniency. His administration is known not as much for crimes or punishment for crimes but rather for two reprieves. On September 8, 1974, in an effort to bring the Watergate scandal to a close, Ford pardoned his predecessor, Richard Nixon, of any wrongdoing he might have done while serving as president. Though Ford's action stopped all investigations into Nixon's conduct, suspicions turned to Ford. However, these theories are baseless, as

President Gerald Ford faces reporters at a White House press conference in Washington, D.C., on October 9, 1974, a month after his controversial pardon of former president Richard Nixon.

no proof ever emerged to confirm that Nixon and Ford conspired to trade elevation to the presidency for a pardon.

Though American ground troops were out of Vietnam before Ford took office, the question remained in America of what ought to be done about those who refused to serve. To these young Americans, the impact and ramifications of the war continued long after the troops left the battlefield. Some served jail time, while others fled into exile, forced to live abroad or lurk in America's shadows. Two weeks after Ford pardoned Nixon, he announced his Presidential Clemency Program. Ford's program allowed Vietnam War resisters to earn reentry into American society by performing alternate service. Nevertheless, Ford's plan was not a pardon, a fact that angered doves and received critiques of hypocrisy from Democrats still frustrated with Ford's full pardon of Nixon. A pardon for draft dodgers (but not deserters) would only come three years later when Ford's successor, Jimmy Carter, did so as his first act as president.

Within Ford's first month in office, he set the tone of his presidency. However, these actions had strong repercussions for his political capital and ability to govern. Two months later, based in large part on frustrations over the twin traumas of the Vietnam War and the Watergate scandal, but also Ford's acts of leniency, the Democratic Party made significant midterm election gains in the House of Representatives and the Senate. Rallying around these new members—known as the Watergate class—Ford's agenda and the plans of his administration often ended up at loggerheads with the Democratic opposition in Congress. Their skepticism of existing presidential power and their paranoia about the abuse of power translated to a fine line Ford had to walk. Moreover, Ford's leniency irrevocably damaged his political capital and was one of the reasons he lost the 1976 election.

Jason Friedman
Wasatch Academy

See Also: 1961 to 1980 Primary Documents; Carter, Jimmy (Administration of); Clemency; Nixon, Richard (Administration of); Presidential Proclamations; Selective Service Act of 1967; Watergate.

Further Readings
Brinkley, Douglas. *Gerald R. Ford*. New York: Times Books, 2007.
Cannon, James M. *Time and Chance: Gerald Ford's Appointment With History*. New York: HarperCollins, 1994.
Ford, Gerald. *A Time to Heal: The Autobiography of Gerald R. Ford*. New York: Harper and Row, 1979.
Friedman, Jason. "Reconciling the Vietnam War: Draft Dodgers, Resisters and the Debate Over Amnesty." In *Our Way Home 2007 Conference Proceedings*. Ottawa: National Research Council of Canada Press, 2009.
Greene, John Robert. *The Presidency of Gerald R. Ford*. Lawrence: University of Kansas Press, 1995.

Mount, Graeme S. and Mark Gauthier. *895 Days That Changed the World: The Presidency of Gerald R. Ford*. Montreal: Black Rose Books, 2006.
Plaxton, Sharon Rudy. "To Reconcile A Nation: Gerald Ford, Jimmy Carter, and the Question of Amnesty." Ph.D. thesis. Queen's University, December 1995.
ter Horst, Jerald F. *Gerald Ford and the Future of the Presidency*. New York: Third Press, 1974.

Forensic Science

From the etymology of the word *forensic* comes a greater understanding of the term's relationship to crime investigation and prosecution. The Latin root, *forensis*, roughly translates to "of the forum." In one way, to mark something as "forensic" means to use evidence and testimony collected with the express purpose of being presented in a public legal forum. In another way, the term *forensic* is bound to notions of public argumentation. "Forensics" is a debate surrounding a question of wide public interest, where two sides of an issue are offered to listeners, and the winner is determined by the compelling selection and presentation of evidence. Beyond these definitional boundaries, forensic evidence or forensic science is more colloquially understood as physical evidence as well as the collection, testing, and identification of that evidence within the context of a criminal prosecution. Thus, "forensics" indicates a type of physical matter as well as the means by which that matter is made probative and admissible in a courtroom through legal and scientific scrutiny.

In one basic definition, forensic science means the application of scientific principles and methods to legal problems or to satisfy legal requirements. Throughout its historical development, forensic science has been caught between the two disciplinary frameworks of law and science. Scientific truth is determined through hypothesis, standardized experimentation/testing supported by technological developments with findings subject to rigorous peer review, and further testing before the theory becomes widely accepted or transformative of previous knowledge. The reproducibility of results is a key component scientific research. The field of science, however, can be perceived as a closed circuit of knowledge production and dissemination, which makes it difficult to communicate complex and sometimes contradictory findings to a larger public with ease and continuity. Such a process is exacerbated in the courtroom, where rules of argumentation dictate the admissibility of testimony and evidence emerges as truth within the course of a legal proceeding.

Against this backdrop, forensic scientists operate, explaining what things are and interpreting what things mean. The discipline is an applied science with the goal of determining truth through what Roger Koppl and Lawrence Koblinsky call a "rule-governed competitive process." While at first glance, the ideas of rules and competing truth link science and law together, the variability of the governing rules and the depth of influence regarding competing interpretations illustrate core tensions among the disciplines that emerge in particular ways within forensic domains. Recent studies have found that these tensions between legal and scientific protocols have allowed forensic science and scientists to operate in a vacuum, bolstered by the air of infallibility conferred upon them by popular-culture crime narratives, without national standards to govern training, testing, and testimony. In other words, forensic science in the United States operates without standardized and rigorous means for officers of the court, not to mention the public at large, to determine which disciplines represent strands of legitimate science and which are using terms and technology borrowed from but not subject to scientific scrutiny to argue their forensic value.

History

It seems logical to locate the beginnings of U.S. forensic science discourse in the rapid expansion of scientific and jurisprudence fields in the late 19th century. The scientific revolution and the increasing reliance upon the scientific method offered fertile ground for experimentation relevant to the development of forensic sciences, particularly in the fields of pathology, chemistry/toxicology, and physical anthropology. By the mid-19th century, medico-legal domains—from the development of an organized and trained police force to the use of "expert" witnesses to consult on cases during investigation and court proceedings—were evolving and developing new technologies and grappling with professional protocols and standards. In the United States, practices regarding scientific criminal investigation were scrutinized by the public through the lens of the rapidly expanding domain of mass media. Such simultaneous development also inspired skepticism and controversy about the scope and accuracy of what would become known as "forensic science."

Large urban centers such as New York and Chicago incorporated from and capitalized on discoveries made by European experts such as Pierre Nysten (a physician who conducted in-depth studies of rigor mortis in 1811), Mathieu Orfila (who linked decomposition and etymology in the early 1830s), Henry Faulds (a Scottish physician who published articles in the 1880s describing fingerprint identification and analysis), Alphonse Bertillon (the father of the criminal photography and measurement classification system known as anthropometry), Ludwig Karl Teichmann (the Polish anatomist whose 1863 test based on color-change reactions to show the presence of blood on an object was used until the mid-20th century), and Hans Gross (a self-taught jurist in 1870s Austria whose view of crime as a scientific problem to be solved by a well-trained observer employing refined research and technical tools became the foundation for the discipline of criminalistics). Perhaps the most foundational forensic concept came from Edmond Locard, the director of the Police Scientific Laboratory of Lyon, France (established in 1912). "Every contact leaves a trace," or Locard's principle, as it came to be known, relates to microscopic trace evidence such as dust, hair, fibers, and soil. Almost 75 years later, the belief that forensic scientists can uncover and analyze physical matter no matter how obscure and degraded and conclusively connect it from victim to suspect still holds sway in the public perception of the power and certainty of forensic science.

In the early 19th century, much of the focus in the United States was on developing the field of legal medicine. In 1813, the College of Physicians and Surgeons of New York City established the first Chair of Medical Jurisprudence. In 1867, the Medico-Legal Society was organized in New York. By the turn of the 20th century, however, forensic focus turned to standardizing and professionalizing police forces and building upon scientific developments to standardize techniques of investigation and incarceration. The proliferation of scientific "experts" with their dramatic but largely untested and unchallenged claims of identification and authenticity fed the public's imagination, which was already whetted by the stories of Sherlock Holmes and Chevalier Auguste Dupin (Edgar Allan Poe's fictional French private investigator). From this time to today, the intermingling of known and developing forensic science innovations and theories with popular culture and mass media narratives has shaped public consciousness about the power and persuasiveness of techniques labeled "forensic science," regardless of whether they employ the rigors of scientific testing, peer review, and reproducibility.

Urban centers with exploding populations and greater financial resources led the way in developing forensic professions and protocols. In 1903, the New York state prison system began collecting and categorizing fingerprints as part of other anthropometric measures and photographs of suspects and prisoners. In 1905, newly elected president Theodore Roosevelt (a former police commissioner of New York City) established the Federal Bureau of Investigation (FBI). In 1910, August Vollmer, the self-educated chief of police in Berkeley, California, organized that city's first public crime lab. Under Vollmer's stewardship, new technologies (the polygraph) and techniques (such as an early prototype of a fingerprint database) were merged with new training practices. In Chicago, Calvin Goddard, a significant figure in the field of ballistics, had greater success

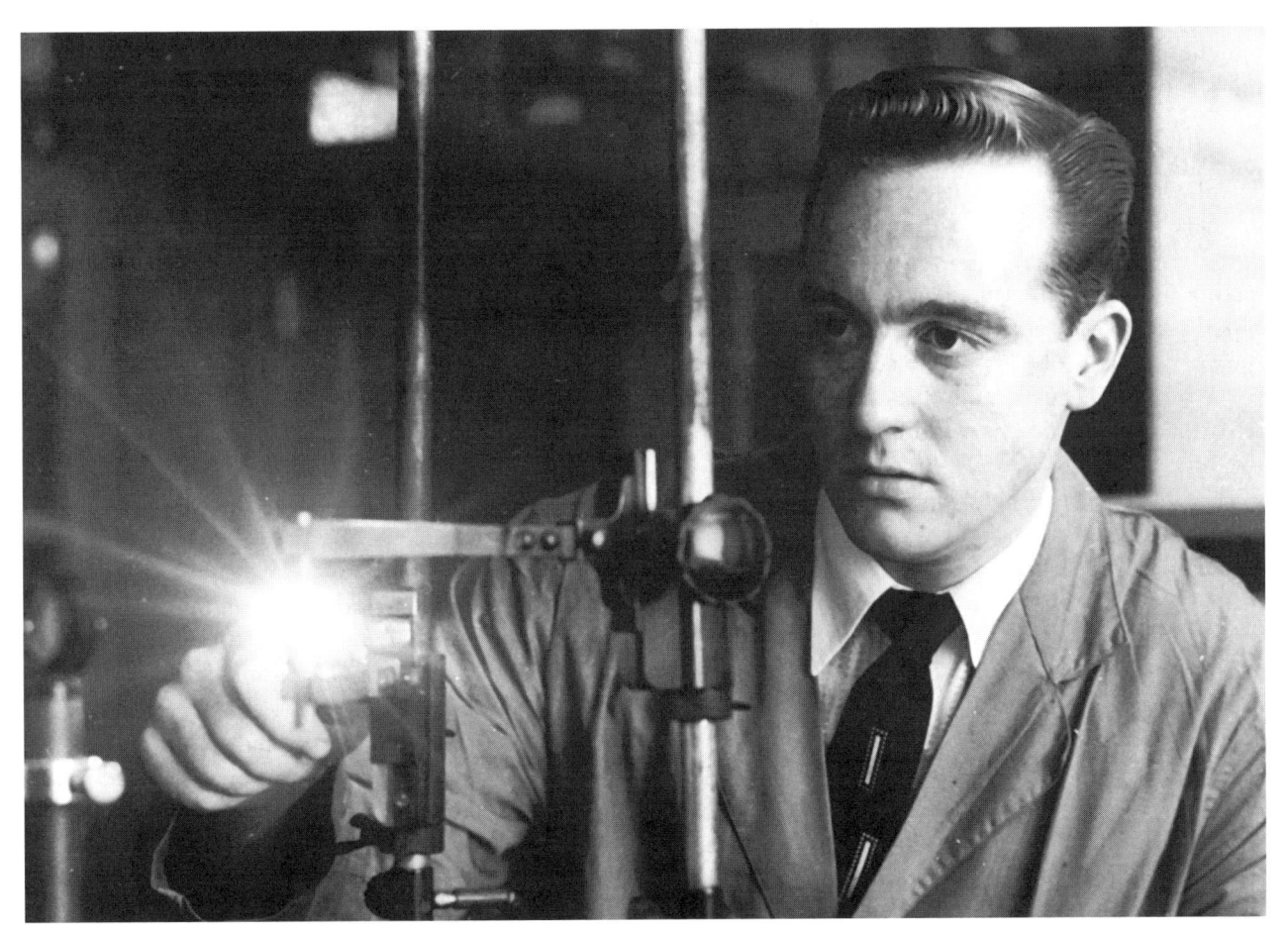

Calvin Goddard, a ballistics pioneer who created the first private crime lab at Northwestern University, went on to establish the Federal Bureau of Investigation's (FBI's) first lab in Washington, D.C. In the 1990s, the FBI moved the lab to Quantico, Virginia, to join the Forensic Science Research and Training Center. The photo shows an FBI laboratory scientist at work in the early years of the FBI lab.

establishing the first private crime lab at Northwestern University, which had its own publication, *American Journal of Police Science*, to report new findings and techniques to the wider forensics community. Goddard's expertise, particularly his comparison microscope study of the bullets and casings that upheld the convictions of Nicola Sacco and Bartolomeo Vanzetti, made him the perfect candidate to oversee the development of the FBI's own technical laboratory. This lab's first site was Washington, D.C., but it was moved in the 1990s to Quantico, Virginia, where the FBI had created, in 1981, its Forensic Science Research and Training Center.

Evolution of Modern Forensics

By the early 20th century, an explosion of new forensic techniques and experts deluged unprepared courtrooms across the United States. Without unified standards to guide rulings or educate judges, prosecutors, or defense attorneys about which applications stood up to scientific or industry scrutiny, rulings were dependent upon the persuasiveness of expert witnesses and the resources of labs and lawyers. Some guidance was given in 1923 with *Frye v. United States*. In the case, the appeals court upheld the ruling of the trial judge, who denied the defendant's request to admit expert testimony regarding his results from a systolic blood pressure deception test (an early prototype of the lie detector). The judge denied the testimony on the grounds that a community of relevant experts had not established the validity and reliability of the test. As a result, the "Frye Standard" would guide rulings regarding expert testimony on forensic science techniques and technology in American courtrooms for the next 70 years.

In 1965, Supreme Court Chief Justice Earl Warren created a committee of lawyers and legal scholars to draft uniform federal rules of evidence. After much delay and redraft by Congress, these rules were adopted in 1975. The 1993 Supreme Court case *Daubert v. Merrell Dow* would turn to Part 702 of the Federal Rules of Evidence to supplant the Frye Standard. The "Daubert Standard" gave the trial judge the task of evaluating the admissibility and relevance of scientific evidence and expert testimony. *Daubert* specified the factors judges must consider when determining whether a scientific methodology is valid, particularly whether the theory or technique in question can be and has been scientifically tested, its known or potential error rate, and the existence of industry or disciplinary standards controlling its operation.

One particular strain of forensic science, DNA analysis, appeared to fulfill the stringent demands of the Daubert Standard. DNA fingerprinting, a technique credited to the 1984 accidental discovery of British geneticist Alex Jeffreys, emerged out of academic science research. Unlike other forensic fields, which developed out of or in conjunction with criminal investigation, developers touted DNA "fingerprinting" as an objective and infallible means to identify a suspect. In reality, identification is not the same as individuation, although these two terms are frequently interchanged in public understandings of forensic science. Many forensic scientists promote the idea of individuation, a set of characteristics and traits (some genetic or biological, some culturally or socially encoded) that are unique to an individual, thus tying physical evidence to a specific suspect definitively.

Private genetic firms (such as Lifecodes and Cellmark Diagnostics, two early industry leaders) found it profitable to promote this probabilistic science as capable of providing desired individuation. Industry publicity coupled with compelling data and claims made DNA a particularly potent weapon in the courtroom. Public failures of forensic evidence, especially DNA evidence, however, dramatized the continued tension between scientific certainty and legal argument.

Perhaps the greatest failure of "certain" DNA evidence happened during the 1995 trial of O. J. Simpson. There were many factors that led to Simpson's acquittal, not the least of which was the background of two members of his defense team: Barry Scheck and Peter Neufeld. Under the auspices of their legal clinic, the Innocence Project (founded in 1992), Scheck and Neufeld championed the accuracy of DNA evidence to overturn wrongful convictions motivated by faulty eyewitness identifications or incompetent or corrupt legal practices. Arguing for Simpson's defense, however, Scheck and Neufeld led the attack on lax standards, testing imperfections, and faulty chains of evidence in the Los Angeles crime lab. They also employed their own forensic expert, Henry Lee (then the chief criminalist for the state of Connecticut), whose dramatic yet understated

Federal Bureau of Investigation forensics students recovering remains at a "body farm" where donated bodies are left to decompose for research and teaching purposes and for comparisons to actual crime-scene conditions. In 2009, a report found that the relatively new field of forensic pathology suffered from a lack of necessary funding and training of personnel, lack of lab accreditation, and the disparity of coroners (who are not always medical professionals) versus medical examiners overseeing autopsies.

testimony supported the defense's interrogation of the statistics that accompanied blood-typing evidence and ultimately undermined what was believed by prosecutors to be a solid case built on persuasive forensic evidence.

Since the Simpson verdict, the public face of forensic science has changed dramatically due in part to the popularity of television crime stories. The Daubert Standard left the assessment of forensic science validity and relevance of expert testimony to the trial judge, a presumed nonscientist. The general public had shows like *CSI: Crime Scene Investigation* (CBS) to help them visualize the technology and techniques behind crime science (e.g., ballistics, toxicology, DNA analysis). In that popular-culture domain, the crime narrative tends to reinforce the notion that forensic science is infallible; heartily funded by local, state, and federal institutions; and that there are legitimate, vetted hypotheses behind tests and conclusions drawn by scientists always in service of (but never manipulated by) the legal system.

Soon after *CSI*'s debut and dominance in the ratings, articles began to appear in the mainstream press arguing about a growing "*CSI* effect." This effect took one of two trajectories. One was positive for the prosecutors: There was no case that could not be uncovered and successfully prosecuted. One was positive for defense attorneys: Jurors who followed *CSI*-like programs would expect prosecutors to provide reams of physical evidence for cases as basic as shoplifting or as complex as serial murder. Spectators have been characterized as susceptible to largely unproven forensic methods such as handwriting analysis, "voice print" comparison, and psychological profiling, which, despite its continued use as a plot device in myriad films and television shows, has no solid foundation in actual case law or scientific testing. Emerging media studies scholarship challenges these characterizations; however, public prosecutors have seized upon the presumed existence of the "effect" to argue for greater funding and training for forensic personnel at the local, state, and federal level.

Criticisms

In 2006, under the terms of the Science, State, Justice, Commerce, and Related Agencies Appropriations Act, Congress authorized

> ... the National Academy of Sciences to conduct a study on forensic science ... [via] an independent Forensic Science Committee. [...] including members of the forensics community representing operational crime laboratories, medical examiners, and coroners; legal experts; and other scientists as determined appropriate.

This study produced the 2009 report *Strengthening Forensic Science in the United States*, which found that despite the impression given by popular culture, the state of forensic science was anything but sound. The authors noted the shocking lack of standardization for forensic practices across specialties. The findings reinforced the post-Daubert state of the field where DNA analysis has led the way for rigor and sound scientific principles; however, the backlog of genetic material for testing grows each year, and there remain unacceptable disparities in efficient and accurate testing from state to state. Even the recently established field of forensic pathology was found in relative disarray because of a lack of necessary funding and training of personnel, lack of lab accreditation, and the disparity of coroners (elected positions not necessarily filled by medical professionals) versus medical examiners overseeing autopsies and collecting and testing trace evidence. In 2011, there is no nationally administered test, board of certification, or training for forensic scientists in the United States on par with those required for licensure of doctors or lawyers.

As one step to remedy this state of the field, Senator Patrick Leahy (D-VT) introduced the Criminal Justice and Forensic Science Reform Act in January 2011, with the stated goal of establishing

> ... a [Federal] Office of Forensic Science and a Forensic Science Board, to strengthen and promote confidence in the criminal justice system by ensuring consistency and scientific validity in forensic testing.

Until the act becomes law, increasing financial and bureaucratic pressures on local, state, and federal law enforcement agencies will hamper the development of coherent systems of forensic science training, testing, and testimony, even as public demands grow louder that the rigorous and regulated forensic science world of *CSI* should be a reality.

Jules Odendahl-James
Duke University

See Also: 1981 to 2000 Primary Documents; Ballistics; Bertillon System; Crime Scene Investigation; Detection and Detectives; Famous Trials; Federal Bureau of Investigation; Fingerprinting; Poe, Edgar Allen; Sacco and Vanzetti; Simpson, O. J.; Television, Crime in; Vollmer, August.

Further Readings

Aronson, Jay D. *Genetic Witness: Science, Law, and Controversy in the Making of DNA Profiling*. New Brunswick, NJ: Rutgers University Press, 2007.

Beecher-Monas, Erica. *Evaluating Scientific Evidence: An Interdisciplinary Framework for Intellectual Due Process*. New York: Cambridge University Press, 2007.

Byers, Michele and Val Marie Johnson, eds. *The CSI Effect: Television, Crime, and Governance*. Lanham, MD: Lexington Books, 2009.

Faigman, David L., et al. *Modern Scientific Evidence: The Law and Science of Expert Testimony*, Vols. 1–4. Eagan, MN: Thomson Reuters/West, 2009.

Koppl, Roger and Lawrence Koblinsky. "Forensic Science Administration: Toward a New Discipline." http://alpha.fdu.edu/~koppl/fsa.doc (Accessed February 2011).

National Research Council. *Strengthening Forensic Science in the United States: A Path Forward*. Washington, DC: National Academies Press, 2009.

Watson, Katherine D. *Forensic Medicine in Western Society: A History*. New York: Routledge, 2011.

Fornication Laws

Although the term *fornication* derives from the Latin word for brothel, *fornix* being the vaults under which prostitution was practiced in ancient Rome, the term typically refers to illicit sexual intercourse. The Bible warns against fornication, and the New Testament lays down the principles of Christian sexuality that had been zealously disseminated by Paul in the Christian circles of the 2nd century. Fornication was not a common law crime, and it has been traditionally associated with morality and religion, although it is formulated and punishable in a variety of ways following different sociocultural contexts.

The Anglican Church punished illicit sex with prison, and adulterers were often executed. In the 17th and 18th centuries, fornication was punished by the Ecclesiastic Courts of the Church of England, the so-called bawdy courts, allegedly exported to the United States by Puritans. Canon law still punishes fornication with the *sbattezzo*, an Italian term indicating the procedure of deregistration or disassociation of the culprit from the registry of the church. However, most secular countries nowadays do not have fornication laws. The United States inherited from the United Kingdom the common law principle on the basis of which consensual sexual intercourse between majors is a matter of privacy and therefore not punishable.

Illicit sex, variably defined as sodomy, adultery, and fornication, was heavily prosecuted in the early colonies—execution and hanging for adultery and other infamous punishment such as being branded with an "A" on the forehead, or being stripped and whipped publicly. Furthermore, as late as the 1970s, 14 states and a district in the United States passed statutes prohibiting fornication: Alabama, Florida, Georgia, Idaho, Illinois, Massachusetts, Missouri, North Carolina, North Dakota, Rhode Island, South Carolina, Utah, West Virginia, Wisconsin, and the District of Columbia. The notion of fornication as an offense has been articulated with concomitant legislation on sodomy, adultery, premarital sex, and cohabitation outside marriage. The application of these laws did not proceed, it should be noted, without debate on both the nature of the offense and the reasons for punishment.

Surveys of case law on fornication usually start with *Poe v. Ullman* (1961), a U.S. Supreme Court case in which Justice John M. Harlan argued the unconstitutionality of a Connecticut statute that declared contraception by married couples to be a crime. The argument, however, was not successful because the law had never been enforced. Four years later in 1965, the same court, in *Griswold v. Connecticut*, ruled that such a statute was an invasion of the right of privacy protected by the Fourteenth Amendment. Since then, the hope of successfully challenging fornication laws on the basis of the right of privacy encouraged the blossoming of legal arguments advocating the rights of sexual privacy. However, the U.S. courts never accepted the right to sexual privacy as a specific right different from the right to privacy.

Legal doctrine reasoned on several occasions that laws prohibiting fornication and cohabitation were not explicitly forbidden by the Constitution; that the right to engage in consensual heterosexual intercourse between adults could only be argued as a right to privacy; but that even in presence of a fundamental right to privacy, fornication laws would be admissible if they served a state interest. Moreover, even Justice Harlan had reasserted the state's right for criminal inquiry in cases of adultery, homosexuality, and fornication. Although the decision on the unconstitutionality of the prohibition of contraception by married couples does suggest that the state should be cautious with attempts to regulate the sexual conduct of its citizens, subsequent case law shows instead that the regulation of sexual conduct has been regarded as a state's prerogative.

Until 2003, attempts to assert the right to sexual privacy were unsuccessful for unmarried couples. However, as many of the statutes punishing fornication affirm "when any man and single woman have sexual intercourse, each is guilty of fornication, a misdemeanor," one could wonder if fornication laws only targeted heterosexual couples. Furthermore, in *Lawrence v. Texas* (2003) the Supreme Court declared unconstitutional the laws prohibiting sodomy, but since fornication laws were still in force, this had curious implications on the notion of fornication by suggesting that fornication may only be related with vaginal sexual intercourse. *Martin v. Ziherl* in 2005 constituted a crucial turning point regarding the legitimacy of fornication laws. The background of the case was that Martin and Ziherl lived together as an unmarried couple when Martin was diagnosed with herpes. She filed a case against her partner, Ziherl, for failure to inform her of the danger of being exposed to a contagious disease.

The precedent had ruled that damages could not be recovered for injuries caused by participation in a criminal offense. The Virginia Supreme Court, however, declared that fornication laws constituted a violation to the Fourteenth Amendment, allowing, as a consequence, Martin to proceed against her partner. The Supreme Court accepted the argument that sexual intercourse is part of the private and personal relationship of any couple, and that the state does not have any legitimate interest in criminalizing it, unless it involves minors, nonconsensual sexual activity, prostitution, and/or it is done in public.

Livia Holden
Lahore University of Management Sciences

See Also: 1600 to 1776 Primary Documents; Adultery; Bible; Bigamy/Polygamy; *Caminetti v. United States*; Incest; *Lawrence v. Texas*; Obscenity Laws; Prostitution, History of; Puritans; Sex Offenders; Sodomy.

Further Readings
Dubler, Ariela R. "Immoral Purposes: Marriage and the Genus of Illicit Sex." *Yale Law Journal*, v.115/4 (2006).
Gaca, Kathy L. *The Making of Fornication: Eros, Ethics, and Political Reform in Greek Philosophy and Early Christianity*. Berkeley: University of California Press, 2003.
Lecky, W. *History of European Morals From Augustus to Charlemagne*. Ann Arbor: Scholarly Publishing Office, University of Michigan Library, 2005.

Fraud

In a legal sense, fraud is defined as intentionally misrepresenting facts with the ultimate intention of cheating another person out of something of value, particularly money or property. The use of

The Federal Trade Commission estimates that around 9 million people are the victims of identity theft every year. In a credit card fraud, thieves may open new credit cards in someone else's name or may change the billing address on an existing account.

the term can be traced back to the 14th century. Fraud may involve force of some kind and may include trickery, embezzlement, or larceny. Under the common law system used by the federal government and by all states except Louisiana, four elements must be present for fraud to occur: (1) the perpetrator must make a material false statement, (2) the statement must be made with knowledge that it was false, (3) the victim must have taken the false statement as truth and relied on it, and (4) the victim must have suffered some damage as a result of the action. The word *fraud* may also refer to one who commits such acts. The Federal Bureau of Investigation (FBI) reports that fraud is the fastest-growing crime in the United States, claiming almost a fourth of its resources.

According to the Federal Trade Commission, most fraud crimes concern credit cards, utilities, banks, employment, loans, and government documents or benefits. In the first case, either a card or the cardholder's identity is stolen. At least 80 percent of all utility frauds target telecommunication providers. In the case of bank frauds, the most common crime is for a perpetrator to empty a victim's bank account and abscond with the money. Banks are a frequent target of frauds by criminals who open accounts in someone else's name or secure loans using false identities. Government documents are used fraudulently to establish false identities or to prove citizenship, and some criminals have long records of receiving government benefits based on false identities or information.

Frauds are often described as confidence schemes because they are perpetrated by con artists who excel at convincing would-be victims of their honesty and legitimacy. Fraud may be committed in person, over the telephone, in a letter, or, increasingly, over the Internet. It may occur without the victim even being aware that a crime has been committed, as in the case of identity theft. Those who commit fraud may also be individuals or businesses that cheat the government, employers, or insurance companies. Fraud committed on a large scale tends to capture the media's attention, and such perpetrators become household names.

The late 20th and early 21st centuries have produced a plethora of financial frauds that range from money laundering, kickbacks, and insider trading to hedge fund, mass marketing, and securities and commodities fraud. An increase in the number of these crimes is often a response to an uncertain market or to the political environment. During the economic crisis of 2009, for instance, the FBI investigated 592 cases of fraud that entailed more than $1 billion in losses. Many of the crimes under investigation involve large corporations that are engaged in manipulating financial data to either hide assets or to indicate large profits in order to drive stocks up. The FBI is the chief governmental agency that bears the responsibility for investigating financial frauds at the federal level and has created the Financial Crimes Section (FCS) to carry out this function. Within the FCS, specific units such as the Asset Forfeiture/Money Laundering Unit, Economic Crimes Unit, Health Care Fraud Unit, Forensic Accountant Unit, and National Mortgage Fraud Team are comprised of expert investigators in their fields.

Experts have identified a "fraud triangle" in which the perpetrator or fraud is under perceived pressure, seizes an opportunity, and develops the ability to rationalize the fraudulent behavior as acceptable. Research indicates that those who commit fraud have different profiles from most criminals. They are older than the average criminal. They are better educated, more religious, and are less likely to abuse drugs or alcohol or to have previous arrest records. Personality-wise, they tend to be more optimistic, have higher self-esteem, are more motivated than the average criminal, and are more likely to live in well-adjusted families. Perpetrators of fraud are also less likely than other criminals to be caught. If they are found out, they are less likely to be arrested, convicted, or incarcerated. Those who do end up in prison rarely serve long prison terms.

Common Frauds Reported to the FBI

The FBI reports that the most common types of fraud committed in the United States are telemarketing frauds, the Nigerian letter fraud, identity theft, and advance pay schemes. Telemarketing fraud usually begins with a telephone call in which a victim is informed that he/she is being offered a once-in-a-lifetime opportunity or has won a free gift, vacation, or prize. The caller states that a specified amount of money should be sent to the caller, and the transaction requires the target to furnish a credit card or bank account number.

The Nigerian letter, also known as "419" fraud because of the habit of emptying a victim's bank account, has been in operation for a number of years, but perpetrators continue to find victims willing to send them money. A letter or e-mail, purportedly originating in Nigeria, offers the recipient millions of dollars to help the sender transfer money out of Nigeria. In order to take part, the target must provide items such as blank letterhead stationery or the name of his/her bank and account number. The victim's "initial output" is to be dispersed in designated installments. Information gained in this way is sometimes used to steal the victim's identity.

In advance pay schemes, criminals convince their victims that they will receive a loan, contract, investment, or gift in return for an outlay of varying amounts identified as "finder fees." Once the fees are paid, the victims discover that they are ineligible for the promised return on their investments. Variations of this scheme include the work-at-home advance fee scheme, in which the victim must pay a small amount on a credit card to obtain information about jobs that purportedly offer large payments for tasks such as stuffing envelopes, and the cancer research advance fee scheme, in which cancer patients or their families are hoodwinked into paying for a mythical cure for cancer. Healthcare and health insurance fraud schemes also find ready victims. These ploys vary from charging insurance companies for products and services that were touted as free and that were never received to "rolling lab" schemes that offer fake health tests in public places and then bill insurance providers or Medicare for the cost. The elderly are particularly vulnerable to fraud, losing more than $2.6 billion each year as a result of scams perpetrated by either family members or strangers.

Con artists have also become adept at using the government and legitimate businesses to commit fraud. One way of doing this is through the redemption/strawman bond fraud, in which victims are convinced to pay large amounts of money for a kit intended to teach them how to recover money from the federal or state government. Letter of credit frauds have also been successful, with perpetrators offering enormous annual interest rates on investment in a letter of credit or erroneously convincing a bank to release a letter of credit in response to false documentation that goods have been shipped. Some Americans have fallen victim to prime bank note fraud perpetrated by international fraud artists who offer large returns on investing in fraudulent bank guarantees through payments transmitted to foreign banks.

Some of the most notorious frauds committed in the 20th and 21st centuries have concerned Ponzi schemes in which the perpetrator appears to be a legitimate member of the business community. Early investors receive dividends on schedule, but they are paid out of funds submitted by subsequent investors. Eventually, the scheme falls apart because no money is left to pay investors. Italian-born Charles Ponzi perpetrated the first of these scams in the United States in the early 1920s. Ponzi's grand scheme involved buying up vouchers for postage in one country and selling them in another country, where the postage was considerably more expensive. Ponzi used investments of newer investors to pay dividends to initial investors. Pyramid schemes are somewhat similar to Ponzi schemes in that initial investors are paid according to schedule. As these investors in distributorships or franchises spread the word about their successful investments, other investors eagerly come on board. When the pool of investors dries up, the scheme falls apart. The market manipulation fraud, also known as "pump and dump," manipulates the market to increase trading volume on a targeted security in order to garner profit for those involved in the scheme and produce losses for innocent parties who buy the artificially inflated stock.

Cybercrime and Telecommunications Fraud

Two of the most common types of cybercrime are auction fraud and identity theft. Criminals have become extremely adept at perpetrating fraud through rigging Internet auctions. One common ploy is using shills to drive prices up. Perpetrators also engage in a host of investment scams and confidence games. As computers became more commonplace in the last five years of the 20th century, identity theft became a major issue. Generally, all that is needed to establish credit is a name, an address, a date of birth, and a Social Security number. Confidence artists set up bogus e-commerce sites or hack into legitimate e-commerce sites, providing them with credit card information and giving them access to personal information that allows them to establish false identities. Perpetrators explain that the address on the account will be different because they are in the process of moving, preventing mail from going directly to the person whose identity has been stolen.

A person's identity can also be stolen without using the Internet. Information can be obtained through stolen wallets or by rifling through garbage cans for personal information. In some cases, the identities of dead people have been used to commit identity theft. Criminals can then easily open bank accounts, procure car loans, and negotiate mortgages in the names of their victims, who may only learn of the crime when they view their credit reports or apply for credit. It may take up to $1,000 for a victim to restore damaged credit after his/her identity is stolen. Merchants who are taken in by the cons are usually the ones who absorb the loss of fraudulent transactions.

The sheer brazenness of these cybercrimes has ensured their initial success in a number of instances. For example, Carlos Salgado, Jr., a 36-year-old freelance computer technician operating out of San Francisco, managed to steal more than 100,000 credit card numbers using widely available computer intrusion software and amassed a credit line of $1 billion. He was caught in an FBI sting in May 1997, when he tried to sell the information for $260,000. One of the most far-reaching hacking schemes occurred in April 2011, when rogue members of the hacking group Anonymous operating out of Spain hacked into Sony's PlayStation Network, giving them access to credit card numbers and personal information on approximately 70,000 people worldwide. The service was down for several weeks so that it could be rebuilt. It is still uncertain how much damage was caused by the stolen credit card numbers.

By the early 21st century, cybercrime had reached epidemic proportions. Congress passed the Identity Theft and Assumption Deterrence Act, making it a violation of federal law to engage in identity theft. In 2000, financial institutions reported approximately $2.4 billion in losses and expenses incurred as a result of identity theft. More than 90 percent of all government agencies reported that they had experienced security breaches in 2001. The majority of those breaches were perpetrated by hackers or con artists, but a large number were the work of disgruntled employees. With partial funding from the Department of Justice, the FBI has partnered with the White-Collar Crime Center to establish the Internet Crime Complaint Center (IC3).

In 2001, IC3 reported that Internet auction fraud was the most common type of cybercrime, comprising 42.8 percent of all complaints. Slightly over a fifth of all complaints dealt with nondeliverable merchandise and payment accounts. Nigerian letter fraud accounted for 15.5 percent of the total complaints received. Victims of this fraud lost approximately $5,575 each, compared with $1,000 lost in investment fraud incidences. According to IC3's profile of victims of cybercrime, they are most likely to be individuals, rather than business, are predominately males between the ages of 30 and 50, and are likely to live in California, Florida, New York, Texas, or Illinois. Losses incurred tend to be higher for businesses than for individuals and for males than for females. Most contact between perpetrators and victims takes place either through e-mail or via a Web page.

According to statistics released by the National Fraud Information Center (NFIC), some $5 billion was lost to telecommunications fraud alone in 2000. The NFIC identifies the 10 most commonly perpetrated frauds as work-at-home schemes (16 percent), prizes/sweepstakes (15 percent), telephone slamming (15 percent), advance-fee loans (11 percent), magazine sales (10 percent), telephone cramming (9 percent), credit card offers (5 percent), travel/vacation frauds (3 percent), credit and loss protection frauds (2 percent), and investment fraud (2 percent). Telephone slamming is the illegal practice of switching someone's telephone service from one company to another without their consent, and telephone cramming is the illegal practice of charging customers for unwanted or unauthorized services.

Government-Targeted Frauds

In the minds of much of the public, welfare fraud is one of the most common types of fraud committed in the United States, and public pressure was in large part responsible for the passage of the Personal Responsibility and Work Opportunity Reconciliation Act by the Republican-controlled Congress in 1996 as part of their Contract with America. The law required recipients to work 30 to 35 hours a week and placed time limits on the receipt of benefits. Some social workers contend that the lion's share of welfare fraud is committed not by con artists, but by recipients, most of whom are single mothers working for minimum wage, who either knowingly or inadvertently underreport or fail to report income that affects their welfare payments. In San Diego in 2007, the welfare fraud diversion program was created as an alternative to prosecuting first-time, low-level offenders through criminal courts.

The National Health Care Anti-Fraud Association estimates that the United States loses about $15 billion each year to healthcare spending fraud and suggested in a congressional hearing in 2011 that actual losses are more likely from $75 billion to $250 billion per year. The Government Accounting Office suggests that fraud may often be involved in the $48 billion that medical insurers improperly pay each year. Most of those frauds are committed through the Medicare program, which critics point out has few checks in place to prevent fraud. Some of those frauds are committed by individuals receiving benefits to which they are entitled, but most involve physicians and others who bill for services not needed or never performed.

Occupational Fraud
Offenses classified as occupational fraud cover a wide range of behaviors that may not seem like fraud to those who commit them. Put simply, it is enriching oneself through the misuse of an employer's or company's resources. In 1996, in its first *Report to the Nation on Occupational Fraud and Abuse*, the Association of Certified Fraud Examiners (ACFE) attempted to clarify the exact meaning of occupational abuse by noting that to qualify as fraud, a behavior must be clandestine, violate an employee's fiduciary duties to the organization in question, either directly or indirectly benefit said employee, and cost the employer assets, revenue, or reserves. By 2004, "skimming" was identified as a major subgroup of occupational fraud. ACFE defined the practice as removing cash without entering it into an employee accounting system. Skimming was generally accomplished by failing to record sales, understating sales and receivables, stealing checks directly from the mail, conducting business after hours, or short-term "borrowing" of funds with the intention of replacing them. "Lapping" is a form of skimming that involves subtracting money from one account to hide the fact that money has actually been taken from a second account.

Experts on fraud have identified three major types of occupational fraud: asset misappropriation, corruption, and fraudulent schemes. At least 85 percent of all cases of fraud deal with asset misappropriation. It is estimated that occupational fraud occurs millions of times each day in the United States and generates losses of at least $600 billion every year. More than half of all cases of occupational fraud are uncovered through tips from other employees. When tips to hot lines, many of which are anonymous calls from fellow employees, are added to the mix, approximately two-thirds of occupational fraud cases are reported by coworkers. Audits unearth 22.6 percent of cases of occupational fraud, and another 5.4 percent are discovered in the course of management reviews. Only 1 percent of all cases are discovered through an employee's lifestyle drastically changing as a result of fraudulent behavior. The 2002 ACFE report suggests that 30 percent of occupational fraud occurs in publicly traded companies, 31.9 percent in privately held companies, 24.7 percent in government agencies, and 13.4 percent in not-for-profit organizations.

At the lower end of the occupational fraud continuum are behaviors such as using company property for personal reasons, payroll and sick pay abuses, taking supplies to be used at home, filing false claims for overtime, or ringing up "no sale" when removing small amounts of cash from a register. At the higher end, occupational fraud may involve slick, sophisticated schemes intended to cheat employers out of large sums of money, making false financial statements, or setting up dummy companies for the purposes of channeling company profits into other accounts. Fraud dealing with representation of company funds may be the result of hiding inventory or profits to underrepresent total profits, or it may be concerned with making a company appear more profitable than it actually is to attract investors. Fraud perpetrators frequently manipulate income by recording revenue before it is earned, creating fictitious revenue, boosting profits through nonrecurring transactions, shifting expenses to later periods, or failing to report liabilities accurately. Vendor and customer fraud are associated with occupational fraud and may occur simultaneously. Vendor fraud occurs when customers are intentionally overcharged for goods, when inferior goods are shipped, or when goods are not delivered, even when the customer has paid for them. Customer fraud takes place when customers do not pay for goods or when they illegally receive services or goods at no cost.

Historical Examples of Fraud
The history of notorious frauds is legendary. According to FBI records, there were extraordinarily large numbers of land frauds committed in the United States in the 19th and early 20th centuries. Many of these involved buying up lands cheaply and luring investors with false promises

of finding oil or precious gems, but others enticed potential buyers by convincing them that they would find the perfect lifestyle in places like California or Florida. The southern areas of both states attracted Americans interested in warm climates, outdoor sports, and the lure of celebrities. One of the most notorious land frauds that took place in the American west occurred in Oregon in 1905. Land areas that were rich in timber surrounded the newly built Oregon and California Railroad. Even so, the price of the land was set at $2.50 an acre in order to entice new settlers to the area. Ned Harriman, a railroad official, devised a plan whereby he sent men to buy the land and then sell it to his accomplice, who then sold it to the highest bidder for timber rights. A falling out between the partners led to exposure, and more than 1,000 people were eventually indicted. The best known of those convicted of fraud was four-term U.S. Senator John H. Mitchell, who was convicted of accepting bribes to expedite the fraudulent land sales. Representatives John N. Williamson and Binger Hermann were also indicted in the scheme.

Because of the lure of untold riches, the field of mining was ripe for fraud, and the Comstock mine in Nevada was particularly associated with this crime. The name derived from Henry "Pancake" Comstock, who tricked his way into a share of the original silver mine discovered by prospectors in 1859. San Franciscans quickly lined up to invest in the Comstock mine. At one point, more than 400 mining corporations were formed and almost none of them sold land that actually contained silver. The complexity of the enterprise led to the creation of the San Francisco Stock Exchange Board, which locals dubbed "the 40 thieves" because of all the chicanery involved. Other mining schemes involved "salting" designated areas to trick victims into investing in nonexistent mines. One of the most elaborate of such schemes, the "Great Diamond Hoax of 1872," was the brainchild of Philip Arnold, who worked as a bookkeeper for a drill company and was familiar with industrial-grade diamonds. In 1870, Arnold added uncut garnets, rubies, and sapphires obtained from Native Americans to a bag of uncut diamonds, and he and his cousin, John Slack, launched a lengthy campaign to defraud a large group of investors that eventually included Civil War heroes General George B. McClellan and Benjamin "Beast" Butler, as well as Horace Greeley, the editor of the *New York Tribune*. Arnold eventually garnered some $550,000 from his schemes, minus the cost of gems purchased in London that were used to salt the mine. The fraud was eventually uncovered by geologist Clarence King, who went public with his findings.

During the Gilded Age, the United States was growing rapidly, fueled in part by expanding railroads. Between 1865 and 1890, railroad mileage expanded from 35,000 miles to 163,000 miles. Railroad tycoons like Cornelius Vanderbilt and Thomas Clark Durant demonstrated that large fortunes could be made rapidly. Monopolies became common, promoted by men like Jay Gould, Jim Fisk, and Russell Sage, who became known as "robber barons," because of their "innovative" business practices. Gould, the president of the Erie Railroad, was known as the "prince" of the robber barons and was the most vilified of them all. He bought railroads that were going under, improved them, and sold them for huge profits. He also developed a reputation for manipulating insider stock trading and using corporate funds to pay for personal speculation. He was known for bribing everyone from the brother-in-law of President Ulysses S. Grant to members of the New York state legislature.

Fraud has continued as a major part of doing business in the United States, and new scandals are constantly reported on by the media and surface on the Internet.

Elizabeth Rholetter Purdy
Independent Scholar

See Also: 1921 to 1940 Primary Documents; Confidence Games and Frauds; Embezzlement; Identity Theft; Larceny.

Further Readings

Albrecht, Steven and Chad Albrecht. *Fraud Examination and Prevention*. Mason, OH: Thomson/Southwestern, 2004.

Branigan, Steven. *High-Tech Crimes Revealed: Cyberwar Stories From the Digital Front*. Boston: Addison-Wesley, 2005.

Federal Bureau of Investigation. "Common Fraud Schemes." http://www.fbi.gov/scams-safety/fraud (Accessed October 2011).

Federal Bureau of Investigation. "White-Collar Crime." http://www.fbi.gov/about-us/investigate/white_collar (Accessed October 2011).

Internet Crime Complaint Center. http://www.ic3.gov/default.aspx (Accessed October 2011).

Madison, Joyce. *Great Hoaxes, Swindles, Scandals, Cons, Stings, and Scams*. New York: Signet, 1992.

Swan, Richelle S., et al. "The Untold Story of Welfare Fraud." *Journal of Sociology and Social Welfare*, v.35/3 (September 2008).

Wells, Joseph T., ed. *Corporate Fraud Handbook: Prevention and Detection*. Hoboken, NJ: John Wiley & Sons, 2004.

Wells, Joseph T., ed. *Fraud Casebook: Lessons From the Bad Side of Business*. Hoboken, NJ: John Wiley & Sons, 2007.

Freedom of Information Act of 1966

The Freedom of Information Act (FOIA) of 1966 is a piece of landmark legislation regarding the ability to obtain information from government agencies that previously was not accessible to the public. This act became law in 1966 over the objections of President Lyndon B. Johnson. The law has been amended several times and is still a powerful tool for Americans who are doing research for both personal and public interests.

Prior to the passage of this legislation in 1966, the public had very limited access to federal government information; over time this has changed, although the information can still be restricted under later amendments to this law. The impetus for the FOIA dates back to 1953 when the book *The People's Right to Know: Legal Access to Public Records and Proceedings* was published by Harold L. Cross at the request of the American Society of Newspaper Editors. During this period, the press found it difficult to obtain information from government sources because most everything was considered classified and related in some way to national security.

In response to the book's publication, Representative John Moss (D-CA) began a debate in Congress in 1954 that continued for the next 12 years. A series of hearings took place in those years that led to the proposal of Senate Bill 1160 in 1965, which revised Section 3 of the Administrative Code, which until that point was used as the reason for keeping all information secret.

The final version of the bill satisfied Congress, the president, and those who sought government information. The 1966 version called for the publication of key documents like federal laws, regulations and notices of changes to regulations, presidential documents, and even descriptions of each federal agency and its organization, programs, and staff. Also, the public could get copies of court case opinions, agency policy, and manuals, among other items. Ultimately, the purpose of the act was to give citizens access to public records unless the information in them was considered private, a threat to national security, or inaccessible for other reasons. Agencies that opted to deny access to the information had to provide a reason for the denial within 10 working days, and the denial could be appealed. This satisfied the needs of the press, who often wrote articles requiring government information that was often not available because it was "secret."

Amendments and Impact

President Johnson expressed some concerns about the law but was satisfied with the final version, signing it on July 4, 1966; the legislation went into effect a year later. The law received its first update in 1974 with the passage of the Privacy Act, which allowed individuals to inquire about investigations relating to them personally. This was in response to news reports that individuals who disagreed with government policy may be under investigation or may have been investigated by either the Federal Bureau of Investigation or the Central Intelligence Agency. In addition to allowing access to these records to make corrections, the act also called for individuals to be able to sue the government for letting others view information about them. In recent years, this has been expanded to include information held by educational institutions, libraries, workplaces, and physicians, among others. The Privacy Act allows individuals to designate who has access to their information and who can talk with others about their case.

The FOIA gained some credibility in 1974 after President Richard Nixon argued both executive privilege and national security as reasons why Congress and investigators should not have access to White House transcripts and other information related to the Watergate scandal; Congress amended the law in 1974 to force federal agencies to release records. President Ronald Reagan used Executive Order 12356 issued April 2, 1982, in an attempt to limit which information could be obtained under the FOIA, calling for close review of the requests weighing national security against the public's right to information. In 1986, further revision to the FOIA by Congress added limitations to what could be released. President Bill Clinton further restricted what could be accessed with his declaration that the National Security Council does not fall under the FOIA because it holds presidential papers that come under different release guidelines. In 1996, the FOIA was amended by Congress with the addition of the Electronic Freedom of Information Act, which addresses electronic formats like discs, Websites, and other electronic forms not in existence in 1966. In 2002, after the 9/11 attacks, Congress passed further restrictions that would prevent foreigners from viewing files held by security agencies in the United States. Access to information is a major issue in today's society, and legislation must address how to keep it secure and how to verify authenticity, particularly in the case of government information.

While the FOIA has increased access to information from government agencies by the public, it remains a subjective process. The release or denial of access to information often depends on who is asking for the information and what it will be used for. The FOIA also allows people to get information that used to be restricted to them, thus putting great strain on the agencies and their resources Another concern is how to monitor the information that has been released while protecting the individuals involved. Still, the FOIA and its amendments have increased access to information. Researchers can access materials in a timely manner and contribute to the scholarship about politics and historical events without having to wait extended periods for the information to be declassified and released. This law fulfills the founding fathers' wish of having a truly informed public.

Theresa S. Hefner-Babb
Lamar University

See Also: Clinton, William (Administration of); Nixon, Richard (Administration of); Reagan, Ronald (Administration of); Watergate.

Further Readings
Franklin, Justin D. and Robert F. Bouchard, eds. *Guidebook to the Freedom of Information and Privacy Acts*. New York: C. Boardman, 1986.
Hernon, Peter and Charles R. McClure. *Federal Information Policies in the 1980s: Conflict and Issues*. Norwood, NJ: Ablex Publishing, 1987.

Frontier Crime

The imagery of frontier violence is pervasive in the American consciousness. From the dime novels of the 1800s to classic western films and TV shows of the 1930s to the present, the cowboy as symbol of the American west is encountered at every turn. The fact the most cowhands were toothless, semi-literate, foul-smelling men who were almost lame and were riddled with health issues such as chronic urinary disorders (from a life in the saddle and sexually-transmitted diseases) is, however, not as cinematic. Also, it is not popularly understood that frontier violence occurred at places other than the scenic environment of John Ford's iconic Monument Valley, and that John Wayne or Clint Eastwood were not invariably present.

The frontier was never static and was really only in the far west for perhaps a generation; the frontier began in the east in colonial times and shifted continually westward. The "frontier" was defined in the 1770s as the Alleghenies, shifted to the Mississippi (the "old southwest") around 1800, then to Texas in the 1830s, and gradually, well after the Civil War, to the area we would all recognize as "true west," the southwest and California. Alaska, of course, touts itself as the "last frontier," and that is largely accurate. Frontiers or border areas are almost always magnets for crime and vice, and all the regions previously mentioned experienced higher rates of crime before or after their respective booms, or frontier eras. Some areas, usually clustered around international borders, literally remained frontiers; some state borders, having earlier been borders between sovereign nations,

This 1937 photograph by Dorothea Lange shows a sign outside Tombstone, Arizona, that lists some of the condemned criminals and murder victims of that town's boomtown era who are buried in Boothill Graveyard. It was said to be called "Boothill" because most people who ended up buried there died "with their boots on" during violent incidents rather than from natural causes.

continued to enjoy frontier conditions and carried on violent traditions. One of the most infamous frontiers was the Sabine Strip, which ran along the Texas-Louisiana border and harbored outlaws, runaway slaves, and ne'er-do-wells from the days when Texas was part of Spain and Louisiana was part of an infant republic. Through Texas's days as an independent nation, through statehood, and even after the Civil War, the area remained a criminal refuge, and violence was common. State legal institutions remained weak in these areas, and they were never successfully cleared of criminal elements and a "frontier mentality."

Conditions Favorable for Crime

The general rule of violent crime on the frontier is that it flourished under certain conditions. One factor was the presence of large numbers of young men, often drawn to the area by economic boom conditions. The second factor was large numbers of available firearms. Men in frontier situations were often armed for a number of reasons, including hunting and defense from animals, snakes, hostile native people, and each other. Alcohol and other drugs such as opium were freely available and promiscuously consumed in supportive group settings, that is, saloons or opium dens (after the 1840s). The bachelor culture of the era put a premium on honor and on defending one's autonomy and self-respect. This led to many quarrels and altercations over personal space, women (always in short supply), and mining claims. Finally, the lack of respectable influential women and the presence of prostitutes contributed to making the west really "wild." The combination of youth, armament, alcohol, (mostly) loose women, and an exacting code of honor was potentially lethal. It is interesting that in all significant situations where violent frontier episodes are known, the above elements are all present. Boomtowns like Sacramento and San Francisco were so disrupted by criminal and civil disorders that businessmen and miners created vigilance committees, formed private armies (militias), and had kangaroo courts. In these venues, thieves and other offenders suffered swift and harsh justice under the iron hand of vigilantes.

Frontier boomtowns in contemporary South America and Siberia have endured similar criminogenic conditions, and there, too, vigilantes appeared. Again, booming economic conditions, young men, alcohol/drugs, arms, and sexual commerce, when combined, create a context for increased criminal and violent behavior, even transculturally. Significantly, it has been argued that these same conditions to one extent or another prevail in the urban frontier of some inner cities today. That is, drug sales and markets represent the economic boom, young men are armed and touchy, and drugs and prostitutes (e.g., "crack whores") are accessible. Additionally, in the recent past, some communities that adjoined large military bases in the United States have enjoyed reputations as vice-ridden boomtowns. That is, bars, prostitution, and other vice industries flourished to exploit young men, many away from home for the first time. The combination keeps the MPs on the go.

The Old West
Much of the development of the ever-westward-moving frontier was the product of sudden economic booms caused by land speculation, gold or silver rushes, or the movement of commodities such as cattle. In the early days of the republic, canal building pushed the development and settlement westward and created frontier conditions that were ideal for crime. River traffic on the Ohio and Mississippi rivers made cities like St. Louis, Natchez, and New Orleans into frontier towns anew. Buffalo, New York, was a frontier boomtown due to the Erie Canal. Rowdy flatboatmen, gamblers, prostitutes, and bars and saloons were known features of these communities. Railroad building rekindled this same pattern as the tracks moved westward in the 1860s, 1870s, and 1880s. Where railroads intersected with the terminal points of cattle drives, the possibilities for violence were compounded.

In fact, many of the most celebrated examples of frontier violence occurred in cow towns or mining communities. The former were boomtowns buoyed by their proximity to the track or to the end of cattle drives. Small towns like Fort Worth, Texas, and Dodge City and Abilene, Kansas, expanded with new businesses to deal with the cattle trade. The latter included places like Tombstone, Arizona, and Sacramento, California. Gambling establishments, saloons, and brothels became prevalent. Law enforcement was problematic, and these nascent cities were forced to hire such shady characters as Wyatt Earp in various policing capacities.

Earp, though often portrayed as heroic (as in *Gunfight at OK Corral*), stoic, and strictly law-abiding, was actually engaged in gambling, and possibly in procuring. He was a careerist and political hack who warred with Democrats, especially in Tombstone, carried on violent feuds, and associated with the thuggish and infamous gambler and reprobate "Doc" Holliday. The cinematic portrayal in the revisionist serio-comic *Tombstone*, in which Earp is portrayed as a gambler living with a drug-addled prostitute common-law wife, is much closer to the reality of boomtown law enforcement. Indeed, much of the dialogue carefully tracks that which we know to have really been uttered by principals in the events of that era. In many respects, the association of law enforcement personnel with hired guns, the criminal element, and political/mercantile interests was the norm. A significant portion of the business community was heavily invested in commercialized vice. This created a continuous criminogenic climate.

To deal with the issue of ongoing drunken violence, not a few frontier boomtowns and cow towns, such as Dodge City, Kansas, established and enforced "deadlines." Firearms were not allowed beyond this arbitrary point. Weapons had to be checked in with a deputy on the scene or in the town marshal's office. The gun owner would be given a metal token, which he would return upon leaving the restricted area, and his firearm would be restored to him. This allowed municipal officials to disarm all and sundry, thus reducing the probably of alcohol-fueled lethal violence.

Brothels, casinos, and saloons were, thus, often protected by lawmen. Indeed, as in the case of Earp, the officer might have a personal pecuniary interest in these establishments. Prostitutes were often very young and not particularly attractive but found many eager customers. Upon retirement, they frequently found equally ardent suitors and vanished into reputability as businesswomen (perhaps running brothels or "hotels" themselves) and wives. But while "in the life," they could provoke fights and were often diseased and the victims of brutality from customers, pimps, and thugs who maintained order in the bordellos. Brothels were often concentrated in areas (red-light districts) that were defined by informal or even legally specified boundaries.

Bars and casinos were in the same areas and were frequently contained within the self-same establishments. As one might imagine, professional gamblers were as problematic as were prostitutes. While attracting "suckers"—inexperienced yokels and gamblers—to the house with their higher level of play, professional gamblers sometimes provoked violence from losers. Occasionally, they provoked mass outbreaks of violence. In 1835 in Natchez, then very much on the frontier, an antigambling vigilance committee lynched five gamblers for the killing of a local citizen. But the city's vice district, Natchez-Under-the-Hill, remained an attraction for travelers along the Mississippi until after the Civil War.

"Doc" Holliday, who had to leave post–Civil War Georgia because of a violent incident, when not acting as a hired gun for large mining corporations, supported himself by gambling. Living with an infamous prostitute in Tombstone, Holliday was in a series of violent incidents culminating in the shoot-out that newspapers of the time, and subsequent books and films, magnified and mythologized into "the gunfight at O.K. Corral." In reality, this was comparable to an armed brawl over turf or drug markets in a dozen contemporary American cities, that is, one gang of toughs simply prevailed over another. So it can be seen that gamblers, even when allied with law enforcement of the day, further destabilized boomtowns, thus contributing to the violence of frontier areas.

Conclusion

Some have argued that the "violent" frontier imagery that is so much a part of the national narrative is a media-fostered myth. However, this construct may have been exaggerated by fiction, cinema, and popular culture; recent scholarship disputes such revisionism. The Wild West may have actually been much wilder than was previously thought. Archaeologists, for example, have unearthed much evidence of violence and trauma in graves along wagon-train trails. Moreover, the historical record is replete with examples of interpersonal violence and collective violence such as shoot-outs, ambushes, massacres, and vigilantism. In the absence of an effective state, private justice was often perceived as the only option open to individuals and communities.

Francis Frederick Hawley
Western Carolina University

See Also: 1851 to 1900 Primary Documents; Arizona; Earp, Wyatt; History of Crime and Punishment in America: 1783–1850; History of Crime and Punishment in America: 1850–1900; Kansas; Lynchings; Prostitution, History of; Sheriffs; Vigilantism.

Further Readings
Ayers, Edward L. *Vengeance and Justice: Crime and Punishment in the 19th Century American South*. New York: Oxford University Press, 1984.
Brown, Richard M. *Strain of Violence: Historical Studies of American Violence and Vigilantism*. New York: Oxford University Press, 1975.
Courtwright, D. T. *Violent Land: Single Men and Social Disorder From the Frontier to the Inner City*. Cambridge, MA: Harvard University Press, 1998.
Cutrer, Thomas W. "Southwestern Violence." In *Encyclopedia of Southern Culture*, C. R. Wilson and W. Ferris, eds. Chapel Hill: University of North Carolina Press, 1989.
Lane, Roger. *Murder in America: A History*. Columbus: Ohio State University Press, 1997.
Moore, Arthur. *The Frontier Mind*. Lexington: University of Kentucky Press, 1957.
Richards, Leonard. *The California Gold Rush and the Coming of the Civil War*. New York: Knopf, 2007.
Wyatt-Brown, Bertram. *Southern Honor*. New York: Oxford University Press, 1982.

Frontiero v. Richardson

Frontiero v. Richardson (1973) heralded the Supreme Court's willingness to consider gender issues seriously, because for the first time, it held a number of federal statutes in violation of the due process clause of the Fifth Amendment. Also significant was the fact that a plurality of the court endorsed gender as a suspect classification. Prior to the 1970s, laws permitting discrimination on the basis of gender were typically upheld by the courts. However, in *Reed v. Reed*, 404 U.S. 71 (1971), the Supreme Court held unconstitutional, on Fourteenth Amendment equal protection grounds, a state statute requiring probate judges to assign males in preference to females as the administrators of decedents' estates. Applying the "rational basis" test, also known as "minimal scrutiny," the court found the differential treatment arbitrary. In choosing this standard of review, the court refused to apply the "compelling state interest" or "strict scrutiny" test, as it would place gender in the same category as race, ethnicity, and religion.

Sharon Frontiero was an officer in the U.S. Air Force who sought to have her husband classified as a dependent so that they, along with other married couples, might qualify for increased housing allowances and so that he, along with other spouses, might receive comprehensive medical and dental care. Pursuant to the congressional statutory scheme, women service members were required to demonstrate that their contribution to their husband's support was in excess of 50 percent, while male service members, in order to secure the same benefits to their spouses, were not. Frontiero brought suit alleging that this difference in treatment was unconstitutional under the Fifth Amendment's due process clause.

While holding the differential treatment unconstitutional, the individual justices did not agree upon the proper standard of review. Only four justices settled upon gender as a suspect classification deserving of strict scrutiny and requiring the government to show both a compelling interest and a narrowly tailored application. Four other justices agreed that the statutory discrimination was invidious and unconstitutional but thought it better to retain the rational basis test for the reasons articulated in *Reed*. Additionally, they thought it the proper role of the judiciary to await the ratification of the Equal Rights Amendment. The final justice, Justice WilliamRehnquist, found no discrimination whatsoever. Subsequently, the court, in *Craig v. Boren*, 429 U.S. 190 (1976), adopted an "intermediate scrutiny" standard of review for gender discrimination. Under that standard, gender-based classifications must serve important governmental objectives and must be substantially related to the achievement of those objectives.

Frontiero, to some degree, addressed the social and political goals of the feminist movement of that era to end what they defined as the paternalistic, separate, and unequal treatment of women in the male-dominated society of the time. Post *Frontiero*, legislative drafting had added Fifth Amendment due process limitations in the civil context. In this way, it transcended the issue before the court as the cases of discrimination against African Americans had in earlier cases. In 1996, the court established a standard of review for sex discrimination cases, heightened or skeptical scrutiny, in an opinion by Justice Ruth Bader Ginsburg.

In the criminal law context, *Frontiero* and its progeny prompted state legislatures to evaluate gender in sexual offenses. Rape law reforms in many states accomplished not only gender neutrality within the statutes but also expanded the definition of the crime to include a larger range of conduct and contact. Penetration by the penis of the vagina, the historical definition, was expanded to include penetration by objects of other orifices. In some states, the term *rape* was replaced with sexual assault, sexual battery, or criminal sexual conduct. These statutes commonly grade the offense based upon injury to the victim, age of the victim, number of assailants, and use of weapons in the commission of the offense. While some of the goals of the reformers were met, gender neutrality and expanded definitions failed to achieve the most important goal, deterrence.

Karen S. Price
Stephen F. Austin State University

See Also: Civil Rights Laws; Gender and Criminal Law; Sex Offender Laws.

Further Readings

Frontiero v. Richardson, 411 U.S. 677; 93 S. Ct. 1764 (1973).

Ginsburg, Ruth Bader. "Constitutional Adjudication in the United States as a Means of Advancing the Equal Status of Men and Women Under the Law." *Hofstra Law Review*, v.26 (1997).

Novotny, Patricia. "Law and Sexuality." *Seattle Journal of Social Justice*, v.1 (2003).

Siegel, Reva B. "Text in Contest: Gender and the Constitution From a Social Movement Perspective." *University of Pennsylvania Law Review*, v.150 (2001).

Fugitive Slave Act of 1793

Among the early structural legal supports for American chattel slavery, Article 4, Section 2 of the U.S. Constitution provided that "[n]o Person held to Service or Labour in one State, under the Laws thereof, escaping into another, shall, in Consequence of any Law or Regulation therein, be discharged from such Service or Labour, But shall be delivered up on Claim of the Party to whom such Service or Labour may be due." However, the Constitution did not provide any mechanism to enforce the recovery of escaped slaves or indentured servants. Slavery, particularly within the southern states, had become an essential piece of agrarian plantation economies. Opposition to recovery in Northern states, unwillingness on the part of northern citizens and officials to participate in what some considered kidnapping, and confusion on what they were required to do contributed to escalating tension between regions.

The Fugitive Slave Act of 1793, signed into law by President George Washington, constructed that enforcement mechanism for interstate and territorial cooperation on fugitives from justice and escaped servants and slaves. The act criminalized assistance to escapees, imposing a $500 fine and imprisonment for up to one year for aiding a criminal fugitive. The penalty for aiding an escaped slave or servant was $500. Moreover, the act empowered slaveholders and their authorized agents and attorneys to seize alleged slaves and petition the courts for removal to the home state. The act ignored the standard elements of due process and merely required appearance before a judge or magistrate and proof to his satisfaction through oral testimony.

The cover of the sheet music for "The Fugitive's Song," published in Boston in 1845, depicts Frederick Douglass during his escape from slavery in 1838. It is dedicated to Douglass and to "the fugitives from slavery in the free states and Canada."

After the act was passed, state laws still varied. Some states specified which judicial officer had to hear claims against alleged escapees and fugitives. Others set high evidentiary standards for the oral testimony, and in some cases the act was balanced by substantial penalties for the crime of kidnapping. Although Pennsylvania vacillated on protections for African Americans, it did require that a judge hear fugitive cases. It also enhanced evidence requirements. The 1793 act is also notable for giving birth to the soon-bustling industry of slave catching. Professional kidnappers roamed northern cities, often seizing both enslaved and free blacks. Historical evidence suggests that they were not discriminating in whom they captured. In 1841, Solomon Northup, an educated New York free man, was enticed by the promise of lucrative work to travel with men who drugged him and turned him over to slave catchers. His kidnappers threatened his life if he revealed his true name and history, and he remained enslaved until 1853. He later sued his kidnappers in New York courts.

African Americans in the north formed vigilance committees, perhaps most notably that headed by David Ruggles in New York, who received the young Frederick Douglass upon his escape from Maryland. The vigilance societies kept up surveillance on slave catchers, drew attention to seizure cases, protected free blacks, and struggled to force jury trials for seized blacks. In some cases, African Americans resorted to violence to free those seized. In the 1842 case of George Latimer, a Virginia fugitive, even Frederick Douglass became involved, arguing to listeners at a New Bedford, Massachusetts, speech that blacks should come to Latimer's aid. He even wrote later to William Lloyd Garrison of the case, but Latimer's case was eventually settled by his purchase into freedom.

The Fugitive Slave Act of 1793 had attention from the Supreme Court that same year in *Prigg v. Pennsylvania* (1842). The court eventually affirmed the supremacy of the act over state laws. Prigg had sought to recover Margaret Morgan, a Maryland slave who had mostly lived in freedom but who had not been formally emancipated. In doing so, Prigg ran afoul of the 1788 and 1826 Pennsylvania laws that protected escaped slaves and regulated the action of slave catchers. In many ways, the *Prigg* decision helped set the stage for the 1850 Fugitive Slave Act. Even though it prohibited state laws and state officials from interfering with the recovery of slaves, it also gave states a way to wash their hands of enforcement and leave it up to federal officials. With this new support for the act, African American opposition and white abolitionist forces were pressed to take bolder and more provocative action on the issue of slavery.

Eric Ashley Hairston
Elon University

See Also: 1777 to 1800 Primary Documents; African Americans; Constitution of the United States of America; Fugitive Slave Act of 1850; Kidnapping; Slavery; Slavery, Law of.

Further Readings
Douglass, Frederick. *Narrative of the Life of Frederick Douglass, An American Slave Written by Himself*. Ed. John W. Blassingame. New Haven, CT: Yale University Press, 2007.
Morris, Thomas D. *Southern Slavery and the Law 1619–1860*. Chapel Hill: University of North Carolina Press, 1996.
Northup, Solomon. *Twelve Years a Slave*. New York: Barnes & Noble, 2007.

Fugitive Slave Act of 1850

With a vibrant abolitionist movement, an active Underground Railroad, increasing northern opposition to slavery, and powerful escaped slave orators and authors decrying bondage, southern states faced formidable obstacles to sustaining their system of bondage. The Fugitive Slave Act of 1793 had given teeth to the constitutional right of slaveholders to recover property, but the Supreme Court decision in *Prigg v. Pennsylvania* (1842) had served to both affirm the supremacy of the federal rule over any state resistance and provide states with the ability to leave the massive undertaking up to federal officers. This state of affairs certainly did not serve to reduce the conflict between northern and southern states, and a political battle seemingly heading toward southern secession was only resolved by the Compromise of 1850. This legislation, crafted by Henry Clay and negotiated by Stephen Douglas, settled caustic debates over the extension of slavery to California, Texas, and future states carved out

An engraving of illustrations from the life of fugitive slave Anthony Burns, published in Boston in 1855. Burns's May 1854 arrest in Boston and trial under the Fugitive Slave Act of 1850 sparked riots by abolitionists and other Boston citizens.

of territorial areas. It also settled land claims by Texas and determined the disposition of Texas's debt. Notably, the compromise also ended the slave trade in Washington, D.C., which housed an enormous slave market. However, slavery itself still existed in the capital. The most controversial provision of the Compromise of 1850 was a strengthened Fugitive Slave Act that sought to give greater assurances to southern states that their escaped human property would be returned, even over northern state political opposition and the individual scruples of officials.

The Fugitive Slave Act of 1850 targeted official resistance in particular. Federal marshals who refused to enforce the act and arrest suspected runaways could be fined $1,000. A force of commissioners was authorized to specifically enforce the act. These commissioners were given broad discretionary powers, including the ability to compel locals to pursue escaped slaves. Intransigence by local officials and state officials and citizens was countered by the requirement that all citizens aid in the seizure of alleged runaways when properly requested. As before, no form of due process existed for African Americans seized under the act. Anyone claiming a person as a slave only had to provide sworn testimony to the arresting officer. African Americans could not demand a trial by jury, and only an affidavit was required of slaveholders as evidence of servitude in the brief judicial formality. Since suspected slaves had no rights in court, free blacks seized under the act could not offer testimony about their status. The only penalty for mistakenly seizing a free person was a $5 fee. The processing fee for a captured slave was $10. The act also targeted the various groups and individuals who had joined together to combat the professional kidnappers. Anyone who offered food or shelter to an escaped slave faced a penalty of six months in jail and a $1,000 fine. Slave catchers roamed free states incessantly, seizing escaped slaves and reportedly ensnaring free African Americans as well. One prominent slave narrative, that of New York's Solomon Northup, chronicles the experience of one such free man kidnapped into slavery under the older act. The evidentiary restrictions placed on accused fugitives made it difficult to ascertain the truth of claims of freedom under the new act. The alleged fugitive was not allowed to testify at the hearing, and a sworn affidavit was sufficient as proof. Since everyone, including the judge, was made an interested party because of the system of fees and fines, the integrity of the courts could not be relied upon. However, by the 1820s, organized kidnapping rings operated in cities like Philadelphia, often targeting children. That established industry suggests the likely truth of claims of free men and women being kidnapped under the Fugitive Slave Act of 1850. In 1852, white abolitionist and author Harriette Beecher Stowe was inspired to write *Uncle Tom's Cabin* by the passage of the Fugitive Slave Act.

The Supreme Court's decision in *Dred Scott v. Sandford* (1857) virtually ended major antebellum legal challenges against slavery, stripping African Americans of citizenship, civil rights, and court standing. With increasing tensions between pro-slavery and antislavery forces, the course toward the American Civil War was largely set. The Compromise of 1850 might have averted an earlier 19th-century secession, but it served to incense northern populations. Vermont reacted by instituting due process requirements that made it difficult to legally remove escaped slaves, and in abolitionist strongholds elsewhere, dissenters on juries disrupted attempts to prosecute slave supporters who protected runaways. Frederick Douglass, who had published his *Narrative* in 1845, fled America for Europe after its publication, fearing the earlier Fugitive Slave Act of 1793, and he returned to America only after his freedom had been purchased. In 1851, Douglass, spurred partly by the Compromise of 1850, the Fugitive Slave Act of 1850, and southern threats of secession, intensified his rhetoric against slavery and the south, illustrating the south's departure from the principles of the founders.

Eric Ashley Hairston
Elon University

See Also: African Americans; *Dred Scott v. Sandford*; Fugitive Slave Act of 1793; Kidnapping; Racism; Slavery; Slavery, Law of.

Further Readings
Brown-Marshall, Gloria J. *Race, Law, and American Society: 1607 to Present*. New York: Routledge, 2007.
Douglass, Frederick. *Narrative of the Life of Frederick Douglass, An American Slave Written by Himself*. Ed. John W. Blassingame. New Haven, CT: Yale University Press, 2007.
Smith, Rogers M. *Civic Ideals: Conflicting Visions of Citizenship in U.S. History*. New Haven, CT: Yale University Press, 1997.

Furman v. Georgia

In *Furman v. Georgia* (1972), the U.S. Supreme Court held that the imposition of the death penalty in the case constituted cruel and unusual punishment in violation of the Constitution. The case, decided along with *Jackson v. Georgia* and *Branch v. Texas*, essentially suspended the death penalty in the United States until 1976. The court's 5–4 majority decision demanded a degree of consistency in the application of the death penalty, which it found lacking in the Georgia statute at issue. While the decision did not ban the death penalty, it did force states and the national government to enact procedures to ensure that the death penalty would not be carried out in an arbitrary or discriminatory manner.

On the night of August 11, 1967, William Henry Furman broke into a house in Savannah, Georgia, with the intent to commit robbery. The owner of the house, William Micke, awoke in the night and went to investigate. He found an armed Furman in his kitchen. As Furman fled the house, he fired the gun that killed Micke instantly. Before his trial, Furman was committed to the Georgia State Central Hospital for psychological testing where he was found to be mentally deficient and suffering from psychotic episodes. Despite this, his insanity plea was refused. Furman received a court-appointed attorney and his trial lasted one day. It took the jury less than two hours to return a guilty verdict and a death sentence against Furman.

In the companion cases of *Jackson v. Georgia* and *Branch v. Texas*, both men were convicted of rape and sentenced to death. Similar to Furman, Branch was judged to have a below average IQ, though this was not seen as a mitigating factor by the juries that convicted them. In each of the cases, the decision regarding whether to impose the death penalty was placed solely in the hands of the juries that had heard the cases. In rendering its decision, the U.S. Supreme Court issued a 5–4 decision, ruling that the Georgia and Texas laws violated the Eighth and Fourteenth Amendments' protection against cruel and unusual punishment. Although Justices William O. Douglas, William Brennan, Peter Stewart, Byron White, and Thurgood Marshall concurred in the outcome, there was no agreement on the legal rationale for the court's decision to invalidate the Georgia and Texas laws nor was there any agreement among the four dissenters (Warren Burger, Harry Blackmun, Lewis Powell, and William Rehnquist). As such, the justices delivered nine separate opinions in the case.

Justice Douglas, after offering a historical view of the Eighth Amendment prohibition on cruel and unusual punishment, found the laws to violate this principle due to the discriminatory manner in which they were often applied. Justice

Douglas located a promise of equal protection within the ban on cruel and unusual punishment and declared it the duty of legislatures to supply laws that are nondiscriminatory and the responsibility of judges to ensure that they are applied in a fair and evenhanded manner. Justice Stewart, joining the court's majority opinion, also condemned the wide disparities in the application of the death penalty, pointing to the countless numbers that had committed the same crimes but had not received the death penalty.

Justices Marshall and Brennan, concurring with the court, were the only two justices to declare the death penalty as cruel and unusual and therefore unconstitutional. Justice Brennan concluded that times had changed to such an extent that contemporary society now rejected capital punishment as antithetical to ideas of human dignity. Justice Marshall found the death penalty to be wanting on almost every level, from its discriminatory application to its excessiveness and failure as a deterrent, and he concluded that the punishment had become morally unacceptable to the American people.

None of the justices in dissent—Burger, Blackmun, Powell, and Rehnquist—felt that capital punishment ran afoul of the Constitution. Justices Powell and Rehnquist argued for deference to the state legislatures that had enacted the death penalty statutes, while Chief Justice Burger was reluctant to remove the decision to impose the death penalty from juries that he described as the cornerstone of the judicial system. With the court's ruling in this case, capital punishment was essentially halted in the United States until 1976, when the Supreme Court in *Gregg v. Georgia* approved a two-stage system for juries to impose the death penalty.

Mary Lou O'Neil
Kadir Has University

See Also: Brennan, William J., Jr.; Capital Punishment; *Coker v. Georgia*; Cruel and Unusual Punishment; Death Row; Electric Chair, History of; Executions; Famous Trials; *Gregg v. Georgia*; Hanging; Prisoner's Rights; Sentencing; Supreme Court, U.S.

Further Readings

Melusky, Joseph A. and Keith Alan Pesto. *Capital Punishment*. Santa Barbara, CA: ABC-CLIO, 2010.

Palmer, Louis J. *Encyclopedia of Capital Punishment in the United States*, 2nd ed. Jefferson, NC: McFarland & Co., 2008.

Gacy, John Wayne

John Wayne Gacy, Jr. (1942–94) was an American serial killer who was responsible for the sex-related slayings of 33 young men and teenage boys between 1972 and 1978. A successful and civic-minded businessman, Gacy was a gregarious and outgoing attention seeker who was heavily involved in local Democratic politics and in organizations such as the U.S. Junior Chamber (Jaycees)—characteristics and attributes that may have enabled Gacy to avoid detection for so long. In addition to hosting elaborate street parties for friends and neighbors, Gacy assisted at local community activities and projects and performed as "Pogo the Clown," a character that he had created for himself, at fund-raising events, parades, and children's parties. Later, he became known as the "Killer Clown." Most of his victims were buried in the crawl space of his home at 8213 Summerdale Avenue in Norwood Park, Illinois—the far northwest side of Chicago.

Crime Spree

Some of Gacy's victims were teenage male runaways or male prostitutes whom Gacy would pick up from Chicago's Greyhound Bus station or New Town—the formerly used community name for the gay-friendly area of Lakeview on the north side of Chicago. Gacy frequently lured teenage boys and young men to his house with either the promise of a job with PDM Contractors, his construction company, or with an offer of drugs or money for sex. At other times, Gacy would invite one of the young men who worked for him back to his house for a drink.

Regardless of the means of enticing his victims, once back at his home, Gacy would tie up his young victim. Sometimes, Gacy accomplished this by rendering the teenagers and young men unconscious with a chloroform-soaked cloth or getting the teenagers and young men inebriated and then overpowering them—Gacy was a strong and corpulent man. On other occasions, Gacy would deceive his victims by claiming to want to show them a stunt with a pair of trick handcuffs that he used in his clown act. Gacy would claim that there was a secret method to unlocking the handcuffs and would challenge the victim to try to figure it out. Once Gacy's victims were restrained, he sexually assaulted them. Death by asphyxiation or strangulation would occur after, during, or even before sexual assault and rape. Gacy then buried the bodies under the floorboards of his home; he often used lime to hasten decomposition of the corpses.

Gacy was apprehended in December 1978 following an investigation into the disappearance of a 15-year-old Des Plaines pharmacy employee, Robert Jerome Piest, to whom Gacy had offered a job with his construction company. After the owner of the pharmacy named Gacy as the contractor with whom Piest had spoken, the Des Plaines Police Department checked Gacy's record and learned that he had served a prison sentence in Iowa for sodomy. An initial search of Gacy's home yielded suspicious items, including other people's driver's licenses, a high school class ring with someone else's initials, dozens of books on homosexuality and pederasty, a pair of handcuffs and keys, and a photo receipt from the pharmacy where Piest worked. An ensuing search of the crawl space under Gacy's home revealed human remains.

Gacy subsequently confessed to murdering at least 30 people and was brought to trial in February 1980, having been charged with 33 murders, including that of Piest—Gacy's last victim. In March 1980, after deliberating for less than two hours, a jury found Gacy guilty of each murder (although not all of his victims were identified). He was subsequently sentenced to death.

Punishment

Gacy was incarcerated at the Menard Correctional Center in Chester, Illinois, where he spent 14 years on death row. While in prison, Gacy began to paint. Although the subjects of Gacy's paintings varied, many were of clowns and some depicted himself as "Pogo." Gacy also devoted his time in prison to studying law and filing numerous appeals—none of which was successful.

On May 10, 1994, Gacy was executed by lethal injection at the Statesville Correctional Center in Crest Hill, Illinois (although clogging of one of the lethal chemicals in the IV tube that led into Gacy's arm forced the execution to be halted for about 10 minutes). He did not express remorse for his crimes.

Ongoing Controversy

Even after his death, Gacy continued to attract attention and spur controversy. In 1996, Plug In Gallery in Winnipeg, Manitoba, Canada, proposed to exhibit three paintings by Gacy as part of an extensive group show called "The Moral Imagination," curated by Wayne Baerwaldt. Following a public outcry—especially from victims of violence and pedophilia—Baerwaldt decided not to exhibit the Gacy paintings. Instead, he framed and displayed two pages from the tabloid *Winnipeg Sun*, which had reproduced one of Gacy's paintings in full color on the front page of its September 17, 1996, issue. The paintings were never displayed at Plug In or anywhere else in Winnipeg. Many have been destroyed by individuals who purchased them for the purpose of burning them.

In May 2011, the Sin City Gallery at the Arts Factory in Las Vegas, Nevada, briefly displayed Gacy's paintings in an exhibition titled "Multiples: The Artwork of John Wayne Gacy." (The exhibition reopened at the larger Contemporary Arts Center Gallery at the Arts Factory in September 2011.) More than 70 pieces were put up for sale, with several fetching between $1,500 and $15,000. While the exhibition was intended to generate funds for those who have been hurt by crime, the National Center for Victims of Crime refused to accept the proceeds.

In October 2011, the Cook County Sheriff's Department resumed efforts to identify the eight unidentified Gacy victims using new DNA technology. In addition, controversy continues to surround the identification of Michael Marino as one of Gacy's victims.

Three films have been made about Gacy: *To Catch a Killer* (1992), starring Brian Dennehy as Gacy, about the investigation of Gacy following the disappearance of Piest; *Gacy* (2003) with Mark Holton as Gacy and Adam Baldwin as his father; and *Dear Mr. Gacy* (2010), starring William Forsythe as Gacy and chronicling the interaction between college student Jason Moss and Gacy, with whom Moss was obsessed. In addition, Gacy has served as the inspiration for *Gacy House* (2010) (also known as *8213: Gacy House*), a mockumentary about a film crew setting out to find the ghost of Gacy, and *Dahmer vs. Gacy* (2010), a comedy horror film about a fictitious competition between Jeffrey Dahmer and Gacy to see which of them is a "better" serial killer. *Dahmer v. Gacy 2: In Space* is in development with a tentative release date of 2013.

Avi Brisman
Emory University

See Also: Capital Punishment; Chicago, Illinois; Famous Trials; Serial and Mass Killers.

Further Readings

Cahill, Tim. *Buried Dreams: Inside the Mind of Serial Killer John Wayne Gacy*. New York: Bantam, 1987.

Linedecker, Clifford L. *The Man Who Killed Boys*. New York: St. Martin's Press, 1980.

Moss, Jason and Jeffrey Kottler. *The Last Victim: A True-Life Journey Into the Mind of a Serial Killer*. New York: Grand Central Publishing, 1999.

Peterson, Kristen. "A Killer Exhibit: John Wayne Gacy's Artwork Is Now on Display." *Las Vegas Weekly*. http://www.lasvegasweekly.com/news/2011/aug/31/killer-exhibit-john-wayne-gacys-artwork-now-displa (Accessed December 2011).

Sullivan, Terry and Peter T. Maiken. *Killer Clown: The John Wayne Gacy Murders*. New York: Pinnacle Books, 1983.

Gambling

Gambling has undergone a considerable evolution in the United States; while it was once almost universally considered a crime, many forms of gambling are now considered businesses and receive sanction from states that are active partners via their tax collections, which can range from 7 percent to as much as 75 percent of the total take. Additionally, many states own lottery operations outright, making states agents of promoting gambling. This shift from criminality to co-option took place over the second half of the 20th century and was the result of both social and economic changes in the United States. Loosening social mores and economic necessity both contributed to turning several American jurisdictions from policing to promoting gambling in many forms.

What is Gambling?

Most authorities define gambling as the act of placing stakes on an unknown outcome with the possibility of gain. They include: betting on the outcome of contests between animals (horse racing, cockfighting) and humans (betting on team and individual sports), betting on lotteries, and betting on games of chance played with cards, dice, and other randomizing elements. Some of the best-known games fall into this latter category, poker, blackjack, baccarat are played with cards, and craps with dice. Slot machines, which were originally mechanical (but are now electronic) devices that award prizes based on the random stopping of the reels, are another popular form of gambling, and today many forms of gambling, most prominently poker and sports betting, can be accessed from the Internet. Betting on games of chance—be they cards, dice, or slot machines—is usually subsumed under the rubric of casino gambling, which may or may not take place in a structure originally intended as a gambling hall.

Often, a single jurisdiction will promote one or more of these gambling forms while continuing to criminalize others. For example, the state of Nevada permits, and at times enthusiastically encourages, casino gambling in a variety of settings, from tourist-oriented casino resorts to small neighborhood gaming taverns, and is the only state in the nation to permit full sports betting, but it does not have a state lottery. Some states sign compacts to permit Indian tribes to run full-fledged casinos without commercial competition. So, it is frequently difficult to trace the evolution from criminal to state-endorsed gambling, since it is often a question of competing forms of gambling receiving sanction rather than a blanket move from total prohibition to complete authorization.

Generally speaking, most gambling was prohibited in most states before 1960, when the development of public-interest gaming, which began in the 1920s, truly flowered. Gambling was legalized for public policy purposes to combat illegal gambling, create jobs, and enhance state revenues. Today, 48 out of 50 states no longer consider gambling a criminal activity but rather one that is subject to regulation and taxation.

Gambling as Crime

From the earliest days of European settlement in North America, gambling policy was ambiguous. In general, gambling was legal, but disturbances arising from gambling—particularly cheating and fighting over the outcome of a bet—became criminalized. It was not until 1646 that Massachusetts passed the colonies' first law banning gambling in public houses. Other northern colonies ranged from strictly antigambling (Quaker Pennsylvania) to nearly indifferent (New York) when it came to gambling at cards and dice. Lotteries, however, were found in every colony except Pennsylvania. Approved by colonial legislatures, these privately run draws funded the construction of roads, colleges, defensive fortifications, and even churches.

Independence from Britain did not much change either gambling behavior or gambling law. Houses devoted exclusively to gambling, a step toward the professionalization of the activity, first appeared in the 1820s and were widespread by the 1830s, particularly in cities like New Orleans, Washington, and New York. Outside of New Orleans (where they alternated between legal and illegal until 1835 when they were outlawed), gambling houses were illegal. Gradually, states began to turn against legal lotteries, revoking charters to operate them. Great Britain, France, Germany, and many other countries also enacted prohibitions against gambling.

American gambling, however, continued to flourish, as its operators merely bought the complicity of local police and political authorities. In the period after the Civil War, as American cities grew, these illegal gambling halls continued to flourish. Starting in the 1870s, gambling on horse racing also grew dramatically, with over 300 tracks open by 1897. At the same time, some states experimented again with lotteries, though a reaction against legal gambling soon began to sweep the nation. This brief flowering of legal gambling did not last. By 1895, the last legal state lottery, that of Louisiana, was shuttered, and in the same period, laws against bookmaking forced tracks to close in many states. In addition, states that had experimented with legal card and dice games, particularly Nevada, criminalized commercial gambling in these years. As a result, by

Spectators watching the one-mile race on Derby Day in 1901 in Louisville, Kentucky. By 1910, the only legal gambling in the United States was betting on horse races in Kentucky or Maryland. Forty years earlier, however, gambling on horse racing had spread rapidly across the country and toward the end of the century, by 1897, over 300 tracks had been open.

1910, the only legal gambling in the United States was betting on horse races in two states, Maryland and Kentucky.

Illegal operators, however, continued to thrive. Illicit lotteries, called both "policy" and "the numbers" boomed in most American cities, particularly among poorer residents. Illegal race betting was even more popular, and it provided an early form of remote entertainment via a national telegraph network called the "race wire" that linked tracks to betting rooms. This lucrative franchise became the object of gang warfare both before and after the better-known battles over liquor distributorship during Prohibition. Following Prohibition's 1933 repeal, many former bootleggers seized upon gambling as their new moneymaker. Although some groups operated or financed illegal casinos, most of the money was to be made in race betting, illegal lotteries, and slot machines. These devices, which had been developed in the 1890s, were found throughout most American cities, though they were usually illegal. By the 1940s, gambling was a thriving business in most American states, often linked to ancillary crimes.

Rise of Public-Interest Gambling
The persistence of gambling despite its official prohibition led some public officials to reconsider its legal status. The "Straus totalisator," invented in 1928, allowed racetracks to mechanically compute the odds that a win, place, or show ticket should pay, thus cutting bookmakers out of the equation. It greatly sped the American adoption of pari-mutuel betting, in which the pot was automatically divided among winners, at the expense of traditional bookmakers, who would set the odds themselves and often profit exorbitantly by interfering with the race's results. Pari-mutuels also allowed states to take a share of the pool. Race betting was thus promoted as both honest and a source of public revenue—a balm to many states during the Great Depression. Horse racing began to spread across the United States, with 24 states legalizing race betting by 1949. In the same years, bingo, hailed as small-stakes gambling for a good cause, also grew. Pari-mutuel betting and bingo were the first fruits of what would become a massive American industry—public-interest gambling.

While pari-mutuels and bingo were in their infancy, another, higher-stakes gambling industry developed in Nevada: legal casino gambling. In 1931, legislators authorized a resumption of the "wide open" commercial gambling that had marked the state from 1869 to 1910, as a way of encouraging tourism. There was initially no state oversight of gambling. In both Reno and Las Vegas, small clubs offering slot machines and table games like craps, roulette, and blackjack appeared. But Nevada gambling set off on a new course in 1941, with the opening of the El Rancho Vegas, the first casino resort on what would become the Las Vegas Strip. As a self-contained resort with fine dining, entertainment, and gambling, the El Rancho Vegas appealed to casual tourists in a way that the smoky downtown gambling halls did not. Within a decade, a half-dozen other resorts joined the El Rancho Vegas, and the Las Vegas Strip was sprawling south of Las Vegas city limits, welcoming at first thousands, then millions of tourists and gamblers a year.

The balance of commerce in Nevada shifted to the south by the 1950s, chiefly due to the growing success of the Strip's casinos, now numbering more than a dozen. In response to organized crime penetration of the industry and as a way to forestall federal intervention, the state legislature created a regulatory body, the Gaming Control Board, to oversee the industry. Its taxes were increasingly important to the state. Many of the financiers, managers, and employees of casinos, however, had extensive experience in illegal operations in other parts of the country and varying connections to those still active in organized crime. The tension between economic development and keeping the industry free from "undesirables" would mark Nevada casinos for much of their early life.

With a national monopoly, however, and Americans becoming more tolerant of gambling, particularly in the vacation milieu of Las Vegas, the industry grew. Thanks to amendments to the gaming code, publicly traded corporations were allowed to own casinos outright in 1967, leading to more mainstream investment in the industry. With its casinos becoming full-fledged, multipurpose resorts, catering to gamblers, leisure travelers, and convention groups, Las Vegas cemented its dominance in the state, and Las Vegas–style

The 1931 decision to resume "wide open" commercial gambling in Nevada led to the development of the Las Vegas Strip, starting with the El Rancho Vegas resort in 1941. A half-dozen similar resorts opened in the city within just 10 years.

resorts became closely associated with gambling in the public consciousness. Today, casinos in Clark County, which includes Las Vegas and its environs, account for more than 85 percent of all state gambling revenues.

Casino gambling remained taboo in other states throughout the 1960s, but lotteries, which had been vilified in the late 19th century, returned. In 1964, New Hampshire started the lottery boom with a semiannual draw game. Three years later, New York legalized its own weekly game, and in 1970, New Jersey began offering weekly drawings and more modestly priced tickets. The success of the Garden State Lottery spoke volumes, and other states, no less pressed for cash, listened. Within a decade, daily draws became the norm. Then instant games, also known as "scratchers," provided instantaneous lottery play and another revenue source.

With states now actively involved in promoting a form of gambling—daily lotteries—that had once been vilified as criminal and parasitic, taboos against other gambling forms began to waver. Legal pari-mutuel betting reached almost complete acceptance in the United States, and, though sports betting remained off limits, some states began considering the economic engine that appeared to be working wonders in Las Vegas, casino gambling. After a failed 1974 referendum, New Jersey voters in 1976 legalized casino gambling in Atlantic City. Two years later, the first legal casino on the east coast opened, to be followed by about 10 others within the next half-decade. The state's success at keeping organized crime out of the industry, and the inarguable economic benefits of casino gaming—jobs, economic development, and revenue enhancement—broadened the casino debate. By the early 1990s, limited gambling in Colorado and South Dakota; riverboat gambling in Iowa, Illinois, Mississippi, and several other states; and gambling on Indian reservations, spurred by the 1987 Supreme Court *Cabazon* decision and 1988's Indian Gaming Regulatory Act, underscored the growing acceptance of gambling throughout the United States. Slots at racetracks, known as "racinos," served to bail out the struggling horse-racing industry, which began to wilt in the face of generational changes and increased competition from casinos. Cities like New Orleans, Detroit, and Philadelphia permitted one or more urban casinos to open, and, in 2010, New York's Aqueduct race course was poised to bring casino gambling to the nation's largest metropolis.

Despite all of this expansion, some forms of gambling remained criminal. In 1992, Congress passed the Professional and Amateur Sports Protection Act, which forbade states without existing legal regimes to authorize new sports betting. As a result, Nevada remains the only state where full-blown sports betting is legal (Delaware, thanks to its 1970s-era sports lottery, is permitted parlays on several games, but not straight-up betting). Today, illegal sports betting is a large and thriving industry, though there is not even an official estimate of its annual revenues. In addition, online gambling remains an illegal frontier, with Congress criminalizing the use of financial instruments for gambling transactions with the Unlawful Gaming Enforcement Act of 2006. In many cases, those who operate "offshore" gambling sites are breaking no laws in the jurisdictions they are located in; several nations actively court Internet gambling businesses. The U.S. Justice Department, however, prosecutes those it can, usually operators with any kind of domestic exposure.

So, despite the growing American appetite for legal gambling, it continues to inhabit an anomalous position in many states: though it is relied upon to fill public coffers, legislators and law enforcement officials continue to insist that some forms of gambling remain harmful to the public health and do not enjoy the sanction of state regulation. For some, gambling is still a crime, even while it is a thriving legal business.

David G. Schwartz
University of Nevada, Las Vegas

See Also: 1921 to 1940 Primary Documents; 1961 to 1980 Primary Documents; Computer Crime; Corruption, History of; Corruption, Sociology of; Criminalization and Decriminalization; La Guardia, Fiorello; Las Vegas, Nevada; Nevada.

Further Readings
Collins, Peter. *Gambling and the Public Interest.* Westport, CT: Praeger, 2003.
Haller, Mark. "The Changing Structure of American Gambling in the Twentieth Century." *Journal of Social Issues*, v.35 (1979).
Munting, Roger. *An Economic and Social History of Gambling in Britain and the USA.* New York: St. Martin's Press, 1996.
Schwartz, David G. *Cutting the Wire: Gambling Prohibition and the Internet.* Reno: University of Nevada Press, 2005.
Schwartz, David G. *Roll the Bones: The History of Gambling.* New York: Gotham Books, 2006.

Gangs, Contemporary

In contemporary American society, the Office of Juvenile Justice and Delinquency Prevention (OJJDP)—a leading state authority on street gangs—defines a street gang as groups of individuals ranging from 12 to 24 years of age. These groups vary in their size and their level of organization and are engaged in criminal and violent behavior. The contemporary street gang is often categorized by economic, communal, or symbolic considerations, including homicide, drug trafficking, burglary, robbery, and auto theft. Over time, communities in America have reacted with increasingly more fear to gang activities, even as law enforcement authorities have reacted to some gang crime by attempting to rid the country of threats, forcing some to leave through deportation decrees. Technology has also made gang activity more interconnected as groups use the Internet to recruit, to intimidate, and to conduct business.

Overview
Gangs can be found in a variety of locales throughout American society. For instance, shifting, changing, and transitional neighborhoods of larger cities such as Los Angeles, Seattle, Denver, Chicago, Nashville, and other locales have traditionally been considered the areas most commonly populated by gangs and are therefore more affected by gang activity. These same cities also comprise neighborhoods, where families remain for generations, that are considered stable slums. The environment of the stable slum is such that it helps to facilitate and maintain the patterns of decay and social disorganization that are conducive to gang activity. In the late 20th and early 21st centuries, gangs have spread from inner city and urban areas to incorporate suburban spaces that have succumbed to decay and disorganization. Though it has been determined that youth gang activity has found its way into suburbs, and even into some rural areas, the inner city and urban neighborhoods of large cities still experience higher rates of youth gang activity because of strong associations with low socioeconomics. Some of the best-known gangs in the United States make their home in these larger inner city and urban areas. Of these gangs, the more infamous include the Crips, the Bloods, the Vicelords, the Latin Kings, Mara Salvatrucha (MS-13), and 18th Street Gang (M-18). The data indicate that the contemporary gang problem in America reaches from the eastern and western to the southern and northern coasts of the country.

The OJJDP reports that data on street gangs is often unreliable, at times because of the inherent secretiveness that characterizes gangs as organizations, and at times because there are definitional discrepancies as to what constitutes a gang; researchers, as outsiders, run the risk of missing or misinterpreting information. Though it has proven challenging to settle conclusively on the total number of gangs at work nationwide, some researchers rely on the National Youth Gang Survey (NYGS), which takes its data from policing agencies countrywide. At the national level, based on the 2004 NYGS, there was a total of 24,000 street gangs with an estimated 760,000 members. These gangs were estimated to be active in approximately 2,900 jurisdictions. The numbers represent a decline from the decade before.

On the regional level, Los Angeles has the highest number of gangs as well as the highest number of gang members of all the states in the Union; there are a reported 600 gangs comprising 100,000 members. Furthermore, 35 percent of homicides in Los Angeles are committed by gangs. Gang membership in Los Angeles has taken on both cross-country and transnational elements, adding a unique nature to that city's gang involvement and contributing to elements of concern for law enforcement and those others who are aware of the complexity of the cross-national and transnational nature of membership in groups like MS-13 and M-18. The alarm is attributed to the spread in the popularity of these two gangs with disaffected Latino youth nationwide, in inner city, urban, suburban, and rural spaces in places such as New York, Texas, and Nashville, Tennessee. Nationwide in 2005, M-18 boasted approximately 30,000 members alongside MS-13's approximately 8,000–10,000. In response to what the media and Congress have deemed a growing threat, the federal government has deported gang members who are not American born. However, this reaction has been identified as contributing to the transnational element cited as an equally, if not more, pressing concern. Links between members who have been deported are reportedly still strong; these links are notable because these gangs are made up of individuals from multiple countries in Central America (El Salvador, Mexico, Honduras, and Guatemala), who when deported continue with the activities in which they had taken part in America. This has raised concerns about illegal re-entry into the United States for the purpose of narcotics trafficking, smuggling, and other criminal activities, including terrorism. Other cross-border relationships of concern include Canadian-based Chinese and Vietnamese gangs that maintain ties with counterparts in the United States. They are said to be responsible for high-potency marijuana supplies to the United States. The use of technology by gangs within the United States has made it possible to see how transnational connections can be made and maintained.

Increasing Fear of Gangs

Street gangs are a source of great concern for contemporary American society. Delinquency, hooliganism, and self-deficiency are often used to explain their activity. These delineations fit squarely within the category of undesired differentness. Some major issues that inspire this alarm include the high levels of violence that are often manifested in the activities in which members take part. For instance, gang members commit levels of crime that are said to be disproportionately high compared to other crimes committed by delinquent young people who are not involved in a gang. One OJJDP self-report survey testifies that 86 percent of serious offenses were committed by gang members. This is true even though gang members represented only 30 percent of the overall respondents in the study.

The 2006 "National Report on Juvenile Offenders and Victims" intimates that street gang activity alarms American society because of an increased level of sophistication that has come to characterize their activities. For instance, gang members have become more efficient in the commission of their activities. Access to resources such as cars and a shift from street fights that involved fists to the use of more lethal weapons such as guns have seen a change in the character of gangs. According to the OJJDP, an increase in the availability of guns has made the commission of crimes by gang members more sensational, which on the surface makes it appear that gangs are committing more crimes. Though the public alarm in response to gangs suggests that criminal activity has increased in absolute terms, the OJJDP recommends that it would be more reasonable to conclude that it is the increased usage of firearms that makes it appear that gangs are committing more crimes; instead, they are taking part in fewer, but more serious, infringements.

According to the 2009 National Gang Threat Assessment, the threat posed by street gang crime has proven significant, since these gangs are represented in all areas (inner city, urban, suburban, and rural spaces) of the country. Serious crimes include firearm distribution, homicide, armed robbery, drug distribution, and theft. Records show that in July 2008, members of the Crips were arrested for 119 counts of firearm distribution. These weapons were sold within and between groups for the purpose of homicides and armed robberies.

Reasons for Gang Activity

One major question explored in the literature looks at why youth join gangs. Some answers incorporate multiple behavioral or environmental characteristics that indicate the probability (likelihood) of future association with a gang. These factors can be determined by the individual youth, the family, the school, the peer group, and the community living space that youth inhabit. The first reason for joining gangs identifies individual risk. Youth who fall within this category tend to have been introduced unnaturally early to drugs, sex, and alcohol. This might or might not lead to trouble fitting in with others of the same peer grouping—from reportedly as early as the first grade. Similarly, as they struggle to fit in, these youth tend to partake in violent acts of delinquency and are more likely to form an affiliation with a gang when the opportunity presents itself. The second factor identifies family mismanagement—where there is limited or no parental supervision. Some of the fallout of family mismanagement includes child abuse, neglect, poverty, limited supervision, and sometimes a family history of gang involvement. The third risk looks

One of 30 arrests made during an antigang sweep of Atlanta, Georgia, on March 8, 2011. The U.S. Marshals Service worked with the Atlanta Police Department's gang task force and other law enforcement, netting a number of guns and a significant amount of drugs. As of 2004, there were thought to be about 24,000 different street gangs in the United States, with an estimated 760,000 members.

at the school environment and identifies poor academic achievement as a major predictor. In addition, the fear for personal safety is also a factor within the school environment. There is thus said to be an increased likelihood of this factor leading to behavior such as truancy—all of which points to a high probability of eventual gang membership. The fourth factor looks at peer group pressure. This is said to be one of the strongest predictors of gang association. An affiliation with peers who themselves are engaged in delinquent activity—whether during adolescence or later on—can serve as a gateway into gang membership. The fifth and final factor that influences the probability of youth joining gangs identifies the community living space. Some of these risk factors include high numbers of neighborhood youth who are in trouble; accessibility to drugs; poor integration in, and attachment to, community surroundings; and little or no informal or formal social controls. These factors do not necessarily exist alone, nor do they necessarily work together. However, it is not uncommon to see evidence of these dynamics manifested in any given youth gang member.

Race and Gender in Gangs
The makeup of a street gang is also an important point for exploration. For instance, a street gang is more often than not composed along racial and ethnic lines. Among racial groups are Hispanics, African Americans, whites, and Asians. Among these racial groupings, Hispanics are said to comprise the largest percentage of youth in gangs; African American youth comprise the second-highest percentage; next come whites, followed by Asians. Only 2 percent of youth who join gangs are racially undetermined. The literature indicates that hate groups are not counted among those youth who make up the percentage in the racial category of "white."

The racial composition of a street gang can also often be an indication of the kinds of activities in which members take part. These activities might include the sale of drugs, property crimes, or fighting over turf. Along with questions of composition come discussions on the language with which specific gangs identify. This phenomenon manifests itself in forms of communication that include a range of things, from the colors gang members wear to the kinds of hand signals they use. Dress codes, symbols such as street art or graffiti, and hand signals can all indicate membership in a particular group. For example, Hispanic gangs are linked to graffiti characterized by three-dimensional designs that indicate power and cultural pride; African American gangs display graffiti around themes of money, weaponry, profanity, and/or power.

Alongside racial distinctions comes gender diversity. When one thinks of street gang membership it is important to think broadly in terms of gender composition, giving consideration to the nature and extent of female gang involvement. Female gang membership is said to account for approximately 10 percent of total numbers nationwide. However, the numbers for female-only gangs are on the rise. This means that previous to this rise in female-only groups, girls who joined gangs were often integrated into mixed-gender crews.

The rise in the instances of female-only gangs alerts us to an important trend: The rate of female youth gang crime has increased. Discussions on female membership include concerns about the initiation techniques that are used in mixed-gender gangs. For instance, male gang members are required to take part in a range of tests that are most often criminal acts intended to prove their loyalty and resilience. These tests could include theft or acts of violence such as inflicting physical assault on another or being physically assaulted by another. Meanwhile, for female gang members, it is often requisite to be tested sexually by the male members of the gang they intend to join.

Impact
In contemporary times, the reaction to street gangs in America has been influenced by the increasingly high levels of criminality and the associated sophisticated and sensationalized levels of violence. This is to say that even though statistics show a decline in the total number of street gangs and street gang membership, the contemporary street gang is now equipped to operate with increased efficiency—given increasingly sophisticated criminal techniques and weaponry. This has revealed a change in the character of the street gang and in how they are perceived by law

enforcement, as well as by those who are attuned to their existence.

Esmorie J. Miller
Queen's University Belfast

See Also: 1941 to 1960 Primary Documents; Crime in America, Causes; Crime in America, Distribution; Gangs, History of; Gangs, Sociology of; Gender and Criminal Law; Juvenile Delinquency, Sociology of.

Further Readings
Bazemore, Gordon and Mara Schiff. *Juvenile Justice Reform and Restorative Justice: Building Theory and Policy From Practice.* London: Willan Publishing, 2005.
Pappas, Carissa. "U.S. Gangs: Their Changing History and Contemporary Solutions." Youth Advocate Program International Resource Paper, 2001.
Shaw, Margaret. *Comparative Approaches to Urban Crime Prevention Focusing on Youth.* International Centre for the Prevention of Crime. http://www.crime-prevention-intl.org (Accessed September 2011).

Gangs, History of

Many contemporary experts on gangs, focused as they are on dealing with the present gang problem, seem to think that serious street gang issues began around 1900. Obeisance, to be sure, may be paid to the gangs of mid-1800s New York—but is as if they existed in a vacuum. Most criminologists ignore the context of the American narrative and the fact that in other cities, gangs were more known, more prevalent, and certainly at least as problematic as those of New York. Perhaps the more or less exclusive focus on New York expresses a discipline-specific ahistoricism, ignorance, or regional bias. It is likely that most experts assume that the past, in this case, does not inform the present in regard to gang history in or outside New York as important or relevant.

Gang Prehistory and Context
Incipient urban gangs in the United States arose from two sources in the early 1800s: neighborhood boy gangs and fireboy gangs. The first were simple congeries of boys, hanging on street corners for lack of better things to do. There they protected their turf from incursions by other boy gangs. This kind of gang usually constituted undersupervised lower-class and occasional middle-class boys. Before the advent of television, video games, and organized sports, recreational opportunities for such street boys were scarce, unsupervised, and often unwholesome. The second type of gang was made up of boys who frequented the environs of firehouses.

Firemen were exciting figures, and the firehouse was a male preserve where masculine values and bachelor culture reigned supreme. Frequently, firemen were allied with political figures and factions. Violence frequently broke out between rival engine companies as they fought over the right to fight specific fires (and loot the premises) but they also fought over political issues. Boy gangs in close proximity to firehouses often evolved into fireboy gangs. While these boys were regarded as potential firemen, they were also seen as junior members of the male adult group and were involved in their rivalries and street fights.

Politicians had much to gain by allying with gangs. Gangs were used as private armies to block voters' access to polls. Alternately, they could be employed to get out the vote and to encourage voters, or even transients, to vote in different polling places for their candidate. Gang members were awarded with patronage jobs in municipal government agencies, a fact that made controlling them all the more problematic. Police, for example, could be gang members in good standing, or tied to a common political boss or party. This process was at work in most east-coast cities beginning early in the 1800s and reached its apogee in the 1850s.

Civic Wars
In the 1840s and 1850s, organized street gangs coalesced with civic groups and political parties, such as the American Party that opposed the immigration and naturalization of the Irish. This put them in conflict with the Democratic machines in cities such as Philadelphia, New York, Baltimore, and New Orleans. The rise of white workingmen was troubling to elites not only in the south but throughout the country. Gang-led civic unrest and

electoral violence followed in all these areas. Riots and extreme violence occurred on election days in New Orleans, New York, Washington, D.C., and other cities in the 1850s. A full-scale coup was attempted by Democratic gangs led by planter elites in New Orleans in 1859. They were, however, unable to topple the elected Know-Nothing municipal government. In Baltimore, they were more successful.

Gang Activities

The politicized gangs of mid-century were products of a highly masculine culture. They often drank heavily in places of commercialized vice. Cockfights, fistfights, gambling, and prostitution were normal recreational activities in their world. They were routinely contemptuous of other races and especially prickly about "honor." In particular, they rejected the ongoing Victorian emphasis on domesticity and the "gentling" of masculine pleasures.

Young unmarried men had been abandoned by the apprentice system and lacked support from traditional families and found themselves reduced to living on the street or in boarding houses. Working largely as wage-slaves, if they had work at all, they joined fire companies, political clubs, and gangs out of boredom and in hope of making political connections. For the young American of British extraction, immigrants were rightly seen as competitors for jobs. In this highly masculine honor-based context, it was regarded as appropriate to challenge the newcomers' pretentions and obstruct their progress by all means possible. This included preventing them from exercising their voting franchise but also involved street fighting and overt violence and intimidation. Opportunistic crimes such as thievery and pickpocketing were specialties of some of these gangs, as well.

Baltimore was known as "mob town" in mid-century due to the sheer intensity of its gangs' activities and prominence. Such gangs as the Plug Uglies, Rip Raps, American Rattlers, and Blood Tubs arose in reaction to Irish immigration. The appellation *Plug Ugly*, taken from the name of a Baltimore gang, became synonymous with a particularly unappealing type of urban tough: Specifically, it meant a politicized urban thug. The most famous of the gangs were anti-Catholic and allied with the American Party and its affiliated fire companies. This linkage was so problematic that the city council, in order to prevent gang violence, attempted to ban "half-grown" boys from hanging around firehouses or following firemen into action. These gangs attacked German and Irish immigrants, sometimes dumping them in tubs of blood, and also singeing their beards with torches. At times, they would imprison Catholics and force them to vote for American Party candidates, a practice called "cooping." Not surprisingly, Irish and Democratic fireboy gangs arose to meet the nativist threat and committed similar outrages. Numerous street battles were held in which revolvers were used and small cannons were fired. Casualties were common; in the elections of 1856, more than 30 were killed and 350 were wounded. In 1858, electoral violence between the factions lasted over a week.

In the 1850s, there were at least 1,000 gang members in 40 different gangs in Baltimore. These gangs, frequently wearing their "colors," attended political and civic rallies, parading in stirring and dramatic fashion. The fire companies were particularly colorful and made an attractive tableau to impressionable youth. All carried pugnacious and frequently obscene banners and often brandished weapons. The awl was seen as a workingman's weapon, and many were made and handed out at rallies. They were used to "plug" Democrats "ugly" and to prevent them from voting. They were also used in street fights and to intimidate the populace in general. American Party gangs and firefighting companies visited other cities and fostered electoral violence there as well. Additionally, "ride-by shootings," from horseback or carriages, were not unknown.

Baltimore's violent political reputation was so firmly fixed in the national consciousness that Abraham Lincoln, fearing violence from Democratic gangs, skulked through the city in disguise on the way to his inauguration in 1860. In 1861, Democratic gangs and citizens stoned Union troops on the way to Virginia and were fired upon. A full-scale riot ensued in which both soldiers and citizens were killed. Union troops occupied the city and put down the gangs and political violence. The gangs never recovered, though politics continued to be corrupt for years.

New Orleans had criminal gangs, to be sure, but its political gangs were in many respects similar to

Wary residents in the "Bandit's Roost," part of gang-controlled Mulberry Bend in the Five Points section of New York City, in 1888. This photograph by Jacob Riis was published in his influential 1890 book How the Other Half Lives. *While the Irish Dead Rabbits and Anglo Bowery B'houys gangs had waged war in the Five Points neighborhood around mid-century, by the 1880s, German and Jewish gangs had joined the mix and were struggling for control of the area.*

those of Baltimore, though not nearly as violent or as infamous. Gangs allied with both factions were noted in the 1840s and 1850s. Election-oriented violence was common, and some street fighting occurred on those days. The unsuccessful coup of 1859 was an example of these factions finally coming to blows. The Civil War ended this rivalry but new violence broke out between supporters of Reconstruction and gangs of Confederate veterans in 1866, and more notably in 1874, when a full-scale insurrection occurred. More problematic and criminologically significant was the emergence of Italian American gangs beginning in the 1860s. After the Civil War, they began an ascendancy that lasted until the rise of African American gangs in the mid-1980s. Italian American organized crime has been a dominant force in New Orleans life and politics for a century.

An exception to the highly politicized gangs of other coastal cities was the case of Richmond, where simple boy gangs prevailed from the 1820s to the 1920s. These gangs, whose activities were often violent—stoning each other, slaves, and passersby—moved on to more serious armed violence after the war. Like classic Chicago-era gangs, the boys in these gangs often had parents who worked in Richmond's meat packing district. Others, however, were scions of some of the city's first families, such as the son of Jefferson Davis. When brought into court, usually for throwing stones in battle-like daylong wars, they were generally released into the custody of their families.

These rock battles were organized and had elaborate rules and etiquette. It is a certainty that these wars were at least partially inspired by the battles at Manassas and those around Richmond in that era. Some of these boys were involved in the infamous Bread Riot of 1863, when they stole commodities while the business district was in chaos.

The gangs of New York, made immortal by the eponymous book and film, were formidable. The Dead Rabbits and Bowery B'houys kept the Five Points neighborhood and surrounding area in a state of war during the mid-century. Allied with fire companies as were gangs in Baltimore, the Bowery B'houys were nativists and fought with the Irish Dead Rabbits for turf and for kicks. Both gangs and others were also involved in a wide range of criminal activities. Various other ethnic gangs were involved in the Draft Riots of 1863, mainly as looters. In the 1880s, Irish, German, and Jewish gangs linked to social and political clubs struggled for prominence, and Chinese tongs emerged, mainly to prey on their countrymen. Italian gangs emerged in earnest in following decades, and these syndicates displaced most other gangs for decades. In the early 1900s, Jewish and Italian gangs made alliances and fought for prominence. Irish gangs such as the Five Pointers were still prominent but faded as Italian American syndicates, who did not relish competition and street fighting, became more prominent.

Recent Gang History

Urban gangs became primarily African American or Hispanic as these groups migrated in large numbers to the cities of the north and west. Such gangs in the south were unreported, or perhaps underreported, until the mid-1980s. While black gangs were noted in New York City and Chicago in the 1930s, it was in the 1950s that their impact was first felt. This led to a veritable wave of criminological speculations on the attraction of gang life in that decade and in the 1960s. Hispanic gangs also came to dominate certain neighborhoods in these same decades. During the 1960s, it seemed as if street gangs had receded from the scene but that proved to be incorrect. The media was more concerned with civil rights, the war in Vietnam, hippies, drugs, and the women's movement, and gangs were simply not on the media's front burner. Research conducted in the 1970s demonstrated that gangs were very much in evidence in ethnic neighborhoods and had never gone away as had been thought. The marketing of crack cocaine brought gangs back into the public consciousness in the mid-1980s as gang wars over drug markets broke out nationwide. The names of gangs from southern California such as the Crips and Bloods became part of the national lexicon. Their distinctive slang, "colors," and hand gestures became boundary maintenance mechanisms with which their neighborhoods and the nation became familiar. Hispanic and Mexican gangs became similarly commonplace. Both African American and Hispanic gangs were involved in local, and sometimes national, drug trafficking. Thrown into the mix were Russian gangsters, Haitians, Dominicans, and Asians, all fighting for a piece of the drug market pie and/or turf and respect. Girl gangs have emerged in small numbers as well. White racist gangs and remnants of a few old Irish and Italian street gangs struggle for daylight, relevance, and life itself in a few urban locations. But their function is mainly for protection from minority gangs while imprisoned. Outside the walls of prison, the day of the European American street gang is mainly over.

Gangs today dominate neighborhoods, creating a climate of "no snitching" zones where law enforcement is not able to operate. While this was somewhat true in the 1800s, gangs today seem to exert a fear-based hegemony that transcends rationality and what would seem to be obvious self-interest of those in the neighborhood. Gangs are more sophisticated and technologically savvy than in the past and will continue to be a major social problem into the future.

Francis Frederick Hawley
Western Carolina University

See Also: 1851 to 1900 Primary Documents; 1941 to 1960 Primary Documents; Gangs, Contemporary; Gangs, Sociology of; History of Crime and Punishment in America: 1850–1900; Juvenile Delinquency, History of.

Further Readings

Asbury, Herbert. *The French Quarter: An Informal History of the New Orleans Underworld.* New York: Thunder's Mouth Press, 1989.

Asbury, Herbert. *The Gangs of New York*. New York: Garden City Publishing, 1927.

Campbell, Anne. *The Girls in the Gang: A Report From New York City*. Oxford: Basil Blackwell, 1984.

Chudacoff, Howard P. *The Age of the Bachelor*. Princeton, NJ: Princeton University Press, 2000.

Courtwright, David. *Violent Land: Single Men and Social Disorder From the Frontier to the Inner City*. Cambridge, MA: Harvard University Press. 1996.

Greenberg, Amy. *Cause for Alarm: The Volunteer Fire Department in the Nineteenth-Century City*. Princeton, NJ: Princeton University Press, 1998.

Knox, George. *An Introduction to Gangs*. Chicago: New Chicago School Press, 2000.

Melton, Tracy. *Hanging Henry Gambrill: The Violent Career of Baltimore's Plug Uglies, 1854–1860*. Baltimore: Maryland Historical Society, 2005.

Ryan, Mary. *Civic Wars: Democracy and Public Life in the American City During the Nineteenth Century*. Berkeley: University of California Press, 1998.

Thrasher, Frederick Milton. *The Gang: A Study of 1,313 Gangs in Chicago*. Abridged. Chicago: University of Chicago Press, 1962.

Towers, Frank. *The Urban South and the Coming of the Civil War*. Charlottesville: University of Virginia Press, 2004.

Gangs, Sociology of

The dominant alternative discourse on contemporary gangs arises from criminology, following the criminal turn in gang studies after the 1960s. Large portions of federal, state, and local law enforcement budgets are devoted to gang suppression, and the 2009 Federal Bureau of Investigation's (FBI) report *National Gang Threat Assessment* attributes as much as 80 percent of crime to gang activity. Criminology is not where gang studies began, and a sociological explanation might ultimately provide a better purchase on the gang phenomenon than a priori criminological assumptions.

Writing a foreword to John Hagedorn's book *A World of Gangs*, Mike Davis makes the point that a profound intellectual fallacy is reflected in the U.S. Library of Congress bibliographic classification of gangs as a subset of social pathology. A more appropriate classification should place them within urban history or street politics. Davis went on to explain that gangs establish a form of social capital (or street capital) for their members, usually deprived, relatively marginalized young people in their communities. Relative monopolies over key spaces and activities allowed gangs some measure of entrepreneurial activity and local prestige. He concluded with the bold claim that, while some gangs might be vampire-like parasites on their communities, others resemble Robin Hood or employer of last resort. It is in this dualistic appreciation of gangs, as both predators and producers, that a sociological approach to gangs exceeds the more limited criminological paradigm.

The Gang

This dual insight is also where gang studies began, back in the 1920s, with Frederick Thrasher's study *The Gang*, published in 1927. Much influenced by the Chicago school sociology of Burgess and Park and the model of urban ecology they developed, Thrasher's analysis has a surprisingly contemporary feel. The book, his editor Robert Park argued, was a study not just of the gang but also of gangland, its habitat. This habitat was a city slum, and it is here that the sociological study of the gang began. Gangs comprised of "predacious adolescents" and "undomesticated males" grew up "like weeds" among the "shadows of the slum" and on the "frontiers and fringes" of civilization.

By firmly setting the study of the gang within the urban context that produced it, Thrasher claimed his subject for urban sociology. What the gang did, morally or legally, was of secondary significance; he was primarily interested in how they were formed and shaped by circumstances. The tone was investigative, not condemnatory: the gang was a protean manifestation, and no two gangs were alike; some were good, others bad; they had to be considered on their own merits. He went on to compare gangs with other, more "wholesome" community institutions such as churches, schools, clubs, and banks. It was this attention to specifics—to context and habits and the role played by the gang—that made them sociologically interesting. Gangs were social institutions embodying social relationships, offering some reassurance that they were neither incorrigible nor uncontrollable.

Thrasher went on to describe the many varieties of gangs forming in the slums of Chicago, divided by socioeconomic status, employment, race, and nationality. Common to understanding them all, however, was an insight from social ecology that the raw material of the gangs (underoccupied adolescents and young men) were the product of deprived and dysfunctional social arrangements that cast off their surplus youth, as so much waste product, and left them to gather unregarded (except to the extent that they caused trouble for the community or attracted the attention of the police) in the interstices, the cracks and crevices of the urban arena. In this sense, the gang members were interstitial in the social order (not children, but not yet men) and interstitial in the urban geography of the city (occupying wild spaces, living "beyond the pale of civil society" in the "poverty belt" or "no-man's land").

According to Thrasher, the gang was little understood, even misunderstood, when viewed solely in terms of the consequences, crime, or violence of its activities. He argued that although conflict, crime, and violence periodically played upon the public consciousness, the places from which gangs emerged had only been poorly understood. Thrasher claimed that sociologists must investigate how gangs arise and develop, what they do, the conditions that produce them, and the problems they created. All this was to equip a practical sociology to supply better methods for dealing with gangs. An especially important question entailed understanding young people's motivation for joining gangs. A whole series of factors were seen to be pushing young people out of mainstream social institutions and relationships. These included the disintegration of family life, educational failure, poor (or only dull, low-waged, and monotonous) employment opportunities, exclusion from social and political processes, and externality to available leisure and recreational options. In such diminished conditions of life, the gang represented a substitute for what society failed to give, while giving relief from drudgery, boredom, and poverty. In Thrasher's terms, gangs represented the efforts of boys and young men to create a society and culture for themselves where none existed. Gangs provided for the "thrill and zest" of daily life. Conflict with other gangs and the police furnished the gang with many exciting group activities and stories to tell.

Street Corner Society

And yet gangs were, in this account, only transitional entities. Age, maturity, responsibility, female companionship, and then, later, employment and families led to a withdrawal from gang activities. Marriage was a significant cause of the disintegration of gangs. At this time, older gang members were relatively uncommon. Even so, a second important contribution to the sociology of the gang, William Whyte's *Street Corner Society* (1943), one of the classic texts of American sociology, provides early insight into the more criminal and harmful aspects of gang life, especially concerning the ways in which the youthful, transitional gang might become more established and intergenerational, a permanent feature of the life of the slum.

Whyte's research, demonstrating the importance of ethnographic methods, was undertaken during the 1930s and revealed in considerable detail how gang members insinuated themselves into the illegal opportunity structures of a poor Italian community in post-Prohibition era Boston. Gangs thrived upon rivalry and opposition; conflict with the police and other gangs became opportunities for young men to gain respect, allowing the establishment of hierarchies of reputation. Very much implicit in this work lies what more contemporary writers might refer to as the construction of a competitive masculine identity, with its hair-trigger sensitivity to imagined slights and perceived disrespect. One of Whyte's key protagonists, Doc, the self-styled leader of the "cornerboys," outlined his appreciation of this social dynamic of the street: He knew that other kids wouldn't like him, but through fighting he'd get their respect. These issues—the violence of competitive masculinity, the illegal economies of the underworld, and the ever-present wary eye of the police—also point toward alternative criminological readings of the gang. They also reinforce a strong sense that this world was inescapably masculine. Perhaps because gang researchers were, almost without exception, men themselves (a situation that, with relatively few exceptions, still

The child labor activist and photographer Lewis Hine identified this group of boys as a street gang after photographing them in June 1916. They were gathered together smoking and playing with a rifle or toy gun (held by the boy second from left) in the late afternoon on a streetcorner in Springfield, Massachusetts. The Federal Bureau of Investigation (FBI) attributed as much as 80 percent of all crime to gang activity in its 2009 report [FBI] National Gang Threat Assessment.

prevails) and feminist ideas had scarcely entered the academy, the behavior of these men, as masculine performance, is scarcely deemed worthy of remark. Even where the behavior of the gang members toward women became abusive (instances of rape, coerced sexual intercourse, and sexual assault are documented), it is represented, as if though a filter of anthropological detachment, as the entirely routine and familiar behavior of the gang boys. For the gang members, women occupied relatively few roles: as mothers, sisters, and fiancées they embodied family and respectability; as girlfriends they were property and sources of status; as local girls and prostitutes they were for sex and amusement; or they could be "trouble" and sources of conflict.

Delinquent Boys: The Culture of the Gang

By the 1950s, when Albert Cohen published *Delinquent Boys: The Culture of the Gang*, the delinquent activities and criminal consequences of gang activity harnessed the attention of social science. Nevertheless, Cohen approached gangs from within a sociological frame of reference, drawing upon Robert Merton's "strain theory" (1938) to explain gang activity as an adaptive and challenging response to the supposed American Dream. Gangs, he argued, emerged as an underprivileged and largely working-class adjustment to the lack of opportunities in mainstream culture. Through conflict and shared experiences of law breaking, gangs fostered a culture of collective peer support (street capital), turning their frustration, anger, and resentment onto the society that had denied them. In place of education, employment, deferred gratification, control of aggression, and respect for order and property, the delinquent culture of the gang promoted instant gratification, living for the moment, and fierce local loyalties.

Subsequent debate with other sociological commentators on the gang, especially Richard Cloward and Lloyd Ohlin in *Delinquency and Opportunity*, made it clearer that gang membership and delinquency were not just oppositional reactions to the values of mainstream American culture but also a lower-class adaptation to it. In this sense, tough masculinity, conflict, and criminal aspiration were as much a part of the American dream as apple pie and hard work. Delinquency was not a reaction against middle class values but rather a means of achieving status within dominant but class-specific cultural expectations about toughness and streetsmartness. Within this cultural milieu, gang membership could bring high status. Cloward and Ohlin developed this analysis by showing that criminality was just one of a number of forms of cultural adaptation possible, depending upon the material circumstances and "opportunity structures" facing people: Some might make criminality pay (career criminality), others might thrive through conflict with mainstream norms and values (using violence to control illegal markets such as the drug trade, gambling, or prostitution), still others might fail and retreat into addiction, alcoholism, or vagrancy. But, above all, what this marked was an increasing tendency to study gangs from the perspective of their violent and criminal consequences rather than their social origins, organization, and purpose.

People and Folks

By the 1980s and the publication of John Hagedorn's important revisionist study of gangs in Milwaukee, *People and Folks,* the "criminal turn" in gang studies had largely been completed. Hagedorn's express ambition was to draw gang scholarship back from criminology and to contest law enforcement and media-led discourses of the gang. He developed an analysis, drawing particularly upon Thrasher's work, to explain the simultaneous criminalization, racialization, and institutionalization of gangs in poor communities. Like Thrasher, he went back to context and opportunity, the deindustrialization and urban decline of the rust belt cities in the wake of Reaganomics, the establishment of an ethnic underclass, white flight, and the social and economic collapse of the ghetto. Furthermore, neoliberal policy making, replacing welfare with workfare in a job-scarce economy, meant that gangs were no longer merely transitional entities; instead, they became institutionalized features of poverty communities reproducing a particular lifestyle. Young people no longer matured out of gang membership, especially when criminal enterprise, in particular drug dealing, offered an exciting and potentially more lucrative alternative to often nonexistent, boring, and low-paid work. Gangs became institutionalized in poor neighborhoods, not only as an adolescent adaptation, but increasingly also as a means for young adults to cope socially and psychologically with a jobless reality. Marginality was further entrenched into a gang lifestyle by the attentions of the local police, while the fact that gangs were overwhelmingly minority and most police departments overwhelmingly white allowed for racism to contribute to these stereotypes and foment even greater hostility and division on the street.

Code of the Street

Compounding this toxic mix, the material circumstances of the hyper-ghetto, the advent of crack cocaine in the 1980s, the toughening of the war on drugs, and a profound weaponization of street culture leading to unprecedented levels of violent death served to strengthen criminology's handle on the gang question. Yet, even in the face of such adversity, sociologists have continued to reassert the value of a sociological and ethnographic approach to understanding gangs and gang members. Central to this work has been a series of debates about identity formation, affiliation, performance, and respect, the establishment of street capital, and the social relations and negotiations of dangerous street environments. Elijah Anderson's work on the *Code of the Street* has been especially important in these discussions.

Anderson's work was designed to penetrate beyond the crude and radicalized stereotypes of an inhumane, hyperviolent gangland culture peopled by thugs and murderers and to insist upon a sociological understanding of how street violence was regulated and negotiated as a social relationship. Rather than violence being random and senseless, Anderson's research suggested that it was governed by an unwritten and yet well-understood set of rules, street etiquette centered upon relations of respect, belonging, and hierarchy, allowing inner-city residents to negotiate dangerous spaces more safely. In other words, knowing and living the code of the street could keep you safer.

However, since the publication of Anderson's work, his conclusions have been challenged by a variety of qualitative sociological and ethnographic researchers. For example, in contrast to Anderson's claim that street codes mediate potentially dangerous encounters and help avoid violence, others have argued that street knowledge of dangerous contexts creates expectations of violence that, while they allow agents situated choices, on some occasions this choice might be to resort to violence. Furthermore, street codes might also provoke violence by requiring gang members, on occasion, to confront one another to reassert their demand for respect.

Yet, aside from the particular conclusions reached by these differing sociologies of the gang, what they have in common is an essential grasp of gang activity and behaviors as situated in social relations, which become understandable in terms of culture, context, and opportunities. Thrasher, nearly a century ago, like a number of contemporary scholars, insisted upon the importance of an ethnography-informed, sociological understanding of the gang as a necessary prerequisite for comprehending the full range of its influence within a community. Many criminologists are also aware of this, and also that flying too close to the enforcement paradigm, eyeing only the criminological consequences of the gang, offers relatively little in the way of understanding and still less in the realm of policy responses.

Peter Squires
University of Brighton

See Also: 1941 to 1960 Primary Documents; Criminology; Gangs, Contemporary; Gangs, History of; Juvenile Delinquency, History of; Juvenile Delinquency, Sociology of; Juvenile Justice, History of; Juvenile Offenders, Prevention and Education; Urbanization.

Further Readings
Anderson, E. *The Code of the Street: Decency, Violence and the Moral Life of the Inner City.* New York: Norton Paperbacks, 1999.

Cloward, R. A. and L. Ohlin. *Delinquency and Opportunity.* New York: The Free Press, 1960.

Cohen, A. K. *Delinquent Boys: The Culture of the Gang.* New York: The Free Press, 1955.

Hagedorn, J. *People and Folks: Gangs, Crime and the Underclass in a Rustbelt City.* Chicago: Lakeview Press, 1988.

Thrasher, F. M. *The Gang: A Study of 1,313 Gangs in Chicago.* Chicago: University of Chicago Press, 1927.

Whyte, W. F. *Street Corner Society: The Social Structure of an Italian Slum.* Chicago: University of Chicago Press, 1943.

Gardner, Erle Stanley

Erle Stanley Gardner (1889–1970) was an American attorney and prolific crime fiction writer. He is best known for creating Perry Mason, his popular champion legal character of print, radio, television, and film media.

Erle Stanley Gardner was born in Malden, Massachusetts, the second of three sons of Charles W. Gardner and Grace Adelma Waugh. The family moved several times, settling briefly in Oregon, Alaska, and California. In 1906, Gardner was suspended from Oroyale Union High School; in 1909, he graduated from Palo Alto High School in the San Francisco Bay area. Gardner then attended Valparaiso University School of Law in Indiana for about a month before being suspended. He then worked as a typist in the law office of E. E. Keech in Santa Ana, California, taught himself the law, and passed the California bar exam in 1911. He then briefly operated his own law office in Merced, California, but closed it shortly thereafter and worked as a lawyer in the law office of I. W. Stewart in Oxnard, California, from 1911 to 1918. During this time, he defended many Chinese and Mexican clients. From 1918 to 1921, he was employed by the Consolidated Sales Company as a tire salesman.

In 1921, Gardner married Natalie Frances Talbert; they had one daughter, Grace. From 1921 to 1933, he resumed his legal career, working in Ventura, California, at the firm of Sheridan, Orr, Drapeau, and Gardner. Gardner and

Natalie separated in 1935; in 1968, he married his second wife, Agnes Jean Bethell, who had long been his secretary and who many have suggested served as the model for Della Street, Perry Mason's secretary.

Writing Career

Gardner began writing mystery and western stories for pulp magazines in the early 1920s to supplement his income. He initially had many stories rejected, but he kept working to perfect his craft. By the early 1930s, Gardner was making very good money as a writer for pulp magazines. In 1933, Gardner published his first two novels, which were the beginnings of his Perry Mason series. His writings sold very well, and he ceased full-time law practice in 1933 to become an even more prolific writer. The first Perry Mason novel, *The Case of the Velvet Claws*, sold 28 million copies in the first 15 years after being released. During the middle of the 1950s, Perry Mason novels were selling at a rate of about 20,000 copies per day.

Gardner wrote crime fiction stories for many pulp magazines such as *All Detective, Argosy, Black Mask, Clues, Detective Action Stories, Detective Fiction Weekly, Detective Story, Dime Detective, Double Detective,* and *Flynn's Detective Fiction*. Gardner created more than 35 protagonists for these crime fiction pulp magazines. Many were recurring characters such as in the series of six short stories published in *Black Mask* featuring Ken Corning, a crusading defense attorney whom many have cited as a prototype for the Perry Mason character. Another crusading lawyer character created by Gardner was Lester Leith, a wealthy attorney who scammed and swindled myriad blackmailers, thieves, and confidence men and then donated most of the proceeds to charity; the Lester Leith stories appeared mainly in *Detective Fiction Weekly*. However, many of Gardner's leading characters were on the other side of the law from lawyers, such as his Ed Jenkins, "The Phantom Crook," who appeared in 73 short stories, most of which were printed in *Black Mask*.

Gardner wrote in genres other than crime fiction. He wrote many western stories for pulp magazines such as *West Weekly, Western Round-Up,* and *Western Tales*. He also had pieces that appeared in magazines like *Cosmopolitan, Country Gentleman,* and the *Saturday Evening Post*. Gardner also published several nonfiction books, including 13 travel books, mostly focusing on his beloved Baja California region, as well as two true crime books, *Cops on Campus and Crime in the Streets* and *The Court of Last Resort*, which garnered an Edgar Award for Best Fact Crime. Gardner was a founding member of the Court of Last Resort, which was a project to reopen cases in which a defendant might have been wrongly convicted.

It is an understatement to refer to Gardner as a prolific writer. He published more than 190 short stories and more than 120 novels. Many of his novels, like his short stories, were written about recurring protagonists; 82 of these novels featured his iconic Perry Mason. Gardner wrote 29 novels in his Bertha Cool and Donald Lam series, which featured a private detective firm. Gardner was such an abundantly productive writer that he published many of his stories under several pseudonyms, including Kyle Corning, A. A. Fair, Charles M. Green, Grant Holiday, Carleton Kendrake, Charles J. Kenny, Robert Parr, and Les Tillray. Profits from his writing made him a multimillionaire. Gardner gained international success as a writer, as many of his works were translated into other languages; his Perry Mason novels alone have been translated into more than 35 languages. Gardner died at age 80 on March 11, 1970, at his home in Temecula, California; his cremated remains were scattered over the Baja Peninsula.

Victor B. Stolberg
Essex County College

See Also: Dime Novels, Pulps, Thrillers; Literature and Theater, Crime in; Literature and Theater, Punishment in.

Further Readings

Fugate, Francis L. and Roberta B. Fugate. *Secrets of the World's Best-Selling Writer*. New York: William Morrow & Co., 1980.

Hughes, Dorothy B. *Erle Stanley Gardner: The Case of the Real Perry Mason*. New York: William Morrow & Co., 1947.

Johnston, Alva. *The Case of Erle Stanley Gardner*. New York: William Morrow & Co., 1947.

Van Dover, J. Kenneth. *Murder in the Millions: Erle Stanley Gardner, Mickey Spillane, Ian Fleming*. New York: F. Ungar, 1984.

Garfield, James (Administration of)

James Abraham Garfield (1831–81) was the 20th president of the United States. However, he had the second-shortest presidential service, with only 200 days in office before he was assassinated. He was the second U.S. president to be assassinated.

James Abraham Garfield was born in a log cabin in Orange, Ohio; he was the last of the so-called log cabin presidents, and his birthplace was later incorporated as Moreland Hills, Ohio. He was ambidextrous, and in his early studies he mastered ancient Greek and Latin. In 1856, he graduated with honors from Williams College in Williamstown, Massachusetts. After graduating college, he became a professor of classics at Western Reserve Eclectic Institute, which was later renamed Hiram College; Garfield served as president there from 1857 to 1861. For a brief period from 1857 to 1858, he served as a preacher at Franklin Circle Christian Church. On November 11, 1858, he married Lucretia Randolph; they had two daughters and five sons.

Garfield distinguished himself with careers in public service, in both the military and politics. From 1859 to 1861, he served as an Ohio state senator; during his tenure as state senator, he was admitted to the Ohio bar. From 1861 to 1863, Garfield served in the Union army, leading the 42nd Ohio Volunteers. In 1862, at age 31, he became the youngest brigadier general in the U.S. Army. He led his troops victoriously at the Battle of Shiloh (1862) and at the Battle of Chickamauga (1863). He was made a major general of volunteers after Chickamauga. In 1862, while serving in the army, he was elected to Congress. President Abraham Lincoln convinced Garfield to resign his military commission so that he could

A print showing the scene at the Baltimore & Potomac railroad station in Washington, D.C., on July 2, 1881, when President James Garfield was shot twice in the back by Charles Guiteau with a .44-caliber revolver. Garfield later died on September 19, 1881, in Elbberon, New Jersey, of blood poisoning. Guiteau was given the death penalty and was hanged within a year on June 30, 1882.

serve as a Republican representative. He served in the U.S. House of Representatives from 1863 to 1880 during the presidential administrations of Abraham Lincoln, Andrew Johnson, Ulysses S. Grant, and Rutherford B. Hayes. In 1876, he became the Republican floor leader; that same year, he served on the Electoral Commission that decided the election between Rutherford B. Hayes and Samuel Tilden.

A Shortened Term
During the 1880 Republican Party convention, Garfield was managing the campaign of Secretary of the Treasury John Sherman (1823–1900). The leading Republican candidates trying to secure the party nomination that year were former U.S. President Ulysses S. Grant and Senator James G. Blaine. John Sherman, brother of Civil War General William Tecumseh Sherman (1820–91), was hoping to become a compromise candidate. However, on the 36th ballot at the convention, James Garfield became the actual nominee. Sherman felt betrayed; nevertheless, he had a distinguished political career. Chester Alan Arthur was nominated as Garfield's vice presidential candidate. On the advice of President Rutherford B. Hayes, Garfield refrained from much campaigning, and he won the election with a total of 214 out of 369 electoral votes.

These were pivotal times with respect to the role of government in law enforcement. Reconstruction in the south was largely being abandoned, and southern states were beginning to establish legal restrictions on African Americans. Federal revenue bureau officers were clamping down on moonshiners, and the U.S. Secret Service was vigorously pursuing counterfeiters, but perhaps, in retrospect, was not sufficiently concerned with what would soon become their main purpose: protecting the president.

James Garfield's term of office as president was from March 4, 1881, to September 19, 1881. However, during the last two months of his presidency, he lingered on his deathbed. Patronage, ironically as it turned out, was one of the major issues Garfield dealt with during his brief period as president. The Star Route Scandal was a major investigation conducted during Garfield's tenure. It involved the fraudulent awarding of mail route contracts with misappropriation of funds by officials, including members of Garfield's own party.

This scandal eventually, after Garfield's death, resulted in major civil service reforms, such as the Pendleton Civil Service Act.

On July 2, 1881, at 9:20 A.M. at the Baltimore & Potomac railroad station in Washington, D.C., Garfield was shot twice in the back by Charles Guiteau with a .44-caliber revolver. Charles Julius Guiteau (1840–82) was an attorney with the delusion that a speech supporting Garfield's campaign that he had written, but never delivered, was responsible for Garfield's victory. Guiteau sought a consular post and was bitter at not getting it. Surgeons, including Dr. Willard Bliss, were unable to locate the bullets lodged in Garfield's body. Alexander Graham Bell, the inventor of the telephone, was called to the White House to help. Bell designed an induction-balance electrical device, essentially a primitive metal detector, for the crisis but was unsuccessful. Garfield died on September 19, 1881, in Elbberon, New Jersey, of blood poisoning, related mainly to the probing of his body by physicians. Chester Arthur was sworn in the next day as the 21st president and he served out the remainder of Garfield's term, but Arthur was never elected to the presidency. Guiteau was convicted of the murder of President Garfield and was hanged on June 30, 1882.

Victor B. Stolberg
Essex County College

See Also: Arthur, Chester (Administration of); Guiteau, Charles; Slavery, Law of.

Further Readings
Doenecke, Justus D. *The Presidencies of James A. Garfield and Chester A. Arthur.* Lawrence: University Press of Kansas, 1981.
Smith, Theodore Clarke. *The Life and Letters of James Abraham Garfield.* New Haven, CT: Yale University Press, 1925.

Gates v. Collier

This case, heard in 1972, is one of the first prisoners' rights cases in American corrections. The case effectively created minimum standards of confinement for inmates in the United States. No longer was it acceptable for states to incarcerate inmates in conditions violating their constitutional rights. Furthermore, the *Gates* decision eliminated the last remaining form of indentured servitude, more than 100 years after the abolition of slavery. The *Gates* case was filed by inmates at Parchman Farm, which was one of the only correctional institutions in Mississippi in the early 20th century. The institution is located on 19,000 acres in northwestern Mississippi and housed approximately 1,900 inmates at the time the suit was filed. Parchman Farm was intended to punish law violators with hard labor on a state-run farm. The institution was designed to minimize the states' correctional expenditures and maximize the severity of punishment.

The conditions at Parchman Farm were so harsh that many equated the prison with a slave-era plantation. The harsh working and poor living conditions resulted in the untimely death of a number of inmates. An investigation into the conditions at Parchman Farm was launched after the death of a white inmate, Danny Bennett. Although the official cause of death listed for Bennett was heat stroke, a postmortem inspection revealed that Bennett was beaten to death. As a result, the state began making policy and procedural changes at Parchman Farm.

Through inmate interviews, civil rights attorney Roy Haber compiled a 50-page, single-spaced list of civil and constitutional rights withheld from inmates. In February 1971, Haber filed law suits for four inmates (Nazareth Gates, Willie Holmes, Matthew Winter, and Zachary Holmes) in federal court alleging that conditions at Parchman Farm violated the inmates' First, Eighth, Thirteenth, and Fourteenth Amendment rights. Judge William C. Keady determined that the suit qualified as a class-action law suit and extended the suit to include all inmates at Parchman Farm. In August 1971, the state of Mississippi admitted to the constitutional violations alleged by the inmates in order to prevent further public embarrassment from a trial; however, this forced the state to comply with all changes set forth by the court.

Several changes were mandated to correct the problems identified by the court. First Amendment rights were ensured by preventing the censoring of inmates' mail by correctional staff except in conditions of extreme necessity. Fourteenth Amendment rights were restored by mandating due process rights for inmates during disciplinary hearings. Eighth Amendment rights were restored by requiring Parchman Farm to more closely regulate the maximum security unit, secure adequate medical treatment (including personnel and facilities) for inmates, implement a classification system separating hardened offenders from nonviolent first time offenders, improve physical facilities (including the degraded housing, sewage, and drinking water infrastructure), eliminate severe corporal punishment, and eliminate the "trusty system" (arming inmates and charging them with guarding other inmates) in favor of trained and paid civilian guards. Finally, Fourteenth Amendment rights were restored with the elimination of racial segregation on Parchman Farm. Prior to the *Gates* decision, African American inmates, comprising two-thirds of the inmate population, were forced to reside in worse conditions solely because of their race. The state of Mississippi began correcting these deficiencies with the assistance of a $1 million grant from the Law Enforcement Assistance Administration. These changes provided inmates with minimal constitutional protections, now treating them as citizens and no longer as state-controlled slaves.

The impact of the *Gates* decision continues to directly influence corrections in the United States. The three most notable changes attributable to the *Gates* decision are elimination of the trusty system, elimination of corporal punishment, and elimination of racial segregation in prisons. Although the *Gates* decision served as a powerful start to combat many of the adverse conditions of confinement, evidence suggests that racial discrimination and corporal punishment continue to plague corrections in the United States.

Jon Maskaly
University of South Florida

See Also: Chain Gangs and Prison Labor; Corporal Punishment; Due Process; Mississippi; Prison Privatization; Prisoner's Rights.

Further Readings
Edge, Laura, B. *Locked Up: A History of the U.S. Prison System*. Minneapolis, MN: Twenty-First Century Books, 2009.

Gates v. Collier, 01 F.2d 1291 (5th Cir., 1972).

Oshinsky, David, M. *Worse Than Slavery: Parchman Farm and the Ordeal of Jim Crow Justice*. New York: Free Press, 1997.

Taylor, William, B. *Down on Parchman Farm: The Great Prison in the Mississippi Delta*. Columbus: Ohio State University Press, 1999.

Gender and Criminal Law

Laws regarding criminal behavior are generally defined as codified regulations that are established to regulate the behaviors of individuals within society. Laws are socially constructed by groups of individuals who hold the highest degree of power within society and thus often reflect the social values of society's elite classes. Thus, socially dominant groups possess the power to define what types of behaviors and groups of people are perceived as criminal and the negative, along with socially sanctioned ramifications for violating the legally codified rules. Throughout history, laws have been applied to and affect various groups differently, including but not limited to gender groups. Gender, as opposed to sex, refers to the ways men and women are expected to behave based on the socially assigned gender category they represent, namely, male and female. Generally in our society, masculine behaviors are characterized by strength, dominance, power, and aggressiveness. Conversely, feminine behaviors are characterized by inferiority, docility, weakness, and dependency. Thus, through societal attributions of appropriate behaviors, inequalities between men and women in society are created and reinforced in all areas of social life, including the areas of crime and criminal law.

Prior to the late 1970s, women were rarely included in criminological studies and theories of crime. Criminal behavior and involvement in the criminal justice system were socially conceptualized as primarily male spheres of life. However, after the ideas of feminism, particularly second-wave feminism, became more widely accepted, researchers and criminal justice practitioners began to understand that gender differences in criminal offending, victimization, and experiences in the criminal justice system exist and are influenced by social, political, and historical occurrences. While contemporary scholars and practitioners acknowledge that men and women engage in different types and amounts of criminal behavior, to some extent, crime and criminal law continue to be perceived as masculine. Correspondingly, the legal responses to criminal behavior are also, generally, based on a masculine standard. Therefore, previous and current criminal laws often fail to take into account the gendered nature of criminal offending and the role that the social construction of gender plays in the commission of crimes and their associated legal responses.

Women and Crime

Women generally commit fewer and less serious crimes than men. On average, women account for less than 20 percent of arrests for violent crimes and less than 25 percent of the total arrests that occur. Women's less frequent and less serious criminality as compared to their male counterparts is not a new phenomenon but a trend that has persisted throughout time. What has changed over time are the types of crimes for which women have been arrested and processed through the criminal justice system.

In the early 1800s, women had few legal rights, worked inside the home, and were subjected to well-defined views regarding appropriate feminine behavior. During this time, women were primarily arrested for petty larceny and theft, especially during the Civil War because of the resulting economic deterioration. With their husbands at war, many women had to steal to survive. Additionally, social concerns regarding female sexuality existed. Thus, many women were arrested for prostitution because this behavior was viewed as violating the normative standards of feminine conduct regarding sexuality.

During the 19th century, women generally were not associated with violent crimes, such as murder. However, notable examples exist. For example, in 1843, Polly Bodine was accused of murdering her sister-in-law and infant niece by breaking many bones in their bodies, including their skulls, and subsequently setting their house on fire in an attempt to cover up the murder.

Laura Bullion, a female member of the notorious 19th-century gang the Wild Bunch, dressed in men's clothing in an early mug shot created by Pinkerton's National Detective Agency after an arrest on November 6, 1901, in St. Louis, Missouri.

After three trials, Bodine was eventually acquitted for the murders due to a lack of evidence and the invalidation of witness testimony by her attorney. However, she continued to be viewed as an infamous female criminal of her time. Not only was she accused and tried for the murders of her sister-in-law and young niece, but she also deviated from acceptable notions of femininity in various spheres of her life. Prior to the murders, Bodine engaged in sexual behaviors out of wedlock and had several abortions, which, at the time, were not socially accepted. As previously asserted, the behavior of women in the 1800s was guided by well-defined standards, many from which Bodine violated.

In the mid-20th century, women continued to be arrested, charged, and incarcerated for nonviolent and victimless public order offenses, particularly prostitution. Arresting and charging women for public order sex crimes illustrates the idea that criminal law works to maintain and reproduce a gendered social organization. Thus, in both the past and today, the criminalization of prostitution is more about social morality and gendered values than about criminal offending, and is one example of the criminalization of behaviors that violate traditional societal expectations of femininity. By creating and enforcing laws against nonviolent, victimless crimes, such as prostitution, the message conveyed is that law-abiding and moral women should not engage in public sexual acts and, if caught doing so, they will be socially sanctioned through the law.

By the late 20th and early 21st centuries, women's representation in the criminal justice system began to increase. The types of crimes women were arrested for and charged with also began to change. Now, women were primarily arrested for minor property offenses, such as larceny, fraud, and substance abuse charges. In addition, the number of women under correctional supervision, including jail, prison, probation, and parole, increased substantially. For example, from 1990 to 2000, the number of women under correctional supervision more than doubled. Currently, well over 1 million women are under some type of criminal justice system supervision. While women have consistently been less likely than men to be incarcerated in the United States, the rate of incarcerated women has increased more precipitously than the number of incarcerated men over the same time period.

As with men's crime, race and economic class play a significant role in women's criminal behavior and experiences with the criminal justice system. Being economically disadvantaged affects one's ability to survive in a society that is based on financial exchange and limits one's opportunity to engage in lawful employment that provides the financial requirements necessary to meet personal needs. Thus, individuals who are financially disadvantaged may turn to crime to help support themselves and their families, particularly women. Generally, women make less money than men and are less likely to be employed in professions that provide opportunities for advancement. Thus, property crimes such as fraud and larceny are some of the most common types of criminal offenses committed by women.

Women of minority racial groups are often overrepresented at various stages of the criminal justice process. Black women make up more than 50 percent of the total number of women who are currently incarcerated, but only a fraction of the total female population, generally about 6 percent. From 1980 to 1991, the percentage of incarcerated black women increased more quickly than that of incarcerated black men. However, women commit less crime and less serious crime than their male counterparts. Thus, negative, racist attitudes that exist within the criminal justice system and within society as a whole seem to affect black women more than black men.

Evolution of Criminal Law Applied to Women

Despite these numerical increases, there is little indication that women have become more criminal over time. Most female offenders commit nonviolent offenses, which, as previously illustrated, has been consistent throughout history. Additionally, most women are arrested, charged, and under some type of correctional supervision for nonviolent property and drug offenses, not more serious violent offenses like their male counterparts. Of incarcerated offenders released from U.S. prison institutions, the proportion of women who recidivate or reoffend is less than the proportion of men who commit future criminal offenses. Thus, the increase in the proportion of women under correctional supervision over the past several decades is more an effect of structural and political factors, than of women's increased criminality.

Over the past several decades, law enforcement agencies have shifted their attention in terms of the types of crimes on which they focus. Law enforcement practices have moved toward targeting nonviolent, less serious types of offending and thus have effectively broadened the opportunity for women to be arrested for minor offenses. One example of the shift in law enforcement practices and objectives is female prostitution. Studies suggest that women continue to engage

This 2011 arrest of suspected drug gang members in Georgia included three black men and one woman. While black women make up only a fraction of the total female population, around 6 percent, they represent more than 50 percent of the total number of women who are currently incarcerated in the United States.

in prostitution and other victimless sex offenses as often as in previous time periods. However, female arrest rates for these crimes have dramatically decreased. Now, as opposed to focusing on female prostitution, law enforcement officials are increasingly focusing on crimes such as female drug offending. While it may seem that women are committing fewer minor sex offenses than in the past, this is most likely only a reflection of the types of crimes that law enforcement officials are targeting, not a reflection of the types of crimes women are committing.

Recently, federal and state government agencies have increased spending for services related to corrections, while funding for health services, education, and other public needs has diminished. For example, the War on Drugs that was implemented by the U.S. government during the politically conservative 1980s increased legal attention toward nonviolent drug offenses. Thus, women who would not have previously come into contact with the criminal justice system were often punished for minor drug offenses. Additionally, the implementation of mandatory sentencing, particularly as it relates to drug offenses, has increased the number of incarcerated women and men in society. Mandatory sentencing laws place limits on judicial discretion, thus requiring judges to rule in favor of more harsh sentences than they probably would have otherwise, particularly for nonviolent offenses.

Gender Bias in the Law

Women primarily commit nonviolent crimes. Of the relatively low proportion of women who do commit violent crimes, approximately 75 percent commit acts of simple assault. Domestic violence, also known as intimate partner violence, is generally defined as acts of violence or patterns of abusive behaviors committed by individuals in an intimate relationship, such as a family members, romantic partners, or friends. Various scholars and activists argue that many current domestic violence laws have patriarchal and misogynistic origins in which women are viewed as subordinate to men and are treated in ways consistent with this idea. Thus, laws that are virtually prejudiced against women such as domestic violence laws produce, reproduce, and maintain patriarchal social organization and elucidate how women are controlled in society. While the perpetual disadvantage of women based on domestic violence laws often occurs unintentionally, the unconscious internalization of societal gender roles maintains and reproduces the subordination of women through the criminal justice system's imposition of these legal practices. For example, historically, women were viewed as the familial property of their husbands. For centuries, husbands were legally allowed to use violence against their wives in an effort to socially control them.

In terms of women and criminal law, a relatively large proportion of the violent acts committed by female offenders are committed in self-defense against continuing patterns of intimate partner abuse or domestic violence. Thus, domestic violence laws also offer an example of criminal law in which gender plays a salient role, and their use reveals another reason why women's increased involvement with the criminal justice system is primarily a result of structural and political changes.

A body of research exists that examines women who use force against their intimate partner as a reaction to being abused. Many scholars argue that violence is often gendered in nature, and that women who are arrested for acts of intimate partner violence based on mandatory arrest policies are disadvantaged because law enforcement officials neglect to take into account the context in which the acts occurred. More specifically, when women commit acts of violence against intimate partners, it is often in self defense and occurs as a reaction to a long-standing history of domestic violence. Additionally, battered women who use self-defensive violence often get entangled in domestic violence laws that are intended for abusers, specifically, male offenders. Women who are arrested for domestic violence as a method of self-defense contest the charges brought against them less often than men for fear of losing their children or families. As a result, these women are often mandated to attend batterer treatment programs, which assume that the problem of violence was solely the fault of the female victim. In this way, treatment programs maintain and reproduce the larger issues of power and control in society that aid in sustaining violence against women. The previous examples illustrate how criminal law is shaped by social factors such as gender, race, and economic class and the ways in which women as offenders are positioned in a criminal justice system that primarily views crime and criminal law from a patriarchal perspective.

M. Kristen Hefner
University of Delaware

See Also: Domestic Violence, History of; Domestic Violence, Sociology of; Women Criminals, Contemporary; Women Criminals, History of; Women Criminals, Sociology of; Women in Prison.

Further Readings
Belknap, Joanne. *The Invisible Woman: Gender, Crime, and Justice*, 3rd ed. Belmont, CA: Thomson Wadsworth, 2007.
Browne, Angela. *When Battered Women Kill*. New York: Free Press, 1987.
Chesney-Lind, Meda and Lisa Pasko. *Girls, Women, and Crime: Selected Readings*. Thousand Oaks, CA: Sage, 2004.
Miller, Susan L. *Crime Control and Women: Feminist Implications of Criminal Justice Policy*. Thousand Oaks, CA: Sage, 1998.
Raffel Price, Barbara and Natalie J. Sokoloff. *The Criminal Justice System and Women: Offenders, Prisoners, Victims, & Workers*. New York: McGraw-Hill, 1982.

Genovese, Vito

Born in Risiglianio, near Naples, Italy, Vito Genovese (1897–1969) immigrated with his family to the United States as a young man and became one of the most powerful American organized crime figures of his era. He was a member the ambitious cohort of criminals born between 1892 and 1900 that historian Mark Haller identifies as ascending in power in the criminal underground during Prohibition, courtesy of their youth and determination. Within this group of predominantly Italian and Jewish immigrants and first-generation American slum-dwellers, Genovese assumed an influential position, though he was decidedly a rung below leaders like "Lucky" Luciano and Frank Costello. During Prohibition, Genovese proved a brutal and effective enforcer, and his star rose along with those of his peers. Following Luciano's 1931 rise to power, Genovese was, some observers believed, third in the underworld hierarchy, behind Luciano and Costello. Following Luciano's 1936 imprisonment on prostitution-related charges, Genovese expected to occupy a position of greater influence. However, Genovese faced indictment for a gangland murder the following year and fled the United States rather than stand trial.

Returning to Italy, Genovese settled near Naples and reputedly became an ally of Italian leader Benito Mussolini, receiving decorations from the Duce for his services to the fascist republic. He may even have used his contacts in the New York criminal underworld to aid Mussolini. In 1943, Genovese allegedly engineered the murder of Carlo Tresca, a New York–based Italian American antifascist publisher, who was gunned down by unknown assailants in Manhattan. The

Vito Genovese, the leader of the Genovese organized crime family, in 1959, the year of his conviction for conspiring to sell heroin. He may have continued to direct criminal activity while serving his sentence in the Atlanta Federal Penitentiary.

commencement of hostilities between the United States and Italy only enriched Genovese, who reportedly masterminded an immense black-market smuggling operation in southern Italy. As Mussolini's hold on power slipped, Genovese reached a rapprochement with American military authorities. Working as an interpreter, he helped U.S. forces apprehend several rival black marketeers. Meanwhile, he extended his own smuggling operations. In 1944, he was arrested on a warrant for a 1934 New York homicide. When the chief witness died while in custody as Genovese was awaiting extradition to the United States, the case collapsed, and Genovese was acquitted of the charge in 1946.

From there, he resumed his place in New York's organized crime hierarchy. In 1957, he reportedly masterminded a failed attempt to murder presiding "boss" Frank Costello, a shooting that nonetheless precipitated Costello's "retirement" from active involvement in criminal activities. In that same year, he reputedly organized the ill-fated "La Cosa Nostra summit" at the home of Joseph Barbara in Apalachin, New York. When many of its participants, reportedly high-profile mobsters from around the country, were apprehended after they failed to elude a police roadblock; public fears of a national criminal syndicate, now specifically identified as the "Mafia," grew. Though he faced no charges connected to the Apalachin meeting, Genovese found himself the target of intense police investigation. In 1959, he was convicted for conspiring to sell heroin after a drug smuggler implicated him and several of his associates. He reportedly continued to direct criminal activity from his cell in Atlanta Federal Penitentiary.

After a falling-out with former underling Joseph Valachi in prison, Genovese is believed to have ordered Valachi's murder. Valachi, learning of the plot, sought federal protection and became the first high-level mob informant to speak freely to investigators about organized crime in America. His 1963 testimony before Senator John McClellan's Permanent Subcommittee on Investigations provided an unprecedented inside look at the organization Valachi called "La Cosa Nostra." Valachi provided details of the structure of New York's five organized crime "families" and described a series of rituals and mores that bound members to the secretive criminal organization. Valachi's testimony buttressed then attorney general Robert F. Kennedy's efforts to "destroy" organized crime in the United States by making the public aware of the extent and power of organized crime families. Thus, Genovese was indirectly responsible for some of the most damning insider revelations about American organized crime. Genovese passed away from heart disease on February 14, 1969, still in custody at the U.S. Medical Center for Federal Prisoners in Springfield, Missouri. He was interred at St. John's Cemetery in Queens, not far from the crypt of former associate and rival Luciano.

David G. Schwartz
University of Nevada, Las Vegas

See Also: Gambling; Italian Americans; Luciano, "Lucky"; Organized Crime, History of; Rothstein, Arnold; Schultz, Dutch.

Further Readings
Haller, Mark. "The Changing Structure of American Gambling in the Twentieth Century." *Journal of Social Issues*, v.35 (1979).
Peterson, Virgil. *The Mob: 200 Years of Organized Crime in New York*. Ottawa, IL: Green Hill Publishers, 1983.

Georgia

The last of the original thirteen colonies, and one of the original seven Confederate states, Georgia is a southern state with a body of law extending back to the colonial era and the English common law tradition.

Crime
Slavery remained legal in Georgia until the Civil War. Although importing new slaves to the state was prohibited in 1817, that law was repealed 12 years later. At the same time as its repeal, the rights of both free and enslaved blacks were restricted by outlawing teaching blacks to read or write, and by imposing a 40-day quarantine on free blacks on board visiting vessels, during which it was illegal

for other free blacks to communicate with them. Abolitionist texts were criminalized, and the law against teaching blacks was enhanced to include allowing a black person to transact any business in writing on behalf of a white. Perhaps the strictest laws came in 1859, when it was made illegal to free a slave upon the death of the master or to bring free blacks into the state.

During Reconstruction, the Ku Klux Klan was formed as a vigilante group targeting Republicans, blacks, and their allies. Founded in Tennessee, the Klan quickly spread through the south, and the Grand Dragon of the Georgia Klan is believed to have been Confederate general and failed gubernatorial candidate John B. Gordon. The Klan's first apparent action in Georgia was the murder of radical George Ashburn, a delegate to the southern Loyalists' Convention who supported Reconstruction and the Fourteenth Amendment. Ashburn was killed upon his return to his Columbus home.

The white "redeemers" who took control of Georgia after Reconstruction in 1872 enacted vengeance on the black legislators who had come to power during Reconstruction, several of whom were whipped and beaten by mobs. Jim Crow laws were enacted to restrict the rights of blacks and segregate public spaces in order to institutionalize white supremacy in a new form, which lasted until the efforts of the civil rights movement in the 1950s, 1960s, and 1970s.

The Klan soon died out, though the name was revived in the 20th century. This second Klan, founded in 1915, was inspired by the glorification of the Klan in the movie *Birth of a Nation,* and by the lynching in Atlanta of Leo Frank, a Jewish man whose death sentence for the rape and murder of white Mary Phagan had been commuted to life in prison. Many of the new Klan's founders were members of the Knights of Mary Phagan, an Atlanta organization, who were gathered up by former Methodist preacher William Simmons. A number of the Knights accompanied Simmons to Stone Mountain, outside Atlanta, along with two elderly members of the original Klan, to burn a cross and announce the formation of the new Klan. The second Klan was as anti-Catholic and anti-Jewish as it was anti-black, a response not to the ills of Reconstruction as in the first Klan but to the racial tensions caused by urbanization and immigration. The new Klan remained powerful in Georgia, and in many parts of the country was considered an innocuous fraternal organization like the Elks or the Shriners. The violence remained, though, and in the early days of the new Klan it was often aimed at black veterans returning from World War I.

The second Klan gained a great deal of political influence, which the first had lacked, but declined by the end of the 1920s and died out completely in 1944, when the organization was unable to pay its back taxes. During the civil rights movement, numerous anti-black groups throughout the country, especially the south, formed with Klan references in their name, but unlike the first two Klans, there was no single hierarchical organization guiding them.

Police and Punishment

The oldest law enforcement agency in Georgia is the Chatham County Sheriff's Office, established in 1732. In many communities, a single sheriff was the only official enforcer of the law, though he was in times of need assisted by male volunteers from the community, who might or might not be officially deputized for a special purpose. Even when they grew in the 19th century, many sheriff's offices consisted only of a sheriff, a permanent deputy, and a jailer. The sheriffs have continued to have an important role in the state, as county government is more powerful and significant in Georgia than in much of the country. In the 20th century, some counties established county police departments, supplementing but not replacing the sheriff.

The first state prison in Georgia was built in 1811 and opened in 1815. Called Prison Square, it was an all-white facility in practice; there were few free blacks in Georgia at the time, and the punishment of black slaves was generally handled under separate laws and administered by slave owners. Prison Square was one of the first state prisons built in the south, which generally preferred cheaper alternatives to imprisonment.

Georgia was the last state to end the practice of prisoner chain gangs (before their 1990s revival), in 1955. While corporal punishment like floggings had been a way to administer punishment without the expense of imprisonment, chain gangs—like prison industries that used prisoner

An armed guard watches over convict laborers in Oglethorpe County, Georgia, in May 1941. Georgia did not end the practice of prisoner chain gangs until 1955, making it the last state to continue the practice until it was revived in the 1990s. Georgia also practiced convict leasing, beginning with the May 11, 1868, lease of 100 black prisoners to the Georgia and Alabama Railroad. That system, however, was phased out in the first decades of the 20th century.

labor for simple manufacturing—were a way to offset the cost of imprisonment. Groups of prisoners restricted by ankle shackles were used for manual labor, either for government jobs such as highway maintenance or for the private sector under convict leasing programs. The 1930s movie *I Am a Fugitive From a Chain Gang*, based in Georgia and adapted from a convict's memoir, turned public opinion against the practice because of the treatment of prisoners and constitutional concerns over forced labor. Further, although both black and white prisoners were put in chain gangs (called "work" gangs when no shackles were used), it was widely recognized that convict leasing had begun in response to the emancipation of slaves, when black prisoners were rented out as laborers by prisons to private businesses, which no longer had slave labor to depend on. In Georgia, convict leasing began with the lease of 100 black prisoners on May 11, 1868, to the Georgia and Alabama Railroad. The system was phased out in the first decades of the 20th century, and until it was abolished completely, chain gang labor was used only for government and local community projects.

Georgia is a capital punishment state (for capital homicide, aircraft hijacking, and treason) and in fact has been key in the history of capital punishment through the two Supreme Court cases that shape modern death penalty statutes. The 1972 *Furman v. Georgia* decision effectively found all extant death penalty statutes to be unconstitutional, forcing those states wishing to keep the death penalty to draft new laws.

Numerous problems were found with the death penalty. Justices William Brennan and Thurgood Marshall believed it to be unconstitutional in all circumstances, constituting cruel and unusual punishment. Other justices found that the problem was the inconsistency of its application, the fact that it was disproportionately used against black defendants while white defendants were more likely to get a lesser sentence, and the lack of any apparent correlation between the severity of a crime and the use of the death penalty. As Justice Potter Stewart wrote,

> These death sentences are cruel and unusual in the same way that being struck by lightning is cruel and unusual. For, of all the people convicted of rapes and murders in 1967 and 1968, many just as reprehensible as these, the petitioners are among a capriciously selected random handful upon whom the sentence of death has been imposed.

Two other death penalty cases had been combined with the *Furman* case, both of them having applied the death penalty in rape cases, and thus the decision in essence ended the use of the death penalty for rape as well, as a disproportionate punishment.

The death penalty statutes that followed had to find ways to avoid these complaints—to be applied more consistently, to make every effort to ensure that the defendant was guilty and to make use of every available legal recourse, and to use the death penalty only for the most heinous crimes. The subsequent 1976 decision, *Gregg v. Georgia* (which was combined with cases from Florida, Texas, North Carolina, and Louisiana), affirmed the constitutionality of the death penalty when properly applied; the decision invalidated some of the death penalty statutes legislated in the intervening time but made clear how states should draft their capital punishment legislation in the future. In particular, in order to address Justice Stewart's complaints, the process must ensure an appellate review of the criteria for applying the death sentence and must take into account the character and record of the defendant. This second requirement was affirmed by later decisions to exempt juvenile and mentally handicapped defendants from the death penalty. In Georgia, the post-*Gregg* capital punishment statute reserves the death penalty for defendants older than 16, requires delaying the execution of a pregnant defendant until after she is no longer pregnant, and suspends the death penalty for the mentally incapacitated.

Modern Georgia has been criticized for the harshness and disproportionality of its sex offense laws. In the 2002 case *Georgia v. Allison*, for instance, Janet Allison was convicted of a sex offense, was entered into the sex offender registry, and was forced to put three of her children into foster care. Her crime had been to permit her pregnant 15-year-old daughter to have sex with her boyfriend (later husband). The court further forbade Allison from any contact with her daughter or grandchild, and because of being a registered sex offender, she was forced to relocate to a new home in order to not be near a church or school.

The *Allison* case and a similarly disproportionate ruling in *Georgia v. Wilson*, in which a 17-year-old was sentenced to 10 years in prison for aggravated child molestation after having consensual oral sex with a 15-year-old, have been used by legal reform advocates to demonstrate the problems with the sex offender registry and with sex offense sentencing guidelines that do not take sufficient context into account.

Bill Kte'pi
Independent Scholar

See Also: 1851 to 1900 Primary Documents; African Americans; Atlanta, Georgia; Capital Punishment; Chain Gangs and Prison Labor; Convict Lease System; *Furman v. Georgia*; *Gregg v. Georgia*; Ku Klux Klan.

Further Readings
Emanuel, Anne. *Elbert Parr Tuttle: Chief Jurist of the Civil Rights Revolution*. Atlanta: University of Georgia Press, 2011.
Lohr, Kathy. "Century-Old Race Riot Still Resonates in Atlanta." National Public Radio. http://www.npr.org/templates/story/story.php?storyId=6106285 (Accessed June 2011).
Morton, William J. *The Story of Georgia's Boundaries*. Atlanta: Georgia History Press, 2009.
Oshinsky, D. *Capital Punishment on Trial:* Furman v. Georgia *and the Death Penalty in Modern America*. Lawrence: University Press of Kansas, 2010.

German Americans

The influence of German Americans can be found in virtually every facet of American society, from agriculture to business, industry, social life, family life, religion, education, music, art, architecture, politics, military service, journalism, literature, and language. Dwight Eisenhower, Albert Einstein, Babe Ruth, and John Steinbeck are a few of the many prominent German Americans who played a leading role in shaping the United States.

Up until the 19th century, the reputation of German Americans was largely one of respectability and productivity. By the early 1900s, however, the prohibition of alcohol and a world war put some German Americans at odds with the criminal justice system in the United States. While individuals such as John Dillinger and "Dutch" Schultz, the son of German Jewish immigrants, took on the role of the gangster, others were the victims of crime in the form public outcry and anti-German sentiment.

Early German Americans

The history of German Americans can be traced back to 1608, when a small group of German immigrants arrived at the English colony of Jamestown, Virginia. These Germans came to Jamestown as contract laborers, and their contributions exemplify the profound role that German settlers played in the shaping of America. These original settlers marked the beginning of the multiethnic and multicultural society that defines the United States to this day.

Between 75,000 and 100,000 Germans immigrated to America during the colonial period, but the mass of German immigration to the United States took place from 1815 to 1914, as more than 5 million Germans crossed the Atlantic in search of new opportunity. Since the end of World War I in 1918, more than 1.5 million have immigrated. The overall estimate of German immigration to America is more than 7 million.

Given the large number of German immigrants, it comes as no surprise that numerous German Americans have been perpetrators or victims of crime. Examining the German American history of crime is not as clear-cut as that of some other ethnic groups. While crime as related to Italian and Russian Americans can be explored through the extensive crime networks of highly organized and infamous mobsters and racketeers, the German American experience is more general to the essence of America. In other words, German Americans were normalized to such a level in American society that their relation to crime is somewhat akin to that of English immigrants. Despite this commonality, German Americans were a unique ethnic group that numerically held the largest share of immigration. In relation to the greater transcontinental migration, however, Germans made up a mere 15 percent of total immigration to America. The ethnic identity of German Americans led to unique experiences with crime and society in the United States.

German Americans who were born abroad experienced many hardships common to most immigrants. Emigrant travel reports provide a good description of the challenges and vulnerability to crime faced by German immigrants. Francis Daniel Pastorious, founder of Germantown, Pennsylvania, set sail from England on June 6, 1683, and docked in America on August 20. He spent 74 days at sea.

The typical German immigrant received only minimal food aboard ship. They had to cook for themselves and bring along any extra provisions that would be needed. Crowded, dimly lighted decks provided little shelter for the passengers. Medical care and formal security aboard the vessels was virtually nonexistent, save for the captain and crew, who would help in case of emergency, given they had the skills or means to do so. The high stress of being at sea for an unpredictable amount of time sometimes led to a shortage of food, which led some to steal the personal stashes of fellow passengers.

During periods of greater immigration, captains simply allowed more passengers to come aboard, which further crowded the already tight passenger quarters. Crew members and the captain sometimes abused passengers. Overcrowded ships, in addition to being breeding grounds for deadly diseases, were prime environments for petty crooks in search of a pocket to pick, as well as fraudsters looking to capitalize on vulnerabilities of fresh immigrants in need of assistance. In Germany, there were even campaigns aimed at thwarting emigration. Political authorities and the church warned of the risks and dangers of being victimized that accompanied emigration.

The American reaction to the many incoming Germans varied. While at times, new flocks of immigrants were welcomed, there were other times when Americans feared being overrun by foreigners, which led to the victimization of German Americans through both criminal intimidation and harsh legislation. In the 1855 Lager Beer Riot of Chicago, German immigrants took to the streets in opposition to the increase of already costly liquor license fees and the strict enforcement of laws against opening saloons on Sunday. While no one was killed during the protest, a Chicago police officer shot and wounded a young German man. Restrictive legislation such as Sunday closings and liquor license fees also led to violence in other cities. In July 1857, several thousand German Americans in New York City clashed with police over the closing of numerous saloons in lower Manhattan's Little Germany neighborhood. The following day, some 10,000 people assembled on Broadway to commemorate a German immigrant worker who had lost his life during the riot. By 1860, American society had shifted its focus from the prohibition of alcohol, to the problem of slavery.

German Americans of the 19th century, like other ethnic groups, had to deal with adjusting to a new society while attempting to maintain the heritage of their homeland. Perhaps the hardships unique to German life in a foreign land, among other things, can help explain the particularly high murder-suicide rate of Chicago Germans compared to other ethnic groups living in the city at the turn of the century. From 1857 to 1910, German Chicagoans committed murder-suicide at rate that more than doubled their proportion to the city's population. While in 1910, German immigrants represented a mere 8 percent of Chicago residents, they accounted for some 23 percent of the city's murder-suicides. One explanation of this overrepresentation rests in the concentration of German immigrants who earned their living as skilled craftsmen, an occupation that was largely undercut by the expansion of factories and industrial production methods.

Prohibition

Beer, an important element of German culture, placed German Americans at odds with the criminal justice system in 1920. The United States passed the National Prohibition and Enforcement Act and went dry. At midnight on January 16, 1920, the manufacture and sale of intoxicating liquors, which ultimately included beer and wine, was outlawed in the United States. Prohibition was partially a result of anti-German sentiment resulting from America's entrance into World War I, during which Germany was an archenemy. Citing that German Americans owned many breweries, some proponents of Prohibition defended the law as a patriotic and necessary wartime measure, while others argued that grains used to make beer would be better utilized to produce bread to feed the hungry American troops who were fighting the war against Germans in Europe.

Prohibition forced many German Americans to close the breweries, pubs, and bier gartens on which they depended for the income to support their families. Given that many Americans, not just German Americans, enjoyed alcoholic beverages despite the new law, demand fueled a new underground industry for beer and liquor in an illegal black market. The illegal branding of breweries had criminalized the livelihood of numerous Americans, many of whom were German Americans. The high profits that resulted from the high demand in this newly illicit market for alcohol led many to take criminal action, which led to a newer, stronger level of organization in crime as depicted by the gangster era of the 1920s.

One of New York's leading Prohibition-era bootleggers was a German-Jewish American named Arthur Flegenheimer, better known as "Dutch" Schultz. While serving a short prison sentence for robbery when he was a teenager, Flegenheimer decided to go by the name of a 19th-century German American gangster from the Bronx known as Dutch Schultz. While little is known about the first Dutch Schultz, his namesake proved to be among the most brutally successful gangsters of his time. Following Prohibition, he opened several illegal but highly profitable bars in the Bronx area. Schultz used intimidation and violence to gain control of the gambling operations in Harlem. He increased revenues of the already profitable gambling houses through innovations such as illegal slot machines with step stools to ensure that children could reach the levers.

While his involvement in organized crime was common knowledge of the day, Schultz paid off police and made cover investments to successfully avoid jail. After Schultz was acquitted of tax evasion in 1933, former U.S. Attorney Thomas Dewey was tasked with organizing a new case for indictment. Concerned that Dewey's experience and determination might actually land him in prison, Schultz and his men planned an assassination. Upon hearing news of the assassination plan, gangster "Lucky" Luciano, who believed that killing a prosecutor would bring too much heat from law enforcement, took action to stop the hit. Schultz and three of his men were gunned down in October 1935 at the New Jersey restaurant from which they ran their operations. In his last moments, Schultz refused to give names of associates or enemies to police. He is thought to have died a multimillionaire; however, most of his money was hidden in cash hoards, so his total wealth remains unknown.

World Wars
During World War I, German Americans faced oppression as many Americans questioned their loyalty at a time when the United States was at war with Germany. This period has been deemed the darkest hour of German American history. Numerous anti-German governmental and volunteer groups sprang up across the country. Such groups expressed anti-German hysteria through various crimes and injustices. Targets included the German language, the German American press, German lessons in schools, German materials in libraries, and German American organizations. Violence, intimidation, and harassment became a reality for German Americans. Some accused of disloyalty faced beatings or even death at the hands of paranoid mobs. More than 6,000 German Americans were placed in internment camps at this time. The repression of German American culture and the decrease of immigration during World War I accelerated the decline of the towns called "Little Germanys" that had been formed in the 1830s.

In 1933, the establishment of the Third Reich prompted more than 1 million Germans to leave their homeland; some 200,000 came to the United States. This is known as the intellectual migration, as it included many artists, doctors, scientists, and writers. German intellectuals such as Albert Einstein and Thomas Mann enriched American society in fields from science and technology to the arts and politics. In contrast to the intellectual enrichment in the United States, World War II brought yet another wave of anti-German hysteria upon German Americans. American paranoia of German espionage resulted in more than 10,000 German Americans being forced into internment camps throughout the United States. The hysteria of World War II never quite took on the mob-like qualities of the World War I paranoia.

The latter half of the 20th century in America was marked by an ethnic heritage revival, during which time the German American element of America received long-overdue recognition. This trend has continued to the present day. Commonplace throughout the United States are German heritage organizations, which promote German culture through various festivals and activities.

Ben Atkins
Sam Houston State University

See Also: 1901 to 1920 Primary Documents; 1921 to 1940 Primary Documents; Dillinger, John; Great Depression; Luciano, "Lucky"; Prohibition; Schultz, "Dutch."

Further Readings
Gish, Theodore and Richard Spuler, eds. *Eagle in the New World: German Immigration to Texas and America.* College Station: Texas A&M University Press, 1986.
Moltmann, Günter, ed. *Germans to America: 300 Years of Immigration 1683 to 1983.* Stuttgart, Germany: Institut für Auslandsbeziehungen, 1982.
Tolzmann, Don H. *The German-American Experience.* New York: Humanity Books, 2000.

Gibbons v. Ogden

In 1824, the U.S. Supreme Court held that the power to regulate interstate commerce was provided to Congress by the commerce clause of the Constitution (found in Article I, Section 8). The case involved determining whether a congressionally approved federal license or a state-supported license took precedence in operating steamboats between New York and New Jersey. Through the case, Chief Justice John Marshall and the Supreme Court made a classic statement of nationalism—finding that competing steamboat operators were protected by a federal license approved by Congress to engage in trade along coastal waters from a New York state license that had been awarded to two individuals.

In 1807, Robert Fulton successfully ran his steamboat up the Hudson River toward Albany, and in response the state of New York granted a monopoly license to Fulton and Robert Livingston to navigate all waters within the state for a period of years with boats moved by fire or steam. Aaron Ogden received a required license from Livingston and Fulton. Thomas Gibbons, on the other hand, ran a competing steamboat service that was licensed by Congress in regulating coastal trade between New York and New Jersey. They came before the Supreme Court to determine whether Gibbons had a right to continue his business or if his license was invalid under the Fulton-Livingston licensing monopoly in New York.

When it came to questions of state and federal relations, Gibbons's attorney, Daniel Webster, believed there to be four options: exclusive national power, fully concurrent powers, partially concurrent state power, or supremacy of a national statute over a contrary state statute. In Ogden's argument (presented by Thomas Addis Emmitt and Thomas Oakley), he contended that states should have fully concurrent powers with the national government on issues related to interstate commerce. Webster and William Wirt (arguing for Gibbons), on the other hand, believed that Congress had exclusive rights to the regulation of interstate commerce through constitutional provisions. Further, they argued that leaving the regulation of commerce to states would lead to conflicting and confusing statutes that would weaken trade throughout the country.

National Versus State Authority

Both the trial and appellate courts had ruled in favor of Ogden. But Chief Justice John Marshall, an ardent nationalist, found in favor of Gibbons (6–0) and the national government's ability to regulate commerce from its perspective. Since an appropriate federal law already existed that appeared to regulate vessels and coasting trade, New York State did not have the ability to enact monopoly regulation on the same general area. The decision of the court was predicated on answering two key questions: (1) Did "commerce" include regulating navigation? and (2) Did Congress hold an exclusive power to do so?

To the first question, the court clearly accepted a broad understanding of commerce, stating in the majority decision that commerce is more than traffic and includes all kinds of business and trade even within nations. This definition, in the court's eye, includes navigation. Marshall wrote: "All America understands, and has uniformly understood, the word 'commerce' to comprehend navigation." To the second question, the majority opinion demonstrates a strong preference to the national power of Congress, saying, "The power over commerce with foreign nations and among the several states is vested in Congress as absolutely as it would be in a single government."

While the Supreme Court's decision was a clear victory for national powers, an interesting nuance was that the Marshall Court opted to not decide the case on grounds of exclusivity despite Marshall's preference. Because of the potential impact of a broad ruling in this case that demonstrated favor toward national exclusivity across the board, Marshall instead was somewhat more direct in his ruling. William Johnson, a South Carolinian nationalist, wrote a concurring opinion that was far more expansive in prescribing national supremacy on all areas of interstate commerce.

The court failed to resolve some issues in the case. First, it did not rule on whether states had the ability to regulate areas of commerce Congress had not regulated. Second, there was no discussion of whether states could concurrently regulate areas of commerce that Congress was also regulating. These issues were decided in later years. *Gibbons v. Ogden* stood until 1895, when the court started to limit congressional power in *United States v. E. C. Knight Co.* The basic precedent set in the case, however, paved the way for future federal regulation of commerce, with little economic activity today being outside the regulatory power of Congress.

William J. Miller
Southeast Missouri State University

See Also: Constitution of the United States of America; Marshall, John; Supreme Court, U.S.

Further Readings

Baxter, Maurice G. *The Steamboat Monopoly: Gibbons v. Ogden, 1824.* New York: Knopf, 1972.

Dangerfield, George. "The Steamboat Case." In *Quarrels That Have Shaped the Constitution*, John A. Garraty, ed. New York: Harper & Row, 1987.

Frankfurter, Felix. *The Commerce Clause Under Marshall, Taney, and Waite*. Chapel Hill: University of North Carolina Press, 1937.

Johnson, Herbert A. Gibbons v. Ogden: *John Marshall, Steamboats, and the Commerce Clause*. Lawrence: University Press of Kansas, 2010.

Gideon v. Wainwright

In the case *Gideon v. Wainwright*, the Supreme Court established the right of indigent defendants in felony cases at the state level to be provided with an attorney. The right extended the right to counsel found in the Sixth Amendment to the Constitution to defendants at the state level via the due process clause of the Fourteenth Amendment. In doing so, the court overturned the special circumstances rule established by *Betts v. Brady (1942)*, which stated that state courts only had to provide attorneys to the indigent if the lack of defense council would render the trial unfair. The right was subsequently expanded in *Scott v. Illinois* to defendants in all criminal trials where imprisonment is a possible punishment.

Clarence Earl Gideon, a 51-year-old, semi-employed, white male was convicted of breaking into the Bay Harbor Pool Room in Panama City, Florida. At his arraignment, Gideon requested that the court appoint counsel to help him prepare his case. At the time, Florida law only required that defense counsel be appointed in capital cases; in all other cases it was left to the discretion of the court to appoint counsel. The trial court denied Gideon's request for counsel and proceeded to trial. At trial, the prosecution called only two witnesses: one who testified that they had seen Gideon leaving the pool hall with a gallon of wine, and the pool hall owner who testified that he had locked up the hall at midnight. Gideon called six witnesses, but failed to sufficiently examine them to bring forth much exculpatory evidence. He was convicted and sentenced to five years in prison.

In his appeal to the Florida Supreme Court, Gideon claimed that his rights to due process of law had been violated by the failure of the trial court to appoint counsel for him. The Florida Supreme Court rejected his argument, stating that the trial court had the option, but not an obligation to provide counsel at its discretion. Gideon filed a writ of habeas corpus claiming that the denial of counsel denied him his rights guaranteed in the Bill of Rights of the United States. The Supreme Court granted certiorari and appointed counsel to assist with his case in order to reconsider its earlier ruling in *Betts v. Brady*, which rested on similar facts. Abe Fortas appeared on behalf of Gideon, arguing that a requirement for counsel to all criminal defendants would be less intrusive to states than a review of the circumstances of the case as suggested under *Betts*. The attorneys for Florida invited the attorneys general of other states to file amicus curiae briefs; however, all but two of the states that filed briefs that supported Gideon, bolstering his cause.

The court described the *Betts* ruling as aberrant in the course of the court's application of the Sixth Amendment to the states. Justice Hugo Black, writing for the unanimous court, stated, "in our adversary system of criminal justice, any person hauled into court, who is too poor to hire a lawyer, cannot be assured a fair trial unless counsel is provided for him." The court further pointed out that the government, state and federal, hires attorneys to prosecute defendants, and that any defendant who can afford a lawyer procures one. Justices John Harlan and Tom Clark concurred in the holding and Justice William O. Douglas wrote a separate opinion to emphasize that the rights itemized in the Bill of Rights do not decline when applied to the states via the Fourteenth Amendment. The ruling in *Gideon* represented a major step in securing due process rights for criminal defendants. Although Gideon was not a minority defendant, the ruling would assist marginal and minority defendants to prepare their cases and ensure due process at trial. In his retrial with the assistance of counsel, Gideon was found not guilty by a Florida jury.

John Felipe Acevedo
University of Chicago

See Also: Constitution of the United States of America; *Miranda v. Arizona*; Trials.

Further Readings
Chemerinsky, Erwin. *Constitutional Law: Principles and Policies*. New York: Aspen Law & Business, 2002.
Gideon v. Wainwright, 372 U.S. 335 (1963).
Gideon's Broken Promise: America's Continuing Quest for Equal Justice, A Report on the American Bar Association's Hearings on the Right to Counsel in Criminal Proceedings. Chicago: American Bar Association, 2004.
Lewis, Anthony. *Gideon's Trumpet*. New York: Vintage Books, 1964.
Scott v. Illinois, 440 U.S. 367 (1979).
Taylor, John B. *Right to Counsel and Privilege Against Self-Incrimination: Rights and Liberties Under the Law*. Santa Barbara, CA: ABC-CLIO, 2004.
Tomkovicz, James J. *The Right to the Assistance of Counsel: A Reference Guide to the United States Constitution*. Westport, CT: Greenwood Press, 2002.

Former New York City Mayor and Republican candidate for president Rudolph Giuliani addressing the Republican National Convention in front of a giant image of lower Manhattan without the Twin Towers on September 3, 2008, in St. Paul, Minnesota.

Giuliani, Rudolph

Law school graduate, chief of Narcotics Unit for the Office of the U.S. Attorney, associate attorney general, U.S. attorney, and most notably, mayor of New York City, Rudolph W. Giuliani (1944–) was born in Brooklyn, New York, the child of Harold Angelo Giuliani (1908–81) and Helen C. D'Avanzo (1902–2002). He attended Catholic school in Garden City South, graduated from high school in 1961, and from Manhattan College in 1965. He went to New York University Law School in Manhattan, where he graduated magna cum laude in 1968. He married Regina Peruggi (his second cousin) that same year, but they divorced in 1982. He then married Donna Hanover (a local television personality) in 1984. They had two children together (Andrew in 1986 and Caroline in 1989). They divorced in 2002, and Giuliani married Judith Nathan (a sales manager) in 2003.

Giuliani began his career as a clerk in the U.S. District Court for the Southern District of New York. He then joined the U.S. Attorney's office in 1970. In 1975, he became associate deputy attorney general of chief of staff to the deputy attorney general in Washington, D.C. He returned to New York to practice law from 1977 to 1981, working for Patterson, Belknap, Webb & Tyler. He became associate attorney general in 1981, and was appointed U.S. attorney for the Southern District of New York in 1983, where he was very successful at fighting corruption and organized crime. He was credited with the prosecution of Wall Street executives, and with patenting the "perp walk," in which suspects are paraded in front of the media.

Political Career

In 1989, Giuliani ran for mayor of New York City, but lost the election. He worked at the law firm White & Case until May 1990, and then joined Anderson Kill Olick & Oshinsky. He ran for mayor again in 1993, and he won, becoming the 107th mayor of New York City. During his tenure, overall crime was reduced, the streets became safer, and the quality of life was improved for New Yorkers. Giuliani cleaned up public places and created a surplus out of the budget deficit. He implemented a welfare-to-work program and was responsible for an innovative law enforcement strategy. Via CompStat, police were able to monitor criminal activity on street corners, and a proactive stance was taken in reducing criminal activity. He created the Administration for Children's Services to monitor and protect children and initiated HealthStat, which enrolled children in health insurance programs.

He worked to raise the standards of the city's schools through improved student-teacher ratios and special education programs while instituting innovative instructional programs to assist with reading skills. He pushed for libraries in schools, computers in classrooms, and arts education in the school curriculum. He served as mayor until 2001 (two terms). Interestingly, he ran on the Republican and Liberal lines, yet he was a Democrat and an Independent in the 1970s.

It should be noted that some critics did not give Giuliani as much credit as his supporters; although some said the drop in New York City crime surpassed that of the nation, critics claim the crime rate was already dropping when he began his administration, and that federal funding and the hiring of additional police officers decreased the crime problem. Further, there was an improvement in the economy and changing demographics, which contributed to the drop in crime. Giuliani ran for U.S. Senate in 2000 but withdrew once he was diagnosed with prostate cancer (at age 55). In 2001, he was credited for his leadership in response to the September 11 World Trade Center attacks. He became known as "America's Mayor," was named *Time* magazine's "Person of the Year" in 2001, and received honorary degrees and public service awards. He received an honorary knighthood from Queen Elizabeth II and made cameo appearances in a number of movies.

In 2002, he founded Giuliani Partners, a security consulting business. He then joined the Bracewell & Giuliani law firm in 2005. In 2006, he started a Website to help elect Republican candidates. He ran for the Republican Party nomination in the 2008 presidential election, but withdrew from the race after a poor finish in the primaries. He returned to work at Giuliani Partners and Bracewell & Giuliani. He considered running for governor and U.S. Senate but decided against both. Today, he is a frequent political commentator on television and remains politically active, campaigning for Republican candidates.

Gina M. Robertiello
Felician College

See Also: New York; New York City; Organized Crime, Contemporary; Violent Crimes.

Further Readings
Barrett, Wayne and Dan Collins. *Grand Illusion: The Untold Story of Rudy Giuliani and 9/11*. New York: HarperCollins, 2006.
Kirtzman, Andrew. *Rudy Giuliani: Emperor of the City*. New York: HarperCollins, 2001.
Polner, Robert. *America's Mayor: The Hidden History of Rudy Giuliani's New York*. Berkeley, CA: Soft Skull Press, 2005.

Glidewell v. State

Robert Earl Glidewell was convicted of first-degree murder after having participated in the robbery of a local convenience store, which resulted in the death of the store clerk. On February 1, 1978, a convenience store was robbed in Oklahoma City around the early morning hours. David Devol, the store clerk, was talking on the phone with an acquaintance who overheard the commotion and the moment the victim was shot. Upon hearing the gunshots, the acquaintance ran from her home to the store, where she identified Robert Glidewell's car. On the night of the shooting, Robert Glidewell entered the store with three other men (Dennis Glidewell, Charles Moseley, and Kenneth Boutwell) to rob the clerk.

It was decided between them that there could be no witnesses because the Glidewells were familiar with the clerk. One of the men, Kenneth Boutwell, agreed to do the shooting. Once they entered the store, the victim was shot five times. The last shot was to ensure that the clerk was dead. Robert Glidewell proceeded to open the registers and safe and to empty them. Soon after, they were all arrested.

When Robert Glidewell took the stand, however, he claimed that he did not expect the clerk to be shot, despite having admitted to discussing the need to kill the victim. Ultimately, the court found Glidewell guilty, beyond a reasonable doubt, of murder in the first degree; he was sentenced to death.

The appellant (i.e., Robert Glidewell; the person seeking to have the decision reversed) presented various assignments of error for the Oklahoma Court of Appeals to review. The first assignment of error was associated with six veniremen who were excluded for not being able to impose the death penalty. The appellant argued that one of the jurors did not clearly state that he would be opposed to the death penalty; however, he was still dismissed. Glidewell also disagreed with the basis on which a juror can be disqualified. More specifically, jurors should not be disqualified based on their views on capital punishment. The appellant argued that the court committed an error by admitting a color photograph of the victim lying dead on the floor. Further, a supposed illegal search was conducted in which the cash and rifle used during the crime were confiscated.

Glidewell also disputed the constitutionality of Oklahoma's death penalty statutes, citing the statutes were a violation of his Eighth Amendment protection against cruel and unusual punishment and his Fourteenth Amendment right to due process and equal protection of the law. However, the court decided that the constitutionality of the death penalty had been established by the decision in *Gregg v. Georgia*. The most significant error presented happened to be Glidewell's argument that the trial court erred by submitting as an aggravating circumstance that the murder was committed in exchange for a reward or ordered to be committed with the promise of a reward.

Upon having read all of the assignments of error presented by the appellant, the Oklahoma Court of Appeals only recognized the potential influence of the aggravating factor on the sentence. Along with this recognition, the court identified three courses of action they could take: (1) convert the death sentence to life imprisonment by remanding the case, (2) determine that the error could be deemed as having no real consequence on the outcome, and (3) remand the case so that a new jury could resentence Glidewell. In order to make their decision, the justices examined the "weighing process" that guides the jury (upon having been presented with the mitigating and aggravating circumstances in the case) in determining whether a defendant should receive the death penalty.

Ultimately, the court decided that the trial court's mistake in presenting an erroneous aggravating circumstance to the jury could not be deemed harmless because the rendering of a death sentence is dependent upon the existence of at least one aggravating circumstance in the case. As such, the notion of having committed murder in exchange for a reward or order to be committed with the promise of a reward would automatically qualify the defendant for the death penalty. For this reason, the court was ordered to conduct a resentencing trial before a new jury.

Amy S. Eggers
University of South Florida

See Also: Capital Punishment; Juries; Robbery, Contemporary; Robbery, History of; Robbery, Sociology of.

Further Readings
Glidewell v. State, OK CR 4 663 p. 2d738 (1983).
Gregg v. Georgia, 428 U.S. 153, 96 S. Ct. 2909, 49 L.Ed.2d 859 (1976).
Justia U.S. Law. "Glidewell v. State." http://law.justia.com/cases/oklahoma/court-of-appeals-criminal/1983/5938-1.html (Accessed September 2011).

Gotti, John

Boss of New York's Gambino crime family, John Gotti was born on October 27, 1940, in New York, the fifth of 11 children of Fannie and John J. Gotti

Sr. Gotti was also known by two nicknames: "the Teflon Don" for his ability to evade several criminal charges lodged against him over the years and "the Dapper Don" for his natty and meticulous appearance, expensively tailored clothing, and an opulent and flamboyant public persona. Gotti was raised in an impoverished neighborhood in the South Bronx, but his family moved to Brooklyn when Gotti was about 12 years old. He had the reputation of a tough fighter with a perpetual chip on his shoulder and he soon became involved in petty street crime with two of his brothers and others in the neighborhood, running errands for local neighborhood mobsters. He did poorly in school and was often truant, quitting in 1956 at the age of 16. Gotti soon became a member of the Fulton-Rockaway Boys, a local teenage gang, where he rose through the ranks to become one of the gang's leaders.

At about 20 years old, Gotti met and fell in love with 18-year-old Victoria DiGiorgio. They were married in 1962, after the birth of their first child, a daughter. Gotti made two attempts at legitimate employment, once as presser in a coat factory and once driving a truck, but stuck with neither. He continued his career as a petty criminal and did a couple of short stretches of jail time. Through Angelo Ruggerio, a friend from his Fulton-Rockaway days, Gotti became involved with a Mafia crew headed up by brothers Carmine and Daniel Fatico. The Faticos' crew worked under Aniello Dellacroce of the Gambino crime family, specializing in hijackings, particularly out of Kennedy International Airport (JFK). In 1967, Gotti was arrested for his part in hijacking $30,000 worth of merchandise from United's cargo area at JFK and was implicated in another theft for which he was also arrested. While out on bond on those charges, Gotti was arrested a third time for hijacking a load of cigarettes in New Jersey worth almost half a million dollars. Gotti's lawyer struck a deal, and Gotti pled guilty to one charge, another charge was dropped, and the remaining sentence was served concurrently with the first. In all, Gotti served less than three years in federal prison.

Gotti continued to climb through the ranks of the Gambino family. After Carlo Gambino's nephew was kidnapped and killed, Gotti was convicted as part of the hit squad that retaliated and killed one of the kidnappers, for which he was sentenced to seven years. After serving a portion of the sentence, Gotti was released and was rewarded by Gambino with privilege and position in the family. By the late 1970s, Gotti had become an underboss under Dellacroce. When Gambino died of a heart attack in 1976, Paul Castellano was handed the reins of the family. Gotti, loyal to Dellacroce, felt that Dellacroce deserved the position and not Castellano, but Dellacroce kept him in check. Two weeks after Dellacroce died of cancer in 1985, Paul Castellano was gunned down in Manhattan. Within days, Gotti moved in and took over the family, at that time one of the largest and most powerful Mafia families in the United States.

With intense scrutiny by authorities, several attempts were made at prosecuting Gotti on various charges. Each time, Gotti escaped prosecution, earning him the "Teflon Don" moniker, as criminal charges did not stick against him. His luck finally ran out when he was convicted of 13 murders and other charges in 1992, with the aid of wiretap evidence and the testimony of his former underboss Sammy ("the Bull") Gravano. Gravano agreed to testify against Gotti and Gambino family consigliere Frank Locascio in exchange for a guilty plea to only one charge to be leveled against him and for admission into the witness protection program. Gotti was sentenced to life without parole and began serving his sentence at the federal penitentiary in Marion, Illinois. In 2002, Gotti was diagnosed with throat cancer. He died on June 10, 2002.

Paul A. Magro
Ball State University

See Also: Italian Americans; New York; New York City; Organized Crime, History of; Organized Crime, Sociology of.

Further Readings
Abadinsky, Howard. *Organized Crime*. Belmont, CA: Wadsworth, 2010.
Capeci, Jerry and Gene Mustain. *Gotti: Rise and Fall*. New York: Onyx, 1996.
Davis, John H. *Mafia Dynasty: The Rise and Fall of the Gambino Crime Family*. New York: Harper Torch, 1993.

"John Gotti: Making the Charges Stick." In *The FBI, A Centennial History 1908–2008*. Washington, DC: U.S. Department of Justice, 2008.

Roth, Mitchell P. *Organized Crime*. Upper Saddle River, NJ: Pearson Education, 2010.

Sifakis, Carl. *The Mafia Encyclopedia*. New York: Checkmark Books, 1999.

Grafton, Sue

Sue Grafton (1940–), author of the popular Kinsey Millhone detective novels, has been a pioneer in the tough female private investigator (PI) genre. With others such as Marcia Muller and Sara Paretsky, Grafton was one of the first female authors to write about a "hard-boiled" female private eye. Featuring a lead character who was both independent and self-sufficient, Grafton's books have been tremendously successful, influencing other novelists, screenwriters, and video game creators.

Born Sue Taylor Grafton in Louisville, Kentucky, in 1940, Grafton was the daughter of crime novelist Cornelius Warren Grafton. Grafton studied English literature at the University of Louisville, graduating with a B.A. in 1961. Beginning writing at age 18, Grafton completed seven early novels, two of which were published in the late 1960s. Due to her novels' relative lack of success, Grafton began working as a screenwriter in Hollywood. For the next 15 years, Grafton wrote screenplays for a variety of television movies, including adaptations of Agatha Christie's *Sparkling Cyanide* and *A Caribbean Mystery*. Grafton's screenplays were successful, and she was able to work steadily. This experience honed Grafton's ability to write tight dialogue, structure fast-moving plots, and depict realistic action sequences.

In 1982, while continuing to work as a screenwriter, Grafton published her first novel featuring Kinsey Millhone. Millhone was portrayed as being in her early 30s when the Alphabet Series began and lived in the fictional California city of Santa Teresa. In choosing the location of the series, Grafton was paying homage to Ross Macdonald, whose fictional detective Lew Archer first worked in the fictionalized version of Santa Barbara in the mystery *The Moving Target* (1949). Grafton considered Macdonald's stylized Southern California settings, literate style, and tough but compassionate detective as significant influences on her own writing. Grafton is an aficionado of detective fiction, with characters as diverse as Christie, Macdonald, and Nancy Drew influencing her work. All of the titles in the series begin with a letter of the alphabet. Grafton has stated that the series will end once she reaches the letter "Z." Titles in the series range from *A Is for Alibi* (1982) to *V Is for Vengeance* (2011).

All of the Alphabet Series books feature Millhone, a single woman who is self-employed, informal in her dress, and an ardent jogger. An orphan since age 5, when her parents were killed in an automobile accident, Millhone's maternal aunt, Virginia, raised her after the death of her parents. Aunt "Gin" was the lone member of Kinsey's mother's family who overlooked a socially disadvantageous marriage. The rapprochement with her extended family is a continuing theme throughout the series.

By her own account something of a rebel in high school, Millhone spent several semesters in community college before dropping out to join the Santa Teresa police department. Several years later, she became a PI, first working with a mentor, later striking out on her own. Unlike other female hard-boiled PIs, Millhone never achieves great wealth or success in her career. To this end, Grafton purposely manipulates the passage of time in the series, so that while *Alibi* is set in 1982, later novels are still set in the 1980s. Grafton has stated that when the series concludes with "Z," Millhone will be 40, which would occur in 1990. Millhone has several intimate relationships during the course of the series, but gains needed emotional support from other friends, such as her octogenarian landlord, Henry Pitts, a retired baker, and his siblings. Late in the series, Millhone reconnects with her mother's family, the Kinseys, from whom she had long been estranged.

Popular with both the public and critics, Grafton's books have sold millions of copies and won three Anthony Awards, given at the annual Anthony Boucher Memorial World Mystery Convention (Bouchercon), three Shamus Awards, given by the Private Eye Writers of America (PWA), the Cartier Dagger from the British

Crime Writers' Association, and the Grand Master Award from the Mystery Writers of America (MWA). Despite repeated offers, Grafton has declined to have the Millhone novels turned into motion pictures. Grafton's work has influenced a host of other writers, such as Linda Barnes, Karen Kijewski, Wendi Lee, and J. M. Redmann.

Stephen T. Schroth
Knox College

See Also: Christie, Agatha; Hammett, Dashiell; Hillerman, Tony; Literature and Theater, Crime in; Literature and Theater, Police in.

Further Readings
Kaufman, N. H. and C. M. Kay. *"G" Is for Grafton: The World of Kinsey Millhone.* New York: Henry Holt & Co., 1997.
Sachs, Andrea. "Q&A: Mystery Writer Sue Grafton." *Time* (December 11, 2009). http://www.time.com/time/arts/article/0,8599,1946841,00.html (Accessed February 2012).

General Ulysses S. Grant outside a tent at his headquarters in Cold Harbor, Virginia, in June 1864 during the Civil War. Early in his administration, he used the Enforcement Acts of 1870–71 to counter Ku Klux Klan harassment of African Americans.

Grant, Ulysses S. (Administration of)

Noted Civil War Union general Ulysses Simpson Grant (1822–85) was the 18th president of the United States, serving two terms from 1869 to 1877. His Reconstruction-era administration was primarily concerned with the restoration of sectional harmony, the readmission of southern state governments, and the protection of African American civil rights. Grant presided over the 19th century's largest federal law enforcement efforts. Grant petitioned Congress for passage of the Fifteenth Amendment and the Civil Rights Act of 1875 to guarantee federal protection of civil rights, and for passage of a series of enforcement acts granting the federal government judicial authority to prosecute groups such as the Ku Klux Klan (KKK) that sought to prevent the exercise of those rights. He also sent federal troops into the south to suppress violence and protect elections. Grant's accomplishments were marred by a series of scandals involving administration officials.

Grant established his national reputation through a military career, rising to the rank of general and commanding the Union army in the last years of the Civil War. He was known for his strategic abilities and strong will as well as his strong stand against secession. After the war, Grant served briefly as President Andrew Johnson's interim secretary of war in 1867 but disagreed with Johnson's approach to the Reconstruction issues of readmitting the southern state governments to the Union while overlooking the civil rights of the newly freed slaves. Grant sided with the radical Republicans dominating Congress in their battle against Johnson's conciliatory policies.

Grant's status as a war hero helped secure the Republican nomination for the presidency in the 1868 election as well as his subsequent victory over Democratic candidate Horatio Seymour. Grant served two terms in office, defeating Horace Greeley to win reelection in 1872. He successfully appointed Joseph Bradley, William Strong, Ward Hunt, and Morrison Waite to the Supreme Court while three other appointees were never confirmed, including Edwin Stanton, who died after his Senate confirmation but before taking office. Grant vacillated on the subject of civil service reform. Reconstruction politics and scandal, however, dominated the Grant administration.

Civil Rights

Grant sought to balance the often-conflicting goals of ending sectional tensions while enforcing the civil rights legislation benefiting the emancipated slaves, commonly known as freedmen. He actively promoted congressional passage of the Fifteenth Amendment in 1870 and the Civil Rights Act of 1875 while seeking to enforce the Fourteenth Amendment granting African Americans rights as citizens. Voting rights were a key concern, as southerners opposed to African Americans' voting used violence and intimidation to keep them from the polls. Grant sent federal troops into the south on numerous occasions to protect the polls.

Grant also utilized the powers of the federal government to suppress the Ku Klux Klan, a vigilante group formed by Confederate veterans and wealthy planters to terrorize and intimidate African Americans and their white supporters. Grant successfully lobbied Congress for passage of a series of enforcement acts in 1870–71 to target the KKK, as well as for the creation of the Department of Justice and the Solicitor General's office to try federal cases. Attorney General Amos T. Akerman was also known for his vigorous prosecution of offenders. Later in his administration, Grant backed off this strong promotion of African American rights as political and social circumstances shifted public attitudes and military troop reductions left fewer men available for federal intervention in the south.

As concerns mounted over economic difficulties, the enthusiasm of northerners for racial issues waned. Southern Democrats, meanwhile, had largely "redeemed" their state governments from Republicans and began passing Jim Crow legislation designed to restrict African American rights. They also began demanding an end to federal military intervention. Grant dismissed Amos Akerman, failed to seek additional enforcement legislation, and refused to send additional federal troops to police southern elections. The Civil Rights Act of 1875 suffered from lack of enforcement before the Supreme Court ultimately struck it down in 1883. Despite this ultimate failure of the Grant administration's Reconstruction policies, they represented the 19th century's most significant federal law enforcement effort.

Scandals

Grant's lack of political experience, poor choice of administration officials, and personal loyalty led to the numerous scandals for which his administration became notorious. These scandals were motivated by the greed of administration officials and did not involve Grant personally. The first big scandal involved administration officials who aided the scheme of financiers Jay Gould and James Fisk to monopolize the gold market by keeping federal gold supplies off the market. Vice President Schuyler Colfax and others were involved in the Crédit Mobilier scandal involving the Union Pacific Railroad and its construction of the transcontinental railroad, accepting stock bribes to overlook improprieties. Private secretary Orville E. Babcock was involved in the Whiskey Ring plot between distillers and Internal Revenue Service agents to avoid collection of federal alcohol taxes. Grant's testimony helped win his acquittal. Secretary of War William W. Belknap resigned after charges of accepting bribes from Native American post traders surfaced.

The numerous federal interventions in the south and scandals hurt both Grant and the Republican Party, allowing the Democrats to regain control of the House of Representatives in 1874. Grant left office in 1877 after apologizing for his administration's mistakes in his farewell address. After a failed candidacy for the 1880 Republican presidential nomination, Grant spent the remainder of his years traveling abroad and becoming involved in an investment firm. A swindle that damaged the firm forced Grant to declare bankruptcy, and throat cancer threatened his health. He worked with friend and renowned author Mark Twain to complete his memoirs to raise funds for his wife and children upon his death. Ulysses S. Grant died on July 23, 1885, in Mount McGregor, New York. His New York City tomb is a national memorial.

Marcella Bush Trevino
Barry University

See Also: Civil Rights Act of 1875; Enforcement Acts of 1870–71; Ku Klux Klan.

Further Readings
Simpson, Brooks D. *Let Us Have Peace: Ulysses S. Grant and the Politics of War and Reconstruction, 1861–1868*. Chapel Hill: University of North Carolina Press, 1991.
Simpson, Brooks D. *The Reconstruction Presidents*. Lawrence: University Press of Kansas, 1998.
Waugh, Jean. *U. S. Grant: American Hero, American Myth*. Chapel Hill: University of North Carolina Press, 2009.

Great Depression

The Great Depression was an era marked by worldwide economic turmoil, including high rates of unemployment, decreasing gross national products (GNP), and declining stock markets. In the United States, the Depression lasted from 1929 until 1941. Scholars reason differently as to the main factors contributing to the Depression, including bank failures, contracted money supplies, and failure of the free market. While reasons for the Depression continue to be debated, the catalyst of the Depression is not. It began in the United States with the stock market crash on October 29, 1929, also known as Black Tuesday. During the next few months, industrial production fell, unemployment increased, and the Depression was under way.

Effects of Prohibition

The decade prior to the crash was one of prosperity that witnessed the creation of the American consumer culture but also a culture of lawlessness. The National Prohibition Act (Volstead Act) was passed on October 28, 1919, and on January 17, 1920, the Eighteenth Amendment was enacted to began the era of Prohibition. A prohibition commissioner under the National Prohibition Bureau was given power to enforce the Volstead Act, and a small force of officers was established. The prohibition commission was not well staffed or well funded. Within a week of Prohibition's passage, illegal bars known as speakeasies were established, and liquor was stolen from government warehouses. The growth of criminal activity related to Prohibition began. Urban gangsters were able to create syndicate crime organizations that took control of bootlegging and other industries and were easily able to fund the corruption of political and law enforcement officials.

The National Commission on Law Enforcement and Observance (Wickersham Commission) was established by President Herbert Hoover in May 1929 to hold hearings throughout the country on enforcement of Prohibition. The most notable points of the Wickersham Commission were that it exposed the rampant corruption, fraud, violence, and bribery taking place among law enforcement and public officials with respect to enforcing Prohibition; the report concluded that Prohibition was potentially a factor exacerbating harsh economic conditions faced by the country. While the Wickersham Commission exposed the problems with enforcement of Prohibition, the public was enthralled with urban gangsters such as Al Capone, Charles Luciano and Louis Buchalter, who ran syndicates in high style. While it was federal law enforcement that eventually took down Capone, it was a state prosecutor and future presidential candidate who took the anti-syndicate crime reins to battle gangsters such as Luciano and Buchalter.

Alphonse "Scarface" Capone ran a crime syndicate in Chicago that focused on bootlegging, gambling, and prostitution, crimes that during Prohibition were not always frowned upon by the public. Capone engaged in bribery and generally had Illinois law enforcement and public officials in his pocket. Capone was a popular figure for some time, even garnering a front-page photograph on the cover of *Time* magazine in 1930. However, many in the public lost their love of Capone after the 1929 St. Valentine Day's Massacre where seven rival gangsters were killed. Eventually, the federal government went after Capone in a strategy led by Prohibition agent Eliot Ness, and Capone was convicted on charges of income tax evasion in 1931.

Charles "Lucky" Luciano was a New York gangster who organized bootlegging, prostitution, and racketeering. Luciano developed connections with mob leaders across the country and developed a nationwide criminal syndicate of mobsters.

Prohibition began on January 17, 1920, and almost immediately, illegal bars known as speakeasies were established. The photo shows New York City deputy police commissioner John A. Leach, right, watching his agents dump seized alcohol into the city sewer following a speakeasy raid around 1921. Franklin D. Roosevelt took office in March 1933 and quickly repealed Prohibition, which some thought was making the Great Depression even worse.

The power Luciano developed was based on the numerous gang connections and small-time gangsters in his employ, along with political connections such as to the Democratic political machine Tammany Hall. In 1935, special prosecutor Thomas Dewey was appointed in New York to help clean up crime. Dewey was eventually able to get a number of prostitutes to testify against Luciano, who was convicted on June 7, 1936.

Louis "Lepke" Buchalter ran extensive extortion rings against industries in New York, alcohol and drug smuggling, and ran Murder Incorporated, a gang handling enforcement for crime syndicates. In 1937, Thomas Dewey set his sights on Buchalter, and after a false deal was made where Buchalter believed he was turning himself over to the Federal Bureau of Investigation (FBI) for a minimum deal, Buchalter was taken in, tried, and convicted. Buchalter was charged with the 1936 murder of candy store owner Joe Rosen. Buchalter was executed in 1944 for the murder. Thomas Dewey, who became governor of New York, later ran campaigns for president but lost to both Franklin D. Roosevelt and Harry S. Truman.

Crime Control

The winter of 1932–33 is considered the darkest period of the Depression. In 1933, unemployment reached an all-time high of 25 percent. The public took a stand against President Herbert Hoover and the administration's policies and elected Franklin Roosevelt in November 1932. Roosevelt took office in March 1933, and the first 100 days of his term saw a barrage of legislation quickly passed. A major step in crime control came when Roosevelt repealed Prohibition. While it was expected that repeal of Prohibition would do away with the type of criminal syndicates that developed during Prohibition, these organizations merely shifted focus and were able to shield themselves from the limelight as other types of crime took center stage, most notably kidnapping and bank robbing.

President Hoover had not wanted to engage in policies that would empower the federal government, including law enforcement. Thus, it was not until the kidnapping of the Lindbergh baby that President Hoover took any federal law enforcement initiative. On March 1, 1932, the son of American aviator and hero Charles Lindbergh was kidnapped from his home. The child, only 20 months old and named after his father, was later found dead. While not the only person kidnapped, the Lindbergh baby was fodder for public news and made national headlines, reaching President Hoover. Unfortunately, the federal government did not have legal authority to take action as no federal laws existed at the time regarding kidnapping. Because of Lindbergh's status, President Hoover pushed for involvement of federal agencies, including the Bureau of Investigation (renamed the Federal Bureau of investigation [FBI] in 1935) that was within the Department of Justice. After the deceased child was found, Congress passed the Federal Kidnapping Act (Lindbergh Law), which allowed the federal government to intervene in kidnapping cases where the victim was taken across state lines. The man later convicted of the Lindbergh kidnapping, Bruno Hauptmann, was arrested on September 29, 1934, with some of the ransom money but maintained his innocence up through his execution.

The first kidnapping case where federal law enforcement was actively involved was the kidnapping of oilman Charles F. Urschel on July 22, 1933, by George "Machine Gun" Kelly (1895–1954) and accomplice Albert Bates in Oklahoma City. Urschel was released after a ransom was received, and on September 26, 1933, Kelly was captured in Memphis, Tennessee. During this arrest, Kelly supposedly shouted the now-famous words "Don't shoot, G-men. Don't shoot!" referring to government men. J. Edgar Hoover, director of the FBI, was a master publicist who was able to use the exploits of agents to increase public acceptance of federal law enforcement.

Crime and Criminals

In the early years of the Depression, certain crimes such as bank robbing were romanticized by the public. Newsreels, competitive reporting, and detective magazines were a growing form of entertainment. The narrative of the bank-robbing bandit was a story the public could relate to. While bandits were generally young white males, women referred to as "molls" sometimes accompanied them as spouses and lovers, and at other times as active participants. The extent of involvement of the molls varies case by case, and the extent of involvement of particular women such as Bonnie Parker has been disputed.

Bonnie Parker and Clyde Barrow, known by the public simply as Bonnie and Clyde, were a notorious couple who used stolen automobiles to commit robberies of banks and stores, killing several people, including law enforcement officers. The couple met in 1930 and formed a loosely constituted gang of five. Public focus was placed on the couple and their crimes for the amount of violence and guns used as well as the couple's desire to be in the limelight. On May 23, 1934, Bonnie and Clyde drove into a trap near Gibsland, Louisiana, and were killed in a hail of 167 bullets by a Texas posse led by former Texas Ranger Frank Hamer. It was assumed that the FBI was going to intervene in the hunt for Bonnie and Clyde; however, they had sent their resources to aid in the capture of another fugitive, public enemy number one John Dillinger.

John Dillinger was a bank robber who made a number of escapes from prison. Dillinger gained additional notoriety when his picture was taken with prosecutor Robert Estill, whose jail in Crown Point, Indiana, he broke out of on March

3, 1934. The jailbreak, originally believed to be accomplished by a wooden pistol, was achieved through a series of bribes. The escape allowed the FBI to enter the picture when Dillinger drove a stolen vehicle across state lines. Dillinger was killed by the FBI on July 22, 1934, led by agent Melvin Purvis, outside of the Biograph Theater in Chicago.

The era of bandit crime closed with the end of the Barker-Karpis gang. The Barker-Karpis gang was supposedly controlled by Kate "Ma" Barker, who was the mother of four sons involved in the gang that enlisted other bandits such as Alvin Karpis. Scholars disagree with the version of Ma Barker's role in the gang as officiated by the FBI. The Barker-Karpis gang came to an end when Ma Barker and one of her sons, Fred Barker, were killed in a shoot-out in Florida on January 16, 1935, by the FBI. The FBI's capture and killing of the various members of the Barker-Karpis gang solidified the FBI as a crime-fighting organization.

Tensions Run High
In the early Depression years, people were passive in their reaction to the Depression, as many believed they were at fault for their unemployment situation. As the Depression ensued, there was some indication that people were becoming more active in their reactions to the economic and social conditions of the Depression. Farmers engaged in minor acts of rebellion, such as refusing to give up land. In 1932, the Bonus Expeditionary Force (BEF), a group of World War I veterans, set up camp in Washington, D.C., to secure bonuses they had been promised for wartime efforts. President Hoover had the FBI investigate BEF members in an attempt to gather information about the veterans. In late July, Hoover ordered the BEF removed. The first morning of the removal went without incident; however, in the afternoon, violence erupted. Several police officers were injured, and two BEF veterans were killed. While Hoover wanted to avoid use of the military to remove the BEF and placed the local police force in charge, General Douglas MacArthur entered the area with a small force, including tanks. The ensuing militaristic removal of the BEF by MacArthur cast a negative light on the decisions made by the administration.

Another incident that took place in 1932 that showed the changing social climate involved a group of strikers in Dearborn, Michigan, who organized a march against the Ford Motor Company. In response, company security and local police teamed up to stop the demonstrating strikers. What ensued was a violent outburst involving tear gas, water hosing of strikers, and shots being fired into the crowd. Dozens were wounded, and four people were killed. The handling of the demonstrators combined with other instances of the mishandling of those suffering from the Depression were believed to be the result of government-initiated action.

Economic and political conditions were not the only areas impacted by the Depression. Racial conditions were exacerbated as well. There was a growth in the Ku Klux Klan and a rise in the number of lynchings in the south. However, as the plight of African Americans became more apparent, the Roosevelt administration realized some action had to be taken. It would have been politically damaging to include lynching as a federal crime, so in 1935, the administration began to provide employment and housing to African Americans under various federal programs. Roosevelt's position on race may, of course, have been politically motivated as he saw an opportunity to gain the black vote by bringing them into the New Deal coalition.

In 1939, while the United States was still struggling through its economic woes, international issues gained importance. In September 1939, Germany attacked Poland, beginning World War II. While the United States did not enter the war at this time, the 1940 Selective Service Act was passed by Congress, followed two months later by the re-election of Roosevelt to a third term as president. Military spending grew rapidly and helped to start a fast-paced economic turnaround. The country left the Depression behind and entered a new era of economic growth, international intervention, increased federal law enforcement, and eventual leadership as a world power.

Cindy Pressley
Stephen F. Austin State University

See Also: 1921 to 1940 Primary Documents; Bonnie and Clyde; Dillinger, John; Hoover, Herbert (Administration of); Luciano, "Lucky"; Prohibition;

Roosevelt, Franklin D. (Administration of); Volstead Act; Wickersham Commission.

Further Readings

Himmelberg, Robert F. *The Great Depression and the New Deal.* Westport, CT: Greenwood Press, 2001.

O'Reilly, Kenneth. "A New Deal for the FBI: The Roosevelt Administration, Crime Control, and National Security." *Journal of American History*, v.69/3 (1982).

Potter, Claire Bond. *War on Crime: Bandits, G-Men, and the Politics of Mass Culture.* New Brunswick, NJ: Rutgers University Press, 1998.

Woodiwiss, Michael. *Gangster Capitalism: The United States and the Global Rise of Organized Crime.* New York: Carrol & Graf Publishers, 2005.

Green, Anna K.

Anna Green (1846–1935) was an American dramatist and author of poetry, short stories, and novels. She is best remembered as one of the first American detective fiction writers and is often credited with being among those who pioneered significant features that led to the popularity of the genre. She was born in Brooklyn, New York, to James Wilson, a prominent attorney, and Catherine Ann (Whitney) Green but was raised by her father and stepmother Grace Hollister in Buffalo, New York, following her mother's death when Anna was only an infant. She attended the Ripley Female College in Vermont, where she earned a B.A. in 1867. Immediately following her graduation, she returned to her beloved New York. There, she crafted poetry early in her writing career, but when her verse failed to gain public attention, she turned to detective fiction rather than forgoing a writing career. It was not until 1878, at the age of 32, that she published her first novel, *The Leavenworth Case: A Lawyer's Story*, which gained popularity and attention among a broad readership and marked the beginning of a successful and lengthy career as a detective novelist.

In addition to a busy professional career, Green was a devoted wife and mother. In 1884, at the age of 38, she married Charles Rohlfs, a stage actor and artist, who was seven years her junior. Green gave birth to their first child, a girl named Rosamond, a year later, followed by two sons, Sterling in 1887, the same year the family moved to Buffalo, New York, and Roland in 1892. Rohlfs, who became a famed artisan in his own right, and Green, who honed her craft while also attending to her domestic duties, remained in Buffalo for the remainder of their lives.

Green's first novel, *The Leavenworth Case*, remains among her best-known works, but it was only the first of 35 detective novels that Green wrote during her 45-year publishing career that included collections of poems and short stories. Her entry into the detective genre was met with both admiration and consternation. According to published accounts of the period, the fact that a woman had crafted such an interesting tale based on what appeared to be intimate and accurate accounts of a coroner's inquest was hard to believe. Her portrayal of the intricacies of the legal system and the use of medical and ballistics experts had much to do with the close relationship she had with her father. With the publication of her second mystery novel, *A Strange Disappearance* (1880), she further developed her style, earned a devoted following, and established important features of the genre that were taken up later by other detective fiction writers, both men and women, including Agatha Christie.

Among the most noted of her contributions to American detective fiction was the creation of a series investigator, a central figure who became as important, and in many instances more important, than the case under investigation. Green's first series detective was Ebenezer Gryce, a weathered member of the New York Metropolitan Police department. Green's Gryce preceded the better-known Sir Arthur Conan Doyle's detective Sherlock Holmes by nearly a decade. Green also created two female serial investigators: Amelia Butterworth, a spinster whose curiosity rather than well-honed skills helped her unravel the mysteries she faced, and Violet Strange, whose youth and tenacity became a model for protagonists in later detective fiction specifically targeting a young, female audience.

Her mysteries often negotiated the complex social terrain of New York life, where individuals who crossed class and ethnic barriers came into contact in the course of their ordinary lives, sometimes with deadly results. Her novels were

Anna K. Green, one of the first American detective fiction writers, in a portrait from between 1870 and 1890. She wrote 35 detective novels, among other works, over a 45-year career.

populated with ordinary people and the people they dreamed of becoming, for whom she believed readers had a natural curiosity. She also believed readers were more interested in exploring the complex motivations that led people to commit criminal acts. Among her other works are *Hand and Ring* (1883), *Behind Closed Doors* (1888), *Marked Personal* (1893), *The Affair Next Door* (1897), *The House in the Mist* (1905), *The Woman in the Alcove* (1906), and *The House of the Whispering Pines* (1910).

Tracey-Lynn Clough
University of Texas at Arlington

See Also: Christie, Agatha; Detection and Detectives; Literature and Theater, Crime in; Literature and Theater, Police in; New York.

Further Readings
Green, Anna K. *The Leavenworth Case*. New York: Penguin Books, 2010.
Maida, Patricia D. *Mother of Detective Fiction: The Life and Works of Anna Katherine Green*. Bowling Green, OH: Bowling Green State University Popular Press, 1989.
Murch, Alma E. *The Development of the Detective Novel*. Westport, CT: Greenwood Press, 1981.

Gregg v. Georgia

Gregg v. Georgia (1976) was the landmark U.S. Supreme Court case that reinstated the death penalty following the moratorium effectively imposed four years earlier in *Furman v. Georgia*. The *Furman* Court had found the use of the death penalty—as it was then being implemented by the states—to be cruel and unusual punishment in violation of the Eighth Amendment to the Constitution. A majority of states responded to the *Furman* decision by rewriting their capital punishment statutes in attempts to address the Supreme Court's concerns with the use of the death penalty. With *Gregg*, the court declared that the death penalty schemes could comport with the requirements of the Constitution so long as capital punishment laws (1) provided objective criteria to direct and limit the sentencing discretion of judges and juries who decided to impose the death penalty, (2) ensured appellate review of all death sentences, and (3) allowed the sentencing judge or jury to take into account mitigating aspects of the defendant's character.

In *Furman*, a deeply divided court had struck down the death penalty on the basis of a number of concerns. While Justices William J. Brennan, Jr., and Thurgood Marshall argued that any imposition of the death penalty violated the cruel and unusual punishment clause of the Constitution, the other justices did not go so far as to say that the death penalty could never again be constitutional. Rather, the justices expressed concern over the way the death penalty was being imposed (four justices dissented from *Furman*, finding no problems with the implementation or use of the death penalty). Justice Potter Stewart wrote that imposition of the death penalty was arbitrary and capricious and likened getting a death sentence to being struck by lightning—there were no statutory measures in place to ensure that only the most egregious offenders received the death penalty. Due to the arbitrary imposition of death, Justice Stewart and four other justices voted to declare the death penalty unconstitutional for the time. States responded quickly, and by the time *Gregg* reached the court just four years later, 35 states and the federal government had passed new laws aimed at remedying the problems identified in *Furman*.

The *Gregg* case arose after Troy Gregg was found guilty of robbing and murdering two individuals and was sentenced to death under Georgia's new statute. The *Gregg* Court, by a vote of 7–2, upheld the new Georgia death penalty law. Writing the lead opinion, Justice Stewart noted that the death penalty had a long history of acceptance in the United States. The fact that over two-thirds of the states had made efforts to remedy the problems highlighted in *Furman* suggested that public support for the ultimate sanction was still strong. The new Georgia law addressed concerns over the arbitrary imposition of the death penalty, for example, by requiring the jury to find at least one aggravating circumstance accompanying the murder before allowing imposition of death. In addition, the law mandated that all death sentences undergo appellate review and gave the defendant the right to present mitigating evidence of his character to the jury. These measures were sufficient to remedy the concerns expressed in *Furman* and exemplified the new requirements for a constitutional death penalty scheme: (1) laws must direct the discretion of the decision maker by providing objective criteria, (2) laws must ensure appellate review of all death sentences, and (3) laws must allow the defendant to offer mitigating character evidence. Justices Brennan and Marshall dissented, once again asserting their view that the standards of decency in the United States had evolved, and that the death penalty, under these modern standards, was always cruel and unusual in violation of the Constitution.

On the same day the court decided *Gregg*, it also ruled on death penalty cases from four other states, upholding new death penalty schemes in Florida and Texas and finding that new laws in North Carolina and Louisiana did not meet the new criteria for constitutionality. The North Carolina and Louisiana laws had attempted to address *Furman*'s arbitrariness concerns by providing a mandatory sentence of death for specified crimes. The court found that requiring mandatory death for all offenders convicted of a particular crime was also capricious, since these laws did not allow decision makers to consider the individual circumstances of each case.

Rhys Hester
University of South Carolina

See Also: Capital Punishment; *Coker v. Georgia*; Cruel and Unusual Punishment; Death Row; Electric Chair, History of; Executions; Famous Trials; *Furman v. Georgia*; Hanging; Prisoner's Rights; Sentencing; Supreme Court, U.S.

Further Readings

Melusky, Joseph A. and Keith Alan Pesto. *Capital Punishment*. Santa Barbara, CA: ABC-CLIO, 2010.

Paternoster, Raymond, Robert Brame, and Sarah Bacon. *The Death Penalty: America's Experience With Capital Punishment*. New York: Oxford University Press, 2008.

Griffin v. California

Griffin v. California, 380 U.S. 609 (1965), was a U.S. Supreme Court case in which the court ruled that it is a violation of a defendant's Fifth Amendment rights for the prosecutor to comment to the jury on the defendant's refusal to testify, or for the judge to instruct the jury that invoking the Fifth Amendment protection against self-incrimination is evidence of guilt (the "no comment" rule). The ruling specified that this applied to the states through the due process clause of the Fourteenth Amendment.

Background

Edward Dean Griffin had been convicted of first-degree murder and sentenced to death in the death of a woman named Essie Mae Hodson.

At trial, the prosecutor, in his summation, said: "Essie Mae is dead. She can't tell you her side of the story. The defendant won't." The trial court judge, in his instructions to the jury, stated that a defendant has a constitutional right not to testify. However, he went on to say that

> As to any evidence or facts against him which the defendant can reasonably be expected to deny or explain because of facts within his knowledge, if he does not testify or if, though he does testify, he fails to deny or explain such evidence, the jury may take that failure into consideration as tending to indicate the truth of such evidence.

This jury instruction was consistent with the California state constitution, "comment practice" clause (Article I, § 13,), which stated that

> [I]n any criminal case, whether the defendant testifies or not, his failure to explain or to deny by his testimony any evidence or facts in the case against him may be commented upon by the court and by counsel, and may be considered by the court or the jury.

The California Supreme Court affirmed the conviction, and the U.S. Supreme Court granted certiorari to determine

> … whether comment on the failure to testify violated the Self-Incrimination Clause of the Fifth Amendment which we made applicable to the States by the Fourteenth in *Malloy v. Hogan.* 378 U.S. 1 (1964).

History

Historically, defendants in criminal trials in the United States were not allowed to testify, since it was believed that they could not be expected to testify truthfully if it were not in their interest to do so. From 1864 to 1900, most states, beginning with Maine, began to allow defendants to testify, leaving only Georgia still barring the practice at the end of the 19th century.

In 1878, Congress enacted a law declaring criminal defendants competent to testify. The statute included the "no comment rule," prohibiting prosecutors from commenting on the failure to testify, and prohibiting any presumption against the defendant based on his failure to testify (18 U.S.C. § 3481.). This federal law applied only to the federal courts, and the states made their own decisions on this matter. The California constitution explicitly permitted counsel and the judge to comment on the failure to testify.

In two earlier cases, *Twining v. New Jersey* (1908) and *Adamson v. California* (1947), the Supreme Court upheld state laws allowing adverse comments, holding that even if adverse comments did violate a defendant's Fifth Amendment rights, the Fifth Amendment did not apply to state action. In *Malloy v. Hogan* (1964), the court overruled the earlier cases, concluding that the due process clause of the Fourteenth Amendment extended Fifth Amendment protections against self-incrimination to state trials.

The case was one of a series of rulings handed down by the Warren Court during its "Due Process Revolution," when the court "incorporated" many of the rights of the accused in the Bill of Rights, and applied them to the states.

Ruling

The question before the court was whether or not the judge's instructions to the jury constituted a reversible error. Associate Justice William O. Douglas, writing for the majority, observed that

> … a prosecutor's or judge's comment to the jury about a defendant's refusal to testify constituted a penalty imposed on the defendant for exercising a constitutional privilege. By making such comments, the court limited the privilege by making its assertion costly to the defendant.

Douglas acknowledged that a jury might find it "natural and irresistible" to infer the guilt of a defendant who refused to testify while possessing facts about the evidence against him, and so a judge's commenting upon the refusal did not "magnify that inference into a penalty for asserting a constitutional privilege." However, Douglas believed that a judge's comments "solemnizes the silence of the accused into evidence against him."

Concurrence and Dissent

Justice John Harlan concurred because, while the "no comment rule" was part of a federal statute, he believed the rule was a "nonfundamental" part of the Fifth Amendment and therefore should not apply to state action. However, because of the precedent established in *Malloy v. Hogan* (Justice Harlan dissented), he concurred with the majority. Justice Harlan did believe that the court's ruling did undermine federalism beacuse state and federal courts need not run by the same rules and that the decision here reflected the tendency of the federal courts to override state courts, which was contrary to the basic idea of federalism. He went on to state that he hoped "that the court will eventually return to constitutional paths which, until recently, it has followed throughout its history."

Associate Justices Potter Stewart and Byron White dissented. Stewart wrote that the Fifth Amendment states that no person "shall be compelled in any criminal case to be a witness against himself," and that California's "comment rule" did not "compel" the defendant nor anyone else to testify. Also, "the California procedure is not only designed to protect the defendant against unwarranted inferences which might be drawn by an uninformed jury; it is also an attempt by the State to recognize and articulate what it believes to be the natural probative force of certain facts." Stewart wrote this rule "is properly a matter of local concern."

Following the U.S. Supreme Court's reversal of Griffin's conviction and remand, he was tried again for murder. It ended in a mistrial because the jury was deadlocked. Finally, in a third trial, Griffin was found guilty of first-degree murder and was given a death sentence. The verdict and sentence were upheld by the California Supreme Court in 1967.

Jeffrey Kraus
Wagner College

See Also: Appeals; California; Constitution of the United States of America; Supreme Court, U.S.

Further Readings

Ayer, Donald B. "Fifth Amendment and the Inference of Guilt From Silence: *Griffin v. California* After Fifteen Years." *Michigan Law Review*, v.78 (1979).

Bradley, Craig M. "*Griffin v. California*: Still Viable After All These Years." *Michigan Law Review*, v.79 (1981).

Bradley, Craig M. "Havens, Jenkins, and Salvucci, and the Defendant's 'Right' to Testify." *American Criminal Law Review*, v.18 (1981).

Graham, Fred. *The Due Process Revolution: The Warren Court's Impact on Criminal Law*. New York: Hayden, 1970.

Griffin, Lissa. "Is Silence Sacred? The Vulnerability of *Griffin v. California* in a Terrorist World." Pace Law Faculty Publications. Paper 469 (2007). http://digitalcommons.pace.edu/lawfaculty/469 (Accessed 2011).

O'Neill, Timothy P. "Vindicating the Defendant's Constitutional Right to Testify at a Criminal Trial: The Need for an Off the Record Waiver." *University of Pittsburgh Law Review*, v.51 (1990).

Griswold v. Connecticut

The Supreme Court decision in *Griswold v. Connecticut* (1965) was the first successful challenge to a state version of the federal Comstock Law. The court had avoided reproductive issues with the exception of sterilization (see *Buck v. Bell*, 1927, and *Skinner v. Oklahoma*, 1942). In *Griswold*, the court invalidated a 19th-century Connecticut law that regulated sexual morality among married couples. For the first time, the court used the Ninth Amendment to find an unenumerated, substantive right of marital privacy.

Similar to many states, Connecticut passed a law in 1879 that prohibited the use of, and counseling about, contraception. By the late 1950s, Connecticut was the only state that still banned contraception, even if a woman's health was at risk from possible pregnancy. In November 1961, Estelle Griswold, executive director of the Connecticut Planned Parenthood League, challenged the law by opening a birth-control clinic in New Haven. Dr. C. Lee Buxton, professor of obstetrics and gynecology at Yale University, served as medical director of the clinic and medically examined wives prior to dispensing contraceptives. Ten days after the opening of the clinic, the police arrested Griswold and Buxton, charged them with providing illegal contraceptives, and fined them each $100. The circuit court, superior court, and state supreme court of errors upheld their convictions.

In the state, a Catholic majority fought to keep contraceptives illegal in the face of mounting activism to repeal the antiquated law. Nationally, this time period witnessed a struggle to define privacy and the rights entailed therein. When the matter reached the Supreme Court, Joseph B. Clark argued for the state, while Thomas I. Emerson argued for the appellants with amicus briefs from Planned Parenthood Federation of America, Inc., the Catholic Council on Civil Liberties, and the American Civil Liberties Union. In a 7–2 decision, the court struck down the statute because it failed the strict scrutiny test whereby a state must prove the compelling necessity of the law. The court found a constitutional guarantee of a "zone of privacy" for married couples.

Justice William Douglas wrote the majority opinion. State-endorsed marriage contained the right to family privacy, including the right to contraceptives within marital relations. Douglas found this right "within the penumbra of specific guarantees of the Bill of Rights." The First Amendment's right of association extended to marriage. The Third Amendment's prohibition of quartering troops in private residences without the owner's permission established a right to privacy in one's home, including married couples' right to practice contraception. The Fourth Amendment's freedom from search and seizure in private homes protected this notion of a "zone of privacy." As Douglas concluded, "Would we allow the police to search the sacred precincts of marital bedrooms for telltale signs of the use of contraceptives? The very idea is repulsive to the notions of privacy surrounding the marriage relationship."

Two concurring opinions located the marital privacy right elsewhere. Justice Byron White found it in the Fourteenth Amendment's due process clause, which protected marital privacy from state action. Justice Arthur Goldberg's argument proved somewhat controversial. Goldberg found the "fundamental right to marital privacy" in the Ninth Amendment, which protects citizens' rights not explicitly delineated elsewhere in the Constitution. While this amendment does not generate rights, it provides guidance that unenumerated rights exist.

Griswold was not the first time the legal realm discussed privacy. The earliest claims for privacy were based on common law tort. In the late 19th century, Boston lawyer Louis Brandeis coauthored with Samuel D. Warren a pivotal article titled "The Right to Privacy" in the *Harvard Law Review* (1890), which lay a basis for a specifically recognized right to privacy. As a Supreme Court justice, Brandeis enunciated this right in *Olmstead v. United States* (1928) based on the Fourth and Fifth Amendments, which he believed the founders intended to be "much broader in scope" than the text implies. He argued that the founders had conferred "the right to be let alone—the most comprehensive of rights and the rights most valued by civilized men." In 1963, the Ninth Circuit Court of Appeals found that police photos of a nude woman in suggestive poses, allegedly taken to show her bruises, violated her privacy. These actions set the stage for *Griswold*. Two justices dissented from this case. Justices Hugo Black and Potter Stewart contended that no written text existed to support the right to privacy. While they considered the Connecticut law to be "uncommonly silly," they did not see where it violated the Constitution. The Ninth Amendment was to be a restraint on the federal government and a guide to the construction of the first eight amendments. They feared this unprecedented use of the Ninth Amendment would cause unforeseen complexity for future justices trying to define new rights.

Griswold is significant for numerous reasons. It placed the burden on the government to justify when it can interfere in citizens' private lives and laid a foundation for cases dealing with sexual intimacy and reproductive rights recognized by the Constitution. Some feminists used the zone of privacy in *Griswold* to argue for the right to legal abortions. By increasing civil liberties, the case set a precedent expanded upon in *Eisenstadt v. Baird* (1972) and *Roe v. Wade* (1973). It also paved the way for additional cases trying to refine privacy on issues such as the right in one's home to possess obscene materials, use drugs, or engage in homosexual sodomy. In 2003, the basis laid in *Griswold* came to fruition in *Lawrence v. Texas*, where the court struck down state sodomy laws.

Simone M. Caron
Wake Forest University

See Also: 1851 to 1900 Primary Documents; *Bowers v. Hardwick*; Comstock Law; *Eisenstadt v. Baird*; Fornication Laws; *Lawrence v. Texas*; *Roe v. Wade*.

Further Readings

Fein, Bruce. "*Griswold v. Connecticut*: Wayward Decision-Making in the Supreme Court." *Ohio Northern University Law Review,* v.16 (1989).

Helscher, David. "*Griswold v. Connecticut* and the Unenumerated Right of Privacy." *Northern Illinois University Law Review,* v.33 (1995).

Johnson, John W. Griswold v. Connecticut: *Birth Control and the Constitutional Right of Privacy.* Lawrence: University Press of Kansas, 2005.

Grutter v. Bollinger

Grutter v. Bollinger (2003) is a U.S. Supreme Court case in which the affirmative action admissions policy of the University of Michigan Law School was upheld. The ruling was rendered in a 5–4 decision on June 23, 2003. A Caucasian law school applicant with residence in Michigan filed the lawsuit against the law school. In the case, the plaintiff, Barbara Grutter, alleged that the law school had violated her Fourteenth Amendment right by denying her admission on the basis of race. Specifically, Grutter argued that the law school used race as the predominant factor in admissions policy decisions, thus giving certain minorities a considerably greater chance of admission than those with similar records from the majority group.

The district court ruled in favor of Grutter, finding the law school's use of race in the admissions policy to be unconstitutional. The 6th Circuit Court later reversed this decision. The 6th Circuit's majority opinion found that the law school's use of race in admissions was narrowly tailored, because it was only being used as a "potential 'plus' factor," an admissions factor that was found to be

The library of the University of Michigan Law School, the school that denied admission to Barbara Grutter, setting in motion the case that became Grutter v. Bollinger *(2003). While the majority opinion found that the Constitution does not prohibit the narrowly tailored use of race to further the compelling interests of educational benefits, it was suggested that the decision may have a limited life span.*

legal in the landmark Supreme Court case *Regents of the University of California v. Bakke* (1978). When admissions committees use the "plus" factor, they are taking race into account along with other factors (e.g., GPA, admissions essays) in making admittance decisions. Following this ruling, the plaintiff asked that the Supreme Court hear the case, and it agreed. On April 1, 2003, oral arguments were heard in *Grutter v. Bollinger*.

A Shift in Affirmative Action
The majority opinion, issued by Justice Sandra Day O'Connor, found that the U.S. Constitution does not prohibit the narrowly tailored use of race to further the compelling interests of educational benefits that are acquired through a diverse student body. However, O'Connor explained that within 25 years, the court expects that race-based affirmative action policies will no longer be necessary to promote diversity, thus giving the decision a potentially limited life span.

The ruling was consistent with the decision in the *Bakke* case, which allowed race as a consideration (i.e., a "plus" factor) in admissions because it furthered the compelling governmental interest of correcting historic discrimination against minority groups, but found that a quota-based admissions policy in regard to race was illegal. In the majority were Justices O'Connor, John P. Stevens, David Souter, Ruth Bader Ginsburg, and Stephen Breyer. The dissenters on the case were Chief Justice William Rehnquist and Justices Antonin Scalia, Anthony Kennedy, and Clarence Thomas.

Chief Justice Rehnquist, along with Justices Scalia, Kennedy, and Thomas, found that there was little validity in the law school's claim that its race-based admissions policy was necessary to create a "critical mass" of minority students. Additionally, citing admissions statistics, Rehnquist noted that the close correlation between number of minority applicants and number of admittees of a given race was far too precise, inferring that the law school had used some sort of race-based quota system in making admissions decisions.

Following this ruling, Michigan residents circulated petitions in an attempt to outlaw affirmative action admissions by changing the Michigan state constitution. Eventually, the petitioners succeeded and passed Proposal 2 in November 2006, which prohibits race-based admissions decisions in public institutions in Michigan. Proposal 2 is comparable to California's Proposition 209 and Washington's Initiative 200, which are other state-based laws passed in an attempt to eliminate affirmative action admissions policies in public universities.

There was some concern that the decision substantially altered the definition of affirmative action. In the past, affirmative action had been understood as necessary to eliminate the effects of historic discrimination against protected classes, a definition upheld in the *Bakke* case. However, in the majority opinion, Justice O'Connor explained that affirmative action was important because of the "compelling state interest" of educational benefits that spawn from a diverse student body. The redefining of affirmation action in *Grutter v. Bollinger* seems to move the focus from the minority students themselves to the student body as a whole, a nuanced change that is important for the interpretation of affirmative action.

Andrew Ninnemann
JoAnna Elmquist
Butler Hospital and Brown University
Gregory L. Stuart
University of Tennessee, Knoxville

See Also: Equality, Concept of; Racism; Supreme Court, U.S.

Further Readings
Allen, Carol M., William B. Allen, and Barbara J. Grutter. *Ending Racial Preferences: The Michigan Story*. Lanham, MD: Lexington Books, 2009.
Grutter v. Bollinger, 539 U.S. 306 (2003).
Regents of the University of California v. Bakke, 438 U.S. 265 (1978).

Guiteau, Charles

On July 2, 1881, Charles Julius Guiteau (1841–82) shot President James Garfield in the Washington, D.C., train station. Garfield died September 19, 1881, in New Jersey. Guiteau's trial began November 14, 1881, and concluded January 25, 1882, with a guilty verdict. An appeal was denied and Guiteau was hanged on June 30, 1882.

Charles Guiteau was one of 11 children born to Luther Wilson Guiteau and Jane Howe. The Guiteaus were French Huguenots. Both Guiteau's mother and father had mental problems, as did Charles and some of his siblings. Luther was a successful businessman, but he also spent some time in a mental hospital and was captivated by the religious teachings of John Humphrey Noyes, the founder of the Oneida community in upstate New York. This community was a utopian-inspired religious commune that encouraged, among other things, a variant eugenics policy, called stirpiculture. A committee would determine which man to unite with a woman, for the purpose of procreation only; each man and woman could be married to someone else. Luther never stayed at Oneida, but he forced Charles to join just before he was about to enter a preparatory school. Charles stayed there 1860–65.

After leaving Oneida, he tried to start a religious magazine but it failed, and he rejoined the community. He left after less than a year. From 1870 to 1875, Guiteau worked in the insurance business, mostly collecting debts and incurring his own. It was also during this time that he took an axe to his sister, for no apparent reason. A doctor pronounced Guiteau insane, but no action was taken. Guiteau then became a preacher. In 1879, he wrote a book called *The Truth: A Companion to the Bible*. His preaching was ridiculed, however; mainstream religious persons thought him insane.

By 1880, his thoughts turned to politics. At the time, the Republican Party was split between two factions. The Stalwarts, represented by Ulysses S. Grant, New York Senator Roscoe Conkling, and soon-to-be Vice President Chester Arthur, favored maintaining patronage and machine politics. The Half-Breeds, represented by Maine Senator James G. Blaine and by Congressman (and soon-to-be president) James Garfield, advocated civil service reform. Guiteau favored the Stalwarts and believed that he could save the Republican Party from factionalism. When Garfield was elected president, in March 1881, Guiteau sent him letters, asking to be his ambassador to Vienna or to Paris. Garfield's secretary of state, James Blaine, told Guiteau to stop writing such letters. In May of 1881, Guiteau began to have ideas of killing the president. On June 8, Guiteau purchased a gun. After a month suffering from what he called "Divine pressure," Guiteau sought out the president and shot him.

Some 36 doctors who specialized in mental illness, called "alienists," were called in as witnesses for both the prosecution and the defense. About 30 thought Guiteau sane and responsible. Some of the original defense witnesses switched sides just before the trial. The ones who stayed could not fit Guiteau into any pre-existing classification of mental illness. The prosecution's medical team insisted that Guiteau knew what he was doing and, despite the fact that Guiteau had syphilis, found no physical basis for his erratic behavior.

The rule governing the case was the M'Naghten rule, named after Daniel M'Naghten, who in 1843 tried to kill the prime minister of Britain, Robert Peel, but missed and killed his secretary. M'Naghten was found not guilty by reason of insanity. After the trial, the House of Lords issued a report that defined what constituted insanity in a criminal case. The M'Naghten rules require that the defendant prove that he knows the difference between right and wrong and that he knows what he did was wrong. It does not account for volitional or impulsive acts. Yet, Guiteau's defense was that he could not resist the impulse to kill Garfield, comparing the assassination to Abraham's sacrifice of his son, Isaac. But in so doing, he demonstrated his awareness of his crime and that he knew it was wrong. After he was hanged, Guiteau's body was removed to the National Museum of Health and Medicine, in Washington, D.C., for further study. Moreover, following Guiteau's execution, Congress passed the Pendleton Civil Service Reform Act, which outlawed patronage for the federal civil service.

Cary Federman
Montclair State University

See Also: Booth, John Wilkes; Czolgosz, Leon; Garfield, James (Administration of); Insanity Defense; M'Naghten Test.

Further Readings
Peskin, Allan. "Who Were the Stalwarts? Who Were Their Rivals? Republican Factions in the Gilded Age." *Political Science Quarterly*, v.99/4 (1984–85).
Rosenberg, Charles. *The Trial of the Assassin Guiteau: Psychiatry and the Law in the Gilded Age*. Chicago: University of Chicago Press, 1968.

Gun Control

The debate on gun control has become inextricably entwined with the debate on the Second Amendment, although these issues have not always been so directly engaged. How this has come about serves as a wider but indispensable backdrop to the more specific examination of the evolution of gun control laws in the United States. Much of the early history of gun control can be seen as largely event driven; in recent years, however, the growth and influence of the U.S. National Rifle Association (NRA) and its partner gun rights organizations have been much more significant. First formed in the 1870s as a special interest firearms membership and training organization, the NRA evolved in the 1970s and 1980s into a much more hard-nosed political lobby, using the courts and the political system to press the case for shooters' rights. Supreme Court judgments in 2008 and 2010 ultimately reflect this more assertive firearm rights advocacy and the fact that the parameters of U.S. gun control policy and even the very meaning of "gun control" have themselves been fundamentally altered.

Second Amendment Rights

Any discussion of gun control must also deal with both the intense political controversy now surrounding this issue and the loaded philosophical character of the concept. Contemporary interpretations of the Second Amendment now emphasize the second part of this much-contested statement—"The right of the people to keep and bear arms, shall not be infringed"—in what is referred to as the standard or individualist interpretation. Even so, it is often acknowledged that there are as many as 20,000 gun control laws, regulations, and ordinances at federal, state, and municipal levels regulating the ownership, possession, purchase and transfer, carriage, and use of firearms. Many such laws are relatively uncontroversial and are designed to restrict the access to firearms of children, convicted felons, or persons with a history of mental illness. Such laws would today be regarded as laws against firearm misuse rather than gun control. This distinction has become vitally important. Gun control, in this sense, is not considered incompatible with widespread but responsible gun ownership: On the contrary, responsible ownership is seen as the most important form of gun control. More guns, it is claimed, can mean less crime, although the evidence remains intensely contested.

The issue has not just preoccupied contemporary social scientists; historians have also entered the fray. For example, intense debate has surrounded the question of the extent of civilian firearm holdings in the antebellum era and likewise concerning the differences between American and European cultures and patterns of gun ownership. Demonstrating widespread ownership of firearms before the Civil War lends credence to a claim that those responsible for the drafting of the Second Amendment sought to give constitutional protection to individual, as opposed to militia-based, ownership and use of weapons. However these thorny questions are resolved (refer to the intense debate surrounding Michael Bellesiles's *Arming America* research), the notion of the U.S. citizen's unique and unrestricted right to possess

A U.S. Army Criminal Investigation Command special agent examines a handgun during crime scene investigation training. As handguns became more widespread in the 1960s, gun homicide increased, rising 89 percent from 1964 to 1968.

firearms still requires qualification. Even though, after the Civil War, widespread firearm ownership had become established, white Americans were still keen to prevent African Americans (former slaves) and others from owning firearms. While firearms ownership in old Europe was overlain by restrictions of rank and religion, in America, it was colored by race, ethnicity, and social class.

Following the Civil War, many new and disorderly frontier towns established regulations forbidding the carrying of weapons within the town limits. Ordinance #9, introduced in Tombstone by Wyatt Earp on April 19, 1881, is an example. Such measures, anticipating the "police powers" public safety and crime prevention provisions later adopted in many local jurisdictions. were not initially seen to contradict firearm rights but were simply viewed as restrictions on the places and occasions firearms might be lawfully and safely carried. Such questions have lately become more controversial, with some commentators seeing any restriction as an infringement of Second Amendment rights. Thus, debates have arisen concerning the legitimacy of restricting firearm carriage in shopping malls, on college and university campuses, in the vicinity of schools, at airports, and at leisure and entertainment venues. Given the fact that large numbers of Americans now carry firearms for self-defense and that more than 40 states permit concealed firearm carriage, NRA-backed campaigns have lately begun to question whether it is right or lawful to ask citizens to risk going unarmed when visiting such locations.

Early Legislative History

One significant piece of conventional gun control legislation in the early 20th century was the Sullivan Law (named after its sponsor, state Senator Timothy Sullivan) passed in New York State in 1911 following the shooting of the city mayor and amid a wave of anti-immigrant and criminal gang hysteria. Although passed as a crime prevention measure, which was typical of many similar provisions, the law closely reflects the social prejudices implicit in earlier gun prohibitions. It put control of firearm licensing in the hands of the local police and allowed them to discriminate against undesirables, the underclass, immigrants, and non-Americans. An underlying problem was the ready supply of cheap pistols, so-called Niggertown Saturday night specials, in high-crime, slum neighborhoods, establishing an urban gun culture in poorer areas that have preoccupied law enforcement ever since. The Sullivan Law has subsequently drawn criticism that it is both un-American and unconstitutional. It may yet encounter the fate of similar restrictions in Washington, D.C., and Chicago.

Until the late 20th century, gun control was not a particularly important policy area for federal legislators. The 1919 War Revenue Act had established a federal manufacturer's excise tax on firearms, which marked the first use of fiscal measures to serve public safety goals by restricting firearm distribution and placing responsibility for this area of policy within the Department of the Treasury. Reflecting state and municipal concerns about criminal access to cheap handguns, the first federal gun controls were introduced in the 1920s and 1930s. These bills initially sought to restrict the sale and transfer of weapons by mail order. Later came bans on the private ownership of machine guns and other "gangster" weapons (National Firearms Act, 1934) and on interstate weapons trafficking (Federal Firearms Act, 1938). Passed shortly after the repeal of Prohibition, the legislation reflected growing disquiet about the violent activities of organized criminal bootleggers and gangsters (including the St. Valentine's Day Massacre in 1929), but they also drew support from an unlikely source: major gun manufacturers, who were keen to avoid being undercut by cheaper competitors.

A Supreme Court case in 1939, the first and, for a long time, the only Supreme Court judgment on gun control and the Second Amendment, *United States v. Miller* (the outcome of which is still subject to contrasting interpretations) appeared to uphold the prohibition against "gangster" weapons (in this case, a short-barreled shotgun transported across state lines) by adopting the "police powers" interpretation that sensible crime prevention measures did not interfere with Second Amendment rights. In more recent years, this interpretation has been stretched to its limits—some might say broken—by a renewed phase of gun rights activism.

Gun Control Act of 1968

The next federal gun controls, which prompted criticism that the process was largely event driven, occurred in the late 1960s following the assassinations of President John F. Kennedy, Robert Kennedy, and Martin Luther King, Jr., in 1963 and 1968. The Gun Control Act of 1968, much watered down after five years of debate, sought to establish a federal firearms licensing system for dealers, manufacturers, and importers through which to regulate interstate sales and distribution of firearms. It became illegal for any person without a license to engage in any substantial firearm sales business. In addition, a number of groups (minors, convicted felons, persons with a history of mental illness, and users of illegal drugs) were prohibited from owning or possessing firearms. Finally, the importation of surplus military firearms was prohibited unless they were considered to have a primary "sporting purpose." Enforcement of these provisions was vested in the Alcohol, Tobacco, and Firearms Division of the Internal Revenue Service (which became the Bureau of Alcohol, Tobacco, and Firearms in 1972).

The act itself was something of a compromise, and by the time it passed, the social context had changed dramatically. Rising crime, riots, and disorder prompted growing demand for self-defense firearms; sales of handguns had quadrupled to 2.4 million weapon purchases per year by 1968. Existing doubts about the ability of the IRS to exercise effective oversight of firearms commerce were renewed. Even though additional resources were allocated, the ATF lacked capacity to scrutinize more than 2 percent of the total annual trade in firearms.

Criminologist Franklin Zimring made a detailed study of the impact of the Gun Control Act of 1968, a time when the market for cheap handguns was expanding rapidly and gun violence was increasing. Between 1964 and 1968, gun homicide increased by 89 percent in the United States. By 1969, a majority of urban homicides were committed with handguns. Even so, Zimring concluded that despite the limitations of the 1968 act, it had curtailed, somewhat, the supply of cheap handguns and could be said to have moderated the steeply rising trend in handgun violence evident during the 1960s. Following these developments, some liberal commentators, Zimring included, predicted that the 1970s would begin to see an end to America's gun violence problems as public safety policy making gained the upper hand. In 1977, following New York's lead, Washington, D.C., banned handguns and established licensing arrangements for rifles and shotguns. In 1982, Chicago followed suit, banning handguns (both laws have since been struck down by the Supreme Court). The commentators could hardly have been more wrong. During the 1970s, the gun lobby began to shift the focus of its gun rights advocacy toward the defense of civilian ownership of personal protection handguns, and this became a key gun control battleground in the final decades of the 20th century—although not the only one.

Into the Twenty-First Century

A further catalogue of largely event-driven issues surfaced during the 1970s and 1980s and preoccupied the federal government. Congress began to reflect the new political contours of the gun control battle. Tougher penalties were established for the use of firearms in crime and for firearm possession by prohibited persons (the Armed Career Criminal Act of 1986) and for banning the sale of so-called "cop killer" bullets capable of penetrating bulletproof vests (the Law Enforcement Officers Protection Act of 1986). Finally, following the killing of five children in Stockton, California—school shootings became a growing issue after 1999—the late 1980s and early 1990s saw the first rounds of a debate about the appropriateness of civilian ownership of so-called military assault rifles. California banned these weapons in 1989, and federal legislation followed in 1990 (the Crime Control Act of 1990), banning the manufacture or importation of such weapons for the civilian market in the United States. The Violent Crime Control and Law Enforcement Act of 1994 banned a series of specified military assault weapons. This federal assault weapons ban expired in 2004, and although new bills have been introduced from time to time, these assault weapon prohibitions have not been reinstated.

Concurrent with these developments, the main gun control debate of the 1980s and early 1990s followed the shooting of President Ronald Reagan in March 1981. It concerned the campaign to introduce a national instant firearms sales check system (NICS) for would-be purchasers of handguns from federally licensed firearms dealers. The campaign was named in honor of James Brady, Reagan's press secretary, who was seriously wounded during the assassination attempt. After years of debate, the Brady Handgun Violence Prevention Act was eventually passed in 1994, requiring a national instant check system to be established by 1998; in the interim, a five-day waiting and checking period was established. An immediate weakness was that the law impacted only the primary handgun sales market; subsequent sales (around 40 percent of handgun sales annually), including firearms sold at gun shows, went largely unregulated.

A second weakness was that the funds and facilities to enable the appropriate checks to take place were often either unavailable or insufficiently prioritized by police departments. Furthermore, record systems were not always fit for this purpose. The 1997 Supreme Court case *Printz v. United States* deemed certain aspects of the Brady Act unconstitutional. By then, however, not only had many states implemented their own versions of a gun purchase check system, but the long-awaited National Instant Check System hosted by the FBI was almost ready. NICS now operates in more than 30 states (some states retained their own system), checking on would-be firearm buyers. In the decade since 1998, the FBI reported having run more than 100 million checks resulting in some 700,000 gun sale refusals.

Gun Rights Campaigns

In the 1980s, during the Reagan presidency, gun control began to develop its contemporary twin-track character. While debates about NICS and assault weapons bans rumbled on, a number of parallel developments were taking shape. Embodying this approach, at the federal level, the Firearms Owners Protection Act of 1986 relaxed some 1968 restrictions on gun and ammunition sales while introducing tougher mandatory penalties for use of firearms during the commission of a crime. A number of states began to pass legislation to permit the carrying of concealed firearms for personal protection. More than 40 states now issue concealed carry permits to entitled applicants, with some requiring prior participation in gun safety courses. This trend toward liberalizing gun availability, further embodied in so-called Castle doctrine laws (which state that attacked persons have no "duty to retreat" before resorting to potentially lethal force), was accompanied by laws demanding greater responsibility from gun owners, for example, requiring guns to be sold with trigger locks or kept in domestic gun safes and strengthening penalties for firearm misuse. Law enforcement–led initiatives such as Project Exile and Operation Ceasefire, both of which addressed firearm involvement in criminal gang violence, also embraced this underlying twin-track strategy seeking to control gun crime rather than control guns and permitting responsible citizens to keep guns for their own personal protection.

A further development in the 1990s saw gun control groups and victim representatives bringing class action cases against particular gun manufacturers, retailers, or dealers for irresponsibly producing, marketing, or otherwise supplying firearms in ways that were alleged to have facilitated their uptake by offenders. Such lawsuits have not generally been very successful and have more recently faced congressional opposition.

Three final strands in the contemporary debate over gun control require mention. One concerns the supposed gun show loophole. The NICS system largely targeted gun sales in the primary market involving federally licensed dealers; private sales and sales at gun shows (40 percent of the market, around 3 million sales per year) were often exempt. Gun control advocates have attempted to bring gun shows further into the regulatory system: The Gun Show Loophole Closing Act was introduced in the House of Representatives in 2009, although, in fact, many states already regulate gun show firearms purchases in various ways.

A second issue concerns school shootings, which have increased in prominence, especially after the Columbine (1999) and Virginia Tech (2007) atrocities (although there have been dozens of other incidents with smaller death tolls). Such tragedies inevitably raise questions about school security; they have also brought gun control and Second Amendment politics head to head. Schools and colleges have long been places where carrying a weapon has been prohibited. In the wake of such tragedies, in a context in which a majority of states permit concealed weapon carrying, firearm advocates have come to question

These stones make up part of the memorial for the 32 students and teachers killed by a single gunman at Virginia Polytechnic Institute and State University in Blacksburg, Virginia, on April 16, 2007. The tragedy led to strengthening of the National Instant Check System managed by the FBI. From 1998 to 2008, the over 100 million checks run through the system resulted in about 700,000 refused sales.

why college campuses should be places where the claimed benefits of Second Amendment protection do not apply. An NRA-supported student campaign, Concealed Campus, has begun to campaign on this issue.

Finally, two recent rulings of the U.S. Supreme Court have pushed this question wider by striking down the handgun bans in both Washington, D.C., and Chicago. With the gun lobby in political and legal ascendancy, further legal attacks on handgun prohibitions in other cities, including New York, are anticipated. For the foreseeable future, protection from the criminogenic consequences of widespread firearm availability in the United States seems likely to be sought only via control of the criminal or the irresponsible misuse of firearms rather than via control over firearms themselves.

Peter Squires
University of Brighton

See Also: Bureau of Alcohol, Tobacco, Firearms and Explosives; Federal Bureau of Investigation; Guns and Violent Crime; Klebold, Dylan and Eric Harris; School Shootings; Serial and Mass Killers.

Further Readings
Bellesiles, Michael A. *Arming America: The Origins of a National Gun Culture*. New York: Knopf, 2000.
Burbick, Joan. *Gun Show Nation: Gun Ownership and American Democracy*. New York: The New Press, 2006.
Jacobs, James B. *Can Gun Control Work?* Oxford: Oxford University Press, 2002.
Lott, John. *More Guns, Less Crime*, 3rd ed. Chicago: University of Chicago Press, 2010.
Spitzer, Robert J. *The Politics of Gun Control*. Chatham, NJ: Chatham House Publishers, 1995.
Squires, Peter. *Gun Culture or Gun Control: Firearms Violence and Society*. London: Routledge, 2000.

Zimring, Franklin. "Firearms and Federal Law: The Gun Control Act of 1968." *Journal of Legal Studies*, v.4/1 (1975).

Zimring, Franklin and Gordon Hawkins. *The Citizen's Guide to Gun Control*. New York: Macmillan, 1987.

Guns and Violent Crime

Violent crime around the world has remained remarkably constant over both place and time. The United States has often been the location of gun violence studies because of the relatively high prevalence and availability of firearms. Much of this research, however, has been criticized for potentially being designed to make an ideological point as opposed to providing an accurate picture of the extent and nature of gun violence. Furthermore, the extant research has oft-times been misused in the gun debate to support the positions of either the pro-gun or anti-gun lobbies.

Extent of Guns in the United States

There are approximately two million firearms in the United States. Every day in the United States, guns claim 84 lives and wound nearly 200, resulting in more than 30,000 people dead and over 70,000 wounded by firearms each year. Gun violence in the United States has been estimated to cost over $20 billion per year; between 50 and 80 percent of the cost is borne by taxpayers. Research on gun violence shows that the greater the density of guns in a population, the greater the level of gun injury and gun death, other things being equal.

Gun crimes have been increasing as a percentage of all violent crime; however, throughout the 1990s, the number of homicides decreased by 36 percent and the numbers of murders by guns decreased by 41 percent. Over this time, the revolver has fallen out of use in favor of semiautomatic pistols that have a greater number of bullets that can be fired before reloading is necessary. Such pistols can have 20 or more rounds in their removable magazines. Semiautomatic pistols also tend to have larger caliber bullets, which, in turn, increase the potential for more serious injury in a shooting incident. In California, sales of guns to people with at least one prior misdemeanor conviction were six times more likely to be followed by a violent offense than sales of guns to people with no prior criminal history. Even removing these purchases by criminals, however, the United States would still have the highest rate of gun violence of all advanced countries because the majority of gun-using criminals have no prior convictions.

Demographics and the Nature of Gun Crime

Gun violence is not evenly spread throughout American society, with gun violence geographically concentrated in the areas of greatest inequality in the nation—the poverty-stricken areas of inner cities. Half of all homicides occur in the 63 largest cities, which contain only 16 percent of the population. Most of those homicides are committed with handguns. Gun violence experienced a downward trend during the 1990s as the rate of other crimes also dropped. During this time, gun crimes declined more rapidly than other crimes. Firearm violence decreased by 63 percent between 1993 and 2001. Those 12–14 years old experienced a 97 percent decline in firearms violence. In general, minority males (primarily blacks and Hispanics) aged between 15 and 24, and those with the lowest household income are the most vulnerable to being the victims of gun crime.

Blacks are nine times more likely to be victims of a firearms-related homicide than whites. Blacks represent 54 percent of the victims of firearm homicide in the United States, while only making up 12 percent of the population. Firearm homicide is the leading cause of death for black men ages 15–34 and is the leading cause of death for all African Americans aged 15–24. The rate of violent firearm victimization for blacks and Hispanics is approximately twice the rate for whites. For both black and Hispanic victims, the greatest rate of victimization was found in the 18–20 years old category. Both whites and blacks aged between 18 and 20 were more likely than whites and blacks of other ages to have been the victims of firearm violence. For blacks, whites, and Hispanics, the victims of gun violence have an average age that is lower than that of the general population. Among all victims, blacks are older than Hispanics at the

These guns were taken from gang members by the U.S. Marshals Service and the San Antonio, Texas, police department in August 2011 as part of a larger operation that led to 212 gang member arrests and the seizure of 38 weapons. The Kansas City Gun Experiment in 1992 found that a 65 percent increase in gun seizures by the police resulted in a 49 percent reduction in crimes committed with guns.

time of victimization. American Indians have a 43 percent higher victimization rate than blacks, 78 percent higher than Hispanics, and 184 percent higher than whites. Males are more likely to be victims of gun crime (about one-third of all violent crimes), whereas females are victims in about one-fifth of crimes.

The effect of household income (which may suffer from a degree of colinearity with race) is also a factor in victimization rates. Individuals who have a household income of less than $7,500 experience gun violence at a rate three times higher than those with a household income of over $50,000. Blacks at all income levels are more likely to be victimized than whites; but, both blacks and whites are more likely to be victimized in the "less than $7,500" group than those in the "more than $50,000" group.

Variations of Violent Gun Crime

Crimes committed with guns are 3.5 times more likely to cause serious injury or death than crimes committed by an unarmed assailant. Roughly 16,272 murders were committed in the United States during 2008. Of these, about 10,886, or 67 percent, were committed with firearms. Based on survey data from the U.S. Department of Justice, roughly 5,340,000 violent crimes were committed in the United States during 2008. These included simple/aggravated assaults, robberies, sexual assaults, rapes, and murders. Of these, about 436,000, or 8 percent, were committed by offenders visibly armed with a gun. The time of the crime seems to influence the probability of a gun being used in a violent incident. Three out of every five violent gun crimes are committed at night. Over 25 percent of all gun crime victimization occurs when the victim is traveling either to or from work. The most common location for gun violence is on the street, which accounts for 30 percent of all gun crime. Victims were confronted with a firearm by strangers at a rate three times higher than by an intimate partner.

Gun Use in Self-Defense

A 1993 nationwide survey of 4,977 households found that, over the previous five years, at least 3.5 percent of households had members who had used a gun for self-protection or for the protection of property at home, work, or elsewhere. This amounts to 1,029,615 such incidents per year. A 1994 survey conducted by the U.S. Centers for Disease Control and Prevention found that Americans use guns to frighten away intruders who are breaking into their homes about 498,000 times per year. Further to this positive picture of defensive gun use, a 1982 survey of male felons found that over 34 percent had been scared off, shot at, wounded, or captured by an armed victim; 40 percent had decided not to commit a crime because they knew or believed that the victim was carrying a gun, and 69 percent personally knew other criminals who had been scared off, shot at, wounded, or captured by an armed victim.

One study showed that when an offender has a gun, the probability that a threatening situation will result in a homicide is 176 in 10,000 incidents. This is five times higher than the overall risk of 36 homicides in 10,000 threatening situations. Other studies, however, have shown that a threatening situation is less likely to lead to a physical attack when the offender has a gun. Also, when a threatening situation does escalate to an attack, there is a lower probability that the victim will sustain an injury if the offender used a firearm. At first, this seems a risk reduction; but it must be borne in mind that there is a much higher probability that any injury will be fatal when a firearm is involved.

Policy Responses

President Bill Clinton signed the Brady Handgun Violence Protection Act into law in 1993, also known as the Brady Bill. The enactment of the Brady law required that every gun sale be subject to a background check carried out by law enforcement. So far, this law has successfully blocked nearly two million attempts by dangerous people to purchase a gun. After the passing of the Brady Act in 1993 and the Assault Weapons Ban in 1994, the United States saw a reduction in both gun crime and gun violence. From 1993 to 2003, gun homicides dropped by 37 percent and other gun crimes dropped by 73 percent. The 1994 Assault Weapons Ban led to requests for Alcohol, Tobacco, and Firearms (ATF) traces of the banned assault weapons. Their use in crime dropped by 20 percent in the first year, steeper than the 10 percent drop in all homicides. Gun murders also dropped 11 percent below projected levels in the 38 states that had not previously passed a similar ban. Gun murders did not drop in the states where such weapons were already banned. Further, there was a reduction in the rate at which police were murdered with firearms. Subsequently, the administration of President George W. Bush allowed the assault weapons ban to expire, despite opposition from many law enforcement agencies at the local, state, and federal levels. In addition, the Bush administration, via federal legislation, gave the gun industry protection from liability lawsuits. This resulted in an increase in gun crime and gun homicide.

The first formal test of uniformed police patrols against guns was the Kansas City Gun Experiment in 1992. Police in a high-crime area worked overtime to increase gun seizures by 65 percent, and found a 49 percent reduction in crimes committed with guns. This study found no change in either gun seizures or gun crimes in a similar area several miles away. A modified replication of the Kansas City study was carried out in 1996 in Indianapolis. Two target areas either maintained or increased the level of gun seizures, while gun seizures dropped in a comparison area by 40 percent. According to one evaluation, gun assaults, armed robberies, and homicides dropped by 50 percent in one area and 25 percent in the other area, even though crimes rose 22 percent in the control area.

Boston's Operation Ceasefire carried out in 1996 and 1997 was part of a collaborative, comprehensive strategy to address Boston's escalating rates of violent crime. It was a citywide operation that used state and federal laws to crack down on gun crime. The program was a focused law enforcement response to illegal gun traffic in Boston to limit the availability of guns, thereby preventing further homicides and injuries. Homicides in Boston decreased after the program's inception. To determine if the program was associated with this decline, researchers carried out an evaluation of the program's effects on gun violence in the city. They found that the interventions resulted in a 63 percent decrease in youth homicides per month, a 25 percent decrease in gun assaults per month, and a 44 percent decrease in the number of youth gun assaults per month. All of these were in the district in Boston with the highest crime rate. Operation Ceasefire Los Angeles was based on Boston's program. The Los Angeles model was used in an area that had a high level of gun violence. The intervention used intensive law enforcement activity to deter gun crime and offered gun and gang prevention services. The operation also sent a strong message that all gang members would be held accountable if any one of them engaged in violence. The results of this program were inconclusive.

In 1999, Florida (followed by several other states) enacted the 10-20-Life law, which was accompanied by the public service announcement slogan "Use a gun, and you're done." This law ensured a mandatory minimum sentence of 10 years for brandishing a gun during certain felonies, a 20-year mandatory minimum for firing a gun during the commission of certain felonies, and a sentence of 25 to life for shooting someone during the commission of certain felonies. Between 1998 and 2004, Florida's violent gun crime rate dropped by 30 percent, a finding that authorities held up as a vindication of the tough-on-crime legislation.

The Supreme Court has also been involved in the gun control issue. In *District of Columbia v. Heller* (2008), the court addressed the central meaning of the Second Amendment and its relation to gun control laws. After the District of Columbia passed legislation requiring licenses for all pistols, and that all legal firearms must be kept unloaded or trigger locked, a group of private gun owners brought suit, claiming the laws violated their Second Amendment right to bear arms. In a 5–4 decision, the court held that the Second Amendment protects an individual's right to possess a firearm unconnected with service in a militia, and to use that firearm for traditionally lawful purposes, such as self-defense within the home. Writing for the majority, Antonin Scalia addressed the problem of gun violence in the United States in ruling against the District of Columbia statute. He stated, "We are aware of the problem of handgun violence in this country, and we take seriously the concerns raised by the many… who believe that prohibition of handgun ownership is a solution … Undoubtedly some think that the Second Amendment is outmoded in a society … where gun violence is a serious problem. That is perhaps debatable, but what is not debatable is that it is not the role of this Court to pronounce the Second Amendment extinct."

There is a link between guns and violent crime in the United States; however, the nature of that link and its magnitude is still a matter of considerable debate. In a country where the right to bear arms is such an embedded part of its culture, any drastic reform remains unlikely. This will continue to be an issue with which both policy makers and the public must wrestle for the foreseeable future.

Gavin Lee
University of Arkansas at Little Rock

See Also: Bureau of Alcohol, Tobacco, Firearms and Explosives; Crime in America, Causes; Federal Bureau of Investigation; Gun Control; Violent Crimes.

Further Readings
Cook, Phillip and Jens Ludwig. *Gun Violence: The Real Cost*. New York: Oxford University Press, 2000.
Lott, John. *More Guns, Less Crime*. Chicago: University of Chicago Press, 2010.
Zimring, Franklin and Gordon Hawkins. *Crime Is Not the Problem: Lethal Violence in America*. New York: Oxford University Press, 2008.

Habeas Corpus, Writ of

The writ of habeas corpus, Latin for "you have the body," requires a jailer to exhibit the live body of the prisoner to a court and to explain why the prisoner is being held. A writ is a command, usually issued by someone with jurisdiction to issue a writ. In the United States, both state and federal prisoners can apply for habeas corpus in federal courts. Federal law and Supreme Court precedent control the petitioning and issuance of the writ at the federal level. State prisoners can also petition state courts for habeas corpus, which is controlled by state law and practice. Habeas corpus appears in the U.S. Constitution in Article I, Section 9. Most prisoners in the United States, whether state or federal, do not use Article I, Section 9 when applying for a writ. Article I, Section 9 confers no power on any court and it suggests, by its placement in an article concerned with congressional power, that only Congress can suspend habeas corpus and only during times of invasion or rebellion. During the Civil War, President Abraham Lincoln suspended the writ three times. Supreme Court justices ruled twice against the suspension, and in 1863, Congress passed the Habeas Corpus Act, which granted the president the power to suspend the writ where the military was in control.

Prior to the Civil War, convicted state prisoners had limited access to writs of habeas corpus. State prisoners alleging unlawful confinement had to attack their convictions in their state's judiciary first and, if unsuccessful, in the Supreme Court on a writ of certiorari, which is a petition for judicial review. The Supreme Court rarely granted such petitions, because the first 10 amendments to the Constitution did not apply to state citizens until the beginning of the 20th century, and again until the Warren Court (1953–69) incorporated the criminal justice provisions of the Bill of Rights through the Fourteenth Amendment's due process clause. Moreover, before the Civil War, the writ of habeas corpus was unavailable to state prisoners because the Judiciary Act of 1789, which contained a habeas corpus provision, applied only to federal prisoners.

In 1867, Congress passed another Habeas Corpus Act. Unlike the 1789 Judiciary Act, this law allowed "any person ... restrained of his or her liberty" in violation of the Constitution to petition the federal courts for habeas corpus. The act also allowed prisoners to file for writs after conviction, whereas the tradition was that prisoners filed for habeas corpus before conviction.

By allowing for post-conviction attack, the act of 1867 contained an implicit criticism of state criminal justice policies. In an 1886 case, however, the Supreme Court restricted the act's power to release prisoners. First, it held that state prisoners must exhaust all state procedures before applying for the writ in federal court. Second, it held that the writ did not issue as a matter of right. The first duty of a federal court on a habeas petition from a state prisoner is to determine whether the state court's judgment was without jurisdiction, not to inquire into the constitutionality of the petitioner's claim. These procedural enactments set up a policy of federal deference to state court judgments, which lasted until the Warren Court era. In *Fay v. Noia* (1963), the Supreme Court held that federal courts were not required to deny a habeas claim based on a failure to exhaust all state remedies. By 1969, the Warren Court had applied all the criminal justice amendments to the states through the Fourteenth Amendment's due process clause. Habeas corpus now appeared as an extension of a prisoner's right to due process.

Out of a regard for federalism and a concern over the failure of the criminal justice revolution of the 1960s, the Supreme Court throughout the 1970s reimposed restrictions on state habeas petitioners, such as eliminating Fourth Amendment claims from habeas petitions and requiring federal courts to show more deference to state court judgments. In the 1996 Antiterrorism and Effective Death Penalty Act, Congress ratified many of the restrictions the Supreme Court had imposed on habeas petitioners since the 1970s. For example, the AEDPA imposes a one-year limit on filing habeas petitions, whereas before there was no deadline, and it limits the number of habeas appeals to one, whereas before state prisoners could file unlimited appeals.

The war on terror has brought new attention to habeas corpus, particularly on the question of what constitutes the suspension of the writ under Article I, Section 9. The Bush administration held combatants captured in Afghanistan and Iraq at Guantanamo, Cuba, because they believed that Guantanamo Bay was outside the jurisdiction of federal courts. In *Rasul v. Bush* (2004), however, the Supreme Court held that federal courts have jurisdiction to issue habeas corpus to foreign nationals held at Guantanamo.

The Supreme Court also ruled, in *Hamdi v. Rumsfeld* (2004), that American citizens detained in the war on terror must have access to federal habeas corpus. In 2005 Congress passed the Detainee Treatment Act, which, among other

Passmore Williamson, the secretary of the Pennsylvania Abolition Society who had helped free slaves belonging to a Philadelphia visitor, in prison in 1855. He was sentenced for contempt of court after "evasive testimony" in response to a writ of habeas corpus.

things, prohibits Guantanamo detainees from petitioning for habeas corpus in U.S. courts. In 2006 Congress passed the Military Commissions Act (MCA). This act, among other things, forbids foreign nationals from petitioning federal courts for habeas corpus. But in *Boumediene v. Bush* (2008), the Supreme Court struck down portions of the MCA and reaffirmed the right of foreign nationals detained at Guantanamo to petition federal courts for habeas corpus. The Supreme Court has not yet decided if prisoners held by American forces in other countries can apply for the writ.

Cary Federman
Montclair State University

See Also: Bill of Rights; Constitution of the United States of America; Due Process; Habeas Corpus Act of 1679; Habeas Corpus Act of 1863; Judiciary Act of 1789; Terrorism.

Further Readings

Federman, Cary. *The Body and the State: Habeas Corpus and American Jurisprudence*. Albany: State University of New York Press, 1996.

Habeas Corpus Act of 1867, 14 Stat. 385.

Halliday, Paul D. *Habeas Corpus: From England to Empire*. Cambridge, MA: Harvard University Press, 2010.

Habeas Corpus Act of 1679

The writ of habeas corpus originated in the early English writ system as the writ of habeas corpus ad respondum. Ironically, it was initially used to compel defendants to appear but evolved by the 15th century into one of several writs that could be used to challenge imprisonment during the medieval era. The validity and scope of the writ were in dispute until the passage of the Habeas Corpus Act of 1679, which finally extended it to most defendants being held in criminal cases. Although not the first act of Parliament to address the writ, it firmly established the writ as a way for judges to ensure that criminal defendants were not being held against their rights.

The act arose out of the political turmoil surrounding the Popish Plot of 1678 in which false rumors were spread by two men, Titus Oates and Israel Tonge, that there was a Jesuit plot to assassinate King Charles II and thereby bring his Catholic brother to the throne (later James II). The accusations culminated in the execution of 16 men, including the Viscount Stafford and an attempt to exclude the Catholic James from the throne. The act seems to have been proposed because of a series of complaints about jailers ignoring the writ or moving prisoners around and even to Scotland to avoid producing them before a magistrate. The passage of the act was surrounded by turmoil in which the House of Lords added several editions to the bill in an attempt to have it defeated in the House of Commons. Despite these attempts, the act passed both houses of Parliament and was approved by Charles II the same day.

The Habeas Corpus Act provided that people held in all criminal matters except treason and felonies, or a third party on their behalf, could apply to the Lord Chancellor, justices on King's Bench, and the Barons of the Exchequer of the jurisdiction for a review of their imprisonment. The jailer was given three days in which to produce the person if within 20 miles, otherwise 10 days up to 100 miles distant and 20 days if more than that. The act also prohibited jailers from moving the prisoner from one prison to another in an attempt to evade the writ or from sending them to Scotland, where the writ of habeas corpus along with the rest of the Common Law did not apply. The act also enabled a writ of habeas corpus to be filed during recess periods.

Once the prisoner was before the judge or magistrate, it was at their discretion to release on recognizance, determine the number of sureties, and the bail amount in order for the prisoner to be released. It was to be based on the crime of which the defendant was accused and their likelihood to appear at the next assize, but the language of the act was vague on the details. The act also established a statute of limitations of sorts: the defendant had to file the writ within two terms of their imprisonment or forfeit the use of the writ. The strength of the act lay in the harsh penalties set out for jailers who failed to produce the prisoner. For the first failure to produce the prisoner, the jailer was fined 100£, and 500£ for the second failure. In addition, the fine was to be paid to the prisoner and could be pursued as an action of debt by the prisoner, which meant that it was not pardonable by the king. Failure to produce the prisoner was also supposed to prohibit the jailer from holding any future office in the realm.

The major defects of the act were that it gave full discretion to judges who held their office at the pleasure of the king. Under James II, this led to excessive bail being given in cases involving his political opponents. The act also failed to encompass the numerous other persons who were being held in prison on civil charges, such as debt. Although, the act did not solve all of the defects in common law criminal procedure, it did mark the beginning of the modern form of the writ.

John Felipe Acevedo
University of Chicago

See Also: Constitution of the United States of America; Habeas Corpus, Writ of; Habeas Corpus Act of 1863.

Further Readings
"An Act for Better Securing the Liberty of the Subject and for Prevention of Imprisonment Beyond the Seas 31 Car. II, c.2" (1679). In *The Statutes of the Realm*. Buffalo, NY: William S. Hein, 1993.

Halliday, Pual D. *Habeas Corpus: From England to Empire*. Cambridge, MA: Belknap Press of Harvard University Press, 2010.

Maitland, F. W. *The Constitutional History of England*. Delanco, NJ: Legal Classics Library, 2000.

Mian, Badshah. *English Habeas Corpus: Law, History, and Politics*. San Francisco, CA: Cosmos of the Humanists Press, 1984.

Sharpe, R. J. *The Law of Habeas Corpus*. Oxford: Clarendon Press, 1976.

Habeas Corpus Act of 1863

The Habeas Corpus Suspension Act of March 3, 1863, authorized President Abraham Lincoln's suspension of the writ of habeas corpus during the Civil War. Lincoln's suspension of the writ permitted the military to arrest and imprison without trial anyone threatening public safety. Congress protected federal officials from being sued for arresting citizens and for enforcing conscription and emancipation policies during the war. Lincoln suspended the writ of habeas corpus at least seven times beginning in 1861. His suspension was criticized as an unconstitutional expansion of presidential power. Article I, Section 9 of the U.S. Constitution seems to convey the power to suspend the writ to Congress alone. "The Privilege of the Writ of Habeas Corpus shall not be suspended, unless in cases of Rebellion or Invasion the public Safety may require it." The writ of habeas corpus, Latin for "may (or let) you have the body," is the traditional legal method to prevent the imprisonment of the innocent and to prevent the government from harassing its critics. The only common law privilege found in the original Constitution, it establishes an individual's right to a hearing before a judge before imprisonment. Absent such a privilege, a person can be held without trial indefinitely.

The Confederate states attacked Fort Sumter in April 1861, barely a month after Lincoln was sworn in as president. This rebellion posed the gravest military and political crisis in American history. Virginia had seceded, and Maryland, a slave state, was threatening to join the Confederacy, thereby separating Washington, D.C., from the rest of the Union. The first casualties of the war were Union soldiers killed as they fought through the streets of Baltimore on their way to Washington on April 19. Eight days later, Lincoln ordered the suspension of habeas corpus along the Philadelphia and Washington rail route.

Massive resistance to the first ever military draft in July 1863 caused the president to suspend the writ throughout the nation. It is estimated that as many as 38,000 civilians were arrested under the suspended habeas corpus writ. Arrests occurred in states facing little serious threat of insurrection, such as New Hampshire, Iowa, and Illinois. Some were arrested for merely opposing the draft. Many were arrested for burning bridges and raising troops and money for the South.

Congress considered bills to authorize suspension at least three times but did not act until 1863. Congress also imposed limitations on the president's authority to do so. The arresting officer had to supply the names of those detained to the local circuit or district judge and those arrested had be released if a grand jury failed to indict them.

The first legal challenge to Lincoln's orders came in *Ex parte Merryman* (1861). John Merryman recruited and drilled Maryland soldiers to serve in the Southern army. When the military arrested him, Merryman's attorney petitioned U.S. Supreme Court Chief Justice Roger Taney to issue a writ of habeas corpus to the military. Taney, sitting as a circuit court judge in Baltimore, criticized Lincoln's action, asserting that only Congress had the constitutional power to suspend the writ. Lincoln ignored his decision, as did Congress. Whether Lincoln's actions were constitutional was never brought before the whole Supreme Court. Later cases such as *Ex parte Milligan* (1866) held that when civilian courts were available, citizens could not be tried and convicted in military courts. *Mitchell v. Clark* (1884) upheld the immunity granted to federal officials abiding by Lincoln's suspension order.

The writ has been suspended a handful of times since the Civil War. President Ulysses S. Grant suspended it during his 1870s campaign to suppress the Ku Klux Klan. The Hawai'i governor suspended it when he placed Hawai'i under martial law during World War II. President George W. Bush ordered the indefinite detention of noncitizens accused of terrorism or of assisting terrorists after the September 11, 2001, terrorist attacks. The U.S. Supreme Court held unconstitutional Congress's effort to support the president by stripping the habeas corpus rights of Guantanamo detainees in *Hamden v. Rumsfeld* (2006). It also declared unconstitutional congressional efforts to deny court jurisdiction over such appeals in *Boumediene v. Bush* (2008). The United States' experience in the Civil War and in the war on terror poses a difficult choice. A crisis may require a strong executive equipped with the authority to act decisively to protect the national existence. The necessities of a national emergency, however, must be weighed against government officials' temptation to expand their powers to a potentially abusive degree.

Timothy J. O'Neill
Southwestern University

See Also: Constitution of the United States of America; Habeas Corpus, Writ of; Habeas Corpus Act of 1679; Lincoln, Abraham (Administration of).

Further Readings
Hyman, Harold and William Wiecek, *Equal Justice Under Law*. New York: Harper & Row, 1982.
Neeley, Mark., Jr. *The Fate of Liberty*. New York: Oxford University Press, 1991.

Hamilton, Alexander

Alexander Hamilton (1755–1804) is immortalized as a founding father of the United States for several reasons: leadership during the Revolutionary War, advocacy of a centralized government structure on a national scale, and service as the first secretary of the treasury. Hamilton's eminence was preceded by a wretched childhood and followed by violent death.

Born to unmarried parents on the Caribbean island of Nevis, Hamilton was orphaned in 1768 after the death of his mother. His paternity is uncertain, although his surname assumes that James Hamilton was his father. Hamilton's fortunes changed in 1773 when he emigrated from St. Croix to the North American British colony of New York. Matriculation at King's College (now Columbia University) followed. After military confrontation with Great Britain began, Hamilton became General George Washington's closest wartime adviser.

As a delegate from New York to the Philadelphia Convention in 1787, Hamilton realized that his call for national consolidation of the 13 states was shared by few others. Hamilton also recognized that the proposed constitution was the best that existing political and economic conditions would allow. New York may have numbered among the nine ratifying states only because Hamilton recruited James Madison and John Jay to write 85 newspaper articles prior to the Poughkeepsie assembly. Now known as *The Federalist Papers* and still read by millions, these essays cemented Hamilton's reputation as a political theorist.

Political Career
Washington nominated and the Senate confirmed Hamilton as secretary of the treasury in 1790, a post he held until his resignation in 1795. While holding that cabinet post in 1794, Hamilton organized military suppression of the so-called Whiskey Rebellion in western Pennsylvania. Hamilton had supported congressional enactment in 1791 of a federal tax on domestic production of whiskey. Armed resistance by economically marginalized farmers to payment of the federal excise tax ensued.

Also in 1791, Hamilton's father-in-law, Philip Schuyler, had lost his U.S. Senate seat to Aaron Burr. Hamilton lashed out at the New York legislature and at Burr personally. Hamilton sought unsuccessfully to prevent the nomination of

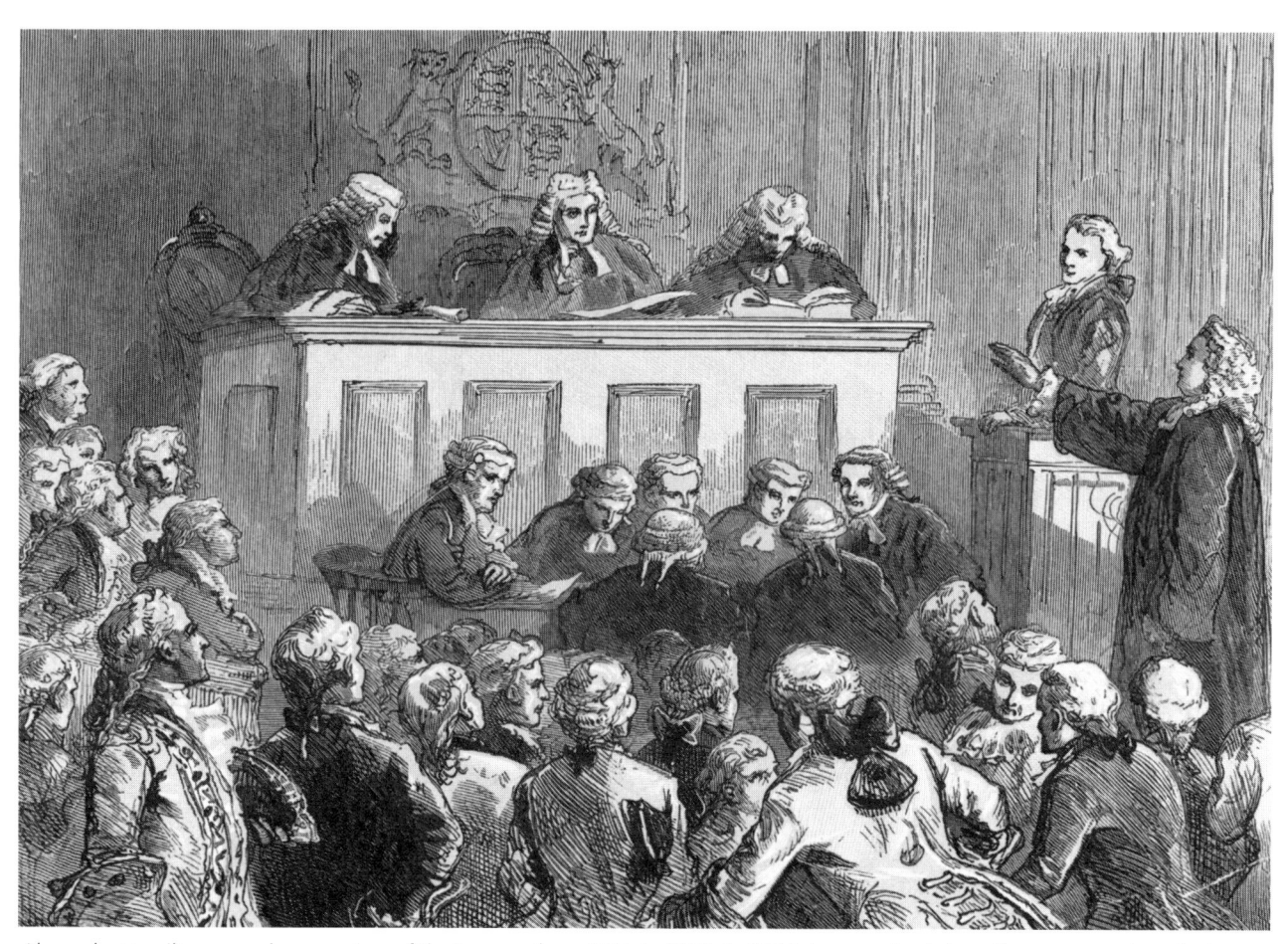

Alexander Hamilton served as secretary of the treasury from 1790 to 1795. In 1794, he organized the military suppression of what became known as the Whiskey Rebellion in western Pennsylvania, which was an armed uprising by farmers protesting a federal excise tax on domestic production of whiskey, a tax Hamilton had supported in 1791. Hamilton was known as an engaging speaker and is shown above addressing a panel of three judges in a courtroom in front of rapt spectators.

fellow Federalist John Adams for the presidency in 1796. In 1800, Hamilton tried again by circulating among Federalist leaders a strident criticism of Adams. Burr, a Republican, obtained a copy and embarrassed Hamilton by having it published. Finally, Hamilton's intemperate opposition to Burr's candidacy for governor of New York in 1804 found its way into print in the Albany *Register*. Smarting from repeated injury to his reputation and political career, Burr challenged Hamilton to a duel.

Dueling as practiced in late 18th- and early-19th-century America originated in Europe a century before. In Europe and the United States alike, dueling occurred outside the court system as a way of seeking restitution for personal insult harmful to one's honor.

On July 11, 1804, near Weehawken, New Jersey, Burr's single shot from a .56-caliber dueling pistol mortally wounded Hamilton. He died the following day. Multiple criminal charges were brought against Burr in New Jersey and New York. No warrant for Burr's arrest was issued to enforce the New Jersey murder indictment or a New York misdemeanor charge for participating in a duel. By fleeing the jurisdiction of both states for the next eight years, Burr avoided prosecution.

By 1800, a regional disparity in public sentiment about dueling was taking hold. Northern law enforcement efforts to prosecute such conduct, while sporadic and inconsistent, were increasingly prevalent after 1804. The Hamilton-Burr duel fortified public distaste, hastening adoption of legislation in Pennsylvania, Illinois, and New England that proscribed causing injury or death of another in a duel as homicidal behavior. Today, 29 states could apply homicide statutes to such conduct.

In the south, dueling continued largely unabated prior to 1840. Governor John Wilson of South Carolina published an official adaptation of the Irish "Code Duello" to his state in the late 1830s. The pamphlet was reprinted until 1858. Twenty-one states now have a provision in their criminal code that defines dueling as a nonhomicide crime punishable by a fine or imprisonment. Notably, eight of them (Alabama, Arkansas, Florida, Mississippi, South Carolina, Tennessee, Texas, and Virginia) were among the 11 Confederate States of America.

Steven H. Hatting
University of St. Thomas

See Also: Adams, John (Administration of); Federalist Papers; History of Crime and Punishment in America: 1783–1850; Murder, History of.

Further Readings
Billacois, Francois. *The Duel*. New Haven, CT: Yale University Press, 1990.
Hogeland, William. *The Whiskey Rebellion*. New York: Scribner, 2006.
Hussey, Jeannette. *The Code Duello in America*. Washington, DC: Smith, 1980.

Hammett, Dashiell

Samuel Dashiell Hammett (1894–1961) was a crime novelist known for creating such classic characters as Sam Spade (*The Maltese Falcon*), Nick and Nora Charles (*The Thin Man*), and the Continental Op (*Red Harvest*). Hammett was employed as a Pinkerton private detective and later in life spent five months in a federal penitentiary. He was a hard drinker, a womanizer with money problems, and the veteran of two world wars. He is also widely considered to be one of the greatest writers of hard-boiled detective fiction to ever live.

Hammett's Writing

Over the course of his career, Hammett produced five novels (*Red Harvest*, *The Dain Curse*, *The Glass Key*, *The Maltese Falcon*, and *The Thin Man*), approximately 90 short stories, and more than 100 reviews. He also published several poems, contributed to radio shows, and created a daily comic strip (*Secret Agent X-9*). His writing is known for being spare and gritty, realistic and fast paced. In *The Simple Art of Murder*, Raymond Chandler praised Hammett for taking murder out of the drawing room and putting it in the alleyway.

Hammett's first story, "The Parthian Shot," was published in 1922 in *The Smart Set* and was followed that year by "The Road Home," published in a new pulp magazine titled *Black Mask*. In 1923, Hammett debuted one of his iconic characters (an unnamed detective from the San Francisco branch of the Continental Detective Agency: the Continental Op) in a *Black Mask* story titled "Arson Plus." Between 1923 and 1930, Hammett published more than 30 Continental Op stories in *Black Mask*, including the four stories collected and published as the novel *Red Harvest*. Between 1929 and 1930, *Black Mask* also published *The Maltese Falcon* as a five-part series.

By 1934, however, Hammett's career was effectively over: He repeatedly failed to deliver promised manuscripts to his publishers, repeatedly failed to deliver screenplays to the studios that hired him, and although he hoped to create something important with his semiautobiographical novel, *Tulip*, that work was never completed.

Hammett's talent, however, distinguished him from other pulp writers. Nobel Prize–winning novelist André Gide proclaimed that the greatest American writers of his age were William Faulkner and Dashiell Hammett. Gide's acclaim has been borne out. *Time* magazine named *Red Harvest* as one of the 100 best English-language novels published between 1923 and 2005. In 2010, *World Literature Today* ranked *The Maltese Falcon* as one of the 10 greatest crime novels of all time (alongside works such as Fyodor Dostoevsky's *Crime and Punishment* and Umberto Eco's *The Name of the Rose*).

Hammett's work has been adapted in a variety of media, including radio, television, and film. In film, Humphrey Bogart's portrayal of Sam Spade in *The Maltese Falcon* is iconic, and William

Powell and Myrna Loy's depictions of aristocratic detectives Nick and Nora Charles sustained five *Thin Man* sequels.

The Pinkerton Agency

In 1915, Hammett joined the Baltimore branch of the Pinkerton National Detective Agency as an operative. He worked in this capacity until enlisting in the army in 1918. After contracting tuberculosis (a condition that plagued him throughout his life) and being discharged, Hammett rejoined the Pinkerton agency in San Francisco. In this capacity, he provided protection to Fatty Arbuckle during the actor's scandalous rape case. He also organized strikebreakers at the Anaconda mine in Butte, Montana. It has been suggested that Hammett was offered money to kill labor organizer Frank Little (who was later lynched) and that these events fomented his leftist views.

Political Controversy

A staunch antifascist, Hammett became politically active during the 1930s, joining the Communist Party in 1937. In 1942, after Pearl Harbor, Hammett, then 48 years old and suffering from tuberculosis, enlisted as a private in the army. He was stationed in the Aleutian Islands, where he edited the camp newspaper *The Adakian*. In 1946, he was elected president of the leftist New York Civil Rights Congress (CRC), but the political climate was changing in the United States. In 1947, the CRC was designated as a communist front group on the Attorney General's List of Subversive Organizations, and in 1951, Hammett was subpoenaed to testify in the trial of four Communists accused of advocating the overthrow of the U.S. government in violation of the Smith Act. Hammett refused to answer any questions about the CRC, invoking the Fifth Amendment. For this, he was found in contempt of court and incarcerated for five months. After his release, he was investigated as part of Senator Joseph McCarthy's anticommunist investigations but refused to cooperate with the Senate Permanent Committee on Investigations and was blacklisted.

Personal Life

While Hammett was an unquestionably talented writer, his personal life was extraordinarily turbulent. Throughout his life, Hammett suffered from serious money problems, frequently running up debts he could not pay, and facing lawsuits from creditors. He often failed to meet the term of his contracts with publishers and film studios, and for this, he was occasionally taken off salary. In 1930, he was also sued by actress Elise De Vianne for battery and attempted rape. Hammett's 1921 marriage to Josephine Dolan was marred by a lengthy series of affairs (most notably with playwright Lillian Hellman), and in 1937, Dolan and Hammett were divorced (although this mail-order divorce proceeding was later deemed illegal). Although he had served in World War I and World War II, his involvement with the CRC had led to his incarceration and his blacklisting. By the 1950s, Hammett was no longer writing, his titles were out of print, and he owed the Internal Revenue Service more than $100,000. His health was poor—he suffered from lifelong tuberculosis and serious alcoholism—and in 1961, he died from lung cancer.

James C. Oleson
University of Auckland

See Also: Dime Novels, Pulps, Thrillers; Literature and Theater, Crime in; McCarthy, Joseph; Private Detectives; Smith Act.

Further Readings

Hammett, Dashiell. *Complete Novels*. New York: Library of America, 1999.
Johnston, Diane. *Dashiell Hammett: A Life*. New York: Random House, 1983
Layman, Richard. *Shadow Man: The Life of Dashiell Hammett*. New York: Harcourt, Brace & Jovanovich, 1981

Hanging

Brought to the United States from England by colonial settlers, hanging as a method of state execution has put more offenders to death than any other method of execution in the history of the United States. Accounting for more than 16,000 executions, hanging was once employed by 48 states. However, with the advent of quicker,

This newspaper engraving from 1859 shows abolitionist John Brown ascending the steps on a wooden scaffold built for the purpose before his public hanging. Scaffolds with trap doors were meant to improve upon early hangings, which were conducted with just a length of rope, a ladder or horse and cart, and a tree branch. More people have been executed by hanging in the United States than by any other method. An estimated 16,000 such executions have taken place in 48 states.

more aesthetically sanitized, and supposedly more humane execution technologies, hanging fell into disfavor over the course of the 20th century and survives now as a method of execution in only two states: as a fallback method, should lethal injection ever be "impossible to administer" in New Hampshire and as an optional method of execution for condemned inmates in the state of Washington.

Procedure of Hanging

To conduct a contemporary hanging execution, the condemned is typically weighed the day before to determine the length of drop necessary to cause a rapid dislocation of the neck and ensure an instantaneous death. If the drop is too long, the offender risks decapitation at the end of the rope; too short, and the offender slowly strangles to death. At the time of the execution, the offender is led to the scaffold and stands on the trap door. His arms and legs are pinioned. His head is placed into a hood and the noose is placed around his neck with the knot behind the left ear. The rope used is between one-quarter and one and one-quarter inches in diameter. Prior to the execution, the rope is boiled and stretched to eliminate any spring or coiling, and the knot is lubricated with wax, or soap, to ensure a smooth, sliding action. At the order of the warden the trap door is released, the offender drops, and if the procedure has been followed correctly, his neck is broken.

History of Hanging

Since revised death sentencing schemes were upheld by the U.S. Supreme Court in *Gregg v. Georgia* (1976) and states were authorized to resume executions, only three people have been put to death by hanging in the United States. The first was Westley Allan Dodd on January 5, 1993, in Washington State, the first execution there in 30 years. Dodd volunteered for execution and chose to be hanged rather than be put to death by lethal injection; however, the American Civil Liberties Union opposed the use of the method and sued the state in an effort to stop the execution. The effort was unsuccessful, however; the Washington State Supreme Court upheld the use of hanging and the execution went ahead as planned. In the following year, May 27, 1994, Charles Campbell was also put to death in Washington State. Campbell failed to choose lethal injection as the method by which he would be executed so, in accordance with state law, he was put to death by hanging. Following the execution, however, the state's death penalty legislation was amended to stipulate lethal injection as the execution method to be used if the inmate fails to make a choice.

The last hanging in the current death penalty era took place in Delaware on January 25, 1996, with the execution of Billy Bailey. In June 1986, legislation had been enacted in Delaware that made lethal injection the primary method of execution in the state with the provision that offenders sentenced before the act were free to choose hanging. However, in 2003, as the last inmate eligible to choose hanging as his method of execution won a new trial and was resentenced to a life term, Delaware dismantled its gallows. All executions in Delaware are now carried out with lethal injection.

That only three hangings have occurred in the current death penalty era is representative of a decline in the compatibility of the method and the evolving standards of decency that have come to govern the mechanics and imposition of capital punishment. Hanging is inherently a relatively crude method of execution, yet even with many of the same tools, the contemporary hanging is markedly different from those conducted in previous centuries when hangings were public spectacles and when the execution was particularly liable to be botched. There were numerous examples from around the country throughout the 18th and 19th centuries of the condemned being left to slowly strangle to death at the end

A photograph titled "What the Sheriff Found" taken in Colorado around 1911 purports to depict a sheriff on horseback discovering a thief hanging from a tree.

of the rope or being decapitated as a result of the executioner, often untrained and unskilled in his role, miscalculating the drop or placing the knot in the wrong place. Early hangings required nothing more than a length of rope, a ladder or horse and cart, and a sturdy tree branch. While hangings have evolved, and executions and executioners have become somewhat more skilled, with the use of gallows built with trapdoors for example, the hanging execution was and is an imprecise science.

Hanging Days

No matter the imprecision of its infliction, hangings of previous centuries were originally structured to be ceremonial events. Hanging days, as they were known, which were common for over two centuries across the country, would frequently bring in spectators far from the locality in which the execution was taking place, with crowds numbering well into the tens of thousands. The execution was underpinned by themes of religion and morality designed to save the soul, not only of the condemned, but also of those in attendance. Like the modern execution, hangings of previous centuries were proclaimed for reasons of deterrence and retribution, but the role played by religion was central. Ideas of repentance and salvation made hanging days wholesome family days to be "enjoyed" by the whole community. Often, hymns would be sung, a sermon given by the minister in attendance, and, providing the condemned played his part in the way sought by the state, the offender would recount how his crimes led him to his execution and how a life of virtue and morality could spare others the same fate. However, themes of morality and religion were slowly subsumed by scenes of drinking and revelry, and hanging executions became a spectator sport for a bloodthirsty crowd.

Slowly, the middle classes began to reject public hangings as distasteful, and the edifying rationale for their continuation slowly lost ground, providing ammunition for the anti–capital punishment movement. This was sustained by the brutality of hangings: upon those in attendance and that inflicted on the condemned by an unskilled executioner. Still, public hangings continued well into the 20th century, the last recorded instance of which was carried out in Owensboro, Kentucky, in 1936 before a crowd of thousands.

Private Hangings and the Movement to Different Forms of Execution

Once hangings were moved behind prison walls and the raucous ceremony disbanded, the process was no more certain to be quick or painless. Like all modern executions, in contemporary hangings the state tried to sanitize the process toward the ideal of a clean, quick, and painless execution, with a minimal amount of ceremony. However, reports from Washington to California, by prison wardens and witnesses alike, recount numerous instances of offenders being slowly strangled to death and, in one instance in Washington, witnesses attending a hanging were sprayed with blood when the drop was miscalculated and the offender's head was nearly detached from his body. It was that risk of the execution being botched, and one in which the infliction of pain was lent credence by the brutal aesthetics of the event, that formed the basis of the suit filed by the American Civil Liberties Union to prevent the hanging of Westley Allan Dodd. As the use of a hood in contemporary hangings hides any facial contortions or distress, it is impossible to know in each execution when the offender loses consciousness or to gauge any experience of his suffering. Descriptions of the effects of hanging, however, regularly include tearing of the cervical muscles and skin, rupturing of blood vessels, engorgement of the face, protrusion of the tongue, micturation, and defecation.

It was the widely circulated stories of hangings that had been botched that threatened the very propriety of capital punishment and underpinned the search for a more humane method of execution that was to see the repeal of hanging across the United States. The trend began in 1885, when the governor of New York, believing that hanging was a relic "handed down from the dark ages," announced to the state legislature that science could provide a more humane and efficient method by which to conduct executions. In the following year, the governor appointed a commission to investigate new possible means of conducting executions and then make recommendations to the legislature. Records of accidental deaths and crude scientific experiments supposedly demonstrated that an offender could be killed quickly and painlessly through the application of electricity.

After consideration of various execution technologies, in 1888, the commission recommended the adoption of electrocution to replace hanging. In 1889, the New York legislature enacted the Electrical Execution Act, which stipulated that anyone capitally convicted after January 1 that year would be put to death by electrocution. Then, in 1890, at Auburn State Prison, William Kemmler became the first person in the United States to be executed by electrocution. Although the execution itself was botched, the legislature remained undeterred and maintained electrocution as its preferred method of putting offenders to death.

Soon after, several other states questioned their retention of hanging as a means of execution, and within 15 years of New York's adoption of electrocution, 14 other states had followed suit; 24 others by 1949. For those states that did not adopt electrocution, the search for a more humane method of execution to replace hanging resulted in the adoption of lethal gas after Nevada first tested the method in 1921. By the time the U.S. Supreme Court struck down existing capital punishment statutes as unconstitutional in *Furman v. Georgia* (1972), only seven states still provided for hanging as a means of execution.

Although hanging as a method of execution has never been reviewed by the U.S. Supreme Court, it has been upheld as constitutional in several state courts: in Iowa (*State v. Burris*), in Delaware (*DeShields v. State*), and in Oregon (*State v. Butchek*). The highest level of judicial review of hanging was the case of *Campbell v. Wood* (1994), in which the Court of Appeals for the Ninth Circuit rejected a claim that hanging was cruel and unusual punishment in violation of the Eighth Amendment. In a 6–5 decision, the court held that any pain inherent in a judicial hanging was not unnecessary and wanton and therefore comported with evolving standards of decency.

That no method of execution has ever been found unconstitutional by the U.S. Supreme Court, and that hanging was the dominant method of execution at the time the American Constitution was drawn up, means that hanging is likely to remain constitutionally acceptable. However, the sanitization of the execution, with methods mimicking those of euthanasia, will surely prevent legislatures from ever returning to hanging. It is in Washington State that any future example of hanging in the United States remains—and will most likely perish.

Mark. N. Pettigrew
University of Manchester

See Also: 1901 to 1920 Primary Documents; Capital Punishment; Cruel and Unusual Punishment; Death Row; Electric Chair, History of; Executions; Lynchings.

Further Readings
Banner, Stuart. *The Death Penalty: An American History*. Cambridge, MA: Harvard University Press, 2002.
Friedman, Lawrence M. *Crime and Punishment in American History*. New York: Basic Books. 1993.
Hillman, Harold. "The Possible Pain Experienced During Execution by Different Methods." *Perception*, v.22 (1993).

Harding, Warren G. (Administration of)

President Warren Gamaliel Harding (1865–1923) was born in the small village of Blooming Grove, Ohio. Little is known of his early years. In 1882, he graduated from Ohio Central College in Iberia with training to be a rural schoolteacher. In 1885, Harding and several friends purchased the *Iberian Spectator,* a nearly defunct newspaper. They changed the paper's name to the *Marion Star*. It rapidly expanded its readership to become an important area newspaper.

In 1920, Harding emerged as the Republican presidential candidate, with Massachusetts Governor Calvin Coolidge as his running mate. The economic and social conditions in the first postwar years contributed to Harding's resounding victory in November 1920. The Harding administration was soon staffed with a mixture of some of the best and some of the worst of choices; the latter seemed to have been better suited for appointment in other positions. The transition between Wilson and Harding at the White House was immediately exciting to the public because the White House was much more open. To many, it seemed as if small town Main Street had come to visit.

Corruption
Harding's personality contributed to the political corruption that marred his administration. He was a very friendly and engaging man who was kind and generous. His kind nature was what prevented him from being hard toward those who were seeking to take advantage of his generosity. He loved golf, playing cards, tobacco, and alcohol. These "vices" were exaggerated in later years to the detriment of his reputation, especially because his consumption of alcohol in the White House took place during Prohibition.

The tolerance of Harding for backroom drinking was mirrored in the emerging public morality that rejected Prohibition (established by the Volstead Act of 1919) and accepted the consumption of bathtub gin and other illegally secured alcohol. The Harding years laid the foundation of the emergence of bootleggers and criminal gangs because of growing public tolerance for the illegal consumption of alcohol. It also nearly killed the American cruise ship industry because American ships went dry and lost their passengers to wide-open drinking on foreign ships.

Harding appointed William J. Burns, a former Secret Service agent and head of the William J. Burns International Detective Agency, to head the Bureau of Investigation. Burns used bureau agents, who were often political hacks, to continue investigating labor union members. His record on enforcing Prohibition was spotty at best. This was in part because of the lack of enforcement funds and the indifference of local officials to a federal law many despised. He eventually involved the bureau in the Teapot Dome Scandal. Probably Burns's most important act was the appointment of J. Edgar Hoover as an assistant: With the succession of Calvin Coolidge as president, Hoover became the head of the bureau.

As president, Harding was faced with numerous postwar problems. Attempts to gain the support of congressional leadership required enormous effort. Between 1921 and 1922, he succeed in seeing tax reduction bills, farm bills, reduced soldier bonus bills, and other legislation through Congress.

Harding's generous nature was exhibited by his pardoning of Eugene V. Debs in 1921. Debs, along with others, had been imprisoned for antiwar activities. Harding also granted a general amnesty to many people jailed during the Red Scare.

Scandals

In 1922, scandals began to emerge that hurt the Harding administration. A congressional investigation of Attorney General Harry Daugherty found nothing, but this was fuel for the fire of Harding's enemies, who alleged that the probe just had not dug deeply enough.

Real scandal emerged when it was discovered that Charles Forbes, director of the Veterans Bureau, had been selling government medical supplies illegally for personal gain. His henchman in this political corruption was Charles F. Cramer, general counsel of the Veterans Bureau. Harding summoned Forbes to the White House and told him to resign, which he did when he was safely out of the country. Cramer committed suicide on March 14, 1923.

Another scandal involved Jess W. Smith, a part of the "Ohio Gang," and a private secretary to Attorney General Daugherty. Smith lived in the same apartments as Daugherty. He was a severe diabetic who may have been depressed when he committed suicide. Smith used his relationship with Daugherty to sell liquor licenses, paroles, and other "fixes." Eventually, Colonel Thomas W. Miller, alien property custodian, was convicted of accepting bribes arranged by Smith in order to illegally transfer German property to American companies. Others also went to prison.

Harding was called upon shortly after his inauguration to suppress labor violence in the coal fields of West Virginia. To stop the fighting in the Blain Mountain Miner War, Harding ordered the aerial bombing of the miners. Soon afterward, he was drawn into suppressing strikers in the Great Railway Strike of 1922 with an injunction that angered many in Congress and suppressed a number of personal liberties. He also supported

Warren G. Harding between 1910 and 1923. His administration has been called the most corrupt in American history and led to the Teapot Dome Scandal, among several other scandals.

antilynching legislation (Dyer Bill) that passed the House of Representatives, but was defeated in the Senate.

On August 2, 1923, Harding was resting in a hotel room in San Francisco when he died instantly from a stroke. Not long afterward, the worst scandal of his administration, the Teapot Dome Scandal, emerged. The Teapot Dome Scandal was unknown to Harding. It involved Harding's secretary of the interior, Albert B. Fall, who accepted bribes from oil companies for leases in the naval oil reserves in the Teapot Dome oil formation in Wyoming and the Elk Hills formation in California.

In the years following Harding's death, his reputation was further degraded by Nan Britton's book *The President's Daughter*, which claimed Harding had fathered her daughter. Rumors also spread that Harding had had extramarital affairs with several women. At least one of these rumors was probably true. These scandals have earned Harding's administration the reputation of being the most corrupt in American history.

Andrew J. Waskey
Dalton State College

See Also: Coolidge, Calvin (Administration of); Corruption, History of; Political Crimes, History of; Prohibition; White-Collar Crime, History of.

Further Readings
Dean, John W. *Warren G. Harding*. New York: Henry Holt & Co., 2004.
Murray, Robert K. *Harding Era: Warren G. Harding and His Administration*. Newtown, CT: American Political Biography, 2000.
Payne, Phillip G. *Dead Last: The Public Memory of Warren G. Harding's Scandalous Legacy*. Athens: Ohio University Press, 2009.
Trani, Eugene P. and David L. Wilson. *The Presidency of Warren G. Harding*. Lawrence: Regents Press of Kansas, 1977.

Harris, Eric

See Klebold, Dylan, and Eric Harris.

Harrison, Benjamin (Administration of)

Benjamin Harrison (1833–1901), the 23rd president of the United States, was born near North Bend, Ohio, on the farm of his grandfather, William Henry Harrison (1773–1841), who was the 9th president of the United States. Benjamin Harrison's great-great-grandfather, also named Benjamin Harrison (1726–91) was a signer of the Declaration of Independence.

In 1854, Harrison opened a law practice in Indianapolis, Indiana. Between 1862 and 1865, he recruited and commanded the 70th Regiment of Indiana Volunteers, rising to the rank of brevetted brigadier general. After the Civil War, he returned to his law practice, where he gained increasing recognition and prestige.

In 1888, Harrison earned the Republican nomination for president. He won the election, defeating incumbent Grover Cleveland with a crushing victory in the Electoral College; however, he was a plurality president, with a popular vote total of 100,000 votes less than Cleveland had. The election was marked by massive vote buying on both sides. It was the result of a system that used ballots that could be secured for wholesale vote-buying purposes. Harrison opposed this type of electioneering, declaiming against it with serious moral concern. Yet without the voting corruption, he would not have won. Cleveland's loss to a plurality presidency was the catalyst for major electoral changes that reduced the ability to buy votes in 38 states.

Harrison himself made no political bargains to gain support; however, many of his top supporters did. These pledges were ignored by Harrison, who offered cabinet posts and other important offices to men of integrity rather than to those who had supported his campaign. This further weakened him politically.

Taking office in 1889, Harrison enjoyed a Republican majority in both houses of Congress during the first two years of his term. The Republican legislative strength enabled him to be an activist president, working to achieve an extensive legislative program; however, he was often faced with disgruntled members of Congress over matters of patronage in the civil

President Benjamin Harrison around 1896. Harrison's support for business interests during the Homestead Strike and other labor disputes helped cost him a chance at a second term.

service. His legislative majority ended in 1892 when the Democrats took control of the House of Representatives and began to stall his legislative agenda.

Important legislation adopted included the Sherman Antitrust Act (1890), which sought to deal with monopolistic business practices that were defined as corrupt combinations hindering commerce. In response to populist demands for an increase in the money supply he supported the Sherman Silver Purchase Act (1890), which required the U.S. Treasury to purchase large quantities of silver. Unfortunately, the treasury notes issued to purchase the silver could be redeemed in either silver or gold. This feature of the law stimulated a financial panic in 1893.

In October 1890, New Orleans Police Chief David Hennessey was murdered. A group of Italians who were tried for his murder were acquitted. Outraged citizens then lynched most of the accused men in the "Mafia Affair." The lynching evoked national concern and talk of war with Italy. Harrison, recognizing that it was a state matter, still appealed to the governor of Louisiana for protection for Italians.

In foreign affairs, Harrison promoted the building of a strong two-ocean navy, the development of a stronger merchant marine, and the negotiation of reciprocal trade agreements that reduced tariffs between the United States and some countries. He promoted an expansion of the Monroe Doctrine with the hosting of the first Pan-American Conference in Washington, D.C., in 1889. He also negotiated a mutual governing agreement of the Samoan Islands with Germany and Great Britain. His attempt to have Hawai'i annexed to the United States in 1893 before leaving office was unsuccessful.

Harrison was nominated for a second term in 1892; however, farmers, upset over low commodity prices, turned to the new Populist Party while working men turned to the Democrats because of the support Harrison had given to businesses during the Homestead Strike and other labor disputes. Harrison did not win reelection. After leaving the White House in 1893, Harrison returned to his law practice in Indianapolis. He died there on March 13, 1901. He was a very articulate individual, a persuasive public speaker, a Presbyterian elder for 40 years, and a moral leader. There were no hints of scandal in his private or professional life.

Andrew J. Waskey
Dalton State College

See Also: Antitrust Law; Hawai'i; Roosevelt, Theodore (Administration of); Sherman Anti-Trust Act of 1890; Strikes; Taft, William Howard (Administration of).

Further Readings
Calhoun, Charles W. *Benjamin Harrison*. New York: Henry Holt & Co., 2005.
Perry, James M. *Touched With Fire: Five Presidents and the Civil War Battles That Made Them*. New York: PublicAffairs, 2003.
Socolofsky, Homer Edward and Allan B. Spetter. *The Presidency of Benjamin Harrison*. Lawrence: University Press of Kansas, 1987.

Harrison Act of 1914

The U.S. Congress passed the Harrison Narcotic Act on December 17, 1914. It effectively made the possession and distribution of opiate and coca-derived products illegal, although the actual provisions of the bill were not worded so directly. The Harrison Act required anyone who imported, manufactured, prescribed, or sold opiates or coca leaves to register with the federal government, pay an annual tax, and keep a record of all drug transactions. Those who failed to register or pay the tax were in violation of the law and could face criminal penalties. Since the act involved the paying of a tax, the enforcement of the new law fell under the auspices of the Treasury Department, within the Bureau of Internal Revenue. Before this law, opiates and cocaine were mostly unregulated products. The act was the culmination of various state and local laws attempting to control these substances as well as international conferences on regulating the trafficking of opiates. While this bill did not directly call for a "war" on drugs, many regard its passage as the actual start of the contemporary war on drugs, since it has become the legal foundation for all drug prohibition.

The precursor to the Harrison Act was the Foster Bill, introduced in 1910 by Representative David Foster of Vermont. The bill attempted to control drug traffic through federal taxation; every drug merchant would need to register, pay a small tax, and record all transactions. Failure to follow these regulations would result in serious criminal penalties. Pharmaceutical industries opposed this bill because they wanted to see certain medical professionals exempt from the bill and less severe criminal penalties. As a result, the Foster Bill did not pass. The discussion around the bill, however, as well as two international conferences on opium, did increase pressure on the federal government to enact a law that would control the sale and distribution of narcotics. President Woodrow Wilson also pushed for a federal narcotics law.

Representative Francis Burton Harrison, a New York Democrat, proposed a 1913 bill that was similar to the Foster Bill, but also alleviated some of the concerns the medical and pharmaceutical industries had about the previous bill. This bill, which became known as the Harrison Narcotic Act, eventually passed both houses of Congress

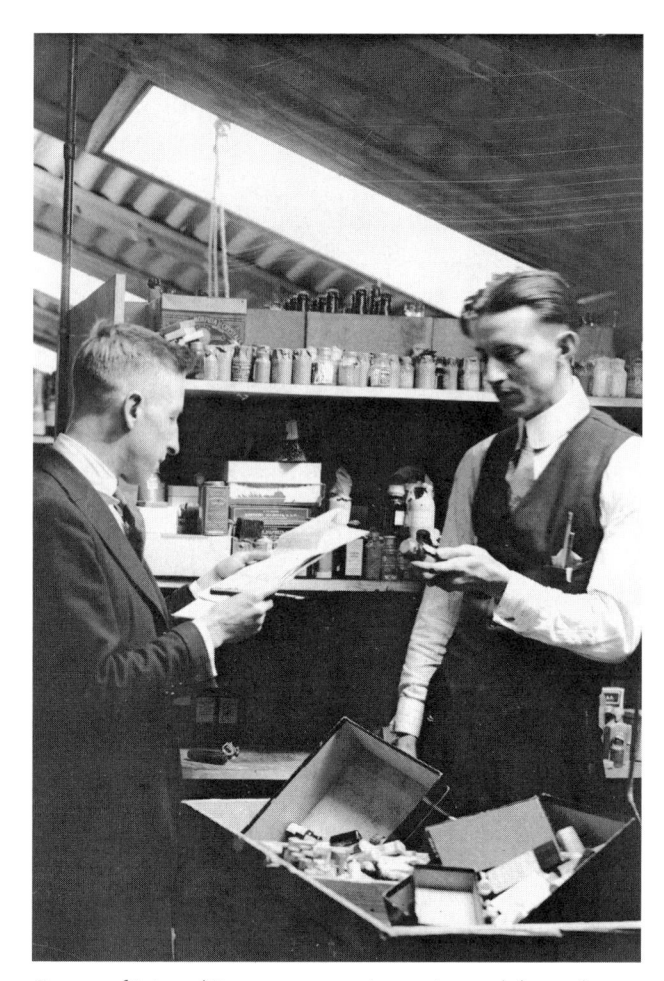

Bureau of Internal Revenue agents inspecting and destroying seized narcotics around 1920 as a result of enforcement requirements created by the Harrison Act of 1914.

and was signed into law on December 17, 1914. The Harrison Act specifies that

> ... every person who produces, imports, manufactures, compounds, deals in, dispenses, sells, distributes, or gives away opium or coca leaves or any compound, manufacture, salt, derivative, or preparation thereof shall register with the collector of internal revenue of the district his name or style, place of business, and place or places where such business is to be carried on.

The initial annual tax the person had to pay when registering was $1. Anyone who registered under the bill also had to record all of their transactions regarding opiates and coca-derived products. The law gave the federal government the ability to determine who could legally deal with these substances. While physicians were explicitly named as a group who could obtain the license, the bill also required physicians and dentists to register the names of their patients and the amount of drugs dispensed to them.

After the law was passed, doctors used the ambiguous wording of the bill to justify their ability to continue prescribing drugs for the purpose of addict maintenance. Those working in the newly created narcotics division of the Bureau of Internal Revenue, who had the charge of enforcing the new law, interpreted it to mean that physicians could not prescribe narcotics for the sole purpose of addiction maintenance. This controversy resulted in two Supreme Court decisions in 1919 (*Doremus v. United States* and *Webb v. United States*) that upheld the provisions of the bill and prohibited doctors from prescribing narcotics to their patients for the purpose of addiction maintenance. The court interpreted the law to mean that the prescription of drugs for addict maintenance was not a "legitimate" medical purpose and therefore not legal. The law also prohibited consumers from registering under the act. Thus, the Harrison Act and the subsequent Supreme Court decisions resulted in the development of a huge illicit drug economy to accommodate the growing number of addicted persons who had previously obtained their drugs from physicians.

Jennifer Murphy
California State University, Sacramento

See Also: Narcotics Laws; *Webb v. United States*; Wilson, Woodrow (Administration of).

Further Readings

Belenko, Steven, ed. *Drugs and Drug Policy: A Documentary History*. Westport, CT: Greenwood Press, 2000.

Lindesmith, Alfred R. *The Addict and the Law*. Bloomington: Indiana University Press, 1965.

Meier, Kenneth J. *The Politics of Sin: Drugs, Alcohol, and Public Policy*. Armonk, NY: M. E. Sharpe, 1994.

Musto, David F. *The American Disease: Origins of Narcotic Control*. New York: Oxford University Press, 1987.

Hauptmann, Bruno

Bruno Richard Hauptmann (1899–1936) was a German immigrant and carpenter. He was convicted in what was called the "Trial of the Century" and executed for the kidnapping and murder of Charles A. Lindbergh, Jr. Bruno Richard Hauptmann was born November 26, 1899, in Saxony, Germany. He served in the German Army from 1917 to 1918 during World War I operating a machine gun. After the war, he was convicted of various criminal offenses in Germany, including breaking and entering in 1919 and possession of stolen property in 1922. He escaped from prison and after two failed attempts entered the United States illegally. Stowing away on an ocean liner, he disembarked in disguise and used a stolen landing card in September 1923. He married Anna Schoeffler (November 19, 1898–October 10, 1994) on October 10, 1925; they had a son, Manfried Richard Hauptmann, born November 3, 1933.

On the evening of March 1, 1932, Charles A. Lindbergh, Jr., the 20-month-old son of famous aviator Charles Lindbergh and his wife Anne Morrow Lindbergh, was kidnapped. The nursery was on the second floor of the Lindbergh's home outside Hopewell, New Jersey. A handwritten note was found in the baby's room demanding $50,000 ransom. Lindbergh soon received a couple of ransom notes mailed from the same part of Brooklyn. In total, 15 handwritten ransom notes were received; all were identified by the same symbol of three interlocking circles. Due to the media attention, it was decided that a go-between was necessary. Lindbergh selected Dr. John F. Condon, a family friend and retired educator. Condon met with the suspect, and on April 2, 1932, handed over $50,000 in ransom, much in gold certificates. On May 12, 1932, a house mover discovered the baby's body with a crushed skull a few miles from the Lindbergh estate.

On September 15, 1934, a $10 gold certificate with a serial number matching the ransom money was used to purchase gasoline from a gas station located at 127th Street and Lexington Avenue, New York City. The gas station attendant wrote the license plate number of the car on the note and recalled that it was a dark blue Dodge sedan. The plate number was traced to Hauptmann. He was arrested on September 19, 1934. Further, at the time of his arrest, Hauptmann had in his possession a $20 ransom bill.

A considerable body of evidence against Hauptmann was collected. Specimens of Hauptmann's handwriting were compared with the ransom notes and related evidence and several experts, including Albert S. Osborn, identified Hauptmann as the writer of the notes. In fact, testimony from eight expert forensic document examiners resulted in 800 pages of the trial transcript concluding that Hauptmann was the writer of the questioned documents. Hauptmann quit working as soon as the ransom was paid and soon began investing in stocks. The wood used to make the ladder used in the kidnapping was forensically analyzed by Arthur Koehler, chief wood technologist of the U.S. Department of Agriculture's Forest Products Laboratory, who found that a piece of wood from the ladder matched by mill markings, grain pattern, and nail holes to a piece of wood cut from Hauptmann's attic. Further, tool marks on the wood matched tools owned by Hauptmann. Hauptmann also appeared to match a composite drawing of the suspect that had been prepared from descriptions by Condon and one of the taxi drivers who had been handed a ransom note to deliver.

On September 26, 1934, Hauptmann was indicted for extortion in the Supreme Court, Bronx, New York; on October 8, he was indicted for murder in Hunterdon County, New Jersey. Hauptmann was extradited to Flemington, New Jersey, on October 19, 1934. His trial began January 3, 1935. The jury of eight men and four women returned a guilty of murder in the first degree verdict at 10:45 P.M. on February 13, 1935, with 11 hours and 24 minutes of deliberation after the 32 court days. An appeal was filed, but on October 9, 1935, the Supreme Court of the State of New Jersey upheld the conviction; an appeal to the U.S. Supreme Court was denied on December 9, 1935. Hauptmann was scheduled to be executed on January 17, 1936, but that day the governor of New Jersey granted a 30-day reprieve and Hauptmann was resentenced on February 17. The Pardon Court of the State of New Jersey denied Hauptmann's petition for clemency on March 30. At 8:47 P.M. on April 3, 1936, Hauptmann was electrocuted.

Victor B. Stolberg
Essex County College

See Also: *Chandler v. Florida*; Famous Trials; Federal Bureau of Investigation; Great Depression; Kidnapping; Lindbergh Law; New Jersey.

Further Readings
Ahlgren, Gregory and Stephen Monier. *Crime of the Century: The Lindbergh Kidnapping Hoax.* Boston: Branden Books, 1993.
Fisher, Jim. *The Lindbergh Case.* New Brunswick, NJ: Rutgers University Press, 1998.
Gardner, Lloyd C. *The Case That Never Dies: The Lindbergh Kidnapping.* New Brunswick, NJ: Rutgers University Press, 2004.

Hawai'i

Hawai'i was annexed by the United States in 1898 and became a U.S. state in 1959. Unique among U.S. states, it consists entirely of islands (eight main islands and about 1,500 smaller islands) and is located in the south Pacific Ocean, about 2,000 miles southwest of the mainland United States. The population of Hawai'i (based on the 2005–09 American Community Survey) is 1,280,241. Hawai'i has an ethnically diverse population with the largest ethnic group being Asian (38.5 percent), followed by white (26.9 percent), Native Hawai'ian or Pacific Islander (4.4 percent), and African American (2.4 percent); 16.8 percent of Hawai'ians are foreign born, and 24.4 percent of people age 5 and above speak a language other than English at home. The median household income (in 2009 inflation-adjusted dollars) is $64,661, higher than the U.S. average of $51,425, and 9.4 percent of individuals live below the poverty line (as compared to 13.5 percent in the United States as a whole). Honolulu is the state capital and major city (population 377,357 in 2006), while the population of Honolulu County, which includes all of the island of Oahu, was 953,207 in 2010 (almost 75 percent of the state's population).

Before contact with the West, Hawai'i was ruled by chiefs, and law enforcement was governed by the *kapu* system. Offenders against the laws of the gods (*kapu akua*) and the laws of the chief (*kapu ali'i*) were judged before the chief, who had absolute power to pass sentence, which could include execution. The *kapu* system was abolished in 1819 by Kamehameha II, and in 1840, Kamehameha III established Hawai'i's first constitution and supreme court. In 1847, Hawai'i had a police force of two officers and 34 men. In 1905, after annexation by the United States, Hawai'i created four county governments, each with an elected sheriff and police department (Hawai'i does not have state or local police forces). The fictional character Charlie Chan was based on Chang Apana, a Chinese-Hawai'ian police officer and detective who served with the Honolulu Police Department from 1898 to 1932.

In the 1920s and 1930s, there was an increase in crime, including several high-profile cases, and in 1932, the Honolulu Police Department was reorganized under an appointed chief of police. During World War II, the territory of Hawai'i was placed under martial law, with police officers operating under the orders of the military governor and criminal trials conducted in the provost court by a military judge. After Hawai'i became a state, and with improvement in air travel in the 1960s, the tourist industry grew rapidly, and there was also concern that Hawai'i would be used as a "cooling-off" spot for criminals, so strict antivice measures were enacted. Women first joined the Honolulu Police Department in 1975, and in 1997, Barbara Uphouse Wong, one of the first female officers, was promoted to the rank of assistant chief. In the 1980s and 1990s, law enforcement technology was upgraded, including the implementation in 1990 of the Automated Fingerprint Identification System managed by the Hawai'i Criminal Justice Data Center and the implementation in 1997 of a digital mug shot system. Hawai'i does not have the death penalty, and no one has been executed in Hawai'i since it became a state.

In 2008, according to the Federal Bureau of Investigation (FBI) Uniform Crime Report statistics, a total of 3,512 violent crimes were reported in Hawai'i (272.6 per 100,000 population), including 25 incidents of murder or nonnegligent manslaughter, 365 incidents of forcible rape, 1,086 robberies, and 2,036 aggravated assaults. In 2008, 48,004 property crimes were reported (3,571.2 per 100,000 population), including 9,379 burglaries, 31,492 cases of larceny-theft, and 5,133 cases of motor vehicle theft. The Hawai'i High Intensity Drug Trafficking Area was created by the U.S. Department of Justice in 1999. Most trafficked drugs pass through Honolulu, which serves as the primary drug market area for the state and is also a transshipment zone for drugs bound for the mainland United States and elsewhere. Marijuana is extensively cultivated in Hawai'i (in 2006, Hawai'i ranked fourth among U.S. states in terms of the number of cannabis plants eradicated), while methamphetamine is generally imported rather than created on the islands. Hawai'i does not specifically track drug-related crimes but analysis of available data indicates that more than half of violent and property crimes in the state are related to drug trafficking, primarily methamphetamine. The National Drug Intelligence Center reported in 2002 that Hawai'i had more than 140 street gangs, which controlled most drug distribution in the state. Most Hawai'ian gangs are organized on ethnic lines, with Filipinos, Hispanics, Native Hawai'ians, Samoans, and Tongans all being represented. Besides gang activity originating in Hawai'i, some gang members have relocated from California to Hawai'i, in particular to Honolulu.

Sarah Boslaugh
Kennesaw State University

See Also: Chinese Americans; Film, Crime in; Film, Police in; Japanese Americans; Native Americans; Television, Police in.

Further Readings
Honolulu Police Department. http://www.honolulupd.org (Accessed June 2011).
Huang, Yunte. *Charlie Chan: The Untold Story of the Honorable Detective and His Rendezvous With American History*. New York: W. W. Norton, 2010.
National Drug Intelligence Center. "Hawai'i High-Intensity Drug Trafficking Area: Drug Market Analysis." http://www.justice.gov/ndic/pubs23/23628/index.htm#Contents (Accessed June 2011).
U.S. Department of Justice, Federal Bureau of Investigation. "Crime in the United States 2008." http://www2.fbi.gov/ucr/cius2008/data/table (Accessed June 2011).

Hayes, Rutherford B. (Administration of)

Rutherford B. Hayes (1822–93), the 19th president of the United States, served one term in a time of political and social unrest during the end of the Reconstruction era. During his presidency, he attempted to rebuild relations with the former Confederate states, reform the civil service system, protect the voting rights of African Americans, and bring honesty back to the government. His efforts were minimized, however, by his controversial election and a sharply divided Congress that did not support many of his proposals.

Hayes graduated from Kenyon College in Ohio in 1842 and Harvard Law School in 1845. He earned a strong reputation serving as a criminal defense attorney, often representing fugitive slaves. He served in the Union during the Civil War and was wounded in battle several times. While serving in the Union army, Hayes was elected to represent Ohio in the U.S. House of Representatives in 1864.

Hayes strongly supported the efforts of his fellow Republicans during Reconstruction, including the passage of the Fourteenth Amendment and the Reconstruction Acts, which placed the former Confederate states under tight restrictions. His popularity allowed him to serve as governor of Ohio from 1868 to 1872 and again from 1876 to 1877. As governor, Hayes supported universal suffrage for African American males and supported the impeachment of President Andrew Johnson. Immediately after he won a third term as Ohio's governor, Republican Party leaders began circulating Hayes's name as a presidential candidate in 1876.

The presidential campaign of 1876 was one of the most controversial in U.S. history. Hayes's opponent, Democratic candidate Samuel Tilden, won the popular vote but did not secure a majority of Electoral College votes. Fraud was rampant, as evidenced by areas where more votes were cast than the number of eligible voters, and bribes were offered to influence vote counts. Congress established a bipartisan Electoral Commission to determine the status of 20 disputed Electoral College votes. After concessions were promised to southern states, the commission, with an 8–7 Republican majority, awarded the votes to Hayes and ensured his victory.

This detail from an 1877 newspaper illustration shows a young convict in a chain gang helping to clean the streets of Richmond, Virginia, in preparation for a visit by President Rutherford B. Hayes.

A One-Term President

Hayes's presidency was influenced by the failures of his predecessor. The administration of Ulysses Grant was marred by scandal and corruption. Hayes championed civil service reform over the spoils system. Entrance examinations were more thoroughly utilized, bureaucrats were ordered not to be involved in overtly political acts, and some offices faced extensive personnel cuts. However, Hayes's attempts at civil service changes were just enough to anger those favoring the old system but not enough to satisfy reformers. His efforts were also thwarted by a lack of support from Congress for reform. While he was largely seen as unsuccessful in these efforts, Hayes's policies laid the foundation for future civil service systems, such as the Pendleton Civil Service Reform Act (1883) and the U.S. Civil Service Commission.

Domestically, Hayes sought to protect minority voting rights in the south. Hayes hoped that southern states would accept African American voting rights, but he was too optimistic in his assessments. He vetoed many bills supported by Democrats that would have removed federal involvement in state elections. A major event during his presidency was the Great Strike of 1877, in which railroad employees in several cities stopped working after repeated salary cuts. Federal troops were dispatched to several areas to quell uprisings and riots. Although federal troops remained out of violent altercations, civilian protesters and state militia members were killed. The strikes showed workers the power of collective action while they also inspired owners to take a harsher stance toward unionization. In addition to strikes, President Hayes also had to deal with Native American unrest, including the Nez Perce War.

Concerning foreign affairs, President Hayes worked out an agreement with Mexico concerning bandits that crossed into U.S. territory, averting conflict between the two nations. Conflicts also arose concerning Chinese immigration, as some whites viewed Chinese immigrants as taking away jobs from native U.S. citizens. Following the Monroe Doctrine, Hayes took a strong stand on the future Panama Canal, stating that no European power should control such a vital U.S. interest.

As he pledged to serve only one term, Hayes did not seek reelection in 1880. Hayes did counsel his Republican successor, James Garfield, helping him win the presidency. Out of the White House, Hayes worked diligently for universal education for the poor, particularly African Americans. He also worked for prison reform and served as an advocate for several universities.

Todd A. Collins
Western Carolina University

See Also: Civil Rights Laws; Grant, Ulysses S. (Administration of); Native Americans; Pendleton Act of 1883; Strikes.

Further Readings
Davison, Kenneth E. *The Presidency of Rutherford B. Hayes*. Westport, CT: Greenwood Press, 1972.
Hoogenboom, Ari. *The Presidency of Rutherford B. Hayes*. Lawrence: University Press of Kansas, 1988.
Trefousse, Hans L. *Rutherford B. Hayes*. New York: Times Books, 2002.

Hays, Jacob

High constable of New York City, Jacob Hays (1772–1850) was born in Bedford, Westchester County, New York, in 1772. Before serving as high constable, Hays served as one of the mayor's marshals from 1798 to 1802. In 1802, Mayor Edward Livingston appointed Hays to the position of high constable. Although the reorganization of the police force in 1844 abolished the position, Hays continued to serve as high constable until his death in 1850. While high constable, he also delivered writs of the court and served as sergeant-at-arms to the board of alderman and crier of the court sessions. By the time of his death, his crime-fighting exploits were known throughout the English-speaking world. During Hays's years as high constable, New York City became the most prominent city in the United States. Its trade, wealth, and population increased exponentially, as did squalor, overcrowding, and crime. As the city changed, Hays's responsibilities shifted from enforcing church attendance on the Sabbath and rounding up vagrants to investigating crimes, detecting forgeries and counterfeits, recovering stolen goods, quelling riots, and arresting countless criminals.

Hays's meticulous record-keeping attempted to impose order on a disordered city and was a forerunner to the official crime statistics and databases of today. In one record book, he noted all the thefts that occurred in the city and described the goods that were stolen. In another notebook, now housed at the Museum of the City of New York, Hays recorded the name, age, race, gender, place of birth, crime, date of conviction, physical appearance, and date of release from prison for every criminal he arrested whom juries convicted and judges sentenced to the New York State Prison in the City of New York, commonly known as Newgate. He also cultivated and maintained a far-flung intelligence network of informers, which most notably helped him capture one of the alleged robbers of New York's City Bank (1830) in Philadelphia.

In addition to arresting bank robbers, Hays became renowned for his uncanny ability to solve murders and suppress riots and disturbances throughout the city. In 1823, his knowledge of New York City's underworld helped him capture John Johnson, keeper of one of the city's many dockside boardinghouses, for the murder of James Murray. Armed with his constable's staff, great physical strength, and apparently no fear of danger, Hays waded into the middle of street brawls and disturbances to diffuse anger and calm the combatants. He rarely used deadly physical force but instead used his constable's staff to knock combatants' hats off their heads and then pushed the men to the ground when they hunched to recover their fallen headwear. When the troublemakers hit the ground, he detained the instigators of unrest and encouraged the rest of the crowd to disperse. Hays's successes in solving crimes and ending public disturbances made him famous throughout the English-speaking world. His name, contemporaries claimed, struck terror into the minds of all American criminals. Newspapers throughout the nation published notices of his yearly reappointment to the position of high constable, especially when he was in his 70s, and of his death in 1850. His exploits were known by some 19th-century Englishmen, who while witnessing a riot in London, allegedly wished for a man like Hays who could impose law and order.

Historians have written little of Hays's early years or personal life. His biographers speculate that since his father David served in the Revolutionary Army and his childhood home was a meeting place for local patriots, young Jacob may have been personally acquainted with General George Washington. History has forgotten the name of his first wife, but remembers the name of his second, Catherine Conroy, with whom he had three children; and his third, Mary Post, with whom he fathered an additional six children. In 1850, Hays died at the age of 78. He is buried at Woodlawn Cemetery in New York City. Although deceased, New Yorkers did not forget "Old Hays." In 1937, the *New York World-Telegram* published a popular six-part series on his exploits. Most recently, Hays figures as a prominent protagonist in Joel Rose's novel, *The Blackest Bird* (2008), a fitting tribute to a man whose exploits many antebellum-era New Yorkers followed, celebrated, and mythologized.

Jonathan Nash
State University of New York, Albany

See Also: Detection and Detectives; Livingston, Edward; New York; New York City; Riots.

Further Readings
Asbury, Herbert. *All Around the Town: Murder, Scandal, Riot and Mayhem in Old New York*. New York: Basic Books, 2003.
Burrows, Edwin G. and Mike Wallace. *Gotham: A History of New York City to 1898*. New York: Oxford University Press, 1999.
Costello, Augustine E. *Our Police Protectors: A History of the New York Police*. Montclair, NJ: Patterson Smith, 1972.
Denlinger, Sutherland. "Old Hays—There Was a Cop!" *New York World-Telegram* (March 1–6, 1937).
Rose, Joel. *The Blackest Bird: A Novel of Murder in Nineteenth Century New York*. New York: W. W. Norton, 2008.
Thompson, George A. "Hays, Jacob." *American National Biography Online*. http://www.anb.org/articles/20/20-01601.html (Accessed December 2011).

Hereditary Crime

Hereditary or genetic explanations of crime date back to the roots of criminology in the 1700s. Early theorists varied considerably on exactly what inherited factors, or combination of factors, were responsible for criminal behavior. They also made little distinction between biological and psychological characteristics. Since virtually all early theorists were trained as physicians, their main focus was on physical features of the human body.

Darwinism and Crime
In 1859, Charles Darwin presented his theory of evolution in *On the Origen of the Species*, which

emphasized inherited traits in both animals and humans. Darwin's ideas inspired additional interest in identifying inherited traits associated with deviant and criminal behavior. One of the first to examine the relationship between crime and heredity was Ceseare Lombroso, an Italian army physician. In 1876, Lombroso published *The Criminal Man,* which described the "born criminal" as a genetically inferior throwback to a more primitive stage of human evolution. Lombroso proposed that criminals could be distinguished by certain telltale physical characteristics, including enormous jaws, strong canines, flattened noses, and supernumerary teeth.

Raffaelle Garofolo (1851–1934), a contemporary of Lombroso, also believed that criminals were born and could be identified by specific physical traits. Lombroso's student, Enrico Ferri (1856–1929) agreed as well, adding some minor social factors to his explanation. Charles Goring (1870–1919), however, disagreed somewhat with Lombroso, claiming that criminality was primarily the result of "defective intelligence," and proposed that crime be controlled by preventing reproduction in families with inherited traits such as "feeblemindedness."

Francis Galton was one of the first researchers to conduct systematic studies of heredity and criminal behavior. In 1907, Galton proposed that several criminal characteristics were inherited, including an underdeveloped conscience, vicious instincts, and an uncontrollable temper. In 1913, Charles Goring studied convicted prisoners and their families, reporting significant correlations between the criminality of siblings, spouses, and parents and children. Goring advocated reproductive regulation for people displaying inherited criminal traits.

William Sheldon is recognized for developing the first systematic theory of hereditary crime. In 1942, Sheldon concluded that certain body types were not only correlated with, but caused the development of particular personality styles and temperaments. Sheldon's work was followed in 1950 by a massive study of delinquency by Sheldon and Eleanor Glueck. The Gluecks, like Sheldon, examined the relationship between body type and delinquency in 500 institutionalized, chronic youthful offenders. Both Sheldon and the Gluecks concluded that muscular, mesomorphic males were most likely to become criminals.

In the early 1960s, a new genetic factor emerged in the study of crime. Some high-profile violent criminals, including Richard Speck who murdered eight student nurses in Chicago, were found to have an extra y sex chromosome. This finding spurred additional studies, reporting that compared to the general population, there were a disproportionate number of prisoners with the xyy pattern. These "supermales" were described as hostile, hyperactive, and prone to violence. Later research, however, questioned this conclusion, reporting that xyy males were no more likely than normal xy males to become serious, violent offenders. In fact, each of the early perspectives that concluded that criminality was caused by inherited biological traits and physical features was severely criticized for its faulty methodology and experimental designs and was virtually dismissed.

Family and Twins Studies

Since the work of Lombroso, Galton, Sheldon, the Gluecks, and other early researchers was discredited, there has been continued interest in hereditary crime. In 1985, for example, James Wilson and Richard Herrnstein in their book, *Crime and Human Nature*, criticized the disparaging view of a gene-crime connection and endorsed the association of crime and heredity. This support spurred additional research on hereditary crime that came from four main sources: family studies, twin studies, adoption studies, and studies of the interaction between genes and the environment.

If criminal tendencies are inherited, the offspring of criminal parents will be more likely to commit crimes. Family crime studies date back to 1877 when Richard Dugdale was the first to study an extended family, the Jukes, in which he found a history of arrests in several generations. Since Dugdale, numerous studies have reported significant correlations between parental criminality and that of their children. These studies made it clear that crime follows family lines and that part of this association may be genetic. The major problem with family studies, however, is their inability to determine the relative contributions of heredity and environment.

As a way to overcome this obstacle, twin and adoption studies emerged. Twin studies compared the criminality of genetically identical twins with

This 1884 illustration, meant to emphasize the dangers of drinking, depicted two grown children of a man held in a criminal lunatic asylum visiting their insane father. The caption identifies the young man as a thief and the woman as a prostitute.

fraternal twins who share only half of their inherited genes. These studies typically found a higher crime concordance rate for identical twins. Twin studies, however, are limited because identical twins may have more shared environmental experiences and may model each other more than fraternal twins. To address this problem, researchers began observing the children of criminal parents who were adopted out to parents with no criminal history. Several adoption studies highlighted the influence of gene-environment interactions, uniformly reporting genetic predispositions to criminality that are either enhanced or inhibited by various environmental factors (e.g., socioeconomic status of adoptive parents). In their review of adoption and twin studies, S. H. Rhee and I. D. Waldman (2002) concluded that while heredity was a significant predictor of future criminal behavior, even strong genetic predispositions could be controlled by exposure to certain positive environmental factors (e.g., functional parenting).

An interest in examining the interaction of genes and environment was also spurred in the mid-20th century by contemporary trait theory. This view characterizes genetic factors as predisposing certain people toward criminality rather than determining crime. Trait theory has two main branches; biosocial theory, which proposes that crime is related to an individual's physical and biological makeup, and a second view that emphasizes genetically influenced psychological traits, characteristics, and illnesses. Both branches propose that people with abnormal biological and psychological traits have more difficulty adjusting to their social environment and, thus, are more vulnerable to crime-producing influences.

Bio-Social Theory

The bio-social view cites certain personality disorders that are associated with criminal behavior and are heritable. These include oppositional defiant disorder (ODD), attention deficit hyperactivity disorder (ADHD), conduct disorder (CD), and antisocial personality disorder (ASPD). These disorders are characterized by behaviors such as noncompliance, aggressiveness, poor impulse control, inability to learn from past behavior, and disregard for social rules. Bio-social theorists also point to studies that have found a higher incidence of genetically influenced mental disorders in criminal populations such as schizophrenia, major depressive disorder, bipolar disorder, and minimal brain dysfunction (MBD). Left unchecked by environmental factors, each of these disorders is thought to increase the likelihood of criminal behavior. For example, youth with both MBD and ADHD have been found to be at extremely high risk for antisocial behavior, which typically persists into adulthood. Bio-social theorists also highlight research that suggests that criminal behavior is influenced by certain neurochemicals such as monoamine oxidase, epinephrine, norepinephrine, serotonin, and dopamine. Low levels of these neurochemicals have been associated with increased aggressiveness and impulsivity, which may increase the likelihood of criminal behavior. Furthermore, arousal theory suggests that the brains of certain people work differently, requiring more stimulation to feel normal or comfortable. Thus, these people may be more prone to taking risks and engaging in stimulating activities that may include criminal acts. Bio-social theorists emphasize, however, that environmental factors may affect gene expression and the neurotransmitters that moderate behavior. Understanding this interaction is essential to more accurately discern the expression of criminal behavior.

Trait theorists propose that individuals with particular traits are more likely to engage in criminal behavior, often high-rate, chronic offending. These traits, which frequently appear together in certain people, include low verbal IQ, learning disabilities, and the "super traits" of low self-control and irritability. Genetic factors are thought to increase the likelihood that people will develop these traits through their effect on the central and autonomic nervous systems.

Molecular genetic studies, for example, have identified specific genes related to the traits of hyperactivity and impulsivity. These and other crime predisposing traits appear not to be the result of single genes but rather the product of several gene variants, not confined to particular groups but spread out through the general population. Thus, the prevailing view of trait theorists is that people who inherit a particular cadre of variant genes and then encounter certain dysfunctional environmental factors are more likely to develop the traits that increase the likelihood of criminal behavior.

In sum, there is considerable agreement that heredity does influence certain personality traits, learning problems, and mental disorders that may predispose certain individuals to criminal and antisocial behavior. It remains difficult, however, to determine the extent to which the expression of these disorders is attributable to heredity and environment. It is likely that modern brain imaging techniques and the recent sequencing of the human genome will enhance the understanding of hereditary crime. It is anticipated, however, that the importance of heredity in explaining crime will continue to focus on the connection between inherited factors and environmental bases of crime rather than on their direct relationship to criminal behavior.

Thomas M. Kelley
Wayne State University

See Also: Child Abuse, Sociology of; Crime and Arrest Statistics Analysis; Crime in America, Causes; Domestic Violence, Sociology of; Drug Abuse and Addiction, Sociology of; Juvenile Corrections, Sociology of.

Further Readings
Rhee, S. H. and I. D. Waldman. "Genetic and Environmental Influences on Antisocial Behavior: A Meta-Analysis of Twin and Adoption Studies." *Psychological Bulletin*, v.128 (2002).
Shoemaker, Donald J. *Theories of Delinquency: An Examination of Explanations of Delinquent Behavior.* New York: Oxford University Press, 1990.
Walters, Glenn D. and Thomas W. White. "Heredity and Crime: Bad Genes or Bad Research?" *Criminology*, v.27 (1989).
Wilson, James D., et al. *Crime and Human Nature.* New York: Simon & Schuster, 1985.

Hillerman, Tony

Anthony Grove Hillerman (1925–2008), better known as Tony Hillerman, was a leading American crime fiction writer. He is best known for his Navajo Tribal Police mystery novels. Hillerman was a second-generation German American born on May 27, 1925, in Sacred Heart, Oklahoma, a rural town of 50 people. Growing up there during the Great Depression, he was sent to Saint Mary's Academy, which was a Benedictine missionary school mainly for Potawatomi and Seminole girls. There, he acquired his lifelong respect for Native American culture. He went to college for one year but left to enlist in the military during World War II. He served in the U.S. Army as a mortarman with the 103rd Infantry Division and was awarded both Bronze and Silver Stars for valor as well as the Purple Heart for injuries sustained from a mine explosion.

After the war, he returned to school and graduated with a bachelor's degree in 1948 from Oklahoma University. In 1948, he married Marie Unzer, and together they raised six children, five of whom were adopted. From 1948 to 1962, he was a journalist, working as a reporter and then editor for newspapers in Borger, Texas, and Lawton, Oklahoma; finally, he served as political reporter in Oklahoma City for United Press International (UPI) and then UPI bureau chief in Santa Fe, New Mexico, and editor of the *New Mexican*, Santa Fe's leading newspaper. In 1966, he earned a master's degree in English literature from the University of New Mexico in Albuquerque. Hillerman taught journalism at the University of New Mexico in Albuquerque from 1966 to 1987.

Hillerman's first novel, *The Blessing Way*, was published in 1970 and initiated his 18 Navajo mystery novels set in the Four Corners region of the American Southwest. His stories often feature conflicts between traditional Navajo conceptions of crime and criminals versus the American criminal justice system. The Navajo appreciation of maintaining tribal harmony as portrayed by Hillerman is often at odds with the legal system. This harmony, known as *hozho*, is, in a sense, the Navajo version of justice; that which destroys *hozho* is, in Hillerman's novels, a crime. The Navajo are generally more sensitive than members of the larger society to moral weaknesses, and they tend to negatively value greed, or efforts to accumulate more than is needed. Hillerman delves into the metaphysical aspects of crime. He draws upon the religious and other cultural value systems not only of the Navajo but also of the Hopi and Zuni peoples. His compassionate efforts to describe people striving to maintain their traditional practices and beliefs in the modern world touched many readers. He wrestled with the discordance inherent in cross-cultural interactions, such as crossing religious taboos.

Hillerman's best-known protagonists in the Navajo crime novel series are Lieutenant Joe Leaphorn and Officer Jim Chee, both members of the Navajo Tribal Police. Lt. Leaphorn was introduced in *The Blessing Way* and is the more experienced policeman of the pair, but he is somewhat skeptical of some of the traditional Navajo beliefs about their rich spiritual world. For instance, although Lt. Leaphorn does not personally believe in witches, he takes reports of witchcraft seriously, because he has learned that the belief in witches can lead to problems. Officer Jim Chee, on the other hand, although younger than Leaphorn, holds a more traditional Navajo worldview. Jim Chee, introduced in Hillerman's 1978 *People of Darkness*, is studying to be a shaman, people called *hathaali* by the Navajo. Signs of witchcraft and other supernatural events are used by perpetrators in several of Hillerman's crime novels to cover up crimes.

Several of Hillerman's works were award winners. His second installment in his Navajo crime novel series was his 1973 *Dance Hall of the Dead*, which garnered the Edgar Award for Best Novel from the Mystery Writers of America. His 1986 *Skinwalkers* won a Golden Spur Award from the Western Writers of America, while his 1988 *A Thief of Time* was a number one best seller and won a Nero Wolfe Award, as did his 1990 *Coyote Waits*. In addition to his Navajo series, Hillerman wrote over a dozen other books, including two novels for children, works on the history and natural beauty of the American Southwest, and a memoir, titled *Seldom Disappointed*, which won an Agatha Christie Award. He was recognized for his outstanding service to other writers by getting the Parris Award from the Southwest Writer's Workshop. He was inducted into the Oklahoma Journalism Hall of Fame in 1993. In 1987, the Navajo Tribal Council granted him their Special Friend of the Dineh Award, of which Hillerman was particularly proud. Hillerman's stories remind us that there is a cultural context that should be appreciated to better understand crime and punishment. He died of pulmonary failure on October 26, 2008, in Albuquerque, New Mexico.

Victor B. Stolberg
Essex County College

See Also: Literature and Theater, Crime in; Literature and Theater, Police in; Native American Tribal Police; Native Americans.

Further Readings
Freese, Peter. *The Ethnic Detective: Chester Himes, Harry Kemelman, Tony Hillerman*. Essen, Germany: Verlag Die Blaue Eule, 1992.
Hillerman Tony, and Ernie Bulow. *Talking Mysteries: A Conversation With Tony Hillerman*. Alburquerque: University of New Mexico Press, 2004.
Reilly, John M. *Tony Hillerman: A Critical Companion*. Westport, CT: Greenwood Press.

Hispanic Americans

Throughout history, a number of different factors contributed to the racial tensions between whites and Hispanic Americans. During World War II, distrust stemming from differences in culture and race led to the imprisonment of Japanese Americans and ill treatment of foreign individuals in the form of segregation and job discrimination. Toward the end of World War II, a surge of patriotism was felt by white Americans, which coincided with an increased fear of Mexican children becoming juvenile delinquents as a result of their believed inability to conform to American standards. The fear was related to the rising popularity of the pachuco style, in the 1940s, which served to anger and further alienate the whites. The appeal of the pachuco style was that Mexican Americans were able to express their sentiments about the segregated norms that were in place. The pachuco style was a subculture to which many Mexican American (Chicano) youth began to adhere, which was seen as an alternative form of American culture that incorporated elements of jazz, slang, and clothing.

The style was associated with the zoot suit, which was publicized by the media as the style of gangsters and rebellious youth. Essentially, whites viewed the pachuco style as a challenge to what were considered established norms. However, the media continued to focus on the pachuco style, thus propagating the gangster affiliation among Mexican Americans. In 1942, the "Sleepy Lagoon murder" further fueled the tension and anger that plagued whites and Mexican Americans at this time. The controversy reached a new high when Jose Diaz, a 22-year-old Mexican American, was attacked on his way home from a party a few days before he was scheduled to leave for war. The attack ultimately led to his death and resulted in widespread hysteria about gang violence within Los Angeles. The attention that this crime garnered resulted in mass investigations in an effort to capture those responsible for the murder; however, the investigations broadened to include all Mexican American and African American communities. In other words, the Los Angeles Police Department (LAPD) used the death at Sleepy Lagoon as a pretense to launch a campaign against zooters, pachucos, and Chicano gangsters.

In 1943, racial tensions erupted between whites and Mexican Americans and resulted in the Zoot Suit Riots. By this point, there was a general fear of uncontrolled gang violence in East Los Angeles, which was fueled by the media. Riots began erupting throughout Los Angeles in areas frequented by Chicanos and returning sailors. For example, a rumor that a group of Chicanos had stabbed a sailor resulted in the development of a mob and, ultimately, a manhunt. A similar incident occurred when a group of sailors accused Chicano youth of attacking them and thus reported the attack to the police. The police then formed the Vengeance Squad in an effort to find the assailants, but to no avail. However, many groups of sailors took it upon themselves to search throughout downtown and East Los Angeles and beat up any Mexican youth who were dressed in zoot suits.

People began to question whether Mexican Americans were simply too different to coexist with whites within American society. The perceived differences in culture, intellect, and biology led to a mentality that continues to permeate American society to this day. More specifically, immigrant groups were viewed as "biologically deficient," meaning there is a genetic tendency that made this group of people more criminally prone. In other words, it was believed that since they were born outside of the United States, these people were the most likely to commit crimes. This perception led to many political debates that centered on immigration. Nonetheless, the perception of immigrants being criminally prone continued to receive public support.

"Criminal" Immigrants

During the 1980s, large numbers of Hispanics immigrated to the United States from various Spanish-speaking countries, for example, an estimated 125,000 Cubans made Miami their home while seeking refuge. However, their arrival was not well received because of reports of people with criminal records and mental disorders among those that emigrated. Because of their visibility and growing size within the population, the media directed much of its attention at them, especially because the rates of gang and drug-related homicides increased during the 1980s. Even though the rates of Mariel Cuban homicide victims and offending increased to levels similar to those recorded for African Americans, they soon decreased to levels reported for other Latinos and non-Latino whites. However, the belief in an immigrant criminal was still prominent.

Young Mexican migrant workers resting at a filling station in Neches, Texas, while on their way home to the Rio Grande Valley from a job picking cotton in Mississippi in October 1939. Studies of immigration and crime have found that adolescent violence was reduced in neighborhoods with high levels of immigrant concentration and that, while most nonwhite communities had higher rates of violence in comparison to white communities, Hispanic communities did not.

Because of this fear of immigrants, many researchers began conducting studies in order to understand the validity of the criminal immigrant. These studies examined the relationship between immigration, Hispanics, and crime from both individual and community perspectives. Individual-level studies demonstrated that first-generation youth (i.e., individuals born outside of the United States) tended to have lower rates of criminal participation, which included hitting someone, throwing objects at someone, carrying a weapon, being involved in a gang fight, or picking pockets/snatching purses in comparison to second- and third-generation youth (i.e., youth born inside of the United States). Similar results were found when incarceration rates were examined. Overall, incarceration rates for second- and third-generation youth were four times greater than that for first-generation youth. Also related to these findings was the age of arrival of youth to the United States. More specifically, those youth who arrived at a younger age to this country were more likely to commit the above acts than those who arrived at a later age. Therefore, researchers concluded that there seems to be no support for the belief that Hispanics arrive to this country with criminal tendencies; rather, Hispanic Americans seem to become more involved in crime the longer they live in the United States.

The Latino Paradox

Another topic related to Hispanic Americans is homicide. Dating back to the 1980s and the reoccurring belief in the criminal immigrant, Hispanic Americans have often been portrayed as dangerous and bloodthirsty. For this reason, Ramiro

Martinez, Jr., analyzed homicide rates between various groups to understand whether first-generation Hispanics and second-/third-generation Hispanics are more criminally prone. Ultimately, the results indicated that despite a slight increase in homicide rates for first-generation Hispanics during the late 1980s; first-generation Hispanics had lower rates of homicide than second- and third-generation Hispanics. Other comparisons specifically focused on the Mariel Cubans to determine the validity of the arguments presented by politicians and the media about the criminality of the "Marielitos." Once again, Ramiro Martinez, Jr., concluded that the homicide rates of the Mariel Cubans in comparison to African Americans, whites, and other Hispanics were high between 1980 and 1984; however, their rates eventually dropped to levels that were even lower than those for whites. Therefore, these studies demonstrate that there does not seem to be much evidence provided for the rationalization behind the criminal immigrant belief.

In an effort to explain these unexpected results, researchers have proposed a concept known as the "Latino paradox." The paradox stems from the success that Hispanics tend to have among different social and criminal outcomes, despite their socioeconomic status. In other words, considering the social hardships (i.e., poverty, language barriers, lower income, and lower education) that many Hispanic Americans face, they are expected to fare much worse among various outcomes. Within the study of criminology, many of these socioeconomic characteristics aid in the understanding of which people are more or less likely to offend and/or to be victimized. Despite having these characteristics present in their lives, Hispanic Americans actually fare quite well. Examples of these outcomes include health, mental health, and crime. Some explanations for the Latino paradox include heavy emphasis on the family, a strong motivation to work and succeed in a new country, and a desire to not be deported. Aside from being used as an explanation for individual-level differences, the Latino paradox has also been studied within community-level studies in criminology.

To better understand the manner in which communities are studied within a criminological perspective, researchers have implemented social disorganization theory. The theory of social disorganization was developed by Clifford Shaw and Henry McKay in an effort to explain the presence of high crime rates in specific neighborhoods or communities. In their original study, the results indicated that high levels of residential mobility (residents constantly moving in and out of the community), ethnic heterogeneity (large amounts of ethnically and racially diverse people residing within the same communities), poverty, and structural disadvantage (a concept that encompasses measures of poverty, female-headed families, and jobless males) were associated with increased levels of crime. Therefore, neighborhoods with these characteristics are described as "socially disorganized" and are expected to have higher rates of crime. In other words, Shaw and McKay determined that, despite the importance of individual characteristics for understanding crime, community characteristics are just as important.

In reference to Hispanic Americans, the popularity of the criminal immigrant once again emerges. According to social disorganization theory, increased levels of ethnic heterogeneity (i.e., large concentrations of Hispanics) in communities are believed to be associated with higher rates of crime. However, community-level studies have also provided evidence of the Latino paradox. These studies incorporate the percentage of foreign-born residents to gauge whether large concentrations of Hispanics contribute to crime. Martinez states that much of the research on immigration and violence reports findings suggesting that this relationship is not as it seems. It is in this capacity that the Latino paradox emerges as a puzzling finding within this type of research. It seems that immigration serves to strengthen the social structure of Hispanics and provide support for those within the neighborhood; rather than to weaken the social structure already in place, causing further deterioration leading to crime. In other words, large percentages of Hispanics within a community seem to protect the community.

One topic that demonstrates the influence of immigrant communities is homicide. Martinez compared homicide rates among five specific Hispanic communities within five different cities (i.e., Chicago, Houston, San Diego, El Paso, and Miami) to determine whether more impoverished communities display higher levels of homicide. A second study examined whether neighborhoods in Miami, El Paso, and San Diego (areas with large immigrant settlements) have high levels of homicide, as did another in San Diego. All three studies concluded that immigration did not increase levels of homicide; instead, it decreased the level of homicide in some cases. These findings challenged the stereotype of a criminal immigrant and the explanation provided by social disorganization.

Similar conclusions have been drawn for other studies of immigration and crime. For example, it was found that changes in crime rates over a period of 10 years were not associated with changes in immigration rates, thereby concluding that reducing immigration is not likely to impact crime rates. Adolescent violence was also reduced in neighborhoods with high levels of immigrant concentration (i.e., larger percentages of foreign-born and non-English-speaking residents). Another group of researchers also recognized that, even after controlling for neighborhood disadvantage, all nonwhite communities had higher rates of violence in comparison to white communities with the exception of one group: Hispanics. Interestingly, the rates for Hispanic communities did not vary significantly from those found in white communities. Therefore, prior research demonstrates that there are elements present within immigrant communities that do not coincide with the expectations of social disorganization.

Amy S. Eggers
University of South Florida

See Also: Arizona; Border Patrol; Customs Service as Police; Deportation; Florida; Immigration Crimes; Miami, Florida; Race-Based Crimes; Racism.

Further Readings
Akers Chacon, Justin and Mike Davis. *No One Is Illegal: Fighting Racism and State Violence on the U.S.-Mexico Border.* Chicago: Haymarket Books, 2006.
Desmond, Scott A. and Charis E. Kubrin. "Immigrant Communities and Adolescent Violence." *Sociological Quarterly*, v.50 (2009).
Diego Vigil, James. *Barrio Gangs: Street Life and Identity in Southern California.* Austin: University of Texas Press, 1988.

Krivo, Lauren J., Ruth D. Peterson, and Danielle C. Kuhl. "Segregation, Racial Structure, and Neighborhood Violence Crime." *American Journal of Sociology*, v.114/6 (2009).
Lee, Matthew T., Ramiro Martinez, Jr., and Richard Rosenfeld. "Does Immigration Increase Homicide? Negative Evidence From Three Border Cities." *Sociological Quarterly*, v.42/4 (2001).
Martinez, Ramiro, Jr. *Latino Homicide: Immigration, Violence, and Community.* New York: Routledge Taylor & Francis Group, 2002.
Martinez, Ramiro, Jr., Jacob I. Stowell, and Matthew T. Lee. "Immigration and Crime in an Era of Transformation: A Longitudinal Analysis of Homicides in San Diego Neighborhoods, 1980–2000." *Criminology*, v.48/3 (2010).
Obregon Pagan, Eduardo. *Murder at the Sleepy Lagoon: Zoot Suits, Race, and Riot in Wartime L.A.* Chapel Hill: University of North Carolina Press, 2003.

History of Crime and Punishment in America: Colonial

The legal system in British America relied on English legal conventions. Considering the relative autonomy of the colonies, however, their legal codes varied from colony to colony and reflected the unique concerns and beliefs of each. The manner in which colonial authorities enforced laws was meant not only to compensate victims and discourage crime but also to promote specific religious and social ideas.

One of the major factors in colonists' perception of crime was their tensions with Native Americans, which often erupted into full-fledged wars and added much anxiety about crime. The Pequot War (1634–38) and the King Phillip War (1675–76) nearly wiped out the European settlements in New England. The region remained volatile in the 18th century, particularly during the Seven Years War (1756–63) against the French. Accounts of those who survived Indian captivity, such as *The True History of the Captivity & Restoration of Mrs. Mary Rowlandson* (1682), typically portrayed Indians as incorrigible criminals who menaced Christian settlers. Conflicts of this sort were also common in the southern colonies, most notably in Virginia, where in the 1670s, frontier settlers felt compelled to form a militia to drive Indians from the region.

Threats of unrest and crime also came from within communities. It was widely assumed that the heathenism and wilderness of America could diminish colonists' respect for laws and spark crime. For this reason, colonial authorities were not inclined to tolerate any manifestation of lawlessness. In fact, during their formative years, settlements like those in Virginia were run almost in a military fashion. The fate of John Smith offers a telling example about the anxiety of authorities; although he was an important figure in the 1607 effort to settle Virginia, Smith came close to being executed for simple insubordination. The colony's second governor, Thomas Dale, introduced a set of stringent laws, which warranted severe punishment even for fairly minor transgressions. Dale's laws also allowed capital punishment for almost two dozen offenses, including illegal trading with Indians, blasphemy, and property damage.

Social and Political Unrest

Leaders in New England were equally concerned about signs of social unrest. In the case of the Pilgrims, who established the colony of Plymouth in 1620, their fears were amplified by the fact that they had no legal claim to the land where they settled. Even before they disembarked in the Massachusetts Bay, a group of the Mayflower passengers declared that they were not obliged to follow their leaders. Episodes like this necessitated the need for an assertive government, which was in place in the first decades of colonization; the authorities deported or prosecuted anyone whose behavior could undermine social order. Several people, most famously Thomas Morton, were consequently removed from the colony for what was perceived as unruly behavior.

The efforts of authorities notwithstanding, the colonies were occasionally disrupted by revolts, which highlighted the weakness of social order in British America. Particularly devastating was Bacon's Rebellion in Virginia in 1676. It was started by frontier farmers who believed that the government did not do enough to protect them from Indians. The rebels burned Jamestown, the seat of the colonial government, and chased the governor away. The rebellion dissipated only after the unexpected death of its leader and the execution of several ringleaders. The anarchical streak of early American culture became even more apparent in the aftermath of the Glorious Revolution in England (1688–89), which saw the overthrow of James II. It inspired several coup d'états and unrests in the American colonies, particularly in Boston, New York, and Maryland.

Slave conspiracies and rebellions started to occur as early as the 1650s and became fairly frequent in the 18th century in both the south and the north. Remarkably, some of the most disturbing revolts took place in New York (one in 1712 and the other in 1741), where the authorities felt compelled to resort to some unusually harsh measures. In 1739–40, South Carolina saw two bloody revolts, one of which, the Stono Rebellion, was the largest in the colonial period.

Crime

Piracy became a serious problem in the early 18th century. It originated in the Caribbean, where Spain's commercial activities created a lucrative environment for English, French, and Dutch outlaws. Some pirate groups flourished with the tacit acquiescence of the English government, which hoped that pirates could keep Spain's empire in check. New York City and other American ports served as safe havens for pirates throughout the 17th century, where they enjoyed some protection from government officials. When piracy started to endanger British trade in the Atlantic, however, the colonial authorities turned against lawlessness of this sort. A number of pirates were publicly executed in New England in the early 18th century.

Most commonly, authorities had to deal with such ordinary transgressions as violations of public order and crimes against property and people. How such crimes were dealt with reflected the religious and political differences among various colonies.

In Pennsylvania, which was established as a refuge for the Quakers, the attitude toward crime and punishment was somewhat different from other British colonies. In contrast to the Puritans and other Protestants, the Quakers never put much emphasis on the concept of original sin. They did not regard criminal behavior as a manifestation of man's innate inclination toward perversity, and consequently were more inclined to try to rehabilitate criminals. Compared to other colonies, Pennsylvania had fairly few capital crimes. To the extent possible, its system of punishments was designed not only to prevent other crimes but also to reform criminals. This approach ultimately put Pennsylvania at the forefront of penal reform.

In the Chesapeake south, the legal system was designed primarily to preserve the social order. Although religious teachings influenced many colonial legal codes in the 17th century, including Virginia's "Articles, Laws and Orders" (1610), religious concerns did not seem to preoccupy the magistrates. In the early stages of the colony's history, religious rules were indeed widely enforced. Blasphemy was punishable by death. All colonists were required to attend church and faced fairly harsh punishments, such as lengthy service in the galleys, if they failed to comply. Once the colonies were firmly established, however, they became fairly tolerant of religious diversity. The magistrates were then primarily concerned about crimes that threatened the power of wealthy colonists or threatened to upset the social order. For this reason, people of lower classes were likelier to be punished than their wealthier compatriots.

Punishment

The most common form of punishment in the colonies was a fine, which could be used to compensate plaintiffs. Those who were unable to pay the fine were often sold as indentured servants to work off the debt. Long-term incarcerations, which entailed supporting prisoners at the government's expense, were not common. Criminals and suspected criminals were imprisoned only in anticipation of the trial, sentencing, or execution. The first correctional facility, which was designed to contain prisoners for lengthy periods of time, was opened only in 1773 in Connecticut. Magistrates also created elaborate public punishment rituals to discourage crime.

Condemned criminals could be confined to a pillory, whipped in public, or subjected to some other humiliating punishment. The customs of branding and forcing criminals to wear various marks of shame were fairly often used in Virginia

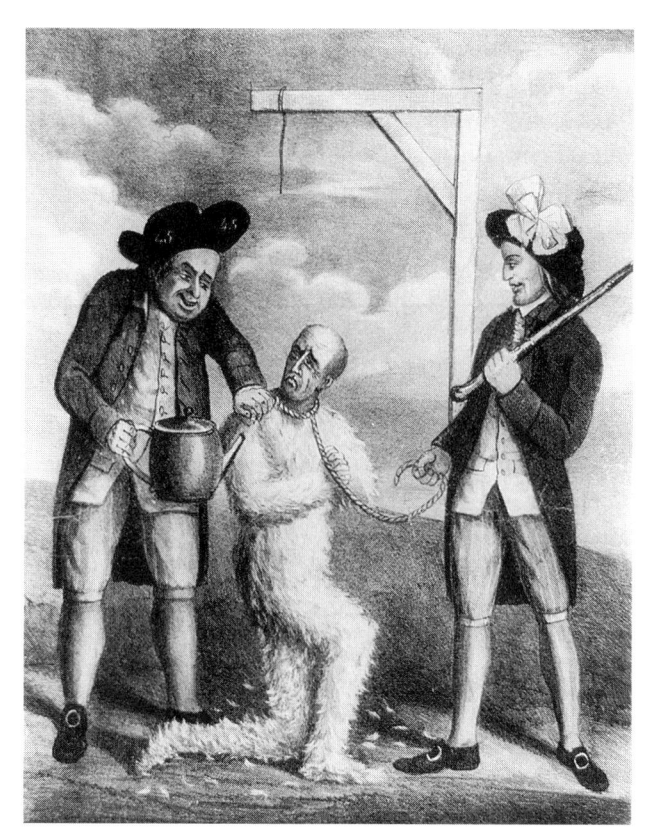

This 1774 print shows the notorious incident of the tarring and feathering of John Malcom, a British customs officer, before the Revolution. He was forced to drink tea and led before a gallows in front of a crowd of 1,200 spectators in Boston.

and New England. Some culprits were adorned with distinct signs, similar to the one described in Nathaniel Hawthorne's novel *The Scarlet Letter* (1850). Others were branded with a hot iron on their hands or faces. The marks were typically letters identifying the crime; "A" for adultery, "T" for theft, and so forth. Such marks of shame reinforced the authorities' prestige for their vigilance and served as constant reminders that crime was a threat to the social order in the colonies.

Religion and Crime

In New England, which was dominated by the Puritans, religion made a far greater impact on the legal conventions than in other British colonies. Although the Puritans nominally believed in the separation of church and state, its leaders were committed to preserving the sense of religious orthodoxy, which affected their attitude toward crime and punishment. In the Massachusetts

Bodie of Liberties (1641), for example, all capital crimes were adopted from the Bible.

Religious tensions were feared because they could have a destabilizing effect. For this reason, religious diversity was to be avoided. In the 17th century, the New England authorities methodically prosecuted and deported individuals who did not share Puritan beliefs, let alone those who showed disrespect for the existing religious order. This was particularly evident in the expulsions of Roger Williams in 1636 and Anne Hutchinson in 1638. The authorities also persecuted entire religious groups, most notably Anabaptists and Quakers, whose religious views were believed to inspire discord in New England. Several Quakers were executed in Boston in 1660–61.

Moral transgressions were considered as serious as crimes against people and property. In the Puritan mind-set, all crimes, regardless of how harmless they were, reflected man's general propensity for sin. This belief was reinforced by the Puritan fascination with the concept of original sin, according to which all people were potentially criminal. What is remarkable about the American Puritans, however, is that they were very successful in exploiting this belief for political purposes. Ministers habitually perpetrated the notion that the colonization of heathen America was a sacred war against Satan, who defended himself by inciting crime among the colonists. They routinely decried manifestations of immoral behavior as signs of the colony's downfall. This strategy was used particularly often at times of crises. In the aftermath of the King Phillip War, which such well-known ministers as Cotton Mather regarded as God's punishment, the synod issued a proclamation that accused colonists of all sorts of crimes: disrespect for the authorities, intemperance, promiscuity, dancing, gambling, idleness, wearing inappropriate clothes, and many other transgressions. It is understandable that this trend obscured crime statistics in New England because religious moralists there tended to exaggerate the extent of crime in order to emphasize the importance of religion.

Executions, which in Massachusetts were warranted for such crimes as idolatry, blasphemy, perjury, adultery, murder, bestiality, homosexuality, and witchcraft, were always conducted publicly. This approach reflected the strategy of exploiting punishment rituals as occasions for moralizing. In the period leading to punishment, the condemned were usually subjected to repeated visits from ministers, who worked with criminals to explain their spiritual condition and, in case of executions, prepare them for God's judgment. This period also afforded the criminal a chance to repent his or her crime. Criminals were also prompted to write didactic confessions, which were published for the benefit of other people.

Colonists were encouraged to attend execution rituals to contemplate their spiritual condition. The day of execution followed a prescribed format. It generally began with a sermon that included a methodical discussion of the culprit's crime and an explanation of its significance in the larger social and religious context. Since the Puritans believed that everyone was innately sinful, ministers always reminded their congregations that seeds of criminality were planted in everyone. Therefore, the public was expected not to distance itself from the condemned but to relate to the criminal condition. The publication of execution sermons, trial records, and related materials completed the cycle of punishment. To ensure their wide circulation, execution sermons were published as cheap pamphlets. Their popularity was enhanced by the fact that they were aggressively promoted as educational publications.

The Eighteenth Century
The crime trends and the colonial legal systems started to change in the 18th century, when the American colonies found themselves more firmly integrated into the British Empire. Their legal system became more formalized and anglicized, while local religious and social concerns started to lose their significance. What's more, the rapid growth of cities, which created a more cosmopolitan environment in the colonies, contributed to proliferation of new forms of crime. Between 1690 and 1775, the population of New York jumped from 3,900 to 25,000, while Philadelphia grew from 4,000 to 40,000 residents. The latter, famous for its diversity, had a reputation as the most dangerous city in British America. Like other cities, it was plagued by typical urban crimes: burglary, pickpocketing, robberies, and prostitution. Philadelphia was also sporadically ravaged by bloody riots, which were sparked by all sorts of grievances.

In the 18th century, we can also discern the first manifestations of vigilantism and other forms of extralegal violence, which blurred the lines between law and lawlessness. It relied on the notion that people can take justice into their own hands. One some level, this popular trend can be seen as a reaction against formalization of the legal system. The trend began with innocent rituals and celebrations, such as the Pope Night in New England. Organized each year by common people with fervent anti-Catholic sentiment, the Pope Night consisted of parading and insulting an effigy of the pope through the streets. This trend undoubtedly contributed to the growing disrespect toward authority, which became particularly apparent in revolutionary America.

In the 1760s and 1770s, Americans reacted with hostility to what they considered unjust policies of Parliament and the king, particularly the Stamp Act (1765). It gave rise to the notion that laws were not always just and that common people were capable judges of all affairs in their communities. Consequently, many Americans felt free to express their anger through protests and rituals in which people could express their dismay.

Symbolic executions, particularly burning and hanging of effigies, were fairly common. One the first victims was Andrew Oliver, the Boston official whose position obliged him to enforce the Stamp Act. In the summer of 1765, when Bostonians learned about the provisions of the new law, a mob ransacked Oliver's house, hanged his effigy on the Liberty Tree, and then, in a brazen act of defiance, paraded in front of the town house.

As the situation in the colonies continued to deteriorate, some protesters went beyond burning effigies and started to harass British officials and loyalists directly. American radicals viewed such acts as a form of direct justice, which they enforced with a dramatic flair. In the fall of 1769, a mob got hold of George Geyser, who was suspected of being an informer for the British; Geyser was not only tarred and feathered but was also paraded through the streets of Boston to inspire terror among people. Jesse Saville, another informer, met the same fate the following year. Particularly infamous was the 1773 case of John Malcom, a customs officer in Boston, whose tarring and feathering gathered an enormous and diverse crowd of 1,200 enthusiasts. This trend helped sustain revolutionary spirit in the 1770s, but in the aftermath of the Revolutionary War, it posed a challenge to the authorities as they sought to re-create the rule of law in the country.

Alexander Moudrov
Queens College, City University of New York

See Also: 1600 to 1776 Primary Documents; American Revolution and Criminal Justice; Bodie of Liberties; Common Law Origins of Criminal Law; *Laws and Liberties of Massachusetts*; Puritans.

Further Readings
Greenberg, Douglas. *Crime and Law Enforcement in the Colony of New York, 1691–1776*. Ithaca, NY: Cornell University Press, 1976.
Meranze, Michael. "Penalty and the Colonial Project: Crime, Punishment and the Regulation of Morals in Early America." In *The Cambridge History of Law in America*, Michael Grossberg and Christopher L. Tomlins, eds. Cambridge: Cambridge University Press, 2008.
Purvis, Thomas. "Law Enforcement and Crime." In *Colonial America to 1763*. New York: Facts on File, 1999.
Vaver, Anthony. "Early American Crime: An Exploration of the Social and Cultural History of Crime and Punishment in Colonial America and the Early United States." http://www.early americancrime.com (Accessed September 2011).

History of Crime and Punishment in America: 1783–1850

American criminal justice underwent profound transformations in the period between the American Revolution and 1850. At the most basic level, moral or religious offenses so prevalent in colonial penal codes were increasingly rare in the north in the period after the Revolutionary War, though they persisted on the books in the south. During the 19th century, property offenses, especially larceny (and variations of larceny like horse theft), and disorderly conduct (including drunkenness and vagrancy) dominated the criminal courts in northern states. Policing was also undergoing transition. In most of this period, large towns and cities were still patrolled by night watchmen and constables; however, beginning in the 1830s and 1840s, large cities like New York and Philadelphia began the process of adopting organized police forces with specific city- or countywide jurisdictions but that operated much like constables. Changes to the criminal trial also began to emerge. Throughout colonial history and the early republic, cases were brought by private prosecutors, private individuals who brought the accused to court, often because the individual himself was victimized by the crime. However, throughout the course of the 19th century, this practice gave way to office-holding prosecutors. At around the same time, the portion of trials by jury began to decline. Throughout the east coast, beginning around the 1830s, the number of guilty pleas rose, a disputed portion of which are believed to have been the result of a primitive form of plea bargain. In these various budding transitions, the modern criminal justice system began to take shape.

Capital Punishment

Among the most important changes, however, were the gradual abandonment of capital punishment and the search for alternative punishments culminating in the adoption of the prison. While states experienced change at slightly different times, change generally came in two major bursts the first directly after the Revolutionary War lasting into the 1810s, the second beginning in the 1810s and continuing well into the 1840s. Moreover, those convicted of crimes had very different experiences of criminal justice based on their gender, race, nationality, and region.

Following the American Revolution, but as early as 1776, several states altered their constitutions to include mandates to change their criminal laws by reducing their use of capital punishment. They had been influenced by several factors. First, Cesare Beccaria's 1763 pamphlet *On Crimes and Punishments* had been translated and slowly made its way across the Atlantic by the outbreak of the Revolutionary War. This tract included arguments against the death penalty, which Beccaria saw as an uncertain sanction that occurred too quickly to leave a lasting impression and took place too long after the crime to be a proper deterrent. Second, as the colonies began to attack monarchy as an institution, they also saw certain practices as monarchical and unfit for a more free and democratic country. The death penalty in particular was attacked as a relic of monarchical excess. Instead of killing its citizens, it was thought that the government's duty was to reform or otherwise improve them. Others suggested that the death penalty was rendered insufficiently useful by jury nullification, the phenomenon in which jurors find an offender not guilty, despite clear evidence to the contrary, simply to avoid sentencing someone to a more severe punishment than thought appropriate or necessary. This was representative of a growing discomfort since the Enlightenment with executing offenders for property crimes, which were becoming more common in the colonies. Finally, others argued that capital punishment was actually counterproductive because it "brutalized" those who witnessed the execution, thereby creating more criminals. There were, of course, some commentators like Benjamin Rush, who advocated the complete abolition of capital punishment; however, they would have to wait until the following century to see real progress on this front. In the meantime, capital punishment was dismantled more slowly.

Thus, as fighting broke out with the British, Pennsylvania (1776), Vermont (1777), and South Carolina (1778) altered their constitutions ordering restrictions on corporal and capital punishments, often in favor of more "proportionate" sanctions. Pennsylvania's law in particular called for the creation of houses of correction to punish previously capital offenders. However, more progress was made in reducing the list of capital offenses than in adopting alternatives. In 1786, Pennsylvania reduced its list of capital offenses by removing robbery, burglary, sodomy, and buggery from capital eligibility. In 1788, Ohio limited capital offenses to murder. In 1794, Pennsylvania went even further and limited capital eligibility to a new category of murder, first-degree murder. This limited capital punishment to murders that were planned or especially heinous, while second-degree murder, including all other murders, would be sentenced to a term of imprisonment at Walnut Street Jail. Many states followed this example, including Virginia in 1796 and Kentucky in 1798.

In 1796, both New York and New Jersey limited capital punishment to murder and treason. Thus, in the first decade of the new United States, several states severely restricted their use of capital punishment legislatively.

Jails

By limiting the number of capital offenses, states were left with a void in their penal schemes. States primarily turned to a heavier reliance on the jail, experiments with hard labor, and attempts at disciplining with corporal punishment. Their searches often followed the Beccarian mantra that the certainty of the punishment was more important than its severity. Thus, in 1785, Massachusetts converted a fortress in Boston to hold convicted criminals as its state prison, at which they would work at hard labor. Confinement at Castle Island looked something like the early workhouses found in England, but unlike those workhouses and even American jails, this was the first instance of an institution devoted solely to the confinement of convicted inmates in the United States. This experiment ended in 1789, however, and had minimal impact on subsequent American developments, which were influenced much more heavily by developments in Pennsylvania.

Pennsylvania filled its penal void by adopting the Wheelbarrow Law in 1786. Henceforth, convicted men would publicly labor on the streets of Philadelphia while tied to a cannonball and wearing unattractive clothing in order to deter others and reform themselves into good laborers. At night, they would be housed in jail. The shame and labor elements were thought to be reformative. This law was soon copied by Rhode Island in 1787, followed by New York, Massachusetts, Maryland, and Virginia. However, this plan backfired when the wheelbarrow men fought among themselves or with the public, were jeered or cheered by passersby, and, in some cases, escaped; the practice was seen as an abject failure. When the law was abandoned, Pennsylvania turned to its Walnut Street Jail in Philadelphia.

Since 1776, comfortably middle-class citizens had been concerned with the state of their jails. Some had read John Howard's 1777 book *The State of the Prisons*, about the grotesque conditions of the local jails in Great Britain. Some citi-

Philadelphia locksmith Patrick Lyon, who in 1798 became a widely known victim of judicial injustice after being falsely convicted of robbery of the Bank of Pennsylvania. A book about his ordeal pled for equal justice for both the rich and the poor.

zens, especially Quaker individuals, experienced American jails firsthand during the revolution when they were jailed for not fighting. However, Quakers generally had a long tradition of concern with incarcerated individuals, in part because of their religious beliefs but also because of a longstanding history of being banished, incarcerated, or executed for their religious affiliation. Thus, in 1776, a group of Philadelphia citizens formed the Philadelphia Society for Assisting Distressed Prisoners, which was later renamed, in 1787, the Philadelphia Society for Alleviating the Miseries of Public Prisons. By 1787, the jails were horribly overcrowded, in part because of recently increased reliance but also because of an increased crime rate following the disbanding of soldiers after the war. The Walnut Street Jail, founded in 1776, was one such institution.

The Walnut Street Jail was remodeled in 1790, designated a state prison, and experienced some changes reflecting contemporary penological thought. While inmates were held in congregate in large common rooms, they were first classified and kept in different rooms according to their classification. The jail contained 16 cells for solitary confinement, but these were used if inmates violated rules and not as a general punishment to which one was sentenced. Inmates were also provided with work in communal workshops. Moreover, a large number of serious offenders were actually sentenced to lengthy periods of time instead of brief stints, as before. While the penological theory underlying Walnut Street was less developed than what followed, there was a belief that simply moving offenders from their environment, and preventing them from getting worse in the process, would reform them. The institution was also thought (especially by Benjamin Rush) to provide a deterrent to would-be offenders, who would be ignorant of what actually went on inside. However, like previous jails, Walnut Street held those convicted of a range of crimes, from second-degree murder to petty larceny, as well as those awaiting trial, witnesses, some vagrants, debtors, and the feeble. Despite some similarities with previous and contemporary jails, though, this represented a significant break from the past. The Walnut Street Jail is generally regarded as the first important development in carceral punishment in the United States, sometimes even referred to as the first prison, the institution at Castle Island notwithstanding. The Philadelphia model was heavily copied: In 1796, New York allocated funds to build Newgate Jail. In 1797, New Jersey completed construction of its new "penitentiary house," as these institutions were sometimes called. In 1800, Virginia and Kentucky also completed their structures, while Massachusetts allocated funds for its penitentiary house. By 1810, Connecticut, Tennessee, Vermont, New Hampshire, and Maryland (10 states in all) had a penitentiary house or jail.

However, the experiment with jails in Pennsylvania and elsewhere was generally a failure. States experienced major resistance on the part of inmates, their family members, and guards. Riots were common. Pennsylvania's Walnut Street Jail experienced four sizable riots between 1817 and 1821, and Newgate in New York had riots in 1818, 1819, 1821, and 1822. In addition to riots, the jails experienced fires and escapes; the escapes and riots especially contributed to the perception that crime was on the rise and that the new jails were contributing to this increase. Moreover, overcrowding, which had contributed to the disorder in the jails, also made workshop labor impossible. Thus, by the 1810s, several states were looking for another alternative not only to capital punishment but to jail-based incarceration as well, for their more serious offenders.

Development of Prisons and Penitentiaries

This search led to the adoption of the first American prisons. The first of these was Auburn State Prison in New York. Its construction was authorized by statute in 1816. Following the failure of Newgate, reformers rejected congregate incarceration in favor of true solitary confinement. It was thought that inmates contaminated one another and this prevented them from reforming themselves and their ways; thus, silent, lonely reflection would enable this end. Initially, beginning in 1821, inmates were maintained in very small cells (3.5 by 7 by 7 feet), were not permitted to talk, and were denied visitors. The experiment had devastating consequences, as many inmates died or became insane, and had to be discontinued in 1823. At that point, New York returned to the congregate style of incarceration seen in the early jails; however, inmates were kept in solitude in their own cells at night. During the day, inmates worked in large factory-like workshops in complete silence; they were not permitted to even look at one another for fear of communication. To both maintain order and prevent contaminating communication among the inmates, Auburn's prisoners were required to walk everywhere in lockstep, a maneuver in which an inmate put his hand on the shoulder of the man in front of him and his foot behind the foot of the man in front of him while his head looked in the direction of the opposite shoulder and foot. Consistent with the theme of order, guards as well as inmates were forced to follow a military kind of protocol, including a strict schedule and uniforms (the inmates wore stripes). Inmates who failed to comply were whipped. This became known as the congregate or New York model of prison discipline.

Not long after New York's reforms, in 1818, Pennsylvania ordered the erection of Western State Penitentiary in what is now Pittsburgh. In 1821, the legislature also provided funds to build Eastern State Penitentiary outside Philadelphia. In both prisons, the initial plan was to use solitary confinement without labor. Still under construction, Western opened in 1826. It was quickly apparent that the new prison was an architectural disaster not equipped for solitary confinement. The inmates were transferred to work on canals and other public works projects in the western part of the state. The prison closed not long after receiving its first inmate. By contrast, Eastern opened in 1829 and remained open for nearly 150 years. Well before its first inmate arrived, the experiment in New York had proven unsuccessful and, while Philadelphia inmates were still held in cells separated from the other inmates day and night, the Pennsylvania plan had changed to allow inmates to work in their cells. Inmates performed tasks like shoemaking, spinning or weaving, and blacksmithing, all of which could be done solitarily within one's own cell. John Haviland, the architect of Eastern State Penitentiary, had also included other amenities to allow for continuous cellular confinement. Cells, which were much larger than those at Auburn, were equipped with small exercise yards or gardens as well as flushing toilets and plenty of ventilation.

A major concern of Eastern's officials was the privacy of the inmates, whom they wanted to return to the free world unharnessed by a reputation as a criminal and a former prison inmate. They were thus escorted to their cells while wearing hoods through which they were unrecognizable by escorts, and food was delivered through a special compartment that prevented the recipient or deliverer from seeing the other party. Religious services, which the inmates could hear from their cells, were also held roughly every two weeks. However, inmates at Eastern did not go long without seeing another person—the warden, the inspectors of the prison, the physician, local ministers, and members of the local reform societies (as well as prominent European tourists like Alexis de Tocqueville and Charles Dickens) regularly met with the inmates. Finally, inmates who misbehaved were punished quite severely by corporal punishments aimed at pacifying the offender, including the water bath (something akin to waterboarding) and the iron gag (a device forced into the mouth and connected to the hands wedged behind one's back, making it very painful to struggle against). This became known as the separate or Pennsylvania model of prison discipline.

These two prisons became vastly influential throughout the national and international penal community. Both were among the top tourist attractions and received prominent European visitors. This attention may have exacerbated what became a vicious debate over which form of prison discipline was best that lasted from the time of the first prison's construction to roughly 1850. The lead competitors were members of the Boston Prison Discipline Society (supporting the New York model) and the Philadelphia Society

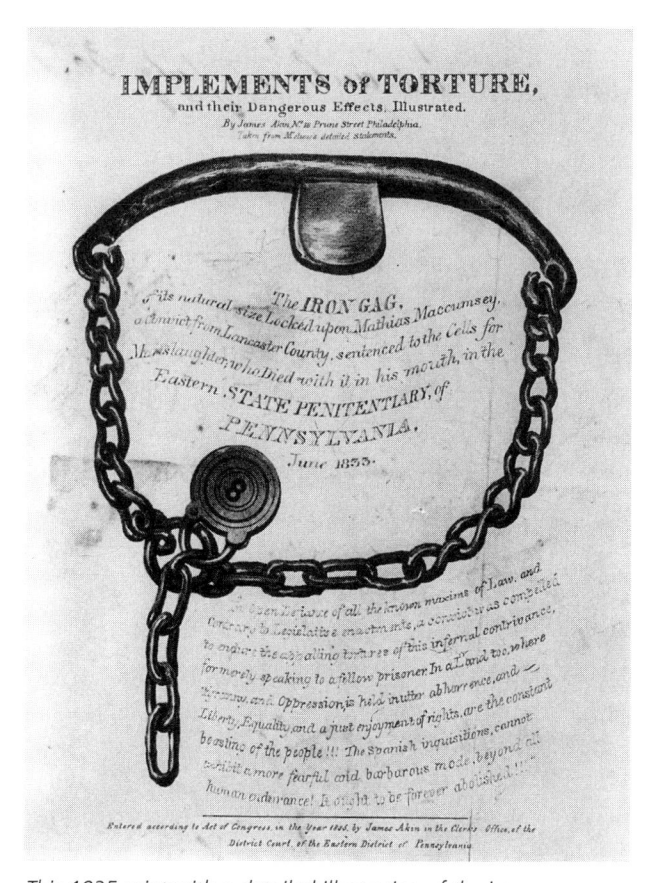

This 1835 print with a detailed illustration of the iron gag torture device used at the Eastern State Penitentiary attributes one prisoner's death to its use and argues for its abolishment.

for Alleviating the Miseries of Public Prisons (supporting Pennsylvania's model). Each took turns explaining how the other was cruel, ineffective, or too expensive. Indeed, while states rarely made a profit on their prisons, many believed the New York model had the potential for positive revenue because wardens could sell the labor of the inmates to the highest bidder. Moreover, the Pennsylvania model, which was in fact much more expensive, was also perceived to be inhumane by some for its use of solitary confinement; it had few supporters outside Pennsylvania. New York built a second prison, Sing Sing, on its own model in 1828, followed by Connecticut at Wethersfield, Massachusetts at Boston, and Maryland at Baltimore. In the 1830s, New Jersey and Rhode Island also adopted prisons largely based on the Pennsylvania model. By mid-century, however, most American prisons had been built on the New York congregate model while most European countries had built prisons on the Pennsylvania separate model.

Regardless of the model, however, inside the prison, not everyone had the same experience. For most of the 19th century, prisons housed both men and women. However, women represented a very small fraction of prison inmates—at Eastern State Penitentiary, they represented about 5 percent of the prison population, with generally a handful admitted each year. Because of their small numbers, officials were not entirely sure what to do with the women. They were generally provided with a separate wing, a large room, an attic, or a separate little house on the property of the prison proper in which they were left to their own devices, which could be both a blessing and a curse, as there was no one to protect them from each other or from unscrupulous guards. Only around mid-century were matrons hired to supervise the women. Because women were generally neglected, their carceral experiences differed from men's in many ways, including a lack of silence or other separations, little if any work to occupy them, and less available exercise or even fresh air. Moreover, female criminals were considered especially bad because of the high moral standards set for women at the time. Additionally, a large portion of female criminals tended to be African American or recent immigrant, groups to which comfortably middle-class individuals often ascribed negative moral attributes. Consequently, in a period that embraced rehabilitation or reformation, even if only in rhetoric at some facilities, female inmates were not frequently intended as the objects of reformation as male inmates were, further differentiating their treatment.

Contrasting Experiences

African Americans and new immigrants also had different experiences with criminal justice generally. Immigrants and African Americans ensnared in the criminal justice system were typically found in northern states as they tended to immigrate to northern states and, in the south, criminal justice for African Americans was largely meted out privately on the plantation. In the north, however, these groups tended to be overrepresented in the prison population (and throughout the larger criminal justice system) relative to their population in the jurisdictions from which they were sentenced. This was likely because of a combination of bias as well as the fact that African Americans and recent immigrants (especially the Irish) were disproportionately poor, uneducated, and members of the lower class, a group that has always been disproportionately represented in the criminal justice system.

The largest difference in experience, however, was that between the north and the south. Most of the developments in criminal law and punishment originated and occurred in the north. Criminal justice in the south was quite different. There were essentially two criminal justice systems in the south. Slaves were generally under the jurisdiction of their owner. Masters had few restrictions on how severe the punishments could be, but the value of their human property typically offered an upper limit; thus, corporal punishment was the primary form of punishment meted out by masters. However, if a slave committed an offense considered especially heinous, or if he committed a crime against someone not in his master's household, the official criminal law held sway. Consequently, well into the 19th century, the south maintained a list of capital offenses that the north had gotten rid of in earlier colonial times, including many petty property offenses and several biblical offenses. As whites were rarely punished, these offered both deterrence and retribution for slaves and free blacks. Some have argued the presence of a sufficiently threatening group—African American slaves—allowed upper-class whites to ignore lower-class whites and the kind of crime threat they were thought to pose in the north. Additionally, the different economic systems—an agrarian slave economy in the south with a more urban, commercial one in the north—led to different goals of the criminal justice system such that the south was less concerned with rehabilitation than the north was. Lacking both a group in need of rehabilitation (like immigrants, lower-class whites, and free blacks in the north) and no economic incentive to have cheap factory-style labor, prisons made less sense in the south. Moreover, southerners saw prisons as antithetical to their celebrated concept of honor, which required men to seek vengeance for crimes against them, and to some extent the southern version of republicanism. Nevertheless, prisons were not unknown in the south. Despite popular opposition to prisons, southern legislators enabled their states to slowly join the north in building prisons, which were primarily reserved for violent white offenders.

Renewed Debate

The emergence of the prison did not entirely quiet the debate over capital punishment. In the early 19th century, reform movements arose against slavery, blood sports, animal cruelty, and other actions considered inhumane, and the movement for the abolition of capital punishment was among them (in some cases, championed by the same sets of individuals). Debates over capital punishment were held live and in the print media of the time. Between 1820 and 1850, states continued to reduce the number of capital offenses. In Maine (1829), Illinois (1832), and Massachusetts (1852), rape was no longer capital eligible. In the north, it was increasingly rare to find anything other than murder or treason listed by 1850. Full abolition was also proposed and was often defeated. The exception was Michigan, which in 1846 abolished capital punishment completely, but only Rhode Island (1852) and Wisconsin (1853) followed suit.

Instead, the major victory in this period won by the anti–capital punishment movement was to relocate executions within the walls of the prison instead of continuing the public spectacle. Not everyone supporting the move was against capital punishment entirely, however. Occasional stories of pickpockets in the crowds at an execution were mentioned by reformers and other interested parties. Commentators also noted that the crowd could be sympathetic to the condemned. Neither of these phenomena showed capital punishment deterring its intended audience. In the early 19th century, as well, arose the concept of the private sphere separate from the public sphere, and increasingly, middle- and upper-class citizens retreated to their homes, avoiding, among other things, the public executions. This changed the demographics of who attended executions, giving the perception that they were immoral, lewd, or disorderly spectacles. Thus, officials began adopting what were called private executions. While these emerged without legislative fiat in some areas, state legislatures began abolishing the public execution, including Connecticut in 1830, followed by Rhode Island, Pennsylvania, New Jersey, New York, Massachusetts, New Hampshire, Iowa, Mississippi, Alabama, Ohio, Vermont, and Delaware, all before 1850—the move was more common in the north than in the south. However, these executions were not exactly private: They were often attended by several hundred upstanding, wealthy, powerful (typically white) male citizens chosen by the sheriff, while onlookers who could not secure an invitation found positions enabling a peek at the execution from beyond the prison or jail yard's walls.

By 1850, the debate between Pennsylvania and New York over prison discipline had cooled, and New York had won. Likewise, the debate over the death penalty was nearing a temporary cessation of activity as the country prepared for more important debates. In the north, nearly every state now had a prison to punish its most serious offenders, but the death penalty had survived, albeit to punish fewer crimes and in a much less public manner.

Ashley T. Rubin
University of California, Berkeley

See Also: American Revolution and Criminal Justice; Auburn State Prison; Capital Punishment; Corrections; Eastern State Penitentiary; Penitentiaries; Walnut Street Jail.

Further Readings

Ayers, Edward. *Vengeance and Justice: Crime and Punishment in the 19th-Century American South.* New York: Oxford University Press, 1984.

Banner, S. *The Death Penalty: An American History.* Cambridge, MA: Harvard University Press, 2002.

Hirsch, Adam J. *The Rise of the Penitentiary: Prisons and Punishment in Early America.* New Haven, CT: Yale University Press, 1992.

Ireland, Robert M. "Privately Funded Prosecution of Crime in the Nineteenth-Century United States." *American Journal of Legal History,* v.39 (1995).

Masur, Louis P. *Rites of Execution: Capital Punishment and the Transformation of American Culture, 1776–1865.* New York: Oxford University Press, 1989.

McConville, Mike and Chester Mirsky. "The Rise of Guilty Pleas: New York, 1800–1865." *Journal of Law and Society,* v.22/4 (1995).

Meranze, Michael. *Laboratories of Virtue: Punishment, Revolution, and Authority in Philadelphia, 1760–1835.* Chapel Hill: University of North Carolina Press, 1996.

Rothman, David J. *The Discovery of the Asylum: Social Order and Disorder in the New Republic.* New Brunswick, NJ: Aldine Transaction, 2005.

History of Crime and Punishment in America: 1850 to 1900

The Civil War era marked an extraordinary period of escalating collective violence throughout the nation. Conservative vigilantism, both urban and rural, and politically oriented gang-related urban violence were omnipresent in most of the country. In the 1840s and 1850s, militant political groups and militias flourished in both the north and the south. Private armies and political militias proliferated. In the election of 1860, Republicans mobilized an army of thousands of uniformed torch-wielding Wide Awakes, whose very existence alarmed both northern Democrats and southern elites. The latter mobilized local militias in preparation for the bloodbath that was to follow. This breakdown in civic trust destroyed the old union and created chaos in the years that preceded secession and the war itself. In such a climate, personal violence and civic warfare escalated and intensified.

While the war put a temporary end to the pattern of urban political warfare, the postwar period was marked by extreme personal and collective violence, especially in the south and the west. While much of the southern violence was related to race and politics and to the devastation that the region had suffered (one-fifth to one-third of southern white males had died in the sectional conflict), collective violence in the west was often tied to battles for hegemony over the region's resources, with range wars or management-labor conflict.

In addition, much of the celebrated outlawry that flourished in the postwar period was tied to the war in some manner: Either the participants were veterans nursing a grudge, battling over political ascendancy in the region, or fighting for specific control over water, grazing, or mineral rights. So while urban gangs became less problematic in the postwar era, outlaw gangs and private armies funded by industrial, ranching, and mining interest became dominant political realities. Some historians call the collective violence of the postwar period the "Western Civil War of Incorporation" and present the period as a continuation of Republican–Democratic political violence.

As the century drew to a close, wealthy plutocrats, aided by sympathetic politicians, had achieved political control and virtual hegemony, and the status of the laborer and the small farmer was in decline. The 1901 assassination of President McKinley, the last Civil War veteran to serve in that office, marked the end of the era. The Progressive Era that followed saw substantial verbiage about change and interest in controlling the manifest abuses of corporate capitalism, though Progressive reform efforts were largely superficial.

Gang and Vigilante Crime and Violence

The decade immediately before the war was dominated by politically oriented urban gang violence. Gangs, almost always affiliated with fire companies, dominated the political process and urban life in many large cities such as New Orleans, Baltimore, New York City, St. Louis, and San Francisco. While gangs like New York City's Bowery B'houys were oriented toward the interests of the workingman and improving his lot and espoused a radical socioeconomic agenda, other voluntary associations like San Francisco's vigilantes were controlled by mercantile interests and were nativist or Republican in focus.

Such political gangs were really private politically oriented and well-organized armies, like the *Freikorps* noted in Weimar-period German history, and fought continuing wars for control of urban politics. They were particularly problematic on election days, when open warfare flourished in some cities. Gangs and allied fire companies marched in uniforms and "colors" featuring patriotic motifs at loud and boisterous political rallies, where overheated and intemperate rhetoric were featured. Voter fraud, bribery, and violent intimidation were the order of the day. For example, during the late 1850s, Baltimore's nativist gangs carried awls with which they intimidated would-be Democratic voters at the polls. Democratic gangs fought back in kind, and both sides continually clashed throughout the decade, using firearms and even small cannons. The city became known as "Mob Town" in the nation's press and developed a fearsome reputation.

Civic warfare was also found in New Orleans, where elected nativists were almost deposed by a revolt of Democratic "vigilantes," led by locals in 1858. Democratic gangs were in the ascendant and ultimately wrested control from nativists at the dawn of the Civil War. The city's endemic civic violence was only temporarily quelled by wartime occupation by Union forces. After the war, New Orleans was the scene of frequent large-scale battles between Democratic ex-Confederates and Union Army of Occupation–controlled municipal police. An unrelated and unique episode of lynching of 11 accused Italian organized crime figures by an elite-controlled mob occurred in 1891. This incident illustrated the fact of Mafia domination of the city's criminal subculture of the era. The general public reacted to impotence of the courts through organized political violence. Eventually, these Italian American syndicates, along with Jewish and Irish gangs, furnished foot soldiers for the Prohibition wars of the Roaring 1920s in New Orleans, and in many other urban locales.

In California, crime flourished in the interregnum between Mexican and American rule. The U.S. Army was spread too thinly, and the territorial-state and federal criminal justice systems were simply not adequate to deal with the crime that occurred in the wake of the 1848 gold rush.

This wood engraving shows a street battle between the rival gangs the Dead Rabbits and the Bowery B'houys at a barricade in Bayard Street in New York City's Sixth Ward. It was published in Frank Leslie's Illustrated Newspaper *on July 18, 1857. Gangs in other cities, such as San Francisco and Baltimore, were often controlled by commercial interests and were more political.*

When the world rushed in to capitalize on the mineral riches of the region, chaos ensued. Groups of citizens, usually funded by mercantile interests, stepped in to enforce a kind of order. In gold rush San Francisco, most vigilante violence was directed against legally elected Democratic office holders or criminal gangs of Australian origin, the Sydney "Ducks." Although civic warfare followed, the mercantile nativist vigilantes prevailed. Their version of what was essentially a seditious rebellion against elected city and state officials prevailed in popular history and mythology. The forces of "law and order" had triumphed over outlawry and corruption. In the nearby gold fields, thieves and violent criminals were subject to the justice of vigilante kangaroo courts and summary execution.

Committees of Vigilance (or Regulators) in the south were instruments of the slaveholding ruling class and were focused on protecting the "peculiar institution" of slavery. This led to using any and all means to reduce the influence of abolitionists and their contrary notions, and quashing real or imagined slave rebellions. Such groups occasionally lynched hapless travelers who muttered reservations about the slave economy, and woe betide slaves who could not give a good account of their actions or whereabouts when questioned by patrols. Actual slave uprisings were suppressed with exemplary medieval cruelty.

The Wild West
Before and after the war, such self-appointed groups, always using extralegal violence, lynched cattle rustlers in Texas and fought range wars such as the Lincoln County War (1878) in New Mexico and throughout the west. Such outlaw luminaries as Billy the Kid and "Doc" Holliday came to notoriety in these conflicts. Holliday, allied with the Earp brothers, was a central figure in Tombstone's famous Gunfight at the O.K. Corral in 1881, but had a history of working as a hired gun and gambler. This particular incident, really a minor skirmish between mercantile-funded Republican gunslingers and populist-oriented Democratic ranchers, has been grossly distorted and immortalized in cinema, television, and even in science fiction. But it was only one episode in a continuing series of battles between ex-Confederates and Unionists in the territories. Lawmen were often gunslingers hired by merchants to impose a version of law and order that strictly supported their interests. Opponents, be they farmers, labor unions, cowboys, or other outlaws, were handled with extreme prejudice.

Outlaw gangs such as the celebrated James and Younger brothers prospered in the chaotic postwar period. During the war, they served as Confederate irregulars with William Quantrill in Kansas and Missouri. After the war, they continued fighting Republican and northern interests in Missouri, Kentucky, Arkansas, and Louisiana. Their many bank robberies drew the attention of the press and the Pinkerton Detective Agency, which began its own reign of terror against the families of the outlaws. In one incident, detectives threw a bomb into the James family home, killing a brother and wounding the Jameses' mother. This only increased their mystique and appeal to southern-oriented farmers who saw the James brothers as latter-day Confederate warriors—a role that the outlaws deliberately fostered and probably believed. On September 7, 1876, the attempt of the James and Younger brothers to rob the First National Bank of Northfield (Minnesota) came to a bad end when they were cut down by armed citizens in the streets. Only the James brothers escaped the shoot-out and the pursuing posse. The Younger brothers were duly imprisoned, while the James gang continued in outlawry but led a low-profile conventional life in Missouri. Jesse James was murdered in 1882, but Frank James lived peaceably until 1915. His passing, coming three years after the admission of old frontier territories Arizona and New Mexico as states, signaled a closing of the chapter of outlawry in the Wild West.

Postwar Racial Violence and Feuding
At the end of the Civil War, much of the south lay in ruins. Many combatants had perished, and their families and dependants were starved, destitute, and demoralized. Additionally, the socioeconomic system had been destroyed, and an army of occupation controlled political and civil institutions. Freed slaves were settling scores within the African American community with unwonted violence. Groups like the Ku Klux Klan (KKK), founded in 1865 in Pulaski, Tennessee, emerged as a source of extreme social control. Its goal was to subjugate newly freed slaves to a status similar to bondage

or peonage. In reality, during their masked night rides, local KKK members (generally not members of any formal or centralized organization) visited violence on blacks, Union sympathizers, and carpetbaggers. Some members also used this opportunity to settle private grudges.

Viewed in a larger perspective, the Klan was a decentralized, poorly organized, extralegal vigilante group intent on enforcing its view of law and order. It was highly effective and not particularly vulnerable to law enforcement efforts because there was no real "head" that could be chopped off by federal efforts, and it was vigorously supported by local whites. Many local sheriffs were supporters or members, and local juries, when primarily comprised of whites, simply would not convict. In some respects, it represented an armed wing of the Democratic Party, and as such, was vigorously suppressed by Union forces and Republican officeholders throughout the Reconstruction period.

The Civil Rights Act of 1871 was specifically aimed at curbing the Klan, but the many decentralized groups of Klansmen had largely ceased their activities by that date. Federal courts in South Carolina continued to successfully try and convict members of the KKK throughout the 1870s. In part, this led to the formation of other, slightly more respectable groups, such as the Red Shirts. This group was formed to engage in public activity to support Democrats and work against any Republican candidates in South Carolina. The efforts of the Klan and groups like the Red Shirts were largely successful in preserving white supremacy as Union troops were withdrawn from the region by 1877. Even the victorious north was at long last exhausted by the continuation of the sectional struggle.

Native Union sympathizers in the south proved vulnerable to state-level pressure during the course of the war and were ostracized by their neighbors immediately thereafter. Much to their chagrin, they were not given much credence by occupying Union forces, and neighbors had long memories. They were generally caught up in the same chaotic forces as ex-Confederates in the postwar period. While some moved west to the territories, others became involved in the famous feuds that plagued the region. The Hatfield–McCoy feud of Kentucky and West Virginia is illustrative of the bellicose tendency of border state denizens. Union loyalists in east Tennessee and North Carolina feuded and fought with former Confederates. Something as mundane as shooting a pig could ignite such a multigenerational conflict. Texas and Louisiana were also inundated by Reconstruction era violence and feuding. In Texas, even the renowned Texas Rangers (not traditional lawmen but a state army that was controlled by large ranching interests) proved inadequate to the task of keeping order in east Texas. Killings involving upper-class citizens were common, some even occurring on courthouse steps. Feuds of this nature lasted well into the 1900s, though the killings eventually abated.

Personal Violence in the Civil War Era

The decades from 1850 to 1900 were some of the most violent and tumultuous in American history. The period saw the erosion of national authority on a number of levels, which contributed to a destabilizing of political discourse and civic culture. Before the war, violent mobs raged in urban centers, guerrilla conflicts tore at the wound of "Bleeding Kansas," and private armies (gangs and vigilantes) kept order by strictly upholding

Mississippi Ku Klux Klan members arrested in 1872 wearing hoods to obscure their identities, but uniforms that are quite different from those used by later incarnations of the Klan.

the interests of the mercantile and slaveholding classes. Moreover, outlawry and violence flourished in California and the territories; in San Francisco, elected officials were overthrown by a commercially funded vigilante coup. Slaveholders believed that the north was intent on eroding their property rights, and some northerners believed that the south would stop at nothing to impose its "peculiar institution" in the territories and would even impose the duty of apprehending and detaining escaped slaves on nonslaveholding states through the Fugitive Slave Act. People of goodwill, north and south, were alienated by overheated secessionist rhetoric of slavery advocates or repelled by absolutist and seditious abolitionist agitation. Slavery and the reaction against it destabilized the already tenuous union between the regions.

Separate cultures and societies had developed and evolved and were moving from a state of cold war into a more militant and less accommodating status. Rumors of slave revolts created a climate of fear and dread among southern whites. The quixotic and bizarre attack on Harper's Ferry by the self-anointed freedom fighter John Brown, an action encouraged and funded by northern industrialists and intellectuals, intensified the anxiety of southern whites and increased their desire to leave the Union. This created a crisis of confidence, or crisis of legitimacy, that filtered downward to all levels of society. Street-level and personal violence became endemic in areas that had formerly been almost violence free, such as the mountain areas of the south. Formerly peaceful farm communities elsewhere were also torn by personal violence. Urban areas, besides coping with the instability that gang violence encouraged, saw increases in personal violence. Violent rhetoric and incidents on the floor of the Senate and the House of Representatives only served to further destabilize the civic climate. After the war, this atmosphere of violence continued to impact the rural south and west, locales where legal institutions remained rudimentary at best.

Management–Labor Violence
Labor unrest, already noted during the early days of the Industrial Revolution, came to the fore in the years following the Civil War. Mercantile interests, in the area of mining and manufacturing, aided by ascendant Republican politicians, exploited labor and violently suppressed workers' efforts to organize. Unions that attempted to obtain humane working conditions and more equitable recompense for their labor were met with lockouts and violent responses from private armies of "detectives," who were actually hired guns. State militias and National Guard troops were also employed to break strikes and protect management strikebreakers. Management–labor disputes metastasized into battles that broke out throughout the nation. In 1886, a peaceful demonstration in support of an eight-hour workday by Chicago workers ended with a bombing that killed one police officer; police gunfire killed seven in the crowd. Several labor organizers, all of whom were probably innocent, were convicted of murder, and four were executed. The Haymarket riot, or "massacre," ended in disaster for the unionists, but created a number of proletarian martyrs and enshrined May Day as a holiday among leftists worldwide.

Another strike in this era ignited a violent struggle between the Amalgamated Association of Iron and Steel Workers and the Carnegie Steel Company in 1892, in Homestead, Pennsylvania. After strikers defeated 300 heavily armed Pinkerton agents, 6,000 state militia troops were imported to retake the factory. In a pattern that became familiar in the following decades, unions were broken due to the use of overwhelming force and other union-busting tactics employed by management. This pattern was repeated numerous times in the post–Civil War period, particularly in coal mining areas and in the west.

The Reformatory Movement
Wartime prisons afforded a point of departure and facilities for the reformation of prisons and the beginning of the concept of "corrections." A former prison for Confederate enlisted men was retooled for the first effort in modern prison reform. The Reformatory movement was a response from the nascent correctional community to increases in crime and the disorders of the era. Begun in the early 1870s at the Elmira Institution in New York by Zebulon Brockway and other penal experts of the era, this movement attempted to build vocational and educationally oriented "reformatories" that would rehabilitate,

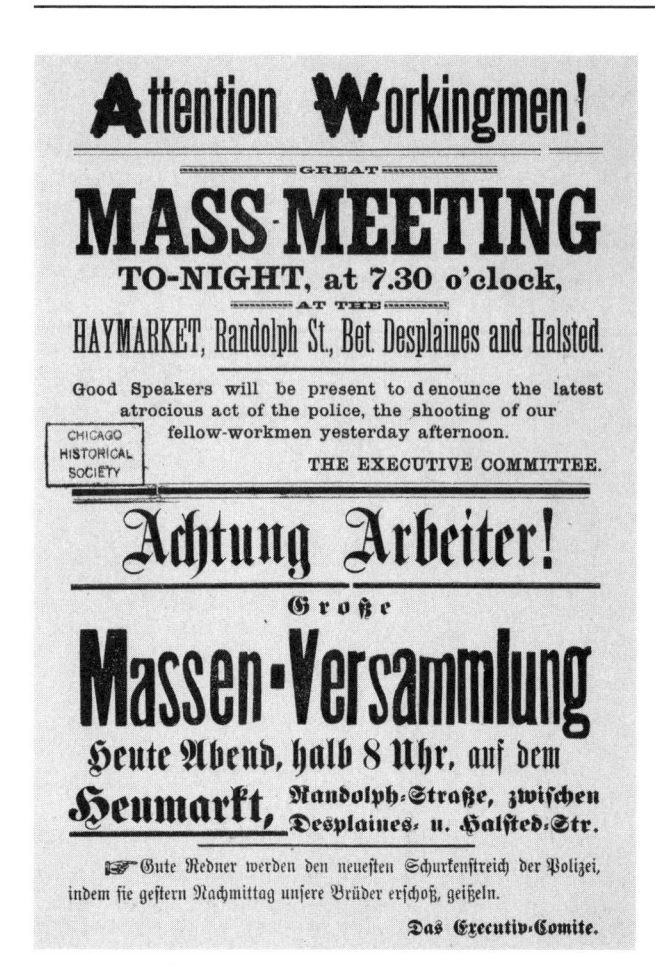

A flier calling for a rally in the Haymarket in Chicago on May 4, 1886, in response to the shooting of seven people the day before. Four labor organizers were later executed for the deaths.

rather than merely punish or confine, the young and first-time offender.

The unstated but nevertheless clear goal was to turn lower-class, mainly immigrant inmates into middle-class-oriented, upwardly mobile, upstanding citizens in the Protestant mold. To that end, a specific plan of progressive steps was developed, aimed at preparing the inmate for a manual labor profession, and efforts were made to ensure employment in the larger community. If inmates were successful in their institutional adjustment, they were granted parole. Parole carried with it certain inviolable conditions involving continued employment and avoiding criminal associations and activities and many inmates failed. When parolees failed on release to community, it produced frustration in the larger community, and by 1900, this experiment was in serious peril. Politicians succeeded in having it so attenuated that true parole and rehabilitation as a goal was effectively abandoned.

Post-Reconstruction Crime and Violence

In the immediate postbellum period, lynching and terrorism were successfully used by some southern whites to reassert political dominance over former slaves. By the mid-1870s, the national government had given up on Reconstruction. After southern whites regained control of the region following the withdrawal of occupying forces in the late 1870s, violent crime rates, like most forms of KKK terrorism, dropped. This was a reflection of a stabilized political climate and the sense, among whites at least, that legitimacy had returned to governance after years of occupation and carpetbag and scalawag rule. The "Redeemers" reestablished Democratic hegemony and white supremacy. This had a calming effect after years of perceived misrule and perceived tyranny. Violence rates among oppressed former slaves continued to be high, however, as they rightly saw the new order as nothing more than old wine in new bottles.

In the years following the Civil War, the use of opiod drugs and alcohol became a major issue in the American narrative for the first time. Racist campaigns against the use of opium by Chinese laborers became a staple of the "yellow press." It was thought that young women were lured into the "white slave trade" by evil Asian criminals who plied them with drugs. Civil War veterans intoxicated on morphine and an easily available cornucopia of patent drugs containing cocaine, opiods, cannabis, poisons, and alcohol became a matter of grave national concern. Respectable housewives and community leaders became addicted to patent medicines and over-the-counter narcotics. A wide variety of laborers—miners, cowboys, sex workers, stevedores, and sailors—frequently used opiods recreationally and for self-medication. The drug industry was extremely influential, and meaningful drug regulation was decades in the future.

Municipal policing, which had begun in eastern and port cities in the 1830s, was still rudimentary and both urban police departments and rural sheriff's offices were often staffed with drunks, incompetents, and political appointees. Ethnic rioting in the 1840s and 1850s gave rise to elite concerns about improving police and putting an end to urban disorder. However, following the war, civil service was not yet a reality and departments were famously inept and corrupt. In fact, one had to bribe politicians in order to get a job as a police officer in some machine-controlled municipalities. Some officers had close associations with urban political gangs. Job security was unknown and officers were at the mercy of elected officials. In some cities, entire departments were fired when a new political party took office. Officers of one ethnicity were typically allied with certain political parties and came to dominate police work. Thus, the Boston and New York Police departments were heavily Irish, while Cincinnati's police were predominately German. Ethnic rivalries were often manifested in police treatment of newly arrived immigrant groups. For example, Jewish merchants were arrested for doing business on Sundays, a violation of Protestant-oriented laws. In addition, police frequently took bribes to protect gambling interests and the sex trade. In general, police were unprofessional and poorly supervised and were not held in high regard by the public.

Cities such as New York, Cincinnati, and New Orleans worked at police reform, but it was only in the first decades of the 20th century that significant change would occur at the local level. On the federal level, agencies such as federal marshals achieved some small successes against racial terrorists in South Carolina in the 1870s and against outlaws on the frontier in that and later decades. In the west, federal marshals were all political appointees and were often heavily influenced by local ranching interests and state-level politicians. Muncipal marshal and sheriffs were similarly controlled by state and local elites and business interests, and generally protected vice in their environs. The cinema-fostered image of the local marshal standing up to irrational forces of violence and disorder is belied by the stark reality of corruption, protection of vice, and gross partisanship that typified law enforcement on the frontier.

Federal revenue agents began serious efforts to combat "moonshining" in this period, but were barely able to contain it. Liquor sales were, and remain, a significant source of federal taxable revenue. On the other hand, federal agents were more successful against mail fraud and counterfeiters, though the Secret Service experienced signal failures in protecting Presidents Garfield and McKinley from assassins.

In the west and throughout the rest of the nation, as old wounds healed and the two-party system returned with a modicum of civility, crime became less problematic as a sense of legitimacy was reestablished. Remaining Native American outliers and dissidents were decimated or pacified; the frontier was secured. Not quite a golden age, as the period experienced depression and labor conflict, the gay 1890s were a period of reconsolidation of the formerly warring regions and a time when ascendant industrialists and ranching interests consolidated control over the vast resources of the west.

Francis Frederick Hawley
Western Carolina University

See Also: 1851 to 1900 Primary Documents; Corrections; Drug Abuse and Addiction, History of; Elmira Prison; Enforcement Acts of 1870–71; Frontier Crime; Gangs, History of; Ku Klux Klan; New Orleans, Louisiana; Penitentiaries; Racism; Slavery; Slavery, Law of; Strikes; Vigilantism.

Further Readings
Ayers, Edward L. *Vengeance and Justice: Crime and Punishment in the 19th-Century American South.* New York: Oxford University Press, 1984.
Brown, Richard M. *Strain of Violence: Historical Studies of American Violence and Vigilantism.* New York: Oxford University Press, 1975.
Courtwright, David T. *Violent Land: Single Men and Social Disorder From the Frontier to the Inner City.* Cambridge, MA: Harvard University Press, 1998.
Cutrer, Thomas W. "Southwestern Violence." In *Encyclopedia of Southern Culture*, C. R. Wilson and W. Ferris, eds. Chapel Hill: University of North Carolina Press, 1989.
Knox, George. *An Introduction to Gangs.* Chicago: New Chicago School Press, 2000.
Lane, Roger. *Murder in America: A History.* Columbus: Ohio State University Press, 1997.
Musto, D. *The American Disease: Origins of Narcotics Control*, 3rd ed. New York: Oxford University Press, 1999.
Richards, Leonard. *The California Gold Rush and the Coming of the Civil War.* New York: Knopf, 2007.

History of Crime and Punishment in America: 1900–1950

By the early 20th century, urbanization and the advent of new technologies meant rapid changes not only for American society but also for American legal culture. With cars to race across state lines, telephones to keep in touch with faraway accomplices, and access to more dangerous weapons like the machine gun, crime could no longer be contained by small, local police forces. The early 20th century saw the expansion of federal involvement in crime fighting, including the creation of the Federal Bureau of Investigation (FBI), and the understanding that crime was a national issue. With new technologies came new crimes such as traffic law, economic and regulatory crimes (so-called white-collar crimes), and the first American drug laws. And finally, new changes in procedure made accused criminals' experience of the legal system dramatically different from their predecessors and much more like the system we have today. The creation of criminal procedure laws and juvenile courts in the early 20th century dramatically shifted how Americans interacted with the criminal justice system, while the idea of constitutional rights and the growing use of probation and parole rendered the process increasingly humane.

With some exceptions such as the Indian Police, U.S. Marshals, postal inspectors, and Internal Revenue Service agents, criminal justice prior to the 20th century was overwhelmingly the business of the states, not of the federal government. To this day, states remain responsible for most matters of crime and punishment. However, since the start of the 20th century, the federal government has increasingly participated in the prosecution of crimes. During the first half of the 20th century, America saw the creation of significant numbers of new federal crimes such as tax evasion, drug offenses, securities fraud, and a variety of regulatory crimes. The early 20th century also witnessed the beginning of an escalating trend of federal involvement, which included regulating interstate crimes, setting national crime policies, and using federal tax dollars to support local law enforcement efforts. In the 19th century, crime was a local problem; by 1950, it was decidedly a national issue.

Legislation

One of the first steps in this direction was the creation of the Mann Act in 1911. Also known as the White Slave Traffic Act, this new federal crime campaign put federal law enforcement efforts into policing the sex lives of Americans—a domain that was previously a state and local concern. While campaigns against prostitution were longstanding, in the early 20th century, fears about immorality mixed with fears concerning immigration. False rumors spread, fueled by muckraking journalists, that foreigners were kidnapping women off the streets, drugging them, and then smuggling the women to brothels across the country in vast, immigrant-controlled networks. The Mann Act made it a federal crime to transport a woman or girl across state lines for purposes of "prostitution or debauchery, or for any other immoral purpose." The broadness of the act and its vague language led to misuse, allowing the prosecution of men for reasons of race or plain old-fashioned adultery. For example, one of the earliest people charged under the act was Jack Johnson, the first African American heavyweight boxing champion, who was found guilty in 1913 of bringing his white girlfriend on a trip from Pittsburgh to Chicago. Another example was the famous *Caminetti v. United States* case decided by the Supreme Court in 1917, in which two young, married men were found guilty of bringing their mistresses on an interstate road trip to California and Nevada.

After the Mann Act, the ratification of the Eighteenth Amendment in 1919 was the next big step in increasing federal involvement in law enforcement. The Eighteenth Amendment made the sale, manufacture, and transportation of alcohol illegal in the United States. While the amendment itself had no teeth, the subsequent Volstead Act or National Prohibition Act packed plenty of bite. The act established the legal definition of intoxicating liquor, as well as the penalties for producing it, and made the sale, distribution, and manufacture of liquor a federal crime. After the passage of the Volstead Act, many states passed their own "little Volsteads," criminalizing the sale, distribution, and

In a photograph taken at the Treasury Department, a man examines moonshine produced by a still that had recently been confiscated by the Internal Revenue Bureau in the 1920s or early 1930s. While enforcement of the Volstead Act was limited, the 13 years of Prohibition led directly to thousands of felony and misdemeanor convictions.

manufacture of liquor at the state level. During the 13 years of Prohibition, thousands of people were tried and convicted of felonies and misdemeanors related to alcohol.

Crime

While acts such as the Mann Act and the Volstead Act signaled the beginning of federal involvement with crime, the 1930s served as the federal government's debutante ball in the world of crime fighting. In his inaugural address in 1929, President Herbert Hoover was the first U.S. president to address crime, proposing the creation of a federal commission to study the problem. The subsequent Wickersham Commission, otherwise known as the National Commission on Law Observance and Enforcement, published 14 reports in 1931 on a variety of criminal justice issues, including police behavior, penal institutions, and the various causes of crime. This commission exposed the abuses of the local and state criminal justice systems and boldly accused them of brutality, corruption, and inefficiency.

The interest of the federal government in crime reflected the new national mood. The Great Depression saw American culture becoming progressively national in a variety of ways. Radio stations began playing more national programs, new chain supermarkets featured national brands making shopping a mass-cultural experience, and Americans increasingly turned to the federal government to solve what was a national economic disaster. Further, long-standing corruption in local police departments had left many Americans jaded concerning law enforcement on the local level. While progressive reformers in this period worked to eliminate police corruption by recommending the centralization of departments, hiring better-qualified personnel through civil service exams and narrowing police functions, the shocking reports of the Wickersham Commission showed how ineffective the efforts had ultimately proven.

Therefore, when on March 1, 1932, the infant son of Charles Lindbergh (the first person to fly solo across the Atlantic and an American hero) was kidnapped and killed by Bruno Hauptmann for ransom, Congress reacted to the national uproar by passing the Lindbergh Act, which created the first federal kidnapping law. Importantly, this act reflected a new national feeling that the federal government and its agencies had a role to play in crime fighting. Further, the rise of national attention to crime syndicates during Prohibition left many Americans with the impression that crime was no longer the mom-and-pop venture it once was. If organized crime was being run along the lines of a business, then America needed a more professional organization to deal with these more professional criminals.

Law Enforcement Professionalization

But when it came to a federal crime-fighting force or facilities, there was little to be found. Prior to 1891, the federal government did not even have any prisons, except for a handful to incarcerate soldiers and sailors in violation of military law. Between 1891 and 1930 only five additional federal prisons were built (one of which was for women.) So in 1930, Congress created the Federal Bureau of Prisons within the Department of Justice and charged it with the management and regulation of all federal penal institutions. Between 1930 and 1940, the federal prison system grew to 24 facilities with 24,360 inmates. The most famous of these new prisons was Alcatraz, built in 1934 in San Francisco Bay. Designed by one of the nation's top security experts, Robert Burge, "The Rock" was as escape-proof as it was forbidding and became the home of such notorious criminals as Al Capone, George "Machine Gun" Kelly, and Robert "Birdman of Alcatraz" Stroud. Even more impressive than the new federal prison system was the start of a new federal bureau to investigate crime. With the expansion of federal crimes in the early 20th century, the head of the U.S. Justice Department, Attorney General Charles J. Bonaparte, asked Congress for the authority to hire investigators in 1908. When Congress failed to give Bonaparte what he wanted, he issued an order from the Justice Department itself organizing a small investigative staff. With the support of President Theodore Roosevelt, who issued an executive order and contributed eight Secret Service agents to this new Bureau of Investigations, the Justice Department made the first steps toward the creation of what is now known as the Federal Bureau of Investigation.

How this small, pencil-pushing group of men would evolve to become a national crime-fighting force is largely found in the story of J. Edgar Hoover. Appointed head of the Bureau of Investigations in 1924, Hoover was determined to shape the bureau into a professional leader of criminal justice. Under his 42 years of leadership, the FBI came to stand for the latest in forensic science and was represented by the new professionalized agent: highly educated, not subject to patronage, and well trained, Hoover's new FBI agents were marketed as new American heroes, only sporting suits instead of cowboy hats. Besides creating the new crime-busting professional, the FBI of the early 20th century pioneered the use of fingerprinting and blood test technology and created the Uniform Crime Reporting (UCR) program—the first program to gather crime statistics from across the country. Further, the new professional law enforcement model was soon emulated by police departments throughout the country, who began to divest themselves of political ties and to focus exclusively on law enforcement activities.

While the earlier progressive reforms had failed to curb police corruption, the movement for professionalization stemming from within local police headquarters met with far greater success. Outside of the development of the federal system, all over the United States the early 20th century saw dramatic changes in criminal justice. Advances in technology and changes in lifestyle quickly brought about new categories of laws to be enforced. For example, the creation of the automobile and the rise of car culture in America led to a new branch of crime: traffic law. In 1905, California became the first state to make driving an unregistered vehicle a crime (soon followed by driving without a license). Most states very

A Federal Bureau of Investigation (FBI) fingerprint analyst in the 1940s. The FBI's other innovations in the early 20th century included blood test technology and the Uniform Crime Reporting program, which collected crime statistics from across the country. Under J. Edgar Hoover's leadership, the FBI furthered the development of forensic science and raised standards for American law enforcement.

quickly followed suit, enacting laws for speed limits and age of licensure and placing restrictions on who could or could not obtain a license (with many barring the "feeble-minded," as well as habitual alcoholics and drug addicts). By 1919, the Dyer Act, or National Motor Vehicle Theft Act, made it a crime to drive a stolen vehicle across state lines or to deal in stolen vehicles that had crossed into another state. And in 1926, New York state created the first in a new category of felonies: drunk driving laws.

Regulatory Laws

The early 20th century also saw the expansion of regulatory crimes—laws that concern the environment, labor regulations, finance, and consumer health and safety. For example, following the stock market crash of 1929, Americans lost most of their faith in Wall Street's ability to police itself. The Securities and Exchange Act of 1934 was designed to restore this faith by demanding financiers "play by the rules" and setting up the Securities and Exchange Commission (SEC) to make sure that they did.

Another of the most important new regulatory laws was the Food and Drug Act of 1906, which made it a criminal act to manufacture and sell dangerous foods or drugs. The act also created the Food and Drug Administration (FDA), although the agency was given little power to criminally prosecute offenders. However, that soon changed as a result of the elixir of sulfanilamide scandal that rocked the nation in 1937. Responding to an outraged public, Congress quickly passed the

1938 Food, Drug and Cosmetics Act, which significantly increased federal authority over drugs by mandating a premarket review of the safety of all new drugs. The act also set new regulatory standards for foods, cosmetics, and therapeutic devices. By the late 1940s, most states had created their own FDAs, and more than 22 states had adopted acts that were patterned after the Food, Drug and Cosmetics Act.

The early 20th century saw the creation of what continues to be some of the most prosecuted crimes in America: drug laws. The very first drug laws were created in local councils and state legislatures, with the first being San Francisco's ordinance against opium dens in 1875. States began regulating drugs under poisons statutes, such as New York's 1905 law that declared cocaine, morphine, and opium to be poisons that could no longer be retailed without a warning label, or California's 1907 amendment of the state's Poison Act to prohibit nonmedical sales of opium and cocaine. However, drugs were quickly picked up as a national concern. In 1909, Congress passed the Opium Exclusion Act, banning the importation, possession, and use of smoking opium. While the act was extremely limited—it banned only opium for smoking but not its use in tinctures and other widely used "medicinal" forms—it was the first federal law banning the nonmedical use of a substance.

Then, in 1914, the Harrison Narcotic Drug Act was passed. Based on the constitutional authority of the federal government to raise revenue as well as tax and to regulate the distribution and sale of narcotics, the act was only a tax statute in form—but its true goal was to end drug trafficking. The act applied to opium and its derivatives as well as to coca leaves and their derivatives and marked the first time that cocaine was placed in the same lethal category as morphine and heroin. Although the Harrison Narcotic Drug Act also included a clause that allowed doctors to continue to prescribe these drugs, the clause was interpreted in the 1919 Supreme Court case *Webb v. United States* as not including prescriptions for those considered to be drug addicts. With the passage of the Harrison Narcotic Drug Act, thousands of Americans who had been legally using narcotics suddenly found themselves labeled addicts and placed on the wrong side of the law. By 1920, an illegal drug economy had emerged in the United States, particularly around cocaine and heroin distribution. In response, Congress passed the Jones-Miller Act, or the Narcotic Drugs Import and Export Act, in 1922, which provided fines of up to $5,000 (equivalent to approximately $65,000 today) and prison sentences of up to 10 years for anyone caught importing illegal narcotics. In 1930, Congress established a Federal Bureau of Narcotics to enforce the Harrison and Jones-Miller Acts. Under the direction of Henry Anslinger, the bureau began a campaign in 1937 against marijuana, modeling the Marijuana Tax Act after the Harrison Narcotic Drug Act. As Anslinger and the bureau stepped up drug enforcement efforts and argued that the illicit drug trade constituted a major national threat, an increasing number of Americans found themselves facing drug charges. By 1935, for example, more than 50 percent of the female inmates in the Federal Industrial Institution for Women in Alderson, West Virginia, were in prison on narcotics charges. The first half of the 20th century was the birth of modern America's war on drugs.

New Takes on Old Crimes

While new crimes were capturing the public imagination, some old crimes were being construed in new ways. One old crime that was "new" again was prostitution. While Congress created the Mann Act to regulate interstate prostitution, reformers in cities across America began vicious crackdowns, which resulted in the destruction of red-light districts and the shutting down of brothels. Prostitution was considered a public health issue, and the tough new stance against it only made the lives of prostitutes more degraded and dangerous. With the closing of brothels, most prostitutes were forced into the streets, where madams were replaced with more brutal male pimps. Labeled as "sex delinquents," prostitutes faced conviction, with first-time offenders often receiving probation while repeat offenders were sent to either workhouses or reformatories. Their male customers, however, were typically given either a small fine or no punishment at all.

Another example is sedition laws, which were dramatically toughened during the first decades of the 20th century. During World War I, Congress passed an elaborate Espionage Act in 1917 and a

Sedition Act in 1918 that outlawed any written or spoken words that were considered "disloyal, profane, scurrilous, or abusive" about the U.S. government, its flag, or its armed forces, or that could potentially cause others to view the American government or its institutions with contempt. But these laws became caught up in a larger campaign against radicals in the United States, particularly against those considered to be associated with socialists, communists, or anarchists. The Industrial Workers of the World (IWW), an international labor organization founded in Chicago in June 1905, was particularly singled out by the new laws. The first prominent cases concerning the right to free speech came out of the prosecutions for these laws, in particular, the illustrious *Schenck v. United States* Supreme Court case of 1919. Charles Schenck, secretary of the Socialist Party in America, distributed 15,000 leaflets to men throughout the United States who were about to be drafted, urging them to resist. In the court's decision, Justice Oliver Wendell Holmes created the infamous "clear and present danger" test, which equated Schenck's assertion of civil rights during a time of war with shouting fire in a crowded theater.

Correctional System
Whether charged with a new crime or an old one, a defendant in the first half of the 20th century faced a different criminal justice system than his or her predecessors. With the increase in federal prosecutions, in 1940 Congress gave the Supreme Court the authority to create procedural rules for the federal courts. Once the federal criminal procedure rules went into effect on March 23, 1946, they were used by states throughout the nation to create procedural regulations of their own. Another feature of the modern criminal justice system was the larger role that constitutional principles, based in the federal and state bills of rights, began to play in criminal law.

Further, dramatic changes had come to fruition in punishment and corrections. While the seeds of parole, probation, and indeterminate sentencing (prison sentences that include a range of time) had been planted in the 19th century, they blossomed in the 20th. By 1925, 46 of the 48 states had adopted parole laws as part of a sweeping national trend to make criminal justice better suited to the individual case, rather than a one-size-fits-all proposition. While the desire to individualize justice was commendable, the results were mixed: Prison sentences actually increased in length, as judges were willing to let people out sooner, but with a variety of conditions. These conditions varied widely and included such measures as those found in Minnesota that barred parolees from buying goods on installment plans, in the state of California that banned parolees from "public speaking," or in Massachusetts that prohibited parolees from living with women to whom they were not married.

But even with conditions attached, most convicted criminals gladly took parole over the appalling conditions of early-20th-century prisons. With epidemic levels of overcrowding, disciplinary measures that included routine floggings and water torture, and infestations of vermin and deadly diseases, early-20th-century prisons were truly horrific places. In 1943, an African American man named Leon Johnson tried to sue for his freedom based on the depraved conditions on a Georgia chain gang. Although the case was eventually overturned by the Supreme Court, the lower federal courts did initially grant Johnson a writ of habeas corpus. The court claimed the conditions on the chain gang were so inhumane, they violated Johnson's Eighth Amendment rights. While overall conditions in prisons did not improve until the 1960s, one reform that did occur during this time was an increase in classifying both prisons and prisoners. The first part of the 20th century saw the rise of maximum-, medium-, and minimum-security prisons, as well as separate facilities for men, women, and children.

Another 19th-century innovation that was realized in the early 20th century was probation. The probation procedure began when either a defendant made a reasonable request for probation or a judge independently decided that probation would likely be the best solution for the defendant. In either case, the judge would turn the case over to a probation officer for investigation. Early probation officers had little to no specialized training, with many states only having vague recommendations that they be over the age of 21, physically and morally fit, and possess a high school education. Probation officers would investigate the prisoner, and often the prisoner's

Secret Service, White House Police, U.S. Coast Guard officers, and Treasury Enforcement Services staff testing out a new target range that had just been completed in the subbasement of the U.S. Treasury Building in Washington, D.C., in June 1940. Increased enforcement of new drug laws in the early 20th century meant growth in both law enforcement and corrections as the century progressed and more and more Americans were being incarcerated on drug charges.

family, and then file a report for the judge's consideration as to whether he felt the defendant would benefit from probation rather than jail. Although the probation system came with its own set of conditions, which often included the scrutiny of a middle-class do-gooder into the intimate details of the lives of the probationer and his or her family, it was a crucial first step to a more professional justice system, as well as a means by which first-time offenders could avoid the horrors of the prison system.

One of the most important innovations of the early 20th century, however, was the creation of the juvenile justice system. The first juvenile law went into effect in Cook County, Illinois, on July 1, 1899, and quickly became the model for juvenile courts throughout the nation and the world. Based on new scientific ideas concerning the development of children and adolescents, the juvenile court was designed to see young offenders brought before it as children in need of help rather than as hardened criminals. This meant that juvenile proceedings did not have the trappings of adult procedures, as every person in the courtroom, from the judge to the probation officer, was supposed to have the child's best interest at heart. Unfortunately, the juvenile justice system conflated delinquency with criminality, and children could be sent to reformatories or subjected to long periods of probation for actions that were not, in fact, crimes—such as skipping school, flirting with strangers, or using profane language. Working-class and immigrant parents also co-opted the courts to help control rebellious children. Parents would sometimes turn in their own children to get help in forcing the child to turn over wages to the family, obey curfew, or act respectfully. For young women, the prevailing sexual double standard meant that most of the girls brought before the courts in the early 20th century were accused of sexual activity, including wearing promiscuous clothing, flirting, and fooling around with boyfriends. Further, probation officers and courts had a highly middle-class perspective of child-rearing and behavior, which often penalized working-class parents and immigrant families who could not conform to their ideals. All this notwithstanding, the creation of the juvenile court system was one of the most important steps to creating a more humane and modern legal system in the United States.

Mariah Adin
State University of New York, Albany

See Also: 1901 to 1920 Primary Documents; Alcatraz Island Prison; *Caminetti v. United States*; Espionage Act of 1917; Federal Bureau of Investigation; Federal Prisons; Great Depression; Harrison Act of 1914; Juvenile Justice, History of; Lindbergh Law; Mann Act; Prohibition; *Schenck v. United States*; Securities and Exchange Commission; Sedition Act of 1918; Uniform Crime Reporting Program; Volstead Act; *Webb v. United States*; Wickersham Commission.

Further Readings
Acker, Caroline Jean. *Creating the American Junkie: Addiction Research in the Classic Era of Narcotic Control*. Baltimore, MD: Johns Hopkins University Press, 2002.
Friedman, Lawrence. *Crime and Punishment in American History*. New York: Basic Books, 1993.
Langum, David. *Crossing Over the Line: Legislating Morality and the Mann Act*. Chicago: University of Chicago Press, 1994.
Lerner, Michael. *Dry Manhattan: Prohibition in New York City*. Cambridge, MA: Harvard University Press, 2007.
Potter, Claire Bond. *War on Crime: Bandits, G-Men, and the Politics of Mass Culture*. New Brunswick, NJ: Rutgers University Press, 1998.
Stolberg, Mary. *Fighting Organized Crime: Politics, Justice and the Legacy of Thomas E. Dewey*. Lebanon, NH: Northeastern University Press, 1995.
Tannenhaus, David. *Juvenile Justice in the Making*. Oxford: Oxford University Press, 2004.

History of Crime and Punishment in America: 1950–1970

Between 1950 and 1970, official crime rates in the United States increased dramatically. During this period, the media brought attention to organized crime and police corruption. In the 1960s, acts previously thought of as private family matters were redefined as domestic violence crimes. Awareness of the victim as the forgotten person in the criminal justice system grew in society, and the victim's rights movement was established. The civil rights movement brought attention to the discriminatory treatment of African Americans by the criminal justice system.

The social response to crime changed in some notable ways. Academics and the general public began questioning the benevolence of the government and the three elements of the criminal justice system—police, courts, and corrections. Police were impacted by several landmark Supreme Court decisions, which dictated that procedural rights be guaranteed to the defendant. In the area of corrections, the prison population grew. Rehabilitation was a dominant approach to treating criminal offenders in the 1960s, and community-based correctional programs grew. Public support for the death penalty dropped, as did the number of convicted offenders sentenced to death.

The Nature of Crime 1950–1970
According to the Uniform Crime Reports (UCR), the rates of both violent (murder and non-negligent manslaughter, forcible rape, robbery, and aggravated assault) and property crime (burglary, larceny-theft, and motor vehicle theft) more than doubled between 1960 and 1970. The violent crime rate rose from 160.9 per 100,000 in 1960 to 363.5 per 100,000 in 1970. Over this 10-year period, the murder rate increased from 5.1 per 100,000 to 7.9 per 100,000. The rate of property crimes skyrocketed from 1,726.3 in 1960 to 3,621 in 1970. Pre-1960 UCR data is not comparable to that collected after 1960. Therefore, UCR statisticians strongly discourage use of these data to compare trends over years prior to 1960.

Criminologists noted that the "official" crime figures from the UCR only counted crimes known to the police. Since many crimes may be unreported, criminologists concluded that the UCR likely underestimated the volume of crime. One approach to understanding the extent and nature of underreporting was to construct victimization surveys, which asked individuals about their criminal victimizations instead of relying on crimes known to the police as the sole source of information about criminal victimization. In 1966, the National Opinion Research Center gave a victimization survey to 10,000 households in the United States for the President's Commission on Law Enforcement and the Administration of Justice. A considerable percentage of persons who told interviewers that they had been victims of crime also told them that they had not reported their victimization to the police. These unreported crimes were labeled the "dark figure of crime." Subsequently, moves to supplement the UCR figures with victimization survey data expanded. These culminated in the development of the National Crime Survey in the early 1970s and the current National Crime Victimization Survey.

Crime and Social Movements

Stemming from the increase in crime rates, the law and order movement of the 1960s emerged. Americans were bombarded with images of political assassinations in the 1960s. Americans became aware of mass murders, as gruesome killings by Richard Speck and the Manson family were broadcast into their living rooms. The law and order movement considered a strong criminal justice system to be the answer to the crime problem. The movement's criticism of the criminal justice system, if any, was that is wasn't harsh enough on criminals. The law and order movement called for various strategies, including strengthening police forces and ensuring that convicted criminals are punished appropriately for their crimes. Their focus was on protecting law-abiding citizens, and they opposed the lenient treatment of criminals that they perceived to be occurring in the United States.

Toward the end of the 1960s, the women's movement formed to advance the rights and roles of women in American society. Part of the mission of the women's movement during this time was to bring attention to the criminal justice system's treatment of women victims of domestic violence and rape. Historically, domestic violence incidents had been viewed as a family matter in U.S. society, and police rarely made arrests in spousal assault cases. In 1965, Morton Bard received a grant from the U.S. Justice Department to advance a method of police response to domestic calls that utilized mediation, not arrest. Bard's work involved the creation of a Family Crisis Intervention Unit that would handle all domestic disputes in a precinct in New York. Officers working in this unit underwent counseling training. When called to a domestic dispute, officers tried to mediate the conflict by separating the couple and speaking to each party separately. Afterward, the couple was reunited as officers tried to have them discuss the situation together and come up with an informal resolution. The training did not involve a directive to arrest the offender (who was usually a male). It was not until the 1980s that arrest was considered an appropriate or preferred strategy for dealing with domestic disputes.

During the 1960s, the women's movement began to bring attention to the crime of rape. Members challenged many myths surrounding the crime and educated the public about the nature of rape. This included dispelling the notion that rape is an act of uncontrolled passion and defining it as a crime of violence. Many feminist groups pointed to a patriarchy and other societal factors as contributing to the prevalence of rape in the United States. A general questioning of male and female roles and the empowerment of women were common themes in the women's movement. The women's movement had a great impact on the definition of crimes and the way the criminal justice system now treats female victims in our society.

Many suggest that it was in the mid-1960s in the context of the children's movement that child abuse was "discovered." Society began to define abuse against children as a social problem. States also enacted legislation outlining the limits to which a child could be physically "disciplined." Children's bureaus within criminal justice agencies were established or expanded to deal with the maltreatment of children. Advocates of the children's movement helped provide living opportunities for children who suffered from abuse in their families. In the 1960s, runaways gained publicity as a serious social problem. During this time, children's rights groups also established runaway shelters in big cities to help youth trying to escape abuse and neglect.

The focus of the civil rights movement was moving toward racial equality in the United States, with a focus on the rights of African American individuals. American history showed overt and covert racially discriminatory practices. The civil rights movement helped educate society about the violence and victimization that African American people have endured, including lynching and other hate-motivated crimes. Like the women's movement, the civil rights movement questioned the legitimacy of our criminal justice system. Both scholars and civil rights activists brought to light racially discriminatory practices of police, courts, and correctional agencies. Research showed how criminal acts against blacks had been ignored by law enforcement and how black victims were in essence devalued. Studies showed that offenders who committed crimes against black victims were given lighter sentences, compared to offenders who victimized white victims. Civil rights activists demanded equal justice, regardless of race. During the 1960s, intraracial crime was "rediscovered," and the impact of rising rates of violent predatory crime was more obvious in black neighborhoods than in white neighborhoods.

The foci of the above movements overlapped with those of the victim's rights movement, which developed in the late 1950s and early 1960s. Social scientists, journalists, government officials, and some members of the criminal justice system brought to light that the victim had become the forgotten person in the criminal justice system, as crime rates continued to rise. At the same time, the Warren Court was handing down one case after another that was viewed by many as letting offenders "get off on a technicality." Victims and their families were dismayed by the lack of attention and respect afforded the crime victim. The victim's rights movement began with several different groups trying to bring attention to the plight of the crime victim and advancing remedies to alleviate the suffering brought on both by criminal victimization and the treatment of victims and their families by the criminal justice system. President Lyndon Johnson appointed a commission to examine crime and the criminal justice system. Victim issues were an important focus of the 1967 President's Commission report. Suggestions for community programs aimed at providing victim services followed.

In the 1950s, legal scholars and criminologists introduced the notion that victims of crime should be compensated financially for the losses they suffered as a result of their criminal victimization. This idea was compatible with the common sentiments in society that the government should aid those suffering from social problems, in this case, crime. Andrew Karmen has noted that public support for victim compensation was triggered by society's outrage to brutal predatory violent crimes happening in the country, which were presented by the mass media during this time. The first state to establish a victim compensation fund was California in 1965. Congress considered arguments for and against establishing federal assistance to state victim compensation funds in 1965.

Police and Corruption

In 1950, a major police scandal was exposed to the general public. On May 10 of that year, a Senate Crime Committee was created and chaired by Senator Estes Kefauver of Tennessee. The Kefauver Committee, as it became known, conducted a widespread investigation into organized crime. Their findings included the revelation that a nationwide crime syndicate existed in the United States. The Kefauver Committee interviewed hundreds of witnesses who testified before them, and people such as Joe Adonis, Frank Costello, and "Lucky" Luciano became known to the general public. Evidence showed that this syndicate was run by the Mafia. The Kefauver Committee also found evidence in many cities across the United States that law enforcement officers were taking bribes to protect gamblers and prostitutes from prosecution. Tales of "gifts" (including thousands of dollars and even a limousine) being given to police chiefs and sheriffs from gamblers outraged Americans who watched the committee's hearings on television. The information gathered by the Kefauver Committee showed the ease with which the underpaid police forces in the nation could be corrupted. The Kefauver Committee called for the end of political domination of police forces.

During this time period, William Parker was appointed chief of the Los Angeles Police Department (LAPD) in 1950. Parker gained a reputation for demanding professional conduct by his officers, and his leadership style served as a role model for many other municipal departments in the United States. In efforts to remedy brutality and corruption by officers in the LAPD and gain public confidence, Parker fired more than 40 officers when he became chief. He also revised selection procedures for police officers, requiring a competitive written examination, physical fitness, and psychological testing. The innovations that William Parker brought to the LAPD were modeled by other American police administrators, whose images had also been tainted by corruption scandals. These strategies included the formation of internal affairs units, the separation of police discipline from politics, the creation of intelligence and research units, the improvement of community relations through innovative programming, and the enactment of a firearms review policy that would review a situation in which weapons were discharged.

Despite significant efforts to professionalize police departments, even toward the end of the 1950s, good police administration concepts applied only to some cities. Community relations programs were lacking in many urban areas. Lingering was mostly white male police officers patrolling predominantly black inner-city neighborhoods.

Although Parker's supervisory style was looked upon favorably overall, the hierarchical form of the department and military style that characterized the police force did receive some criticism.

Frank Costello testifying in 1951 before the Kefauver Committee, which was created and chaired by Senator Estes Kefauver of Tennessee in order to investigate police corruption and organized crime. The committee exposed the existence of a nationwide Mafia syndicate and interviewed witnesses such as Costello and "Lucky" Luciano, who became known to the public because of their testimony.

During the Watts riot in 1965, issues of institutionalized racism and brutality came to the forefront and highlighted lingering problems in police-community relations.

The Civil Rights and Antiwar Movements

The civil rights movement and antiwar movement in the 1960s brought new challenges to police across the nation. During the 1960s, civil rights demonstrations escalated, and riots and civil disturbances often ensued. Student unrest manifested itself in protests of the war in Vietnam and American social conditions and often turned into violent protests on campuses and city streets.

The police were the most visible representatives of formal social control. The way police handled demonstrations and riots was an issue for police departments throughout the country; police across the nation came across as unprepared. The police were ill trained and badly equipped to handle riots. They were criticized by conservatives for being too permissive and accused by liberals of police brutality.

One of the most notable riots was the 1965 Watts riot. The Watts community in Los Angeles suffered from unemployment, substandard schools, high crime rates, and drug problems. In August 1965, Watts was likened to a war zone. It took 16,000 police, highway patrol officers, and National Guard troops to stop the violence. More than 4,000 rioters were arrested in five days; 1,000 people were injured and 34 were killed. There were millions of dollars in property damage, including 250 buildings that were completely destroyed. The Watts riot was not an isolated example of rioting. In 1966, at least 38 major riots occurred in the country. Cities including Chicago, San Francisco, and Cleveland experienced riots. The American public saw police openly discriminating against African Americans in race riots and rarely arresting white perpetrators.

In 1964, a student sit-in demonstration at the University of California, Berkeley, exploded into mass civil disobedience as 830 police officers from a variety of agencies arrested more than 700 people. The students were parts of various groups that held a common goal to protest the Vietnam War. Some groups and individuals went underground and engaged in isolated terrorist tactics. Explosions of governmental buildings killed several innocent people. Violent student unrest swelled, and thousands of demonstrators clashed with the police during the Democratic National Convention in Chicago in 1968. Conservatives blamed student protest movements for problems, and liberals complained of abusive and excessive police action.

The Columbia University protests in April 1968 involved multiple student demonstrations that incited police response. One involved the Students for Democratic Society (SDS) protesting Columbia University's ties with the Institute for Defense Analysis, which conducted research on weapons and was associated with the U.S. Department of Defense. The other involved the construction and design of a university gym that was close to the university in Morningside Park, which protesters (Columbia students and the African American Harlem community) believed was designed to limit access by neighborhood residents and was interpreted as promoting segregation. Both protests escalated to students' occupying several buildings on campus, and counterprotests also developed. On April 30, 1968, several days after the occupation of university buildings, the New York Police Department (NYPD) used violence and tear gas and stormed university buildings. Police response resulted in more than 100 students, four faculty members, and a dozen police being injured and more than 700 students being arrested.

Law enforcement's response to political dissidents was not confined to just local police. Several Federal Bureau of Investigation (FBI) counterintelligence programs, with the acronym COINTELPRO, operated from the mid-1950s until they were revealed publicly in early 1971 by the Citizens Committee to Investigate the FBI in 1971. The activities of COINTELPRO included the covert surveillance and sabotage of political activity that the FBI deemed threatening but that was protected under the U.S. Constitution. Targeted groups included, but were not limited to, the American Indian movement, the Community Party, the Socialist Worker's Party, and black nationalist groups.

Because the Communist Party was illegal in the United States in the 1950s, the Senate and House of Representatives set up committees to investigate and "out" communists. Senator Joseph McCarthy headed the House Committee on Un-American

In the aftermath of riots in Washington, D.C., in April 1968, these National Guard soldiers patrolled the streets. In 1966, at least 38 major riots broke out in cities such as Chicago, San Francisco, and Cleveland, Ohio.

Activities and the Senate Internal Security Subcommittee. When the Supreme Court rulings in the mid-1950s challenged the work of these committees and the constitutionality of the prosecutions related to the Smith Act was questioned, COINTELPRO was established. The FBI was involved in more than 2,000 COINTELPRO missions before it was dismantled in April 1971. When the activities of this domestic counterintelligence program were exposed, there was public outcry, which served to question the benevolence of law enforcement on the federal and local levels.

The Courts

Several landmark decisions concerning the actions of criminal justice actors were handed down by the Supreme Court in the 1960s. Earl Warren served as chief justice of the U.S. Supreme Court from 1953 to 1969 as a liberal majority formed on the highest court in the land. The "due process revolution" described many court decisions that dictated that state and local law enforcement officers and prosecutors be bound by the specific provisions in the Bill of Rights. The decisions made by the court during this period have guided the actions of police officers in arrest and investigation stages and have dictated the circumstances under which evidence can be considered by the courts. Many decisions of the Warren Court ensured the rights of those accused of crimes, and the decisions directed policies of those working in the criminal justice system, as due process became a paramount concern.

Under Chief Justice Earl Warren, the Supreme Court sent a message that criminal convictions would be voided if they were obtained in violation of key amendments to the Constitution. Evidentiary rules concerning the admissibility of evidence involve the Fourth Amendment, which protects against unreasonable searches and seizures, and the Fifth Amendment, which protects the accused against self-incrimination.

In *Mapp v. Ohio* (1961), the Supreme Court overturned Dollree Mapp's conviction, citing the Fourth Amendment's prohibition of unreasonable search and seizure. In this case, the evidence against Dollree Mapp was gathered without a proper warrant, and the court decided it should have been excluded from state trial. This represented the first time the Supreme Court imposed detailed constitutional restrictions on the actions of state law enforcement officials. *Mapp* held that the Fourth Amendment of the Constitution applies to all the states through the due process clause of the Fourteenth Amendment.

In *Gideon v. Wainwright* (1963), the court required that states must appoint counsel for indigent defendants in both capital and noncapital cases.

In *Miranda v. Arizona* (1966), the Supreme Court held that police must advise suspects of certain constitutional guarantees in order to make a confession admissible as evidence. The *Miranda* case involved a 25-year-old mentally handicapped man who was arrested in Arizona and charged with kidnapping and rape. After the police asked him questions for about two hours, he signed a written confession. He was convicted of the crimes and sentenced to 20–30 years in prison. During an appeal, attorneys claimed that Miranda was not told that the statements he made would be used against him. The Supreme Court decided that the statements that Miranda made while in custody and deprived of freedom were inadmissible. Citing the Fifth Amendment provision that no one should be compelled to be a witness against himself (or herself), the majority in a 5–4 decision overturned Miranda's conviction. If the suspect is not warned, subsequent evidence given (spoken or written) can't be admissible in trial.

The implication of this case for law enforcement is that the Miranda warnings must be read to the accused before custodial interrogation and include informing the accused of the right to remain silent, that his or her statements may be used as evidence against him or her, that he or she has a right to an attorney, and that if he or she is unable to afford an attorney, one will be provided.

Police actions in many of the earlier landmark cases had been considered legal by lower courts and appellate courts. Usually by a 5–4 vote, these Warren Court decisions negated earlier precedents and lower court rulings. A police action that was legal one year was often ruled illegal retroactively a year or so later by the Supreme Court. By the 1970s, public opinion polls showed that a most Americans felt that the "pendulum had swung too far to the left," and that court was in effect "coddling criminals."

Imprisonment
Between 1950 and 1960, the prison and probation populations rose, yet prisons offered few professional programs to prisoners. Overcrowding was a major concern within prisons, and the conditions of many prisons were deplorable. Between 1950 and the mid-1960s more than 100 major disturbances or prison riots erupted in U.S. prisons.

Until 1964, the Supreme Court did not rule on the rights of people confined in prison but instead adopted a "hands-off" approach. This followed *Ruffin v. Commonwealth of Virginia* (1871), a Supreme Court decision that established the slave of state doctrine, which characterized inmates as slaves of the state who had no rights, other than those granted to them by the state in which they were incarcerated. Between the time of this ruling and the mid-1960s, the Supreme Court did not accept lawsuits regarding violations of the constitutional rights of inmates.

It wasn't until 1964 in *Cooper v. Pate* that the Supreme Court intervened in the treatment of inmates. This case dealt with religious freedom. Black Muslim inmates said that they were not being allowed to congregate, eat their prescribed religious diet, or wear distinctive clothing. These were important parts of their religion, and prison actions violated Section 1983 of the Civil Rights Act of 1871. The court said that because they are an organized religion and their practicing did not pose a clear and present danger to the security and running of the prison, they should be able to practice. This case signified an end to the hands-off doctrine and recognized that inmates could sue prison officials for violation of their rights under the Constitution. Since this ruling, federal courts have heard many cases on prison conditions.

Between 1960 and 1970, the dominant goal of corrections was rehabilitation. Corrections followed the medical model, in which the offender was viewed as sick and in need of treatment. The focus of rehabilitation is on treating the offender, as opposed to punishing the criminal. Rehabilitation assumes that there are treatment modalities that work to, in effect, "cure" the offender from what caused him or her to commit crime. Some rehabilitation programs focused on individual-level causes of crimes, such as alcoholism, drug addiction, or anger issues.

Alcoholics Anonymous, Narcotics Anonymous, and group therapy programs were instituted in prisons throughout the country during this time. Some prisons offered educational programs ranging from GEDs to college degrees. Others implemented different individual and group counseling programs in an effort to understand and treat the psychological problems that may have contributed to the individual's criminality. The emphasis was on giving the offender tools to become a productive member of society so he or she would not return to crime upon completion of his or her sentence.

Rehabilitation programs go hand and hand with indeterminate sentencing strategies, which were also the norm between 1950 and 1970. Upon conviction for a serious crime, the judge could sentence between a minimum and maximum range, which was often very wide. For example, an offender convicted of robbery could face a sentence of 10 to 20 years. The exact length of the sentence, whether it be 10 years, 20 years, or somewhere in between, would depend on the offender's behavior within prison, plans for the future, and evidence that he or she had been rehabilitated. A discretionary parole board would make this decision and ultimately determined the exact length of the sentence.

Community-Based Corrections

The term *community-based corrections* was introduced in the 1960s. As the term implies, offenders could serve their sentences in the community, under some form of probation supervision, instead of behind bars. The growth of community supervision grew in the 1960s and was compatible with the sentencing goal of rehabilitation, as offenders could take advantage of a wide range of occupational and educational programs and services that were available in the community. Sentenced offenders could also avoid the stigma of "prisoner" by avoiding incarceration. This was a desirable goal in the 1960s, when labeling theory was popular among criminologists. The secondary deviance hypothesis of labeling theory suggests that once an offender is labeled as "prisoner," he or she will internalize that label and act in a way to live up to that label. Serving one's sentence in the community is less stigmatizing for the offender than serving time in prison.

Capital Punishment

The general trend from 1950 to 1970 was a decrease in the number of executions carried out in the United States. While there were 715 executions in the 1950s, only 191 executions were carried out in the 1960s. Public support for the death penalty began to decline in the 1950s and dropped to its lowest level in 1966. A Gallup poll that year indicated that only 42 percent of Americans supported the death penalty.

Challenges to the legality of the death penalty arose in the 1960s. The question of whether the death penalty was per se, or in and of itself, cruel and unusual punishment unconstitutional under the Eighth Amendment was explored in the early 1960s. In *Trop v. Dulles,* a non–death penalty case decided in 1958, the Supreme Court concluded that the Eighth Amendment contained an "evolving standard of decency that marked the progress of a maturing society." Advocates of abolishing capital punishment tried to apply this decision to the use of capital punishment in modern society and suggested that society should no longer tolerate the death penalty.

Liz Marie Marciniak
Nicholas A. Hall
University of Pittsburgh at Greensburg

See Also: Civil Disobedience; Civil Rights Laws; Corrections; *Gideon v. Wainwright*; *Mapp v. Ohio*; *Miranda v. Arizona*; Organized Crime, History of; Riots; Violent Crimes.

Further Readings
Death Penalty Information Center. http://www.death penaltyinfo.org (Accessed September 2011).
Johnson, Herbert A. and Nancy Travis Wolfe. *History of Criminal Justice*. Cincinnati, OH: Anderson Publishing Co., 1996.
Karmen, Andrew. *Crime Victims*. Belmont, CA: Wadsworth Cengage, 2010.
Seiter, Richard P. *Corrections: An Introduction*. Upper Saddle River, NJ: Pearson Prentice Hall, 2011.
Siegel, Larry and Clemes Bartollas. *Corrections Today*. Belmont, CA: Wadsworth Cengage, 2011.
Wadman, Robert C. and William T. Allison. *To Protect and Serve*. Upper Saddle River, NJ: Pearson Prentice Hall, 2004.
Walker, Samuel and Charles Katz. *The Police in America*, 7th ed. New York: McGraw-Hill, 2010.

History of Crime and Punishment in America: 1970–Present

Crime and punishment became fundamental issues in national politics during the 1960s and early 1970s. Amid deep social and economic change and increases in crime, contending political forces sought to change criminal justice policy: Liberals argued that crime was a social phenomenon and that the criminal justice system reproduced and deepened social stratification. Conservatives countered that crime was a matter of individual will and that the system coddled criminals. By the 21st century, incarceration had increased sixfold from its 1973 level, despite the fact that crime rates had returned to pre-1970 levels. Grappling with how this world of crime and punishment emerged is one of the major tasks for those who hope to understand the recent past.

Changing Crime Patterns
Violent crime multiplied in the 1960s and 1970s, with the homicide rate—the most reliable crime statistic—doubling from 1958 to 1974. The belief that violent crime continued to rise unabated thereafter until the 1990s is probably a product of crime statistics, especially the Uniform Crime Report (UCR), rather than reality. The UCR consists of crimes known to the police, collected by the Federal Bureau of Investigation (FBI) from local police. From 1973 to 1994, the total number of UCR crimes doubled, driving this rate steadily upward. This increase was at least in part the ironic product of efforts to professionalize law enforcement that made crime reporting more accurate but also—on paper—made crime rates appear higher. The increased attention to crime led to the 1972 development of the National Crime Victimization Survey (NCVS), which provides more accurate estimations of national crime trends by using surveys of crime victims and sampling techniques. Nonetheless, because only the UCR provides statistics for individual cities, it remains widely relied upon by law enforcement and is a benchmark for most crime reporting.

Homicide statistics and the NCVS show that crime rates were stable between the mid-1970s and mid-1990s. Homicide peaked in the 1930s at a rate of 10 per 100,000 persons; it fell to less than half that level by the end of the 1950s; and it rose back up to the same level in the early 1970s. From 1970 until 1995, the homicide rate fluctuated only 22 percent from its 1980 peak of 10.7 per 100,000. It fell by 20 percent between 1980 and 1984, before it rocketed up again following the arrival of crack cocaine in the mid-1980s to a relative peak rate of around 10 in 1991. Thereafter, a new decline began before it stabilized around 6 per 100,000 persons from 1999 to 2006 (excluding 2001)—55 percent of its peak. Similarly, the nonfatal NCVS violent crime rate varied less than 20 percent from a maximum of 52 violent victimizations per 1,000 persons age 12 or older from 1973 to 1994, with the trends loosely tracking the oscillations of the homicide rate. It peaked from 1979 to 1981, followed by a decline of 20 percent over five years. In the mid-1980s, victimization increased for eight years to a second relative peak near a rate of 50 in 1994, when the present decline began. By 2000, crime was reduced to less than 55 percent of its 1994 high; by 2009, it was less than 33 percent of that high. The rate of property crime as measured by the NCVS (burglary, theft, automobile theft) decreased approximately as much as nonfatal violent crime but demonstrated a slightly different pattern: It declined slowly and steadily from the mid-1970s until it stabilized at less than 30 percent of its high in 2001.

These aggregate trends obscure a host of changes for subsections of the population. The spike in homicide that began in 1958 corresponded with a 42 percent increase in the number of people age 15 to 24 from 1958 to 1967—the young men who would commit and suffer a disproportionate amount of the increased violent crime. Since 1980, there has been an ongoing downward trend in violence among what has become a much larger population of people over age 35 (baby boomers).

As baby boomers aged out of crime, a new group aged in; the rise in violent crime after 1984 consisted almost entirely of an extraordinary increase in violence committed by and against young men.

Over the next 10 years, the homicide rate for African American adolescents age 14 to 17 more than doubled; the rate for African American men from 18 to 24 increased nearly as much. For African American men over 25, however, the rate stayed nearly the same. 1991, the peak homicide year of this period, illustrates the interplay of age, race, and gender. As has been true since 1974, African American victims accounted for 50 percent of all homicides, despite being about 12 percent of the population. The homicide rate was much higher among African American men than white men (71 per 100,000 persons versus 9); much higher among African American men than African American women (72 versus 14);

and much higher among white men than white women (9 versus 3).

The Politics of Criminal Justice

Even the most prescient observer could not have imagined the changes in criminal justice policy after 1970. In 1970, the United States was a world leader in criminal justice reform. Building on an understanding of crime as a by-product of residual social inequalities, Lyndon B. Johnson's Great Society programs sought to reduce crime by incorporating racial minorities and the poor into mainstream society. Government acted to rationalize and professionalize various aspects of criminal justice: protecting the rights of suspects during evidence-gathering by police; passing new criminal laws in areas ranging from reproductive and sexual choices to partner battery; improving the conditions and nature of confinement; and eliminating the death penalty. Many of these actions were the culmination of social movement organizing that demanded the extension of constitutional guarantees to all people, including those in prison. They were supported by growing efforts at criminal justice experimentation and research to provide new evidence on which to base policy choices.

By contrast, crime, riots, and civil disobedience made "law and order" a potent theme for Ronald Reagan in California in 1966 and Richard Nixon nationally in 1968. Opponents of civil rights had long believed that African Americans were predisposed to criminality. As victories against Jim Crow delegitimized outright racism, promoting law and order became a way of identifying racial liberalism and civil disobedience with social disorder. To this chorus were added the voices of criminologists who doubted rehabilitation, and others who believed that "root cause" solutions that saw social reform as the key to reducing crime were incompatible with the continued rise in crime. As conservatives re-evaluated the government's basic capacity to address social problems and called instead for the rollback of the social state, they announced punishment and control, rather than the care and rehabilitation of offenders, as the legitimate aims of penal policy.

This debate over the proper role of the state in social life took place in a moment of dramatic transformation. Over the second half the 20th century, new patterns of inequality were created as racial and class differences became embedded in increasingly sprawling metropolises. Even as the civil rights movement brought gains for some African Americans, including increased political power and new pathways into the middle class, changes in the national (and global) political economy also produced, intensified, and concentrated poverty.

In 1973, wage inequality began to grow for the first time since the 1930s as real wages stagnated for those in the bottom quintiles. Amid these new patterns of stratification, increased social distance, and rising crime rates, Americans engaged in a course of political struggle that transformed the nature of contemporary crime control and criminal justice.

One consequence of the polarization of the 1970s was a punitive turn in public opinion. Just as important, though, was how the political system channeled this change. The weakness of the American social state left the nascent victims' rights movement to focus on punishing offenders, rather than on other methods of redressing crime victims' injuries (like compensation or social assistance). Rights were imagined as a zero-sum game: Criminal procedure decisions that enforced suspects were criticized as injurious to crime victims. Sociological understandings of crime—especially the claims of some prisoners' rights advocates that cast incarcerated people as victims of social injustice—came under withering attack. Within the institutional matrix of American politics, even the efforts of political projects traditionally associated with the political left, such as the women's movement's efforts to reduce domestic violence and rape, were channeled toward punishment-oriented solutions.

Elections of prosecutors and judges similarly focused on punishment as they became increasingly politicized and expensive. Labeling one's opponent "soft on crime" became a devastating tactic, as illustrated by the defeat of California Supreme Court justice Rose Bird, a 1977 appointee of Jerry Brown, in her 1986 retention election. Although it is unusual for judges to lose retention elections, Bird received only 34 percent of the vote after a series of political groups, including one called Crime Victims for Court Reform, spent between $7.5 million and $10 million to defeat her with ads that focused almost exclusively on her opposition to capital punishment.

Expanded crime control and federal involvement were intertwined. The number of congressional hearings on crime each term more than tripled over the second half of the 20th century, and budget allocations grew sevenfold. Federal legislation worked both by giving monetary assistance to the state and by broadening the scope of federal crime control. The Omnibus Crime Control and Safe Streets Act of 1968 marked an unprecedented level of involvement with local crime control. Its administrative creation, the Law Enforcement Assistance Administration, awarded more than $8 billion in grants over 12 years. Since 1968, there have been three omnibus crime bills: the Comprehensive Crime Control Act of 1984, the Crime Control Act of 1990, and the Violent Crime Control and Law Enforcement Act of 1994. Each of these offered financial assistance to state and local government. The 1994 act provided them with more than $30 billion in financing, including almost $9 billion for additional police officers.

Narcotics regulation has been the most important area of federal criminal enforcement since President Nixon declared a "war" on drugs. The organization of federal regulation was set out by the Controlled Substances Act of 1970, which organized drugs into five categories ("schedules") and placed heroin, marijuana, and LSD in "schedule one," as having a high potential for abuse with no legitimate use. Nixon also created the Drug Enforcement Agency in 1973, which saw its budget increase from $74.9 million in 1973 to $1.4 billion in 1999. Illustrating the more fluid politics of the early 1970s, Nixon also passed the Comprehensive Drug Abuse Prevention and Control Act (1970), which reduced penalties for possession of a controlled substance for one's own use to

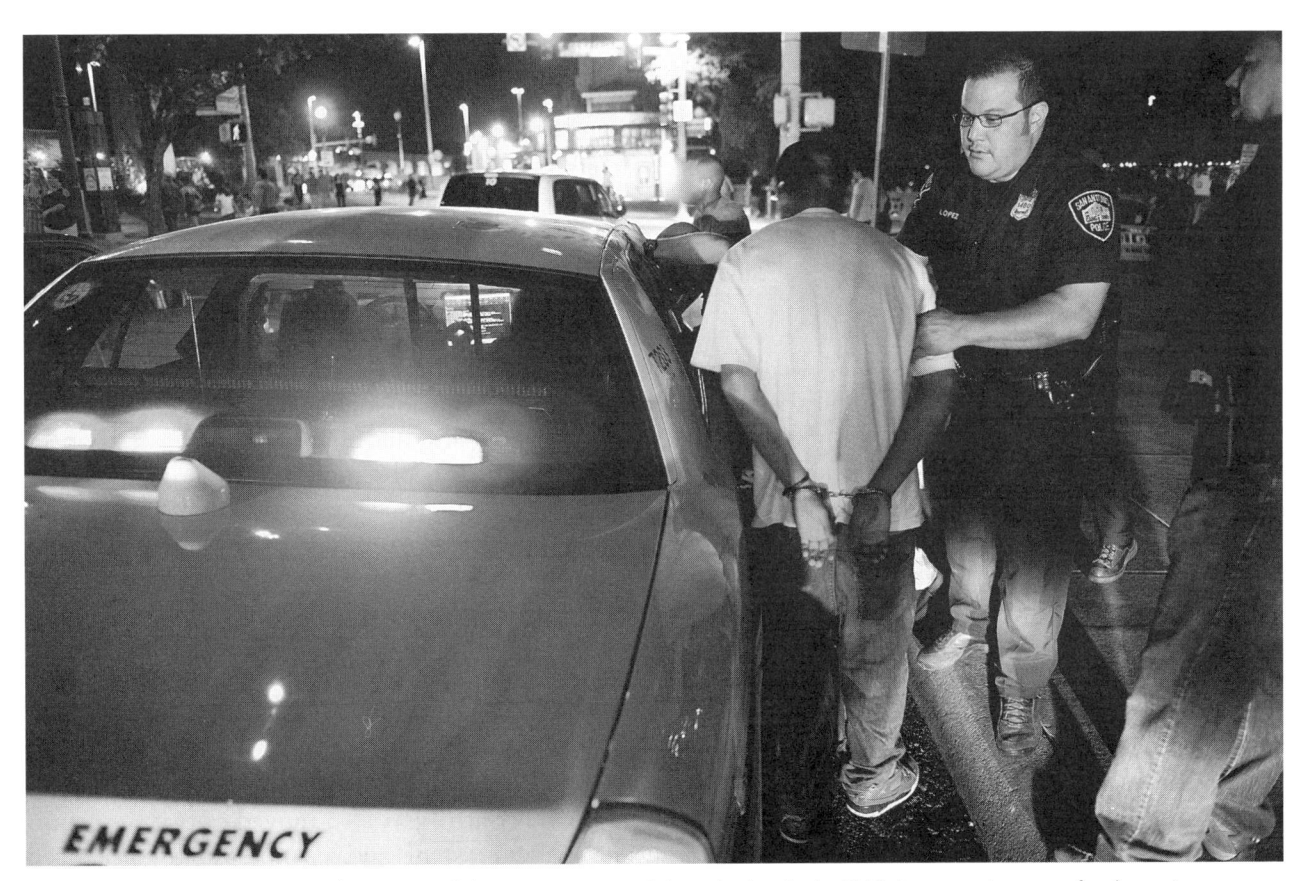

An arrest in San Antonio, Texas, during a crackdown on gangs and drugs in the city in 2010. Incarceration rates for drug crimes since the mid-1980s have increased by a factor of 10 in the United States. In the state of California alone, the number of prisoners incarcerated on drug charges rose from 115 in 1950 to 3,609 in 1985 to 13,741 in 1990.

a misdemeanor. By contrast, in 1973, New York's famously liberal Governor Nelson Rockefeller took the approach that would eventually come to dominate: mandatory minimum sentences of 15 years to life for selling (two ounces) or possessing (four ounces) common street drugs. Mandatory minimums only emerged in federal law more than a decade later out of furor over crack cocaine in the Anti-Drug Abuse Act of 1986 and the Omnibus Anti-Drug Abuse Act (1988).

Federal gun regulation and, since September 11, 2001, fighting terrorism have also been important areas of crime control. Gun regulation began during the Johnson administration and was continued by his successors, including President Reagan. Although the growing political strength of the National Rifle Association was unable to prevent a ban on assault weapons from inclusion in the 1994 Violent Crime Control Act, it prevented the provision's reauthorization a decade later. Changes in constitutional interpretation have further made such regulation more uncertain. The USA PATRIOT Act addressed perceived shortcomings in intelligence gathering and sharing. It authorized the attorney general to intercept communications pertaining to terrorism and allowed greater sharing of matters of foreign intelligence and counterintelligence among agencies. The creation of the Department of Homeland Security in 2002 transformed the organization of federal law enforcement.

Diversity and Innovation

Local police were central to the explosive criminal justice politics of the 1970s, and they remain a focus of conflict today. Police generally have faced two different demands since the 1970s. The first grew out of decades of civil rights activism that accused them of racial bias and sought greater African American control over police departments. These efforts resulted in increased diversification, even if few departments reached parity with the African American or Latino populations of their cities. African American officers now make up 18 percent of policemen, up from 6 percent in 1960. In cities of more than 250,000 residents, officers are 20 percent African American and 18 percent Latino. For women, the story has been more dramatic: from less than 2 percent of officers in *any* major department in 1970, they now comprise 12 to 13 percent of officers. The police have adopted new tactics to address these concerns as well. Strategies like "team policing" in the 1970s and community policing in the 1990s and 2000s developed greater rapport and cooperation between officers and the neighborhoods they police.

Despite improvements, survey research demonstrates that there are still wide gaps in the way whites and blacks view the police, with Latinos falling in the middle. The video recording of Rodney King's beating by Los Angeles Police Department (LAPD) officers in 1991 provided a public demonstration of the excessive use of force about which police critics had complained for years. Although civilian review boards have been proposed since the 1960s as a method of controlling such excess, they have proven largely ineffective and often sustain fewer claims than internal review agencies. The departments that have been most successful at limiting excessive use of force—especially firearms—have been those with strong internal procedures and leadership that is intolerant of brutality. Racial profiling is another persistent issue. Some studies since 2000 have discovered racial profiling in the stopping of cars, while others have identified black drivers as more likely to be given citations, pat-downs, and longer than average stops.

The second demand has been for police to control crime. The past two decades have seen a fervor for police innovation. Although all police departments continue to rely on the standard model of reactive policing to some extent, some have tried new approaches and have demonstrated openness to empirical observation. These include public order policing, such as zero tolerance, in which minor problems are addressed in order to show community intolerance of disorder, and the use of real-time data analyzed by computers (Compstat) or graphic information systems mapping to organize resources and target hot spots. A growing body of evidence supports the effectiveness of various forms of focused policing that target specific types of crimes and locations in reducing crime.

Crime control has also moved out of the criminal justice system and is increasingly practiced by a variety of other institutions. Private police forces, such as corporate security guards, are one such manifestation. The extension of surveillance into the social body includes neighborhood watch groups that began in the late 1960s and multiplied in the 1980s, the proliferation of gated residential communities, and the spread of closed-circuit cameras. Following the spike in adolescent and young adult violence that began in the mid-1990s, other grassroots programs like Operation Ceasefire have tried to prevent youth gun violence.

The Rise of Mass Incarceration
Undoubtedly, the most striking transformation of the period beginning in 1970 is the vast expansion in the number of incarcerated people. For the five decades before 1970, the rate of imprisonment in the United States remained relatively steady, hovering around 100 per 100,000 persons. By 1970, there were more than 300,000 individuals under carceral control in American prisons and jails. Within institutions, prisoners rebelled and used violence to demand changes. These prisoners and their allies used litigation to challenge incarceration and the conditions of confinement, with the belief that they might end the practice altogether. They were highly successful in convincing the federal courts that the constitution did not stop at the wall of the state penitentiary. As recently as 1993, 40 states were under court orders to reduce overcrowding or eliminate unconstitutional conditions.

Such litigation did not result in decarceration. Instead, by 1980, the incarceration rate doubled. More than 25 years later, it had risen more than sixfold, eclipsing 750 per 100,000. Today, there are more than 2.3 million people in prison and jail. More than 7 million people are either in prison, on parole or probation, or under some form of community supervision. Around 8 percent of state and federal inmates are currently incarcerated in privately run prisons, reflecting a precipitous growth rate of more than 1,600 percent since 1990. These institutions are disproportionately concentrated in the south and west. Women make up only 7 percent of inmates, but their rate of incarceration increased twice as fast as men's from 1980 to 2008, growing from 11 to 69 per 100,000. The rate of incarceration in the south is 180 percent of that in the northeast (with the west and the midwest falling between). At the extremes, Louisiana incarcerates its residents at a rate five-and-a-half times greater than Maine. Spending has tripled nationally since the early 1970s.

The great paradox of the post–civil rights era is why African American incarceration has expanded so disproportionately to that of whites after 1970, such that the ratio is now seven to one. This is particularly evident since 1980: At the then prevailing rate of imprisonment, only one-third the number of African Americans would be incarcerated today. Among African Americans, class and likelihood of imprisonment are increasingly intertwined. From the 1970s to the 1990s, the chance that an African American man without a high school education would go to prison by age 35 rose from 17 to 59 percent; with some college education, it fell from 6 to 5 percent. Whites show similar shifts: a high school dropout's chances of going to prison expanded from 4 to 11 percent; with some college, it fell to 0.5–0.7 percent. Latinos are incarcerated at rates lower than African Americans but the rate is still disproportionate to their percentage of the population.

Three mechanisms drove this growth: more imprisonment, longer imprisonment, and changing drug policies. The growth in incarceration rates during the 1980s was caused largely by an increasing likelihood that an offender would receive prison time. More complaints resulted in arrests, and, for violent crimes, the chances that an arrest would lead to time in prison doubled between 1980 and 2001. Later increases were the product of longer sentences. Whereas the ideology of rehabilitation once advised vesting almost complete discretionary authority with trial judges and parole boards, determinate sentencing schemes, such as the federal sentencing guidelines, now dominate. The attack on discretionary sentencing came from liberals, who attacked arbitrary disparities—especially racial disparities—in punishment, and conservatives, who charged that nothing worked in penal rehabilitation and called for greater emphasis on incapacitation. Until the Supreme Court declared mandatory guidelines schemes unconstitutional in 2005, they had become the rule in 17 states since 1978. Other sources of discretion, such as parole, no longer exist in a dozen states beginning with Maine in 1975. Mandatory minimum sentences are widely used, including the mandatory minimums for habitual offenders that flourished in the 1990s. The harshest of these 24 state laws is California's three-strikes provision, which imposes an almost

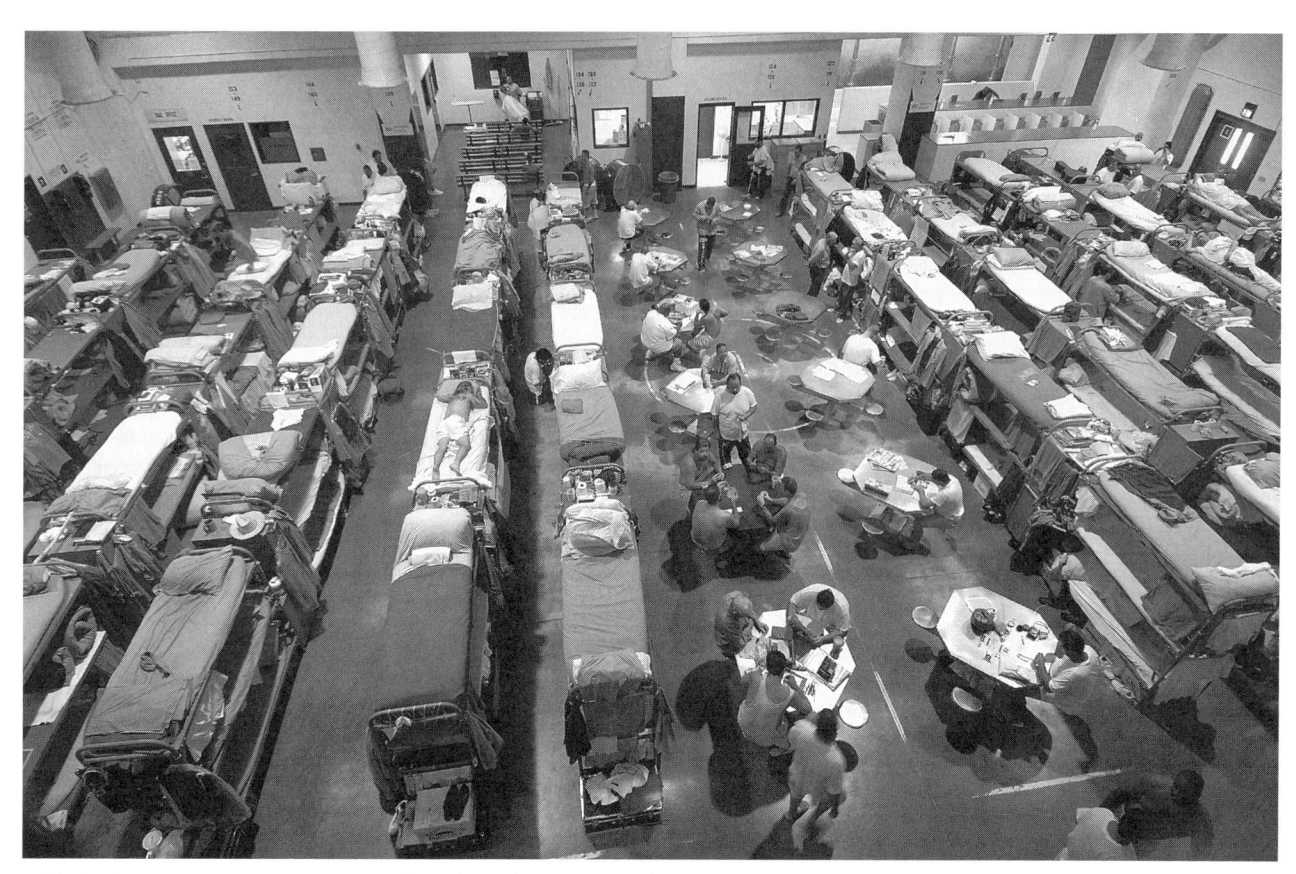

With the increase in incarceration rates throughout the country, Mule Creek State Prison, a California state prison in Ione, California, has suffered from serious overcrowding. This photograph from July 19, 2006, shows bunk beds set up in a common area in order to house some of the prison's population of 3,769. It was originally designed to house only 1,700 prisoners when it was built in 1987.

de facto life imprisonment for a third felony conviction. Truth-in-sentencing laws proliferated after Congress passed the Violent Crime Control and Law Enforcement Act of 1994, providing financial incentives for states to incarcerate prisoners for at least 85 percent of their sentences. Prior to the act, only four states would have achieved its benchmark; this increased to 17 in 1995 and to 27 in 1998.

Prosecution and incarceration for drug crimes since the mid-1980s increased dramatically. Despite public health studies showing decreasing drug use since 1980, the incarceration rate for drug offenses has grown by a factor of 10. In California alone, the number of prisoners incarcerated on drug charges went from only 115 in 1950 to 3,609 in 1985 to 13,741 in 1990. While drug arrests increased 17 percent from 1980 to 2001, prison admissions increased sixfold. Parole revocation because of drug violations doubled as well. Drug offenders are also serving more time. As a result, although drug courts and other programs to divert offenders from incarceration exist, an increasing number of prisoners—more than 20 percent of state prisoners and more than 50 percent of federal prisoners—are now drug offenders.

Racial disparities in incarceration for drugs are a particularly troubling phenomenon. Unlike homicide, where African American men are more likely to be in jail for murder but are also more likely in equal ratio to have committed homicide, increases in drug arrests have little to do with drug usage. African Americans are arrested for drug crimes more often than white people, despite higher rates of drug usage among whites. The ratio of black-to-white arrest rates for drug crimes grew from two to one around 1974 to more than four to one in 1989 before dropping to a little more than two and a half to one in 2000. The increasing predominance of drug offenders among prisoners, their longer sentences, and rates of racial disparity have meant disproportionate increases in African American incarceration.

The Death and Life of Capital Punishment

The course of American criminal justice is perhaps best symbolized by the disappearance and re-emergence of the death penalty. Americans were once world leaders in death penalty abolition, with Michigan being the first sovereign to outlaw it in 1846. While capital punishment remained in use throughout the 20th century, the number of executions steadily declined, from a high of 199 in 1935 to just 21 in 1963. Public opinion turned against it, with support falling from 70 percent in 1953 to just 42 percent in 1966. In *Furman v. Georgia* (1972), the Supreme Court declared the death penalty unconstitutional in its current application and cast its future into deep doubt. Instead, *Furman* opened the door to refining but preserving the maximum penalty. In its aftermath, 38 states reinstated the death penalty, and the Supreme Court found many of these schemes to be constitutional in *Gregg v. Georgia* (1977). A decade later, the court turned back the strongest remaining challenge to capital punishment when it rejected the argument in *McCleskey v. Kemp* that the death penalty was racially discriminatory because it was imposed on people who killed white victims at a disproportionate rate. Post-*McCleskey* challenges have merely rationalized the usage of capital punishment, limiting it to murder and outlawing it for juveniles and the mentally disabled.

Federal and state governments have consistently sought to limit the appeals process in order to make execution quicker and easier. But putting someone to death remains a complicated and expensive process, and states have to be willing to fight in court for years for the right to do so. Since Gary Gilmore's execution on January 17, 1977, American governments have put more than 1,200 people to death. Yet the number executed is a mere fraction of those sentenced to death, which eclipsed 7,700 by the end of 2009. As with other aspects of crime and punishment, state-by-state variation is notable. Texas executes far more often than any other state, with 464 executions since 1977. Virginia (108 executions) and Oklahoma (93 executions) follow closest behind, with the latter executing people at a higher rate per capita than Texas. There remains perhaps some hope for abolitionists. After rising to a post-*Furman* high of 98 in 2000, executions have declined in almost every year. As well, state political and judicial processes have added four states and the District of Columbia to the ranks of the 12 that never reinstated the death penalty.

Peter Constantine Pihos
University of Pennsylvania

See Also: 1981 to 2000 Primary Documents; Capital Punishment; Clinton, William (Administration of); Community Policing and Relations; Crime and Arrest Statistics Analysis; Drug Enforcement Administration; Gun Control; Homeland Security; Johnson, Lyndon B. (Administration of); Nixon, Richard (Administration of); Prisoner's Rights; Reagan, Ronald (Administration of); Sentencing: Indeterminate Versus Fixed; Terrorism; Victim Rights and Restitution; Wilson, James Q.

Further Readings

Bureau of Justice Statistics. http://bjs.ojp.usdoj.gov (Accessed December 2010).
Garland, David. *Cultures of Control: Crime and Social Order in Contemporary Society.* Chicago: University of Chicago Press, 2001.
Gottschalk, Marie. *The Prison and the Gallows: The Politics of Mass Incarceration in America.* New York: Cambridge University Press, 2006.
Simon, Jonathan. *Governing Through Crime: How the War on Crime Transformed American Democracy and Created a Culture of Fear.* New York: Oxford University Press, 2007.
Wilson, James Q. *Thinking About Crime.* New York: Basic Books, 1975.

Holden v. Hardy

Holden v. Hardy was a Supreme Court case argued before the court on October 21, 1897, and decided on February 28, 1898. In this case, the Supreme Court upheld a Utah state law that limited the number of work hours for miners and smelters as a legitimate exercise of the state's police power. The majority held that such a law is legitimate, provided there is a rational basis, supported by facts, for the legislature to believe particular work conditions are dangerous. In making this decision, the court distinguished *Holden* from other cases it had decided up to that time concerning state efforts to limit "liberty of contract." In prior cases, the court had often held such statutes unconstitutional, finding that they violated "liberty of contract" under the due process clause of the 14th Amendment. The opinion was written by Associate Justice Henry Billings Brown (joined by Chief Justice Melville Fuller, John M. Harlan, Horace Gray, George Shiras, Edward D. White, and Joseph McKenna).

The act of March 30, 1896, c. 72, of Utah, provided that "the period of employment of workingmen in all underground mines or workings shall be eight hours per day, except in cases of emergency where life or property is in imminent danger." The statute also provided for "the period of employment of workingmen in smelters and all other institutions for the reduction or refining of ores or metals shall be eight hours per day, except in cases of emergency where life or property is in imminent danger." The law also provided that "any person, body corporate, agent, manager or employer who shall violate any of the provisions of sections one and two of this act shall be deemed guilty of a misdemeanor."

On June 20, 1896, a complaint was made to a justice of the peace of Salt Lake City that Albert F. Holden had unlawfully employed John Anderson as a miner in the Old Jordan mine in Bingham Canyon, in Salt Lake County, for 10 hours a day, in violation of the statute. A second complaint involved Holden employing William Hooley to work as a smelter for 12 hours a day.

Holden was arrested and admitted to employing Anderson and Hooley for more hours than permitted under the statute. However, he argued that he was not guilty because the men had voluntarily agreed to the arrangement, and that the act of the state of Utah establishing the maximum hours limit was unconstitutional. A trial court found Holden guilty, imposed a fine of $50 and costs, and sentenced him to a term of 57 days in the county jail or until the fine and costs were paid.

Holden sought a writ of habeas corpus from the Supreme Court of Utah. The state supreme court denied his application and remanded him to the custody of the sheriff of Salt Lake County. Holden then appealed to the U.S. Supreme Court, seeking a writ of error by challenging the constitutionality of the state law, contending that it deprived him of his property and liberty without due process of law.

In rejecting Holden's petition, Associate Justice Henry Billings Brown wrote that

> This court has not failed to recognize the fact that the law is, to a certain extent, a progressive science; that, in some States, methods of procedure which, at the time the Constitution was adopted, were deemed essential to the protection and safety of the people or to the liberty of the citizen have been found to be no longer necessary; that restrictions which had formerly been laid upon the conduct of individuals or classes had proved detrimental to their interests; and other classes of persons, particularly those engaged in dangerous or unhealthy employments, have been found to be in need of additional protection.

The court concluded that

> Upon the principles above stated, we think the act in question may be sustained as a valid exercise of the police power of the State. The enactment does not profess to limit the hours of all workmen, but merely those who are employed in underground mines or in the smelting, reduction or refining of ores or metals. These employments, when too long pursued, the legislature has judged to be detrimental to the health of the employees, and, so long as there are reasonable grounds for believing that this is so, its decision upon this subject cannot be reviewed by the Federal courts.

As to Holden's argument that the law violated his employees' liberty of contract, the court responded

> It may not be improper to suggest in this connection that, although the prosecution in this case was against the employer of labor, who apparently under the statute is the only one liable, his defense is not so much that his right to contract has been infringed upon, but that the act works a peculiar hardship to his employees,

whose right to labor as long as they please is alleged to be thereby violated. The argument would certainly come with better grace and greater cogency from the latter class. But the fact that both parties are of full age and competent to contract does not necessarily deprive the State of the power to interfere where the parties do not stand upon an equality, or where the public health demands that one party to the contract shall be protected against himself.

While the case established the precedent for states to limit the hours of workers in dangerous occupations, the Supreme Court did not necessarily defer to the states to determine whether danger existed. In a subsequent case, *Lochner v. New York*, 198 U.S. 45 (1905), the court struck down New York state law limiting the working hours of bakers, holding that New York had not demonstrated how longer hours for bakers either harmed them or the public at large.

Jeffrey Kraus
Wagner College

See Also: *Lochner v. New York*; *Muller v. Oregon*; Utah.

Further Readings
Frankfurter, Felix. "Hours of Labor and Realism in Constitutional Law." *Harvard Law Review*, v.29/353 (1915–16).
Freund, Ernst. "Limitation of Hours of Labor and the Federal Supreme Court." *Green Bag*, v.17/411 (1905).
Holden v. Hardy. 169 U.S. 366 (1898).
Summers, Clyde W. "Labor Law as the Century Turns: A Changing of the Guard." *Nebraska Law Review*, v.67/7 (1988).
van Alstyne, William. "The Demise of the Right-Privilege Distinction in Constitutional Law." *Harvard Law Review*, v.81/1439 (1968).

Holmes, Oliver Wendell, Jr.

Oliver Wendell Holmes, Jr., (1841–1935) was a jurist and scholar, and one of the most influential sources of American common law. After serving as an associate and chief justice of the Massachusetts Supreme Judicial Court of Massachusetts and as Weld Professor of Law at Harvard Law School, Holmes served as an associate justice of the U.S. Supreme Court from 1902 to 1932. In these roles, Holmes shaped thinking about crime, punishment, and criminal justice institutions. A proponent of legal realism, Holmes opposed the doctrine of natural law, marking a profound shift in American jurisprudence. A popular figure with American Progressives, Holmes retired from the U.S. Supreme Court at the age of 90, making him the oldest justice in the court's history. His opinions and dissents influenced a great deal of subsequent American legal thinking regarding pragmatism and critical legal studies, both areas that have shaped how criminal justice is conceptualized.

Holmes was born on March 8, 1841, in Boston, Massachusetts, the son of Oliver Wendell Holmes, Sr., an influential writer and physician, and Amelia Lee Jackson, an abolitionist. After studying literature at Harvard University, where he was elected to Phi Beta Kappa, Holmes graduated in 1861 and enlisted in the 4th Battalion of the Massachusetts Militia, then was commissioned as a first lieutenant in the 20th Regiment of the Massachusetts Volunteer Infantry. Holmes saw action in the American Civil War. At the conclusion of hostilities, Holmes again enrolled at Harvard to study law, was admitted to the bar in 1866, and went into private practice in Boston. Holmes's practice focused primarily upon admiralty and commercial law, and he frequently traveled to London, where he became acquainted with the founders of the sociological school of jurisprudence. The sociological approach favored incorporating diverse perspectives, such as sociology, psychology, economics, and political science, into discussions regarding jurisprudence. Holmes became an editor of the *American Law Review* in 1871, and published widely on the common law. During this period, Holmes also formed his view that judicial decision is the only source of law, with the judiciary forced to sometimes draw on premises from outside the law. Holmes briefly served as a professor at Harvard Law School, resigning in 1882 to accept an appointment as an associate justice of the Massachusetts Supreme Judicial Court, of which he was named chief justice in 1899.

Supreme Court justice Oliver Wendell Holmes, Jr., challenged many traditional views of the U.S. Constitution and although he retired in 1932, his influence over American law continues.

While serving on the Massachusetts Supreme Judicial Court, Holmes consistently followed legal precedents, buttressing his views of the common law. When writing about criminal law during this period, Holmes demonstrated his sensitivity to diverse perspectives when contemplating sentencing. Although the law had traditionally supported the position that criminals must be punished, Holmes queried whether the quest to punish criminals might not have the result of degrading them and plunging them further into crime. Holmes suggested that in determining sentences, it might be advisable to focus on the criminal rather than the crime, as traditional methods of punishment and deterrence had little effect upon the "degenerate," yet served chiefly to harm the weak and impressionable. These ruminations, frequently posited in articles or dissents, had great influence.

In 1902, Theodore Roosevelt nominated Holmes to replace Justice Horace Gray on the U.S. Supreme Court. Holmes was unanimously confirmed by the U.S. Senate two days later and has been seen as one of the few such appointments based solely upon the nominee's merits rather than political considerations. Holmes wrote numerous opinions and dissents, many of them relatively short and frequently quoted by lower courts. An ardent supporter of the right to free speech, Holmes limited that right with his opinion in *Schenck v. United States*. The *Schenck* case involved a leader of the Socialist Party of America who had mailed 15,000 leaflets to prospective military draftees entreating them to resist the draft. After being convicted of violating the Espionage Act of 1917, the defendant appealed, asserting that his constitutional right to free speech protected his actions. A unanimous Supreme Court affirmed the conviction, asserting that during wartime, the government possesses extraordinary rights to prevent a clear and present danger that would bring about substantial evils. The following year, however, in the case of *Abrams v. United States*, 250 U. S. 616 (1919), Holmes dissented when the majority of justices upheld the conviction of defendants who had thrown two leaflets denouncing American involvement in World War I from an open window. Holmes explained the difference between the cases as centering on the defendants' requisite intent to cripple the United States' war efforts. He emphasized his belief that the First Amendment only allowed the government to suppress free speech where an imminent threat existed. Although a dissent, Holmes's views have had a wide range of authority.

Holmes challenged many traditional views of the U.S. Constitution, believing that law must develop along with society and that judicial restraint was necessary so that the judiciary would not interpret the Constitution according to their own social philosophy. Holmes felt that for constitutional interpretation, judges must consider experience, including the necessities of the time, the prevalent moral and political theories, and public policy considerations to determine the rules by which the citizenry should be governed. These ideas resonate today, and Holmes remains one of the most influential arbiters of American law. Retiring from the Supreme

Court in 1932 at the age of 90, Holmes died on March 6, 1935.

Stephen T. Schroth
Jason A. Helfer
Cale T. Dahm
Knox College

See Also: *Abrams v. United States*; Blackstone, William; Massachusetts; Roosevelt, Franklin D. (Administration of); Roosevelt, Theodore (Administration of); *Schenck v. United States*.

Further Readings

Holmes, O. W., Jr. *The Common Law*. Mineola, NY: Dover Publications, 1991.

Posner, R. A., ed. *The Essential Holmes: Selections From the Letters, Speeches, Judicial Opinions, and Other Writings of Oliver Wendell Holmes, Jr.* Chicago: University of Chicago Press, 1997.

Schenck v. United States, 249 U.S. 47 (1919).

White, G. E. *Justice Oliver Wendell Holmes: Law and the Inner Self*. New York: Oxford University Press, 1993.

Holt v. Sarver

Holt v. Sarver was a landmark court case that produced a lasting effect on the administration of prison systems in the United States. In the case, the inmates of an Arkansas prison farm filed suit against the state over conditions at the prison, charging that they were exposed to beatings for insubordination, were forced to live in unguarded communal sleeping arrangements, and were supervised by unpaid guards and staff who were themselves prisoners. After years of legal and political wrangling, the federal district court found the Arkansas State Penitentiary System unconstitutional in its administration of the prison and called for striking reform in three specific areas: the trusty guard system, the barracks-style housing of inmates, and the use of isolation cells as punishment. Ultimately, the outcome of the case served to modify how inmates are housed and guarded, and the case represents a significant step in the prisoners' rights movement.

Prior to the decision in *Sarver*, the vast majority of the staff and guards running the prison farm at the Cummins unit, and the smaller but linked Tucker unit, were inmates themselves. Called "trusties," these inmates were in charge of almost every aspect of the prison's day-to-day operations (e.g., monitoring inmates as they worked the farm and preventing escape through the threat of harm). In fact, the criteria for choosing an inmate for trusty status was not based on his criminal record or good behavior, but rather on his willingness to obey the "free-world" staff and employ violence to prevent escape. The control maintained by trusties in the prison over regular, powerless inmates led to an environment in which the trusties could take advantage of other prisoners. Some trusties were even allowed to guard other inmates—occasionally while armed. Extortion, thievery, and sexual assaults were perpetrated and tolerated by trusties with impunity, as they vastly outnumbered the paid, free-world staff. Another problem with the trusty system was that it allowed inmate trusties to restrict access to services and authority figures. Trusties' control of things like phone time or granting access to medical services led to further abuse and victimization of inmates of the Arkansas prison.

Eighth Amendment Rights

The idea of violent inmates guarding other inmates, some of whom were certainly less violent and dangerous, produced an additional problem for the court. In this situation, nonviolent criminals could be housed alongside murderers, rapists, or other violent criminals. A clear example of this was the barracks-style sleeping arrangements referred to in *Sarver*. In open bunkhouses, all sleeping prisoners were at the mercy of their fellow inmates. This placed a great deal of importance on diligent guardianship on the part of the prison staff. Yet at the Cummins and Tucker farms, 90 percent of the staff was made up of inmates, and at night, only two paid civilian guards were on duty. Perhaps not surprisingly, the risks to a sleeping inmate in such a situation were manifested in the form of a high number of stabbings and sexual assaults.

A final specific area of constitutional concern for the federal court was the use of isolation cells as punishment. After a previous court case declared the use of whippings unconstitutional, the isolation cell became the new preferred method to punish poor behavior, refusal to work, or insufficient production. This led to so-called isolation cells that were actually crowded with inmates—sometimes 10 men in a 10-by-8-foot cell. With one concrete, lidless toilet, and men sleeping on cot mattresses on the floor, conditions at such capacities approached cruel and unusual punishment for the court.

The bottom line for the court in *Holt v. Sarver* was inmate safety. The court acknowledged that prison administration is not a simple or pleasant task, that reform takes time, and that insufficient funds are always an issue. Although it was also recognized that prison is inherently a dirty and dangerous place, the findings in *Sarver* established the idea that state governments (as well as prison officials) are obligated to take actions to prevent dangerous situations and unsanitary conditions. In short, *Holt v. Sarver* was at the forefront of a reconsideration of modern correctional justice by emphasizing inmate safety within the conditions of their confinement.

Gabriel T. Cesar
Kevin A. Wright
Arizona State University

See Also: Arkansas; Corrections; Prisoner's Rights; Reports on Prison Conditions.

Further Readings
Boston, John and Daniel E. Manville. *Prisoners' Self-Help Litigation Manual,* 4th ed. New York: Oxford University Press, 2010.
Feeley, Malcolm and Edward Rubin. *Policy Making and the Modern State: How the Courts Reformed America's Prisons.* Cambridge: Cambridge University Press, 1998.
Friedman, Lawrence M. *Crime and Punishment in American History.* New York: Basic Books, 1993.

Homeland Security

Homeland security is a generic term used to refer to efforts designed to protect the American people from terrorist attacks within the United States. Following the 9/11 terrorist attacks, the administration of George W. Bush placed a renewed emphasis on homeland security as a key component of the administration's war on terror. Extensive government resources were poured into the homeland security effort in an attempt to prevent future terrorist attacks. In 2002, the U.S. Department of Homeland Security (DHS) was created to serve as a focal point for federal government actions in this area. Still, homeland security remains an issue that federal, state, and local government officials all must address. The concept of homeland security continues to evolve and now also encompasses government efforts to respond to large-scale natural disasters (e.g., hurricanes and earthquakes) that might also raise security issues on U.S. soil. Homeland security also remains a controversial topic as Americans debate which policies should be adopted to maximize security while still protecting the civil liberties of American citizens.

Institutionalizing Homeland Security
The concept of homeland security did not originate with the 9/11 terrorist attacks. The same functions that today's DHS performs were instead highly decentralized and spread across dozens of federal agencies with little overall coordination. The 9/11 attacks forced the United States to rethink this decentralized approach. Eleven days after 9/11, President George W. Bush announced that he would create an Office of Homeland Security within the executive branch and that it would be led by Pennsylvania Governor Tom Ridge. Bush also proposed a Homeland Security Council staffed by cabinet-level officials that would function as the domestic equivalent of the National Security Council. Senators Joe Lieberman and Arlen Specter introduced a bill in October 2001 designed to establish a Department of Homeland Security, but the bill, opposed by the Bush administration, never passed. Several months later, President Bush came out in support of a cabinet-level DHS. Its main missions would be (1) border and transportation security, (2) emergency preparedness and response, (3) chemical/biological/nuclear countermeasures, and (4) information analysis and infrastructure protection. In June, the Homeland Security Act of 2002 was introduced in Congress and the act was signed into law on November 25, 2002.

While homeland security is a coordinated effort by all levels of government, the focal point at the federal level has become the Department of Homeland Security. DHS began operations in 2003. The government reorganization that created the department was the largest overhaul of the federal bureaucracy in decades. The new department absorbed the functions of 22 agencies and houses such familiar names as U.S. Customs, the Coast Guard, the U.S. Secret Service, the Transportation Security Administration, and the Federal Emergency Management Agency (FEMA). With over 200,000 employees, it constitutes the third-largest cabinet department behind the Department of Defense and the Department of Veterans Affairs. DHS is also responsible for the Homeland Security Advisory System, a color-coded threat level assessment tool ranging from severe (red) to low (blue). The advisory system is designed to provide public awareness when intelligence indicates that terrorist attacks may be more likely to occur.

The creation of DHS has not been without controversy. The agency's budget has grown at an extraordinary pace since its inception. This was especially true in the wake of the 9/11 attacks when safety was at a premium and the government was willing to spend considerable sums of money on homeland security. In 2003, the agency's budget was $29 billion, while the proposed budget for 2011 approaches $45 billion, an increase of roughly 50 percent in a few short years. DHS has been criticized for disorganization and wastefulness. In 2008, Congress estimated that DHS had wasted over $15 billion in agency contracts where services were delayed, over budget, or never delivered at all. Other critics take issue with the allocation of agency resources, worried that the agency focuses too much on defending against civilian air attacks while largely ignoring other potential threats.

One of the most important balancing acts that the United States must consider as it develops homeland security policies is doing so in a way that protects the constitutional liberties of its citizens. Officials are forced to address the question of whether the country is truly at war. To what degree should the military be used in the name of homeland security? Can conventional law enforcement agencies and mechanisms be the primary means to prevent terrorist attacks and bring terrorists to justice? Historically, the United States has primarily treated terrorism as a law enforcement matter. However, since 9/11, Presidents Bush and Obama have used all the government's military and law enforcement resources to identify, apprehend, and punish suspected terrorists. Americans are still engaging in a debate about whether conventional constitutional protections (e.g., warrants for searches, and the right to counsel) should be reduced or even eliminated when individuals are suspected of terrorism.

Observers marking the first anniversary of 9/11 in New York City on September 11, 2002. The terrorist attacks and a move toward centralization led to the creation of the Office of Homeland Security within the executive branch 11 days after the attacks.

Failed Terrorist Attacks

While there have been no successful major terrorist attacks on U.S. soil since 9/11, there have been a number of attempts. Among the more noteworthy is the attempt by Richard Reid, often referred to as the "Shoe Bomber." In 2002, Reid's failed attempt to detonate explosives hidden in his shoes resulted in a life sentence in federal prison. On Christmas Day 2009, Umar Abdulmutallab attempted to detonate plastic explosive hidden in his underwear. Authorities foiled the plot of the "Underwear Bomber" and he remains in federal custody. Government agencies have also been quite active in attempting to identify and apprehend domestic terror groups. One of the more publicized successes involved the capture of the "Lackawanna Six," a group of Yemeni Americans who had attended an Al Qaeda training camp together in 2001. All pled guilty to terrorism-related charges. Some officials have argued that these captures and the lack of another 9/11 is a sign that the United States has been successful in its homeland security policies, while critics often emphasize how these episodes expose many of the flaws in the government's homeland security programs.

Legislation and Government Policies

In the immediate wake of 9/11, the U.S. government passed a number of laws designed to enhance homeland security. On September 14, only three days after the attacks, Congress passed the Authorization to Use Military Force (AUMF). This broad, open-ended mandate authorized President Bush to use force if/when he believed necessary to bring the perpetrators of 9/11 to justice and prevent future terrorist attacks on the United States. The AUMF was subsequently invoked in a war against the Taliban government and Al Qaeda in Afghanistan. The U.S. objectives were to prevent Afghanistan from being a base for future terrorist operations and to capture Al Qaeda leader Osama bin Laden, who was thought to be hiding in the country. Arguing that the federal government needed expanded investigatory powers to fight the terrorist threat, the Bush administration convinced Congress to overwhelmingly pass the USA PATRIOT Act of 2001. The act greatly expanded the power of many government agencies to obtain telephone, electronic, financial, and other records of suspected terrorists. It also eased restrictions on foreign intelligence gathering in the United States while at the same time greatly enhancing the ability of different agencies to share information with one another.

In addition to the new antiterror laws passed by Congress, President George W. Bush's administration also adopted a host of controversial policies as a part of its war on terror. These policies were controversial both because of their subject nature (e.g., warrantless wiretapping and interrogation) and because they were often adopted by the administration unilaterally and in secret. In addition to launching wars in Afghanistan and Iraq, the Bush administration unilaterally decided to use the American naval facility at Guantanamo Bay, Cuba, to house suspected terrorists. The interrogation policies practiced at that facility generated a firestorm of criticism by those who argued that the United States was torturing many of the detainees. Despite repeated public denials, substantial evidence emerged documenting mistreatment of detainees by U.S. personnel. A similar problem at the Abu Ghraib prison in Iraq also revealed the mistreatment of detainees. The Bush administration also adopted a secret warrantless electronic surveillance program shortly after 9/11. The Terrorist Surveillance Program (TSP), as it came to be known, allowed executive branch agencies great leeway to gather electronic foreign intelligence without any judicial supervision or legislative oversight. The program was eventually discontinued when its existence became public.

Sometimes antiterror policies were unilaterally initiated by the Bush administration and then subsequently endorsed by Congress. In November 2001, President Bush announced that some suspected terrorists would be subject to trial before a newly created military tribunal system. Critics of the new system argued that it was a system rigged to produce convictions for the government and that the military tribunals contained insufficient protections for potential defendants. In *Hamdan v. Rumsfeld* (2006), the U.S. Supreme Court struck down this system of tribunals, concluding that they violated both domestic and international law. Congress responded to the court's decision by passing the Military Commissions Act of 2006, creating a military tribunal system that was in many ways similar to the one the court had struck down.

President Barack Obama (center) meeting with the Homeland Security Council at the Federal Emergency Management Agency (FEMA) headquarters on May 29, 2009. He is accompanied by council president John O. Brennen (to his right), Department of Homeland Security secretary Janet Napolitano, and FEMA administrator W. Craig Fugate. Obama was briefed on response and recovery plans for the upcoming 2009 hurricane season.

Future of Homeland Security

For years after 9/11, the focus of homeland security has been the prevention of another terrorist attack with a special focus on Osama bin Laden and Al Qaeda. However, time is likely to change the nature of the threats. Al Qaeda may remain an important threat, but others may emerge as well. For this reason, DHS is slowly transforming its focus from preventing Al Qaeda attacks to a more generic "all hazards" approach to homeland security, which includes responding to large-scale natural disasters such as Hurricane Katrina. Many of the agencies absorbed by DHS have functions that have little to do with terrorism. Emergency management is, and will continue to be, a crucial part of homeland security. This means that DHS and other federal agencies will need to work extensively to integrate their security efforts with state and local institutions and actors. Since 2001, billions of dollars in federal grants have been distributed to state and local agencies to improve their emergency response capabilities. Defining roles and coordinating efforts among different government, nongovernment, and military groups will continue to be an important component of homeland security in the future.

Darren A. Wheeler
Ball State University

See Also: 1981 to 2000 Primary Documents; Bush, George W. (Administration of); Obama, Barack (Administration of); Terrorism; USA PATRIOT Act of 2001.

Further Readings

Bullock, J., et al. *Introduction to Homeland Security*. Oxford: Butterworth-Heinemann, 2008.

Kettl, Don. *System Under Stress: Homeland Security and American Politics*. Washington, DC: CQ Press, 2007.

The 9/11 Commission Report: Final Report of the National Commission on Terrorist Attacks on the United States. New York: W. W. Norton, 2004.

White, Jonathan R. *Terrorism and Homeland Security*. Belmont, CA: Wadsworth, 2011.

Homestead Act of 1862

The Homestead Act of 1862 established one of the most influential models for disposing of public land in American history. Signed by President Abraham Lincoln on May 20, 1862, the Homestead Act entitled settlers to enter a quarter section of undeveloped federal land (160 acres), resulting in the eventual transfer of some 285 million acres of the public domain to private citizens over the course of nearly 125 years. Any head of a family or individual 21 years of age, including both citizens and immigrants filing declarations of intention to become such, were eligible under the act, provided they had never borne arms against the government or aided its enemies. Women who were heads of families, unmarried women, freed slaves, and Native Americans who abandoned tribal affiliations were also eligible to homestead when the act became effective on January 1, 1863.

Prospective homesteaders paid filing and commission fees totaling $14 to claim 160 acres temporarily, after which they were required to continually occupy the land for five years. During this period, the land could not be encumbered and taxes could not be collected, but the homesteader was required to build a dwelling and cultivate the surrounding land. After the payment of a final $4 fee and the voucher of two witnesses attesting that the homesteader had actually resided on the land, the homesteader was granted a title deed for a total amount of $18. Although individuals were entitled to only one homestead under the act, families regularly acquired larger plots by using older sons and daughters to claim adjacent homesteads. In 1872, Congress modified the act, allowing veterans to count up to four years of military service toward the five-year residency requirement. In 1912, Congress reduced the residency requirement to three years. Homesteaders could alternately purchase the land from the government, after six months of residency, for $1.25 per acre.

Like many national policies in the first half of the 19th century, homesteading was embroiled in regional controversy. By 1850, the federal government had gained 1.2 billion acres of public domain land through land purchases and cleared Indian lands. Although the federal government initially used sales of these lands to help bolster the federal treasury, the demand for free land from those hoping to settle the west soon overwhelmed the government's plan. By the mid-1830s, early versions of homesteading legislation had been introduced to Congress. The first bills, however, were met with considerable resistance from the south, which opposed homesteading as unwelcome competition to plantation farming. When homestead legislation finally passed in 1860, the sectional division was clear: In the House, only one supporting vote came from a slave state, and only two free states voted against the bill. Every Republican voted for the bill.

In an attempt to pacify the south, President James Buchanan vetoed the bill. Additionally concerned about the financial stability of the United States, Buchanan justified his veto by alleging the unconstitutionality of the homesteading bill: The low price for the public land was tantamount to giving the land away, a power Congress lacked. Buchanan's veto became an important campaign issue in the subsequent presidential election and was one of the first issues addressed when the next congressional session began in 1861. Although southern opposition remained robust, the secession of several states from the Union following Lincoln's election enabled the Republican majority to pass the final version of the Homestead Act, which became effective the same day the Emancipation Proclamation became law. Notably, the act excluded southern settlers from free lands until after the end of the Civil War.

By prompting the population of rural regions, supporters argued that homesteading would help combat the evils of urban indigence and vice. The act was also considered a remedy for economic harms, in part by benefiting the working class. By producing a new class of small farmers, the provision endeavored to eliminate excess labor and stabilize wages while promoting the economic development of the nation.

Opponents of homesteading feared that giving away vast expanses of land would result in mass migration from the east, leading to an insufficient workforce and depressed land values. Many in the west, conversely, worried eastern states would unfairly profit from their public lands. Others feared that immigrants, whom town developers recruited directly from Europe, would soon overrun the newly available land.

Settlers, too, criticized homesteading, complaining that the 160-acre quarters could not be successfully ranched or farmed.

By the late 19th century, much of the desirable land had already been claimed by war veterans and settlers from eastern states. The remaining quarters lay largely in the arid west, far from water, woods, and markets and transportation. Furthermore, because claims were not systematically evaluated under the Homestead Act and witnesses could easily be bribed, the potential for abuse was high. Land was often claimed to control resources, especially water, and speculators, railroad barons, and swindlers exploited the act to gain control of much of the public domain. In addition to the harsh climate and poor soil, homesteaders also faced hardships from Native Americans, pests, and natural disasters. As a result, only 40 percent of homestead claims resulted in the successful transfer of title. To make farming and ranching more feasible, Congress eventually increased land claims in arid regions to 320 and then 640 acres of public land in 1909 and 1916, respectively.

Notwithstanding the difficulties, homesteading helped expand the western growth of the nation. In all, the Homestead Act made the expansive public domain available to more than 1.5 million people, who claimed and settled a total of 285 million acres, or 10 percent of the landmass of the United States. The Homestead Act remained effective until 1976, when the Federal Land Policy and Management Act was passed, except for Alaska, where homesteading was permitted until 1986.

Matthew H. Birkhold
Princeton University, Columbia Law School

See Also: Buchanan, James (Administration of); History of Crime and Punishment in America: 1850–1900; Lincoln, Abraham (Administration of); Livestock and Cattle Crimes; Native Americans.

Further Readings
Gates, Paul W. *History of Public Land Law Development.* Washington, DC: U.S. Government Printing Office, 1968.
Johnson, Dennis W. *The Laws That Shaped America.* New York: Routledge, 2009.

Hoover, Herbert (Administration of)

Herbert Hoover was the first American president to mention rising crime rates in an inaugural address. Delivered on March 4th, 1929, the speech paid homage to the efforts of Calvin Coolidge's administration to make the United States an influential and respected nation around the world. After the tragedy of World War I, Hoover praised the United States for its achievements in restoring hope abroad and creating a new civilization at home. However, he also expressed concern for the increasing "disregard and disobedience of the law" and the parallel decreasing "confidence in rigid and speedy justice." The president called for a wide-scale investigation in the "entire Federal machinery of justice" and a speedy "reform, reorganization and strengthening of [the] whole judicial and enforcement system."

Only two months after this speech, Hoover appointed George W. Wickersham, the former attorney general in President William Howard Taft's administration, to lead the National Commission on Law Observance and Enforcement (NCLOE). This commission remains Hoover's most significant legacy to the American legal system. Although the president had the merit of proposing a task force to promote a scientific approach to the study of the judicial system and law enforcement, the federal government failed to adopt the findings of the commission as guidelines in a possible reform strategy. In addition, Hoover's judicial appointment of Judge John Parker to the Supreme Court, his constant refusals to accept appeals for anti-lynching laws, and the patent contradictions in the Scottsboro Trials revealed the president's acceptance of a justice system that was discriminatory against African Americans.

Prohibition and the Great Depression

The 1920s and 1930s have been widely referred to as "the lawless decades" or "the crime control decades" because crime became a major political and social concern. The Eighteenth Amendment, which prohibited the making, selling, and possession of alcoholic beverages, and the onset of the Great Depression were largely responsible for making crime and the failure of enforcing existing legislation an obsession for Americans. Historians have concluded that what rose in the 1920s and 1930s was not so much the actual homicide rate or the numbers of property offenses but the perception of these in the minds of American citizens. Because the concentration of famous criminals and their exploits was so great, gangsters, bootleggers, and public enemies became the focus of media and popular attention through highly publicized cases such as the Lindbergh kidnapping and the St. Valentine's Massacre. Although in his inaugural address Hoover maintained that the confidence of American citizens in law enforcement had been declining well before the passing of the Eighteenth Amendment, Prohibition was a big blow to the credibility of the justice system. Not only criminals but also the general public found ways to overwhelm weak enforcement; as with other businesses with eager customers, such as gambling and prostitution, drinking was difficult to outlaw. The attempts to enforce Prohibition unintentionally helped criminal organizations exploit public demand.

Wickersham Commission

Hoover initially formed the Wickersham Commission to investigate ways to more effectively enforce Prohibition. The commission, formed of 11 members, mostly educators and legal experts, soon addressed other important issues in its 14 official reports published throughout 1931. These included the growth of organized crime, abuses in law enforcement practices, deportation laws, child offenders, the American justice system, criminal procedure, penal institutions, the financial burden of crime, and the causes of crime. Although the reports made some recommendations, such as the use of uniform criminal laws and crime statistics,

President Herbert Hoover (third from right in front) with his crime commission in May 1929. The commission went on to publish 14 official reports through 1931, covering such topics as the growth of organized crime, deportation laws, child offenders, the American justice system, criminal procedure, penal institutions, the financial burden of crime, and the causes of crime. The reports made some innovations in their attention to police brutality and their challenge of the presumed connection between foreign citizens and crime.

the commission avoided interpretation of the data in favor of a mere presentation of statistics. The reports were innovative in their criticism of police brutality and in their challenge of the equation between foreign citizens and crimes. However, they failed to suggest ways in which the judicial system could be made fairer and more efficient. In addition, they stubbornly supported the enforcement of the Eighteenth Amendment, even if its poor results were apparent, and the commission denounced abuses linked to Prohibition. The commission also devised the Mooney-Billings Report, which was published privately in 1932 due to political pressures not to make it public. The report denounced the grave violations in the investigation, trial, and conviction of labor activists Thomas J. Mooney and Warren K. Billings for a bomb explosion in San Francisco in 1916 that killed eight people. Although the commission did not claim that the defendants were innocent, it did argue that the law practices to which they had been subjected to were unfair.

Entrenched Racism

After encouraging the establishment of the Wickersham Commission, Hoover and his administration largely ignored its call for a fairer justice system for all citizens. When, at the beginning of the first Roosevelt administration in 1934, the attorney general's Conference on Crime took place, the statistics of the commission went mostly unnoticed. Hoover's administration also showed little attention to the legal protection of African American rights. In 1930, the president appointed Judge John Parker of North Carolina to the Supreme Court, in spite of the judge's endorsement of the disenfranchisement of blacks 10 years earlier. The joint opposition of the National Association for the Advancement of Colored People (NAACP) and the American Federation of Labor (AFL) succeeded in making the appointment so controversial that the Senate rejected it. The Scottsboro Trials, which began in 1931, also provided evidence that the American justice system and society were still deeply racist. The nine African American defendants collectively known as the Scottsboro Boys were accused of raping two white women and were imprisoned for years, although medical evidence showed that the women had been lying and their guilt could not be established irrefutably. Herbert Hoover's State Department had to start an investigation in the face of international outrage and petitions from communists, civil rights activists, and liberals in the United States and around the world. Hoover refused to pardon the defendants.

Luca Prono
Independent Scholar

See Also: African Americans; Prohibition; Racism; Scottsboro Boys Cases; Wickersham, George; Wickersham Commission.

Further Readings

Friedman, Lawrence. *Crime and Punishment in American History*. New York: Basic Books, 1993.
Hatfield, Mark O., ed. *Herbert Hoover Reassessed*. Honolulu, HI: University Press of the Pacific, 2002.
Hoover, Herbert. "Inaugural Address." March 4, 1929. The Avalon Project. http://avalon.law.yale.edu/20th_century/hoover.asp (Accessed June 2011).

Hoover, J. Edgar

J. Edgar Hoover (1895–1972) was born in Washington, D.C., to Anna Marie and Dickerson Naylor Hoover, Sr. He attended George Washington University, where he received his law degree in 1917. Hoover never married and had no children and lived at home with his mother until her death in 1938. Hoover was romantically linked to both Dorothy Lamour, an actress, and Ginger Rogers's mother, Lela Rogers. Many believe Hoover was romantically involved with Clyde Tolson, who was his sole heir and worked for him in the Federal Bureau of Investigation (FBI). These two men rode to and from work together daily and frequently dined and vacationed together. Critics of the homosexual rumors reported that the two men were more like brothers.

Hoover was a member of the Freemasons for 52 years, beginning in 1920, and was awarded several honors by that organization, including being made Master Mason shortly before his 26th birthday. As a lasting tribute, the J. Edgar Hoover Room within the Masonic lodge in Washington, D.C., contains many of Hoover's papers. During

World War I, Hoover went to work for the Justice Department. He was quickly moved to head of the Enemy Aliens Registration Section. He then took over running the General Intelligence Division of the Bureau of Investigation, which would later become the FBI. At the age of 29, Hoover was appointed director of the Bureau of Investigation by President Calvin Coolidge. He remained director until his death on May 2, 1972.

The Ultimate G-Man

Bank-robbing gang members like John Dillinger crossed state lines in stolen cars, opening the door for Hoover and the FBI to investigate them for federal crimes. The FBI did not do a particularly clean job in these investigations, and at least once, the robbers escaped while multiple people were injured and two were killed. When Hoover realized he might lose his job, he paid more attention to the situation, and Dillinger was eventually killed in 1934. During this same time frame, while Hoover denied that organized crime existed, Mafia shootings increased due to the Volstead Act, which prohibited the making, moving, and selling of alcohol throughout the United States. Even into the 1950s, Hoover denied the need for the FBI to focus on the Mafia, which led to much criticism. Jack Anderson, a columnist, exposed the huge crime network. Anderson's reporting linked Hoover to the Mafia as well, for which Hoover harassed him for the next 20 years.

Hoover had the Bureau of Investigation renamed the Federal Bureau of Investigation and given more power in 1935. This was a result of the publicized killings and captures of gangster bank robbers. Within four years of these changes, the FBI excelled in domestic intelligence. Under Hoover, the FBI assembled the largest collection of fingerprints in the world. He also grew the FBI Laboratory, which was created for evidence examination in 1932.

Hoover maintained detailed and controversial secret files on politicians, coworkers, acquaintances, and a number of other powerful people. Because of these files and their possible political repercussions, it is reported that Presidents Harry Truman, John F. Kennedy, and Lyndon Johnson were all leery of firing Hoover. Also contained within these files was the result of surveillance conducted on Eleanor Roosevelt in an attempt to prove she was a lesbian. These files were key in Hoover's ability to gain promotion and avoid negative consequences for his sometimes questionable behavior.

Hoover was obsessed with the idea of subversion. In 2007, documents belonging to Hoover were declassified. In these documents, there was a list maintained by Hoover of approximately 12,000 Americans he suspected of subversion. He had plans to arrest or detain them by suspending the writ of habeas corpus; however, there is no evidence that President Truman accepted his plan.

Hoover believed that citizens should be punished for political affiliations no matter the means of prosecution. To this end, he formed COINTELPRO, or Counter Intelligence Program, which utilized covert operations against American groups that were suspected of subversion or disloyalty. The FBI frequently forged documents or presented false propaganda to aid in this program until 1971, when it became public. Organizations that were infiltrated included the Communist Party, the American Nazi Party, the Ku Klux Klan, the Southern Christian Leadership Conference and Martin Luther King, Jr., the Black Panthers, Students for a Democratic Society, and anti-Vietnam War groups

Espionage

In the late 1930s, the FBI's priority became counterespionage. The FBI began collecting information on German spies, culminating in arrests beginning in 1938. These activities continued during World War II. The FBI was even able to stop a group of Nazi agents when one of these men contacted the agency about a plan to land German U-boats at Florida and Long Island in the Quirin Affair. The Verona Project was a joint endeavor between the FBI and the British government to spy on Soviet spies. The project led to the ability to break some Soviet codes and established that the Soviets were involved in espionage. Hoover reportedly kept the deciphered intercepts from the FBI. He kept them in a safe in his office and only disclosed them in 1952 to the Central Intelligence Agency (CIA).

In 1958, Hoover penned the book *Masters of Deceit: The Story of Communism in America and How to Fight It*. The book was written during the cold war and has a slightly paranoid feel to it with statements such as:

The Party's attack is geared to the wide variety of American life. Communism has something to sell to everybody. And, following this principle, it is the function of mass agitation to exploit all the grievances, hopes, aspirations, prejudices, fears, and ideals of all the special groups that make up our society, social, religious, economic, racial, political. Stir them up. Set one against the other. Divide and conquer. That's the way to soften up a democracy.

This passage only further illustrates Hoover's obsession with subversion and gives a unique insight into his mind.

President Johnson made an exception for Hoover to remain director of the FBI for the rest of his life, waiving the mandatory retirement age of 70. This waiver took place just before Hoover testified in the hearings held regarding the Warren Commission, which was the name by which the investigation of President John F. Kennedy's assassination was known. The FBI, under Hoover's leadership in this investigation, was criticized by the House Select Committee on Assassinations in 1979 for failing to properly investigate any possibility of a conspiracy to kill President Kennedy.

Recognition

J. Edgar Hoover received many awards and honoraria throughout the years from various agencies. These included but were not limited to an honorary doctorate from Oklahoma Baptist University in 1938 and an honorary knighthood by King George VI in 1950. President Dwight Eisenhower gave him the National Security Medal in 1955, and President Johnson gave him the Distinguished Service Award in 1966.

Hoover had requested that he be interred in a Masonic ceremony; however, this request was ignored at the time of his death. In fact, Congress voted that Hoover be allowed to lie in state in the Capitol Rotunda. At Hoover's funeral in 1972, Tolson accepted the folded American flag. Upon Tolson's death, he was interred close to Hoover in the Congressional Cemetery.

Jennifer M. Miller
University of Arkansas at Little Rock

See Also: 1901 to 1920 Primary Documents; 1921 to 1940 Primary Documents; Dillinger, John; Espionage; Federal Bureau of Investigation; History of Crime and Punishment in America: 1900–1950; History of Crime and Punishment in America: 1950–1970; Political Dissidents; Uniform Crime Reporting Program.

Further Readings
Hack, Richard. *Puppetmaster: The Secret Life of J. Edgar Hoover.* Beverly Hills, CA: New Millennium Press, 2004.
Hoover, J. Edgar. *Masters of Deceit: The Story of Communism in America and How to Fight It.* New York: Henry Holt & Co., 1958.
Powers, Richard G. *Secrecy and Power: The Life of J. Edgar Hoover.* New York: The Free Press, 1987.

Hurtado v. California

Hurtado v. California (1884) is an important piece of Supreme Court jurisprudence dealing with the doctrine of incorporation, due process, and the Fourteenth Amendment. The facts of the case surround Joseph Hurtado, who first assaulted and then later killed José Estuardo for an alleged affair Estuardo was having with his wife. Charges were brought up against Hurtado by the state of California, not the federal government, an important fact because Hurtado was eventually convicted by the state and sentenced to death without the initial grand jury indictment that would accompany a federal charge of a capital offense per the Fifth Amendment. Instead of a grand jury proceeding, the state of California had indicted Hurtado under its constitutional provisions that prosecutions as such could proceed based on a prosecutor's statement of information, a procedure that the Supreme Court would later rule is a sufficient substantiation for a grand jury indictment.

Hurtado brought his case to the Supreme Court, arguing that the state of California had denied him his grand jury protections under the Fifth Amendment to the Constitution. At this time, the Bill of Rights did not apply to the states and were binding restrictions only on the federal government. States at the time relied on their own constitutions and legislatures to delineate criminal procedures and rights of the accused. It was not until the early 20th century that the Supreme Court started to incorporate the Bill of Rights onto the states, affirming that the Fourteenth Amendment intended to do as much. Hurtado argued for the doctrine of incorporation, a legal argument dating back to the early 1800s in a Supreme Court case law. Stronger arguments for applying the Bill of Rights to state governments gained more traction after the passage of the Fourteenth Amendment in 1868 but still did not strongly capture the court's attention until the Warren Court (1953–69), known for its protection of civil rights and criminal procedure, began to rule that parts of the Bill of Rights did apply to the states.

The basic argument behind the doctrine of incorporation rests on the language of the Fourteenth Amendment, which emphasizes explicitly that no state shall deny its citizens due process along with the "privileges and immunities" and equal protection of the law. Supporters of the doctrine of incorporation argue that the phrase *no state* by implication meant that state governments were now bound by the Bill of Rights and that this was the intent of the Fourteenth Amendment's framers. Others argue to the contrary and assert that the original purpose of the Fourteenth Amendment was to protect freed slaves from abuse by state and local governments who tried to alienate their black citizens through Jim Crow laws designed to uphold de jure segregation, restrict voting rights, and reaffirm the inferiority of the black race.

Early Supreme Court rulings on the doctrine of incorporation sided with the latter argument. In *Barron v. Baltimore* (1833), for example, the court denied a claim made by a man who had lost business due to actions by the city government on the grounds that there was no indication that the Bill of Rights applied to the states. Even after the passage of the Fourteenth Amendment, the court still did not buy into the doctrine of incorporation argument, ruling in 1873 that the Bill of Rights only applied to the states after a group of butchers filed suit under the Fourteenth Amendment when they had been forced by the City of New Orleans to consolidate their individual slaughterhouses into one central operation.

Hurtado's specific argument was that the grand jury indictment of the Fifth Amendment was incorporated onto the state of California and, additionally, the state had violated the due process clause of the Fourteenth Amendment that clearly applied to states. The majority opinion in *Hurtado*, authored by Justice Stanley Matthews, found that California's provisions for indicting Hurtado were sufficient "due process" to satisfy the Fourteenth Amendment, and the Fifth Amendment separated "grand jury" from "due process" in its language, thus implying the two could be read as mutually exclusive and a grand jury trial was not necessarily a part of due process per se. Also, without an express declaration that the grand jury provisions applied to the states, there was no basis for incorporating them. The dissent in *Hurtado*, written by Justice John Harlan, argued that due process did not mean one thing to the states and another to the federal government and that due process means the same rights are protected in every context.

Jacob Day
Washington State University

See Also: *Barron v. Mayor of Baltimore*; California; Due Process.

Further Readings
Hurtado v. California, 110 U.S. 516 (1884).
O'Brien, David M. *Constitutional Law and Politics: Civil Rights and Civil Liberties*, Vol. 2, 7th ed. New York: W. W. Norton, 2008.

Idaho

A northwestern state admitted to the union in 1890, Idaho is one of the largest and most sparsely populated states in the country. It originated as the Idaho Territory, a remnant of the Oregon Territory after a large chunk of that territory was turned into the state of Oregon. Crime in Idaho is fairly low, in large part because of the small population. In the territorial days, the territory—like the frontier in general—had a reputation for lawlessness, but the sort of frontier chaos detailed in dime novels really depended on some kind of dense settlement like Deadwood or Tombstone, or a disproportionate amount of people and wealth like in gold rush towns, in order to provide sufficient opportunity for crime. Idaho, even in its early statehood, did provide a good hideout for outlaws, rustlers, and train and stagecoach robbers because of its sparseness.

Police and Punishment

The Old Idaho State Penitentiary, also known as the Idaho Territorial Prison, was constructed in the early days of the territory in 1870 and continued to operate for the next 100 years. Originally a single-cell jailhouse to serve the sparsely settled territory's occasional need, it was expanded into a complex of multiple buildings within a sandstone wall built by inmates. The architecture of the new buildings reflects the Romanesque Revival then popular in the country. Its maximum capacity after expansion was 600 inmates. When living conditions in the prison degraded, two violent prison riots in 1971 and 1973 prompted the state to close the Old Pen down, relocating the 416 inmates then incarcerated there to a new, modern penitentiary. The Old Pen was closed at the end of 1973, was placed on the National Register of Historic Places, and is now managed by the state's historical society.

Idaho's sparse population distribution has influenced the development of its police forces, as many settlements, especially in the first decades of statehood, lacked the resources to staff and fund their own modern police department. Even today, most rural communities depend on state agency assistance to handle serious crime when it occurs; the Boise and Coeur d'Alene areas, with the greatest concentration of population, are the exceptions. In 1919, the new state Department of Law Enforcement included the Bureau of Constabulary, which was tasked with criminal investigations, dealing with public nuisances and riots, enforcing court orders, and preventing wrongs to children and animals. The Idaho State Police (ISP) was created 20 years later, with both a patrol division and an investigation division. ISP detectives typically investigate the state's major crimes, like murders, kidnappings, and large-scale drug operations. Other divisions deal with computer crime (Cyber Crimes Unit), commercial trucking laws (Commercial Vehicle Specialists), liquor laws (Alcohol Beverage Control), and forensics support to both state and local police. Only five Idaho state troopers have died in the line of duty since the force's 1939 inception, and of those, one died of a heart attack and two in vehicular accidents.

Crime

During the Progressive era of the late 19th and early 20th centuries, a conflict grew in Idaho centered around the emerging labor unions. In 1896, Frank Steunenberg was elected governor of Idaho, nominated by both the Democratic and Populist parties and supported by the labor unions. He was re-elected in 1898 and oversaw a period marked by labor disputes; because of his administration's support for the unions, many corporations increased wages and gave in to other labor demands because they feared that the government would support the unions in the event of a strike. The Bunker Hill Mining Company was one of the exceptions, and the mining industry in general was the most marked by unrest; when strikers destroyed one of the company's mills, Steunenberg declared martial law and used federal troops to quell the uprising. The unions considered it a betrayal of his promises and ideals, and he did not seek a third term.

Four years after leaving office, Steunenberg was assassinated when a bomb was set off at his front gate. Pinkerton agent James McParland led the investigation at the request of Chief Justice Charles O. Stockslager. A man named Albert Horsley, aka Tom Hogan and Harry Orchard, had set the bomb and had not attempted to flee arrest, but McParland suspected an "inner circle" in the miners union and pitched the Pinkerton agency's services to the mining companies. The subsequent investigation led to the arrest of three of the Western Federation of Miners union leaders using falsified extradition papers, but no case could successfully be made against them, and Horsley was the only one convicted of any crime connected to the assassination.

Idaho made headlines in the 1990s for its sodomy laws, first for the case *Idaho v. Limberhand*, in which a man was arrested for masturbating in

Western Federation of Miners general secretary Bill Haywood and president Charles Moyer with Idaho miner George Pettibone waiting outside the Boise, Idaho, sheriff's office during their trial for the murder of ex-Governor Frank Steunenberg in 1907.

a closed toilet stall by police without a warrant patrolling a rest stop for homosexual activity. The court of appeals ruled that the closed restroom stall constituted sufficient privacy that no crime had been committed. In 1992, the court of appeals evaluated the decision in *Idaho v. Hayes*, in which Brian Hayes had been sentenced to 5–12 years in prison for consensual homosexual sex. Idaho was the only state that still permitted a life sentence for sodomy, and that maximum sentence had impacted the sentence given to Hayes. The appellate court ruled that it was appropriate to issue such a sentence for consensual sex because the wording of the law made no mention of violence or harm but rather was grounded in the premise that homosexual sex is harmful to society inherently, and that the century in which the law had stood on the books without change demonstrated that it represented the wishes of the citizenry of Idaho.

The American Civil Liberties Union (ACLU) began an attempt to repeal Idaho's sodomy law, without success. In fact, subsequent sex offense laws in Idaho reinforced the law's condemnation of homosexuality, including sodomy, on the list of crimes requiring the offender to register with the sex offender registry for life.

Bill Kte'pi
Independent Scholar

See Also: American Civil Liberties Union; Sodomy; Strikes.

Further Readings
Schwantes, Carlos Arnaldo. *In Mountain Shadows: A History of Idaho.* Lincoln: University of Nebraska Press, 1991.
Stapilus, Randy. *Outlaw Tales of Idaho.* Augusta, GA: TwoDot, 2008.
Young, Virgil. *The Story of Idaho.* Caldwell, ID: Caxton Press, 1990.

Identity Theft

Identity theft has become a major crime in the United States, negatively affecting individuals and businesses alike. The Federal Trade Commission (FTC) estimates that around 9 million victims are affected annually. According to the FTC, identity theft is the unauthorized use of ones personally identifying information such as name, Social Security number, and credit card number by someone to commit frauds or other crimes. Identity theft can cause major disruptions to a person's health, business, finance, and life. It is important to detect identity theft as soon as possible by monitoring one's credit report regularly. Identity theft will require a great deal of time, energy, and resources for the victims to recover from the theft.

While there is no established record of the first case of identity theft, the *Oxford English Dictionary* notes that the phrase was coined in 1964. Identity theft can happen in different ways. The thieves can use the victim's name to rent housing, set up phone lines, or open a credit card account. Unless one monitors credit reports diligently, the victim might not know about the theft until a debt collector contacts them or he or she receive bills for charges they did not make.

Identity theft has become a lucrative business, and causes adverse financial burdens for its victims. Some victims might have to pay hundreds of dollars and spend days recuperating their credit and life from the theft. As a result of identity theft, some victims can also be denied housing or job opportunities, education loans, and the like.

Methods
Identity thieves have several ways to obtain a victim's information. The FTC lists the following methods: dumpster diving, skimming, phishing, address changing, old-fashioned stealing, and pretexting. With dumpster diving, the identity thieves search through garbage for bills and other documents with the victim's personal information on it. The thieves can also use skimming to extract information from ones credit or debit card numbers with a special storage device when processing your card. In phishing, they are disguised as financial institutions or businesses sending the victim spam or pop-up messages to get he or she to give out their personal information. The thieves can also change a victim's address to redirect billing statements to a different location by filing a change of address. Thieves also use old-fashioned stealing, including misappropriating wallets, purses, bank and credit card statements, preapproved credit offers, new checks, or tax information. They can also steal personal records or bribe those with access to them. Pretexting takes place when thieves make false pretenses to acquire personal information from financial agencies, telephone companies, and other places.

After the thieves have stolen the victim's personal information, they can use it in a multitude of ways. Some of the most common ways include credit card fraud, phone or utilities fraud, bank/finance fraud, and government documents fraud. In a credit card fraud, the thieves may open new credit cards in the victim's name, whose bills they might not pay, resulting in delinquent accounts listed in your credit report. They may change the billing address on the victim's credit card and incur charges. Since the victim no longer receive bills, he or she would not notice the problem immediately.

Phone or utilities fraud takes place when an account is opened in a victim's name or when charges take place in an existing account without his or her knowledge. The thieves can use this name to sign up for utility services such as electricity, heating, cable TV, or gas. Bank/finance frauds involve the thieves' creating counterfeit checks with a victim's name and account number, or opening a bank account in his or her name and writing bad checks. They might also clone ATM or debit card and withdraw money from bank accounts, or get a loan in the victim's name. Thieves can use personal information in government documents fraud, to get a driver's license or official ID card issued in the victim's name but with the thief's picture, to get governmental benefits, or to file a fraudulent tax return.

Identity thieves may use a victim's information to get a job using his or her Social Security number, rent a house, get medical services, or to give personal information to the police during an arrest. When they fail to show up for their court date, a warrant will be issued for the victim's arrest.

Consumer Sentinel Network
Once a person suspects that he or she is a victim of identity theft, his or her credit report needs to be investigated. If such is the case, the victim should issue a fraud alert on his or her record. In particular, to protect consumers from identity theft, the FTC has established measures to help the organization detect, deter, and defend against this crime. These three steps help consumers take charge of the situation and prevent or battle identity theft effectively. The Consumer Sentinel Network (CSN) is a secure online database with millions of consumer complaints available only to law enforcement. Besides storing complaints received by the FTC, the CSN also keeps tracks of complaints filed with the Internet Crime Complaint Center, Better Business Bureaus, Canada's PhoneBusters, the U.S. Postal Inspection Service, the Identity Theft Assistance Center, and the National Fraud Information Center, among others. Law enforcement partners, wherever they may be in the nation and around the globe, can access the database for investigations.

The CSN was set up in 1997 to collect fraud and identity theft complaints and has received more than 5.4 million complaints. In 2009 alone, the CSN received more than 1.3 million consumer complaints. Since the CSN also stores complaints transferred from other organizations, the total number of complaints is usually higher than that found in the initial annual reports.

Federal Efforts
Because of the extensive impacts that identity theft has had on the American public, President George W. Bush established the President's Task Force on Identity Theft by Executive Order 13402 on May 10, 2006. The task force was to spearhead the combat against identity theft and to help ease the tremendous financial and emotional burden that identity theft victims experience. The task force was also to work with other governmental agencies to eradicate this crime.

The task force aims at crafting a strategic plan to optimize federal government's efforts in creating awareness about, forging prevention against, instigating detection of, and carrying out prosecution against identity thefts. The task force is chaired by the attorney general and cochaired by the chairman of the FTC.

The task force focuses on various areas, including law enforcement, education, and government safeguards. In the area of law enforcement, the task force looks at the legal tools that can be used in preventing, investigating, and prosecuting identity theft crimes. The task force also examines ways to recover the proceeds of these crimes and to make sure that the punishment of identity thieves is just and effective.

In the area of education, the task force reviews the education efforts carried out by governmental agencies and the private sector on how individuals and businesses can protect their personal information. In the area of government safeguards, the task force works in tandem with several federal agencies in determining how the government can augment the regulations to maximize the security of personal data kept by the government and private businesses.

The task force also engages in a wide range of activities to involve and inform the public in the fight against identity theft. The task force organizes meetings, talks with stakeholders, and solicits public comments on major issues pertaining to identity theft. The strategic plan aims to strengthen efforts of federal, state, and local law enforcement officers; to inform individuals and businesses on how to deter, detect, and defend against identity theft; to aid law enforcement officers in capturing and prosecuting identity thieves; and to amplify the measures employed by federal agencies and the private sector to guard the personal data they hold.

As part of its responsibility to help resolve problems caused by identity theft, the FTC has developed the Guide for Assisting Identity Theft Victims, which can be found on the task force Website, to aid attorneys and victim service providers when working with pro bono clients.

Internet-Based Crime

Of all the methods employed by identity thieves, phishing—also known as Web spoofing or carding—is the most current and is likely the most prevalent in the future given the usage and business activities conducted online. Looking at client-side defense against Web-based identity theft, Neil Chou et al. from the Computer Science Department at Stanford University predict that phishing will continue to be a problem in the years to come.

Web spoofing is a major form of Internet crime, affecting as many as thousands of individuals on a daily basis. Typically, a bulk e-mail will instigate the fraud, urging unsuspecting consumers to click on a link that leads them to a spoofed site. The consumer will then be asked to log in, and once username and password are entered, the identity thieves can access the consumer's account, usually to make withdrawals or to cause other harm.

It is necessary to pay special attention to Web spoofing because phishing can become more sophisticated in the future, while nonexpert Internet users might not be up to speed with the new tactics employed by spoofers. There has also been an exponential increase in phishing cases over the years. The agents of the U.S. Secret Service San Francisco Electronic Crimes Task Force received more than 75,000 complaints in 2002, three times the amount filed the previous year. The estimated monetary loss was $54 million, compared to $17 million in 2001. Most of the $37 million increase in loss in 2001–02 was attributed to Web spoofing.

Victim Advocacy

Several nongovernmental organizations have stepped in to assist identity theft victims in restoring their identity. The Identity Theft Assistance Center (ITAC) provides assistance to victims at no charge. The ITAC has helped tens of thousands of victims defend against identity theft. According to the ITAC, it is not possible to eradicate identity theft, but it is possible to manage it.

A consumer advocate on identity fraud and the financial services industry's identity management solution center, the ITAC is affiliated with the Financial Services Roundtable and is supported by the industry as a free service to its clients. Since 2004, ITAC has aided tens of thousands of consumers in restoring their identity.

Members of the ITAC provide free ITAC victim assistance service to those who surmise that their identity might have been stolen. ITAC minimizes the time to resolve a case by assigning a single point of contact to each case. A trained agent will help the customers recognize questionable transactions and inform all the companies with possible frauds. The client will receive documentation of the related incidents, which can be useful to law enforcement or other account holders. Becasue of its quality services, the ITAC has a 98 percent rate of customer satisfaction.

With ITAC Sentinel, consumers can be proactive in protecting their identity. This service alerts consumers to changes in their credit report, signaling them to act before serious harm takes place. The ITAC Sentinel includes ITAC Victim Assistance and gives immediate help to those who need it but are not a customer of an ITAC member company. ITAC Sentinel subscribers receive ongoing protection.

ITAC Sentinel is a useful way to manage the risks found in data breaches. Because of its services, the ITAC is seen by law enforcement as an important resource in combating identity theft. The ITAC has data-sharing agreements with the FTC and the U.S. Postal Inspection Service, hence making relevant information about identity theft available to investigators and prosecutors across the states.

To equip its customers with the right knowledge and skills to combat identity crimes, the ITAC emphasizes consumer education. On this front, ITAC partners with national education initiatives, including the Alliance for Consumer Fraud Awareness, National Cyber Security Alliance, the Identity Theft Council, and Protect Your Identity Now.

As a source of fact-based information on identity theft, ITAC offers news, information, and opinion through its consumer Website and the official ITAC blog. The blog provides a space for the exchange of opinion, ideas, and best practices among industry professionals, policy makers, attorneys, information security and privacy experts, law enforcement, and academics.

In spite of the availability of services such as the ITAC, the best defense for each consumer is knowledge and awareness about identity theft. Consumers should also be aware of their rights in order to protect themselves and to take the proper actions toward having a credit report free of fraudulent accounts.

Trangdai Glassey-Tranguyen
Stanford University

See Also: 1921 to 1940 Primary Documents; Computer Crime; Embezzlement; Fraud; Larceny.

Further Readings
Federal Trade Commission. "Fighting Back Against Identity Theft." http://www.ftc.gov/bcp/edu/microsites/idtheft/index.html (Accessed November 2011).
Identity Theft Assistance Center. http://www.identity theftassistance.org (Accessed November 2011).
Identity Theft Resource Center. "Working to Resolve Identity Theft." http://www.idtheftcenter.org (Accessed November 2011).
IDtheft.gov. "Resources From the Government." http://www.idtheft.gov (Accessed November 2011).

Illinois

Early European settlement in Illinois clustered around the riverine lands that form a U shape at the state's tip and was tied to the commercial life of the Mississippi River system. Beginning in the mid-19th century, canal, railroad, and automobile transportation continually shifted the state's center of population north. While Chicago's gangsters, molls, notoriously corrupt policemen, and politicians have stolen most of the headlines, inhabitants in the rest of the largely rural state long have faced criminal justice challenges based on their distinct demographic, social, political, and institutional realities.

By the 1850s, advances in communication and transportation helped to integrate rural Illinois into the vast system of exchange that was developing around the Empire City of the west. This provided the means by which the state's population grew and spurred the building of institutions of criminal justice. The 1818 state constitution set up four judicial circuits with legislatively appointed, circuit-riding judges; to hear lesser criminal cases, the legislature soon created a system of justices of the peace for each county. In 1848, a new constitution established a supreme court, nine circuit courts with elected judges, and county courts with jurisdiction over lesser criminal cases (justice of the peace courts persisted). Appellate courts were added in 1870. For all counties except the Chicago area, this overlapping warren of courts persisted until 1964, when the state consolidated all trial courts into unified circuit courts.

While the legislature pared down capital offenses to only the most egregious crimes in the 19th century, it continually expanded the law's criminal provisions. By one count, offenses multiplied from 131 in the 1850s to 460 nearly a century later. By the early 1960s, there were 800 sections of substantive law and more than 300 sections of procedure. The Criminal Code of 1961 shrank the substantive law to less than a quarter of that size. A characteristic change was the repeal of 74 sections dealing with theft in favor of a single comprehensive offense. A new code of procedure was adopted two years later. Nevertheless, codification has not restrained subsequent legislatures.

Law Enforcement
In early Illinois, sparse settlement left geographical gaps in the authority of state and federal law. Prior to the coming of the steamship, for example, the notorious pirates at Cave-in-Rock along the Ohio River preyed on Illinois travelers. The existence of other sovereigns posed another challenge. Although European settlement led to the diminution and displacement of native peoples, there was more than a century and a half of cohabitation. In cases of cross-cultural homicide, peace required negotiation. In 1811, Pottawatomie leaders refused to hand over a group of native men to face trial in Illinois courts or to kill the warriors themselves, on the grounds that the Euro-Americans refused to reciprocate by handing over white suspects. This was an important factor that led the territorial governor to make war on the

recalcitrant tribe in 1811 and 1812. By contrast, when two Winnebago suspects were handed over to the Illinois authorities and executed 10 years later, the U.S. War Department paid reparations to their kin in an improvised version of the indigenous practice of "covering" the dead.

Even after questions of sovereignty were resolved, limited institutional capacities and a reliance on popular sentiment presented challenges for law enforcement in Illinois. In the late 1860s, a family feud known as the Bloody Vendetta resulted in a spate of murders in Williamson County—the first in a long series of lawless tragedies that gave the county the nickname "Bloody" Williamson. In this case, the county sheriff could rely on a few employees and the ability to call out a *posse comitatus*, with only the nonprofessional state militia in reserve, and was effectively powerless to intervene.

In other cases, thorough integration into broader political and criminal networks compromised law enforcement. By the last third of the 19th century, the Chicago Police Department was part of a ward-based system of political authority that typically tolerated—instead of fought—the city's many gambling dens, houses of ill repute, and criminal syndicates. To mitigate the outcry of the city's middle classes, vice districts were located in the city's immigrant (and later, African American) neighborhoods. The most notorious of these districts was the Levee, located within the south side First Ward, which flourished in the two

This 1851 print published in New York depicts the June 27, 1844, murder of Mormon leader and founder Joseph Smith by a mob who broke into Carthage Jail in Hancock County, Illinois, where Smith was being held on charges of treason. The Mormon leader and his followers had only recently moved to Illinois after suffering harassment in Missouri.

decades around the turn of the century under the watchful eyes of aldermen Michael "Hinky Dink" Kenna and "Bathhouse John" Coughlin. While prospering from the graft paid by saloons, brothels, and gambling halls, they also sponsored the rise of Chicago's first big mob boss, "Big Jim" Colosimo. Of course, corruption was not exclusive to Chicago. A gang war between "Bloody" Williamson's rival bootleggers, Charlie Birger and the Shelton brothers, resembled nothing so much as Chicago's beer wars of the 1920s, in which Colosimo's former lieutenant, Johnny Torrio, and his protégé from Brooklyn, Al Capone, rose to bootlegging prominence. In both cases, the decentralized infrastructure of law enforcement left individual officers and police districts vulnerable to outside influence. When vice interests corrupted local ward (or county) officials, there was no centralized authority that could effectively prosecute.

The enforcement of the will of majorities against minorities in violation of law represented a problem of a different order. Joseph Smith and the Mormons created Nauvoo in 1839 after fleeing from Missouri. Almost immediately, they became embroiled in conflict with their Hancock County neighbors, who feared Smith's political domination. In 1844, a mob consisting of many of the county's best citizens stormed the jail where Smith was being held on treason charges and murdered him.

Similarly, in Williamson County, conflicts over the unionization of coal mines repeatedly spurred deadly violence from the 1890s through the 1920s. The worst of these battles, outside the town of Herrin in 1922, began when 500 striking union miners pinned down 50 professional strikebreakers and prison guards in a gun battle in which two union miners were killed. When the owner's men surrendered, based on a promise of free passage out of the county, the angry strikers took their vengeance. On the march to town, they killed and mutilated 18 prisoners. Elected to office by the unionized miners, the sheriff did little to stop them; moreover, juries condoned the massacre by finding everyone who was prosecuted not guilty.

Black history, as first charted by Ida B. Wells's studies of lynching, recapitulates this theme. Wells recorded three lynchings in Illinois in 1893 and 11 others from 1893 to 1924. During 20th-century race riots, black people were indiscriminately murdered by whites in Springfield in 1908 (seven dead), twice in East St. Louis in 1917 (at least 48 dead), and in Chicago in 1919 (38 dead). These acts resembled the Herrin massacre in the frenzied nature of the violence and in the failure of authorities to hold anyone responsible.

Moral conflicts have divided the populace and hamstrung law enforcement. Between 1830 and 1850 in Massac, Pope, Ogle, and DeKalb counties, armed citizen groups calling themselves "the Regulators" took the law into their own hands. They justified their actions by claiming that criminal justice officials in their counties were affiliated with lawless elements, including murderers and horse thieves. The line between the just and the criminal blurred quickly. Temperance and prohibition movements produced similar divisions, as advocates attempted to impose greater restraint on a masculine subculture of violence. In Williamson County, skepticism about the sheriff's willingness to enforce Prohibition led the Ku Klux Klan to take matters into its own hands. Many Klansmen were at one point deputized by S. Glen Young, a former federal agent. However, Young far exceeded his minimal authority, leading Klansmen into a virtual war with bootleggers, Catholics, and others, before dying in a drugstore shoot-out. Unlike spasms of popular violence, the Regulator and Klan wars stymied law enforcement by pitting popular factions of equal strength against one another.

When crimes have made it into the courts, they have rarely gone to trial. This is well known for Chicago's overburdened courts, but it is also true in rural Illinois. From 1870 to 1960, less than 15 percent of criminal cases went to trial in the courts of rural Menard and Bond counties. Prosecutors dropped a plurality of cases (46 percent in Bond, 45 percent in Menard); a quarter ended in guilty pleas (28 and 23 percent, respectively). While the number of guilty pleas rose considerably over time, this was in large part because of the changing composition of charged offenses. In the 1870s, criminal dockets were dominated by moral offenses and interpersonal violence, which declined over time in favor of property and public safety offenses, including serious traffic violations.

Punishment

In early Illinois, the scarcity of labor augured against imprisonment as punishment in favor of

The Blue Ribbon mine in Williamson County, Illinois, in 1939. The county was plagued by violence and labor conflicts in the 1920s. In the most violent incident of that era, a strike by 500 union miners led to a gun battle in which two miners were killed, and 18 guards and strikebreakers were then murdered in retaliation. Local juries later acquitted everyone who was prosecuted.

the pillory and public whippings, accompanied by fines. Officials auctioned the labor of offenders who could not pay. The building of Alton prison in 1833 reflected the settling of the state. Beginning with the conviction of Sally Jefferson in 1835, women were imprisoned in the same institutions as men; after 1896, women's prisons were built. At Alton, the state leased the entire prison to a contractor, with license to use the labor of its prisoners for profit. Convict labor was used to build a new prison at Joliet, which opened in 1860. When Joliet became too small, a second state penitentiary was built at Menard in 1878—a particularly advantageous location because it could be reached by water in the event of a railroad strike. The convict-leasing system came under attack in the 1860s, when the legislature put the prison under the control of a commission that had no financial interests in the prisoners. This led to a massive increase in expenses and destroyed the basic system of prison discipline, heretofore oriented around work.

In the 20th century, prison wardens employed diverse strategies to control their institutions. In building Stateville in 1925, the state employed architecture as a medium of authority. All prisoners in the round, four-deck structures could be observed from a central point. The awarding and withholding of benefits were common solutions. The 1922 Classification Act was intended to separate offenders by type, according to their treatment needs. By integrating the entire system, the act created a threat—transfer to a less desirable location—that wardens could use as a tool of control. Indeterminate sentencing provided incentives as well. From 1833 until 1872, the jury decided sentence length. Thereafter, Illinois adopted "good time" credits and, in 1895, went to a scheme of indeterminate sentencing in which prison officials could release prisoners at any time. Though the system was occasionally modified, it remained in place until 1978, when the state created a system of determinate sentencing. This change was later reinforced by a truth-in-sentencing law that permitted less use of "good time." Finally, punitive segregation and other highly authoritarian forms of discipline, like that imposed by Joseph Ragen at Stateville from 1936 to 1961, played an important role. Control strategies reached their apex with the invention of the "supermax" at the federal prison in Marion. Built in 1963, the prison went into total lockdown after an eruption of violence in 1983 in which an inmate killed two officers. Pioneering a model that subsequently has been adopted all over the country, Marion isolated its prisoners in their cells for 23 hours a day. The state of Illinois opened up its own supermax facility, Tamms Correctional Center, in 1998.

Although Illinois prisons were often overcrowded, the rate of incarceration was relatively stable before 1970. Thereafter, the number of prisoners grew from 7,300 to 47,000 by 2005, at an incarceration rate of more than 370 per 100,000 persons. Moreover, this was a fraction of all people under state supervision: 188,000 were in county jail, state prison, or on probation or parole. By 2005, blacks were imprisoned in state prison at a rate more than nine times that of whites (2,020 per 100,000 compared with 223), and Latinos nearly double the rate of whites (415 to 223). Since 1990, the female inmate population has grown at more than double the rate of the male, largely because of the drug sentences that by 1999 made up 40 percent of all Illinois prison sentences (up from 17 percent in 1988). To handle this growth, the Department of Corrections built nine new facilities in the 1990s, raising to 48 the total number of facilities, of which 35 are for confinement.

In the past decade, the death penalty became a major subject of controversy. Between 1818 and 1962, Illinois executed 348 people. Following the Supreme Court's ruling in *Furman v. Georgia* (1972), the state almost immediately enacted a new capital punishment statute, although there were no executions until 1990. Over the next decade, 12 prisoners were executed, before Governor George Ryan declared a moratorium in 2003 following a rash of exonerations of innocent people and concerns about the role that torture by Chicago police commander Jon Burge played in securing the convictions of others. In 2005, Ryan commuted the sentences of the remaining 167 death row prisoners. In 2011, the Illinois legislature abolished the death penalty.

Peter Constantine Pihos
University of Pennsylvania

See Also: 1801 to 1850 Primary Documents; Chicago, Illinois; Ragen, Joseph; Strikes; Supermax Prisons.

Further Readings
Angle, Paul M. *Bloody Williamson: A Chapter in American Lawlessness*. New York: Alfred A. Knopf, 1952.
Cunard, Nancy. *Asylum, Prison, and Poorhouse: The Writings and Reform Work of Dorothea Dix in Illinois*. Carbondale: Southern Illinois University Press, 1999.
Daniels, Stephen. "Continuity and Change in Patterns of Case Handling: A Case Study of Two Rural Counties." *Law & Society Review*, v.19/3 (1985).

Immigration Crimes

U.S. immigration has gone through the following four distinct periods: colonial, mid-19th century, the beginning of the 20th century, and post-1965. Each of these waves differs by the racial and ethnic groups migrating to the United States. During the colonial period of migration, most immigrants were from Europe and arrived as indentured servants. During the mid-19th century, there was a sharp increase in migration from northern Europe. In the next period of immigration, there was an increase in migration from eastern and southern Europe. Finally, during the last period of immigration post-1965, the majority of immigrants came from Asia and Latin America.

During periods of migration, there have been restrictions placed upon who is admitted into the United States. During U.S. history, there have been quotas based on national origins. Other restrictions have included excluding anarchists and polygamists.

Entering a country without legal authorization is a crime against immigration laws. Those who enter a country illegally the first time can be charged with a misdemeanor. Committing that same offense more than once can result in a felony. Another type of immigration offense includes evading inspection by an immigration official. Misleading immigration officials in an attempt to enter the country is also an immigration offense. These offenses are punishable by fines or incarceration.

Penalties for immigration violations increase once a person who has been deported reenters the United States illegally. Those who are deported on criminal grounds face imprisonment for 10 years should they choose to reenter the United States illegally. Under United States Code (U.S.C.), those who are convicted of an aggravated felony and reenter the United States illegally after being deported face a 20-year prison sentence. Using false documents, harboring undocumented immigrants and falsely claiming U.S. citizenship are also punishable by incarceration. Once apprehended, undocumented immigrants are more at risk of being incarcerated because of their treatment by the criminal justice system.

Enforcement

The federal government has jurisdiction over immigration policy. Policies set at the federal level must be enforced at the state and local levels. State and local agencies are obligated to set up programs designated by the federal government with little to no financial support from the federal government. Federal immigration policies have a direct impact on government spending and resource allocation at the state and local level. States and local governments take on numerous costs because of the regulations created at the federal level.

There has been a debate over whether state and local law enforcement agencies should enforce federal immigration laws. Those opposed to law enforcement taking on the role of immigration enforcement include people in the immigration community and local law enforcement officers. Local law enforcement officials work extremely hard to build a relationship with the immigrant community. The immigrant community needs to have a level of trust in law enforcement to report crimes and to serve as witnesses. One of the other worries regarding state and local law enforcement agencies aiding in immigration enforcement is that it can create the potential for racial profiling

U.S. Customs and Border Protection agents searching an offender, whose face has been obscured, during a drug-related arrest at Arizona's border with Mexico. In 2003–04, there were 9,500 border agents like these protecting the U.S. borders.

and civil rights violations because of their lack of training. Even though the agencies that participate in immigration enforcement receive some training, it is not to the extent that they need. They do not have the experience or knowledge of how to approach immigration enforcement. In order to address some of the training issues, the Department of Justice (DOJ) proposed that state and local agencies who wanted to enforce immigration laws could enter into a Memorandum of Agreement (MOA) with the DOJ.

As of early 2007, numerous counties and states, including the Arizona Department of Corrections, enlisted in an MOA with the DOJ. Agents who are given additional immigration enforcement authority are only permitted to investigate someone under typical law enforcement duties.

Law enforcement officials are not supposed to stop people for the sole purpose of investigating their legal status. Some believe that if state and local officials are trained by federal officials, it will reduce the likelihood of racial profiling.

In communities where state and local agencies have taken on the role of immigration officers, there has been controversy surrounding this partnership. Racial profiling has been a claim asserted by many in communities where state and local law enforcement have been enforcing immigration laws. Discrimination and abuse of power have both been alleged against numerous state and local agencies assisting in this cause. Racial profiling by law enforcement for purposes of immigration enforcement can lead down a dangerous path. Racial profiling can lead to negative stereotypes about a particular race and ethnicity. Even though racial profiling does not increase efficiency, studies have shown that it is actively used by many state and local law enforcement agencies.

Legal residents and citizens have felt targeted by these programs simply because of their race or ethnicity. This can lead to feelings of resentment against all agencies of law enforcement. As these types of programs continue in some communities, those who feel targeted may decide to leave their communities because of feeling discriminated against. In some states, there is a target group; in Arizona, the target group is Hispanics. Groups of undocumented immigrants will resort to living in the shadows.

Historical Perspective
One of the earliest U.S. immigration policies targeted Chinese immigrants. In 1882, the Chinese Exclusion Act, set by Congress, limited immigration from China, prohibited Chinese immigrants from acquiring legal status, and mandated the deportation of Chinese workers. One of the consequences of the mass deportations of Chinese workers was that it created a shortage of low-skilled workers. In the southwest region of the United States, where Chinese workers had been predominantly employed, growers in the agricultural industry began to look for other sources of cheap labor. Growers began recruiting Mexican laborers to take the place of recently deported Chinese workers. During the 1920s, Americans began to express concerns over illegal immigration from the southern border.

The 1920s were marked by the introduction of legislation aimed at decreasing immigration altogether. The 1924 Immigration Act required anyone who wanted to enter the United States to obtain a visa, and also set a quota system for immigrants from every country. Public and political concern began to grow over immigration. In response to immigration concerns, the U.S. government founded the Border Patrol Agency (BPA) in 1924. The BPA became responsible for guarding the border in order to deter illegal immigration. During the 1920s, there were countless deportations of Mexican undocumented immigrants. The concern over undocumented immigrants did not last long because in 1942, the U.S. government initiated the Bracero (temporary worker) program to provide agricultural labor.

Border Security
Most of the attention and resources allocated by government have gone toward securing the U.S.-Mexico border. Securing land borders is a complex and expensive task. There are several issues that need to be addressed when examining current border security measures. Perhaps one of the most influential factors in the way that border security measures are implemented and carried out is through immigration policy. Immigration policies can be used to potentially mitigate the amount of activity that takes place around the border. Some of the strategies that could be used to lessen activity around the U.S.-Mexico border are to increase security measures, emphasize the legal means of entering the United States, enforce the laws already in place, and support economic activity in Mexico.

Border security is one of the central issues at the forefront of national security. Securing the borders plays a significant part in maintaining protection from unauthorized individuals and other potential threats. Increasing security measures around the southern border has not deterred immigrant motivation to cross the border; additional security measures only make the journey more difficult for them. Deaths around the border have increased over the past decade because in order to avoid detection, undocumented immigrants attempt to cross the most dangerous,

A Mexican contract worker weighing cotton picked in Perthshire, Mississippi, in 1939. After a crackdown on undocumented immigrants in the 1920s, waves of new workers would still be occasionally invited when labor needs dictated.

unguarded, treacherous mountain and desert terrain. Strict border security measures along the California and Texas borders have resulted in increased activity along Arizona's most notorious terrain. The increase in the number of deaths along the U.S.-Mexico border has caused both national and international human rights groups to declare this a humanitarian crisis.

Workplace Enforcement
Immigrants are vilified for trying to obtain employment while bypassing the visa program, but their employers typically escape with little or no punishment for hiring them in the first place. American businesses are partly to blame for the current state of the broken immigration system. Jobs are part of the reason that individuals immigrate illegally. Many employers do not do enough to investigate an employee's legal status. Businesses who hire undocumented workers need to be held to higher standards. Politicians choose to punish immigrants while turning the other way when big businesses break the law. Congress does not want to disrupt the economy, so instead it focuses attention on immigrants.

Border security is given higher priority than workplace enforcement. From 2003 to 2004, the Immigration and Customs Enforcement Agency requested $23 million for worksite enforcement and received only $5 million, while the BPA received $74 million. There are substantial staffing differences between border and workplace enforcement agencies. There were a total of 124 full-time employees assigned to workplace enforcement while there were 9,500 border agents assigned to border security from 2003 through 2004. Government agencies have not shown that worksite enforcement is as much a priority as border enforcement or that American businesses should be held as accountable as undocumented immigrants for breaking the law.

The current law simply states that employers are not permitted to knowingly hire undocumented workers. The claim of ignorance allows employers to escape without suffering many consequences. In 2007, only 2 percent of workplace arrests were of employers and the other 98 percent of arrests were of undocumented immigrant employees.

E-Verify is an employment verification program that is administered by the U.S. Citizenship and Immigration Services and supported by the Social Security Administration. In April 2008, an estimated 61,000 of the 7.4 million nation's employers had registered for the program but only half of those actively used it. E-Verify is a voluntary program but in Arizona and Mississippi, employers are mandated to use the system when determining the eligibility of potential employees. There has been some discussion about making E-Verify a mandatory nationwide program. There are estimates that using the E-Verify program from 2009 through 2012 would cost approximately $765 million if recently hired employees were the only ones checked.

Mercedes Valadez
Arizona State University

See Also: Border Patrol; Chinese Americans; Customs Service as Police; Deportation; Hispanic Americans; Racism; Xenophobia.

Further Readings
Arnold, C. L. "Racial Profiling in Immigration Enforcement: State and Local Agreements to Enforce Federal Immigration Law." *Arizona Law Review*, v.49 (2007).
Chiswick, B. R. "Illegal Immigration and Immigration Control." *Journal of Economic Perspectives*, v.2 (1998).
Cornelius, W. A. "Controlling 'Unwanted' Immigration: Lessons From the United States." *Journal of Ethnic and Migration Studies*, v.31 (2005).
Hagan, J. and A. Palloni. "Sociological Criminology and the Mythology of Hispanic Immigration and Crime." *Social Problems*, v.46 (1999).

Incapacitation, Theory of

Incapacitation refers to physical restrictions used to mitigate or eliminate a person's ability to commit a criminal offense. It is generally recognized as constituting one of the four primary justifications for the use of punishment in criminal justice systems—the other three being deterrence, retribution, and rehabilitation. Along with deterrence and rehabilitation, it is a "forward-looking" philosophy that seeks to prevent future offenses, whereas retribution is used to redress social inequity caused by past offenses. Unlike deterrence or rehabilitation, however, incapacitation is aimed at not merely dissuading would-be offenders, nor mitigating the likelihood of crime through rehabilitation, but at physically restricting the possibility of an individual to commit criminal activity.

Rehabilitative Model

Historically, the use of incapacitation dates back to the earliest recorded uses of punishment. However, prior to the modern age, the logic of incapacitation was less prevalent than that of retribution, although forms of punishment such as banishment, physical amputation and branding, and capital punishment frequently served dual purposes. In the 18th century, the emergence of deterrent uses of punishment was popularized by the Italian Cesare Beccaria, who argued that imprisonment was a more effective form of deterrence than torture or death. Incarceration became an increasingly common form of punishment throughout the 19th century in Europe and the northern United States, influenced first by deterrence theorists and later by reformers and physicians who believed that criminals were a product of poor social environments and thus could be reformed given the proper motivation and guidance. This rehabilitative model of punishment became the dominant one, at least in northern states, by the middle of the 19th century. Under this approach, it was common for criminals to receive wide-ranging sentences; for example, five years to life, and the use of such indeterminate sentencing was standard in the United States throughout much of the 20th century. Beginning in the 1970s, however, criticism of this model had begun to grow, both from conservatives who argued that rehabilitation was ineffective and from liberals who argued that it led to wide racial disparities in sentencing. In the late 1970s and 1980s, several states as well as the federal government adopted the use of determinate sentencing, which replaced indeterminate-range sentences with much narrower ranges or fixed terms. This constituted in part a return to a more retributive approach to justice, characterized, for example, in the rise of "just deserts" that took the position that punishment should reflect only the seriousness of the offense. However, determinate sentences were also supported by criminologists such as James Q. Wilson, who argued that increasing the use and length of incarceration would reduce crime by incapacitating a larger number of offenders for longer periods of time.

Determinate Sentencing

This general incapacitation effect was popular among many conservatives and was a central part of their support for determinate sentencing. However, it was also criticized by policy makers, prosecutors, and judges who viewed such a strict use of incapacitation as a blunt and costly means of crime control. A primary criticism was that offenders who posed little risk of reoffending were given similar sentences to those who posed much greater risks of reoffending. A shift in the use of incapacitation emerged in the 1980s, partially as a result of Marvin Wolfgang's earlier cohort research that had suggested a smaller number (roughly 6 percent) of individuals were responsible for a much higher number of serious crimes. Following this logic, other research, particularly that of Peter Greenwood and his colleagues in the 1980s, found that the early identification of such serious offenders would allow for a more precise, or selective, use of incapacitation to the degree that offenders more at risk to recidivate could be identified and given longer sentences or more intensive supervision. Greenwood's research has been criticized for several reasons, most directly for methodological errors that may lead to false positives in the identification of high-risk offenders. However, the use of risk prediction in sentencing was already passively employed in some determinate sentencing models that took into account the number and type of past offenses (long recognized as a strong predictor of future recidivism) in determining the length of sentences. In the 1980s and 1990s, several states moved to adopt more refined sentencing schemes such as "three-strikes" or "habitual offender" laws that gradated the seriousness of sentences according to past criminal histories.

Selective Incapacitation

However, the future of selective incapacitation lay not in the use of sentencing schemes that responded to past offenses but rather in the rise of risk-assessment models that sought, as Greenwood did, to more accurately predict future offending. The use of risk-assessment instruments is today commonplace within juvenile and adult justice systems, where offenders are assessed on a range of demographic, social, environmental, and behavioral factors to determine the degree of supervision required for incarcerated offenders, the possibility of community corrections in lieu of incarceration, and the provision of treatment or rehabilitation services for offenders. Risk assessments are also used in many states without determinate sentencing schemes to determine eligibility for parole. Yet, perhaps the most decisive turn in the use of selective incapacitation exists in the rise of what is called "actuarial sentencing," which moves beyond determining levels of supervision

or parole eligibility toward the determination of sentences based on risk of serious future or violent offending. Currently, three states—Missouri, Pennsylvania, and Virginia—are using some form of this type of sentencing, and it is likely other states will follow.

Today, the most prevalent form of incapacitation is the use of incarceration. Other commonly used methods include the use of "house arrest," accompanied by an active monitoring device. The use of alcohol monitoring and ignition interlock devices is also common. The use of chemical castration for repeat sex offenders has been a controversial application of the use of incapacitation. It has been used for repeat offenders convicted of child molestation in California since 1996 and in Florida since 1997. More recently, Louisiana has allowed for its use for convicted rapists since 2008. It has also been used in varying frequencies within the last 10 years in Argentina, England, Germany, Israel, Poland, and Russia. Finally, the ultimate

An ignition-interlock breath analyzer from 2004. As a form of incapacitation, such devices require a driver to pass a breath alcohol test before they can start their car and also makes a record of the driver's blood alcohol level from each test.

incapacitant remains that of capital punishment, which has been discontinued in most Western industrialized countries but remains in use (with strong public support) in the United States.

William R. Wood
University of Auckland

See Also: Capital Punishment; Deterrence, Theory of; Electronic Surveillance; Parole; Rehabilitation; Retributivism; Sentencing: Indeterminate Versus Fixed; Three Strikes Law; Wilson, James Q.

Further Reading
Greenwood, P. W. and A. Abrahamse. *Selective Incapacitation*. Santa Monica, CA: Rand Corporation, 1992.
Zimring, F. and G. Hawkins. *Incapacitation: Penal Confinement and the Restraint of Crime*. Oxford: Oxford University Press, 1997.

Incest

The legal definition of incest is the act of sexual relations between two individuals who are related by blood or affinity. Incest is a sexual crime. Most states prohibit incest under criminal law and marriage law. Marriage unions between parent and child, siblings, uncle and niece, and aunt and nephew are prohibited in the United States. The laws for marriage between cousins vary by state. Twenty-six states allow first-cousin marriages, and all states allow marriage between second cousins. Maine allows first cousins to marry if they submit to genetic counseling. The United States is the only Western country that prohibits cousin marriage. Cousin marriage is legal in both Canada and Mexico, as well as throughout Europe. In the United States, criminal penalties for incest range from fines to incarceration depending upon the state.

Theoretically, the discourse concerning incest is divided along two lines. The first, historically older perspective is represented by bloodlines and the newer perspective on incest is defined by desire. Michel Foucault's definition of sexuality helps to construct the older perspective. He describes a definition of sexuality wherein the family is solely defined by biological relationships. Therefore, the goal of sexual relations is procreation to expand the family. According to this perspective, incestuous behavior crosses the boundaries of kinship and its inherent goal. The contemporary perspective of organizing sexuality frames incest within broadening definitions of family relations and pleasurable sexual acts. The recent changes in kinship and family structure have led to many questions regarding the definition of incestuous behavior. Increasingly, the family structure has changed so that the definition of family is not solely based upon bloodlines. The diversity of the family unit now includes adoptive parents, stepparents, and informal ties.

Sibling Incest
Types of incest include parental and sibling incest. Contrary to popular belief, research has found that cases of sibling incest are more common than parental incest. Sibling incest has been defined as a range of behaviors that can include touching, indecent exposure, masturbation, oral sex, anal sex, digital or object penetration, and intercourse between brother and sister or same sex siblings. Sibling incest is sometimes difficult to differentiate from developmentally normal exploration and sexual curiosity. Several factors need to be considered in order to decide if the crime of incest has occurred, such as the age difference between parties, the type of sexual behavior including frequency and duration of this behavior, motivation of the offender, and voluntariness of the parties. Specific prevalence rates of sibling incest are difficult to determine because there is a dearth of research on this phenomenon, and the information that has been gathered is mainly from case studies and clinical files. Additionally, research has found that cases of sibling incest are underreported. The typical age difference between the victim and offender involved in sibling incest crimes ranges from two to 10 years. The most common pairing found among incidents of sibling incest is the brother-sister dyad, and the majority of these crimes are initiated by the brother. One possible explanation that sexual relations among siblings are more common than parental incest is that the taboo against sibling incest is weaker. Taboos against incest are generally found in most cultures throughout the world.

Phillip Jenkins, noted sociologist, argues that crimes involving children, particularly those deemed immoral by the public, are eminently newsworthy. Crime stories that focus on child victims are said to be morality campaigns that serve to ensure the media's commitment to the preservation of the ideal image of the archetypal family. Crimes committed by adults against children seemingly cross a higher threshold of perception of victimization than adult-on-adult crime. Nonetheless, research has found that sexual crimes against children are underrepresented by the media, compared to other crimes involving children, thus preserving the image of the model family. Public abhorrence of incest and the assertion that this crime only occurs among families of low social status is reflected by the popular media.

Effects of Sexual Abuse

Sexual abuse behavior has been documental by mental health professionals as both serious and traumatic. Incest as a type of sexual abuse is particularly damaging because it disrupts the victim's primary support system, which is the family. The victims of incest typically experience profound psychological, sexual, and relationship problems. Severe depression, increased anxiety, suicidal thoughts, and sexual promiscuity are very common among sexually abused women. Victims of sibling incest endure continuing difficulties such as mental health challenges, low self-esteem, and subsequent sexual, emotional, and physical victimization. Research has found a connection between incest victimization and future incidents of abuse later in life. Victims of sibling incest experience a greater likelihood of victimization as an adult compared to other nonabused children. Studies have found up to 75 percent of incest victims report incidents of abuse after the age of 18.

Recent literature has linked incest and self-mutilation behaviors. Incidents of self-mutilation among incest survivors range from a low of 17 percent to a high of 58 percent. Self-mutilation can be viewed as a psychological adaptation behavior among incest survivors. Self-mutilation, while punishing the body, helps to counter the dissociative tendencies found among these victims. Moreover, incest survivors sometimes have difficulty establishing trust in relationships. Cognitive behavior therapy (CBT) techniques have been suggested to aid survivors. The characteristics of sibling incest and the linked psychological problems among victims are similar to those found among victims of father-daughter incest. Therefore, the psychological costs of sibling incest should not be construed as less severe than those experienced by victims of parental incest. In addition to the psychological issues associated with incest behavior, scientists have raised concerns about the offspring of partners in an incestuous blood relationship and the possible biological deficiencies that result from this sexual behavior. Higher incidences of birth defects are found among this group.

Melissa E. Fenwick
Western Connecticut State University

See Also: Child Abuse, Sociology of; Children's Rights; Rape, Sociology of; Sex Offender Laws; Sex Offenders.

Further Readings
Carlson, B. E. "Sibling Incest: Adjustment in Adult Women Survivors." *Families in Society*, v.92/1 (2011).
Cyr, M., Wright, P. McDuff, and A. Perron. "Intrafamilial Sexual Abuse: Brother-Sister Incest Does Not Differ From Father-Daughter and Stepfather-Stepdaughter Incest." *Child Abuse and Neglect*, v.26 (2002).
Foucalt, M. *The History of Sexuality*, Vol. 1. New York: Random House, 1978.
Jenkins, P. *Moral Panic: Changing Concepts of the Child Molester in Modern America*. New Haven, CT: Yale University Press, 1998.

Indecent Exposure

Indecent exposure, often referred to as public indecency, is bodily exposure or parts of bodily exposure within a public domain. Specifically, A. Young states that "indecency laws apply to conduct or misconduct taking place in a public or quasi-public domain whereby individuals are invited to or pay for admission." However, the complexity of understanding indecent exposure is arguably rooted in defining the term and the shifting of perspectives. As early as the 1700s, societal norms viewed the exposure of legs, ankles, and shoulders as an indecent act—an act against the moral fabric of the prevailing cultural norms. These beliefs were upheld by the status quo throughout the Victorian period (1837–1901).

Throughout the 20th to the 21st century, the laws of public indeceny predicated on both social and sexual tolerance. The transformation of sexual imagery and tolerance is predicated on what society deems sexually appropriate or inappropriate in a time-laden and cultural context. Often, what is considered by a society to be indecent is rooted in the social stigmas adhering to, reflective of, and defined by traditions, morals, and the religious genesis of that society. As such, the concept of indecent exposure is variable, culturally sensitive, and relevant.

What is considered indecent, inappropriate, sexually deviant, or offensive in one culture may not mirror the expectations and tolerance levels of another culture. For example, the definition of indecent exposure has evolved throughout history from the revealing of ones' genitalia to one or more person in a public domain to evoke shock, to the exposure of any female body part (i.e., the public exposure of a female breasts), which is deemed unlawful in ultra-conservative states. In New York, the law extends to those who willfully expose themselves and urinate in public.

Consequently, the media has also played a visible role in carving the public's perception of and attitudes toward indecent exposure. Contemporary platforms of communication such as social networking forums, coupled with traditional forms of communication such as television and print media, have embodied other avenues that have heightened awareness in the public domain of defining lewd and indecent acts globally. For example, while Canada does not provide a statutory definition of indecency, the law denotes that the exposure of genitalia or female nipples to anyone under the age of 14 is decided by judicial discretion and thus variable in nature. Moreover, the mere act of public nudity is not considered indecent within the general population.

The Role of Media

Media, particularly social media, facilitates shaping the landscape of how society and individuals view and react to public indecencies. Reactions to indecency are contingent on whether a particular act receives high or low visibility and coverage. When public domains such as YouTube, Facebook, and Twitter sensationalize such acts, the lens of the public tends to shift and subsequently frames judicial attitudes. Hence, laws are codified by judicial officers to define the parameters of what is deemed unlawful and harmful to the general public. For example, Young argues that three types of harm have been established supporting a finding of indecency: "(1) harm to those whose liberties have been violated when confronted with inappropriate conduct; (2) harm to society given the predisposition to others via anti-social conduct; and (3) harm to individuals participating in the conduct." Given the inadequacy of the aforementioned constructs, recent studies have particularly focused on indecencies involving minors, although women historically have been most often impacted and victimized.

Patrick Pflaum conducted a study on indecent exposure, "Shocking and Embarrassing Displays Online: Recent Developments in Military Crimes Involving Indecent Conduct via Webcam," and found that the military fails to provide the protection of a minor under what laws have been established and deemed harmful for minors in the general public. Pflaum further argues that the military's defining characteristics of indecent exposure are peppered with ambiguities requiring the physical presence of an exposure with a minor, yet ignoring the harmful nature such acts have on minors. Consequently, the laws that currently embody the military justice system are suffering from a cultural lag by not maintaining a technological stride with the epoch of the Internet. Additionally, the challenge of defining indecent exposure is currently in the wake of another paradigmatic shift whereby public breastfeeding by women is categorized in some Western cultures as indecent exposure, which challenges and questions (as feminist would argue) the social freedoms of women.

Conclusion

Indecent exposure greatly reflects cultural ideologies and practices within a societal perspective.

While the definition of indecent exposure is tautological in nature and is sculpted by the evolution of societal values and the passage of time, D. Finkelhor posits that society and lawmakers would benefit by contextualizing the offense within the parameters of a given society, not by just examining the idiosyncratic nature of individual offenders.

Anita Bledsoe-Gardner
Johnson C. Smith University

See Also: 1921 to 1940 Primary Documents; 1941 to 1960 Primary Documents; Children's Rights; Juries; News Media, Crime in; Sex Offender Laws; Sex Offenders.

Further Readings
Finkelhor, D. *Sexually Victimized Children*. New York: Macmillan, 1979.
Pflaum, Patrick D. "Shocking and Embarrassing Displays On-Line: Recent Developments in Military Crimes Involving Indecent Conduct via Webcam." *The Army Lawyer* (March 2010).
Riordan, S. "Indecent Exposure: The Impact Upon the Victim's Fear of Sexual Crime." *Journal of Forensic Psychiatry*, v.10/2 (1999).
U. S. Department of Health and Human Services, Human Resources and Services Administration, Maternal and Child Health Bureau. "Breastfeeding Laws." http://www.ncsl.org/default.aspx?tabid=14389 (Accessed September 2011).
Young, A. "The State Is Still in the Bedrooms of the Nation: The Control and Regulation of Sexuality in Canadian Criminal Law." *Canadian Journal of Human Sexuality*, v.17/4 (2008).

Independent Treasury Act

The Independent Treasury Act, first passed in 1840 at the urging of President Martin Van Buren, and again in 1846, formally separated the U.S. Treasury and its policies from commercial banking. It required all federal revenues to be placed into several regional depositories, called subtreasuries, rather than in national, state, or private banks as had generally been federal practice since

This 1840 cartoon uses the figure of a woodcutter chopping down a hickory tree to portray the opposition to the independent treasury system and its subtreasuries, which Andrew Jackson originated and Martin Van Buren continued.

the 1790s. The measure also required that future payments to the national government be made in specie (gold or silver) only. Paper currency such as banknotes would no longer be accepted. This federal treasury system would generally stay in effect until the establishment in 1913 of the Federal Reserve System, which again tied the federal treasury to commercial banking. The last subtreasuries were closed in 1920.

Creation of the Independent Treasury System resulted from a long-standing political argument between Whigs and Democrats over the merits of the Second Bank of the United States (commonly called the National Bank). Besides acting as an agent of the Treasury Department and a repository for federal revenues, this semiprivate institution conducted commercial business as well. While Whigs viewed the National Bank as essential to financing national economic development, preventing dangerous financial bubbles, and sustaining a stable currency, Democrats believed it constituted an unconstitutional, powerfully corrupt, and sinister threat to democracy and determined to eliminate it.

The conflict came to a head when Democrat Andrew Jackson assumed the presidency. Determined to "kill the monster," Jackson vetoed the National Bank's charter renewal in 1832, four years prior to its expiration, and then effectively defunded it by withdrawing federal revenues and placing them in numerous private state-chartered banks (derisively dubbed "pet banks" by Jackson's opponents). Congress followed with a Distribution Act that required all surplus federal funds be distributed to the states each year.

Soon after the National Bank's demise, the nation witnessed a dangerous overspeculation in federal land sales and certain commodities. The state banks, recently fattened with federal deposits, which they used to increase their lending capacity, fueled this behavior. Through speculative lending, they flooded the economy with paper currency. Land and commodity prices were rising dangerously and without the defunct National Bank to rein them in. Recognizing the danger of a growing financial bubble that could result in economic collapse, in 1836 Jackson issued an executive order, called the Specie Circular, requiring all payments to the federal government to be in gold or silver. Rather than head off a crisis, as Jackson had hoped, the new policy led to a drain of specie from the banks and eventually to a severe economic collapse and depression, dubbed the Panic of 1837.

A New Federal System

Jackson's Democratic successor, Martin Van Buren, proposed that Congress create a new method for maintaining federal funds that would be totally divorced from the banking system. He reflected a desire of many Democrats for an alternative to either reestablishing the National Bank as Whigs were demanding or continuing the policy of depositing revenues in state banks as some "soft money" Democrats (those who favored inflating the currency with paper money) allied with state banking interests preferred. The onset of severe economic distress convinced many Democrats to end the policy of depositing federal revenues in state banks.

After several failures, Congress passed and Van Buren signed the Independent Treasury Act in 1840. It created the system that, except for the Civil War, generally governed the handling of federal funds until the creation of the Federal Reserve System in 1913. All federal revenues would be maintained by the Treasury Department in several regional vaults called subtreasuries and thereby would be unavailable for speculative ventures by bankers. The measure also included a specie clause requiring payments to the federal government to be only in specie. The Whigs successfully repealed the law in 1841, after briefly winning control of Congress for one term, but the Democrats reenacted it in 1846.

Although it helped to limit excessive financial speculation, the Independent Treasury System seemed to create new problems for the economy. The specie requirement and the stockpiling of specie in the subtreasuries often served to freeze up currency circulation, resulting in excessive credit tightening. The Lincoln administration temporary suspended the requirements of the Independent Treasury Act, finding it nearly impossible to finance the Civil War while adhering to its restrictions. Rapid industrialization of the later 19th century seemed to require a more flexible financial system while distressed debtors, particularly farmers, sparked the Populist movement, demanding relief through increasing the currency in circulation. Many blamed the severe depressions of 1893 and 1907 on lack of currency flexibility.

In 1913, Congress replaced the Independent Treasury with the Federal Reserve System, again tying the U.S. treasury to the banking system. The government gradually transferred federal funds from the subtreasuries to Federal Reserve district banks.

John Kelly Damico
Georgia Perimeter College

See Also: Corruption, History of; Jackson, Andrew (Administration of); Lincoln, Abraham (Administration of); Securities and Exchange Commission.

Further Readings
Kinley, David. *The History, Organization and Influence of the Independent Treasury of the United States*. Charleston, SC: Nabu Press, [1893] 2010.

Platt, John David Rolands. *The United States Independent Treasury System*. Washington, DC: U.S. Office of Archaeology and Historic Preservation, 1968.

Rothbard, Murray N. *A History of Money and Banking in the United States: The Colonial Era to World War II*. Auburn, AL: Ludwig von Mises Institute, 2002.

Indian Civil Rights Act

The Indian Civil Rights Act of 1968 (ICRA) applies many of the provisions of the U.S. Bill of Rights to Indian tribes (U.S.C. 25, sections 1301–3). Growing out of concern for Native Americans abused by both non-Indian and tribal agencies, the ICRA ostensibly gave federal courts jurisdiction to hear civil rights claims against tribal nations. Ten years after its enactment and considerable litigation under the act, the Supreme Court found that the court lacked jurisdiction to hear ICRA cases, considerably limiting the reach of the ICRA.

Prior to 1968, tribal governments were exempted from the limitations outlined in the Bill of Rights based on the notion that tribal sovereignty predates the Constitution. During the 1960s, however, the perceived lack of legal protections for tribal members garnered increasing attention. Abuses by federal and state non-Indian agencies, including the Bureau of Indian Affairs and local police departments, prompted several Indian organizations to voice concern for civil rights. Federal lawmakers also expressed an interest in securing rights for tribal members but focused on violations by tribal governments. Fearing that tribal governments, not bound by the Bill of Rights, might restrict the freedoms and rights of citizens under tribal jurisdiction, Congress began drafting the ICRA. Because the ICRA seeks to limit tribal self-government to reflect the Bill of Rights, some representatives of Indian tribes opposed the act, protesting that the ICRA was an infringement on tribal sovereignty. In response to this objection, the final version of the act does not incorporate the Bill of Rights in full.

Several guarantees of the Bill of Rights are modified or excluded in recognition of the diverse cultural and political practices of the various tribes. The establishment clause of the First Amendment, for example, was omitted from the ICRA to respect the religious-based governments of some tribes. Unlike the Bill of Rights, the ICRA also does not guarantee the right to appointed counsel or the right to a jury trial. Moreover, the act originally prohibited tribes from imposing sentences of more than six months in prison and $500 in fines. Since its enactment, the ICRA has been amended twice: in 1986 to increase sentencing limitations, and again in 1991 to overturn the Supreme Court decision in *Duro v. Reina*, 495 U.S. 676 (1990), holding that tribes did not have criminal jurisdiction over nonmember Indians. As a result, the ICRA now includes the exercise of criminal jurisdiction over all Indians (members and nonmembers) in the powers of tribal self-government.

Following the passage of the ICRA, federal courts began hearing cases involving civil rights violations by tribal governments. In the decade after its enactment, federal courts decided nearly 80 cases covering a wide array of civil rights issues, including civil and criminal proceedings in tribal courts, tribal voting, tribal police activities, and equal protection cases. The first case to reach the Supreme Court, *Santa Clara Pueblo v. Martinez*, 149 U.S. 49 (1978), challenged tribal membership decisions. Instead of addressing the merits of the case, however, the court disposed of the case on a jurisdictional basis. The Supreme Court held that the ICRA did not grant federal courts broad jurisdiction to review tribal government civil rights claims except those complaints arising under section 1303 as writ of habeas corpus actions. The Supreme Court's decision thus greatly circumscribed the impact of the ICRA. As a result, tribal courts are the only forum in which most ICRA protections can be enforced.

Tribal courts, therefore, bear the primary responsibility for enforcing the civil rights protections set forth in the ICRA. Although the Supreme Court's decision in *Martinez* is considered a victory for the recognition of tribal sovereignty, the case also prompted concern that there might not be a judicial forum to enforce the ICRA because tribal sovereign immunity prohibits a tribe from being sued in tribal court. As the U.S. Commission on Civil Rights noted in its 1991 Report on the Indian Civil Rights Act, the vindication of rights guaranteed by the ICRA is contingent upon the extent to which tribal governments waive their immunity from suit. Tribal governments have accordingly been called upon to acknowledge the civil rights of their tribal members by passing legislation explicitly waiving their sovereign immunity from suit under the ICRA or by passing additional tribal civil rights laws. After *Martinez*, many tribes began amending tribal constitutions to incorporate their own version of the Bill of Rights.

Matthew H. Birkhold
Princeton University, Columbia Law School

See Also: Bill of Rights; Civil Rights Laws; Courts of Indian Offenses; Indian Removal Act; Native Americans.

Further Readings
Johansen, Bruce E. and Barry Pritzker. *Encyclopedia of American Indian History*. Santa Barbara, CA: ABC-CLIO, 2008.
O'Brien, Sharon. *American Indian Tribal Governments*. Norman: University of Oklahoma Press, 1989.
Richland, Justin B. and Sarah Deer. *Introduction to Tribal Legal Studies*. Lanham, MD: AltaMira Press, 2010.

This 1838 print depicts Sauk leader Black Hawk, who led an unsuccessful 1832 uprising in an attempt to push back against white incursion into Native American lands in Ohio. He was taken prisoner and displayed in New York as a prisoner of war.

Indian Removal Act

The Indian Removal Act of 1830 authorized the president of the United States to exchange unorganized land west of the Mississippi River for Indian-held land within existing states and territories. The act granted Indians perpetual title to the western land and compensated Indians for improvements made to the exchanged land in the east. In addition, the act provided for the aid and assistance of the relocated Indians for the first year of removal. All expenses associated with transportation to the west were to be assumed by the federal government, for which the act appropriated $500,000. The act itself did not order the forced removal of the Indians or sanction the abrogation of treaties that guaranteed land rights to Indians within the states but simply empowered the president to negotiate such exchanges. Accordingly, removals of specific Native nations were concluded by individual treaties.

The wholesale removal of the Indians was not a new idea in 1830 but had been proposed as early as 1803 by President Thomas Jefferson. Although the earliest land exchange and removal was concluded in 1817, America's policy had largely been to allow Indians to remain within the states if they assimilated or became "civilized." Increased contact, especially between the Five Civilized Tribes—the Chickasaw, Choctaw, Creek, Seminole, and Cherokee—and white settlers in the southeast, however, exacerbated existing tensions between Indians' claims to sovereignty and states' rights.

Cherokee Claims of Sovereignty in Georgia
The adoption of a federal act to address the conflict was precipitated by the Georgia legislature, which in 1828 extended Georgia's jurisdiction

over Indians within the state. After ceding lands to the federal government in 1802 for a pledge to extinguish all Indian titles to land within the state, Georgia began to doubt whether the federal government would uphold the deal when, in 1827, the Cherokee adopted a constitution asserting the independence and sovereignty of their nation. The Cherokee had negotiated treaties with the United States protecting their right against encroachment by Georgia. Like other southern states, however, Georgia claimed that Indians did not have a right to occupancy and sought to expropriate Indian lands, despite the constitutional provision authorizing the United States alone to make treaties with the Indian tribes and to acquire their territory. The Georgia legislature delayed enforcement of the policy until June 1, 1830, giving Congress and the president time to devise a plan.

In his 1829 State of the Union address, President Andrew Jackson discussed the constitutional issues raised by the Cherokee claims to political sovereignty within Georgia, expressing his belief that Indians were subject to the laws of the states in which they resided. Recommending new legislation, the president concluded that removal to western territory was the only action that could save the remaining tribes from extinction. The ensuing debate in Congress over Jackson's proposed legislation quickly divided along political and geographic lines, with Democrats and southerners supporting the act. The opposition argued that treaties with the Native Americans were the law of the land and that the Jackson administration, by refusing to enforce existing treaties, was violating the Constitution. In addition to protesting the unfair treatment of the Indians, opponents also insisted that Jackson's active participation in the legislative process was an attempt to control congressional affairs and was therefore an assault on the constitutional system.

Political Support for Removal

Proponents of the act argued that removal was the only way of ending violence against the Indians and defended the constitutional right of the states to exercise sovereignty over all residents within their borders, including Indians. Pointing to a clause in the proposed act guaranteeing that no provision would be construed as authorizing the violation of any existing treaty between the United States and Indian tribes, Jackson and his supporters maintained that Indians were welcome to remain behind as citizens of the states, where they would be both protected in persons and property, and subject to all state laws. Emigration, while championed as the best solution for the Indians, would be voluntary.

In the end, the act narrowly passed and was signed on May 24, 1830, by President Jackson, who immediately began negotiating with the tribes. Indian removal was ultimately carried out on a forcible basis as treaties with Indians were often negotiated under duress and fraud. While some tribes peacefully relocated, many resisted the relocation policy through both legal channels and violent measures. After Georgia extended state jurisdiction, the Cherokee and Creek rejected negotiation talks with President Jackson, choosing instead to take their case directly to the Supreme Court. When the Mississippi legislature, following Georgia's lead, voted to exercise jurisdiction over Indian lands in the state, the Chickasaw similarly sought legal recourse. Forbidden from exercising tribal power and threatened with fines and imprisonment, the Chickasaw protested the contravention of treaties ratified by the United States, appealing to President Jackson to enforce federal law. In response, the Chickasaw were told that they had no alternative to submitting to Mississippi law but to move. Other tribes, including the Seminole, waged guerrilla wars against federal authorities.

Trail of Tears

In September 1830, the Chocktaw in Mississippi became the first tribe to formally conclude a land exchange and removal treaty. Less than two years later, the Creek abandoned their legal challenges, the Seminole consented to relocation, and by 1832, the Chickasaw decided they could no longer live under Mississippi law. By the end of Jackson's first term, all of the Five Civilized Tribes had moved but the Cherokee. Although in 1831 the Supreme Court ruled in *Cherokee Nation v. Georgia* that the Cherokee had no standing in court to appeal Georgia's seizure of their lands, Chief Justice John Marshall wrote one year later in *Worcester v. Georgia* that the Cherokee nation was a distinct community, occupying its own territory in which the laws of Georgia had no force. Nevertheless, President Jackson continued pursuing his removal policy and the Cherokee were forcibly evicted from their lands in Georgia by federal troops. Under increasing pressure from American intrusion and settlement, the Cherokee were finally forced to undertake a forced march west, joining the mass migration of Indians known today as the Trail of Tears of the 1830s and 1840s.

Matthew H. Birkhold
Princeton University, Columbia Law School

See Also: 1801 to 1850 Primary Documents; 1851 to 1900 Primary Documents; Indian Civil Rights Act; Jackson, Andrew (Administration of); Marshall, John; Native Americans.

Further Readings
Johansen, Bruce E. and Barry Pritzker. *Encyclopedia of American Indian History*. Santa Barbara, CA: ABC-CLIO, 2008.
Remini, Robert Vincent. *Andrew Jackson & His Indian Wars*. New York: Viking, 2001.
Wallace, Anthony F. C. and Eric Foner. *The Long, Bitter Trail: Andrew Jackson and the Indians*. New York: Hill & Wang, 1993.

Indiana

Originally a French territory in the Midwest, Indiana became a state in 1816. In the 19th and early 20th centuries, it had a perennial problem with vigilante groups and lynchings. The term *White Caps* is used to refer to several Indiana groups that lynched known and suspected criminals after the Civil War. The first famous incident involving the White Caps was the lynching of 10 members of the Reno Gang, which ended the gang's activities in 1868; the gang had begun its train robberies during the Civil War and continued in the years following, inspiring other train robbery gangs. Two of the gang members were in federal custody when they were taken away by a White Cap mob and lynched—the only time in American history that federal prisoners have been lynched before a trial.

Further White Cap activities ranged beyond violent criminals like the Reno Gang and included lynching of horse thieves (one such group was called the State Horse Thief Detective Association). Other "moral groups" apprehended and flogged public drunks, the unemployed, and men unwilling to provide for their families, in order to encourage better behavior among the populace. As the reputation of such groups grew, they got bolder and even harassed women thought to be straying from their home and domestic duties, as well as truant schoolchildren. White Cap groups died out toward the end of the century, as the state and local sheriff's departments made it a higher priority to punish members.

Police and Punishment

One reason vigilante groups arose in Indiana is because law enforcement was sparsely distributed, and the proximity of the frontier—with its outlaws and Indian wars—was a constant source of concern for settlers. Town marshals became more common after the 1853 passage of the second Indiana constitution; while serving the same role as the modern local police force, town marshals were elected officials, not professional law officers. In many places, especially growing cities like Indianapolis and Lafayette, they were supplemented with private "merchant police," who could be compared to either security guards or mercenary soldiers, depending on the situation. Cities and large towns typically had a formalized city watch as well, and over the course of the 19th century, paid police forces were eventually adopted, their jurisdictions overlapping with those of the county sheriffs and in some cases township constables. Early police departments were overseen by the town marshal rather than a dedicated police chief, but this changed by the end of the 19th century in most jurisdictions.

Indiana's first state prison opened in 1821 in Jeffersonville and was later known as Indiana State Prison South, in contrast with State Prison North, built in 1860 in Michigan City. Both prisons expanded their capacity over time, and from 1897 to 1918, State Prison South was used to house male inmates age 16–30, in the belief that young men should not be kept in the same prison as older career criminals. When a 1918 fire damaged most of the prison, it was replaced with a new, more centrally located prison in Fall Creek Township, near Pendleton. The new prison served

The Jefferson County Jail in Madison, Indiana, was built in 1848–50 and survived nearly unchanged into the late 20th century as a prime example of a 19th-century American jail. The photo shows its heavy cellblock doors and iron catwalk.

as the Indiana Reformatory until 1996, when it was renamed the Pendleton Correctional Facility. One of the most famous inmates of the prison was bank robber John Dillinger, who was sentenced to 10–20 years for the robbery of a grocery store and beating of its owner.

Around the turn of the century, police departments throughout Indiana began to be modernized. In 1893, Lafayette established a Metropolitan Board of Police Commissioners to run the department independently of the Lafayette mayor. The commissioners appointed and oversaw a superintendent and two captains (one to run the night shift, the other the day shift). This was a significant shift in sophistication of organization and bureaucracy from the loosely organized city watch overseen by the town marshal, which had been the norm only 30 years earlier. The Indiana State Police was created in 1921, originally as the 16-man Motor Vehicle Police Force (MVPF), given statewide jurisdiction over traffic laws. In 1933, the MVPF was turned into the Indiana State Police.

Ku Klux Klan

The second Ku Klux Klan, inspired by the portrayal of the first in the movie *Birth of a Nation* and responding to Protestant white fears of Catholic immigrants and the Great Migration of blacks, was founded in Georgia in 1915 but quickly spread. While the original Klan had been a vigilante group fighting against those then in power in the south, the second Klan was treated by many as a fraternal organization like the Elks, and amassed considerable political power—despite its role in lynchings, cross-burnings, property destruction, harassment, and other acts of violence. It was also strongly allied with the temperance movement in the years before Prohibition.

Nowhere was the second Klan more influential than in Indiana, which had rapidly industrialized in the preceding decades and become home to an influx of newcomers of many ethnicities previously unrepresented in the state. The Indiana Klan broke away from the national organization in 1923, led by Grand Dragon D. C. Stephenson, and quickly reached its peak of power, with 30 percent of white men in the state members of the Klan, as well as half of the legislators, many government officials, and Governor Ed Jackson, who served 1925–29. Many former White Caps were now Klansmen, but the Klan had a political influence not seen in the state before or since.

The Klan's efforts in Indiana were aimed primarily at Catholics, and they used their political power to shut down numerous Catholic schools. Street fights broke out regularly between Klansmen and minority groups. The group's power waned quickly after Stephenson was arrested for the rape and second-degree murder of Madge Oberholtzer, an Indiana teacher who was in charge of the state's literacy programs. The night of Jackson's inauguration, Stephenson repeatedly raped Oberholtzer on a train ride, until she poisoned herself in order to induce an illness that would convince him to return her home. After telling several people what had happened, she died, either of the poison or the injuries Stephenson had given her. He was immediately arrested.

Because Jackson had been elected only because of Stephenson's support, Stephenson assumed he would be pardoned, but no pardon came (in fact, he spent the next 30 years in prison). So Stephenson himself, out of apparent spite, undercut the Klan's power by revealing to reporters many instances of the Klan's bribes and behind-the-scenes work in Indiana politics. Jackson was brought to trial, which resulted in a hung jury, and he refused the many demands for him to resign, but his political career ended decisively when his term as governor did. Attempts to revive the Klan in Indiana when Klan groups in the south were founded in response to the civil rights movement failed.

Crime

In the 1960s, Indiana was home to one of the worst child abuse cases in American history. Gertrude Baniszewski was a divorced woman who agreed to take in two teen sisters as boarders while their parents, traveling carnival workers, went on the road for work. When their parents' payment failed to show up on time, she beat the children for a minor infraction, and over the course of the summer, the abuse grew. She enlisted her own children and their friends in the neighborhood to torture and abuse the eldest sister, Sylvia Likens, who was kept naked in the basement. She was sexually abused with Coke bottles and red-hot needles, doused with scalding hot water, beaten regularly, and eventually killed.

In 2010, the first comprehensive review of Indiana's criminal code since the 1970s was conducted, with the goal of both reducing recidivism and reducing the cost of imprisonment to taxpayers by enacting prison reforms. In particular, community-based programs and stronger rehabilitation programs—giving long-term inmates skills to embark on a crime-free life after prison—were emphasized, along with more sensible sentencing guidelines. The call for reform had increased after a spike in Indiana's prison populations and the realization that $1 billion would be needed to build new prisons from 2011 to 2018 in order to address the system's growing needs. Many of the recommended changes in sentencing dealt with reducing the jail sentences for nonviolent drug offenses, which accounted for a sizable portion of the prison population.

Bill Kte'pi
Independent Scholar

See Also: 1921 to 1940 Primary Documents; Child Abuse, History of; Frontier Crime; Ku Klux Klan; Lynchings; Women Criminals, History of.

Further Readings
Bodenhamer, David J. and Randall T. Shepard, eds. *The History of Indiana Law*. Athens: University of Ohio Press, 2006.
Madison, James. *The Indiana Way*. Bloomington: Indiana University Press, 1990.
Moore, Leonard J. *Citizen Klansmen: The Ku Klux Klan in Indiana, 1921–1928*. Chapel Hill: University of North Carolina Press, 1997.

Infanticide

Perhaps one of the most underreported causes of death in the United States, infanticide takes the lives of between 100 and 300 infants annually. Despite the availability of contraceptives and abortion, as well as new laws in all 50 states that allow parents to abandon without legal repercussion unharmed infants within seven days of birth, cases of infanticide have remained fairly constant. Nearly every civilization has practiced infanticide, from ancient Greeks and Persians to medieval Europeans. Parents used it to control family size as a means to avoid starvation. The economic stress and social disorder of the American colonial period led to an increase in infanticide; officials reacted with harsh laws that included the death penalty to prevent the practice.

By the 19th century, judges and juries were often lenient toward single women who committed infanticide, considering them as seduced and abandoned victims. In Chicago between 1870 and 1930, 185 cases of infanticide occurred. Police solved 21 cases, and prosecutors brought 11 cases to trial; courts convicted only one woman. This attitude reflected a societal view of women that had evolved from the colonial lustful temptress to the 19th-century woman of Republican virtue and morality who fell prey to male sexual behavior. As society developed an increasing sense of the centrality of motherhood to women's identity, infanticide increasingly came to be seen as unnatural. Some medical professionals deemed mothers who killed to be temporarily insane, while others saw their actions as an abomination against nature.

Perceptions of these women varied according to circumstances. Evidence of preparing for the infant's arrival often led to acquittals based on the assumption that the death was accidental. Women who had made no preparations often faced charges because officials believed they had planned to kill the infant at birth; some women deflected such accusations by claiming that the infant came a month earlier than expected. Married women tended to avoid prosecution more than single women: With husbands to support them, officials often believed these women had no excuse to commit infanticide and thus deemed the death unintended.

Proving infanticide was difficult. An infant could have been strangled accidentally by the umbilical cord or intentionally with string. Bruising could have been caused by the woman going through a difficult birth alone or by premeditated blunt force trauma. The hydrostatic test, introduced into American courts in the 19th century, was unreliable. The test could be useful if doctors did not draw unwarranted conclusions from it; the test, for example, could prove a false positive for live birth if decomposition had accumulated gases in the lungs.

Over time, the reasons for infanticide remained relatively constant. Many women feared social ostracism: Pregnancy was a visible sign of premarital sex. Others faced dire economic circumstances: Unwed pregnant women had difficulty holding respectable jobs. As such, many hid the pregnancy and gave birth alone. Some women denied the pregnancy, leading them to deliver in bathrooms because they had convinced themselves that the cramping of labor pains was caused by a need to defecate. Others simply panicked. A minority suffered from postpartum psychosis, a diagnosis that emerged in the 19th century and divided professionals into the 21st century.

Punishment

The American legal approach to infanticide differed from that of Europe; 15th-century courts in France and 18th-century courts in German states often granted leniency to women based on mental disturbance. Austria abolished the death penalty for infanticide in 1803. The British M'Naghten Rule of 1843 stated that defendants could not be held responsible for their actions based on their mental state; Parliament specifically applied this principle in the Infanticide Acts of 1922 and 1938, which stated that women who killed their infants within 12 months of birth were mentally ill. The German code of the early 20th century mandated no more than three years' hard labor for mothers who killed illegitimate infants. By 2000, 29 countries had separate laws governing infanticide, with most mandating treatment versus punishment. In the United States, no separate law applies to mothers. With no presumption of mental illness, defense attorneys must prove mental illness. Although the American Psychiatric Association recognized postpartum disorder in 1994, no formal diagnostic criteria exist for it.

Simone M. Caron
Wake Forest University

See Also: 2001 to 2012 Primary Documents; Abortion; Child Abuse, History of; Child Abuse, Sociology of; Children, Abandoned; Gender and Criminal Law; Prostitution, History of; Smith, Susan; Women Criminals, Contemporary; Yates, Andrea.

Further Readings
Barton, Brenda. "When Murdering Mothers Rock the Cradle: An Overview of America's Incoherent Treatment of Infanticidal Mothers." *Southern Methodist University Law Review* (March/April 1998).
Hoffer, Peter C. and N. E. H. Hull. *Murdering Mothers: Infanticide in England and New England 1558–1803.* New York: New York University Press, 1981.
Jackson, Mark, ed. *Infanticide: Historical Perspectives on Child Murder and Concealment, 1550–2000.* Aldershot Hants, UK: Ashgate Publishing, 2002.
Oberman, Michelle. "Understanding Infanticide in Context: Mothers Who Kill, 1870–1930." *Journal of Criminal Law and Criminology*, v.92 (2002).

Insanity Defense

The insanity defense is one of the most controversial and misunderstood topics within criminal law, raising difficult questions about whether, and to what extent, mental illness should absolve a defendant of criminal responsibility. When defendants are found "not guilty by reason of insanity" (NGRI), it means that mental illness or defect prevented them from possessing the "guilty mind" (mens rea) required to hold them legally responsible. Thus, insanity is a legal term, not a medical one. Those acquitted on grounds of insanity are normally committed to psychiatric facilities (for rehabilitation and treatment) instead of being incarcerated (for punishment). In many states, commitment to a mental facility is automatic upon the rendering of a NGRI verdict. In some states, commitment is discretionary. In these states, trial judges have the authority to detain insane individuals for examination and observation (to determine whether they should be committed). The insanity defense has an extensive history in Anglo-American law. Despite this long tradition, the insanity defense is viewed with suspicion by the public, and after the 1982 insanity acquittal of John Hinckley, Jr., several jurisdictions either modified or abolished it.

Historic Evolution of Insanity Tests

The insanity defense has been traced to the works of Homer and Aristotle. Under ancient Roman law, insane persons were treated like wild beasts: they could not be held responsible for their actions, but their keepers could be liable in tort for failing to restrain them. Lenience for the insane was sometimes justified on the grounds that "the madman is sufficiently punished by his madness" (*furiosus satis ipso furore punitur*). In England, precursors to the insanity defense appeared as early as the 10th century, and insanity became recognized as a complete defense during the early 14th century. Over time, in England and later in the United States, a number of influential legal tests for insanity were developed.

One of the earliest tests for insanity was the "wild beast" test, developed from the writings of eminent 13th-century jurist Lord Bracton. This test was applied in the 1812 attempted homicide case, *Rex v. Arnold*, where Justice Tracy told the jury that when a man is totally deprived of his understanding and his memory and does not know what he is doing, he is like an infant or a wild beast and not an appropriate object for punishment. The "child of 14" test, developed by 17th-century jurist Matthew Hale, was an attempt to address the jurisprudential dilemma of "partial insanity" (conditions where the reason is impaired, but not entirely absent, such as in cases of severe depression). Hale suggested that if the afflicted person possessed the understanding that an ordinary 14-year-old has, then punishment was appropriate. Absent such understanding, an insanity acquittal was appropriate.

The insane delusion test was articulated in the 1800 case *Rex v. Hadfield*. James Hadfield, a former soldier who had sustained brain injuries, believed that Jesus Christ was returning to Earth to save humanity, but that in order to precipitate Christ's return, Hadfield had to die. A devout Christian, he could not commit suicide. Hadfield's solution was to fire a shot at King George III, allowing himself to be arrested and executed. Under the prevailing wild beast test, an insanity acquittal looked unlikely. After all, Hadfield knew what he was doing, knew that treason and murder were wrong, and planned his offense. He appeared rational. But Hadfield was defended by brilliant lawyer Thomas Erskine, who argued that the total incapacity required under the wild beast test does not in fact exist, and that actual insanity is different. Reason is not absent in cases of insanity but is compromised by distraction. The court agreed with him, stopping the proceedings to instruct a compliant jury that Hadfield was unequivocally insane and that an insanity acquittal was in order.

Forty years later, in the case of *Regina v. Oxford*, the irresistible impulse test was formulated. In some ways, the case resembled *Hadfield*. Like James Hadfield, Edward Oxford fired a shot at a royal (Queen Victoria, in this case). But unlike Hadfield, Oxford was not trying to trigger a global event. In fact, he could not even say why he fired a pistol at Victoria, whom he considered to be a very nice lady. Because the court found that, at the time of the offense, Oxford lacked the will to control his actions and acted from an irresistible and uncontrollable impulse, he was found not guilty by reason of insanity.

It is generally agreed that the M'Naghten (McNaghten) rule has been the most influential test of insanity. In 1843, Daniel M'Naghten, believing that he was being persecuted by the English government, attempted to assassinate Prime Minister Robert Peel. But M'Naghten did not what know Peel looked like and killed Peel's secretary, Edward Drummond, by mistake. M'Naghten had excellent lawyers who persuaded the court to stop the trial and effectively direct the jury to acquit. M'Naghten was acquitted, but the House of Lords took the unusual step of requiring the justices in the case to explain their reasoning. Their answers collectively yielded the now-famous M'Naghten test: "To establish a defense on the ground of insanity it must be clearly proved that, at the time of the committing of the act, the party accused was laboring under such a defect of reason, from disease of the mind, as not to know the nature and quality of the act he was doing, or if he did know it, that he did not know he was doing what was wrong." Although the M'Naghten test was widely adopted throughout the United States as the de facto standard, it was criticized on at least three grounds. First, it is entirely cognitive, focusing upon what the defendant knows. It ignores conditions that impede volition. Second, it does not recognize degrees of incapacity, but requires a total

This wooden cage invented in Belgium to restrain the severely mentally ill reflects some of the historical attitudes toward the insane, which equated them with "wild beasts." However, insanity had been recognized as a complete defense in England as early as the 14th century. While the "Belgian Cage" was demonstrated as a curiosity at a national exhibition in Brussels in 1880, it had not been legal for use since a government overhaul of insane asylums in 1850.

lack of awareness. Third, it does not define its key terms (e.g., "know," "nature," or "wrong"), and different jurisdictions have applied these terms in very different ways.

In the 1954 case *Durham v. United States*, Judge David Bazelon formulated the product test. Judge Bazelon rejected the M'Naghten rule and developed an expansive new test: If the defendant's actions were the product of a disease or defect of mind, the defendant was to be found not guilty by reason of insanity. While noteworthy for its break from M'Naghten, the product test was scrutinized and criticized (for conferring too much authority on psychiatric experts, among other things), and was replaced by the 1962 Model Penal Code test developed by the American Law Institute (ALI). The ALI test drew upon the M'Naghten and irresistible impulse tests and bears some resemblance to the product test, but it combined them and used new terms to express the core concepts. The ALI concluded that a defendant is not responsible for his criminal conduct if at the time of the act he lacks substantial capacity either to appreciate the criminality of his conduct or to conform his conduct to the law as a result of mental disease or defect. The ALI standard is more expansive than the M'Naghten rule, since "appreciating" implies emotional as well as intellectual understanding. It is also more precise, since the term *criminality of his conduct* specifies a legal breach, whereas M'Naghten's reference to "wrong" was ambiguous as to whether it implied moral or legal wrongness. The ALI test was adopted by most federal courts and approximately half of the state courts.

Hinckley and the Call for Reform

In 1982, however, the U.S. landscape changed. After John Hinckley, Jr., attempted to assassinate President Ronald Reagan on March 30, 1981, in a bid to impress actress Jodie Foster, a high-profile trial took place, and Hinckley was found not guilty by reason of insanity. The verdict resulted in public outrage. People felt that Hinckley had beaten the rap and that the insanity defense had been abused. Research, however, suggests that such suspicion is misplaced: The insanity defense is rarely invoked (in only about 1 percent of felony cases and even fewer misdemeanor cases) and when insanity is claimed, the plea does not usually succeed (it is rejected in about 75 percent of cases). Even then, when it is successful, the victory is pyrrhic. Most NGRI defendants spend about twice as much time in psychiatric facilities than they would have spent in prison, had they been convicted of the crime.

But the post-*Hinckley* public was incensed, and around the United States, legislatures responded. Jurisdictions restricted the defense, shifted the burden of proof to the defendant, or modified their rules of evidence, and three states (Idaho, Montana, and Utah) abolished the defense entirely. Kansas later abolished it in 1996. In abolitionist states, defendants may introduce evidence of mental disease or defect to rebut the prosecution's claims that they possessed the requisite mens rea to be found guilty of the crime. Thirteen states adopted an alternative verdict, "guilty but mentally ill" (GBMI). If a defendant was guilty of a crime, was sane at the time of the offense, but is "mentally ill" during the trial, juries can return a GBMI verdict. If this verdict is imposed, the defendant receives the sentence that would normally be imposed (e.g., incarceration in a prison) but may receive psychiatric care while in the correctional setting. One exception to this general rule would be the execution of a defendant after committing a capital crime. In 1986, in *Ford v. Wainwright*, the Supreme Court held that executing an insane person violates the Eighth Amendment.

The federal government reacted to the Hinckley case. In 1984, Congress passed the Insanity Defense Reform Act, creating a new standard for federal courts. This statutory test is different from, and stricter than, the ALI test. Under this standard, the burden of proof rests with the defendant. Additionally, the defendant must prove that he suffered from a severe mental disease or defect when he committed the crime and that his mental disease or defect prevented him from appreciating the nature and quality or wrongfulness of his conduct. Both prongs of the test must be proven by clear and convincing evidence. Any other proof of mental disease or defect does not constitute a defense. By requiring "severe mental disease or defect," the test excludes conditions that might have been exculpated under the ALI's substantial capacity standard and approaches the wild beast standard. Similarly, by eliminating the volitional prong of the ALI test, the statute established a test resembling the purely cognitive M'Naghten rule.

Research suggests that these legislative reforms, while ominous sounding, did little to change actual outcomes. Even in states that abolished the defense, mentally ill defendants continued to claim that they lacked the requisite mental state for criminal responsibility (rebutting the prosecution's claim of mens rea). Instead of finding them not guilty by reason of insanity, many of these defendants were found incompetent to stand trial. Most (two-thirds) were committed to the same psychiatric facilities where patients who had been found NGRI were housed. It seems as if post-*Hinckley* legislative reforms changed legal labels but did little to change underlying actual practices.

James C. Oleson
University of Auckland

See Also: 1941 to 1960 Primary Documents; 1961 to 1980 Primary Documents; Capital Punishment; M'Naghten Test; Rehabilitation; Trials.

Further Readings
Bonnie, R. J., et al. *A Case Study in the Insanity Defense: The Trial of John W. Hinckley, Jr.*, 3rd ed. Mineola, NY: Foundation Press, 2008.
Durham v. United States, 214 F.2d 862 (1954).
Ford v. Wainwright, 477 U.S. 399 (1986).
Hans, V. P. "An Analysis of Public Attitudes Toward the Insanity Defense." *Criminology*, v.24 (1986).
Oleson, J. C. "Is Tyler Durden Insane?" *North Dakota Law Review*, v.83 (2007).
Regina v. Oxford, 173 Eng. Rep. 941 (H.L.) (1840).
Rex v. Arnold, 16 How. St. Tr. 695 (1724).
Rex v. Hadfield, 27 How. St. Tr. 1281 (1800).
Robinson, Daniel N. *Wild Beasts and Idle Humours*. Cambridge, MA: Harvard University Press, 1996.
United States v. Hinckley, 525 F. Supp. 1342 (D.D.C. 1981).
Walker, Nigel. *Crime and Insanity in England*. Edinburgh: Edinburgh University Press, 1968.

Internal Revenue Service

The Internal Revenue Service (IRS) is an agency of the U.S. Department of the Treasury, and is charged with collecting taxes and interpreting and enforcing provisions of the Internal Revenue Code. While its primary charge is to act as the revenue service for the federal government, failure to pay taxes on income is a crime, and the IRS frequently becomes involved in criminal prosecutions against those who have acquired monies by illegal means, because this is sometimes the most efficacious approach to punishing wrongdoers. With its thousands of agents and enormous access to financial data relating to individuals, corporations, organizations, and other entities, the IRS is in a prime position to instigate, or assist with, investigations of financial crimes. The IRS has recently been involved with the national security community in an effort to address and prevent terrorist threats associated with illicit finance and the international financial system.

Background
In 1862, during the administration of President Abraham Lincoln, the U.S. Congress authorized the Office of the Commissioner of Internal Revenue and created an income tax to assist with expenditures incurred as a result of the American Civil War. Although the Revenue Act of 1862 was passed as a temporary and emergency solution to a wartime exigency, the position of commissioner of internal revenue has continued to the present day. The Revenue Act of 1862 was modeled upon the British system of generating revenue from income, rather than taxing trade or property. The initial rate of taxation, passed in 1861, was a 3 percent assessment on incomes over $800 per year, which exempted most Americans because they earned an annual income below this amount. In 1862, this was changed to a 3 percent assessment on incomes between $600 and $10,000 per year, with the taxation rate increasing to 5 percent on incomes in excess of $10,000. By the end of the Civil War, approximately 10 percent of households in the Union states had paid this income tax, and this source of revenue allowed the federal government to raise slightly more than 20 percent of the funding needed for the war cause. The Revenue Act of 1862 also created a host of excise taxes, with those imposed on liquor and tobacco surviving the wartime income tax. Much of the activity of the Bureau of Internal Revenue in the latter half of the 19th century involved enforcing these laws against bootleggers, moonshiners, smugglers, and others

After the Harrison Act of 1914 gave drug enforcement authority to the Department of Treasury, the Internal Revenue Service kept laboratories such as this to use in enforcing restrictions on narcotics, which were based on taxation, not criminal punishment.

who conspired to evade paying taxes on liquor. Prior to the imposition of the modern income tax, the tax on liquor trailed only the tariff as the federal government's primary source of revenue.

Although income tax revenues were used after the Civil War to finance Reconstruction, railroads, and other government projects, the temporary income tax provisions were permitted to expire in 1872. Income taxes continued to be seen as an important source of revenue, and in 1894, Congress authorized a new income tax, which was ruled unconstitutional by the U.S. Supreme Court in *Pollock v. Farmers' Loan & Trust Co* (1895). As a result of this ruling, the federal government was unable to impose an income tax again until passage of the Sixteenth Amendment to the U.S. Constitution, which permitted Congress to assess taxes on incomes, "from whatever source derived." The Sixteenth Amendment was quickly ratified by 42 of the then 48 states, and the IRS created its first Form 1040 in 1913, instructing all of those with incomes in excess of $3,000 per year to file. The IRS publishes an enormous number of tax forms from which taxpayers can choose the proper documents and calculate and report their federal tax liability. Although the IRS collects withholding tax from many workers' paychecks and has other ways to gather revenue, it requires individual taxpayers to file an annual tax return stating their income and any deductions permitted under the tax code. Failure to file correct information with the IRS is a criminal offense.

The IRS has grown into an enormous government agency, with its headquarters in Washington, D.C., and service offices located in Austin, Texas; Cincinnati, Ohio; Fresno, California; Kansas City, Missouri; and Ogden, Utah. The IRS collects more than $2.4 trillion in revenues (exclusive of refunds) and processes in excess of 170 million income tax returns every year. Although in 2011, the IRS had a budget of $12.8 billion and more than 105,000 employees, it estimates that the U.S. Treasury is owed more than $350 billion more in tax revenue than the IRS is able to collect. The IRS is authorized to pursue those individuals and entities who cheat on their taxes and is permitted to enforce liens and seize assets without obtaining a judgment in court. Since the failure to pay income taxes is a crime, the IRS is often involved in criminal investigations of those it suspects are illegally withholding revenue owed the federal government.

IRS Response to Tax Evasion

The IRS possesses the authority to investigate those who do not pay the appropriate amount of taxes for tax evasion, which is a federal crime. Occasionally, the federal government chooses to pursue tax evasion charges against criminals who would otherwise be difficult to prosecute, since this is often easier to prove than other allegations. One of the most famous prosecutions involving charges of tax evasion concerned mobster Al Capone, who was in charge of an organization known as the Chicago Outfit, and who was involved in bootlegging, gambling, prostitution, and other criminal activities. In 1928, Frank J. Brown, a former accountant, was assigned by Elmer L. Irey, the chief of the Enforcement Branch of the Bureau of Internal Revenue (the predecessor to the IRS), to investigate Capone on allegations of tax evasion. While Capone had successfully defended several racketeering prosecutions, Irey believed that he might be susceptible to tax evasion charges in light of a 1927 U.S. Supreme Court holding in *United States v. Sullivan* that income from criminal activities was subject to income taxes.

Capone's behavior made the tax evasion investigation complex and challenging because it was difficult to account for his income. Capone did not file federal or state tax returns, maintain a bank account, endorse checks, own property, or provide receipts. Wilson arranged to have federal agents infiltrate the Chicago Outfit to document Capone's dealings. After three years of gathering evidence, Wilson was able to document that Capone had earned millions of dollars that he had not declared, resulting in his 1931 prosecution by the U.S. Department of Justice. Capone was convicted and sentenced to 11 years in prison.

Unreported income in the United States is estimated by the IRS to amount to approximately $2 trillion per year, nearly 20 percent of total reportable income. The IRS has developed a profile of the typical tax evader who does not, contrary to stereotypes, generally earn his or her living through illegal activity. Instead, the typical tax evader is male, under the age of 50, a member of the highest tax bracket, and files a complicated return, frequently with many overstated charitable contributions. An individual meeting this profile has a higher than normal chance of being audited by the IRS. Since the failure to pay the proper amount of income tax is a crime in the United States, individuals and corporations who purposefully or inadvertently evade taxes are, if found guilty, subject to fines, penalties, and in extreme cases, imprisonment.

The IRS's role in investigating and dealing with alleged tax evaders has been criticized. In 1998, for example, the U.S. Congress passed what is popularly known as the Taxpayers Bill of Rights III. This legislation shifted the burden of proof from the taxpayer to the IRS in certain situations and ordered the IRS to engage in more taxpayer-friendly behaviors. Recently, the IRS has also been condemned for allowing plea agreements for some involved in a tax shelter scheme, while vigorously prosecuting others engaged in the same activity.

Combating Terrorism and Financial Crimes

Although the IRS works with other government agencies to investigate criminal activity, it is primarily focused upon collection of revenue owed the U.S. government, pursuant to the tax code. In an effort to combat terrorism and global financial crimes, the U.S. Department of the Treasury established the Office of Terrorist Financing and Financial Crimes (OTFFC) to better coordinate efforts between law enforcement agencies, financial institutions, and the IRS. The OTFFC serves as a policy development and outreach office and works with all elements of the national security community.

The undersecretary for terrorism and financial intelligence supervises the OTFFC. Law enforcement agencies, regulatory groups, policy organizations, members of the diplomatic corps, and intelligence operatives work with the OTFFC to examine financial data provided by the IRS, financial institutions, and foreign governments to detect and prevent threats and all forms of illegal finance from being hidden by the international finance system.

The OTFFC and its partners are most concerned with money laundering, weapons trafficking, terrorist financing, drug smuggling, and financial crimes. The IRS, which collects massive amounts of data regarding possible financial irregularities, sometimes coopeates with the OTFFC to provide evidence of financial malfeasance. As a result of these initiatives, global standards have been developed for combating money laundering and terrorist financing.

Stephen T. Schroth
Knox College

See Also: 1921 to 1940 Primary Documents; 1941 to 1960 Primary Documents; 1961 to 1980 Primary Documents; Bootlegging; Bureau of Alcohol, Tobacco, Firearms and Explosives; Capone, Al; Drug Enforcement Administration; Federal Bureau of Investigation; Harrison Act of 1914; Ness, Eliot; Organized Crime, History of; Tax Crimes; White-Collar Crime, History of.

Further Readings

Glenny, M. *McMafia: A Journey Through the Global Criminal Underworld.* New York: Vintage Press, 2009.

Robinson, J. *The Merger: The Conglomeration of International Organized Crime.* Woodstock, NY: Overlook Press, 2002.

Shafiroff, Ira. *Internal Revenue Service Practice & Procedure Deskbook,* 3rd ed. New York: Practising Law Institute, 2004.

Internal Security Act of 1950

The Internal Security Act of 1950, also referred to as the McCarran Internal Security Act of 1950 and the Subversive Activities Control Act of 1950, became law on September 22, 1950, by congressional resolution. The act required that all communist and related political organizations be registered with the U.S. attorney general. Because of the constitutional questions with requirements of the act, President Harry S. Truman vetoed the law and sent it back to Congress. The law went into effect after both houses voted to override the veto.

In the early 1950s, at the beginning of the cold war, Americans feared the spread of communism into the United States. Congressional hearings under the Dies Committee and the House Un-American Activities Committee kept the anticommunist rhetoric in the public consciousness. In 1950, Congress chose to resurrect the Mundt-Nixon legislation proposed in the previous session. Hearings were held for almost two weeks with testimony from opponents of the legislation. However, the mood in Washington was influenced by the Korean War and the outcome of the Alger Hiss trial. Congress looked to a revised version of the Mundt-Nixon act proposed by Republican Senator Patrick McCarran (Nevada) as the solution. The act would ultimately become known as the McCarran Internal Security Act.

Title one of the act on controlling subversive activities calls for the registration of communist-action and communist-front organizations with the U.S. attorney general. Recognizing the failure of prior laws to enforce this mandate, McCarran alternately required the registration of the officers of non-compliant organizations. Other prohibited acts concerned government employees, conspiracies against the government, properly communicating classified information, and the penalties associated with these crimes. The State Department could not issue passports to registered party members once the law went into effect. Communist parties also had to submit annual reports to the Board of Communist Activities, including a statement of address for individuals, accounting of all monies received, and other membership details. These records had to be kept, and the attorney general was required to notify persons listed. They also had the opportunity to deny membership. The law required annual reports by the attorney general to Congress and the president. The act also amended the Immigration Act of 1917 and the Nationality Act of 1940, where it referred to persons who sought citizenship who had affiliation with the communist government or promoted the spread of communism in the United States in any form.

Concerned about potential problems with the legislation, President Harry Truman asked Congress to only strengthen the espionage and sabotage laws and to caution that any other proposals would be vetoed if they endangered basic constitutional freedoms covered by the First Amendment. Congress did not heed Truman's warning and passed the McCarran Act by large margins in both houses of Congress. Truman vetoed the law, and Congress overrode the veto by the required two-thirds majority in the House and Senate. The McCarran Act would not go into full effect because of immediate challenges brought against the law in the courts. In 1953, President Dwight Eisenhower appointed members to a five-man Subversive Activities Control Board, and all were approved by the Senate. Soon after, the Communist Party was the first to appeal the registration requirements, lost in the Court of Appeals, and spent the next few years going back and forth between the appeals court and the U.S. Supreme Court. In June 1961, the Supreme Court ruled against the Communist Party and determined in a 5–4 vote that the registration requirement was constitutional.

During this same time, another court case concerning 10 individuals was brought to the courts by the attorney general. In May 1962, charges were filed against 10 Communist Party members who refused to register when their party did not. The Supreme Court ruled in 1965 that the party members did not have to register and could not be required to because it might lead to further prosecution under other federal laws. These two decisions resulted in no individuals or groups registering under the law's mandates. During this 15-year period of litigation, Congress continued to investigate espionage cases and kept the country focused on the communist threat with the McCarthy hearings and the House Un-American Activities Committee hearings. In 1968, major amendments to the McCarran Act became law.

Major Pedro Luis Díaz Lanz, the former commander in chief of the Cuban airforce before the Castro takeover, testifying on the communist threat to the United States before a Senate subcommittee on the Internal Security Act in July 1959.

Most of the Title 1 section was repealed in 1968 after court decisions ruled them unconstitutional.

Parts of the McCarran Act are still in effect today. The law revised the quotas for those wanting to immigrate to the United States as established in the Immigration Act of 1940. The major influence was the change from emphasis on admission of Europeans and broadening the definitions to include people from any country, each with an established quota limiting the number of people accepted each year.

In 1965, Congress revised the section of the McCarran Act with the Immigration and Nationality Act of 1965. This legislation abolished the quota system and replaced it with a system that stressed skills of immigrants and gave preference to those who already had relatives in the United States. Seven criteria were established for immigrants from Eastern Hemisphere countries allowing them to immigrate to this country. The law also set a restriction on visas to 170,000 per year, with quotas for each country, with some exceptions for persons from Western Hemisphere countries and those related to American citizens.

Other sections govern federal employees and how they are screened for various security-sensitive positions. When Congress passed the McCarran Act over Truman's veto, they were reacting to events at the time. In 1950, a midterm congressional election saw a trend toward more conservative members. The investigation and conviction of Alger Hiss and the invasion of South Korea by North Korea caused concern about persons with communist leanings getting involved in government and other positions of authority. The intent was to make these groups and individuals register so that their actions could be traced and so that the communist threat would be limited.

Theresa S. Hefner-Babb
Lamar University

See Also: 1941 to 1960 Primary Documents; Eisenhower, Dwight D. (Administration of); McCarthy, Joseph; Political Dissidents; Political Policing; Truman, Harry S. (Administration of).

Further Readings
"An Act to Protect the United States Against Certain Un-American and Subversive Activities by Requiring Registration of Communist Organization, and for Other Purposes." 64 Stat. 987. Washington, DC: Governmental Printing Office, 1952.
Goodman, W. *The Committee: The Extraordinary Career of the House Committee on Un-American Activities*. New York: Farrar, Straus & Giroux, 1968.
Haynes, John E. *Red Scare or Red Menace? American Communism and Anticommunism in the Cold War Era*. Chicago: Ivan R. Dee, 1996.

International Association of Chiefs of Police

Today, the International Association of Chiefs of Police (IACP) serves as a global nonprofit leadership organization of more than 20,000 police executives from more than 100 countries, as well as a resource and advocate organization for advancing police technology, operations, and services.

Established in 1893 as the National Chiefs of Police Union, the founding organization of the IACP was created primarily to locate, apprehend, and return wanted persons who had fled local agency jurisdiction to escape the law, which was an increasing problem during this time. As such, in November 1892, Webber S. Seavey, police chief of Omaha, Nebraska, mailed invitations to 385 heads of the major police agencies in the United States requesting them to convene as a matter of urgency the following year in Chicago, Illinois, with the aim to form a national police organization and to "explore ways in which they could join together to fight crime and improve police services." Fifty-one accepted and subsequently worked together over three days in 1893 to create this new organization. Renamed in 1902, the IACP over the decades has evolved and expanded considerably to include an array of other activities, services, and responsibilities. In the United States and globally, the IACP embraces a rich and respected reputation for improving police practices.

In rising to their motto—"global leadership in policing"—the IACP's mission encompasses a number of key objectives pertaining to all facets of policing. On the whole, this organization works to professionalize and advance the science and practice behind police services in a number of ways. For example, the association seeks to develop and disseminate new methods to improve police organizations internally, technologically, and operationally—for example, in areas of administration, leadership, and management—and well as to provide police with new, sophisticated methods, expertise, and technology for investigating crime and locating offenders. It also helps foster police cooperation and communication on many levels—local, statewide, federal, and international—in order to facilitate the exchange of information and experience among police administrators and agencies. Additionally, the IACP establishes standards for recruiting and training of qualified candidates, including ethics for police professionalism and community interaction. In terms of legislative activity, the IACP has historically taken a conservative stance on drug policy and reducing both the minimum drinking age and availability of firearms, and has long supported legislation in areas to improve policing—for example, through advanced technology, research, and community and partnership initiatives—along with new laws on hate crime, identity theft, and child protection in order to enhance public safety.

Achievements

Since its inception, the IACP has made a number of key achievements in American policing. In 1904, the association helped to encourage the science of using fingerprints as a means of identification through exhibits in various member communities around the country. The IACP played an imperative role in the early days of the Federal Bureau of Investigation (FBI), having created the Uniform Crime Reports in 1922, thus providing the foundation work for the creation of the FBI's Identification Division in 1924. The IACP eventually turned over these files to the FBI in 1930, and then in 1934, began working with the FBI to establish the FBI National Academy. In the same year, the IACP was officially recognized as a source of information for legislators, which helped to establish 12 laws through its recommendations. In 1935, the IACP began to offer consultant services to police agencies and in 1940, established official headquarters in Washington, D.C. The International Police Academy was developed in 1955, followed by minimum training standards for police officers in 1960. The association also played a key role in World War II with the creation of mobilization plans and guidelines for handling disorders, sabotage, and transportation of troops and materials.

After Quinn Tamm became executive director in 1962, the IACP embarked on an extensive expansion campaign. During the 1970s, international training programs were developed, police apparatus was tested, and police organization research was conducted. Additionally, two centers were established—the Police Assessment Center and National Bomb Data Center—the latter of which was eventually handed over to the FBI. The United Nations also conferred consultative status to the IACP in recognition of work performed in various member states. In the 1980s, the World Regional Division was opened in Europe, and a number of International Policing Executive Seminars were conducted there and in Asia. In the United States, the IACP collaborated with the Bureau of Justice Assistance to establish the National Law Enforcement Policy Center and the Commission on Law Enforcement Accreditation in collaboration with the National Organization of Black Law Enforcement Executives, the National Sheriffs' Association and the Police Executive Research Forum. Since the 1990s, interests have centered on international drug trafficking, drunk driving, police use of force, civil disorder, illegal aliens, community policing initiatives, nonlethal weapons training, and operations strategies for managing police agencies. In 1992, the IACP moved its headquarters to a historic five-story building located at 515 North Washington Street in Alexandria, Virginia.

Structure

A number of offices and services make up the IACP. An 85-page constitution and an eight-member elected board of officers govern the association. These officers are both experienced former police chiefs of large municipalities and nationally recognized leaders in law enforcement. As of April 2011, the chief executive of the IACP is Mark A. Marshall, chief of police in Smithfield, Virginia. Presently, 41 committees are devoted to a number of specialized topics, crimes, and practices of relevance to policing and the IACP itself. Similarly, 19 sections embody a number of specialized staff—analysts, instructors, counselors—and various groups—retired, transportation, and university police—associated with law enforcement. There are also divisions devoted to representing both state and international police agencies, which hold meetings annually to develop relationships, foster communication, share information, identify problems, and explore solutions in their respective jurisdictions. In 1986, a psychological services section was created, which today includes more than 100 recognized experts in various areas of police psychology. Although the IACP is largely funded through federal grants, other sources of income—membership dues, conference fees, and public and private donations—also help finance the organization.

The IACP engages in a number of activities. Mainly, the association exists to share good practice, techniques, strategies, and tools utilized by police agencies, in order to improve police services and investigation of crimes. Annually, the IACP convenes a five-day conference both nationally and internationally as a vehicle to achieve these objectives, which brings together thousands of police executives from all over the globe who attend presentations, training workshops, and exhibitions of tools and services for policing provided by hundreds of manufacturers. Similarly, the IACP provides training seminars more frequently on a variety of policing topics, which are supplemented with many published guides and resources. It also provides other services such as mentoring, guidance, and information resources to new police leaders; performs research surveys on behalf of agencies to evaluate services and operations; assesses candidates for promotion through job simulations, interviews, and examinations; and maintains a police search database to advertise executive-level positions for profiling, recruiting, and screening candidates. The IACP's monthly magazine, *The Police Chief*, dates back to 1934 and provides a voice for the global law enforcement community.

Michael J. Puniskis
Middlesex University

See Also: Fingerprinting; Professionalization of Police; Training Police; Uniform Crime Reporting Program.

Further Readings

International Association of Chiefs of Police. http://www.theiacp.org (Accessed January 2011).
Reppetto, Thomas A. *American Police: A History, 1845–1945*. New York: Enigma Books, 2010.
Wadman, Robert C. and William Thomas Allison. *To Protect and to Serve: A History of Police in America*. Upper Saddle River, NJ: Prentice Hall, 2003.

Internment

Internment has been a subject often overlooked in texts that examine criminal justice issues. Despite this omission, internment has implications for a central component of the criminal justice system: due process. In times of emergency, the United States has detained aliens and citizens without having to face a court of law.

The Cherokee experienced internment into various military forts and eventual forced removal. For the Cherokee, in the 1830s, multiple stockades were utilized for forced confinement, and then they were forced into three "emigration depots" for forced removal west. Unsanitary conditions aided the spread of disease in these facilities and increased the number of deaths. Many died in detention before embarking upon the Trail of Tears.

Similarly, the Navajo also experienced an atrocious event known as the Long Walk, which by Navajo accounts, resulted in numerous extrajudicial executions. After being forceably relocated near Ft. Sumner, New Mexico, into an area of 40 acres, the Navajo were closely monitored in the mid-1860s. Under this "controversial experiment," food rations were inadequate or rotten, and the Navajo had to shelter in small pits covered with branches for a period of four years. During the same time period, the Apache were interned at San Carlos, Arizona; early in the internment, movement was restricted, daily roll calls were utilized, and neck tags were assigned for administrative purposes.

Effects of War

During World War I, President Woodrow Wilson issued two sets of regulations in 1917 that required males to report to the post office, obtain a registration card, and report any address changes. During World War II, more than 100,000 Japanese, most of them U.S. citizens, were interned. This was conducted under Executive Order 9066, signed February 14, 1942. The Supreme Court affirmed such action with its decisions in *Hirabayashi* in 1943 and *Korematsu* and *Endo* in 1944.

Before this, however, aliens of Italian, German, and Japanese nationality were subject to arrest and internment. Immediately after the Japanese bombings in 1941, President Franklin Roosevelt declared under sections 21–24 of Title 50 of the U.S. Code (USC) that aliens were subject to arrest and detainment. The result was that thousands of

Apaches lined up outside the San Carlos agency building in Arizona in 1899. Native Americans and Americans of German, Italian, and Japanese descent all experienced internment within the United States either in the 19th century or during wartime. The issue of internment has returned with the detention of suspected terrorists at Guantanamo Bay in Cuba after the terrorist attacks of 2001.

Germans and Japanese, and a few hundred Italians, were interned in the United States. Roosevelt also interned "subversive" or "potentially subversive" Germans from Latin America within the United States. Only a small percentage of the Latin American Germans interned had loyalty to the Nazi cause.

After World War II, the threat of the Axis powers shifted to the Red Scare. Because of the supposed threat of communist "domestic subversion," the McCarran Act, passed by the U.S. Congress in 1950, allowed the denial of habeas corpus and for U.S. citizens to be interned during an "internal security emergency." Such an emergency could be enacted during invasion, war, or national threat to public safety. The act allowed the detention of persons where there is a "reasonable" belief that person will engage, or "probably will conspire with others to engage in, acts of espionage or sabotage." The act was unique and without statutory precedent since it allowed the indefinite detention of U.S. citizens who had not committed crimes, but might because of their political beliefs. The U.S. government maintained six camps for mass internment as envisioned by the act, until the act was repealed in 1971. These six facilities were expected to hold thousands of U.S. citizens, if deemed necessary.

Operation Garden Plot
During the 1960s, Operation Garden Plot, a master martial law plan, was created. It was first discovered in 1971 by Senator Sam Ervin's Subcommittee on Constitutional Rights. The intention was to develop contingency plans in the event of civil unrest. This plan was practiced through exercises known as Cable Splicer, in which military and local police were coordinated to contain and suppress civil insurrection. In the simulated scenarios, violence erupted simultaneously in 25 cities, and coordinated measures were taken by police and military forces. These observers and participants were addressed directly by California Governor Ronald Reagan in 1969.

The plans were partially disclosed, but only recently have the documents been declassified. Both the U.S. Army and Air Force had procedures under Garden Plot. Accordingly, arrest and detainment could occur in conjunction with local authorities, and officials would be able to operate, maintain, or provide for detention facilities in extreme emergencies.

Garden Plot was a plan developed by the U.S. Air Force and Army; a very similar plan was practiced by the Federal Emergency Management Agency (FEMA). Before the signing of Executive Order 12148, by President Jimmy Carter, on July 20, 1979, these military organizations would have been the agencies to respond to civil unrest and detain people if necessary. Under Jimmy Carter, FEMA was established to coordinate with the Department of Defense and implement plans for civil emergencies. FEMA would be the agency to detain groups under a presidential order.

Mass internment of U.S. citizens was a dormant issue until the Iran-Contra hearings. While Oliver North was being questioned about illegal supplying of arms to Iran, the sales of which were used to supply material support to the Contras in Nicaragua, a couple of newspaper stories appeared that disclosed plans to intern certain American groups in the event of civil unrest. When Oliver North was questioned about the plans by Representative Jack Brooks on July 13, 1987, the representative was admonished by committee chair Daniel Inouye. The next day, Senate Intelligence Committee Chair David Boren reported the "so-called Martial Law Plan" had been discussed in executive session. Oliver North denied the existence of any plan, and no official disclosure was presented.

One newspaper that initiated this inquiry was the *Miami Herald*. One component of this plan, Readiness Exercise 1984, or Rex 84, was detailed in a memo dated June 30, 1982, by FEMA's deputy director of national preparedness programs, John Brinkerhoff. Supposedly, the *Miami Herald* was able to secure a copy of the memo, which discussed the possible internment of African Americans. This plan resembled a document authored by the chief of FEMA, Louis O. Giuffrida, "National Survival—Racial Imperative," at the U.S. Army War College, which examined the feasibility of interning African Americans in the event of urban unrest.

Another component of the plan, as Ross Gelbspan (1991) of the *Boston Globe* addressed, was a joint exercise with the Immigration and Naturalization Service (INS), FEMA, Pentagon, and state and local agencies that would be ignited into action by a major U.S. intervention in Central America, in which thousands could be detained. These activists included environmentalists, nuclear energy opponents, and refugee assistance advocates. Fifty state defense forces, which consisted of local law enforcement and military reserve units, would be deputized.

Contemporary Issues

The internment issue was dormant until the events of September 11, 2001. Afterward, hundreds of aliens were detained indefinitely and were denied access to an attorney. Many were deported. There were several problems noted by the Office of the Inspector General in 2003: indefinite detention, notice of charge a month after arrest (the usual procedure requires 72 hours), a "no bond" policy was implemented, terrorism and illegal alien distinction was not met, many were held in lockdown for 23 hours per day, inconsistent phone access was granted, and lights were illuminated 24 hours a day. In addition, those who inquired about detainee confinement were told by the Metropolitan Detention Center (MDC) in New York City, that he/she was not at the facility, when the detainee was actually being held there. These abuses were also noted by the United Nations Working Group on Arbitrary Detention.

The issue of internment has been highlighted with the detention of suspected terrorists at Guantanamo Bay in Cuba. Central to this issue has been the denial of habeas corpus and other minimal protections as presented in the Geneva Convention. Habeas corpus allows the courts, either domestic or international, to evaluate the lawfulness of their detainment. The Supreme Court ruled in *Hamdan v. Rumsfeld* (2006) that detainees were allowed such minimum safeguards. Many of the prisoners released have alleged that various forms of torture were used at the facility.

Other public internment concerns have been raised through the granting of a contingency contract to Halliburton to build internment facilities within the United States for immigration and other programs. Also, there was some public alarm that HR 645, the National Emergency Centers Establishment Act of the 111th Congress, would have allowed a number of military bases to become FEMA detention centers. In addition, S. 3081, the Enemy Belligerent, Interrogation, Detention, and Prosecution Act, also of the 111th Congress, would have allowed the possible detention of U.S. citizens, if connected to terrorist organizations. Neither of these bills made it out of committee, and hence were not enacted into law. However, the National Defense Authorization Act was signed into law December 31, 2011, by President Barack Obama, allowing U.S. Citizens to be detained, indefinitely if it is believed that he or she has a connection to terrorist activity.

J. Michael Botts
Belmont Abbey College

See Also: Due Process; German Americans; Habeas Corpus, Writ of; Indian Removal Act; Internal Security Act of 1950; Japanese Americans; *Korematsu v. United States*; Native Americans; Terrorism.

Further Readings

Carley, Kenneth. *The Sioux Uprising of 1862*. St. Paul: Minnesota Historical Society, 1961.

Churchill, Ward. *A Little Matter of Genocide: Holocaust and Denial in the Americas 1492 to the Present*. San Francisco, CA: City Light Books, 1997.

Cotter, Cornelius and J. Malcolm Smith. "An American Paradox: The Emergency Detention Act of 1950." *Journal of Politics*, v.19/1 (1957).

Dunbar, Leslie W. "Beyond *Korematsu*: The Emergency Detention Act of 1950." *University of Pittsburgh Law Review*, v.13 (1951–52).

Goldstein, Robert Justin. *Political Repression in Modern America: From 1870 to the Present*. Cambridge, MA: Schenkman Publishing, 1978.

Helms, Harry. *Inside the Shadow Government: National Emergencies and the Cult of Secrecy*. Los Angeles: Feral House, 2003.

Johnson, Broderick H. *Navajo Stories of the Long Walk Period*. Tsaile, Navajo Nation, AZ: Navajo Community College Press, 1973.

Lichtblau, Eric. *Bush's Law: The Remaking of American Justice*. New York: Pantheon Books, 2008.

Simpson, Christopher. *National Security Directives of the Reagan and Bush Administrations: The Declassified History of U.S. Political and Military Policy, 1981–1991*. Boulder, CO: Westview Press, 1995.

Interrogation Practices

Throughout history, from the religious inquisitions and witch hunts of old to modern-day DNA exonerations, interrogations have been a key component of the criminal justice system. The power of the police to interrogate suspects in order to investigate crimes is a crucial tool for their ability to clear cases and thereby protect citizens from further victimization. But pressure on police to solve crimes and put offenders in prison can lead to overzealous interrogation practices that may have unintended negative effects. As a way of limiting this discretion, Supreme Court decisions during the 1960s such as the now-famous 1966 decision in *Miranda v. Arizona* limited the autonomy of police interrogators and required police to inform suspects of their rights regarding interrogation. Subsequent Supreme Court decisions have tended to cut away at the protections provided by cases like *Miranda*, and subtle loopholes accompanied by a diverse interpretation of these protections have created variation in their implementation. Emerging trends like the increasing frequency of exonerations because of exculpatory DNA evidence, as well as heightened interrogation practices employed in the fight against terrorism, have kept interrogation practices at the forefront of criminal justice topics.

Suspect Rights and Interrogation

Corporal punishment and harsh interrogation tactics were legitimately employed by American police and prison officials well into the 20th century, perhaps most famously by New York City chief of detectives Thomas Byrnes in the 1890s. But although the Wickersham Commission's report of 1930 detailed many problems with so-called "third-degree" interrogation tactics, little changed with regard to police procedure until a series of precedent-setting court decisions during the 1960s added to the protections of criminal suspects. Specifically, under Chief Justice Earl Warren, the Supreme Court initiated the requirement of police to inform suspects of their rights regarding police interrogation in adherence to the spirit of the Constitution. The court also required investigators to stop interrogations if a suspect invoked his or her right to counsel by attorney and obligated trial courts to appoint lawyers to represent indigent defendants in serious criminal cases.

Many Supreme Court decisions under Chief Justice Warren, and the policies that emerged from them, were a product of the social and political upheaval of the 1950s and 1960s. During this time, the civil rights movement was initiated by African Americans as a counteraction to segregation and discrimination in the south. As African American civil rights groups lobbied, protested, and sued for equal inclusion into American policy, the court increasingly found that the Fourteenth Amendment extended constitutional protection to every citizen of the United States. Since then, the idea that each American is worthy of equal protection and due process under the law (as provided by the Fourteenth Amendment) has been extended to other political, ethnic, and social groups—including suspects of crime and convicted criminals.

Generally speaking, the decision in *Miranda* was indicative of the broader context of social justice and equality commonly associated with the African American and youth movements of the 1960s. Specifically, the Supreme Court enacted *Miranda*'s limitations on police and prosecutorial power in a reaction to third-degree interrogative tactics employed against suspects of crime. As indicated above, third-degree tactics include high-pressure and violent actions designed to frighten and brutalize a suspect into compliance, such as threats of violence, aggressive confrontations, and badgering, as well as beatings with fists, rubber hoses, or other weapons. Prior to the 1960s, police—especially in poor, crime-ridden neighborhoods—could employ third-degree tactics with almost absolute impunity and little risk of reprimand.

Surely, aggressive, confrontational interrogations may be appropriately called for in dealing with violent crimes and brazen criminals. To the extent that such interrogations elicit usable information without violating the constitutional (or human) rights of the suspect, they may be viewed as valuable investigative tools for investigators. Nevertheless, simply beating, badgering, or torturing a confession out of a suspect may not only be unconstitutional but might not render accurate, reliable information.

The decision in *Miranda* signaled the start of a reconsideration for proper police procedure

A U.S. Border Patrol agent reads the Miranda rights to a Mexican national arrested for drug smuggling. The 1966 decision in Miranda v. Arizona *limiting the autonomy of police interrogators and requiring police to inform suspects of their rights regarding interrogation was one of several Supreme Court decisions from the 1960s that have had a lasting impact on how interrogations are conducted.*

and led to the now-famous recitation of Miranda rights to each arrested suspect as one means of limiting capricious police behavior. Today, the idea of informing a suspect of his or her rights before initiating interrogative questioning seems elementary. The right to remain silent during questioning, the right to have an attorney present during questioning, and the idea that anything said by an interrogated party can and will be used against that party in court are now established in American legal and social lexicons. The court's decision in *Miranda* placed a spotlight on police tactics and procedures and led to more stringent requirements of police in the field. In many ways, this can be seen as the implementation of reform recommendations suggested by the Wickersham reports three decades earlier. Subsequent cases, however, have increasingly limited the scope of *Miranda*'s protections.

Subsequent Court Decisions

The first right mentioned in the well-known and often-cited *Miranda* litany is the right to remain silent, but the Supreme Court found in *Michigan v. Moseley* (1975) that police interrogators (upon a suspect's invocation of this right) need not permanently discontinue the interrogation. Instead, the court ruled that the interrogation could resume after a time, as long as the interrogators continue to adhere to *Miranda*'s requirements. This allows room for a level of police discretion in interpreting the intentions of a suspect under interrogation. Similarly, in *Edwards v. Arizona* (1981) the court found that police questioning must stop immediately if a suspect states that he wants an attorney present on his behalf during the questioning; yet *Davis v. United States* (1994) clarified that the invocation of the right to counsel must be clear enough so that a reasonable interrogator in the same context would interpret the request for attorney as just that. The decision in *Davis* is thus another example of limitations placed on the reform instituted by *Miranda* and again illustrates an increase in police discretion in regard to criminal interrogations. In some television representations, police questioning stops immediately upon the mere suggestion by a suspect of an attorney. In practice, however, suspect requests for an attorney that are posed in the form of a question, are mumbled, or are otherwise not forcefully and repeatedly stated may legally go ignored by police interrogators.

From the time an officer places a suspect under arrest, during the drive to the police station, and throughout the following processing and interrogation, the rights afforded by *Miranda* are interpreted by the arresting and investigating officers. The reading of the Miranda rights might be recited by an officer in an articulate, informative manner, or they may be quickly rattled off to an agitated and uncooperative suspect. Likewise, a request for attorney or invocation of the right to remain silent may be accepted at face value, or the true intention of the invocation could be questioned by officers—allowing the interrogation to continue virtually endlessly. Savvy interrogators, intent on eliciting information that might help close a case, may intentionally prolong an interrogation for hours in an attempt to exhaust the resistance of a suspect to police questioning. In the worst cases, interrogators may even threaten violence or the arrest of family members in an effort to dislodge useful information from unwilling suspects.

The Influence of DNA Evidence

One current example of the power of interrogation techniques to impact criminal justice outcomes is the growing number of exonerations of individuals falsely convicted of violent crimes. Over the past 20 years, as DNA technology has expanded and improved, there have been a growing number of convictions that have been reversed once bodily fluid or tissue evidence from old, closed investigations has been processed or reprocessed with techniques not available at the time of the original investigation. While faulty eyewitness testimony and intentional perjury are among the most common causes of false convictions in America, it has been suggested that as many as 15 to 20 percent of DNA exonerations are the result of false confessions due to police coercion and overaggressive police interrogations. To be sure, false confessions can often be the product of the aggressive interrogation of at-risk populations such as young or mentally ill suspects over long periods of time.

The increasing frequency of exonerations of individuals convicted of serious violent crimes because of exculpatory DNA evidence has shed light on modern police interrogation and investigation tactics. Law enforcement agencies and officers generally operate with considerable latitude and discretion over the particulars of an investigation. The intricacies of a criminal investigation are many, and the benefit of the doubt is often given to officers in the performance of their duty. Nevertheless, care must be taken to keep in check the power of police to unilaterally detain, aggressively interrogate, and possibly coerce information from suspects of crimes. In addition to the ongoing interpretation of the protections granted to suspects by the Constitution, there is the risk that overly abusive, prolonged interrogation will render information that is neither useful nor accurate.

Serious violent crimes such as rape and homicide are the cases most likely to include DNA evidence, which is partly because of the often personal and physical nature of the act. Another component, however, is that the seriousness of violent crimes elicits a strong reaction from law enforcement that encourages the unfettered use of agency resources. In short, serious violent crime investigations are those most likely to be fully pursued from an investigational and forensic standpoint.

For example, semen samples are often taken routinely during rape investigations, yet lesser sexual offenses may not produce a fluids exchange between victim and offender. Similarly, blood and tissue samples are collected and stored at agency expense where warranted by a homicide scene whereas blood from a domestic dispute or other assault may not be collected for analysis. The broader point is that only the most serious crimes are available to exoneration by DNA. Given this limitation, and the growing rate of convictions based on false confessions that have been overturned, it is plausible that many less serious crimes that have been officially cleared by police via interrogation and confession have been wrongfully prosecuted. This represents an inconsistency between high American ideals of due process, by which all people are afforded equal protection under the Constitution, and the economy of justice, which requires the speedy and cost-effective resolution of criminal offenses. Overall, then, it could be expected that the increased use of DNA evidence will only serve to further question the appropriateness of aggressive interrogation techniques in the American criminal justice system.

Terrorism and Interrogation Techniques

Another contemporary example of the high-stakes nature of modern interrogations is the use of "enhanced interrogation" techniques by the Central Intelligence Agency (CIA) and other agents of the U.S. government in the ongoing effort to combat terrorism. In the wake of the terrorist attacks of September 11, 2001, President George W. Bush authorized American interrogators and their agents to use tactics such as sleep and sensory deprivation, verbal and physical humiliation, and simulated drowning as a means of obtaining valuable information from suspected terrorists. While the use of such methods clearly contradicts some of the constitutional concepts and protections referred to previously, the administration justified their use on terrorists by defining them as "enemy combatants" instead of prisoners of war. With no uniforms, no organized rank and file, and no official country of residence, the United States deemed Al Qaeda members and other terrorists not to be legally entitled to the protections of the Geneva Convention or the U.S. Constitution. The use of these heightened interrogation tactics was therefore viewed by the administration as both legal and justified.

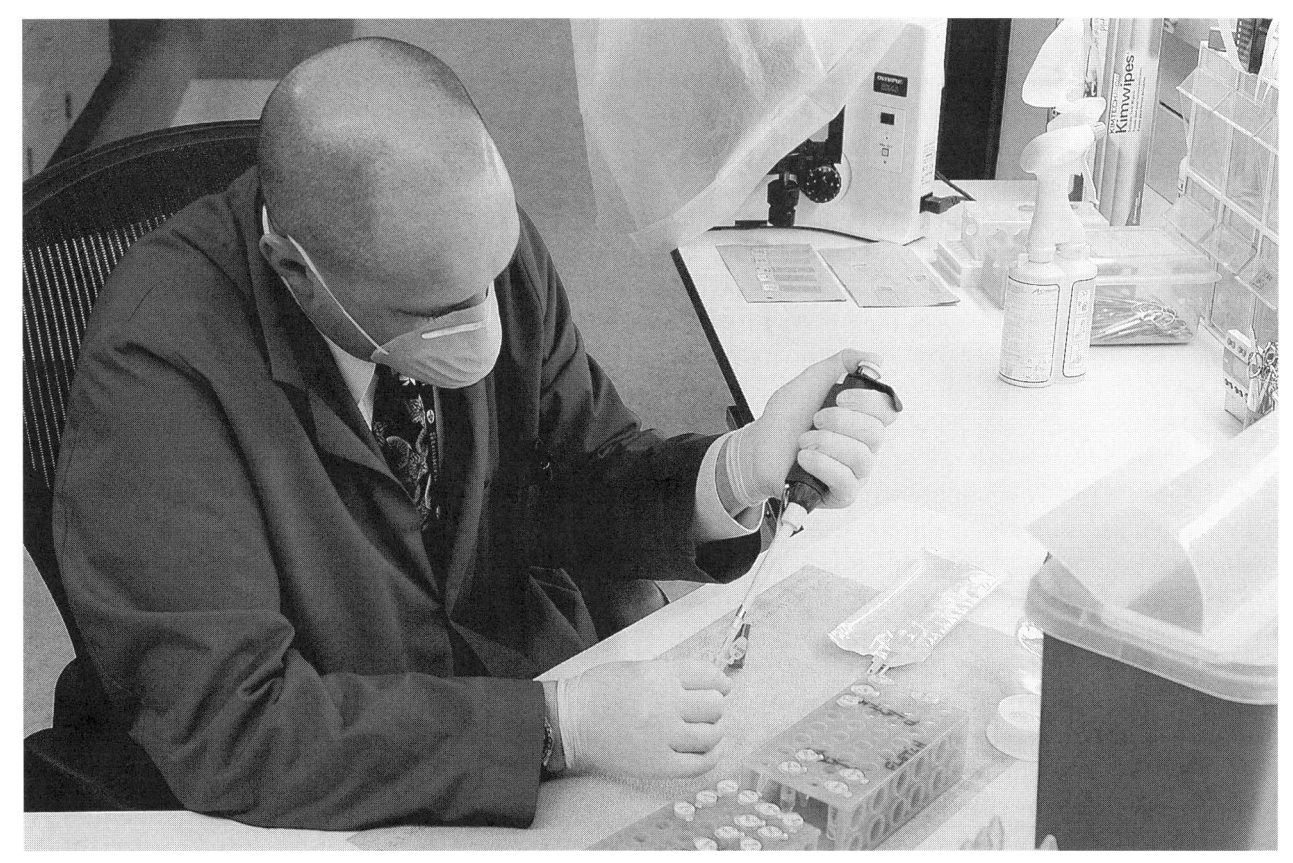

A forensic scientist at the U.S. Army Criminal Investigation Laboratory at Fort Gillem, Georgia, processing evidence in a DNA extraction room. It is thought that as many as 15 to 20 percent of DNA exonerations are connected to convictions that were the result of false confessions made because of police coercion and overaggressive police interrogations.

The use of enhanced interrogation tactics divided Americans ideologically when the public became aware of their existence. Some believed that American ideals of due process and human rights should apply to all American actions—both at home against suspected criminals as well as abroad in the fight against terrorism. Others believed that the fluid, unpredictable nature of modern, large-scale terrorist operations like Al Qaeda, combined with their proven willingness to kill civilians, justified the use of the most severe interrogation techniques as a means of securing usable intelligence and foiling would-be terrorist attacks. Similarly, there is disagreement as to whether the use of these tactics has elicited any useful information. While proponents asserted that these techniques prevented further terrorist attacks during the period following 9/11, opponents contended that it was not clear that any specific attack was averted by the use of enhanced interrogation tactics. Whatever the arguments for or against the use of such methods, it is clear that efforts to thwart terrorism have had a major impact on interrogation practices in America.

When President Barack Obama took office in 2009, he ended the official use of enhanced interrogation techniques in the fight against terrorism. This did not, however, ease the conundrum presented by the nonmilitary combatants captured by coalition forces in places like Iraq and Afghanistan and detained indefinitely by the United States. A military tribunal for these terrorists would contradict their established status as nonmilitary "enemy combatants." Prosecution in a civilian court would avail the defendants of many rights, such as due process and a protection against cruel and unusual punishment, and could cause the trials to drag on for years. While some domestic and lower-level terrorists have been successfully tried in civilian courts, having high-level international terrorists tried in civilian courts and housed in domestic prisons is troublesome for many, both in government and in the public. For others, trying terrorists in the fairest, most humane way possible offers a chance to display both the effectiveness and impartiality of American justice on a world scale.

The legal, social, and moral complexities indicated by the interrogation of accused terrorists and the increase in DNA exonerations in modern criminal justice highlight the fact that interrogation practices are close to the core of the American criminal justice system. Americans rely heavily on the police and the government to maintain order and social stability by solving crimes and sanctioning offenders. However, it is important that a collective, implicit insistence on the speedy, economical clearing of crimes does not lead to overzealous or abusive interrogations, which contradict the American Constitution and ideals. It is also important that the interrogation practices that are allowed law enforcement agents are proven to be effective at rendering valid, usable information. Ultimately, interrogations are, and always have been, an integral component of law enforcement. But through the evolution of interrogation practices over time, there is presented a view into ongoing legal and social culture and the competing values of security and freedom in America.

Gabriel T. Cesar
Kevin A. Wright
Arizona State University

See Also: Confession; Due Process; *Mapp v. Ohio*; *Miranda v. Arizona*; Suspect's Rights.

Further Readings
Gross, Samuel R., et al. "Exonerations in the United States 1989 Through 2003." *Journal of Criminal Law and Criminology,* v.95 (2005).
Hopkins, Ernest Jerome. *Our Lawless Police: A Study of the Unlawful Enforcement of the Law.* New York: Da Capo Press, 1972.
Rychlak, Ronald J. "Interrogating Terrorists: From Miranda to 'Enhanced Interrogation Techniques.'" *San Diego Law Review,* v.44 (2007).
Skolnik, Jerome H. and Richard A. Leo. "The Ethics of Deceptive Interrogation." *Criminal Justice Ethics,* v.11 (1992).

Interstate Commerce Act of 1887

The Interstate Commerce Act of 1887 became law on February 4, providing regulation for the railroads in the United States that, prior to the law's passage, had no established form of regulation at the national level. The legislation created the Interstate Commerce Commission (1887–1995) to oversee and investigate violations of the law by individuals and companies.

The origins of the Interstate Commerce Act go back to 1869, when railroads connected the United States from coast to coast. Prior to passage of the law, the regulation of the railroads came under state control, making it a confusing and costly process as railroads crossed state lines. An even greater problem was the competition between railroads for long-haul routes and the lack of competition for short routes. A serious problem of monopolies developed, leading to rate differences, special rebates, and unfair business practices. States could not keep up with the policing of the railroads, and in many cases, the practices of state officials were as corrupt as those of the railroads. In 1877, the Supreme Court decision in *Munn v. Illinois* ruled that the states had regulatory authority over the railroads. Between 1871 and 1887, over 100 bills were introduced in Congress seeking to federalize regulation of the railroads. Legislative proposals from Congressman John Reagan (D-Texas) and Senator Shelby Cullom (R-Illinois) contributed to the final version of the 1887 act.

Reagan's proposals, beginning in 1878, featured four key areas that needed regulation. Under his version, discriminatory rates and rebates would be prohibited and the market fairly divided. He also addressed the issue of fair pricing on long hauls versus short hauls, making them proportionate, and required that railroads post their rates for the public. Reagan opposed the establishment of a commission to regulate the industry and he sought penalties from the various companies when found in noncompliance. The second version considered by the Senate originated with Senator Cullom in 1883. He sought the creation of a commission appointed by the president and approved by Congress, but this measure failed. A committee was formed to study the issues, and their findings led Cullom to sponsor another version of the bill in 1883. The railroads preferred this bill to Reagan's because it allowed them more freedom with only government oversight via the commission. Ultimately, the two bills caused great debate in Congress but no final resolution developed until the Supreme Court handed down the *Wabash* decision in 1886, which declared that the states did not have the power to regulate the railroads—a reversal of the *Munn* decision.

With the removal of regulation from the states, it became necessary to establish a regulatory organization for the railroads. Congress reached a compromise and used the short- and long-haul clause and the anti-pooling guidelines from the Reagan bill and established the commission recommended by Cullom. The Interstate Commerce Commission (ICP) was made up of five people appointed by the president with approval of the Senate. It became the first independent agency under the federal government. It quickly became necessary to amend the law to increase the authority of the ICC, including two laws enacted in the early 1900s. The ICC regulation powers were increased and railroad rates were placed under the commission's purview under the Elkins Act of 1903. Commission powers were increased further under the Hepburn Act of 1906, which allowed the ICC to set railroad rates. The commission continued to regulate the railroads and later the trucking industry until the 1970s and 1980s, when Congress deregulated the railroad industry and reduced the powers of the ICC. The Interstate Commerce Commission ceased as an independent agency in 1995 and its remaining duties were transferred to the Surface Transportation Board.

The Interstate Commerce Act of 1887 was the first legislation to regulate an industry at the national level in the United States. Through regulation, railroads were forced to end unfair business practices that included bribery, special rates and discounts based upon the length of routes, and allowed increased competition in the markets. Amendments strengthened the agency's power and it continued until 1995 when deregulation made the Interstate Commerce Commission obsolete.

Theresa S. Hefner-Babb
Lamar University

See Also: Antitrust Law; Elkins Act of 1903; Federal Policing; *Munn v. Illinois*.

Further Readings
Eisner, M. *Regulatory Politics in Transition*. Baltimore, MD: Johns Hopkins University Press, 1993.

National Archives and Records Administration. "Transcript of Interstate Commerce Act (1887)." http://www.ourdocuments.gov/doc.php?doc=49&page=transcript (Accessed January 2011).

Ripley, William Z. *Railroads: Rates and Regulation.* New York: Arno Press, 1973.

Intolerable Acts of 1774

Also referred to as the Coercive Acts, the Intolerable Acts of 1774, enacted under King George III, were crucial in the process of America gaining independence from Britain. The four acts represented a punitive response from the British to the events of the Boston Tea Party. Colonists destroyed cargos of tea in response to the taxation without representation imposed on them. There was common resistance to the arrival of the tea and payment of the threepence duty imposed by the British; however, resistance developed into action in Boston.

Far from achieving the intended outcome of putting down the rebellion, the series of coercive measures that followed the Boston Tea Party served to unite the American colonies and proved pivotal in the buildup to the American War of Independence and eventual independence. The four acts were the Boston Port Bill, the Massachusetts Government Act, the Administration of Justice Act, and the Quartering Act. The Boston Port Bill was a punitive measure aimed at closing the port until the East India Company had been remunerated for the tea that had been destroyed.

This cartoon, published in London in 1774 and titled "The Able Doctor, or, America Swallowing the Bitter Draught," satirizes the Intolerable Acts. The scene centers around a female Native American figure who represents America and is being forced to drink tea by British lawmakers, while another female figure representing Britannia stands in the background hiding her face in her hand.

The act was also intended to close the port until order resumed. The effects of this served to punish all of the port workers and impacted the local economy. This duly angered colonists, and many saw this as a needless breach of their rights and an example of indiscriminate punishment.

The Massachusetts Act was highly controversial because it changed the government within Massachusetts, dictating that members of the council were to be appointed by the governor as opposed to being elected. This effectively brought Massachusetts under the control of the British government. This further strained tensions between Britain and the colony. The Administration of Justice Act enabled officials to have their trials moved from Massachusetts in order to receive a fair trial, which was not deemed to be the case in Massachusetts. This was perceived by some as allowing the British to escape justice for their crimes. Finally, the Quartering Act required colonists to feed and even accommodate British soldiers. This piece of legislation related to all colonies, but in America it was most problematic. An additional piece of legislation, the Quebec Act, is also often linked to the Intolerable Acts.

Jack Sosin has written authoritatively on the matter, demonstrating that history has had a tendency to frame the acts as exercises in capricious infringements of civil liberties and repression of the Boston population. However, such a position can be questioned. For instance, in relation to the Boston Port Act, Sosin remarks that the British government's aims were limited; to "*legally* put down what appeared a revolutionary movement aimed at overthrowing its authority." Also, "The ministers did not act arbitrarily or order arbitrary use of military force. Nor did they attempt to 'render the military independent of and superior to the Civil Power' as the Americans were to charge in the Declaration of Independence."

Through the establishment of the First Continental Congress, delegates from the American colonies met to discuss appropriate responses to events in Boston. One such response was the boycott of British trade; this included a refusal to import, consume, and export goods, and this was successful in greatly reducing British imports. From this position events escalated. The acts were intended as a tough response to events in Boston in 1773, in effect to stamp out unrest and enforce rule. King George III and his advisers, including the commander in chief in America, General Thomas Gage, believed that "resolute action" was required; otherwise the colonists "will be lyons, whilst we are the lambs." This was in the context of the recently repealed Stamp Act and Townshend Acts, which had already weakened the British position. However, the acts served to do the exact opposite of what the British had hoped. The Intolerable or Coercive Acts of 1774 united the American colonies against Britain. The American War of Independence followed in 1775, and subsequently independence was declared.

Tony Murphy
University of Westminster

See Also: American Revolution and Criminal Justice; History of Crime and Punishment in America: Colonial; Proclamation for Suppressing Rebellion and Sedition of 1775; Stamp Act of 1765; Townshend Acts of 1767.

Further Readings
Draper, Theodore. *A Struggle for Power: The American Revolution.* New York: Time Books, 1996.
Sosin, Jack. "The Massachusetts Acts of 1774: Coercive or Preventive?" *Huntington Library Quarterly,* v.26/3 (1963).

Iowa

Deep in America's heartland, the landlocked state of Iowa has been a central player in American agriculture since shortly after the Louisiana Purchase. Close to the middle whether states are listed by area, population, population density, or median income, settled by both southerners and northerners, Iowa is the picture of middle America. It is frequently praised as one of the safest states in which to live. Despite this, in the late 20th and early 21st centuries, the state was also central to the growing meth epidemic throughout exurban America.

Despite staunch opposition to the Civil War by the vocal Copperhead minority, Iowa was long a progressive state in civil rights matters, outlawing slavery in the state in the very first decision of the Iowa Supreme Court, in 1839. Interracial marriages were legalized in 1851, and segregation (in public schools and public accommodations) was ended in theory in a series of court decisions from 1868 to 1875. In practice, discriminatory practices against African Americans continued at state universities until the mid-20th century. Similarly, women's rights were granted early—the first public university admitting women and men on an equal basis was the University of Iowa in 1847, In 1869, Iowa became the first state to rule that women had the right to practice law—but until the Nineteenth Amendment, women's right to vote was limited to ballot issues, not the election of officials. In the 21st century, the state became the first midwestern state and the third in the country to legalize same-sex marriage.

Iowa also led the Union in Prohibition, passing its first laws restricting the sale and consumption of alcohol in 1847. The Whigs pushed through a law against "dram shops" (bars) in 1851, and in 1882, Iowa was briefly made a dry state—the following year, the Supreme Court ruled the state's law against the manufacture and sale of alcoholic beverages unconstitutional. But Iowa laws continued to strongly restrict alcohol, with a local option adopted in 1893 and a strong statewide prohibition law adopted in 1916, shortly before federal Prohibition.

Police and Punishment

The Iowa court system began with the establishment of the territorial government of Iowa by act of Congress in 1838, which established the territory's supreme court, probate court, district courts, and justices of the peace. The first Iowa Supreme Court judges, of which there were three, also served as district judges. A fourth judicial district was added after statehood in 1846, during the Iowa General Assembly's first legislative session. The constitution adopted subsequently in 1857 increased the judicial districts again, to 11, to account for the population spike after statehood.

The earliest town and city police in Iowa, outside of the federal marshal presence and the county sheriffs, were town marshals and night watchmen. In many Iowa towns, the holder of one of these jobs might hold several other town government positions, like jailer, clerk, treasurer, dogcatcher, and so on. Over time, as the state became more populated, police departments were modernized and the position of police officer was professionalized. The sparseness of law enforcement coverage in the 19th century led to occasional bursts of vigilante justice, and in the 1880s and 1890s, Iowa was one of the states where the "White Cap" movement was popular—vigilante justice in the form of lynch mobs, often but not always directed against African Americans or transients.

The Iowa State Penitentiary, patterned after the Auburn Penitentiary in New York, was established in 1839, the year after Iowa was made a territory. It remained the state's primary corrections center, and today is a maximum security men's prison with a maximum capacity of 550 inmates. The old design was modernized in 1982, when unitization was introduced.

In 1982, the Iowa Department of Corrections began a restitutions program that it has successfully defended in both state and federal court. Initially, the state deducted a small amount from allowances paid to inmates for work they'd done, in order to fund restitutions paid to victims. In 1992, these deductions were extended to include credits deposited into inmates' accounts from the outside; the following year, the Department of Corrections also began making deductions in order to collect on legal debts from inmates as ordered by federal courts.

That was the first of Iowa's victim and restorative justice programs. Other programs have been established since, including a victim notification program (established in 1986) to notify the victims of violent crimes when their offender is released from prison, if a request has been registered in advance; a 1995 policy to notify victims of sexual assault if the offender, while an inmate, tests positive for human immunodeficiency virus (HIV); and victim impact panels, which since 1994 have been held as part of classes in which inmates are taught the effects that their crimes have had on their victims and the victims' families.

In 1993, the Department of Corrections began its Victim Offender Intervention Sessions (VOIS) program. In this program, a safe, controlled environment is provided, mediated by a trained facilitator, in which an inmate's victim may meet face to face with his/her offender. The program is aimed to help victims with closure and, to a lesser degree, to help rehabilitate criminals by forcing them to confront the consequences of their actions. However, not every victim petitioning for participation in the program is approved; it is considered a program to be handled with extreme care.

Crime

In 1985, Lone Tree farmer Dale Burr was one of many who had gone broke during the farm crisis that had hit rural America harder than any economic crisis since the Great Depression. Over $500,000 in debt, he was pressured by the bank to sell his livestock and machinery in order to pay off a portion of his debts, and to rent his land out to pay the rest—to abandon the farm the 63-year-old farmer had inherited from his father and grandfather. Instead, he snapped, killing the bank president, a fellow farmer (Richard Goody, who had won a judgment from Burr's son in a land dispute), and his own wife before turning his gun on himself. While shocked, many Iowans worried that the shooting spree would be the first of many—indicating that on some level Burr wasn't a lone psychotic but a symptom of the region's larger problems.

Increasingly, Iowa, like much of the midwest, has had a methamphetamine problem of epidemic proportions. Declining briefly after 2004—having made national news and been the focus of several books and magazine news programs—meth use and manufacture began rising again, as meth manufacturers ("cooks") found ways to skirt the law. Limits of pseudoephedrine purchase quantities, for instance, were circumvented by visiting a succession of pharmacies and buying the maximum amount at each. Further, a technique from money laundering called smurfing could be used, in which many individuals each make small purchases on behalf of another party amassing large quantities. Meanwhile, with the help of the Internet, new formulas for meth were adapted and circulated. Meth cooks dealing with pseudoephedrine purchase limits could simply manufacture smaller amounts of meth at a time, for instance, and as large-scale meth dealers declined, the prevalence of small-scale meth cooks increased to meet the demand—often their own. Many small-time cooks had learned to manufacture the drug simply to meet their own needs for the drugs, selling any excess to friends in order to fund their habit and operating expenses. In 2010, Iowa pharmacies began reporting pseudoephedrine sales in real time to an electronic system monitored by law enforcement authorities.

In 2011, a new "one pot" meth cooking technique began to catch on in Iowa, using ammonium nitrate—from fertilizing stakes or cold compresses, for instance—as a precursor, instead of anhydrous ammonia or red phosphorous. The one-pot technique cooks meth in a two-liter soda bottle, and as more of the one-pot labs were discovered in the summer, officials worried that the combination of flammable chemicals, pressurized cooking, fragile containers, and drug use could lead to serious residential fire problems.

Bill Kte'pi
Independent Scholar

See Also: Drug Abuse and Addiction, Contemporary; Drug Abuse and Addiction, Sociology of; Victim Rights and Restitution.

Further Readings

Bryan, Patricia and Thomas Wolf. *Midnight Assassin: A Murder in America's Heartland*. Des Moines: University of Iowa Press, 2007.

Schwieder, Dorothy. *Iowa: The Middle Land*. Ames: Iowa State University Press, 1996.

Vos, Betty, Mark Umbreit, and Robert Coates. "Victim Offender Mediation: An Evolving Evidence-Based Practice." In *Handbook of Restorative Justice*, Dennis Sullivan and Larry Tifft, eds. New York: Routledge, 2006.

Irish Americans

In the early 19th century, the Irish people lived in squalor and servitude at the behest of the British Crown. They worked the land for British landlords with no property ownership or social mobility. From 1845 to 1855, the Great Potato Famine forced thousands of Irish to immigrate to the United States. The potato famine was a desolation of Irish culture, was severely mishandled by the British government, and reduced the Irish people to subhuman levels of existence. During the 10 years of the potato famine, 1 million Irish people died and another 1.5 million left the country for survival, many to the United States.

Early Struggles

Upon arrival in the United States, Irish immigrants faced negative stereotypes imported from England characterizing the Irish as pugnacious, drunken semi-savages. The Irish Americans were seen as boss-controlled, violent, voting illegally, prone to alcoholism, and dependent on criminal street gangs. These stereotypes endured through the 19th century as terms such as *paddy-wagons*, *shenanigans*, and *shanty Irish* gained popularity. The Irish Americans faced rampant discrimination with a plethora of signs and job postings stating "No Irish Need Apply." The Irish were often forced into low-paying and extremely dangerous occupations and were often arrested simply for being drunk or disorderly.

Despite the effects of offensive stereotypes, discrimination, and poverty, Irish immigrants possessed great numbers, the ability to speak English, and a western European culture similar to American culture. A turning point for negative Irish American sentiment was the Civil War. Irish units, including the all-Irish 69th New York Regiment, participated in monumental battles at Bull Run, Antietam, and Gettysburg, earning them a reputation for dependability and bravery. Following the Civil War, Irish laborers provided the hard work for the expansion of industrial America. The Irish Americans ran factories, built railroads, and worked in the mines. The Irish organized the first trade unions and fought for better wages, shorter hours, and safer working conditions.

Many Irish Americans also found themselves working as police officers and firefighters. Irish Americans became an urban cultural icon, one that was dedicated to public service, keeping the peace, enforcing the laws, and providing public safety. Even though these occupations were harsh, offered low pay, and lacked benefits during the 19th and early 20th centuries, many believe that if not for the Irish, organized and fully functioning fire and police departments would not be in existence today. For example, in the 1860s, more than half of those arrested in New York City were of Irish descent, but nearly half the city's law enforcement officers were also Irish. By the turn of the 20th century, five out of six New York Police Department officers were Irish American. Today, virtually every major police and fire department in the United States has its own Emerald Society to celebrate and honor police officers and firefighters of Irish heritage.

Tammany Hall and Five Points

Irish Americans also became involved in politics and organized crime in the United States. The Irish brought with them a natural sociability and an understanding of the importance of human interaction. They found social advancement and political involvement in the saloon, parish hall, and political clubhouse. One such place was Tammany Hall. Tammany Hall was a political organization established in New York in 1786. It was a Democratic political machine that sometimes distorted the democratic process but played a crucial role in controlling New York City politics and helping Irish immigrants advance in American politics from the 1790s to

An Irish American policeman in New York's Central Park in September 1942. By 1900, as many as five out of every six New York City Police Department officers were Irish American.

the 1960s. Tammany Hall's electoral base was primarily with New York's growing immigrant constituency, most notably the Irish. Tammany Hall offered public welfare to Irish immigrants in exchange for patronage and votes, and Irish immigrants were more than able to work their way into the Tammany political machine. The first gangs of New York City worked on behalf of Tammany Hall—they were the force behind the Tammany apparatus bullying for votes on Election Day. According to T. J. English, the criminal rackets that surged from the everyday workings of the Tammany machine became the basis of organized crime in the United States.

The term *mob boss* originated in the Irish-dominated Five Points from a type of political activity known as a mob primary. According to English, mob primaries comprised the most basic form of political organization known to man. Basically, an aspiring political leader orated until he gathered a crowd or mob willing to sign his petition for candidacy. The mob pledged loyalty to the orator, who was also usually a saloonkeeper, willing to offer his rough and unsavory constituents room, food, and drink. Thus, the mob boss became the leader of a gangster constituency that was a powerful force in many elections and often operated at the behest of political organizations such as the Tammany Tiger.

John Morrissey could arguably be considered the first Irish mob boss in the United States. Morrissey arrived in Five Points, New York, the infamous slum neighborhood that dominated the Sixth Ward at the lower tip of Manhattan Island in 1849. He was a brawler, a troublemaker, and a gangster, and by the age of 18 had been indicted for burglary, assault, and assault with intent to kill. His first job was to greet new immigrant arrivals and direct them to kitchens and boarding houses controlled by the Rynders organization. Captain Isaiah Rynders was a local political fixer for the Democratic Party. Morrissey developed a reputation as a tough though fair man who directed desperate immigrants to food and lodging, and in exchange, they signed voter cards and pledged their support to the political organization Morrissey represented (i.e., Tammany Hall). By 1851, John Morrissey had established himself as an honest immigrant runner, political organizer, saloonkeeper, and professional boxer, and was the people's champion in Five Points. He had fought William Poole ("Bill the Butcher") to a standstill, and eventually two of Morrissey's henchmen gunned down Poole.

During Morrisey's time, Five Points was well known for licentiousness and depravity with saloons, speakeasies, organized thievery, and prostitution. However, the physical environment was nothing compared to its reputation for gangs and gangsters. The mostly Irish gangs were a salient feature of Five Points. The Irish gangs included the Forty Thieves, Kerryonions, Shirt Tails, Chichesters, Patsy Conroys, Plug Uglies, Roach Guard, and the notorious Dead Rabbits. The rival native-born American gangs—the Bowery Boys, True Blue Americans, and American Guard—were in constant battle with the Irish gangs of Tammany Hall.

Organized Crime

Within this framework of criminal enterprise and politics, both Irish criminal organizations and prominent political figures continued through the following decades. Below is a truncated list of the most notable and notorious Irish gangsters, mobsters, and criminal syndicates.

In the years following Morrissey's death to the end of the century, the Whyos were by far the most notorious gang in New York. The Whyos, who were predominately Irish, were led by Danny Lyons and Danny Driscoll and presided over Lower Manhattan. The Whyos were racketeers. The term itself comes from the word *racket*, which was a public function held by criminals under the pretext of being an event for a worthy cause. Ultimately, the term was extended to include the use of physical intimidation or political pressure to procure protection money out of the merchants. Lyons and Driscoll were both hanged in 1888 for murder. The Whyos communicated with a variety of bird and animal sounds, and their name was derived from a sound made by a bird or owl.

Timothy Daniel "Big Tim" Sullivan (1862–1913) was a New York politician and prominent figure of Tammany Hall who controlled Manhattan's Bowery and Lower East Side districts. He is credited as being one of the earliest ward representatives to use his position to enable the activities of criminal street gangs. Sullivan owned four local bars, one of which he opened on Christie Street, just east of the Bowery. One of Sullivan's bar customers was Thomas "Fatty" Walsh, a notorious ward leader in Tammany Hall. Sullivan fell under Walsh's political wing, and in 1894, Sullivan was elected to the Third District's State Assembly. Sullivan was involved in illegal activities in the Lower East Side, including prostitution, gambling, loan sharking and "voter influence." He also had legal endeavors, including a partnership in the MGM and Loews cinema operations. Sullivan passed the Sullivan Act in 1911, which made it illegal to carry guns, unless you could afford a registration fee. In 1911, Sullivan contracted syphilis, was judged mentally incompetent, and was removed from his senate seat. In 1912, his family placed him in a mental institution.

Michael "King Mike" Cassius McDonald (1839–1907) made his fortune in Chicago through gambling, specifically faro, and the success of Mike McDonald's faro game energized gambling operations in Chicago unlike anything seen before. An Irish immigrant, King Mike ran Chicago's first crime syndicate. He oversaw the construction of a gigantic, four-story gambling house. This casino-like palace, "the Store," was located close to city hall, and it provided a gathering place for Democratic politicians as well as gamblers. McDonald obtained the cooperation of the police force, politicians, and an army of skilled confidence men to run his rigged games. McDonald's criminal activities predated those of Al Capone and other Chicago gangsters.

Dean O'Banion (1892–1924) was an Irish American mobster and the main rival of Johnny Torrio and Al Capone during the Chicago bootlegging wars of the 1920s. The O'Banion mob, known as the North Side Gang, ruled the North Side and Gold Coast areas of Chicago. At the height of his power, O'Banion was supposedly earning $1 million a year in alcohol sales. Although O'Banion had an agreement with Torrio and Capone over bootlegging control in various parts of the city, an eventual rift between Torrio, O'Banion, and the Genna Brothers led to his murder on November 10, 1924. The O'Banion murder sparked a five-year gang war between the North Side Gang and the Chicago Outfit that led to the killing of seven North Side gang members in the St. Valentine's Day Massacre in 1929.

Owen Vincent "Owney" Madden (1891–1965) was a gangster and underworld boss in New York City in the 1920s. Born in Leeds, England, to Irish parents, he rose to lead Hell's Kitchen's most violent gang, the Gophers. By the late 1920s, Madden was a millionaire, chief of an underworld empire that included real estate, boxing, gambling, bootlegging, breweries, and entertainment. With Frank Costello and other mob figures, he organized a "crime commission," or syndicate, whose objective was high profits, a businesslike operating style, and a minimum of bad publicity.

The Westies were an Irish American gang originating in Hell's Kitchen on the west side of Manhattan, New York. The Westies' most notorious members included Eddie McGrath, James Coonan, Mickey Featherstone, and Edward "Eddie the Butcher" Cummiskey. According to English, although never comprising more than 12 to 20 members, the Westies became tantamount to the last generation of Irish gangsters in the birthplace of the Irish mob.

The Winter Hill Gang

The Winter Hill Gang is a confederation of Boston-based organized crime figures. Members of the Winter Hill Gang have included such infamous Boston gangsters as Howie Winter, James McClean, James "Whitey" Bulger, and Stephen "The Rifleman" Flemmi. The Winter Hill Gang originated in the 1960s and derives its name from the Winter Hill neighborhood of Somerville, Massachusetts. The Winter Hill Gang has been involved in criminal activities such as murdering rival mobsters, illicit gambling, protection for hijackers and bookmakers, rigging horse races, and drug trafficking. Leaders of the Winter Hill Gang have included James "Buddy" McClean (1960–65), Howard "Howie" Winter (1965–78), James "Whitey" Bulger (1978–95), Kevin Weeks (1995–2000), and George "Georgie Boy" Hogan (2000–present). Kevin Weeks became a cooperating witness in 2000 and was released from federal prison on 2005. James "Whitey" Bulger, perhaps the most infamous of Irish mob bosses, fled Boston in 1994 pending a federal indictment. Bulger was on the Federal Bureau of Investigation's (FBI's) Ten Most Wanted list with a $2 million reward for information leading to his capture until June 22, 2011, when Bulger was arrested outside an apartment in Santa Monica, California. Arrested with him was his longtime girlfriend, Catherine Greig. Bulger was 81 years old at the time of his arrest.

Patrick O'Brien
University of Colorado Boulder

See Also: 1801 to 1850 Primary Documents; Boston, Massachusetts; Italian Americans; New York City; Organized Crime, Contemporary; Organized Crime, History of; Organized Crime, Sociology of.

Further Readings
Asbury, Herbert. *The Gangs of New York: An Informal History of the Underworld.* New York: Random House, 1927.
English, T. J. *Paddy Whacked: The Untold Story of the Irish American Gangster.* New York: Harper Collins, 2005.
Lehr, Dick and Gerard O'Neill. *Black Mass: The Irish Mob, the FBI, and a Devil's Deal.* New York: PublicAffairs, 2000.
Nee, Patrick. *A Criminal and an Irishman: The Inside Story of the Boston Mob–IRA Connection.* Hanover, NH: Steerforth, 2006.

Italian Americans

The people of the Italian peninsula have come to America since its earliest days as English colonies. Although they came from every region and every province of Italy, most of the immigration from Italy has been from southern Italy and Sicily, the so-called *mezzogiorno*. Most occurred during the period of the great, or "new," migration period that lasted from about 1880 to the 1920s. Italian Americans, as with every other immigrant group that has arrived on America's shores, have been useful, productive, and law-abiding citizens in their new homeland, and the list of notable accomplishments by prominent Italians and Italian Americans is a long and respectable one. However, as with every other immigrant group, a small number of immigrants and/or their descendants have been involved in criminal activities. For most people, this fact conjures up images of the Mafia and organized crime that they have acquired through the popular media, such as *The Godfather, The Sopranos, Goodfellas*, and other movies and TV programs. These images and negative stereotypes do not tell the entire story of Italian American immigrants or the criminals who came with them. By the late 19th century, millions of *contidini*, or peasants, began leaving southern Italy and Sicily in search of new opportunities overseas, many of them coming to the United States to realize their dreams. More Italians (4.6 million), in fact, came to the United States between 1880 and 1930 than from any other country.

Life in the *Mezzogiorno*
To understand those who came to the United States from Italy, it is necessary to understand the sociohistoric context from which they came, particularly southern Italy and Sicily, or the region now called the *mezzogiorno*.

With its subtropical climate, Italy for much of the year is the object of intense and scorching heat in the afternoon. The word *mezzogiorno* in Italian means noon, or literally "half-day." The origin of the term as applied to southern provinces remains murky; however, it was in common usage by the late 1800s, after the unification of the kingdoms of Italy. One version of the term as applied to southern Italy is that culturally, the afternoon in Italy, especially in the south, is the time for shops to close for the afternoon respite, a time for inactivity until the heat begins to pass in the late afternoon. The word *mezzogiorno*, then, came to be associated with the south of Italy (including Sicily), when not much was accomplished and the people relaxed and did not do much. In time, the term took on a pejorative connotation, applying to the southern provinces and the people.

From ancient times, southern Italy and Sicily were coveted areas, strategically important both militarily and commercially because of their geographic location, jutting out into the middle of the Mediterranean Sea. As such, southern Italy and Sicily was a frequently invaded and often-conquered land, coveted for its strategic location. Going back some 3,000 years, this part of Italy was conquered and held by Greeks, Romans, Spanish, Arabs, Normans, and Carthaginians, to name just a few. This series of conquerors had several effects that made the *mezzogiorno* unique. One was that,

Italian markets in New York City's Little Italy in the late 20th century, one of which boasts that it has been there for "over 100 years." From 1880 to 1930, Italians immigrants, of which there were 4.6 million, outnumbered those from any other country.

after intermarriage with many of the conquering nations, over time, the people became of mixed ethnic heritage. Particularly through the influence of Greek, Spanish, Arab, and North African blood, the people became swarthy in appearance—dark hair and eyes and dark complexions, which was seen as inferior by the people of the north, who tended to be lighter skinned and influenced more by the peoples of northern Europe. The north was also the cultural, industrial, and academic center of Italy, influenced by the art and music of the Renaissance, the religious influence of Rome, and later, by the Industrial Revolution that swept through Europe. The south, on the other hand, was rural, agricultural, feudal, and geographically isolated for much of the same time. In turn, the people were seen as ignorant and uneducated by many in the north. The unification of Italy in the 1860s at first held promise for the people of the *mezzogiorno*. Hopeful of achieving equality, the peasants of the south soon came to see the government of the north as just as oppressive as the foreign governments from the outside that they had dealt with for millennia. At worst, they were maltreated, and at best, they were ignored by the government; they were taxed and conscripted into the military at higher rates, with fewer and poorer schools, and with less recourse in the law and its enforcement than their northern counterparts had. The vendetta, then, became the norm—dealing with one's enemies oneself, rather than taking the dispute elsewhere.

The occupation of foreign armies also affected the culture of the people of the *mezzogiorno*. One such effect was the distrust of outsiders, who were all seen as potential oppressors. In the south, the concept of *campanellismo* became the norm—the distrust of anyone who came from outside the sound of the church bells. *Omerta*, often incorrectly labeled as a formal code of silence in the Mafia, also emerged from this culture of distrust. Originally, the code of *omerta* carried a similar connotation as the Hispanic value of *machismo*— a "real man" took care of his own problems and needed no help or interference from outsiders. Further, he minded his own business and did not repeat anything he heard from others. Later, after immigration began en masse, this was a trait seen as clannishness among those of the host country. The family, the primary unit of most societies, took on an extra special meaning to the peasants of the *mezzogiorno*. Inside the family, one could find protection, trust, and insulation from outsiders.

National allegiance was rarely seen among the peasants of the *mezzogiorno* as well. Even after the unification, people generally gave their allegiance to their local cities and regions, and not to the national government. Thus, they saw themselves more as citizens of Palermo, or Naples, or Bari; of Sicily, Calabria, or Puglia; and less as "Italians" in the national sense. It is often noted in the academic study of Italy and Italian immigration that Italians did not even know they were Italians until they came to the United States (or to other countries), when they were labeled as such by their hosts.

The Mafia

The origin of what is now called "the Mafia" began with the end of feudalism in the early 19th century and was centered on the island of Sicily, specifically the western portion. Much of the island was transformed into large private estates. Owned by the aristocracy who eventually began leaving their land, the peasants, or *contidini*, depended on the overseers appointed and hired by the former feudal lords to look over their interests. These overseers, or *gabelloti*, over time became powerful and important people in the former feudal society. With few opportunities available to them, people turned to the *gabelloti* to lease small parcels of land to farm for their subsistence or for a sharecropping arrangement. One needed to curry the favor, then, of the *gabelloti*, who often took advantage of the peasants who were dependent upon them. The relationship of the *contidini* and the *gabelloti* came to be a symbiotic network of favors, tribute, and patronage, with the advantage and power on the side of the overseers. In time, the *gabelloti* became men of power who were owed the deference and respect of the peasants.

They also became power brokers of sorts, who provided protection and subsistence to the peasantry in exchange for loyalty and the ability, for many of them, to take unfair advantage of the peasants. Many of the overseers hired henchmen to help protect their interests and insulate themselves from potential opposition by disgruntled peasants seeking revenge, or from the government, seen as interlopers by peasant and overseer alike. It was this system of patronage and power that many scholars and criminologists now see as the origin of what we now call the Mafia, more, in its original sense, a method or a way of doing things than a formal criminal organization.

The etymology of the word *mafia* is unclear. Theories abound that the term may have originated in the many different dialects of Italy, or the languages of the many conquerors that once occupied the *mezzogiorno*, specifically. It appears that original connotation of the term meant "bold," "daring," or "exciting," and a mafioso (*mafiusu* in the Sicilian dialect) grew to mean a person who displayed those characteristics. The term then evolved to mean what, in the vernacular of modern English, would mean "an attitude," not originally applied to one with a criminal background but rather to those who exhibited the characteristics of boldness, daring, and excitement. Those were characteristics certainly displayed by the *gabilloti* as they grew in power and strength and demanded the respect and evoked the fear of the local peasantry.

Coming to America

As the end of the 19th century drew near, the peasants of the *mezzogiorno* began to see a way out of the bigotry and oppression they had suffered for years, first at the hands of foreign governments, then from their own, and eventually from the patronage system of the *gabelloti*. As the technology of sea travel improved, the importation of crops and other farm goods from far-away lands such as America became cheaper than those that could be grown locally. This began to lead to economic collapse of the largely agricultural south. The same technology, however, made it easier for any peasant who could scrape together the fare to travel and move to other lands with more promise of opportunity. The great migration thus began.

The peasants of the *mezzogiorno*, most of whom had lived in small and isolated mountain villages and farmed the plots of land leased or shared with the *gabelloti* for their subsistence in the old country, became urban dwellers when they arrived in the United States. With no ties to the land or to farming, they settled wherever they had the promise of work or moved to the places where relatives and friends had already settled and could help them get established. For the most part, they crowded into urban tenements and became city dwellers, a much different existence than the rural village life from whence they came. A majority settled into the large cities of the northeast, particularly in New York. With them they brought their customs, food, and culture—and the patronage system, the "mafia" method of doing things that they learned in the *mezzogiorno*.

Most of these immigrants worked at low-paying manual-labor jobs. Sometimes their children, who in the old country had played with cousins and friends on narrow cobblestone streets or courtyards under the watchful eyes of parents, relatives, or neighbors, roamed the streets in urban neighborhoods with little or no supervision. Some of the immigrants, who had grown up unschooled themselves, saw little practical value for their children in schools that taught subjects like literature or history. Left to their own devices, the mischief of boys and their schoolyard chums could easily grow into youth gangs, with boyhood pranks escalating into skirmishes with the police and the legal system.

The Black Hand (*la mano nera*), often described as "the" precursor to the Mafia, in reality were groups of independent extortion gangs rather than a single unified and monolithic criminal organization. Relatively unsophisticated, Black Hand gangs would extort money from their fellow immigrants, particularly those who were doing well financially, in exchange for "protection," or being left alone. Black Hand gangs were relatively small, ranging usually from 3 to 20 members, who were able to, or perceived to be able to, carry out their threats.

As the sons of the immigrants grew and their playgroups coalesced into gangs, they became involved in various criminal activities. These gangs were usually profit driven rather than territorial. Often they were involved in burglary, robbery, or other forms of theft involving stolen goods that could be easily resold for a profit. In 1920, the Eighteenth Amendment, and the Volstead Act, which enabled its enforcement, provided the groundwork for what eventually would become the Mafia. Passed largely as a response to and under the pressure of the temperance movement in the United States, Prohibition created an unprecedented money-making opportunity for criminal entrepreneurs who satisfied the thirst of a large part of the American public that was unwilling to do without alcohol. It also required a great deal of organization in order to provide the service, putting the "organized" into organized crime.

Italian American Crime: New York and Chicago

In New York, the early gangsters were primarily Irish and Jewish, with the Italians arriving on the scene as latecomers. With the opportunity provided by Prohibition, the Italians soon rose to either push their Irish and Jewish counterparts out of the picture or began to cooperate and work with them, dividing the Prohibition pie up among all. Still, during the 1920s, there was no unified structure among the groups involved in bootlegging activities. As such, rivalries and disputes were common.

By the late 1920s, war had broken out in New York between the two most powerful of these groups, one led by Joe "the Boss" Masseria and the other by rival Salvatore Maranzano. In 1931, with the war beginning to take its toll, Masseria henchmen Charles "Lucky" Luciano and Vito Genovese met with Maranzano and agreed to betray Masseria in a plot to bring an end to the war and allow Maranzano to ascend to leadership as the "boss of all bosses" over everyone in New York. Maranzano, by all reports, made an insufferable boss and was soon killed as well. With Luciano as the impetus, the position of boss of all bosses was eliminated, the five-family structure was set up, and "the commission" was put in place to settle disputes, establish rules, and ensure cooperation between the New York families and other families across the country. This is usually considered the beginning of the Mafia as an organization, rather than as the method brought from the *mezzogiorno*, with the same basic structure that remained in place throughout the years and up until today.

The organization in Chicago, usually referred to as "the Outfit," evolved a bit differently. James (Big Jim or Diamond Jim) Colosimo had risen to the top of the Chicago underworld primarily by managing the prostitution enterprises of his wife. Colosimo, who also owned a prominent restaurant/nightspot, enjoyed a flashy and opulent lifestyle and soon attracted the attention of a local Black Hand gang that attempted to extort money from him. Colosimo sent for a distant relative of his wife's from New York, John Torrio. Torrio arrived and, with the help of gangster associates from New York, had the Black Handers killed. With extraordinary business acumen, Torrio remained in Chicago as an aid to Colosimo and soon was running the entire operation, allowing Big Jim to move in the legitimate social circles of Chicago. To assist him, Torrio brought in a former protégé from New York named Al Capone. When Prohibition took effect in 1920, Torrio, with his talent for business, quickly recognized the enormous profit potential that awaited in bootleg liquor. Colosimo, however, content with his prostitution enterprises, would have none of it. Unable to convince him, Torrio set Colosimo up to be killed, again by former associates from New York, and along with Capone set up alcohol manufacturing and distribution in Chicago and throughout the region. Other gangs, however, again primarily Irish and Jewish, also availed themselves of the opportunity afforded by Prohibition and competed with the Torrio-Capone organization for the profits to be made in alcohol. Torrio and Capone were soon involved with rivals in a war for domination of Chicago. When North Side leader Dion O'Banion was murdered in his florist shop, the North Siders retaliated with a planned hit on Torrio. Torrio was severely wounded in the attack but eventually recovered and decided that he had had enough. Torrio officially retired, leaving the entire organization in the hands of Capone. Capone built his criminal enterprise into a multimillion-dollar business, with income not only from bootlegging, but also prostitution, gambling, usury, and other criminal activities. In 1932, Capone was convicted on income tax evasion charges and was sent to prison, where he later died. The Outfit continued throughout the years under the leadership of such notorious gangsters as Frank Nitti, Paul Ricca, Tony Accardo, and Sam Giancana.

Italian American Crime in the United States

Similar social conditions affected the immigrants from the *mezzogiorno* in similar ways, no matter where they settled. As in New York and Chicago, most of the immigrants who came to America along with their descendants led normal, productive, and law-abiding lives. Also in a similar fashion, the sons of some immigrants grew into organized crime groups in urban areas in similar, although not identical, ways. The Federal Bureau of Investigation (FBI) eventually identified 26 Mafia "crime families" in various cities throughout the country. While the history and evolution of each is unique, it is fair to say that at one time the Italian American Mafia had a ubiquitous presence in the United States.

As with other European ethnic groups, however, ethnic identity as "Italian" has changed over the years, affected by the passage of time, intermarriage with other ethnic groups, and assimilation into the mainstream culture, now a century or more removed from the great European migration of their grandparents and great-grandparents.

These changes have also affected Italian American organized crime, held together more by profit and less by the bonds of ethnic identity. Italian organized crime, while still in existence, has been considerably weakened by this lack of ethnic unity, the rise of organized crime groups of other ethnicities, the passage of anti–organized crime laws such as the Racketeer Influenced and Corrupt Organizations Act (RICO), and concerted efforts by both federal and local law enforcement authorities.

Paul A. Magro
Ball State University

See Also: 1941 to 1960 Primary Documents; 1961 to 1980 Primary Documents; 2001 to 2012 Primary Documents; Capone, Al; Chicago, Illinois; Irish Americans; Jewish Americans; Luciano, "Lucky"; New York City; Organized Crime, Contemporary; Organized Crime, History of.

Further Readings

Albini, Joseph L. *The American Mafia: Genesis of a Legend*. New York: Appleton-Century-Crofts, 1971.
Ellis Island. "The Peopling of America." http://www.ellisisland.org/immexp/wseix_5_3.asp? (Accessed December 2010).
Gallo, P. J. *Old Bread, New Wine: A Portrait of the Italian Americans*. Chicago: Nelson-Hall, 1981.
National Italian American Foundation. http://www.niaf.org (Accessed December 2010).
Raab, Selwyn. *Five Families: The Rise, Decline, and Resurgence of America's Most Powerful Mafia Empires*. New York: St. Martin's Griffin, 2006.
Reppetto, T. A. *American Mafia: A History of Its Rise to Power*. New York: Holt Paperbacks, 2004
Roth, Mitchell P. *Organized Crime*. Upper Saddle River, NJ: Pearson Education, 2010.

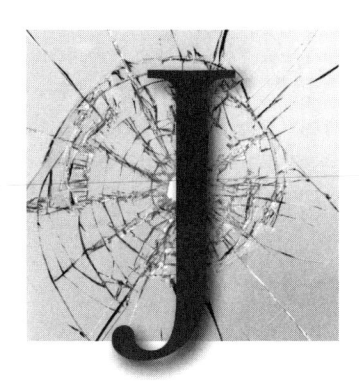

Jackson, Andrew (Administration of)

Andrew Jackson (1767–1845) was the seventh president of the United States (1829–37). Jackson's two terms ushered in a new era of American politics with an ideology known as Jacksonian democracy. His presidency encouraged more government participation by the population. At the same time, he expanded executive power. Jackson's presidency occurred during an era when state penitentiaries were established, and his opponents, the Whigs, were working for prison and punishment reform. Jacksonian democracy, however, influenced judiciary reform at the federal and state levels and helped to establish city police forces.

Jackson believed that it was the president's job to defend the Union, even if he supported states' rights. This belief was demonstrated during the Nullification Crisis in 1832. The crisis emerged over disagreements over tariffs and compounded the growing sectional tension between the northern and southern states. Southern planters believed the tariffs that placed high taxes on imported European goods, making them more expensive than goods produced by northern industrialists, benefited the northern states at the expense of southern farmers. John C. Calhoun supported his home state of South Carolina, resigning as vice president in December 1832 and saying that states had the power to nullify a federal law that hurt the state's interests. South Carolina threatened to secede if the national government tried to enforce the new tariff in 1832. To protect the nation, Jackson signed a Compromise Tariff in 1833, which stalled further discussion of secession.

President Jackson further demonstrated executive power through his use of vetoes, successfully vetoing 12 bills in eight years. The use of the presidential veto is notably recognized in Jackson's dispute with the Second National Bank, an issue that came to be known as the Bank War. In July 1832, Jackson vetoed a bill that would renew the charter for the National Bank four years before the existing charter was scheduled to end. Jackson disliked the bank in part because it concentrated the national wealth in a single institution, made the rich richer, and favored the northern states over those in the south and in the west. With this veto, Jackson argued that a president should be able to veto any bill that he felt would be detrimental to the nation. As a result, legislators had to begin to factor into their negotiations how the president might feel about a bill. After his reelection to a second term, Jackson decided to abolish the National Bank. In 1833, he removed the federal government's deposits and put them in numerous state banks. The subsequent rise of credit and speculation eventually led to high inflation and created a demand for specie that could not be met. The new banks collapsed, and the nation descended into a deep depression after the Panic of 1837.

Jackson's policy of Indian removal is one of his administration's more controversial stances and shows how presidential authority tangled with the federal judiciary. In 1830, he signed the Indian Removal Act to relocate Native American tribes west of the Mississippi River. The president was authorized to make land exchange treaties with the tribes in order to facilitate removal. The Cherokee took their case to protect their land to the U.S. Supreme Court. In 1831, in *Cherokee Nation v. Georgia*, the court stated that the Cherokee were a sovereign nation. The 1832 case *Worcester v. Georgia* declared that the state had no jurisdiction on tribal lands. Jackson refused to enforce the court mandate of *Worcester v. Georgia* that would have removed Georgia's authority from tribal lands. Jackson also denied that as president, he had the power to enforce laws against individual states. This stance is interesting considering how Jackson handled the Nullification Crisis. In 1835, a small faction of Cherokee signed the Treaty of New Echota with the U.S. government, resulting in the forced removal of the Cherokee from the southeast in 1838 in what was called the Trail of Tears.

Jacksonian Democracy

While Jackson and his fellow Democrats had respect for American law, they also wanted to protect the autonomy of the American public. Jacksonians believed that the power of judges and lawyers came from legal ambiguities, so Jacksonians wanted to simplify legal codes and procedures to eliminate a judicial aristocracy. Jackson's friend, Edward Livingston of Louisiana, pushed for codification of common law and statutes, and his ideas for legal reform became important to the Democratic Party. Several states, including Pennsylvania, Ohio, and Massachusetts, revised their legal codes in the 1830s as a result of Livingston's efforts. When new western states were admitted to the Union, their constitutions were influenced by Jacksonian legal reforms. Jackson also signed the Judiciary Act of 1837, setting the number of justices on the Supreme Court at nine, and adding two new appeals circuits to cover the growing number of western states.

The rise of Jacksonian democracy led to more rioting in the United States in the 1830s. Riots occurred as a result of elections, racial and ethnic relations, and labor unrest. Hundreds of riots in American cities occurred in the 1830s and 1840s. In response, cities created professional police forces. New York City organized its first professional police force in 1845. Democratic politicians controlled the police department, as well as many aspects of the city's government, causing the state legislature to create a state-run police force for the city in 1857 in an attempt to quell Democratic power.

Jackson's administration expanded the presidential power in many ways, as illustrated by his use of the veto, his stance on nullification, his policy on Indian removal, and reforms to the judiciary. The executive power exhibited by his administration shaped the presidency for the next several terms, and the ideals of Jacksonian democracy influenced American society for decades.

Erica Rhodes Hayden
Vanderbilt University

See Also: 1801 to 1850 Primary Documents; Adams, John Quincy (Administration of); Independent Treasury Act; Indian Removal Act; Livingston, Edward; Native Americans; Riots; Supreme Court, U.S.

Further Readings
Cole, Donald B. *The Presidency of Andrew Jackson*. Lawrence: University Press of Kansas, 1993.
Remini, Robert V. *Andrew Jackson and the Course of American Democracy, 1833–1845*. New York: Harper & Row, 1984.
Remini, Robert V. *Andrew Jackson and the Course of American Freedom, 1822–1832*. New York: Harper & Row, 1981.
Schlesinger, Arthur M., Jr. *The Age of Jackson*. Boston: Little, Brown, 1946.

Jackson, Mississippi

Jackson, founded in 1821, is the state capital and largest city in Mississippi. In 2006, the population

James Meredith, the first African American student to enroll at the University of Mississippi, is seen here flanked by U.S. marshals while he walks to class in October 1962. Meredith later led a march from Memphis, Tennessee, to Jackson, Mississippi, in June 1966 as part of a drive to register African American voters and build support for civil rights legislation.

of Jackson was 176,614, a 4.1 percent decrease from 2000. The majority (70.6 percent) of the population of Jackson is African American, and 27.8 percent is white, with smaller numbers of other ethnic groups. Median household income in 1999 was $30,414, slightly below the state average of $31,330, and 23.5 percent of the population lived below the poverty line. After the Civil War, Jackson (and Mississippi as a whole) resisted the efforts of Reconstruction, remaining segregated into the 1960s. A variety of measures, from a violent paramilitary organization called the Redshirts to administrative measures such as poll taxes and literacy tests, were used during these years to deprive African Americans of the right to vote and thus of political power. In addition, an estimated 500 African Americans were lynched in Mississippi between 1800 and 1955.

Jackson was significantly damaged during the Civil War and earned the nickname "Chimneyville" after being burned in 1863 by Union forces. After the war, Mississippi exerted considerable resistance to Reconstruction, passing restrictive "Black Codes" meant to control the newly freed African Americans (including vagrancy laws and laws against intermarriage). Violence was also used to suppress the rights of African Americans; this violence was often aimed at institutions (e.g., schools and churches) serving African Americans as well as toward individuals. The city government was notable for its corruption in the postwar period but the city continued to grow, aided by the increase in railroad activity near the end of the century and the discovery of natural gas in the early 20th century. Jackson was a center for the civil rights movement in Mississippi, with some of the earliest efforts to defy segregation made by students from the historically black Tougaloo College. In 1961, more than 300 Freedom Riders were arrested in the city, and many boycotts and acts of civil disobedience took place in Jackson in the early 1960s. On June 12, 1963, civil rights activist Medgar Evers was shot and killed in his driveway in Jackson by Byron de la Beckwith, a member of the White Citizens' Council (a white supremacist organization founded in Mississippi in 1954). Evers's murder (or assassination) drew national attention to the civil rights cause in Mississippi. De la Beckwith was tried twice for Evers's murder, both times with all-white juries, but both ended as mistrials as the juries were unable to reach a verdict (he was retried in 1994, based on new evidence, and he was convicted of murder). In June 1966, James Meredith, the first African American student to enroll at the University of Mississippi, led a march from Memphis, Tennessee, to Jackson to register African American voters and gain support for civil rights legislation. In 1967, the Ku Klux Klan bombed the Beth Israel Congregation in Jackson as well as the home of Dr. Perry Nussbaum, rabbi of Beth Israel and a civil rights worker who founded the first city and state interracial organizations in Mississippi. In May 1970, two African American students at the historically black Jackson State College (now Jackson State University) were shot and killed by state police during a Vietnam War protest.

The first state prison in Mississippi was built in Jackson in 1843, but it was heavily damaged during the Civil War and was not rebuilt because of a lack of funds. Until the construction of the Mississippi State Penitentiary in Sunflower County (also known as Parchman after its first warden, J. M. Parchman) in 1901, convicts were leased out to farmers and other private individuals. The Jackson Police Department was established in 1822, one year after the founding of the city of Jackson. Uniforms and badges for police officers were introduced in 1873, and specialization began in 1878 when the first police detective was appointed; further specialization such as patrol officers and desk sergeants were later introduced. The Police Training Academy was constructed in 1965. In 1972, the first female police officer was sworn in, and in 2006, Shirlene Anderson became the first female chief of police for Jackson. Today, the Jackson Police Department is comprised of about 430 officers and 250 civilian support personnel.

According to the CQ Press rankings, based on Federal Bureau of Investigation (FBI) statistics from 2009, in 2010, Jackson had the 14th-highest crime rate in the country with a score of 218.91 (where 0 would indicate an average crime rate and a positive number a higher than average rate) and the ninth-highest crime rate among cites with a population of 100,000 to 499,000. According to FBI statistics, in 2008, 1,515 violent crimes were reported in Jackson, including 37 murder or non-negligent manslaughters, 124 forcible rapes, 958 robberies, and 396 aggravated assaults. There were 13,182 property crimes reported in that year, including 4,569 burglaries, 6,994 larceny-thefts, 1,619 motor vehicle thefts, and 113 cases of arson.

Sarah Boslaugh
Kennesaw State University

See Also: African Americans; Ku Klux Klan; Mississippi; Race, Class, and Criminal Law; Race-Based Crimes; Racism; Segregation Laws.

Further Readings

City of Jackson, Mississippi. "Jackson Police Department." http://www.jacksonms.gov/government/police (Accessed May 2011).

"City Crime Rankings 2010–2011." CQ Press. http://os.cqpress.com/citycrime/2010/citycrime2010-2011.htm (Accessed June 2011).

Evers, Medgar Wiley. *The Autobiography of Medgar Evers: A Hero's Life and Legacy Revealed Through His Writings, Letters, and Speeches*, Myrlie Evers-Williams and Manning Marable, eds. New York: Basic Civitas Books, 2005.

Vollers, Maryanne. *Ghost of Mississippi: The Murder of Medgar Evers, the Trials of Byron de la Beckwith, and the Haunting of the New South*. Boston: Little, Brown, 1995.

James, Jesse

Jesse James (1847–82) was an infamous outlaw of the American West in the 1860s through the 1880s. He committed dozens of robberies and murdered at least six men. Jesse Woodson James was born in Centralville, Missouri, which is now known as Kearney. His father, Robert James (1818–50), was a Baptist minister who left the family in 1850 to minister to gold miners in California, but died soon after arriving there. Jesse's mother, Zerelda Elizabeth Cole (1825–1911), remarried twice and thus Jesse, his two brothers, Alexander Franklin (1843–1915) and Robert Jr. (1818–50), and their sister, Susan Lavenia (1849–89), gained two half-brothers, two half-sisters, and a stepbrother. The James family had its origins in Kentucky, and they were slave owners and southern sympathizers; James's father owned seven slaves. With the outbreak of the Civil War, James became a member of the notorious Confederate guerrilla unit led by William Quantrill and William "Bloody" Anderson; they allegedly perpetrated brutal acts against the Union army along the Kansas-Missouri border.

While surrendering at the end of the war, James was shot through one of his lungs. He had a long, slow recuperation and was nursed mainly by his first cousin, Zerelda Mimms. On April 23, 1874, after a nine-year courtship, Jesse and Zerelda married; they had two children, a son, Jesse Edwards, and a daughter, Mary Susan, as well as twin boys who died soon after birth.

Life of an Outlaw

After the end of the Civil War, Jesse and Frank James returned home, but they found that Missourians were bitter and belligerent toward former Confederates, particularly former guerrilla fighters, and terrorized the James brothers and their families, robbing them of their material possessions in retribution. Accordingly, in 1866, the James brothers joined with the Younger brothers to form an outlaw band. Thomas Coleman "Cole" Younger had initially ridden with Quantrill's Raiders, but later left to join the regular Confederate cavalry, just like Frank James had done. The example of the James brothers has been cited by criminologists as evidence in support of the violent veteran model of the theoretical relationship between war and violent crime, which suggests that the experiences of warfare make soldiers more accepting of violence, as well as more proficient at it. Jesse James certainly became very proficient with pistols and was an accomplished horseman as a result of his wartime activities.

The James-Younger gang robbed banks, stagecoaches, trains, and a fair in Kansas City. On

A portrait of Jesse James from around 1882. That year, Missouri Governor Thomas T. Crittenden offered $10,000 for the capture of the James brothers. The reward led to his shooting on April 13, 1882. His killer was sentenced to death but was pardoned.

February 13, 1866, they robbed the Clay County Savings Bank in Liberty, Missouri; on October 30, 1866, they robbed the Alexander Mitchell Bank in Lexington, Missouri. In March 1867, the gang unsuccessfully tried to rob a bank in Savannah, Missouri. On May 22, 1867, they robbed the Hughes and Wasson Bank in Richmond, Missouri, and on March 20, 1868, they robbed Nimrod and Cin banking house in Russellville, Kentucky. On December 7, 1869, they robbed the Daviess Savings Bank of Gallatin, Missouri, where Jesse James shot and killed a cashier. On June 3, 1871, they robbed the Ocobock Brothers Bank in Corydon, Iowa. On July 21, 1873, the gang conducted the first successful train robbery in the Old West by getting away with about $3,000 from the Chicago and Rock Island Express train near Adair, Iowa. They had removed part of the tracks to stop the train, and during the heist Jesse James shot and killed the train engineer. On January 15, 1874, they held up the Concord Stagecoach near Malvern, Arkansas. Other train robberies included the St. Louis Iron Mountain and Southern Railroad (January 31, 1874) and the Missouri-Pacific Railroad (July 7, 1876). On September 7, 1876, the gang attempted to rob the First National Bank of Northfield, Minnesota; after the manhunt that followed this raid, only Jesse and Frank James were free—the rest of the gang were dead or captured.

In 1882, James and his family were living in a rented home in St. Joseph, Missouri. James had recruited brothers Robert and Charles Ford to help with a planned robbery of another bank. The governor of Missouri at the time, Thomas T. Crittenden, had offered the substantial reward of $10,000 for the capture of the James brothers, dead or alive. This reward allegedly tempted Robert Ford on April 13, 1882, to shoot James in the back of the head and kill him as he was climbing onto a chair to straighten a picture. Jesse James was buried on the James family farm, but in 1902, he was reinterred at Mt. Olivet Cemetery in Kearney, Missouri. Robert and Charles Ford were convicted of James's murder and were sentenced to hang, but were pardoned by the governor of Missouri. Two years later, Charles Ford committed suicide; in 1892, Robert Ford was killed in Creede, Colorado, in a barroom brawl.

Conclusion

Journalists and writers of pulp fiction have portrayed Jesse James as a romanticized Robin Hood figure. James helped to cultivate this heroic image of himself and his deeds, including sometimes even writing letters to newspapers attempting to justify his actions. Former southern sympathizers commonly rallied to his defense. Rumors persisted that Robert Ford had not actually killed James, but someone else. One J. Frank Dalton, who died in Granbury, Texas, in 1951 at age 103, claimed to be Jesse. However, in 1995, the body buried in James's grave in Missouri was identified by forensic specialists using mitochondrial DNA as highly likely to be that of Jesse James.

Victor B. Stolberg
Essex County College

See Also: 1851 to 1900 Primary Documents; Dime Novels, Pulps, Thrillers; Frontier Crime; Missouri; Robbery, History of.

Further Readings

Love, Robertus. *The Rise and Fall of Jesse James*. Lincoln: University of Nebraska Press, 1990.

Settle, William A. *Jesse James Was His Name, or, Fact and Fiction Concerning the Careers of the Notorious James Brothers of Missouri*. Lincoln: University of Nebraska Press, 1977.

Stiles, T. J. *Jesse James: Last Rebel of the Civil War*. New York: Alfred A. Knopf, 2002.

Japanese Americans

Japanese Americans are a racial, ethnic, and cultural group making up part of the landscape of U.S. citizenry. While distinguished by their perceived cultural and geographical tie to Japan, Japanese Americans are also identified as part of a broader Asian American community. Historically, Japanese American difference from, and sameness to, other Asian American ethnic communities (like Chinese Americans) has fluctuated depending on the political climate. U.S. law and policy as well as social attitudes have shaped Japanese Americans into a distinct and marginalized category that was historically criminalized and racialized as perpetual foreigners, and later as wartime enemies, despite citizenship status.

Immigration

The category of Japanese American was in part created and defined through the policing of early U.S. immigration and citizenship laws. Immigration laws passed during the late 19th century restricted entry and naturalization along racial lines, helping to distinguish Japanese Americans as outside the boundaries of U.S. citizenship. The Page Act of 1875 is one notable immigration law that in application targeted Japanese and Chinese women hoping to gain entry into the United States. This law identified morally suspect character as a reason for denial, detention, and deportation, and enforcement of the law often targeted Japanese women. Japanese immigrants during this period occupied a tenuous position. They were welcomed as an undervalued labor force (especially in agriculture on the West Coast and on plantations in Hawai'i) even as they were targeted by nativists as threats to the nation, for instance in San Francisco, where the board of education ruled to segregate Japanese students from white students in 1906. Criminalization of Japanese Americans in this early period thus hinged on their perceived racial and cultural difference, which was understood by immigration officials, politicians, and ordinary (white) citizens as a marker of immorality and sexual deviancy.

However, the relative strength of the Japanese government helped Japanese Americans gain ground as U.S. residents in contrast to Chinese immigrants. With passage of the Chinese Exclusion Act of 1882 prohibiting almost all persons of Chinese origin from entry into the United States, Japanese immigrants, encouraged by the Japanese government, attempted to distinguish themselves from the Chinese. Constructing Japanese immigrants as ambassadors rather than laborers, Japanese immigrant leaders pushed Japanese Americans to adopt so-called American clothes and customs. The Gentleman's Agreement (1908) negotiated by the Japanese government allowed Japanese immigrant men already in the United States to send for wives and thus enabled Japanese American heterofamily formations, further differentiating Japanese from Chinese immigrants and residents. The agreement ended immigration and legal entry of laborers from Japan; however, it was conceived of by the Japanese government as a measure to help protect Japanese already in the United States. The resulting wave of "picture brides" from Japan during the early 20th century was not without anti-Japanese and nativist activism, nor was it without accompanying anxieties over perceived immoral sexualities. Much of the public discourse of the time played on anxieties over Asian immigration in general (and Japanese in particular) by casting the Japanese "picture bride" as a potential prostitute in hiding. Furthermore, nativist concerns over Japanese women immigrants also involved fears that once allowed entry, Japanese mothers would rear inassimilable Japanese American children who were loyal not to the United States, but to Japan.

These immigration laws were not just about regulating and policing entry; they were also a means through which "Japanese American" emerged as a distinct and criminalized category. Laws over entry and citizenship were applied unevenly across racial, national, and class categories, where the criminalization of some groups in contrast to others not only justified their legal exclusion but helped fuel (and was shaped by) popular sentiments around criminal physiology. For example, author of several pamphlets and publisher of the *Sacramento Bee* newspaper V. S. McClatchy was one prominent figure in the anti-Japanese movement during the early 20th century. McClatchy was a member of the Japanese Exclusion League, one of several such groups dedicated to the exclusion and deportation of Japanese and Japanese Americans on the basis of their assumed racial, cultural, and psychological inferiority.

Publishing such views of Japanese American inferiority and criminality in venues like the *Bee* helped shape public sentiments that eventually enabled passage of Alien Land Laws in California, which targeted Japanese (and Chinese) Americans, keeping them from owning land (1913). Anti-Asian and anti-Japanese sentiments on the national level helped pass the 1917 Immigration Act, which established the Asiatic Barred Zone. With the subsequent passage of the Cable Act (1924), immigration of peoples from this geographic region (the Asiatic Barred Zone), which included Japan, was ended. The ban was not lifted until passage of the Immigration Act of 1965.

Citizenship

Thus for Japanese Americans, citizenship and naturalization served as key sites through which the community was shaped during the late 19th and early 20th centuries. Testing existing naturalization laws as well as challenging stereotypes of Japanese Americans as criminally suspect and inassimilable, Takao Ozawa, a 26-year resident of the United States born in Japan but educated in California, filed what eventually became a Supreme Court case challenging the racial clause for naturalization. In his case, Ozawa argued that "at heart I am a true American," defining himself as a "free white person" who was "without negro blood," the requirement for naturalization. Decided in 1922, *Ozawa v. United States* denied

Ozawa's claims to being a "free white person," restricting the definition of *white* to those persons of the Caucasian race.

Internment

The criminalizing of Japanese Americans as unworthy of U.S. citizenship extended beyond immigration and naturalization bans. Japanese Americans who were native-born citizens also experienced similar policing around their identity. Japanese Americans were racialized as what Lisa Lowe terms *foreigners-within*; both the U.S. government and white, nativist citizens questioned Japanese American claims to citizenship and national loyalty. Such suspicions formed the crux of government action during World War II to contain Japanese Americans living on the West Coast in designated internment camps out of fear that Japanese Americans were potential spies of the Japanese government. The Federal Bureau of Investigation (FBI) arrested and detained many first-generation Japanese American community leaders during World War II on suspicion of working for the enemy.

By 1942, Executive Order 9066, adopted by Franklin Roosevelt at the suggestion of General John Dewitt, instigated the removal of all peoples of Japanese descent from the west coast. Executive Order 9102 and Public Law 503 implemented what the government then termed "voluntary relocation" by assigning a war relocation authority and establishing criminal sanctions. Criminalized for being inassimilable immigrants and unpatriotic U.S. residents, more than 120,000 Japanese Americans residing on the west coast were evacuated from their homes and relocated into 10 internment camps situated in rural, often desolate locations (often, camps were located on Native American reservations).

U.S.-born Japanese American citizens were included in these orders, and several Japanese Americans challenged the legality of the removal orders in court. Notably, *Hirabayashi v. United States* (1943) and *Korematsu v. United States* (1944) challenged the constitutionality of the relocation orders. As U.S. citizens, Japanese Americans like Korematsu argued the violation of their rights. The decisions in these cases rationalized that the need to protect the nation during war overrode the individual rights of citizens like Korematsu. After he refused to relocate, Korematsu was sent to one of three FBI prisons established to hold those refusing Executive Order 9066. Ironically, the fear of Japanese American disloyalty did not dissuade the U.S. government from recruiting detainees to fight in the U.S. Army.

Internment of Japanese Americans began to wind down in 1944, with the relocation order rescinded in 1945 as the war ended, though it was not until 1976 during the civil rights era that Order 9066 was formally repealed. The loss of property that resulted from internment left many Japanese Americans to resettle in new places. Psychological studies of the time found that the trauma of internment impacted many Japanese Americans, and the period after World War II saw the rise of stereotypes of Japanese

Japanese American Corporal Jimmie Shohara, who served in the U.S. Army during World War II, was visiting his interned U.S.-born parents at the Manzanar internment camp in California in 1943 when Ansel Adams took this photograph of him.

(and Asian Americans more generally) as "model minorities" who were characterized as quiet and hardworking. Even though the model minority figure emerged in state and media discourses as a wartime tool to distinguish Chinese Americans (as allies) from Japanese Americans (as enemies), the impact of internment on the social, political, and economic position of Japanese Americans quickly shifted the association of the model minority stereotype to Japanese Americans. The figure of the model minority emerged as a way to decriminalize Asian Americans, and for many Japanese Americans, the geographic dispersal, economic loss, and psychological impact of internment resulted in internalized pressures to assimilate.

Additionally, U.S. national guilt over internment after the war (when internment was quickly paralleled to Nazi practices) created a national sentiment of victimization and decriminalization toward Japanese Americans, which further solidified the stereotype of the Japanese American model minority.

One of the political outcomes of the model minority stereotype was to provide rationalization for the criminalizing of African Americans against Asian Americans in the state's efforts to resist structural changes being advocated as part of the civil rights movement. However, the bifurcating of Asian Americans as model minorities against African Americans as "monitored minorities" fails to recognize the active participation of Asian Americans in the civil rights movement, for instance, the work of Japanese Americans in establishing redress for internment, which was both influenced by and influential to other kinds of organizing around equal access and rights taking place during the 1960s and 1970s.

The criminalization of Japanese Americans has historically shared many similarities with Chinese and other racialized minority American populations in that racial and cultural differences worked as external indicators of internal propensities (toward immorality or criminality). However, the legal treatment and cultural representations of Japanese Americans was often a result of the contrasting of Japanese Americans against other ethnic and racial categories. The category of Japanese American continues to be shaped in relation to Chinese and other Asian ethnic (as well as African American, Latino, and Native American) difference as well as through decriminalization.

Julietta Hua
San Francisco State University

See Also: Chinese Americans; Internment; *Korematsu v. United States*; Racism; Xenophobia.

Further Readings
Kurashige, Lon. *Japanese American Celebration and Conflict: A History of Ethnic Identity and Festival.* Berkeley: University of California Press, 2002.
Okihiro, Gary. *Cane Fires: The Anti-Japanese Movement in Hawaii.* Philadelphia: Temple University Press, 1991.
Spickard, Paul. *Japanese Americans: The Formations and Transformations of an Ethnic Group.* New Brunswick, NJ: Rutgers University Press, 2009.
Yamamoto, Traise. *Masking Selves, Making Subjects: Japanese American Women, Identity and the Body.* Berkeley: University of California Press, 1999.

Jefferson, Thomas

Thomas Jefferson's legacy to subsequent generations has been vast, including political theory, philosophy, architecture, and education. Jefferson's influence on American thought regarding crime and punishment has been especially great. Conceptualizing crime and punishment as a consequence of the social contract under which citizens live, Jefferson believed that punishments must be carefully related to the crime committed. His strong belief in public service informed his commitment that government's most sacred duty is to provide equal and impartial justice to all citizens.

Jefferson was born April 2, 1743, in Shadwell, Virginia. His father, Peter Jefferson, was a planter and his mother, Jane Randolph, was descended from one of Virginia's most distinguished families. Thomas Jefferson inherited a significant estate, including slaves, from his father. At age 26, Jefferson began building his estate, Monticello. For most of his adult life, Jefferson owned about 200 slaves. After serving as a delegate to the Second

A painting depicting Thomas Jefferson (standing), Benjamin Franklin (left), and John Adams working on drafts of the Declaration of Independence in Philadelphia in 1776.

Continental Congress from 1775 to 1776, where he drafted the Declaration of Independence, Jefferson was elected to the Virginia House of Delegates. In that role, he drafted 126 bills, many dealing with issues of crime and punishment. For example, Jefferson attempted to simplify the judicial system, believing that too often, needless delays obstructed justice in criminal cases. Jefferson also sought to abolish the death penalty in Virginia for all cases excepting those involving murder or treason. Although unsuccessful in this attempt, Jefferson was elected governor of Virginia in 1779, serving until 1781. Primarily focused on the Revolutionary War, Jefferson was instrumental in moving the state capital from Williamsburg to Richmond, a more central location, so that all residents of Virginia would be better heard. Jefferson also served as the second vice president and third president of the United States. After his retirement, he founded the University of Virginia in 1818. Jefferson died on the 50th anniversary of the signing of the Declaration of Independence, on July 4, 1826.

Toward the end of the 18th century, the death penalty's use in the United States had grown exponentially. Murder and other conventional law offenses were mostly punished by hanging. Certain minority groups, such as blacks and Indians, were routinely punished by burning or lynching for even minor infractions. Petitions and forgiveness for any defendant facing the death penalty were unusual. For example, slave policies in the south encouraged the use of the death penalty for many crimes, including those that, if committed by a white person, would have been punished less severely. Many freed slaves were denied a trial and faced mob justice. This inequity bothered Jefferson, who argued for accommodating the sternness of a punishment to the magnitude of the crime—this led him to oppose the death penalty for all crimes except murder and treachery. He believed that cruel and sanguinary laws defeated their own purpose, encouraging society to withhold prosecutions, smother testimony, or listen to testimony with bias. Thus, Jefferson sought to reform sentencing laws, and was especially concerned with prosecutions related to crimes such as rape and the punishments that accompanied them. Jefferson was also skeptical about imposing harsh sentences for crimes that relied upon the testimony of a single witness, such as rape or assault, as he believed some prosecutions could stem from impure motivations on the part of a disgruntled former lover or friend. Such ambiguity in evidence caused Jefferson to oppose the use of capital punishment for all but the most severe crimes: murder and treason. Although he was unable to secure passage of these reforms, they shaped subsequent generations' efforts.

Jefferson believed that harsh punishments should be meted out only rarely. If used, harsh punishments should only occur in those few cases where the circumstances merited their implementation. Jefferson asserted that punishments should match and fit the executed crime. Many modern discussions related to sentencing guidelines are predicated upon Jefferson's belief that criminals deserve accurate and proper justice even when they have committed an infraction. Jefferson maintained that justice is served only when convicted defendants' punishment corresponds to their crime. Jefferson believed that the law is effective only when it restores order. That is, the law can only punish the people involved in crimes justly, as dictated by the circumstances surrounding their crimes. Jefferson thus felt that imposing the death penalty for a wide variety of actions was inhumane and considerate only of the law's makers and not the law-abiding citizens who were often silenced through fear of capital punishment.

Jefferson believed that the human conscience works with individuals' instincts to guide citizens in making the right choices. Laws and regulations that do not provide this guidance to assist individuals to shape their own lives and be responsible for their actions were consequently ineffective. As a believer in the individual's power and ability to choose right over wrong, Jefferson believed a major purpose of criminal laws must be to educate the public regarding the reasonable consequences for violating those laws. Although Jefferson believed that punishment was an effective means of deterring crimes and criminal behavior, he felt that those in power too often misused and overused punishment. Jefferson's writings regarding crime and punishment have resonated throughout American history, and his philosophy of crafting appropriate sentences to specific actions has affected sentencing guidelines and discussions about the purposes of the penal system.

Stephen T. Schroth
Jason A. Helfer
Celestina D. Agyekum
Knox College

See Also: 1777 to 1800 Primary Documents; American Revolution and Criminal Justice; Bill of Rights; Declaration of Independence; Jefferson, Thomas (Administration of); Slavery, Law of; Virginia.

Further Readings
Malone, D. *Jefferson and the Ordeal of Liberty.* Boston: Little, Brown, 1962.
Malone, D. *Jefferson the Virginian.* Boston: Little, Brown, 1948.
Peterson, M. D. *Thomas Jefferson Writings: Autobiography, Notes on the State of Virginia, Public and Private Papers, Addresses, Letters.* New York: Library of America, 1984.

Jefferson, Thomas (Administration of)

The influence of the legal and political thought of Thomas Jefferson (1743–1826) was felt by America in its earliest days. Lawyer, landowner, and slave owner Thomas Jefferson began his political career as a representative for Albemarle County in the Virginia House of Burgesses. There he served from 1769 to 1774, during which time he began to argue in favor of independence from Britain. In 1775, Jefferson began his participation in the Second Continental Congress, where he was named, along with John Adams, Benjamin Franklin, Robert R. Livingston, and Roger Sherman, to write to the British government a declaration of independence. The draft of the Declaration of Independence is attributed to Jefferson where, following theorist John Locke, he wrote of unalienable rights and consent of the governed and outlined complaints the colonists had against King George III of Britain. Jefferson's document was ratified by Congress on July 4, 1776. In 1776, Thomas Jefferson was elected as a member of Virginia's House of Delegates, where he advocated religious freedom and opposed primogeniture. He remained a member of that body from 1776 until 1779, when he prevailed in an election for governor of Virginia.

In subsequent years, Jefferson served in a variety of other offices, including member of Congress, minister to France, and secretary of state under George Washington. Throughout the latter half of the 1770s, Jefferson emerged as a leader of the Democratic-Republicans. This led to his nomination by the Democratic-Republicans for the presidency; he ran against John Adams in the election of 1793. Despite Jefferson's loss to Adams in that election, he placed second in the Electoral College vote count, which, at the time, meant he would serve as his opponent's vice president. As vice president, Jefferson opposed the highly unpopular Alien and Sedition Acts enacted by the Federalist incumbent, Adams. The election of 1800 resulted in a tie between Jefferson and his running mate, Aaron Burr. A tie enabled the Federalist-controlled House of Representatives, which opposed both Jefferson and Burr, to ultimately choose Jefferson to be the third president of the United States.

First Term

The early years of Jefferson's presidency were focused on foreign affairs. During his first few months in office, Tripoli declared war on the United States, alleging that the United States owed them tribute for the prevention of piracy of American ships. President Jefferson refused payment, and Congress followed with a formal recognition of the war against Tripoli in 1802. Consistent with his interest in academics and foreign affairs, the president established the West Point United States Military Academy in the midst of the international disputes and negotiations of the time.

Of particular note is that in 1803, President Jefferson received news that Napoleon Bonaparte of France was willing to sell the Louisiana Territory to the United States for roughly $15 million. On April 30, 1803, Jefferson agreed to the exchange that came to be known as the Louisiana Purchase. Later that year, Jefferson sent Meriwether Lewis and William Clark on an expedition to chart the new territory. Just before the completion of Jefferson's first term, Congress amended the U.S. Constitution and added the Twelfth Amendment, stipulating that the Electoral College could cast votes for president and vice president as separate offices. The election of 1804 was conducted according to the new law of the land.

Second Term

Thomas Jefferson won reelection in 1804 against Federalist Charles Pinckney of South Carolina and continued his presidency in 1805 with a new vice president, George Clinton of New York. Also spanning the years 1804 and 1805 was the impeachment of Supreme Court justice Samuel Chase, who had been nominated to the court in 1796 by President George Washington. Justice Chase was thought by many to be a devout Federalist. This was exhibited by his strong and public support of Jefferson's predecessor, President John Adams, and by his criticism of the Democratic-Republican policies of the Jefferson administration. In 1804, the House of Representatives voted in favor of Justice Chase's impeachment on the grounds of misconduct and bias. Ultimately, the members the Senate acquitted Justice Chase; he remained a Supreme Court justice throughout the remainder of the Jefferson presidency. To date, Samuel Chase is the only Supreme Court justice to have been impeached by the House.

In midyear 1805, the war with Tripoli came to an end with the Treaty of Tripoli. As the war with Tripoli ended, hostilities over territory and trade with Spain, France, and Britain arose over the following few years and continued until the end of Jefferson's presidency. In 1806, Jefferson lobbied Congress successfully to place a ban on slave trade to begin in 1808. In 1807 Jefferson signed the controversial Embargo Act, which restricted trade even further so as to completely prevent all ships from going to foreign ports. This act and others that followed were precursors to the War of 1812.

Also in 1807 was the dramatic trial of Jefferson's first vice president, Aaron Burr, for misdemeanor and treason. Just years after Burr killed Alexander Hamilton in a duel in 1804, he was brought to court in front of Chief Justice John Marshall. In 1807, Burr was charged with conspiring to commit acts of war against the Spanish-owned territories to the south of the United States. The case forced new legal questions of what constitutes treason and war, and of the evidentiary responsibility the president of the United States has when subpoenaed. In the end, Burr was acquitted and left to exile in Europe. Soon after, in the election of 1808, it was determined that President Thomas Jefferson would be succeeded by Democratic-Republican James Madison, fourth president of the United States, who continued federal governance with Vice President George Clinton.

Sierra J. Powell
University of California, Irvine

See Also: 1777 to 1800 Primary Documents; Declaration of Independence; Jefferson, Thomas; Madison, James (Administration of).

Further Readings
Bailey, Jeremy D. *Thomas Jefferson and Executive Power*. New York: Cambridge University Press, 2007.
Gordon-Reed, Annette. *Thomas Jefferson and Sally Hemings: An American Controversy*. Charlottesville: University of Virginia Press, 1997.
Malone, Dumas. *Jefferson and His Time*. Charlottesville: University of Virginia Press, 2007.

Jewish Americans

Jewish Americans, once distinguishable as an ethno-religious group of immigrants from primarily European ghetto communities, initially sought out social and economic niches at the periphery of urban American society. They have since found success in shaping certain critical moments in social activism, the criminal underworld, and urban culture more broadly. Now largely assimilated, most Jews in the United States have lost ties to European immigrant communities and are now firmly rooted in American culture and politics.

Prior to the middle of the 19th century, the United States' Jewish population was relatively small and concentrated largely in urban areas. Germany, eastern Europe, and Russia were the main centers of Jewish settlement. As a result of increased persecution and anti-Semitism beginning in the 1870s, European Jewry began a long period of immigration, primarily to Palestine and the United States. This occurred in the same period as other large migrations to the United States, including German, Irish, and Italian immigrants. This influx of immigrants led to a large expansion of the American population and caused some Americans political and social discomfort. This political and social discomfort on the part of the American populace created a generally hostile environment against immigrants of all types, including Jews. Popular media played on the participation of small numbers of Jews in criminal and radical political endeavors to bolster anti-Semitism and xenophobia.

Immigration and the Mafia

The early experience of Jewish immigrants to the United States followed a similar pattern of that of other immigrant communities: In the face of discrimination and limited socioeconomic opportunity, insular communities developed and, within them, underworld activity became prominent. Especially in the New York area, Jewish Americans organized into gangs engaged in low-level illicit activities such as racketeering, prostitution, and gambling. One of the most prominent members of the Jewish Mafia, Arnold Rothstein, had a significant impact on the development of organized crime in the United States. In addition to his alleged role in fixing the 1919 World Series—the Black Sox Scandal—Rothstein is credited as one

Jewish American gangster Meyer Lansky leaving court in Manhattan in February 1958. At the time he was fighting a ban on his return to his gambling operations in Havana, Cuba. He also worked with "Bugsy" Siegel on casinos in Las Vegas.

of the pioneers of organized crime, among the first to transform underworld activity into a business venture. Rothstein and other Jewish American gangsters were among the first to synthesize capitalism with crime and, in the context of Prohibition and the Roaring Twenties, fused them into ventures not unlike corporations in terms of profitability and top-down control.

As the 20th century progressed, other names rose to prominence in the Jewish American underworld, and new forms of criminal ventures were created. Under the guidance of men like Meyer Lansky and Benjamin "Bugsy" Siegel, the original fissures that existed between the underworlds of immigrant communities were bridged, resulting in greater cooperation between Jewish and Italian organized crime groups. This increased cooperation ultimately contributed to the growth of crime organizations throughout the United States, particularly during the Prohibition era. As Prohibition came to an end, the partnerships that had sustained the ties between Jewish and Italian crime groups persisted and evolved into new forms. In the mid-20th century, Siegel and Lansky became involved in ventures in establishing casinos in Las Vegas, a higher-stake version of some of the very gambling endeavors that had spurred the emergence of Jewish American criminal organizations.

Radical Politics

By the mid-20th century, like other immigrant communities, Jewish Americans found themselves more integrated within their country; there was one feature, however, in which the Jewish American experience was markedly different. Many of the European Jews who immigrated to the United States brought with them a tendency toward countercultural political traditions. The Pale of Settlement, a broad territory in modern-day Poland and Ukraine, was one of the primary homes of the Zionist movement. Similarly, some European and Russian Jews, unable to participate in the daily political life of their countries of birth, became involved in a number of reformist or revolutionary movements, especially forms of anarchism or communism. The involvement of Jews in such movements was overstated by anti-Semitic propaganda in post–Bolshevik Russia and Nazi Germany, but some tradition of involvement in radical politics, especially Zionism, did exist among European Jewry, and both the tradition and the stereotypes moved to the United States with Jewish immigrants.

Some Jewish Americans continued these links to radical politics; Jewish American intellectuals especially developed a reputation for supporting communist ideals. In the mid-20th century, with the rise of the Red Scare and McCarthyism, major Jewish organizations made an attempt to repudiate such connections. The specter of anti-Semitism rose as the investigations of the House Un-American Activities Committee proceeded. Though Jews were never a specific target of McCarthy, some organizations were concerned about association with communism, especially after the execution of Julius and Ethel Rosenberg. These attempts were largely successful in avoiding a direct association between Jewish Americans and communist parties, allowing Jewish Americans to instead become involved in new causes more oriented toward social justice and civil rights reform.

Civil Rights Movement

Jewish Americans, cognizant of their recent history as oppressed minorities, fought alongside African Americans for racial justice throughout the civil rights movement. The earliest example of the Jewish–black alliance was Joel Spingarn and his brother Arthur, who dedicated their professional careers to making the National Association for the Advancement of Colored People (NAACP) a viable advocacy group in the 1910s and 1920s. Arthur served as the president and Joel the legal adviser for the nascent organization, which would have many more Jewish allies in its long life span.

As the civil rights movement gained ground and the stakes grew higher, Jewish activists continued to fight for equality with their black brothers and sisters. The majority of the white students who traveled to Mississippi in the 1964 voter registration drive were of Jewish descent, and many of them either witnessed or experienced the police brutality and vigilante violence that was directed against civil rights protesters in the south That summer, two of the students, Michael Schwerner and Andrew Goodman, were reported missing along with their African American colleague James Chaney, and their bodies were later found in a ditch. Jesse Jackson later invoked the triple murder to indicate the solidarity that bound together the struggles of Jewish and African American activists in the civil rights movement. Other individuals who figured prominently during this period included Howard Zinn, a historian and author of the *People's History of the United States* who worked with the Student Nonviolent Coordinating Committee (SNCC); Stanley Levison, Martin Luther King, Jr.'s friend and speechwriter; Kivie Kaplan, president of the NAACP; and Marvin Rich, fundraiser and coordinator for the Congress of Racial Equality (CORE). Rich was later persecuted for being a member of the Communist Party. Older and wealthier Jews also contributed significant sums of money to SNCC, CORE, and the Southern Leadership Christian Conference (SLCC), among other organizations working for racial justice in the south.

Mainstream American Identity

Despite the successes of the civil rights movement, Jewish Americans did not continue to ally themselves in significant numbers with the struggles taking place in communities of color. Resegregation of urban and suburban residential areas, as well as gentrification within the Jewish community, caused solidarity with African Americans to wane, with New York neighborhoods in particular becoming sites of tension. Jewish teachers, who had replaced African American teachers during desegregation, launched strikes that were seen as a threat to certain schools; Orthodox Jewish residents protested public speeches by Nation of Islam leader Louis Farrakhan; and the Crown Heights neighborhood witnessed in rapid succession both the tragic death of 7-year-old Daren Cato and ensuing murder of Yankel Rosenbaum.

On a national level, conservative Jewish leaders spearheaded a number of efforts that served to distance themselves from communities of color, including legal challenges to affirmative action; dismissal of Ambassador Andrew Young for meeting with the Palestinian Liberation Organization; and the escalation of anti-Islamic rhetoric in the neoconservative movement of the late 1990s and early 2000s. While citizens of Jewish heritage continue to support racial justice movements in large numbers and anti-Semitism continues to paint Jews as outsiders, cultural assimilation and socioeconomic advancement have led Jewish Americans into a more mainstream, white American identity. Though centuries of life on U.S. soil have rendered Jewish Americans a less culturally distinct group than they once were, their history tells much about the dynamics of immigration and assimilation of newcomers in American society.

Sarah Combellick-Bidney
Augsburg College
Eric van der Vort
Ball State University

See Also: African Americans; Immigration Crimes; McCarthy, Joseph; National Association for the Advancement of Colored People; Organized Crime, History of; Rothstein, Arnold; Xenophobia.

Further Readings

Diner, Hasia R. *The Jews of the United States, 1654 to 2000*. Berkeley: University of California Press, 2004.

Fried, Albert. *The Rise and Fall of the Jewish Gangster in America*. New York: Holt, Rinehart and Winston, 1980.

Kaufman, Jonathan. *Broken Alliance: The Turbulent Times Between Blacks and Jews in America*. New York: Touchstone, 1995.

Johnson, Andrew (Administration of)

Few presidents have been as poorly understood and regarded as Andrew Johnson (1808–75). Born in poverty in North Carolina, Johnson moved to eastern Tennessee with his family as a boy. He was apprenticed to a tailor in South Carolina and learned that craft in his teens but never received any formal education. Until his marriage, he was completely self-taught but his wife encouraged him to read more widely and taught him mathematics and some computational skills. As a result of his hardscrabble childhood and continuing struggle, Johnson came to identify intensely with the plight of the white workingman and dislike the planter elite in the south. He believed in the manifest necessity of white supremacy and had a distrust of policies imposing racial equity. A strong advocate of states' rights, he opposed big government and postwar federal interventionism in principle. He was a Jacksonian Democrat who celebrated the common (white) man and held utopian prescriptions for reconstituting the postwar south in ill-disguised contempt. He stood foursquare against extending full constitutional rights to freed slaves and was against federal policing of the South. As president, he used executive power to obstruct congressional attempts to force Republican ideologically based retributive policies on the defeated southern states. He was also a stubborn and difficult man with whom to deal and was ill-equipped to compromise.

Rise to Power
Johnson's political career began with a stint in the Tennessee House of Representatives in 1835. Thereafter, he served in various capacities in state elective office until 1843, when he was elected to the U.S. House of Representatives. After 10 years of service in that office, he was elected governor of Tennessee. He served as U.S. senator from 1857 until 1862, when he became the only senator from a seceding state not to resign. His reasoning was that although a state's rights were paramount, they did not include secession. Therefore, the seceding states were fictitious entities, and all acts under secession governments were null and void. Johnson viewed secession as a fiction and saw himself as continuing to represent the legal government of the state of Tennessee. This "unionism" did not make him a Republican, however. He remained a staunch Jacksonian "War Democrat"—Andrew Jackson also opposed secession. Johnson stubbornly held these views through his life. Both his views and his obstinacy brought him into conflict with Radical Republicans in Congress. Though he was a Democrat, Johnson's opposition to secession brought him to the attention of President Abraham Lincoln, who appointed him occupation governor of Tennessee, a political move that carried with it the rank of brigadier general. In another political move, Lincoln chose Johnson as his running mate in the election of 1864 because of his status as a pro-Union "War Democrat." Inaugurated as vice president on March 4, 1865, Johnson became president when Lincoln was assassinated just a few weeks later. His presidency got off to a rocky start when it was alleged that he gave his inaugural address in a state of intoxication. Recovering from a bout with typhoid fever, he unwisely used some spirits medicinally and appeared to be drunk. Most historians reject the notion that Johnson was an alcoholic, as some of his opponents alleged at the time.

Presidency
As president, Johnson initially took a hard line toward former Confederates and secessionists. But he soon began granting wholesale pardons and refusing to support or endorse more draconian retributive prescriptions proposed by the Radicals in Congress. He also reined in the Freedman's Bureau and reversed confiscations of lands owned by some southerners. Furthermore, the policy of some Union generals and officials of granting of seized lands to former slaves was rescinded. Johnson's view was to restore property and political rights to poor and yeoman whites while hindering the former planter class from dominating the politics of the former Confederate states. Again, Johnson regarded secession as having never really occurred, and he felt that the status quo that existed before the war—minus slavery and the planter aristocracy—should be restored as much as possible. He later saw that restoring certain elites from among Unionists in the old elite class would be necessary to restore order and confidence in any new state government.

Thus, the utopian plans of Radical Republicans, based on creating a completely free market–based economic system in the south that was devoid of the vestiges of the paternalistic plantation economic order, were in substantial conflict with the more "restorative" Reconstruction foreseen by Johnson. Johnson vetoed a Civil Rights Act in 1866 but his veto was overridden. He then tried to block the passage of the Fourteenth Amendment, which gave voting and civil rights to freed slaves. In the midterm election of 1866, Johnson made a disastrous campaign journey through the north—the "swing around the circle." The subsequent elections were viewed as repudiation, as the Republicans took control of Congress and dominated Reconstruction.

A major structural break occurred when Johnson replaced Secretary of War Edwin Stanton, an ally of the Radicals, against stipulations of an act passed by Congress, the Tenure of Office Act. Johnson alleged that it was unconstitutional (the U.S. Supreme Court supported his contention in *Myers v. United States* in 1926) but at the time, Congress disagreed. On March 5, 1868, impeachment proceedings against Johnson began in the Senate with 11 articles enumerated against him. The trial, which lasted three months, was ultimately decided by one vote—Johnson was not convicted. The unabashedly political nature of this trial exhausted the Congress, the executive, and the nation and is regarded as a blot on the history of Reconstruction and of the presidency itself.

In his last year in office, Johnson was forced to stand by as the Republican Congress took a harder line toward the south. Johnson had rejected federal policing of racial conflicts in the south. Much of Congressional ire was aimed at white supremacist gangs such as the Ku Klux Klan (KKK), which began a reign of terror in the mid-1860s. Many of Johnson's efforts at rebuilding the region's political culture were undone. Military occupation and Republican attempts to control elections through fraud were met with more political and terroristic resistance. Violence flourished as the KKK, local affiliates, and other militia-type groups created chaos and restored white supremacy through intimidation and terror. Northern political elites eventually tired of this "fool's errand," as one writer called it, and allowed the southern elites to return to power. Toward the end of Reconstruction, Johnson was elected to the Senate in 1874; he died in 1875.

Andrew Johnson has been regarded among the worst of American presidents, though some historians admire his uncompromising devotion to certain principles. It was, however, that very inability to compromise that earned him the enmity of his contemporaries and the condemnation of most historians. The Radical Republicans took control, and their candidate, General Ulysses S. Grant, won the next election and presided over

This wood engraving depicts the powerful chairman of the House Ways and Means Committee Thaddeus Stevens delivering a final speech on Andrew Johnson's impeachment in the House on March 2, 1868. When the proceedings against Johnson began in the Senate on March 5, 11 articles were enumerated against him in a trial that lasted three months.

one of the most corrupt administrations in American history.

Francis Frederick Hawley
Western Carolina University

See Also: Grant, Ulysses S. (Administration of); Lincoln, Abraham (Administration of); *Mississippi v. Johnson*.

Further Readings
Brown, Richard M. *Strain of Violence: Historical Studies of American Violence and Vigilantism.* New York: Oxford, 1975.
Foner, Eric. *Reconstruction: America's Unfinished Revolution: 1863–1877.* New York: HarperCollins, 2005.
McDougall, Walter A. *Throes of Democracy: The American Civil War Era 1829–1877.* New York: HarperCollins, 2008.

Johnson, Lyndon B. (Administration of)

In convening the President's Commission on Law Enforcement and the Administration of Justice on September 8, 1965, Lyndon B. Johnson declared to its members, "Crime is a sore upon the face of a nation. It is a menace on our streets. It is a drain on our cities. It is a corruptor of our youth. It is a cause of untold suffering and loss. … [L]et the nation know today that we have taken a pledge not only to reduce crime but to banish it." With no intention to intervene in this local matter when he unexpectedly took office in 1963, the increasing political salience of "street crime" led him to address crime control on multiple fronts. His most important action was the passage of the Omnibus Crime Control and Safe Streets Act of 1968, which inaugurated the contemporary regime of criminal justice and federal involvement in criminal law.

Johnson was not the first president to intervene in criminal justice issues. The federal government periodically expanded its institutional capacity through its enforcement of the Mann Act and Prohibition, the growth of the Federal Bureau of Investigation (FBI) and Department of Justice, and President John F. Kennedy's programs to combat juvenile delinquency and organized crime. Johnson built upon his predecessor's record, but he also laid the groundwork for a vast expansion of federal spending and assistance to states and localities.

Johnson came to crime control defensively. George Wallace and Barry Goldwater, his presidential opponents in 1964, distilled a concatenation of political and social forces into a new politics of law and order. The power of their rhetoric derived from its blending of distinct issues of crime, civil disobedience, and urban racial disorder into a general framework of lawlessness. Increased crime was a real phenomenon, even if its perception was exaggerated. The number of violent crimes reported to the police used to make up the FBI's Uniform Crime Report far outpaced the growth of more definitively measureable crimes, such as homicide. To this, Wallace and Goldwater added the argument that the government helped create lawlessness by accepting civil disobedience. Goldwater lamented that American citizens had come to accept as normal the use of a variety of pressure tactics in order to influence national debate, including civil disobedience, demonstrations, and boycotts, but extending as well to violence, civil disorder, and riots. Both charged liberals, especially the Supreme Court, with coddling criminals. These arguments became more potent when redoubled government efforts in civil rights and the war on poverty were followed by the long, hot summers of 1965 through 1968.

Preconceptions of black criminality were part of the rich vein of fear tapped by law-and-order politics. Conflation of the "Negro problem" and the crime problem was a long-standing staple of social analysis, and the black freedom struggle only intensified this association for the opponents of civil rights. The most virulent southern opponents of integration made black criminality a straightforward argument against integration. But there were also more subtle versions of this association. For example, many moderate, northern, urban white homeowners opposed the integration of their neighborhoods, articulating racial difference in ways that embraced the growing fear of crime.

Johnson's rebuttal sounded themes that in retrospect increased his vulnerability to criticism over the next four years. In Dayton, Ohio, on October 16, 1964, he criticized Goldwater, who "bemoans violence in the streets but votes against the war on poverty, votes against the Civil Rights Act, and votes against major educational bills that have come before him as a legislator. The thing to do is not to talk about crime; the thing to do is to fight and work and vote against crime." Johnson incorporated crime reduction into the aims of his Great Society. By demanding that the federal government act to end crime, Johnson complicated his own task and helped spawn the disillusionment with federal action that would follow.

Johnson made the first of four major addresses on crime to Congress on March 8, 1965. His plans recognized the states as the "right and proper" repository of police authority but also claimed, "crime is a national problem." He proposed new efforts in four areas under federal control. While he acted with less zeal than Kennedy in one of these areas—organized crime—he expanded the federal role in the three others. New drug laws tightened control on depressant and stimulant drugs, coupling greater penalties for drug sellers with treatment for heroin addicts. The comprehensive Federal Gun Control Act of 1968 prohibited interstate handgun shipment, restricted firearms sales for certain categories of individuals, required dealer licensing, created a gun registration system, and restricted ownership of certain weapons. In the District of Columbia, direct federal control allowed the administration to test crime control policy. Over the course of his tenure, Johnson added to these four issues the reform of the federal bail system and greater use of federal criminal law to prosecute white southern vigilantes.

Johnson also created a new role for the federal government in assisting states. This began with the creation of the Office of Law Enforcement Assistance by the Law Enforcement Assistance Act of 1965, which was funded with $20 million for demonstration projects. The federal government spent additional millions in the area of juvenile justice. But it was the President's Commission on Law Enforcement and the Administration of Justice that did the heavy lifting in the name of reform. Over the two years of its existence, the commission engaged in groundbreaking research; for example, it pioneered the use of surveys of crime victims to provide a more accurate assessment of the nature of the crime problem. It issued *The Challenge of Crime in a Free Society* in 1967, with more than 200 recommendations to improve law enforcement and the administration of justice, providing a foundation for the Safe Streets Act that Johnson proposed in 1967.

By the time Congress considered this crime control proposal, Johnson's legislative power had begun to unravel with his credibility. Although Johnson ultimately signed the bill that Congress passed in June 1968 as the Omnibus Crime Control and Safe Streets Act, it differed in important ways from his ideas. Only the fourth of the bill's four titles, addressing the sale of handguns, was substantially in accord with the administration's intention. His disagreement with congressional modifications to Titles II and III of the act was particularly vehement. The former challenged the Supreme Court's rulings on the admissibility

This March 1965 photograph shows an African American man carrying a child on his shoulders and holding a sign telling President Johnson to go to Selma, Alabama, to show support for civil rights marchers confronting violence and intimidation there.

of confessions, substituting the rule that preceded the Warren Court's announcement of the prophylactic warning requirement in *Miranda v. Arizona*; the latter loosened the rules governing federal wiretaps.

The core provision of the bill, Title I, created the new Law Enforcement Assistance Administration, and Congress also revamped it. Southern Democrats and Republicans in the Senate swapped out a grant-in-aid program that would have given money directly to police departments and other institutions in exchange for a block grant scheme that anticipated the new federalism of Richard Nixon. Under the new Title I, money was placed under the control of state planning agencies that would pass it on to local institutions. As well as being grant makers, these new state agencies were to engage in comprehensive criminal justice planning to end the Balkanization of the various elements of their criminal justice systems—courts, law enforcement, and corrections—identified by the president's commission.

Johnson left a mixed legacy. Although the Law Enforcement Assistance Administration has been criticized as a failure in many ways, it did inaugurate a new era of federal assistance to state and local governments for crime control. Beginning with a little more than $300 million of grants in its first two years, which went largely toward the purchase of riot control equipment for the police, the agency would go on to grant over $8 billion in 12 years. By and large, the state planning agencies did not have the leverage or clarity of ideas to wholly reform criminal justice institutions. Nonetheless, the programs were responsible for aspects of modernization in many different areas. For criminal justice study and planning, the act's creation of the National Institute of Law Enforcement and Criminal Justice (now the National Institute of Justice) spurred greater standardization and rigor in the gathering of crime statistics. Perhaps most significant was the political inheritance left by Johnson's opponents. Lawlessness became a major plank in Richard Nixon's campaign in 1968 and his legislative policy and judicial appointments reflected a desire to definitively break with the root causes approach espoused by Johnson.

Peter Constantine Pihos
University of Pennsylvania

See Also: Civil Rights Laws; Law Enforcement Assistance Act; Law Enforcement Assistance Administration; President's Commission on Law Enforcement and the Administration of Justice.

Further Readings
Flamm, Michael W. *Law and Order: Street Crime, Civil Unrest, and the Crisis of Liberalism in the 1960s.* New York: Columbia University Press, 2005.
Speeches of Lyndon B. Johnson. "The American Presidency Project." http://www.presidency.ucsb.edu (Accessed December 2010).
Weaver, Vesla. "Frontlash: Race and the Development of Punitive Crime Policy." *Studies in American Political Development,* v.21 (2007).

Johnson v. Avery

Johnson v. Avery (1969) was a landmark case for "jailhouse lawyers"—prisoners who engage in legal actions on their own behalf or on behalf of fellow inmates. In *Johnson*, the Supreme Court held that prisoners have the right to give legal advice to other prisoners and to receive legal advice from other prisoners, unless the prison system provides a reasonable alternative means by which illiterate prisoners can obtain assistance with their legal actions. *Johnson* also established that prisons can restrict such rights to limit abuse and can limit jailhouse lawyering to certain times and places. Limitations must have legitimate penological foundations and may not be imposed in an arbitrary manner. Jailhouse lawyers have standing to challenge prison regulations that restrict them from assisting other prisoners.

The *Johnson* case stemmed from regulations imposed by the Tennessee State Penitentiary that prohibited inmates from assisting one another with writs or other legal matters. In 1965, William Joe Johnson was transferred to a maximum-security facility for violating this regulation. Johnson then filed a motion for law books and a typewriter and was again disciplined by the penitentiary system. The Supreme Court's decision in *Johnson* is based on its respect for the importance of the writ of habeas corpus and the need to maintain it unimpaired. The primary function of habeas corpus is to enable people who are wrongly imprisoned to win back their freedom; hence, prisoners must have access to the courts in order to ensure their ability to protect their constitutional rights.

The *Johnson* decision cited precedents that prohibited prisons from charging prisoners to file a writ, or from compelling prisoners to submit their writs for approval to prison officials before filing them. It mandated that the state provide prisoners with transcripts of prior hearings to refer to in future proceedings. These precedents implied the existence of a right to engage in jailhouse lawyering on one's own behalf. The *Johnson* decision also states that it is unconstitutional for the state to enforce regulations that forbid illiterate or poorly educated prisoners from filing writs of habeas corpus. However, if Tennessee prevents literate prisoners from assisting illiterate prisoners with writs, then—in the absence of any other means of legal assistance—the state has effectively denied illiterate prisoners access to habeas corpus.

There is no constitutional right to counsel for postconviction proceedings. Some states do provide access to public defenders or law students to assist prisoners in postconviction proceedings. However, in states that do not provide such resources, inmates who lack the financial wherewithal to retain a lawyer must rely on their own efforts to file writs of habeas corpus or on the resources available to them within the prison itself. Thus, without jailhouse lawyering, potentially valid constitutional claims might never be heard by a court, and people who are wrongly convicted may have no means of winning their freedom.

Wolff v. McDonnell (1974) expanded the rights established in *Johnson* to include civil rights actions brought by prisoners. *Ervin v. Ciccone* (1977) bounded the rights established in *Johnson* by holding that a prisoner's complaint citing *Johnson* failed because he did not allege that prison officials had never established alternate means of legal assistance other than jailhouse lawyering. In *Bounds v. Smith* (1977), the court held that habeas corpus requires prisons to assist prisoners in filing legal papers by either providing adequate law libraries or assistance from trained personnel. However, *Lewis v. Casey* (1996) upheld Arizona's severe restrictions on prisoners' access to law library materials and held that prisoners must demonstrate injury in order to sustain a complaint about adequacy of prison law libraries or about restrictive access to legal research materials. *Lewis* creates a potential catch-22 for inmates. If their access to legal research is inappropriately restricted, they may not be able to bring and win an effective complaint, because they lack the access they need to research such a complaint in the first place.

Courts since *Johnson* have noted that the rights to receive and to give legal assistance are related and that unreasonable restrictions on the right to give assistance may infringe on First Amendment liberties. The rights established in *Johnson* still prevail today and are acknowledged to exist in order to protect habeas corpus for prisoners who do not have the capability to engage in legal research and legal actions on their own behalf.

Thomas F. Brown
Virginia Wesleyan College

See Also: Habeas Corpus, Writ of; Legal Counsel; Prisoner's Rights; *Procunier v. Martinez*.

Further Readings
Anderson, James F., et al. *Significant Prisoner Rights Cases*. Durham, NC: Carolina Academic Press, 2010.
Johnson v. Avery, 393 U.S. 483 (1969).
Palmer, John W. *Constitutional Rights of Prisoners*. Cincinnati, OH: Anderson Publishing, 2010.

Judges and Magistrates

Judges and magistrates, who are vested with the authority to hear and decide legal matters brought to a court or other venue, are public officials who are either elected or appointed to their positions. In the United States, judges and magistrates may serve at the federal, state, county, or municipal level. Judges and magistrates have since colonial times worked to resolve disputes and to enforce the law. While some judges and magistrates are appointed by presidents or governors, others are elected. Judges and magistrates serve terms set by their local jurisdiction, which in the case of the federal judiciary are appointments for life. Depending upon the type of criminal matter heard, judges and magistrates may rule on motions made before or during trial, make determinations regarding the admissibility of evidence, craft jury instructions, and in some cases make determinations of guilt. Judges and magistrates are also involved in the sentencing of defendants convicted of crimes. The American jurisprudence system varies somewhat from the civil or common law systems in place in other parts of the globe—this can cause some confusion for defendants not familiar with the U.S. policies and procedures.

Colonial Judges and Magistrates
Soon after colonists settled in North America, judges and magistrates began working to help solve disputes, including those that involved allegations of criminal behavior. After the establishment of Jamestown, the Virginia colony was the earliest to adopt a criminal justice system and practices, based on the English system, including establishing a series of judges, doing so in the early 17th century. Virginia established a system of county courts that were similar to the English system, with each court having a sitting judge. Judges assisted with establishing traditional English practices and procedures for dealing with criminal proceedings, including arrest, indictment, bail, trial, juries, judgment, and execution. Beginning in 1623, the House of Burgesses also established a five-member appellate court to hear appeals from lower courts, also known as the Quarter Court, as it met four times per year. Although not all judges had legal training, most were from business or farming backgrounds and had experience in dealing with disputes.

Farther north, in New Holland, which was established in 1614 by the Dutch West India Company, a different sort of justice system evolved. The Dutch West India Company gave certain of its large stockholders, called patroons, large tracts of land, called patroonships. In addition to land, the patroons were given manorial rights and privileges that permitted them to set up civil and criminal courts and to appoint judges. These courts were quite a bit more liberal in their administration of justice than those in Virginia, and indeed the rest of the colonies. While New Holland permitted slavery, slaves were allowed to sign legal documents, could bring legal actions against whites, and were allowed to testify in court. Even after the colony became known as New York in 1674, some of these more liberal practices persisted. More restrictive were Puritan magistrates in the Massachusetts Bay Colony, established in 1630. When allegations of criminal mischief arose, Puritan magistrates heard the pleas of the defendant, and if satisfied that charges were grounded, suspects were handed over to a superior court, which then called a grand jury. Since many of the Puritan magistrates were clergymen or respected members of their congregation, they tended to adopt a no-nonsense, clerical approach, which proved problematic during the Salem witch trials.

Origins of the Federal Judiciary
American experiences during the Revolutionary War and the period immediately preceding it resulted in tremendous interest in the rights of those charged with criminal offenses. In particular, Americans felt many of their compatriots had been ill-treated by British authorities seeking to quell rebellious acts. Protections for criminal defendants were memorialized in the Articles of Confederation, the U.S. Constitution, and the Bill of Rights. After American independence, and even before, citizens became much more ready to disregard English legal precedents and rules in an effort to improve the implementation of the criminal justice system. Interest was great in providing a judiciary who would ensure the efficiency and equity of the judicial system, especially with regard to the independence of judges and magistrates. As a result of these concerns, Article III of the U.S. Constitution established a judicial system that was to coexist with the executive and legislative branches of the federal government. While the Constitution itself is rather vague about the powers and scope of judges within the judiciary, stating only that the judicial power shall be vested in one supreme court and other unnamed inferior courts, the Judiciary Act of 1789, which established the federal courts, was much more specific regarding these issues. Article III did, however, provide federal judiciary with lifetime appointments, which was seen as necessary to establish their independence. This was conditioned on the judges exhibiting "good behavior," which means that members of the federal judiciary may be impeached, although this has seldom occurred.

William McAdoo, whose previous career included serving in Congress in the 1880s and as New York City police commissioner, was appointed chief magistrate of the New York City magistrates' courts and served from 1910 to 1930.

The congressional leaders who drafted the Judiciary Act of 1789 were most familiar with the British judicial system, which was organized into three separate divisions, Admiralty, King's (criminal), and Chancery. Instead of using this model, Congress chose to establish a system of federal trial courts (known as U.S. District Courts) with broad jurisdiction permitting these to hear both civil and criminal matters. The act also created the U.S. Supreme Court, which originally was comprised of a chief justice and five associate justices, and circuit courts, which heard appeals. Justices and judges of the federal judiciary were appointed by the president and confirmed by the U.S. Senate. The Judiciary Act of 1793 modified the earlier act slightly, mandating that only one, instead of two, Supreme Court justices needed to sit on circuit court panels, reduced the number of circuit courts from 13 to 3, and also authorized courts to create and promulgate their own rules, which was a codification of extant practices. The Judiciary Act of 1801, sometimes referred to as the Midnight Judges Act, was an attempt by the Federalists to assert power over the federal courts after their defeat in the elections of 1800. The act reduced the number of Supreme Court justices from six to five upon the next vacancy on the court, an issue that proved moot. The act also increased the number of circuits from three to six and created a number of new circuit judgeships, all for Federalist appointees of John Adams. The landmark case *Marbury v. Madison* (1803) was heard as a result of the Judiciary Act of 1801 and established the Supreme Court's right to invalidate a law by declaring it unconstitutional, thereby establishing the practice of judicial review.

After Thomas Jefferson succeeded Adams, the Democratic-Republicans worked to diminish the effects of the Judiciary Act of 1801, which resulted in the passage of the Judiciary Act of 1802. This later act maintained the structure of six circuit courts and assigned a Supreme Court justice to each circuit. Unlike the earlier act, however, the Judiciary Act of 1802 created no new circuit judgeships, so justices were forced to resume riding circuit, a practice that was to continue technically until the creation of the U.S. Court of Appeals in 1891, although the practice had informally ended by the 1840s. The number of justices serving on the Supreme Court also was adjusted periodically during the 19th century, growing to seven in 1807, nine in 1837, and 10 in 1863. In 1866, the U.S. Congress passed an act reducing the number of justices to seven, and two were removed by 1867, but the Judiciary Act of 1869 returned the number of justices to nine, where it has remained. Although members of the federal judiciary have been appointed continuously since 1789, at times there have been efforts made to have elected judges, most notably during the terms in office of Andrew Jackson. Jackson, a great populist, believed that the people should directly elect judges. Although he was unsuccessful in persuading Congress to make this change, he was able to convince the Georgia state legislature to permit the direct election of state judges there. Although there has never been a successful effort to have federal judges and magistrates elected, the issue does arise from time to time and continues to be an issue of contention in various states.

At times, the political goals of various administrations have clashed with the outlook of the majority of Supreme Court justices, often when great change is happening. For example, during the administration of Franklin Delano Roosevelt, a great many programs were set up to deal with the Great Depression facing the nation. Many pieces of the Democratic Roosevelt's New Deal agenda were ruled unconstitutional by a Supreme Court majority who were largely conservatives appointed by Republican presidents. In an effort to circumvent these rulings, in 1937 Roosevelt suggested that the number of justices serving be expanded to as many as 15, as he would appoint one justice for every justice who reached the age of 70. This scheme, often referred to as the "court packing plan," was ultimately unsuccessful, although a wave of retirements permitted Roosevelt to nominate justices who were more sympathetic to his agenda. Occasionally since Roosevelt's plan, expressions of discontent have been made regarding perceived prejudices of the federal judiciary, such as when many southern members of Congress took issue with certain civil rights decisions during the 1950s and 1960s.

Federal Courts

The U.S. Supreme Court comprises a chief justice and eight associate justices. The U.S. Court of Appeals is divided into 13 circuits, 11 of which are numbered, the DC Circuit, and the Federal Circuit. The 179 judges of the court of appeals are, like all members of the federal judiciary, nominated by the president and confirmed by the Senate, and have lifetime tenure. The various courts of appeal hear more than 10,000 cases per year, of which roughly 100 per year are selected by the Supreme Court for further hearing. Courts of appeal hear disputes arising from the district courts within its boundary. The U.S. District Courts comprise 89 districts spread across the 50 states and an additional five districts in the District of Columbia, Puerto Rico, the U.S. Virgin Islands, Guam, and the Northern Mariana Islands. All states contain at least one district, and the following states have two or more districts: Alabama, Arkansas, California, Florida, Georgia, Illinois, Indiana, Iowa, Kentucky, Louisiana, Michigan, Mississippi, Missouri, New York, North Carolina, Ohio, Pennsylvania, Tennessee, Texas, Virginia, Washington, West Virginia, and Wisconsin. The 94 districts are served by the 678 district court judgeships that are authorized by Congress. U.S. District Court judges hire magistrate judges, who hear certain preliminary matters, for eight-year renewable terms.

Judges and magistrates working within the federal system must frequently make rulings regarding jurisdiction, as their power to hear cases and controversies is limited by statute. Congress has granted the federal courts subject matter jurisdiction over the following types of cases: criminal prosecutions brought by the United States against defendants; actions involving disputes arising under the U.S. Constitution, laws, and treaties; certain civil actions involving the citizens of different states; actions within the admiralty jurisdiction of the United States; and many other assorted cases and controversies.

In many of these actions, litigants could have also brought their actions in state courts. In these cases, judges and magistrates must determine whether the federal court is the proper venue for the case and will remand the case to state court if improper. In recent years, the district courts with the most federal felony filings were the District of New Mexico, the Western District of Texas, the Southern District of Texas, the District of Arizona, and the Southern District of California. All five of these districts share a border with Mexico, and an upsurge in illegal immigration has caused such filings to multiply. In 2007, for example, these five district courts amounted for 75 percent of the criminal cases filed in the entire district court system.

State Courts

All of the 50 states have judicial systems that hear criminal and civil cases. While all states have both trial and appellate courts, not all of these use the same terms to identify these. Many states mirror the terms used by the federal courts and have district courts for trials, a court of appeals, and a state supreme court. Others use different terms, however, such as California where trials are heard in the superior court and New York, the trial court of which is known as the supreme court and the highest appellate level known as the court of appeal. Several state court systems use magistrate courts, which are sometimes called justice of the peace courts. Magistrate and justice of the peace courts typically have jurisdiction to handle small civil matters, applications for bail, petitions for arrest and search warrants, and the adjudication of petty or misdemeanor criminal offenses.

A majority of states allow judges to be selected through elections, a decision that is controversial insofar as many critics believe it pressures the judiciary to make decisions that align with popular opinion. Elections in some states are fully partisan events, including all the trappings of television and radio advertisements, banners, and campaign literature. Many states also use appointments by the governor, although these selections are subject to confirmation by members of the state legislature. To address dissatisfaction with either of these approaches, a third method of judicial selection has arisen, known as the Missouri Plan. The Missouri Plan attempts to reduce partisan considerations, to give more control of the process to the state bar association, while maintaining a measure of popular control over the selection of judges. The plan uses an independent nominating committee that screens candidates and then submits a short list of qualified candidates to the governor or other appointing authority. The governor then selects one person from the submitted list, who becomes a judge for a limited time. At the conclusion of this period, the judge stands for reelection for a longer term, running not against other candidates but as part of a vote that asks whether the judge should be retained. The system pleases many because it strikes a balance between judicial independence and democratic accountability.

Most state judges have legal backgrounds, although a number of states use lay judges, magistrates, and justices of the peace to hear preliminary pleas and set bail; most trial judges, however, are members of the bar. At trial, judges make evidentiary rulings, provide jury instructions, and sentence those defendants found guilty. Unlike the continental system, where a panel of judges asks questions of witnesses, judges in the United States allow the American adversarial system to do this, even in cases where the judge, not a jury, is making the determination of guilt.

Stephen T. Schroth
Daniel O. Gonshorek
Knox College

See Also: Constitution of the United States of America; Federal Common Law of Crime; Federal Rules of Criminal Procedure; Judiciary Act of 1789; Juries; Jurisdiction; Sentencing; Supreme Court, U.S.

Further Readings

Carp, R. A., R. Stidham, and K. L. Manning. *The Judicial Process in America*, 8th ed. Washington, DC: CQ Press, 2011.

O'Brien, D. M. *Judges on Judging: Views From the Bench*, 3rd ed. Washington, DC: CQ Press, 2009.

O'Brien, D. M. *Storm Center: The Supreme Court in American Politics*, 9th ed. New York: W. W. Norton, 2011.

Judiciary Act of 1789

Creation of a national court system as well as establishing a federal Office of Attorney General and the U.S. Marshals Service were the objectives achieved when the Judiciary Act was signed into law in 1789. While Article III of the U.S. Constitution had suggested that a federal judiciary should be created, the framers did not dictate a specific structure, nor did they designate jurisdictional authority for new courts. The intent of Article III would be addressed later by the U.S. Congress when it would create courts of original, trial, and appellate jurisdiction and would specify the numbers and locations of federal courts. The specific wording in the act was crafted primarily by Senator Oliver Ellsworth of Connecticut with assistance from William Patterson of New Jersey and Caleb Strong of Massachusetts. However, the concepts embodied in the legislation resulted from a compromise between Federalists and Anti-Federalists, who had disagreed bitterly over the necessity for a dual court system.

Ratification of the U.S. Constitution had been a prize sought by the Federalists, but the Judiciary Act, as the first bill under consideration in the new Congress, created another opportunity for Anti-Federalists to oppose the diminishment of state court powers. The drafters of the Judiciary Act had the challenge of coming up with a charter that would ensure the supremacy of federal laws within a dual court system. Anti-Federalists like

Richard Henry Lee and William Grayson from Virginia pushed to restrict all the powers of any new national courts. Samuel Livermore, from New Hampshire, moved to limit jurisdiction in the federal courts to only questions of admiralty law. But the Federalists prevailed. Final approval of the bill was completed without a recorded vote and the Judiciary Act of 1789, titled "An Act to Establish the Judicial Courts of the United States" was officially signed by President George Washington on September 24.

Effects

The act created three tiers of national courts. A U.S. Supreme Court was to assemble in the nation's capital and would have original trial jurisdiction in cases involving controversies between two or more states, ambassadors, public ministers, consuls, and their domestics. It would have appellate jurisdiction for cases received from the federal district and circuit courts. The Supreme Court would be staffed with a chief justice and five associate justices according to the original act.

Thirteen district courts were also created by the act. These courts would hear cases regarding admiralty and maritime, revenue collection, misdemeanors, and civil actions involving federal matters. Three circuit courts were also created. These courts were to have trial court jurisdiction over serious criminal cases and three types of civil matters, including cases where the United States was a plaintiff, cases where at least one party in the suit was an alien, and cases between parties of different states (diversity cases) for litigation over $500. Diversity cases could be reviewed concurrently by federal circuit courts or state courts.

The circuit courts were designated to meet twice annually in each state. Thus the term *riding the circuits* evolved because each circuit was to be staffed with two Supreme Court judges plus the local district judge. Some historians contend that this was done to ensure that even Supreme Court justices stayed in touch with local issues and did not become too distanced from citizens. To appease the Anti-Federalists and their followers, the Judiciary Act provided that litigation arising from the U.S. Constitution, federal laws, and treaties should be heard in state courts.

As the United States later increased in size and complexity, the number of circuit courts was increased by Congress, and judges were added to reduce the requirement that Supreme Court justices serve in these courts. The number of Supreme Court justices was also increased to nine in 1869. Similarly, the structure of the other federal courts was expanded.

Today, federal district courts handle all federal cases and the former circuits are now referred to as U.S. courts of appeals and no longer have any trial functions. The number of circuits is fixed at 11. The Judiciary Act also established the Office of Attorney General and provided for the appointment of a lawyer. The new attorney general was to prosecute and conduct all litigation in the U.S. Supreme Court to which the United States was a party as well as give advice and counsel on legal questions posed by the president or other heads of U.S. agencies.

The act did not make the attorney general a cabinet level officer, but then President George Washington asked the attorney general to appear so often at cabinet meetings that by custom, the office gained cabinet rank. Today, the attorney general is appointed by the president and is subject to confirmation by the U.S. Senate. Finally, the act also created the U.S. Marshals Service, which is the enforcement arm for federal law and provides security services to the federal court system.

Andrea G. Lange
Washington College

See Also: Anti-Federalist Papers; Federal Rules of Criminal Procedure; Federalist Papers; Supreme Court, U.S.; United States Attorneys.

Further Readings

Marcus, Maeva, ed. *Origins of the Federal Judiciary: Essays on the Judiciary Act of 1789*. New York: Oxford University Press, 1992.

National Archives and Records Administration. "Federal Judiciary Act of 1789." http://www.ourdocuments.gov/doc.php?doc=12 (Accessed January 2011).

Office of the Attorney General. "Selected Bibliography." http://www.justice.gov/jmd/ls/agbib.htm (Accessed January 2011).

Surrency, Erwin C. *History of the Federal Courts*. Dobbs Ferry, NY: Oceana Publications, 2002.

Juries

Being judged by a jury of your peers is a central tenet of the American criminal justice system. One reason the settlers originally chose to flee England and seek refuge in America was that King George III failed to allow juries the ability to function effectively in the English legal system. Once settlers arrived and formed the colonies, King George III continued his assault on their legal rights by filling colonial juries with royal sympathizers or sending them back to England to face juries. As a result, the existence of juries has always been a concern for many Americans. Even during the witchcraft trials of the 1690s, Americans still attempted—to varying degrees—to preserve due process rights and the ability of the accused to receive a fair treatment.

Types of Juries

A jury is a group of individuals brought together to make an impartial ruling on the guilt or innocence of someone or to set a judgment or penalty. According to Article III and the Sixth Amendment of the U.S. Constitution, criminal cases must be tried by a jury of peers. Upon the passing of the Fourteenth Amendment, this requirement was also passed on to all states. While criminal trials were covered, civil trials were originally not. In response to immediate public pressure, the Seventh Amendment was added to the proposed Bill of Rights and required jury trials for civil cases involving disputes over $20. The Seventh Amendment, however, has not been incorporated to the states through the Fourteenth Amendment. Despite not legally being required, all states except Louisiana have provisions for civil juries in monetary cases. The importance of impartiality originates from early 18th century Britain, where sheriffs were charged with appointing juries. Realizing the issues with such a system, the British opted to attempt to guarantee impartiality through selection methods. The debate on whether jurors should be unaware of a case or locally acquainted with it has lasted nearly as long. Consider that in 1807, Aaron Burr's attorney argued to the court that it was impossible to get a fair jury because of the publicity surrounding his client's treason case.

Modern juries find their roots in the ancient Germanic tribes, in which groups of men would come together and judge individuals accused of committing crimes. As time went on, the role of juries evolved in different geographic areas. For example, in Anglo-Saxon England, juries were actually used to investigate crimes in lieu of the police. Modern juries actually emerged in 12th-century England. Rather than being neutral citizens, however, jurors were pulled from around the area of the dispute or crime and heard very little—if any—evidence. Instead, they relied on what they already knew, what they investigated on their own, and rumors. From these traditions, the current American system of juries developed.

While the existence of juries is viewed as a paramount protection in the United States from potential judicial indiscretions, it is worth noting that most criminal cases and a vast majority of civil cases never go before a jury. On the criminal side, the trend toward plea bargaining has removed juries from the decision-making process in more and more cases every year. Plea bargains are more efficient in the criminal justice system but opponents believe the deals remove the ability of the public (through juries) to ensure justice is being served. Civil cases see even fewer cases going to jury. In many cases, civil affairs end up being settled or decided by a single judge or mediator. Regardless, Americans still appear to firmly believe in the importance of trial by jury.

At a most basic level of consideration, there are two types of juries in the American system of justice: grand and petit. Grand juries have become less prevalent over time—today being constrained to select state and federal cases. The job of the grand jury is to decide whether enough evidence exists to bring charges. However, depending on the state, not every case must go through a grand jury. If a grand jury believes there is enough evidence to indict, the case is sent to trial before a petit jury.

The grand jury—typically between 16 and 23 jurors—decides based on evidence presented solely by the prosecution. In a grand jury, there is no defense, and all proceedings are ex parte. If jurors believe the prosecutor has made a strong enough argument, they issue an indictment for the arrest of the suspect(s). In terms of burden of proof, a juror must only believe that there is probable cause to vote to indict. The individuals facing indictment do not need to be notified of

In certain cases, a grand jury is first convened in order to decide whether enough evidence exists to bring charges. Grand juries like this all-male one seen in a May 1922 photograph are larger than petit juries and are typically made up of between 16 and 23 jurors. Grand jurors need only believe that there is probable cause in order to issue an indictment for the arrest of the suspect(s).

grand jury proceedings as grand juries can issue sealed indictments to be served by police at the time of arrest. If a grand jury opts not to indict, it is known as a "no bill" while the decision to indict involves the jury returning a "true bill." A vast majority of grand juries vote to indict. Even if a no bill comes back from a grand jury, it is important to note that double jeopardy does not apply to grand jury proceedings.

Petit juries are the seated juries at the time of trial (both civil and criminal). In this setting, the jury hears from both the prosecutor/petitioner and the defendant/respondent. They hear evidence and instructions before deliberating among themselves. In most cases, there are 12 members of a trial jury in the United States. Depending on the jurisdiction, different majorities are required to reach a verdict. It can be a simple majority, some form of supermajority, or possibly even a unanimous verdict. If a verdict cannot be reached, the jury is said to be "hung."

Composition, Size, and Selection of Juries

In the United States, jury duty is required of all eligible citizens. To be eligible, citizens must be 18 years old. Most locations pull jurors from voter registration records (which allows some individuals to skirt service), while others look to property records, phone books, and vehicle registration lists. In terms of requirements, individuals who understand English, are able to be neutral, and are capable of analyzing the facts of the case are suited to sit on juries. The ability to avoid jury duty depends on where a potential jurist is located. Some jurisdictions grant exemptions for individuals in school, individuals with health problems, or individuals who are sole care providers for children or adult relatives. Others offer almost no exemptions and will instead only delay a reporting date until a potential juror has the ability to undertake jury duty. Jurors typically receive token payment amounts for their service. Failure to appear in response to a summons for jury duty can lead to a warrant being issued for the potential juror's arrest.

The Supreme Court ruled in 1898 that there had to be at least 12 individuals on a jury, although this requirement never fully trickled down to the state level. In 1978, the court revisited the issue in *Williams v. Florida*. Florida had sat a jury of only six individuals, and the defendant filed suit that he had his Sixth and Fourteenth Amendment rights violated. The Supreme Court disagreed, finding that the requirement of 12 jurors was nothing more than a historic accident and not a legal requirement. Small juries, however, remain quite controversial. The Supreme Court has ruled subsequently that five-person juries are too small, but has declined to require any set number larger than that. Smaller juries are largely believed to be more efficient and quicker to reach a decision. Opponents, on the other hand, believe these smaller juries can suffer from groupthink and make decisions that fluctuate from case to case. In the end, they may reach verdicts in less time, but that does not necessarily equate to the best outcome.

Original jury pools are chosen at random from the eligible population. Depending on the size of the jury that is needed for the trial, between 15 and 40 jurors are selected from the pool and called to the courtroom to undergo the voir dire process. Voir dire is used to allow both sides to question jurors and ensure they can be unbiased, fair evaluators of the proceedings. The judge asks each prospective juror for some basic information, including items like occupation, income, and potential time conflicts. More than anything, these questions are used to see if any biases, relationships, or experiences may make it impossible for a juror to be neutral. Once the general questions have been answered, attorneys can ask follow-up questions of their choice to as many jurors as they choose. Through these questions, attorneys hope to determine how a potential juror is likely to view aspects of the case. Each side is given a certain number of peremptory strikes that it can use to remove prospective jurors from consideration without offering an explanation as to why. Historically, attorneys had an unlimited ability to strike potential jurors, but the Supreme Court has issued decisions explaining that there are limits to the usage of peremptory strikes in jury formation. If a juror does not get seated for the case for which he/she has undergone voir dire, he/she is returned to the jury pool and subject to going through the same process for another case.

The selection of jurors is an oftentimes tense process—particularly for high-profile trials or trials of more serious acts. In these cases, lawyers are also attempting to determine how much the potential jurors already know of the actual crime in question. If a potential juror has already established an opinion regarding the potential guilt or innocence of someone, the opposing side will quickly ask for that juror to be removed. But what actually constitutes a reasonable objection once peremptory strikes have been used is not clear. Demographic traits like race, education, and income cannot be used legally against someone outside of peremptory strikes. For example, if a Caucasian male shoots and kills a Hispanic police officer, a Caucasian male potential juror cannot be told he is ineligible to serve based solely on those factors.

Role and Behavior

The role of a judge in a jury trial is to interpret appropriate laws and instruct the jury accordingly. The jury, however, is supposed to determine the facts of the case and render an appropriate ruling based on those facts. In criminal cases, jurors decide whether a defendant is guilty or innocent, while in the civil arena they determine liabilities. Historically, juries were supposed to understand community norms and be able to apply them appropriately to the case at hand. The issue remains that juries are determiners of facts. One jury can hear a case and decide a defendant is guilty. A separately selected jury in the same location, however, could hear the same case verbatim, come to the opposite conclusion, and still technically be correct in its decision. Unlike the decisions of the Supreme Court, there is no binding precedent created by juries.

Given the goal of jurors to be impartial fact-finders, most courts have clear rules regarding what kinds of outside information jurors are allowed to access during a trial. It is the decision of the judge what jurors are allowed to do and who they are permitted to talk to. Typically, they will be told not to learn about anything related to the case from outside sources—particularly from the media. Likewise, they will often be told not to conduct their own independent investigations. Jurors have been found visiting crime scenes, calling family members of individuals involved, and consulting with uninvolved attorneys regarding facts of the case. All of these scenarios could potentially lead to mistrials being declared or to jurors being dismissed. There can be no contact between jurors and anyone affiliated with the trial outside of the foreman and the judge. If a judge is concerned that a case is too high profile or important to risk potential outside influences on jurors, he/she has the option of sequestering them for the length of the trial. In this circumstance, jurors have no outside contact and typically live in hotels until a verdict is rendered.

While jurors are expected to not be influenced by outside factors during a trial, they are likewise expected to keep all information confidential from others not affiliated with the case. For the system to operate as intended, the media and general public are not supposed to be aware of what the jury is thinking or how deliberations are proceeding. If the goal is blind justice, the less outside parties know, the less likely the system is to experience any type of jury tampering. If juries

The jury box in the East Courtroom of the Howard M. Metzenbaum U.S. Courthouse in Cleveland, Ohio, in 2009. There are no set standards or format for jury deliberation so it is up to each set of jurors to determine how best to reach a verdict. One method many juries use is an anonymous poll taken during deliberations to determine how close they are to a verdict and what areas of the case present the most questions. The initial reactions to the case revealed during polling may predict how deliberations will proceed.

are not being tampered with, the system will run more smoothly and public confidence will remain intact for this portion of the criminal justice system. As discussed above, there are benefits to having juries with between six and 12 individuals on them. If they function properly, multiple jurors means multiple perspectives and hopefully a more careful and critical analysis of the facts. If there are 12 people sitting around the table, chances are increased that all possibilities will be presented by someone present. Twelve people can work to formulate their individual perspectives into a collective idea before delivering a verdict.

On each jury, there is a foreman or presiding juror. This individual is typically selected prior to the trial or at the beginning of deliberations, and it is his/her job to ask questions, facilitate discussion, and, depending on the jurisdiction, to read the decision of the jury. In a sense, he/she is the spokesperson for the jury and the only member permitted to seek clarification of legal questions from the judge during the trial and deliberations that follow. Many times, a court will opt to seat a small number of alternate jurors (one to three) who will hear the entire trial but will not partake in deliberations unless one of the jurors must leave or is dismissed prior to the rendering of a verdict.

In 1897, the Supreme Court ruled in *Springville City v. Thomas* that unanimous verdicts were necessary to convict a suspect. Almost a century later, however, in *Apodaca v. Oregon* (1972), the court overturned its precedent. To begin, the court found that the Sixth Amendment guarantee of a jury trial—made relevant to the states by the Fourteenth Amendment in *Duncan v. Louisiana* (1968)—did not require unanimity and only an appropriate proportion of a jury comprised of a cross-section of the community. One novel argument raised in *Apodaca* was that nonunanimous verdicts would violate the Fourteenth Amendment requirement that racial minorities not be systematically excluded from the jury selection process. It was argued that if verdicts did not have to be unanimous, minority members of a jury would not have their opinions taken as seriously (especially if they were not in agreement with the majority of the jury). The Supreme Court, however, saw no merit as to why that would be the case and ruled that unanimous verdicts would no longer be required. At the turn of the 21st century, all states except Oregon and Louisiana still require unanimous decisions by juries when considering criminal cases. Almost 40 states, however, have provisions that allow for less than unanimous decisions in civil cases. When a jury cannot reach the required majority in either circumstance, the case results in a hung jury. With a hung jury, a mistrial is declared and the case can be retried with a new jury.

There have long been questions regarding the appropriate role of judge and jury in a trial. Traditionally, the jury determined guilt and the judge determined the appropriate penalty/punishment. While this has not been abandoned, there have been Supreme Court rulings that alter this relationship. For example, in *Ring v. Arizona* (2002), the court ruled that the jury must decide on aggravating factors that may lead to a defendant being subject to the death penalty. Previously, the judge had made such rulings in Arizona. In many states, though, the jury merely gives an advisory sentencing opinion, which the judge can choose to accept or alter. Some states go a step further—particularly with death penalty cases—and seat a new jury to determine the penalty. This serves as another check on the system and ensures that defendants are given a group of jurors not already invested in the decision.

Deliberation and Nullification

Each jury deliberation is different. With no set standards or format, it is up to the particular jurors to determine how best to reach a verdict. Deliberations can run from minutes to weeks. Jurors oftentimes will take anonymous polls during deliberations to determine how close they are to a verdict and to help determine what areas of the case present the most questions. By measuring the initial reaction to the case, the jury can often tell how deliberations will proceed. If the initial poll reveals the jury is split 11–1, it will likely take less time to determine a verdict (if one can be reached at all) than if the initial split is 6–6. Ultimately, a decision is typically reached once jurors agree on the most reasonable interpretation of the case. At that point, a verdict is rendered and that portion of their work is complete.

Some juries have taken the law into their own hands rather than simply determining the facts of the case and properly determining guilt or liability accordingly. Through the process of jury nullification, juries have the ability to make a law void through their decisions. They can acquit a defendant even if they believe he/she is guilty because they do not believe the action should be criminal. In short, the jury becomes a form of legislative veto. Typically, jury nullification occurs when sympathy or bias drives decisions rather than the instructions of the judge. The more infamous examples in American history involve issues of slavery, freedom of the press, and freedom of religion.

Jury nullification tends to become a popular media topic when it appears in cases. Nullification has occurred throughout American history. It began with juries refusing to convict for violations of the Fugitive Slave Act prior to the Civil War and became even more prevalent during Prohibition, when juries nullified alcohol control laws more than half of the time. In the 1980s, nullification made the news as a series of juries in urban areas acquitted African American shooters despite clear evidence on the grounds that African Americans were treated more negatively in the criminal justice system than their Caucasian counterparts. Morally, many wonder about the implications of jurors choosing to willingly allow someone they believe to be guilty to walk away free on a case because of their beliefs about the law they have pledged to uphold. While the concept of jury nullification often is viewed negatively, it is acceptable according to the Fourth Circuit U.S. Court of Appeals. In *United States v. Moylan* (1969), the appellate court held that jurors were permitted to practice nullification and that courts must abide by the decision. It should also be noted, however, that in *Sparf v. United States* (1895), the Supreme Court ruled that a judge had no responsibility to tell jurors about their right to nullify laws through their decisions. Judges can even go further and remove jurors who they believe are looking to nullify.

Conclusion

Juries will forever remain a heavily examined portion of the American criminal justice system. Through juries, common citizens come together and determine the fate of their fellow citizens in criminal and civil matters. Studies have shown that juries tend to come to the same decision as the median juror, meaning that extreme jurors rarely have as much sway as some may believe. Looking back at the goals of the system, the fact that the median juror's opinion is typically in line with the jury's verdict shows that common citizens have an appropriate say, as the Sixth and Seventh Amendment direct.

William J. Miller
Southeast Missouri State University

See Also: 1941 to 1960 Primary Documents; 1961 to 1980 Primary Documents; Bill of Rights; Citizen Participation on Juries; Courts; *Duren v. Missouri*; Trials.

Further Readings

Jonakait, Randolph A. *The American Jury System*. New Haven, CT: Yale University Press, 2006.

Levy, Leonard W. *The Palladium of Justice: Origins of Trial by Jury*. Lanham, MD: Ivan R. Dee, 2000.

Vidmar, Neil and Valerie Hans. *American Juries: The Verdict*. Amherst, NY: Prometheus Books, 2007.

Jurisdiction

Jurisdiction in general refers to the authority or legal power to decide cases or to issue decrees. In the context of criminal law, it refers to the power of the courts to hear and decide an action brought by the state or federal government against an individual for a wrongdoing classified as a felony or a misdemeanor. Valid criminal judgments require (1) subject-matter jurisdiction, (2) personal jurisdiction, and (3) territorial jurisdiction. States enjoy sovereign immunity from criminal prosecution, and visiting foreign government officials are exempt from the criminal jurisdiction of the host country. In both cases, immunity may be waived. Special considerations aside, every state has personal jurisdiction over those within its territory, and criminal proceedings may be brought only in the state where the criminal acts were committed.

History

Fairly early in the nation's history, the case of *Barron v. Baltimore* separated clearly the jurisdictional role of the states in the nation's governance. Holding the Bill of Rights inapplicable to the states, the jurisdiction of the federal courts was circumscribed until the passage of the Fourteenth Amendment extending the jurisdiction of the federal courts over governmental threats to the rights and privileges defined in the Bill of Rights. Political and social counterforces to expanding federal power, grounded in federalism and the Ninth Amendment, resolved into the principle of dual federalism, the notion that the state and national governments were coequal, each operating autonomously within separate jurisdictions.

Dual federalism dominated jurisdictional thinking through the economic crises of the 1880s, even though the federal government began to exercise broad regulatory power over large business enterprises engaging in practices or agreements that restrained commerce unduly by way of forming trusts. With the economic collapse of the 1930s, however, the federal government, by way of Franklin Roosevelt's New Deal policies, worked in tandem with state and local governments to address economic decline. The formerly distinct jurisdictional divisions of authority blurred first into what was termed a *layer cake* federalism and then into a cooperative federalism, which distributed grants in aid to states and localities, expanding federal government control over state and local government. At the state level, courts were generally considered to lack jurisdiction absent service of process upon a defendant while within the geography of the rendering state in order to protect state sovereignty from incursions by other states, and to protect the defendant's right to be heard. Jurisdiction was eventually expanded over cases where the property of an absent nonresident regardless of whether the suit dealt with the property so long as the claim could be satisfied out of the property. For practical reasons, jurisdiction was expanded eventually to include any person with minimum contacts with the state, a rule under which jurisdiction could be exercised regardless of a party's territorial location, so long as the party could have been reasonably brought into court were he or she present in the state.

Subject-Matter Jurisdiction

Subject-matter jurisdiction refers to a court's constitutional authority over particular *actus rei*, the statutorily defined behavioral elements of particular crimes. A court acquires subject-matter jurisdiction in criminal cases once a subpoena, indictment, or information issues from a court sitting within the geographic locale wherein an alleged crime occurred. The subpoena or accusatory instrument must set forth the basis for subject-matter jurisdiction, including the nature and the statutory penalty for the offense. While defective subpoenas or accusatory instruments do not deprive the court of jurisdiction, a court may dismiss a case on its own initiative for lack of subject-matter jurisdiction.

The federal district courts have original and exclusive subject matter jurisdiction in federal criminal cases. The general jurisdiction of most state courts includes the authority to prosecute violations of state-enacted criminal laws. At both the state and federal level, however, some courts may have specialized jurisdiction as defined by statute. For instance, federal bankruptcy cases, including criminal offenses arising from bankruptcy issues, have proper subject matter jurisdiction only in federal bankruptcy courts per 28 U.S.C. § 1334.

Because of the federal system in the United States, courts may have concurrent personal jurisdiction over a defendant. In such situations, either court has the legal authority to hear the case. For instance, a person accused of a drug-related offense might face state drug charges as well as federal drug trafficking charges for the same course of conduct. Normally in such circumstances, the relevant law enforcement agencies will come to an agreement about which agency takes primary jurisdiction. It is possible, however, that the defendant could face prosecution in both federal and state courts.

Personal Jurisdiction

Personal jurisdiction refers to a court's constitutional authority over those accused of engaging in some particular *actus reus* while in some particular territorial locale and includes the court's power to compel the attendance of witnesses at trial. In conspiracy cases, the courts of several states may have personal jurisdiction over the same individual as the agreement to engage in illegal behavior may involve two or more persons residing in separate states, and as the agreement would then occur in both states simultaneously. While subject-matter jurisdiction may not be waived, the parties to a case may grant personal jurisdiction voluntarily.

Territorial Jurisdiction

Territorial jurisdiction refers to a court's constitutional authority to enforce criminal laws that apply to *actus rei* that are accomplished within its territorial boundaries. State and federal court territorial jurisdictions are determined by the due process clauses of the Fourteenth and the Fifth Amendments, respectively. Politically, jurisdiction is a means of dividing up power among the states and between the states and the federal government. Accordingly, the power to define crimes and their punishment is generally reserved to the states under the Tenth Amendment. However, the Constitution does invest Congress with the power to define crimes and to provide for their enforcement under several clauses, including the commerce clause, the taxing and spending clause, its power to regulate the mail, and its power over locales reserved as federal property.

While territoriality continues as a primary consideration in much of the criminal law, its workability in the context of growing areas of contemporary criminal conduct is in question. International terrorism, environmental concerns, drug trafficking, genocide, and Internet crime, for example, have spawned a number of exceptions. These include (1) the effects doctrine whereby criminal conduct by people outside a state's territorial jurisdiction may be tried by that state's courts if the conduct generates an "effect" within the state's territory, (2) the protective principle whereby a state may have jurisdiction to try acts performed outside its territory yet aimed at overthrowing the state or threatening the integrity of its governmental functions, and (3) the universality principle whereby any state may prosecute alleged crimes that are recognized universally as crimes against humanity.

Extraterritorial Jurisdiction

One state is generally precluded constitutionally from enforcing the criminal laws of another state. However, a state may define behaviors as criminal offenses when committed beyond its territorial jurisdiction, though they are unenforceable against the offenders so long as they remain outside the state. There are two theories of enforcement when the *actus reus* is committed in more than one territorial locale, as when a citizen of one state murders a citizen of another by firing across a state line. The initiatory theory claims jurisdiction where the *actus reus* begins. To avoid prosecuting conduct that does not constitute a complete *actus reus* (e.g., the mere firing of a pistol at a legal time and place), the sequence of behaviors constituting the *actus reus* must be defined statutorily either as activities undertaken when the harm occurs (e.g., speeding in one state that extends across a state line) or in terms of the consequences of the behavior (e.g., making false representations by e-mail that are relied upon by a person online in another state, to their detriment). Inchoate offenses, crimes committed in preparation of another crime (e.g., conspiracy), are considered to continue across time and borders until the failure of the criminal act intended.

The terminatory theory claims jurisdiction when the injury affects a citizen within the territory of a state. As no initiating action defining the *actus reus* is taken within the territorial locale, the wording of the *actus reus* must permit jurisdiction explicitly under the theory that a wrongdoer should not able to escape prosecution by intending harm only to those outside the state where the *actus reus* is initiated. This justification weakens when the harm's locale is accidental.

Concurrent and Special Jurisdiction

Some behaviors are defined as criminal by both federal and state statutes. Either might defer to the other but, alternatively, an accused might be tried in both state and federal trial courts. Concurrent jurisdiction applies most notably in any action seeking to declare a state law unconstitutional.

Some courts are accorded by statute or the Constitution a particular limited jurisdiction. Military courts have jurisdiction over specific cases involving military personnel, tribal courts have jurisdiction over offenses occurring on tribal reservations, and most states provide separate juvenile courts. Some states provide special courts for drug offenses, and most states direct all matters relating to the administration of decedents' estates to special probate courts.

Charles Frederick Abel
Stephen F. Austin State University

See Also: 1961 to 1980 Primary Documents; Courts of Indian Offenses; Criminalization and Decriminalization; Environmental Crimes; Fraud.

Further Readings

Barron v. Baltimore, 32 U.S. 243 (1833).

Charles River Bridge v. Warren Bridge, 11 Pet. (36 U.S.) 420 (1837).

Garadner, T. and T. Anderson. *Criminal Law,* 11th ed. Belmont, CA: Wadsworth Cengage Learning, 2011.

Inbau, F., J. Thompson, J. Zagel, and J. Manak. *Criminal Law and Its Administration,* 6th ed. Westbury, NY: Foundation Press, 1997.

Legal Information Institute: Cornell University Law School. "Jurisdiction." http://topics.law.cornell.edu/wex/Jurisdiction (Accessed September 2011).

Legal Information Institute: Cornell University Law School. "Personal Jurisdiction." http://topics.law.cornell.edu/wex/personal_jurisdiction (Accessed September 2011).

Legal Information Institute: Cornell University Law School. "Subject Matter Jurisdiction." http://topics.law.cornell.edu/wex/subject_matter_jurisdiction (Accessed September 2011).

Justice, Department of

Established in 1870, the Department of Justice (DOJ)—otherwise referred to as "Justice Department" or "USDOJ"—is the legal executive branch of the U.S. federal government. As the combined law, policing, and justice workhorse of the nation, it is tasked with three main functions—upholding federal laws, administering justice, and safeguarding American society—with the overall mission:

> To enforce the law and defend the interests of the United States according to the law; to ensure public safety against threats foreign and domestic; to provide federal leadership in preventing and controlling crime; to seek just punishment for those guilty of unlawful behavior; and to ensure fair and impartial administration of justice for all Americans.

Other key areas of work include protecting and promoting civil rights and liberties, collecting and recording crime statistics, and providing funding for training and research. The head of the DOJ—the attorney general—is currently Eric H. Holder, Jr., who assumed office on February 3, 2009, and is the 82nd official to fill this position. The second in command and chief operating officer—the deputy attorney general—is currently James M. Cole, who assumed office on December 29, 2010. Both officeholders are appointed by the president and confirmed by the Senate. Headquarters are based in Washington, D.C., in the Robert F. Kennedy Department of Justice Building at 950 Pennsylvania Avenue between 9th and 10th Streets. The building was renamed in 2001 in honor of the 64th attorney general of the United States—Robert F. Kennedy—although it is still informally referred to by many as "Main Justice." Appearing on the official seal of the Department of Justice, the Latin motto *Qui Pro Domina Justitia Sequitur* has often been debated, however, many experts have interpreted the phrase to mean "who prosecutes on behalf of justice (or the Lady Justice)."

The Department of Justice is one of the oldest branches of the federal government, dating back to the late 18th century—nearly a century before it officially came into existence. Held in New York City on September 24, 1789, the first session of the U.S. Congress convened to sign the Judiciary Act of 1789 and thus established the federal judiciary for the country. Among other things, this statute created the first Office of the Attorney General, which was to be filled by a person "learned in the law" in order to serve as the chief law enforcement officer for the United States. The purpose of this position was to provide "advice and opinion upon questions of law when required by the president, or when requested by the heads of any of the departments, touching any matters that may concern their departments."

Additionally, this officeholder was to prosecute cases, both civilly and criminally, "in which the United States shall be concerned," and in exceptional circumstances, to appear in person before the Supreme Court to represent the federal government. Appointed by the president and thus a member of the executive cabinet, this office was a one-person, part-time position during its infancy, with incumbents typically holding private law practices while executing public duties.

The U.S. Department of Justice is headquartered in Washington, D.C., in the Robert F. Kennedy Department of Justice Building, shown here. The Department of Justice has 43 specialized departments and the two largest, the Federal Bureau of Investigation and the Bureau of Prisons, had employees totaling 34,926 and 37,485, respectively, in September 2010. As the country's chief combined law office and policing agency, its total annual budget is greater than $27 billion.

In addition, the Judiciary Act of 1789 created several assistant attorneys general and established district attorneys for each federal district, thus laying the new legal framework for the nation while also granting the attorney general with supervisory authority over these offices and others, such as those of clerks, marshals, accountants, and other court officers.

Origin

Understandably, the attorney general's position involved years of dedicated work before an established office took shape. Edmund Randolph, previously the second secretary of state, was first to serve in the office, from September 26, 1789, to January 26, 1794, appointed by President George Washington. Randolph and his six immediate successors—William Bradford, Charles Lee, Levi Lincoln, Sr., John Breckinridge, Caesar Rodney, William Pinkney, and Richard Rush—all undoubtedly made noted contributions to further develop this office. However, and perhaps as a consequence of the increasingly growing workload, they all devoted limited efforts to maintaining detailed and accurate records and notes of the daily workings and services provided by the office during their respective terms, which presented a challenge for successors. As such, the first "great" attorney general was William Wirt, who held office from November 13, 1817, to March 4, 1829—the longest term since inception, spanning two presidencies—who made record maintenance a priority, primarily as a duty to help successfully guide future incumbents after he found there was limited information to work with. Over the following decades, extensive archives began to accumulate as the country began to experience rapid growth and expansion, which naturally resulted in an escalating workload. Consequently, a new problem arose—there was no established executive government department to effectively and efficiently perform many of the orders, services, and activities required of this office, which led to an overburdened staff and a lack of uniformity in the administration of law and the delivery of justice.

Nearly a century later, the idea was born to establish a justice department. The mounting workload was exacerbated by another dilemma—the influx of litigation overwhelming the federal government during Reconstruction following the Civil War, which ravaged the United States from 1861 to 1865. This required a "very expensive retention of a large number of private attorneys to handle the workload," and perhaps only helped to facilitate creation of the new executive branch.

On December 12, 1867, the U.S. House of Representatives formally instructed the Judiciary Committee to "consider the propriety of reporting a bill to consolidate all law officers of the government into one department." In response, Congressman William Lawrence of Ohio was charged to lead an inquiry on the matter of creating a new Department of Justice, which would be headed by the attorney general. Shortly after, Lawrence introduced a bill to the U.S. House Committee on the Judiciary on February 19, 1868, for the creation of the Department of Justice. Initially, this bill was unsuccessful, leading another member of Congress—Republican representative Thomas Jenckes of Rhode Island—to introduce an amended bill two years later.

On April 29, 1870, both the Senate and the House of Representatives approved the bill, which was signed into law by President Ulysses S. Grant on June 22, 1870. Following this, Congress then passed the Act to Establish the Department of Justice, with operations officially commencing on July 1, 1870. This act also created the Office of the Solicitor General, tasked specifically with supervising and conducting all litigation in the Supreme Court on behalf of the United States, as well as to oversee all litigation for federal appellate courts. Appointed by the president in the same year, Benjamin Bristow was the first official to hold this office, from October 1870 to November 1872.

Early Challenges

In the early days, the Department of Justice, of all things, was plagued by instances of corruption. Mainly, this stemmed from the freedom of the attorney general to employ staff of his own political party, which presented him with a frequent conflict of interest between serving the administration of government and the political ambitions of his party. As such, when a new president was elected, existing attorneys were normally replaced with those of members of the successor's own political party. These political distractions thus laid the ingredients for cases of corruption, for example, when two attorneys general, Wayne MacVeagh and Benjamin Brewster, who each served separate terms between 1880 and 1883, faced investigation and prosecution for bureaucratic wrongdoing. In response, MacVeagh resigned, which allowed Brewster to take office. Ironically, after assuming duties, Brewster discovered a DOJ slowly being defrauded by corrupt marshals and commissioners. In light of this, he appointed his nephew Brewster Cameron to investigate and prosecute department officials engaged in misconduct, which led to a high-profile case in which U.S. Marshal Paul Strobach and fellow deputies in Alabama were convicted of committing frauds and falsifying charges on arrested citizens for purposes of collecting fees. Naturally, tension began to ensue among political parties, which led President Chester Arthur to remove Brewster from his cabinet due to "political necessity." Still, in 1884, an extensive investigation conducted by the House Committee on Expenditures and chaired by Democrat William Springer of Illinois concluded to blame the attorney general's administration for the corruption. A number of reforms were subsequently implemented such as requirements for maintaining detailed records of daily office activities, submitting financial reports, instituting an employee merit system, and establishing fixed salaries to eliminate the need for officers to make frivolous charges on arrested citizens for the sake of collecting fees.

From the late 19th century onward, new problems began to plague the DOJ. During Reconstruction, the emancipation of thousands of black slaves enraged some patriotic nationalists of the former Confederacy. Consequently, a new group began to emerge—the Ku Klux Klan (KKK)—

beginning in 1867 in Tennessee, with members working to overturn Reconstruction efforts by the DOJ through acts of violence, rioting, assassinations, as well as torturing and killing of black people. The Department was on the front lines of the Grant administration's efforts to suppress the Ku Klux Klan in 1871–72. At first, the district attorneys and marshals were successful, capturing hundreds of Klansmen, but continued Southern resistance and growing northern apathy failed to eliminate white supremacist vigilantism.

The Department of Justice acquired its own Detective Force in 1908, the Bureau of Investigation, through an executive order of President Theodore Roosevelt. At first, it had little to do because of the lack of federal crimes, but the 1911 Mann Act, World War I, and Prohibition with its mobsters and other criminals, gave the bureau considerable work. In 1924 J. Edgar Hoover became director of the bureau (Federal Bureau of Investigation, or FBI, after 1933) and launched a war against bank robbers, kidnappers, and other public enemies. Generally the FBI stayed away from organized crime and focused on communists and other "subversives." The bureau was hesitant to enforce 1960s civil rights laws, even though the DOJ established a Civil Rights Division in 1957, which made the department responsible for combating racial discrimination. Hoover actually tried to destroy Martin Luther King, Jr., whom he believed threatened a revolution. Finally, another hallmark of the DOJ—the Attorney General's List of Subversive Organizations (AGLOSO)—dating back to 1903 and used during World Wars I and II, was a compilation of organizations regarded as threats to the federal government, such as the KKK and the Nazi Party. From 1947 until it was abolished in 1974, administrations publicized these lists, which had damaging effects for the more than 300 organizations listed with no advance notice, evidence, or hearings.

Evolution

As with any organization, the Department of Justice has faced challenges over the years and has evolved considerably to include new offices, divisions, and positions in order to effectively deal with a multifaceted workload while standing firmly on the foundations established in 1870. Comprising 43 specialized departments, powered by an annual budget exceeding $27 billion, and armed with a staff of more than 116,000 highly trained lawyers, investigators, and agents as of September 2010, the DOJ today essentially serves as the nation's chief combined law office and policing agency. Specifically, two components—the Federal Bureau of Investigation and the Bureau of Prisons—comprise the bulk of the DOJ's manpower, with employees totaling 34,926 and 37,485 respectively, as of September 2010.

Today, the DOJ is managed through leadership offices—the attorney general, deputy attorney general, and the associate attorney general—all of whom are nominated by the president and confirmed by the Senate, and the solicitor general, who is nominated by the Supreme Court and confirmed by the Senate. These offices are supported by five separate divisions responsible for legal policy, legislative affairs, tribal justice, intergovernmental and public liaison, and public affairs. According to the Department of Justice's strategic plan, priority areas today "reflect the reality of law and justice these days," which includes detection and prevention of terrorism as a chief concern; combating crimes of violence, especially crimes committed with firearms and gang violence; computer crime, especially child pornography, obscenity, and intellectual property such as online piracy and identity theft; drug trafficking and substance abuse, especially of methamphetamines, including drug diversion; and white-collar crimes such as corporate fraud and public corruption. The DOJ also promotes civil rights and civil liberties, for example, by eliminating discrimination and human trafficking.

A number of services and operations of the Department of Justice are executed through the following departments. For state and local assistance, there are offices dedicated to community-oriented policing services, community relations services, violence against women, and justice programs, the latter of which houses the Bureau of Justice Assistance; Bureau of Justice Statistics; Community Capacity Development Office; National Institute of Justice; Office of Juvenile Justice and Delinquency Prevention; Sex Offender Sentencing, Monitoring, Apprehending, Registering, and Tracking Office (SMART); and Office for Victims of Crime. Legal representation and advice is provided by a variety of offices: Office of Legal Counsel, Tax Division, Environment and Natural Resources Division, Antitrust Division, Civil Rights Division, Office of Dispute Resolution, National Security Division, and Executive Office for the U.S. Trustees. Law enforcement operations are conducted through the FBI; Drug Enforcement Administration; Bureau of Alcohol, Tobacco, Firearms and Explosives; U.S. Marshals Service; National Drug Intelligence Center; Interpol's National Central Bureau, Criminal Division; Executive Office for U.S. Attorneys; Executive Office for Organized Crime Drug Enforcement Task Forces; and Office of the Federal Detention Trustee. Prisons are overseen through the Federal Bureau of Prisons (includes National Institute of Corrections), Office of the Pardon Attorney, and U.S. Parole Commission. Finally, the Department of Justice is managed and overseen through the Justice Management Division, Office of the Inspector General, Office of Professional Responsibility, and Professional Responsibility Advisory Office.

As of March 2003, the U.S. Immigration and Naturalization Service was transferred to the newly established Department of Homeland Security, although other similar offices—Executive Office for Immigration Review and Board of Immigration Appeals—are still under DOJ command. Other offices include Foreign Claims Settlement Commission and Office of Information Policy. During World War II, a specially created war division operated in order to help coordinate war-related activities but ceased operations in December 1945.

Michael J. Puniskis
Middlesex University

See Also: 1901 to 1920 Primary Documents; 1921 to 1940 Primary Documents; 1941 to 1960 Primary Documents; 1981 to 2000 Primary Documents; 2001 to 2012 Primary Documents; Drug Enforcement Administration; Federal Bureau of Investigation; Federal Policing; Federal Prisons; Homeland Security; Judiciary Act of 1789; Supreme Court, U.S.

Further Readings
Bell, Griffin B. "The Attorney General: The Federal Government's Chief Lawyer and Chief Litigator, or One Among Many?" *Fordham Law Review*, v.46/6 (1978).

Chaitkin, Anton. "How the KKK Got Into the U.S. Department of Justice." *Executive Intelligence Review*, v.25/12 (1998).

Goldman, Ronald M. "The 'Weakened Spring of Government' and the Executive Branch: The Department of Justice in the Late 19th Century." *Congress & the Presidency*, v.11/2 (1984).

Goldstein, Robert J. *American Blacklist: The Attorney General's List of Subversive Organizations*. Lawrence: University Press of Kansas, 2008.

Landsberg, Brian K. *Enforcing Civil Rights: Race Discrimination and the Department of Justice*. Lawrence: University Press of Kansas, 1997.

Langeluttig, Albert. *The Department of Justice of the United States*. Baltimore, MD: Johns Hopkins University Press, 1927.

U.S. Department of Justice. http://www.justice.gov (Accessed January 2011).

Juvenile Corrections, Contemporary

As the United States entered the 21st century, it faced a crisis in juvenile corrections. Due to get-tough sentencing policies enacted in the 1980s and 1990s, juvenile incarceration was at an all-time high. On any given day, there were over 100,000 youths held in juvenile correctional facilities. Reports began to surface, indicating that abuse and poor conditions were endemic in many of these facilities. Court-mandated investigations in both California and Texas uncovered serious levels of mistreatment and violence. Research revealed three-year recidivism rates as high as 50 percent in many states. Today, while the majority of these problems still exist, there are also a number of hopeful trends.

U.S. Correctional System
Describing the American juvenile correctional system is complex because each state system is unique. For example, some states coordinate their systems through a state-level agency, while others share responsibility for incarceration with localities (generally, counties). There is also variation among states in their level of dependence on

private corporations to run correctional centers. States use different types of confinement; some place youths in large institutions, while others use a cottage model with small groups of youths living together. The population of youths in custody in each state also differs widely. Some states incarcerate high numbers of status offenders (youths who violate laws, like truancy, that only pertain to minors) while others try to reserve incarceration for those who have been convicted of a delinquent act. Similarly, states vary in how they handle youths who violate the terms of their parole. Some rely on incarceration, while others have found noncustodial ways to handle these violations.

Despite variation among the states, it is possible to make a number of generalizations about the American system. About half of all youths who come through the juvenile courts are put on probation. Probation generally involves monitoring, programming, and restrictions. Of the approximately 20 percent of youths who are sentenced to confinement, a full 85 percent are male, although the rate of female incarceration has grown steadily over the last 20 years. Disproportionate minority confinement has led to an overrepresentation of blacks and Hispanics in the incarcerated population. Research suggests that this overrepresentation can be traced partly to racial/ethnic variations in crime patterns, but it is also explained by discrimination embedded in the justice process. Youths who are released from confinement are generally put on parole (called "aftercare" in some states) unless they have aged out of the system. Parole, like probation, involves monitoring along with other conditions. Typical requirements include periodic meetings with an agent, curfews, bans on drugs and alcohol, and restrictions relating to school or work.

Rehabilitation, Education, and Counseling

Because one of the goals of the juvenile justice system is rehabilitation, most correctional facilities offer some form of rehabilitative or educational programming. Virtually all states require that juvenile correctional facilities provide a minimum level of education to those youths who do not have a high school diploma or GED. Unfortunately, many of these programs are mired in problems due to underfunding, overcrowding, and insufficient teacher training. Additionally, the

The Louisville, Kentucky, Metro Youth Detention Services building in 2008. Since 2000, the number of youths held in juvenile correctional facilities like this one has declined from about 100,000 to 90,000 on any given day.

incarcerated population is particularly challenging to teach. Most youths arrive in the system considerably behind grade level and many have been diagnosed with learning or behavioral disabilities. As a result of these factors, prison classrooms tend to be chaotic spaces. Special education students have a particularly difficult time because there are insufficient resources to meet their needs.

Most correctional institutions in the United States provide some form of substance abuse treatment, although the type, quality, and amount vary widely. Services to youths on parole or probation, however, are much more limited. The most common forms of treatment within institutions include classes, support groups, and one-on-one counseling. Most correctional facilities also offer general mental health services. Incarcerated youths have disproportionately high rates of mental health problems (particularly, depression and anxiety). While there has been increasing attention paid to these problems in recent years, reports suggest that there are still high rates of self-injurious behavior among correctional center residents. On an encouraging note, several female-specific therapeutic programs have been created. These programs are a response to research showing that females who have been sexually abused have specific therapy needs and tend to be disproportionately represented in juvenile prisons. Overall, however, this type of gender-specific programming is rare and incarcerated females continue to be overlooked by both researchers and practitioners.

The last 10 years have seen a number of new trends in programming offered to incarcerated and paroled youths, as well as to those on probation. For example, there has been a dramatic increase in the number of classes in anger management and victim awareness. Because youths who are parents tend to be overrepresented in the juvenile correctional system, parenting skills courses have become more popular. In response to research showing that families are an important component of juvenile rehabilitation, some correctional programs have begun to include family members in therapy sessions. This is more common in community-based programs because incarcerated youths are sometimes housed too far from their families to make regular visitation possible.

Decrease in Incarcerated Juveniles

The most notable trend in juvenile corrections since 2000 has been the decrease in the number of incarcerated youths. While juvenile incarceration levels are still extremely high—with approximately 90,000 juveniles in custody on any given day—numbers have consistently declined during the last decade. This is partly a result of decreasing crime rates (particularly among black youth), but it can also be traced to policies enacted at the state level. Because of judicial mandates, outrage over abuse, and large budget deficits, many states have enacted initiatives to lower custody levels. For example, Missouri has developed a highly praised and emulated model of juvenile corrections. Youths are incarcerated in facilities no more than 50 miles from their homes and are placed in small-group settings, rather than in large institutions. Youths wear street clothes and participate in decision making in their residences. Missouri in particular is having notable success in lowering recidivism as well as custody rates.

Some states are moving toward increased use of performance-based standards. These standards provide a way for institutions to monitor practices inside facilities (like the use of restraints) with the goal of making targeted and rapid changes to policies. It also appears that states are increasingly using risk assessment in youth placement decisions. Finally, states are reducing their use of incarceration as they experiment with community-based programs such as intensive probation, restitution, community service, and outpatient treatment.

Anne M. Nurse
College of Wooster

See Also: Children's Rights; Juvenile Corrections, History of; Juvenile Justice, History of; Juvenile Offenders, Prevention and Education.

Further Readings

Annie E. Casey Foundation. "A Road Map for Juvenile Justice Reform." http://www.aecf.org/~/media/Pubs/Initiatives/KIDS%20COUNT/123/2008KidsCountEssayARoadmapforJuvenileJustice Reform/KC08Essay_Road_Map.pdf (Accessed March 2012).

Krisberg, Barry. *General Corrections Review of the California Youth Authority*. Sacramento, CA: California Youth Authority, 2010.

Nurse, Anne. *Locked Up, Locked Out: Young Men in the Juvenile Justice System*. Nashville, TN: Vanderbilt University Press, 2010.

Snyder, Howard M. and Melissa Sickmund. *Juvenile Offenders and Victims: 2006 National Report*. Washington, DC: U.S. Department of Justice, Office of Justice Programs, Office of Juvenile Justice and Delinquency Prevention, 2006.

Juvenile Corrections, History of

Juvenile corrections is a term that refers to the system and the philosophies behind the system that detains juveniles who have been processed through the juvenile justice system and found to be delinquent. The evolution of juvenile corrections has historically followed the development of the broader juvenile justice system. One of the most significant factors in the development of juvenile corrections has been how societies have historically defined what it means to be an adult compared to what it means to be a child. Prior to the Industrial Revolution, young individuals were seldom recognized as being different from adults. In fact, they were often treated as little adults. Juveniles were often processed through the justice system and punished in the same manner as adult offenders. This correctional philosophy slowly began to change as societies began to industrialize. The social change that came about as a result of industrialization not only changed the structure of the labor market; it also changed broader ideologies concerning the roles of young people. These two factors fueled the social change that shapes the juvenile justice system to this day.

Until the early 1800s, correctional policies and practices throughout the world generally did not give consideration to a juvenile's age. The first attempts to change juvenile correctional policies and practices occurred in England in the 1820s and in the United States during the mid-1800s. One of the first accounts of juvenile corrections can be traced back to 1820s England when courts held Warwickshire Quarter Sessions—periodic courts that sentenced young offenders to a single day in prison. Following the completion of their

Uniformed African American juvenile convicts, most of them in chains, at work in a field in an unknown U.S. location in a photograph dated 1903. While these young men and boys may have been treated much like adult convicts of that era in the south, during the 20th century, secure juvenile correctional facilities were eventually reformed through legislation such as the American Law Institute's Model Youth Correction Authority Act and social movements to deinstitutionalize juvenile offenders.

sentence, juveniles were released back into the custody of their parents or another responsible adult.

Some of the first historical records of juvenile corrections within the United States date back to the 19th century. In 1824, New York officials opened the House of Refuge, which was a facility that housed juveniles with the intent to rehabilitate instead incapacitate and punish. The establishment of the New York House of Refuge is one of the first official correctional programs that had the goal of diverting the juvenile away from the adult correctional system.

During the mid-1800s, juvenile justice practitioners from the state of Massachusetts were often tasked with finding juveniles suitable living arrangements and to occasionally visit them to ensure that they were refraining from vagrancy and delinquency. The programs established by the state of Massachusetts are recognized as the first official form of probation. In addition to the efforts of officials in Massachusetts, other states slowly began to recognize the need to separate the punishment of juveniles and adults.

During the later part of the 19th and into the 20th century, societies continued to change how juveniles were seen with reference to roles and responsibilities within broader society. During this time, it became widely recognized that juveniles were historically exploited within the labor market. As changes in industry continued and social reform boomed, the concept of adolescence became popular among citizens of the United States. Officials were beginning to recognize that a gray area existed between childhood and adulthood. The recognition of the period of adolescence allowed juvenile justice advocates to argue for an entirely separate juvenile justice system. Although generally recognized as a positive step in juvenile jurisprudence, the creation of the concept of adolescence led to many dilemmas and raised many questions. For example, who defines juvenile, who defines delinquent, and at what age does one cross from childhood to adolescence and from adolescence to adulthood?

The philosophies behind juvenile corrections were greatly impacted in 1899 when criminal justice practitioners in the United States took the first step toward creating a separate juvenile justice system and established the first juvenile court in Cook County, Illinois. Soon after Illinois created the first juvenile court, juvenile courts were created throughout the country. These initial courts established a correctional philosophy that was grounded in the actions of earlier programs established in Massachusetts, New York, Oregon, and other states. The courts approached juvenile corrections according to the legal doctrine of *parens patriae*—the idea that courts should act as parental figures in the absence of capable guardians. In accordance with the doctrine of *parens patriae*, judicial officials were required to consider "the best interest of the child" when assigning correctional treatment. This ideology led to correctional programs that were geared toward correcting adolescent behavior with the goal of returning a rehabilitated, law-abiding citizen to society. The rapid expansion of juvenile courts based on the doctrine of *parens patriae* encouraged the creation of less punitive correctional programs. Despite this approach to corrections, some juveniles have been found to be unresponsive to informal, community-based correctional programs such as probation. This created a two-tiered juvenile correctional system that can be labeled as community-based corrections and more formal or secure corrections.

Community-Based Corrections

Within the juvenile justice system, community-based corrections are favored over more formal treatment in secure facilities. This preference exists because a community-based approach to juvenile corrections is better aligned with the overall philosophy behind the juvenile justice system. Community-based corrections programs became the main line of effort in the juvenile correctional system when the Juvenile Justice and Delinquency Prevention Act was passed in 1974. The act called for the "deinstitutionalization" of all juvenile offenders. After the passing of the Juvenile Justice and Delinquency Prevention Act, advocates for community-based corrections developed a number of programs that allowed for rehabilitation without incarceration. The most common form of community-based corrections is probation.

Probation is a form of correctional treatment that allows a juvenile to remain within the community while being required to follow certain rules and remaining under close supervision by a representative of the state. Probation began in the United States in the mid-1800s. Probation has been the dominant disposition of juvenile cases since its inception. It has been the correctional treatment of choice by criminal justice practitioners because the conditions established for each individual can be tailored so as to help rehabilitate the individual offender. In addition, probation is a common disposition for less serious crimes such as status offenses. When probation fails or is not an option, other common community-based correctional programs include house arrest, restorative justice, intensive supervision, and residential programs.

Established in the early 1980s, house arrest is a correctional program that requires juvenile delinquents to wear a type of electronic monitoring device. During the assigned period, the juvenile delinquent is not allowed to leave the assigned location. The effectiveness of these programs has long been a point of debate among criminal justice practitioners.

The basic concept of restorative justice has existed for thousands of years, as revealed in the Code of Hammurabi. Contemporary restorative justice programs are typically aligned with the philosophy of juvenile justice in that they aim to "restore" all parties involved to their statuses prior to the offense. Restorative justice approaches are different than other correctional programs in that they involve an intimate collaboration between the victim, offender, and justice officials. Research on restorative justice programs is mixed as far as the effectiveness of the programs. However, studies on restorative justice tend to show that there is a relationship between positive victim satisfaction and future offending.

More restrictive community-based approaches to juvenile corrections include intensive supervision and residential programs. Intensive supervision programs require daily interaction with a probation officer or similar judicial representative. Juveniles are often referred to intensive supervision programs when the only alternative is detention in a secure correctional facility. The main goal of this type of program is to provide rehabilitation to juveniles as a last chance alternative to imprisonment while allowing the juvenile delinquent to remain in the community. Residential programs are one of the most aggressive types of community-based corrections. Examples of residential programs include programs such as group homes and camps. A typical group home is operated as an open environment where juveniles live, work, and attend school while taking advantage of specialized correctional services such as group counseling. Group homes are typically staffed with a team that includes counselors, probation officers, and educators. Juvenile camps rose to popularity during the 1980s along with "scared straight" programs, including wilderness camps and militaristic boot camps.

Secure Correctional Facilities

Sometimes, a juvenile court decides that community-based treatment is not in the best interest of the juvenile. Another approach to juvenile corrections that became popular during the early 1800s is detaining youthful offenders in a secure youth correctional facility. Prior to this time period, young offenders were housed with adult offenders in adult facilities.

In the early 1800s, the cottage system was established in New York, Ohio, Massachusetts, and Maine. By the early 1900s, a majority of states followed suit and created some sort of secure correctional facility specifically for juveniles. Facilities included in the cottage system operated as secure facilities under the direction of a headmaster. Although some may consider secure juvenile correctional facilities to be punitive in nature, secure juvenile correctional facilities such as cottages still operated under the doctrine of *parens patriae*. The philosophies that drive secure youth correctional facilities are markedly different than those that drive adult correctional facilities. Secure juvenile correctional facilities have historically operated in a militaristic manner with an emphasis on rehabilitation. This has not always been the case with secure adult facilities. During the 20th century, secure juvenile correctional facilities were greatly reformed through legislation such as the American Law Institute's Model Youth Correction Authority Act and social movements such as the push to deinstitutionalize juvenile offenders.

Today, the major trend in juvenile corrections reflects the "get tough on crime" ideology. Unfortunately, this trend has included the implementation of legislation that allows many juvenile offenders to be waivered to adult courts. The waiver of juveniles to adult courts has revived the age-old questions "How do we define juvenile delinquency?" and "At what age does someone become an adult?" Debates concerning these questions and the current trends in social change will guide practitioners and policy makers throughout the 21st century. The hope is that practitioners and policy makers alike will remember the ideas behind the doctrine of *parens patriae*.

Michael J. Reed
Mississippi State University

See Also: 1921 to 1940 Primary Documents; Children's Rights; Juvenile Corrections, Contemporary; Juvenile Corrections, Sociology of; Juvenile Courts, Contemporary; Juvenile Courts, History of; Juvenile Justice, History of; Juvenile Offenders in Adult Courts; Probation.

Further Readings
del Carmen, Rolando V. and Chad R. Trulson *Juvenile Justice: The System, Process and Law*. Belmont, CA: Thomson Wadsworth, 2005.
Fagan, Jeffrey. "The Contradictions of Juvenile Crime & Punishment." *Daedalus*, v.139/3 (2010).
Ruddell, Rick and Matthew Thomas. *Juvenile Corrections*. Richmond KY: Newgate Press, 2009.
Siegel, Larry and Brandon Welsh. *Juvenile Delinquency: The Core*, 3rd ed. Belmont, CA: Thomson Wadsworth, 2008.
Thompson, William and Jack Bynum, eds. *Juvenile Delinquency: A Sociological Approach*, 8th ed. London: Pearson, 2010.

Juvenile Corrections, Sociology of

The sociology of juvenile corrections refers to the systematic application of the knowledge, concepts, methods, and techniques of sociology to the study of juvenile corrections. In broad terms, the sociology of juvenile corrections refers to the ways in which social structures (groups, organizations, communities), social categories (age, class, sex, and race) and social institutions (political, economic, and religious) affect the development of how society deals with delinquent or status offending minors. The role social factors play in sanctioning and rehabilitation of minors is an important component of the sociology of juvenile corrections. The sociology of juvenile corrections is concerned with the etiology of juvenile corrections along with the impact of social history on juvenile correctional philosophies. It focuses not only on the purposes, structures, and procedures of formal sanctioning of juveniles but also on the practices, historical backgrounds, developments of juvenile corrections, and impact of historical changes in society on how society deals with juvenile offenders.

Children Seen as Adults

The importance of structural functional, interactional, historical, and cultural aspects of society is part of the sociology of juvenile corrections. The evolution of juvenile corrections is embedded in the social structure of any society. A society's human social interaction, rules, and processes impact the evolution and application of juvenile corrections. This can be seen in the sociological evolution of societies, from mechanical to organic societies. The concept of juvenile corrections focusing on nurturing and protecting the young is relatively new. Historical evidence shows that during the Middle Ages, children were viewed as miniature adults or property and were treated as such. By the age of 5 or 6, children were expected to occupy similar roles as adults in the society. Modern conceptions of the distinctiveness of age did not exist. The juvenile correctional system did not exist, and punishment of minors did not differ from punishment of adults. During this time period, childhood was not seen as a prescribed period in human development. There was no different legal system or correctional system to deal with children who violated societies' laws.

Development of correctional institutions designed for children did not emerge until the 1600s. These steps were based in socially formulated rationales about the distinctiveness of age and the importance of status differentiations. The change in the social structure of societies as they evolved over time also changed age-connected statuses. As societies evolved, so did definition of age and adolescence.

Amsterdam House of Corrections

By 1595, the Amsterdam House of Corrections was created to deal exclusively with wayward youths. The hallmark philosophy of juvenile corrections was instituted in this first juvenile-only correctional institution. This philosophy advocated rehabilitation of minors over punishment. The idea was to try to rehabilitate minors who were delinquent in some manner, and not treat them as adults, because they were malleable and could become productive citizens. This philosophy still guides juvenile corrections today.

Sociology of juvenile corrections is centered on the structural, functional, and cultural aspect of any society. Changes in social organization due to economic, social, and political changes that accompanied the end of the Middle Ages dramatically impacted the definition of childhood and treatment of children. Economics is important in understanding the sociology of juvenile corrections. Political and economic arrangements in a society influence inequality in the society, and this is reflected in differential treatment in juvenile corrections. The rise of the Industrial Revolution contributed to the erosion of certain practices. Most poor children were the occupants of early correctional institutions. Poverty was treated as a crime, and poor children were seen as rogues and vagabonds and usually institutionalized or banished from communities.

House of Refuge, New York City

During the early 1800s, the notion of childhood continued to change, and even poor children were deemed to have qualities that could transform them into productive citizens. Within the United States, there was a movement to create correctional institutions specifically for minors. However, House of Refuge, established in New York City in 1825, focused on the activities of lower-class children. The reform was led by wealthy white men who were concerned with protecting their way of life and particular moral codes. They wanted to separate youths from the influence of adult criminals, but they also wanted their moral values and beliefs to dominate the society. Lower-class children were routinely confined to these institutions based on middle-class morality and not necessarily delinquent behaviors. Not unlike the makeup of the early correctional institutions, class plays a major role in contemporary juvenile corrections. There are continued differences in how poor youths are sanctioned compared to middle-class or more advantaged juveniles. The research shows that lower-class youths' overrepresentation in the juvenile justice system is a factor of institutionalized bias evident in the major social institutions in the society.

A delivery boy for a pharmacy in Houston, Texas, photographed by Lewis Hine in October 1913. He had recently been released after one year in a reform school for an unknown offense.

Females

The role of gender socialization is important because what happens in society affects juvenile corrections. The difference in the treatment of male and female juvenile offenders has always been evident in juvenile corrections. Historically, there has always been a differential societal response to female and male juvenile offending. There is a differential rate of offending, but patterns of admission to juvenile correctional facilities have always maintained a chivalrous slant toward women. Males are the majority of offenders, but certain female offenders were treated more harshly than male offenders based on the category of offense. Traditionally, female juvenile offenders have been given harsher sanctioning for moral or values behavior, such as status offending, compared to males engaging in similar behaviors. For example, historically, female status offenders were routinely institutionalized; this was not the case for male status offenders. This is a reflection of the social norms and societal beliefs that influence juvenile correctional policies.

Gender roles are reflected in juvenile corrections as societal expected behaviors for females and males are played out in juvenile sanctioning. Juvenile corrections throughout history have reflected the traditional patriarchal values of the society, highlighting a gender bias. Gender influences juvenile corrections decisions, with the juvenile justice system taking a paternalistic stance toward female delinquents. Exceptions exist, based on race. The literature is consistent that minority females have not been the recipient of this chivalrous treatment. The stereotypical notion of proper female behavior has not been extended to minority female juveniles. The evidence points to juvenile justice personnel adhering to "racialized gender expectations" in which minority girls are more likely to be treated harshly. For example, minority girls are more likely to be detained compared to white girls who are more likely to receive placement in a treatment facility.

Minority Juveniles

The etiology of juvenile corrections is interested in the role race plays in juvenile sanctioning. Minority juveniles at all stages of the juvenile justice process are placed at a disadvantage relative to whites because of court officials' subjective assessments. Minorities are subjected to greater and harsher social control. Starting with the slave trade, slave children were seen as more threatening and were dealt with as harshly as adults, long after the movement to recognize the importance of childhood and adolescence had become widespread throughout juvenile corrections and the society. Race effects are still prominent in juvenile corrections. Racial stereotypes that were evident during colonial times as they relate to slave children tend to still be evident in contemporary society.

The idea that minority juvenile offenders are more dangerous is evident in juvenile sanctioning options, such as deferring prosecution or referral to diversion programs. These options are more likely to be given to white juveniles than minority juveniles, taking all legal factors into consideration. Minority juveniles receive more severe sentences and minority juveniles are more likely to be institutionalized in the juvenile justice system. Juvenile court officers view minority juveniles as posing a threat to the middle-class standard. This racial stereotype has been consistent in juvenile corrections and has continued to influence sanctioning decisions.

Within the sociology of juvenile corrections, the values and beliefs of decision makers are impacted by the larger society, and this is reflected in perceptions about minority juveniles. According to the research, this seems to impact sanctioning. Disproportionate minority confinement is an issue that supports researchers' argument that minority juveniles are treated differently than whites. Minority juveniles detained in detention facilities, secure correctional facilities, jails, and lockups exceed their proportion in the population. At every stage in the juvenile justice process, minority juveniles are overrepresented. The subjectiveness of juvenile justice decision makers and the social construction of realities about minority group members are instrumental factors in the sociology of juvenile corrections.

Denise D. Nation
Winston-Salem State University

See Also: 1921 to 1940 Primary Documents; Gender and Criminal Law; Juvenile Corrections, Contemporary; Juvenile Corrections, History of; Juvenile Delinquency, History of; Juvenile Delinquency, Sociology of.

Further Readings

Barak, Gregg, Paul Leighton, and Jeanne Flavin. *Class, Race, Gender & Crime: The Social Realities of Justice in America*, 3rd ed. Lanham, MD: Rowman & Littlefield, 2010.

Elrod, Preston and R. Scott Ryder. *Juvenile Justice: A Social Historical, and Legal Perspective*, 2nd ed. Sudbury, MA: Jones & Bartlett, 2005.

Leiber, Michael and Kristin Mack. "The Individual and Joint Effects of Race, Gender, and Family Status on Juvenile Justice Decision-Making." *Journal of Research in Crime and Delinquency*, v.40/1 (2003).

Ruddell, Rick and Matthew Thomas. *Juvenile Corrections*. Richmond KY: Newgate Press, 2009.

Thompson, William and Jack Bynum, eds. *Juvenile Delinquency: A Sociological Approach*, 8th ed. London: Pearson, 2010.

Juvenile Courts, Contemporary

Juvenile courts were created and operate on the principle that juveniles are fundamentally and developmentally different from adults. Thus, different forms of intervention techniques are used in the treatment of juvenile offenders. However, various changes in the nature of family units, juvenile delinquency, and the problems that juveniles face today have led to a number of changes in the contemporary juvenile court system. Instead of a one-system-fits-all approach, many juvenile and family courts across the nation are taking a more specialized approach to addressing the needs of delinquent youth.

Juvenile courts vary with each jurisdiction in structure, format, and characteristics. Some juvenile courts focus on therapeutic practices that center on the juvenile, whereas other juvenile courts lean toward a more punitive approach toward juvenile delinquency. Jurisdictions with courts that take a more therapeutic stance on juvenile delinquency employ the use of specialty courts, whereas punitive-based jurisdictions have courts that lean more toward a more formalized version of the juvenile court. At the onset of the 21st century, juvenile courts across the nation were faced with the fallout from increased delinquent activity and violent crime from youthful offenders during the 1980s and 1990s. Public outcry for tougher sentencing, along with criticism of juvenile and family courts for inappropriate sanctions of the various types of crimes committed by juvenile offenders, prompted the creation of specialty courts to address the specific needs of juvenile offenders.

By 2002, juvenile courts across the United States saw 41 percent more delinquency cases than had been seen in 1985, and in 2005, juvenile courts in the United States processed 1.6 million delinquency cases. The types of cases processed through the juvenile court system were also undergoing a drastic change. Drug offense cases seen by the courts rose 179 percent since the 1990s, public order offense cases rose by 102 percent, and person offense crimes experienced drastic increases as well. As a result of changes in the characteristics of the juvenile offender and the cases processed by the courts, many contemporary juvenile courts began to use specialty courts to address the specialized needs of modern youthful offenders. These specialty courts include drug courts, gun courts, teen courts, and mental health courts.

Juvenile Drug Courts

Drug courts began as a response to the overwhelming number of drug-related offenses appearing as a result of the crack cocaine epidemic of the 1980s. The most prominent and publicized of the new form of juvenile courts is the juvenile drug court. Courts of this nature were developed using a similar format as the adult version of such courts, which first appeared in Miami, Florida, in 1989. The first juvenile drug court, which began as a response to alarming rates of drug and alcohol use among high school–age children, is believed to have appeared in the mid- to late 1990s. In 2006, there were 411 juvenile (up from 172 in 2000), 166 family, and 14 family and juvenile drug courts in the United States. Juvenile drug courts differ across jurisdiction, but they have similar goals and objectives. These courts seek to provide immediate intervention and treatment to juveniles with crimes stemming from substance abuse. Additional objectives of these courts include improving the lives of juvenile substance abusers, addressing the source of the drug problem, providing these youthful offenders with coping skills while strengthening families, and promoting accountability on behalf of the juvenile and his or her care providers.

The general process of the contemporary juvenile drug court begins with the drug-related arrest of the juvenile. Following arrest, eligible juveniles are referred to the drug court and subsequently agree to participate in the prescribed program. Juveniles who refuse the treatment or don't follow the court's rules are transferred to regular juvenile court. Participants in the program attend regularly scheduled court-appointed treatment, drug tests, and court dates. In this type of court, judge and staff serve as a team and support group that is specifically designed to meet the needs of youthful offenders and substance abusers. These programs are not for all juvenile offenders; youth entering these programs must meet eligibility requirements specific to each court. For most of these types of courts, the juvenile must be a first-time offender whose crime is not overly violent in nature. For early juvenile drug offenders, the juvenile drug court serves as a replacement to the normal juvenile and family court that deals with delinquent youth.

Juvenile Gun Courts

A second type of specialty court is the juvenile gun court. Although not as well publicized or widespread as the juvenile drug court, juvenile gun courts serve a similar need and purpose. The juvenile gun court assists regular courts as a form of intervention for youthful offenders who commit gun offenses that do not result in serious injury to others. Unlike the juvenile drug court, which is an alternative to traditional juvenile courts, some juvenile gun courts are a supplement to juvenile court proceedings. As of 2007, there were six juvenile gun court programs in the United States. Although there are only a few of these programs in place, the Office of Juvenile Justice and Delinquency Prevention is taking steps to develop more of these programs. Though primarily for gun-related offenses, juveniles charged with other weapons-related offenses and young offenders involved with gangs, drug dealers, or whose codefendant was armed are also referred to these courts. The general process for these courts is as follows: The juvenile is (1) arrested, (2) sent through court intake and subsequently detained, (3) a youth who goes to trial and does not contest the charge is sent to an intensive boot camp to improve social skills, academics, and physical ability, (4) parents/guardians are required to attend workshops while the juvenile is in boot camp, and (5) after release from boot camp, the juvenile is placed on close supervision for a specified amount of time.

Juvenile Mental Health Courts

Due to an increasing number of juveniles entering the court system with some diagnosable mental illness, programs that specialize in the needs of these offenders were initiated during the early part of the 2000s. As of 2006, there were a total of 11 juvenile mental health courts scattered throughout the United States, with at least 20 more planned or considered in jurisdictions across the nation. The Court for the Individualized Treatment of Adolescents (CITA), the first of these courts, was implemented in Santa Clara County, California, and it has served as the model for subsequent juvenile mental health courts. Juvenile mental health courts require voluntary participation. Some jurisdictions require the defendant to plead guilty, yet others simply require that the defendant participate in the program and no criminal charges are placed against the offender. Juvenile mental health courts utilize teams of mental health and criminal justice professionals to coordinate and supervise the youth who enter the programs. These teams consist of the prosecution, defense, probation officers, and mental health coordinators.

Teen Courts

Teen courts have been in place the longest of all juvenile specialty courts, and they comprise the largest number of juvenile specialty courts throughout the United States. As of 2002, 900 teen court programs were in operation around the United States. These courts were developed to address minor delinquency issues that were clogging up and slowing down the juvenile justice system. Juveniles who agree to this form of justice are subject to an informal sanction placed on them by a judge or a panel of their peers.

Characteristics of Regular Juvenile Court

While some courts have turned to the therapeutic approach of the specialty courts, many others have answered public outcries to treat juvenile offenders more like their adult counterparts.

Thus, many juvenile courts have undergone a more formalized process, which is a direct result of legislation brought about in previous decades. Formal processing in juvenile courts involves handling a case in a way that leads to a formal court hearing with a formal outcome. Informal processing includes alternative forms of justice such as teen courts. At present, juvenile and family courts are processing more cases formally than informally. As a result of this formalization process, many juvenile court proceedings have offenders who are represented by counsel, and records of the juvenile court proceedings and detailed rights of the youth and parents are made and maintained. Additionally, many contemporary juvenile courts use the same or similar procedural rules as adult criminal courts.

Robin D. Jackson
Sam Houston State University

See Also: Children's Rights; Juvenile Corrections, Contemporary; Juvenile Corrections, History of; Juvenile Courts, History of; Juvenile Justice, History of; Juvenile Offenders in Adult Courts.

Further Readings
Cocozza, Joseph J. and Jennie L. Shufelt. *Juvenile Mental Health Courts: An Emerging Strategy (Research and Program Brief)*. Delmar, NY: National Center for Mental Health and Juvenile Justice, 2006.
Elrod, Preston and Scott R. Ryder. *Juvenile Justice: A Social, Historical and Legal Perspective*. Salbury, MA: Jones & Bartlett, 2011.
McShane, Marilyn D. and Frank P. Williams, III, ed. *Youth Violence and Delinquency: Monsters and Myths*. Westport, CT: Praeger, 2007.
Whiteacre, Kevin. *Drug Court Justice: Experiences in a Juvenile Drug Court*. New York: Peter Lang, 2008.

Juvenile Courts, History of

Juvenile courts were created as innovative legal institutions aimed at protecting young offenders rather than punishing them. They were local courts, typically organized at the county level and authorized by state legislation that provided juveniles with hearings and detention facilities separate from those for adults. The first was established in Cook County (Chicago), Illinois, in 1899. Juvenile courts typically have had jurisdiction over young people ages 17 and under (although some courts have placed the maximum age at 16 or 15). They handled young offenders accused not only of delinquency—actions that would have been considered criminal for adults—but also offenses defined by the status of being a juvenile, such as truancy or incorrigibility. In some cases, juvenile courts also handled dependency or issues involving financial need or lack of parental support.

Parens Patriae
Juvenile courts originated from a goal—characteristic of late-19th- and early-20th-century social reform movements—of safeguarding young people and thereby improving society. Prior to the creation of juvenile courts, most young people who were arrested were kept in jails together with adults, tried in criminal courts, and potentially subject to criminal penalties. By the 1890s, however, reformers increasingly viewed juveniles as different from adults. They criticized existing courts for mixing young offenders with older ones who could both cause younger ones harm and train them to be more adept at crime. As an alternative, turn-of-the-century reformers advocated the creation of separate courts for juveniles. A basic goal of juvenile courts was diversion, removing young offenders from criminal courts, jails, and prisons. Reformers also saw juvenile courts as a means of resolving the fundamental sources of delinquency.

A coalition of Chicago reformers—including the Chicago Women's Club, attorneys from the Chicago Bar Association, and activists from the Hull House social settlement—sponsored the Illinois Juvenile Court Act in the state legislature beginning in 1898. They interpreted juvenile delinquency as rooted in the social environment. They particularly blamed poverty and family disruption for delinquency, and they believed that the juvenile court would be able to address these problems by helping individual young people. In thinking this, they exhibited characteristic early-20th-century beliefs in the ability of expert social scientific knowledge to assess the source of problems and in the ability of government to provide solutions. The passage of the Illinois Juvenile Court Act in 1899 created the world's first official juvenile court in Cook County (Chicago). As the concept spread, almost every state established some sort of juvenile court for its major cities by 1920.

Juvenile courts were originally designed as protective institutions. They relied on the legal doctrine of *parens patriae*, the concept that the state had the right to intervene in a family if a child's welfare was at risk. Juvenile courts differed from criminal courts both in their broad reach over behaviors that were not necessarily criminal and in their diagnostic and preventive goals. They sought to combine punishment with treatment, seeing dispositions as operating in the best interest of the child. In the early years of juvenile courts, many advocates saw judicial procedure itself as a way to rehabilitate young offenders.

Leading judges of the early 1900s such as Richard Tuthill in Chicago and Benjamin Lindsey in Denver sought to utilize a friendly manner and informal procedure to earn boys' trust and to correct them personally. The courts also relied on probationary supervision—both of young offenders and of their families—to address the perceived social and environmental sources of misbehavior.

Trying to implement these ideals required juvenile courts to gradually accumulate bureaucratic and institutional mechanisms. At first private efforts, mainly by women's groups, supplemented juvenile courts. For example, an offshoot of the Chicago Woman's Club, the Juvenile Court Committee, initially provided 15 probation officers, ran a detention home, and transported youths to the court. Gradually, these functions shifted from private efforts to public responsibilities. Only several years after the establishment of the juvenile court did the Illinois General Assembly

A judge and lawyers surround a small boy in an early U.S. juvenile court around 1902. The world's first official juvenile court began in Cook County (Chicago) after passage of the Illinois Juvenile Court Act in 1899. The concept spread throughout the country, and almost every state had established some sort of juvenile court in major cities by 1920.

authorize Cook County to fund a juvenile detention facility. Similarly, a 1905 amendment to the Illinois juvenile court law allowed the court to hire professional probation officers, supplementing and eventually replacing the volunteers and police officers who had done the job until then. In addition, juvenile courts added systems for filtering the many complaints they received and established closed hearings for juveniles to protect them from public scrutiny.

Early juvenile courts handled both dependency cases and delinquency cases. Dependency cases involved children of all ages, both boys and girls. In these cases, courts administered social welfare services, either providing guidance for families or sometimes removing children from homes to care for them in private facilities or public institutions. The delinquency cases focused largely on teenage boys, often of immigrant backgrounds, accused mainly of minor crimes or status offenses. Again, Chicago is a typical example. Between 1899 and 1909, approximately 80 percent of the Cook County Juvenile Court's delinquency cases involved boys. Of these, theft comprised roughly half of the offenses, while status offenses such as incorrigibility and disorderly conduct made up most of the rest. In a few juvenile cases involving serious criminal offenses, the Cook County Juvenile Court allowed prosecutors to pursue cases in the criminal courts.

In contrast to boys' cases, large majorities of early-20th-century delinquency cases involving girls focused on immorality and sexuality. Girls were accused of behaviors ranging from staying out late to being found in houses of prostitution. Juvenile courts took an interest in these cases even when they did not involve actual criminal violations because court officials—particularly female reformers—envisioned juvenile courts as a means to help protect girls and young women from the temptations and hazards of urban life.

Probation and Reform
Early 20th-century juvenile courts preferred to resolve cases—at least those involving white male offenders—by placing youths found delinquent on probation. In cities that historians have studied such as Chicago, Los Angeles, Memphis, and Milwaukee, courts typically used probation as much to get at the perceived causes of delinquency as to address particular offenses. They placed a relatively small minority of white male offenders in juvenile correctional institutions. Early-20th-century juvenile courts, however, had fewer options in dealing with African American youth. Because private homes and facilities often refused to accept African Americans, juvenile courts placed disproportionate numbers of African American delinquents in state-run reform schools. Juvenile courts were also more likely to institutionalize girls than boys in order to provide what they saw as appropriate supervision. According to one study, nearly half the girls who appeared before the Los Angeles Juvenile Court on delinquency charges in 1920 were removed from their homes.

Juvenile courts struggled almost from the beginning to balance their idealistic goals with the practical realities of reforming troubled youth. In the 1910s and 1920s, a handful of cities established court-based psychiatric clinics aimed at uncovering the root causes of delinquency—psychological as well as social—and addressing them through individual therapies. The emergence of these clinics highlighted an emerging sense among child welfare advocates that juvenile courts alone were not sufficient to solve the problem of delinquency. In the 1920s, a series of reports and conferences criticized juvenile courts for having high rates of recidivism, maintaining detention facilities that resembled jails, struggling to establish proper jurisdiction for youths accused of the worst offenses, and failing to extend beyond big cities. During the Great Depression of the 1930s, juvenile courts also experienced financial cuts that forced staff reductions and, at least in the case of the Cook County Juvenile Court, increased pressure to make hiring and promotion decisions on the basis of political patronage. In the 1940s, World War II helped prompt a perceived increase in juvenile delinquency that continued into the 1950s. In this context, juvenile court systems grew larger and, in the eyes of their critics, more bureaucratic.

Due Process Rights of Juveniles
In a series of cases in the 1960s, the U.S. Supreme Court constrained the informality of juvenile court procedures and expanded the due process rights of young offenders. The Supreme Court applied a new premise that when cases could lead to institutionalization, all suspects deserved

some constitutional protections. In *Kent v. United States* (1966), the Supreme Court—while aware of the special protective functions of juvenile courts—found the informal practices in juvenile court to be deficient in terms of legal procedure. The Supreme Court's specific decision in the *Kent* case found that suspects were entitled to a waiver hearing before being transferred from juvenile to criminal court, and that in these hearings juveniles were entitled to an attorney and formal rules of due process. The Supreme Court went much further in the case *In re Gault* (1967), asserting that juvenile courts neither offered appropriate treatment for young offenders nor provided adequate due process protections. As a result, the Supreme Court found that, in hearings that could lead to institutionalization, juveniles had the right to notice of the hearing, access to legal counsel, the ability to confront witnesses, and protection against self-incrimination. The *Gault* decision largely rejected the premise derived from *parens patrie* that, because juvenile courts had diagnostic and preventive functions, they were not obligated to follow the rules of due process. Later decisions, however, still distinguished juvenile courts from criminal courts, maintaining a lower standard of proof in status-offense cases and not requiring jury trials.

The outcome of the judicial revolution in juvenile courts was mixed. Critics contend that these reforms delivered neither the protections intended by the juvenile court model nor the due process rights appropriate for a criminal court. Studies showed that many juvenile courts complied poorly with the *Gault* decision's procedural safeguards. Many juvenile courts continued to function with the overt goal of helping young people; as a result, hearings routinely found young people delinquent and focused mainly on what sort of treatment should be provided. The procedural changes in juvenile courts also had little effect on the trend toward disproportionate confinement of minorities in juvenile institutions.

Juveniles in Criminal Courts

Since the 1970s, as the public became increasingly concerned about serious crimes committed by juveniles, states have shifted their laws to facilitate transfer of young offenders into criminal courts. One common method has been automatic trans-

Judge Mary Bartelme, shown here around 1913, was the first woman judge of the Circuit Court of Cook County (Chicago) and the Cook County Public Guardian. While working to reform the juvenile justice system, she also founded group homes for girls.

fer or direct waiver, in which certain categories of offenses by juveniles were handled in criminal courts. In 1978, the state of New York passed one of the first automatic transfer laws following a highly publicized double homicide by 15-year-old Willie Bosket. In 1981, Florida became one of the first states to explicitly give prosecutors the option to file cases against juveniles directly in criminal courts. Other states passed blended sentencing laws, allowing courts to impose juvenile and adult sanctions simultaneously. This trend toward pursuing juvenile cases in adult criminal courts accelerated following a sharp increase in youth violence in the late 1980s and early 1990s. At least 47 states changed their juvenile transfer laws between 1990 and 1999, seeking to impose greater criminal sanctions on juvenile offenders. In many instances, states replaced the earlier stated premise of acting in the best interest of the child with a more balanced model aimed at also protecting society and victims. Although only a small percent of the total number of possible juvenile court cases were transferred to criminal court, this shift nonetheless led to the number of juveniles in adult prisons roughly doubling in the 1990s.

David B. Wolcott
Independent Scholar

See Also: 1921 to 1940 Primary Documents; Children's Rights; Juvenile Courts, Contemporary; Juvenile Justice, History of; Juvenile Offenders in Adult Courts; Supreme Court, U.S.

Further Readings
Bernard, Thomas J. *The Cycle of Juvenile Justice*. New York: Oxford University Press, 1992.
Breckinridge, Sophonisba and Edith Abbott. *The Delinquent Child and the Home* New York: Arno Press, [1912] 1970.
Getis, Victoria. *The Juvenile Court and the Progressives*. Urbana: University of Illinois Press, 2000.
Manfredi, Christopher P. *The Supreme Court and Juvenile Justice*. Lawrence: University Press of Kansas, 1998.
Tanenhaus, David S. *Juvenile Justice in the Making*. Oxford: Oxford University Press, 2004.

Juvenile Delinquency, History of

Juvenile delinquency refers to violations of criminal laws or statute violations committed by youth, usually less than 18 years of age. Unlike adult offenders, in most states adjudicated youth offenders are not sentenced for specific crimes per se but rather given dispositions reflective of their delinquent status that may include diversion, restitution, community service, probation, or even incarceration.

To speak of juvenile "delinquency" in any strict sense prior to this is anachronistic, as with few exceptions young offenders were treated the same as adult offenders, including the use of severe and even capital punishments. For centuries prior, in both the United States as well as Europe, the "age of culpability" had been as young as 8, which reflected the reality of early adulthood in agrarian and early industrial societies where youth of this age were regularly employed in adult labor and expected to adhere to adult laws. In his dissent of *In re Gault* (387 U.S. 1 [1967]: 1471) for example, Justice Potter Stewart noted that in the 19th century,

> ... there were no juvenile proceedings, and a child was tried in a conventional criminal court with all the trappings of a conventional criminal trial. So it was that a 12-year-old boy named James Guild was tried in New Jersey for [murder]. A jury found him guilty ... and he was sentenced to death by hanging. The sentence was executed. It was all very constitutional.

One exception in the treatment of younger offenders was the establishment of "houses of refuge," beginning in 1825, for criminal and wayward children. The purpose of these houses was to separate younger offenders from the influence and predation of older criminals in adult prisons. However, these were often nothing more than workhouses, and the abhorrent conditions of many of these facilities were part of the reform movement that began in the late 19th century to establish a separate system of justice for youth offenders.

Aside from the conditions of refuge houses, there were several factors that led to the reform of juvenile justice in the United States. The industrial revolution and growing immigration in the 19th century had led to the common use of forced child labor in factories, in some cases for youth as young as 4 years old. At the same time, however, social attitudes toward children were slowly changing. Increasingly, children were seen as more malleable and easily influenced than adults, and less capable of rational decision making. Theories of crime were also shifting toward explanations that viewed such behavior as a result of both heredity and social environment. Taken together, these factors (harsh refuge houses, child labor, and changing social attitudes toward youth) were instrumental in what Anthony Platt has called the establishment of the "child savers" movement, a confluence of liberal and religious reformers who sought both to mitigate the social effects of delinquency as well as to establish a separate system of justice focused on the rehabilitation of young offenders.

The first juvenile court in the United States was established in Cook County, Illinois, in 1899, under the common law doctrine of *parens patriae* to invoke states' rights and duties to intervene in the lives of children who were neglected, abandoned, or in need of special care. Juvenile courts in the early 20th century were less formal than adult criminal courts and guided not by the premise of determining guilt but rather by the overriding goal of meeting "the best interests of the child." By 1925, all but two states had established juvenile courts, and compared to adult criminal courts, they differed in several respects. Primarily, juvenile court judges were given wide latitude in assessing the "best interests of the child," including decisions on placement, parental supervision, and rehabilitation. Also, judicial decisions often reflected a heightened role of psychologists and social workers in recommending dispositions. Finally, as juvenile courts were not part of the criminal court system, and in many ways drew their auspices from civil jurisprudence, due process was not afforded to youth offenders.

To the degree that each state's juvenile court system varied, the basic structure and administration of juvenile justice did not change markedly between the 1920s and 1960s. Concerns over juvenile crime rose and fell, sometimes related to real increases in youth crime and other times less so, but it was arguably not until the 1940s that the "problem of youth crime" became framed as a distinct one within American culture. During World War II, while crime rates generally fell due to the number of young men at war and the relatively high employment rate, in 1941, delinquency rates began to rise in relation to massive population shifts, less parental supervision, and decreasing community and social resources. In response to the growing problem of youth crime, the U.S. Department of Labor Children's Bureau issued a report in 1943 that detailed community responses to delinquency.

Similar reports and commissions followed throughout the 1940s. However, the 1950s saw a heightened shift away from concerns over delinquency as a result of wartime conditions or the effects thereof, and toward the emergence of a distinctive youth culture and the perceived influence of mass communication. Rock and roll and comic books, in particular, were targeted for their ability to "seduce the innocent." In 1953, the Senate Subcommittee on Juvenile Delinquency, sometimes referred to as the "comic book hearings," developed into what many sociologists have called a "moral panic" about the content of such works and their purported influence on youth. Yet while juvenile delinquency was seen as an increasing social problem in the 1950s and early 1960s, the overall administration of juvenile justice did not change markedly during this time. The Standard Family Court Act in 1959 functioned in part to standardize the informality of states' juvenile court proceedings.

Rather, the single biggest change to juvenile delinquency came not from policy makers but from the Supreme Court case *In re Gault* in 1967. The ruling in this case afforded youth offenders

This 12-year-old boy photographed in St. Louis, Missouri, in May 1910, had two brothers who were already in reform school. He had begun shoplifting and staying out late himself.

The New York City Housing Authority, under Mayor Fiorello La Guardia, commissioned this poster in 1936 that suggested that new public housing could cure juvenile delinquency. By the 1940s, delinquency was seen as a growing problem nationwide.

certain aspects of due process, including the right to confront witnesses, the right against self-incrimination, and the right to counsel. The effect of this ruling was the beginning of the formalization of juvenile court proceedings in the United States, and later cases such as *In re Winship* (1970), which elevated proof of delinquency to "beyond a reasonable doubt," and *Breed v. Jones* (1975), which found that transfer to the criminal court after adjudication constituted double jeopardy, only served to further this formalization.

These Supreme Court decisions were premised in part on the long history of arbitrariness in juvenile court dispositions throughout the United States. However, combined with changing public and political views on crime and delinquency that had begun to question the effectiveness of rehabilitation for adults and young people alike, throughout the 1970s and 1980s, juvenile courts increasingly resembled adult criminal courts in many respects. Such changes were more than a reflection of *In re Gault*. Beginning in the early 1960s, America had begun a long and precipitous rise in crime that lasted until the early 1990s. Much of the blame for this rise in crime was placed squarely on the shoulders of youth: in the rise of social and countercultural movements in the 1960s and early 1970s, in the growing crack epidemic and proliferation of street gangs in the 1980s, and in the rise of the so-called youth superpredators of the 1990s. The effect of these changes resulted in a gradual but ultimately massive shift in legislative responses to delinquency. In 1977, for example, Washington State adopted the use of determinate sentencing for all youth offenders, a move intended to both decrease arbitrary dispositions as well as to hold youth accountable for specific crimes. In response to Willie Bosket, a 15-year-old who killed two people in 1978 and was sentenced to a maximum of five years in a youth facility, New York State changed its laws so that youth as young as 13 could be tried as adults for serious offenses.

Throughout the latter 1980s and early 1990s, in response to growing youth crime rates, state legislatures moved in the direction of harsher punishments. Between 1983 and 1995, the rate of incarceration for youth offenders grew by 25 percent. During this same time, the rate of youth transferred to adult criminal courts doubled in the United States. Many states also moved to expand sentencing discretion for judges and sentencing recommendations for prosecutors and reduced or eliminated confidentiality regarding juvenile offenses and dispositions. In the early 1990s, the Office of Juvenile Justice and Delinquency Prevention predicted a continued increase in youth crime, and youth crime dominated both headlines and political election campaigns at local, state, and federal levels.

Beginning in 1995, however, youth crime began one of its longest and most protracted declines in U.S. history. This decline continued until 2006, rose slightly, and then decreased again in 2008. Explanations for this decrease have been myriad, including the aging of the population, decrease in crack-cocaine markets, decreases in poverty, and increases in the number of police officers and changes in policing strategies, and increases in punitive responses to serious youth crime. The result of this decline has been mixed in terms of social responses to youth crime. For example, California, which had one of the highest rates of incarcerated youth by the late 1990s, has more recently seen a massive reduction in the number of youth sent to residential facilities. Beginning in the late 1990s as well, the number of youth transferred to adult criminal courts in the United States has rapidly declined. On the other hand, relative to the falling rates of serious youth crime in the latter 1990s and early 2000s, the United States saw an increase in the rates of incarcerated youth.

In this regard, the punitive shift beginning in the late 1970s has arguably begun to swing, however slightly, back toward an emphasis on rehabilitation. Approaches such as restorative justice, which seek to discourage the use of incarceration when possible in lieu of holding youth offenders "accountable" by means of repairing harms caused to victims, have also grown in popularity. However, it is equally clear that this shift has not been equal for all youth. Black youth especially remain highly overrepresented in all facets of the juvenile justice system, particularly in rates of incarceration. Thus, while it may be less punitive today for some delinquents than a decade ago, the juvenile justice system faces the problem of becoming a two-tiered system of justice where the delivery of rehabilitative programs and second chances are routine for some youth populations, but the use of incarceration and largely punitive measures remain routine for others.

William R. Wood
University of Auckland

See Also: 1921 to 1940 Primary Documents; African Americans; California; Children's Rights; Due Process; Gangs, History of; Juvenile Corrections, Contemporary; Juvenile Corrections, History of; Juvenile Courts, Contemporary; Juvenile Courts, History of; Juvenile Justice, History of; Juvenile Offenders in Adult Courts; New York; Rehabilitation.

Further Readings
Field, B. *Bad Kids: Race and the Transformation of the Juvenile Court*. New York: Oxford University Press, 1999.
Gilbert, J. *A Cycle of Outrage: America's Reaction to the Juvenile Delinquent in the 1950s*. New York: Oxford University Press, 1986.
In re Gault, 387 U.S. 1 (1967).
Platt, A. M. *The Child Savers: The Invention of Delinquency*. Chicago: University of Chicago Press, 1977.

Juvenile Delinquency, Sociology of

Juvenile delinquency is defined as criminal and/or deviant behavior that is committed by minors. This includes criminal offending that is prohibited for anyone to engage in as well as status offending, which consists of various acts prohibited only for those under the legal age of adulthood (e.g., smoking cigarettes, drinking alcohol, and running away), usually age 18, that otherwise would be legal if committed by an adult. Any child or adolescent who engages in such behavior is referred to as a "juvenile delinquent." Various theories have been proposed to explain such offending in an effort to identify, target, reduce, and even prevent its occurrence in society. The study of juvenile delinquency is important because the problems perpetrators face and the damage suffered by its victims raise a growing and serious concern. A significant portion of youth face challenges in the home, school, and neighborhood, which place youth at risk for delinquent behavior.

Social Construction of Juvenile Delinquency
The concept of childhood as it is known today has not always existed. Historically, children were expected to take on adult roles at an early age. They were also treated harshly by both adults and the law. Over the years, the treatment of youth shifted as society became more sensitive to their special needs. Given that youth are still developing cognitively and socially, they have officially been recognized as a distinct group and thought of as less culpable in understanding the consequences of their actions. They have also been seen as malleable and able to change their ways. As a result, a new legal definition of childhood has emerged, and new laws and courts have been created for wayward children under the concept of *parens patriae*, which suggests that the state should act

in the best interest of children in order to guide and rehabilitate them into productive citizens.

In modern days, delinquent juvenile behavior tends to be sanctioned less heavily than adult crime because of the underlying notions that changed the view on what constitutes childhood. In some rare but extreme cases, however, juvenile delinquents can be treated as adults by being waived to adult courts. Nonetheless, the socially defined position of youth today is characterized by certain expectations and duties. Youth are subject to copious rules and regulations across a variety of institutions, but a general norm is that of conforming to the values set forth by adults in mainstream society. However, adolescence is a stressful and tumultuous period in life that often places individuals at conflict with this ideal. Numerous biological and psychological changes are occurring, and individuals are trying to establish an autonomous sense of identity while simultaneously fitting in among their peers. Consequently, risky and adult-like behaviors are often partaken in; first-time alcohol use, drug experimentation, sexual activity, and curfew violations are familiar examples of delinquency.

Nature and the Extent of Juvenile Delinquency
Three primary methods have been used to measure the nature and extent of juvenile delinquency: official data, self-reports, and victimization surveys. Official data includes data that comes to the attention of authorities (e.g., police arrests, court records, and juvenile corrections data). One of the most widely used sources of official data is that of the Uniform Crime Reports (UCR). Each year, the Federal Bureau of Investigation (FBI) compiles information on crime gathered by police departments across the United States in the UCR, which includes information about the number of offenders arrested for a particular crime along with their age, sex, and race. However, this source underestimates the amount of crime, given that not all crime is reported to police and many crimes are not cleared or solved by arrest, namely, for minor forms of delinquency and "victimless" crimes. Nonetheless, it still reveals that over two million juvenile arrests occur each year, with some offenders being arrested on more than one occasion.

Given that the UCR only includes crimes reported to police, a lot of crime is not captured. Therefore, other methods have been use to get at the "dark figure" of crime. Self-reports are common in the study of juvenile delinquency. This technique asks individuals if they have committed certain crimes or engaged in certain behaviors. The end result is a more accurate estimate of the extent of juvenile offending, especially since self-reports often include minor behaviors that may otherwise be overlooked. Self-reports have also been reliable in eliciting information about unlawful activity, and reports have been validated via comparison criteria (e.g., arrest records, drug tests, and school records), to determine whether individuals are being honest in their reports. Numerous self-report sources exist, and in general, they have found that the extent of juvenile delinquency is much greater than what appears in official sources of data. The vast majority of youth have engaged in some form of delinquency, not only in their lifetime, but also in the past year. The National Youth Survey (NYS) is an example of a common self-report survey. It examines status offenses, minor crimes, and serious crimes.

One more popular source is that of victimization surveys. Victimization surveys, like the National Crime Victimization Survey (NCVS), ask individuals to report on their experiences of crime as victims. Like self-reports, victimization surveys are used to supplement what is known about crime since it is not always reported to police. If individuals report having been a victim of a particular crime, they are typically asked further questions about it (e.g., relationship to the perpetrator, time of day, and other details of the incident). Data gathered using this method have shown that the rates of juvenile delinquency are drastically higher than found in official records. Many youth (as well as adults) have fallen victim to crime.

Further, data from these three sources have yielded important information regarding the characteristics of offenders and the nature of their crimes. Specifically, they have found age, sex, and race to be related to crime. Age is inversely related to crime so that most juvenile offenders will "age out" of crime as they become adults; only a small portion of these individuals will persist. The earlier the age is for the onset of crime, the more likely one is to continue on a trajectory of offending. However, offending is most common for those between the ages of 16 and 24. In regard to sex, males have been found to commit more delinquent acts than females, although the arrest rates for female delinquents have been rising at a faster rate than that of their counterparts. Racial minorities and those in the lower class have also been found to be disproportionately represented in arrest statistics, even though delinquency has been reported across all racial groups and social classes. Some experts contend that while all groups engage in delinquent acts, it is members of the lower class who are responsible for the majority of serious offenses, which is why arrest rates are elevated for these groups.

The sources of data have also shed light on the nature of juvenile behavior. Juveniles are inclined to co-offend (i.e., act delinquent with other juveniles). They tend to victimize someone of the same sex, someone with whom they are acquainted, and someone who is also a member of their own racial/ethnic group. Often times, youth who perpetrate crime against others have also been victimized by crime, in large part because of their risky lifestyle. Many other correlates exist.

Theories of Crime and Implications

Numerous theories have been proposed to understand the underlying causes of crime. Two general classifications of theories have been commonly used in the study of juvenile delinquency: social process and social structure. These theories focus on external forces that influence crime and they attempt to explain why some individuals are more likely to engage in crime than others. Social process theories argue that criminality is the function of individual socialization or interactions with people surrounding them. This branch is comprised of social learning, social control, and societal reaction theories.

Social learning theories contend that human behavior is learned by others, with the family serving as a primary influence. Here, behavior may be imitated when observed, engaged in when approved, or repeated when rewarded. Alternatively, social control theories maintain that everyone has the potential to be delinquent, so such behavior is not learned; rather, the bonds we have with others inhibit such behavior. Lastly, societal reaction, also known as labeling theory, alludes to stigma-producing encounters as the reasons for criminal behavior. Once a juvenile acquires a label, he or she will act in a manner consistent with it.

Social structure theories, on the other hand, argue that social and economic forces are responsible for crime. This perspective consists of strain, social disorganization, and cultural deviance theories. Strain theories hold that anger or frustration can lead to offending. There are several sources of strain: when individuals do not have the means to achieve their goals, when they fail to meet expectations, and when there is the presence of something negative or removal of something positive in one's life. One way to cope with strain is through engaging in delinquent acts. Next, social disorganization states that a breakdown of informal social control in a community produces criminogenic forces. Cultural deviance theories combine the concepts of strain and social disorganization. They state that groups form within society that have their own norms and values; when individuals are not adequately socialized and do not meet middle-class standards, they experience strain and may react by forming delinquent groups, particularly in lower-class neighborhoods. These theories can be applied to experiences that occur within the family, among peers, in school, and in the community at large.

Social Groupings and Institutions That Influence Youth

Families, peers, schools, and communities exert powerful influences on juveniles. Youth spend the majority of their time with these social groupings and institutions. Starting with the family, researchers have stated that family dynamics serve as a large determinant of behavior. Families that contain negative features like family violence (e.g., intimate partner violence, parent-to-child violence, and neglect), marital stress, and/or poor parenting practices are much more likely to produce delinquent offspring than families without such characteristics. Research has linked such factors to the inability to regulate one's own behavior, thereby contributing to delinquency, juvenile arrests, and even similar offending later in life. However, experts have suggested that households characterized by stability and parental efficacy (i.e., consistent, adequate, and appropriate parenting practices) are effective in producing children that refrain from such misbehavior. In addition, family structure has been linked to juvenile delinquency. Families that experience divorce, lose a parent due to death, or are otherwise single-headed households increase the risk for delinquency among youth residing in such homes, although this relationship is less robust than the factors previously mentioned. Reasons underlying delinquency in these homes can include less supervision and more financial strain. Lastly, family criminality has also been linked to juvenile offending. Parents who abuse drugs or alcohol and those who engage in other criminal acts are more likely to have children who do the same; this relationship has also been sustained for sibling criminality.

Peers groups also influence behavior. As children age, peers take on a central part of their lives. They function as a strong source of emotional support and sway their beliefs, attitudes, and conduct. Youth want to be positively regarded by others and accepted into groups. Social success among peers has been linked to conformity, whereas social ineptitude has not. Those who are bullied, rejected, or do not have close friends are often at risk for engaging in delinquent behaviors and experiencing a host of negative psychological consequences.

In some cases, they may engage in such acts in an attempt to fit in (i.e., "peer pressure") or commit egregious acts as a means of revenge (e.g., fighting or shooting). Conversely, youth with close ties to others are much less likely to engage in delinquency than those without these ties. Nonetheless, the presence of strong bonds does not negate delinquent behavior. Research has found that being attached to deviant youth heightens the risk of delinquency. Thus, the type of youth to whom a juvenile is attached must also be considered, along with the frequency, intensity, and duration of contact.

Peer interaction mostly occurs at school. Youth spend the majority of their time at school with peers as well as with teachers and coaches. Schools aim to foster learning and promote healthy development. They subject students to a variety of rules and regulations, including compulsory school attendance, codes of conduct, and daily schedule routines. Success within school has been identified as a crucial determinant of juvenile delinquency. Specifically, research has associated low academic achievement and failure to conform to rules with numerous forms of offending. Students who do poorly are more likely to get suspended, drop out of school, get involved in substance abuse, and engage in other delinquent acts. Along these lines, research has found low IQ to be predictive of delinquent behavior, potentially due to the strain associated with poor performance in school or the weakening of bonds to school, which causes the juvenile to act in a negative manner.

The communities that schools reside in have also been found to influence behavior. Disorganized communities characterized by transient populations, poverty, physical and social disorder, and other incivilities often contain higher rates of juvenile delinquency. Gangs, which are notorious for offending, flourish in schools and neighborhoods with these characteristics. Nevertheless, they have been increasingly found in more rural areas and have numerous consequences for children exposed to them. Therefore, safety has been made a priority in many institutions to quell such activity. Although research has examined the noted social groups and institutions independently, it is often the interaction between all of them that best predicts delinquency. Knowing about social groupings and institutions that influence behavior, along with theoretical explanations, helps to understand the problem and provide a holistic comprehension of the subject matter that can assist in reduction and prevention efforts. With continued research, the threats that underlie adolescent misbehavior can be better addressed.

Alison Marganski
Virginia Wesleyan College

See Also: 1921 to 1940 Primary Documents; 1941 to 1960 Primary Documents; Child Abuse, Contemporary; Child Abuse, Sociology of; Child Murderers, History of; Children, Abandoned; Children's Rights; Hereditary Crime; Juvenile Corrections, Contemporary; Juvenile Corrections, History of; Juvenile Corrections, Sociology of; Juvenile Courts, Contemporary; Juvenile Courts, History of; Juvenile Delinquency, History of; Juvenile Offenders, Prevention and Education; Juvenile Offenders in Adult Courts; School Shootings; Theories of Crime.

Further Readings

Agnew, Robert. *Juvenile Delinquency: Causes and Control*, 3rd ed. New York: Oxford University Press, 2008.

Anderson, Elijah. *Code of the Streets: Decency, Violence, and the Moral Life of the Inner City.* New York: W. W. Norton, 1999.

Becker, Howard. *Outsiders: Studies in the Sociology of Deviance.* New York: The Free Press, 1963.

Berger, Ronald. *Sociology of Juvenile Delinquency*, 2nd ed. Chicago: Nelson-Hall, 1996.

Institute of Medicine and National Research Council. *The Science of Adolescent Risk Taking: Workshop Report.* Washington, DC: National Academies Press, 2011.

Wolfgang, Marvin, Robert Figlio, and Thorsten Sellin. *Delinquency in a Birth Cohort.* Chicago: University of Chicago Press, 1972.

Juvenile Justice, History of

The history of juvenile justice in the United States can be divided into distinct periods, and each can be viewed in relation to a fundamental question: To what extent should the American system of justice view juveniles differently than adult offenders? That question has been resolutely and inexorably tied to how American society has throughout its history viewed "infants," "children," "youth," and "juveniles."

Child-Saving Movement

American justice has long been influenced by the English common law, which, until the colonies and states passed their own laws, was the law that governed the thirteen colonies. In his *Commentaries on the Laws of England*, Sir William Blackstone, a British jurist, judge, and politician, much admired and read in American judicial circles, wrote that "infants" were incapable of being classified as criminals because they lacked what Blackstone described as "a vicious will." Blackstone differentiated between "infants" and "adults" and their liability at law on the basis that children were too young to understand their actions and therefore lacked the necessary "intent" to commit unlawful acts. According to the social and legal conventions of Blackstone's time (he died in 1780), an infant was a person under 7 years of age, while a child over 14 was punished as an adult if convicted of a crime. Exceptions were made for children between the ages of 7 and 14 who were judged to understand the nature of their actions; these unfortunate youths could and were punished as adults, including for capital crimes permitting execution.

Ideological shifts in American culture's conception of youth and children, however, at the end of the 19th and early 20th century, saw distinct changes in how the American society and its justice system viewed the rowdy and sometimes unlawful acts of youth. In Manhattan, the Society for the Prevention of Juvenile Delinquency founded the New York House of Refuge for juvenile delinquents

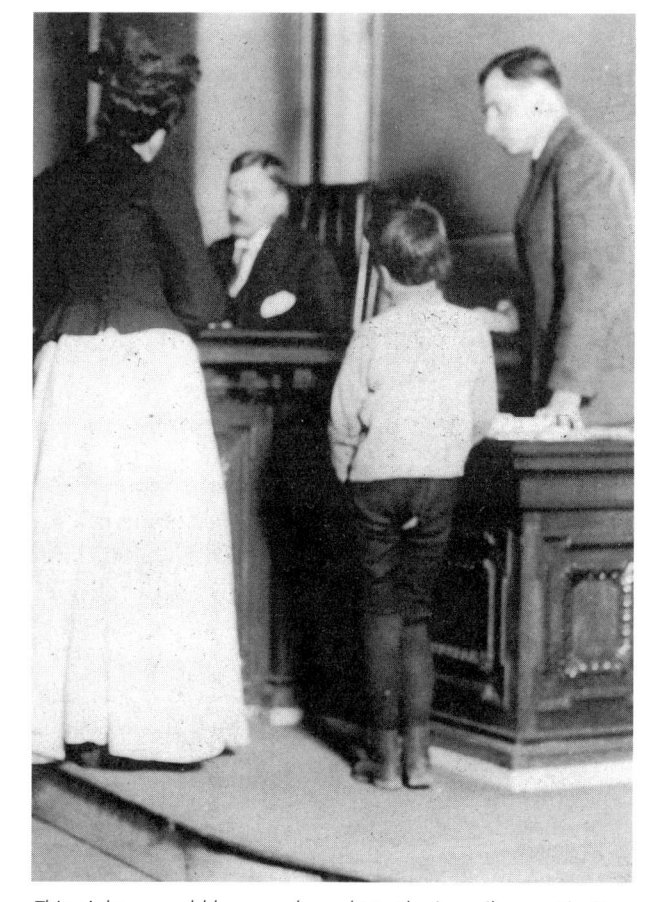

This eight-year-old boy was brought to the juvenile court in St. Louis, Missouri, on May 5, 1910, to answer charges of stealing a bicycle. Judges at that time were making an attempt to keep the courtroom imposing, but also a place of "care and solicitude."

in 1825. Chicago opened the doors of its Reform School in 1855. The country's first juvenile court was established in 1899 in Cook County, Illinois. Soon, other jurisdictions created their own juvenile justice systems where the focus was on understanding the root causes of offending juvenile behavior, rehabilitation, and helping juveniles avoid a life of crime. A social movement took root that did not separate youth from the economic and social conditions that produced them. The establishment of juvenile courts was a crucial component of the rise of the "child-saving movement" of the late 19th century and early 1900s. The activists and reformers who backed these institutions with their time and finances subscribed to a model that protected juveniles by separating them from adult offenders upon incarceration and viewed their offenses in context.

Young people who ran afoul of the law were considered victims of their circumstances and perceived to be delinquents whose offenses were the result of neglect and poverty; these unfortunate youths were guilty of acts contrary to the public interest, but certainly, they were not guilty at law of criminal acts. At this time in American history, focus on the "indiscretions of youth" was on the root causes of offending behavior, usually indicting parents for inefficiently rearing their children. Middle-class women who believed that the future of society was crucially bound to instilling "proper values" in youth were in large part responsible for promoting these views.

Doctrine of In Loco Parentis

At the same time, the doctrine of in loco parentis, an invention of 19th century patriarchy, governed the relationship between the state and youth, both in the justice system and in schools. The doctrine of in loco parentis was cultivated in various contexts, including the law of wills and estates as well as the law of tort. Derived from the Latin and meaning "in the place of the parent," in loco parentis, both in the context of juvenile courts and schools, served as the doctrinal basis and source of the state's legal authority for many decades and underscored the paternal approaches taken by the state institutions and policies. As Judge Julian Mack, an early judge of the juvenile court of Cook County, observed in 1909 of the juvenile court in the United States, the juvenile justice system was vital to ensuring that errant youth was treated in such a way as to ensure that he or she did not return to the justice system as an adult. Judge Mack's description of the workings of juvenile court from that time:

> The child who must be brought into court should, of course, be made to know that he is face to face with the power of the state, but he should at the same time, and more emphatically, be made to feel that he is the object of its care and solicitude. The ordinary trappings of the courtroom are out of place in such hearings. The judge on a bench, looking down upon the boy standing at the bar, can never evoke a proper sympathetic spirit. Seated at a desk, with the child at his side, where he can on occasion put his arm around his shoulder and draw the lad to him, the judge, while losing none of his judicial dignity, will gain immensely in the effectiveness of his work.

These kinds of reforms were also taking root in Canada. In 1908, the Juvenile Delinquents Act was passed by the federal parliament to deal with the offenses committed by youth, also emphasizing reform and rehabilitation, not punishment. Nonetheless, many commentators have pointed out that the "child saving" origins of early judicial responses to juvenile "delinquents" represented merely one of two contrary lines of thought respecting how best to deal with young people when they engage in criminal behavior that have percolated for decades. The ongoing tensions persist today: Should the emphasis in response favor the protection of youth from the cruelties of culture or the protection of society from the disruptions of antisocial youth? A survey of the historical development of the juvenile justice system reveals this ongoing tension and its persistence today.

While the doctrine of in loco parentis had dominated the development of American law and policy in the early 1900s, its prominence had nearly disappeared toward the last half of the 20th century. Youths were no longer conceived merely as juvenile delinquents not responsible for their own behaviors but as potential threats and possible sources of danger. They were focused targets of "tough on crime" efforts of legislators and politicians.

Juvenile Court System

By the 1960s, juvenile courts across the U.S. Supreme Court adjudicated almost all criminal cases involving young people under the age of 18. Young offenders were rarely transferred to the adult criminal justice system, and only when the juvenile court agreed to waive its jurisdiction. A 1967 decision by the Supreme Court, *In re Gault, 387 U.S. 1 (1967)*, made a significant impact on how juvenile cases were administered. The decision of the Supreme Court affirmed that juvenile courts had to respect the due process of law rights of juveniles guaranteed under the Fifth and Fourteenth Amendments to the U.S. Constitution. The ruling was the result of a consideration of Arizona's decision to place 15-year-old Gerald Francis Gault in detention for violating probation by making an obscene call to one of his neighbors.

The Arizona juvenile court ordered that Gault be confined in a state industrial school until he turned 21 or was "discharged by due process of law." The Supreme Court ruled that young offenders had a right to receive fair treatment under the law, including the right to receive notice of charges, the right to legal counsel, the right to confront and to cross-examine their accusers, and the right to the privilege against self-incrimination. When Gault had been apprehended, his parents had not been notified of the charges against their son. In a dissenting judgment, Justice Potter Stewart warned that the court's decision would "convert a juvenile proceeding into a criminal prosecution," preferring the historical purposes of the juvenile justice system, which had up until the *Gault* decision followed a looser model styled after civil proceedings. Justice Stewart presaged that by assuring youth were extended the same due process rights and guarantees in juvenile court as adults in adult criminal court, the majority might very well be transforming juvenile court into criminal courts.

In 1968, Congress passed the Juvenile Delinquency Prevention and Control Act intended to encourage states to develop community-level programs aimed at curtailing juvenile delinquency. In 1974, the Juvenile Justice and Delinquency Prevention Act replaced the 1968 legislation, underscoring the prevention of juvenile delinquency. To qualify for federal funding, states were obliged to maintain a separation between juvenile and adult offenders.

Threats to Society and Superpredators

However, the perception of appreciably rising crime rates among juvenile offenders in the 1980s and 1990s, and the perception that offences committed by youth were becoming increasingly violent, significantly impacted conceptions of juvenile justice. This shift in conception would influence the discussions of juvenile justice in the coming decades and refigure the "hunker down" mentality that would come to inform discussions of juvenile justice ever since. In public consciousness, rehabilitation ceased to be a priority associated with offending youth and the emphasis shifted to "get tough on crime" approaches in which young offenders were no longer perceived as juvenile delinquents free from responsibility for their own actions, but situated young offenders as potential threats and possible sources of danger to the rest of the society.

Discussions about juvenile justice have unfolded in a context of extreme violence. In the late 1990s, a highly publicized series of school shootings and other incidents of extreme violence committed by youths have given rise to a moral panic and a fear of offending youths. No longer portrayed as "juvenile delinquents," some researchers described the rise of the "superpredator" generation in the new millennium. Distinguished from previous generations by the Office of Juvenile Justice and Delinquency Prevention as a generation for whom brutal responses and violence were a way of life, the myth of the superpredator has taken root and will be difficult to turn aside. Recent research disputes these depictions and suggests that youth violence and delinquency was greatly exaggerated in the 1990s; however, the fear experienced at the time resulted in significant changes to the United States' approach to juvenile crime.

As the emphasis on extreme violence and the rise of the superpredator was based in large measure on fear and repeated images in popular culture of youth as perpetrators of ongoing extreme violence, it may be deflected by reference to data that indicate that in the 21st century, youth crime is on the decline and less punitive, and more contextualized measures are needed when it occurs.

Donn Short
Robson Hall Law School

See Also: 1921 to 1940 Primary Documents; Children, Abandoned; Children's Rights; Juvenile Corrections, History of; Juvenile Courts, History of; Juvenile Delinquency, History of; School Shootings.

Further Readings

Biscontini, Tracey Vasil, ed. *Youth Violence*. Detroit, MI: Greenhaven Press, 2007.

Doob, Anthony N. and Carla Cesaroni. *Responding to Youth Crime*. Toronto: University of Toronto Press, 2004.

Leverich, Jean, ed. *Issues on Trial: Juvenile Justice*. Detroit, MI: Greenhaven Press, 2009.

Mack, Julian. "The Juvenile Court." *Harvard Law Review*, v.23 (1909).

MacKay, A. Wayne and Lyle (Chip) Sutherland. *Teachers and the Law*. Toronto: Emond Montgomery Publications, 2006.

McShane, Marilyn D. and Frank P. Williams, eds. *Encyclopedia of Juvenile Justice*. Thousand Oaks, CA: Sage, 2003.

Platt, Anthony. "The Rise of the Child Saving Movement: A Study in Social Policy and Correctional Reform." *Annals of the American Academy of Political and Social Science*, v.21 (1969).

Scott, Elizabeth S. and Laurence Steinberg. *Rethinking Juvenile Justice*. Cambridge, MA: Harvard University Press, 2008.

Snyder, Howard N. and Melissa Stickmund. *Juvenile Offenders and Victims: 1999 National Report*. Pittsburgh, PA: National Center for Juvenile Justice, 1999.

Zimring, Franklin E. *American Youth Violence*. New York: Oxford University Press, 1998.

Juvenile Offenders, Prevention and Education

Juveniles committing criminal offenses at first received the same punishments as adult offenders, but in the late 1800s, courts and groups began to advocate separate considerations for children. Juvenile justice encouraged children's treatment and rehabilitation over incarceration with adults. In part, this attitude continues today, though its value gets questioned as violent crimes appear to increase and the public seeks more accountability and punishment. Multiple programs attempt to prevent youth from becoming delinquents and from becoming further part of the juvenile justice system.

Evolution of Juvenile Programs

Early examples of juvenile programs included reformatory schools, which brought structure, education, work, and even religious instruction to youth. The first reformatory school opened in New York in 1825, but by the late 1800s, the purpose of such schools was called into question because of suspected abuse, labor exploitation, and their general ineffectiveness. Training schools opened in the later 1800s as alternatives to the overcrowded reformatory schools, and these schools offered education and vocational training in rural areas. They, too, got called into question for their effectiveness. Both of these programs serve as precursors for today's juvenile detention facilities.

More recent programs that remove children from their homes include boot camps and wilderness camps. Boot camps run three to six months, and they use military-style training to shock juveniles into proper behavior, though with mixed results. Wilderness camps, such as Tucson-based VisionQuest or Minnesota-based Thistledew Camp, teach juveniles to survive in nature and teach them skills in teamwork, leadership, and confidence. Similarly, the Scared Straight programs attempt to frighten juvenile delinquents in behaving.

Community-based programs allow children to remain at home and attempt either to keep them from jail or to keep them from becoming delinquent. Since children spend a significant part of their lives in school, many programs work with schools. Some programs bring officers into schools to work with juvenile offenders. The Pennsylvania Commission on Crime and Delinquency started a program titled the School-Based Probation Services program, which brought full-time officers into Allentown schools in order to connect the institutions better and to confront drug-use problems. Other school-based programs work to prevent delinquency, prevent alcohol and drug use, and handle attitude and conduct problems, truancy, and dropping out.

Other example programs include the Resolving Conflict Creatively program, established in New York in 1985, and the Violence Prevention Program, established in 1986. One of the most popular school-based programs is DARE, or Drug Awareness Resistance Education. Started in Los Angeles, this program brings police officers into schools to talk about the dangers of drug use. The program uses a combination of techniques, including lectures, role-playing, visual aids, and even program graduation certificates. Starting in Phoenix and targeting primarily seventh-graders, the Gang Resistance Education and Training program focuses on reducing gang membership, and it works much the same way as DARE.

Juvenile Programs by Age and Gender

Other programs attempt to intervene with high-risk groups at various ages. Recognizing the variety of situations and problems in children's lives, these programs focus on multiple problems in multiple areas by integrating multiple agencies. Programs that focus on preschool youth address both children and their parents, particularly those in low-income, single-parent households. In the 1970s, the Perry Preschool Project pinpointed intellectual and social development in children ages 2–4 as being critical. As part of the program, children also received home visits from teachers. The Prenatal/Early Infancy Project worked with teenage mothers in the Appalachian area of New York. Similar programs included Yale Child Welfare Project and the Houston Parent-Child Development Center.

Other programs centered on children ages 6–12 in the classroom and on the playground by attempting to prevent certain behaviors. Example programs include the Fast Track Program for

Daren the Lion, official mascot of the DARE program, greets children at an elementary school on October 28, 2010. While the DARE program has been popular, critics say that it fails to address the real causes of juvenile delinquency. Programs such as family-school cooperation programs, victim-offender mediation, and social skills development programs appear to have had more success by addressing the problems of more types of juvenile offenders and covering a greater range of juvenile delinquency issues.

kindergarteners, the Seattle Social Development Project, and the Child Development Project. The Fast Track Program addressed both children and parents. Children learned academic and social skills, while parents gained lessons in parenting and building relationships. Using a combination of modeling, role-playing, and rewards, Second Step and PeaceBuilders teach antiviolence messages to middle-schoolers.

Programs for youth ages 13–17 address mentoring, dating violence, and gateway drug use. Big Brothers Big Sisters of America pairs each youth with a single mentor, and the two meet multiple times each month. JUMP, or the Juvenile Mentoring Program, also provides one-on-one mentoring between an adult and an at-risk youth. School-based program Safe Dates raises awareness about abuse and violence that might occur in teen relationships. The Midwestern Prevention Project (now Project STAR) attempts to keep seventh- and eighth-graders away from gateway drugs such as alcohol and marijuana.

Some programs recognize that girls and boys have different needs. Adolescent girls face greater risks of sexual abuse, sexual assault, pregnancy, and teen motherhood. Girls are more likely to run away to get away from violence at home, to steal for food or drugs, and to turn to prostitution. Children of the Night, which began in California in 1979, specifically helped young prostitutes through a phone hotline, a walk-in center, professional counseling, and outreach programs. Other girl-oriented programs include the Center for Young Women's Development, Friendly PEERsuasion; Preventing Adolescent Pregnancy, and Operation SMART, which attempts to build girls' interests in science, math, and technology.

Conclusion
The successes of juvenile programs vary, but research points to some clear failures and successes. For some, DARE fails in addressing the root problems of juvenile delinquency, while area projects, which focus on high-risk neighborhoods and geographical areas, offer recreational programs but also fail to address the deeper influences. Programs that attempt to frighten children into behaving, such as boot camps or Scared Straight, offer some possible short-term corrections but not long-term solutions. The programs that offer the most successes attempt to avoid incarceration, seek probation first, use community-based programs, and involve the parents or other family members in the process. Programs that address broader ranges of juvenile offenders and juvenile delinquency issues see more success as well, such as family-school cooperation programs, victim-offender mediation, and social skills development programs.

Heather McIntosh
Boston College

See Also: 1981 to 2000 Primary Documents; Crime Prevention; Juvenile Delinquency, History of; Juvenile Delinquency, Sociology of; Juvenile Justice, History of.

Further Readings
Chesney-Lind, Meda and Randall G. Sheldon. *Girls, Delinquency, and Juvenile Justice*, 3rd ed. Belmont, CA: Thomson Wadsworth, 2004.

Hoge, Robert D., Nancy G. Guerra, and Paul Boxer, eds. *Treating the Juvenile Offender*. New York: Guilford Press, 2008.

Howell, James C. *Preventing and Reducing Juvenile Delinquency: A Comprehensive Framework*. Thousand Oaks, CA: Sage, 2003.

Lawrence, Richard. *School Crime and Juvenile Justice*, 2nd ed. New York: Oxford University Press, 2007.

Penn, Everette B., Helen Taylor Greene, and Shaun L. Gabbidon, eds. *Race and Juvenile Justice*. Durham, NC: Carolina Academic Press, 2006.

Juvenile Offenders in Adult Courts

The modern basis behind trying juvenile offenders in adult court can be traced to the 1966 Supreme Court case *Kent v. United States*, which dictated the process to be followed in juvenile court by the judge to waive, transfer, or certify the matter to an adult criminal court. In other words, the charge(s) against the juvenile would be subject to criminal court procedures and sanctions should the juvenile judge decide in a judicial waiver hearing that the case was better suited for adult court.

Methods of Transfer

The judicial waiver hearing is a nonjury proceeding in which the juvenile judge essentially addresses the current charges, prior delinquent history, amenability to treatment (if the juvenile remains in the juvenile justice system), and public safety in determining whether the matter should remain in juvenile court or instead be tried in criminal court. The decision has important implications to the juvenile because adult criminal court processing subjects one to potentially harsher penalties and stigmatization. Some states have statutes providing that a juvenile can be waived to adult court at any age, although most cases concern juveniles who are 16 or 17.

Other than the traditional judicial waiver, two other methods of trying juveniles in criminals courts were statutorily established by the 1980s and 1990s in a number of states in a variety of formats, and are commonly known as (1) direct file (prosecutorial transfer) and (2) legislative exclusion (essentially, automatic transfer). Either method bypasses traditional judicial waiver; both were instituted, in part, because of an increase in juvenile violent crime in the mid-1980s through the early 1990s. During the mid- and late 1990s, violent juvenile crime actually decreased nationwide, yet additional states continued to legislate these measures. The media's ability to sensationalize juvenile offender homicide cases contributed to the public and legislative leaders mistakenly perceiving that violent juvenile crime was still escalating.

Direct file provides prosecutors the authority to initiate charges, usually for serious violent offenses but sometimes for property offenses, against juveniles who in their discretion ought to be tried in criminal court. Prosecutors can rather effortlessly accomplish what under conventional judicial waiver is a rather formal procedural process. Florida, in particular, overwhelmingly uses direct file. Under legislative exclusion, the state legislature carves out selected serious crimes for which the juvenile offender will be held accountable in criminal court, without any initial judicial or prosecutorial oversight or discretion. The thinking is that some crimes are so heinous that all such offenses should be addressed in a criminal court. Of course, even under legislative exclusion, prosecutors always retain the power, under their discretionary authority, to not prosecute such cases.

In many states, a juvenile waived to adult court is thereafter always deemed an adult for any subsequent offenses committed, regardless of age. However, various states permit the criminal courts to send, in their discretion, an initially waived juvenile back to juvenile court in what is referred to as a reverse waiver. The thinking is that the interests of justice are best served in this manner. Additionally, some states provide for a blended sentence whereby the juvenile can be placed in a secure juvenile facility until perhaps age 21 and then incarcerated in an adult prison. Even under this process, juveniles can sometimes be reevaluated and released prior to entry into the adult prison.

The number of juveniles waived to criminal court escalated between 1985 and 1994, when it reached nearly 13,000. From 1995 through 2001, the number dropped significantly, while during the mid-2000s the number increased somewhat, finally leveling off at around 8,000 in 2007.

Arguments For and Against Waivers

Those who support waivers assert that juveniles who commit serious crimes should be held accountable and punishable in an adult court setting, and that the waiver itself will act as a specific deterrent, discouraging the juvenile from engaging in any further criminal behavior. Additionally, proponents believe the waiver will serve as a general deterrent to serious juvenile offender crime. In other words, other juveniles will not contemplate committing serious crimes because of an appreciation of the adult sanctions that can be imposed. An emphasis on crime control and victim's rights, and a strong adherence to maintaining public safety are paramount under this perspective.

Those with reservations about the propriety of waiving juveniles to adult court maintain that too many juveniles are waived for property offenses such as burglary or for drug-related offenses. Further, research studies on the deterrent effect are either ambiguous on this issue or show that juveniles processed in the adult court are more likely than similarly situated juveniles processed in juvenile court to be rearrested at similar or higher rates. Likewise, opponents argue that adult courts are ill-equipped to deal with juveniles and don't always view such transferred juveniles as being major offenders. In fact, sometimes adult courts sentence juveniles to adult incarceration that is no longer than what would be imposed in juvenile court, and yet at the same time expose them to the risk of severe battery, sexual assault, inadequate juvenile programs, and thoughts of suicide in adult prisons. Additionally, opponents declare that statistics show extralegal factors such as race and ethnicity are improperly considered in waiver decisions; hence, African American juveniles are disproportionately waived. Moreover, opponents argue that juvenile offenders are less culpable for their actions because of decreased cognitive brain development, which results in immature decision making. Hence, they conclude that juveniles are more suitably managed within the traditional juvenile justice system.

Two Supreme Court opinions addressing the significance of decreased juvenile offender brain development were the 2005 case *Roper v. Simmons*, which held that the death penalty for juveniles is unconstitutional; and the 2010 case *Graham v. Florida*, which held that life imprisonment without the possibility of parole for juveniles who committed offenses lesser than homicide is unconstitutional. These cases may have a future impact on the waiver of juvenile offenders to adult court insofar as providing a window of opportunity for revisiting and reassessing when and under what circumstances waiver to adult court is appropriate and for which particular types of juvenile offenders.

To gain an overall perspective of the historical development of juveniles and the law, an examination of the landmark case of *In re Gault* (1967) is necessary, as it formalized due process procedure in the juvenile court, thus replacing in large part the old paternalistic approach in dealing with juveniles. *Gault* extended due process rights to juveniles charged with delinquent offenses by mandating their right to counsel, to protection against self-incrimination, to confront and examine accusers, and to adequate notice of the charges.

Rick M. Steinmann
Southern Illinois University

See Also: 1981 to 2000 Primary Documents; Child Murderers, History of; Juvenile Courts, Contemporary; Juvenile Courts, History of; Juvenile Justice, History of.

Further Readings
Griffin, Patrick. *Different From Adults: An Updated Analysis of Juvenile Transfer and Blended Sentencing Laws, With Recommendations for Reform*. Pittsburgh, PA: National Center for Juvenile Justice, 2008.
Iselin, Ann-Marie R., et al. "Maturity in Adolescent and Young Adult Offenders: The Role of Cognitive Control." *Law and Human Behavior*, v.33 (2009).
Schubert, Carol A., et al. "Predicting Outcomes for Youth Transferred to Adult Court." *Law and Human Behavior*, v.34/6 (2010).

Kaczynski, Ted

Theodore John "Ted" Kaczynski (1942–) is an American domestic terrorist, social critic, neo-Luddite, and anarchist. In 1996, federal agents arrested and a federal grand jury indicted Kaczynski, also known as the Unabomber, for mailing bombs over the course of almost two decades that killed three people and wounded 23 others. The Federal Bureau of Investigation's (FBI) pursuit of the Unabomber was one of the most famous and costly ones in American history.

Kaczynski pleaded guilty to the charges against him in 1998, although he later claimed the guilty plea was coerced and he requested to have it withdrawn. This appeal was denied. He is currently serving a life sentence without parole in the U.S. Penitentiary Administrative Maximum Facility—the supermax—in Fremont County, Colorado. This facility has also housed such famous prisoners as Timothy McVeigh, Zacarias Moussaoui, Terry Nichols, Jose Padilla, Richard Reid, Eric Rudolph, and H. Rap Brown.

Kaczynski was born in Chicago, Illinois, to Theodore Richard and Wanda Kaczynski. From an early age, he showed a high degree of intelligence and aptitude for academic studies; however, Kaczynski rarely interacted with his peers. At the age of 16, he entered Harvard, where he earned his undergraduate degree. During his tenure there, Kaczynski took part voluntarily in a psychological, mind-control experiment that measured stress. Kaczynski's lawyers argued this study had a lasting effect on his emotional stability. Kaczynski ultimately received his doctorate in mathematics from the University of Michigan. In 1967, the University of California, Berkeley, hired the 25-year-old Kaczynski as an assistant professor, but he resigned two years later without explanation.

In 1971, Kaczynski relocated to a remote, one-room cabin near Lincoln, Montana. Here, Kaczynski fashioned a simple and self-sufficient life, learned survival and wilderness strategies, and subsisted without running water or electricity. In spite of this, he found his primitive way of life encroached upon by developers. Seeking the dissolution of what he later called the industrial-technological system, and believing violence to be the only viable method in achieving this collapse, Kaczynski began his terrorist activity.

Initially engaged in minor acts of sabotage on the machines of developers near his cabin, Kaczynski sent his first mail bomb in 1978 to a Northwestern University professor of materials engineering. Suspicious of the package, the professor alerted a campus police officer who opened it and received injuries to his hand from the ensuing explosion. After this first attempt on a human life, Kaczynski began mailing bombs to airline officials and in 1979 attempted to bomb a domestic airliner. The defective bomb did not explode, but this federal crime made the unknown suspect a priority for the FBI, which created a UNABOM (the code name for university and airline bombings) task force that included the U.S. Postal Inspection Service and the Bureau of Alcohol, Tobacco, and Firearms (ATF).

Between 1978 and 1995, Kaczynski sent homemade explosive devices to various targets. The first casualty—the owner of a computer store—did not occur until 1985. No bombings were attributed to Kaczynski between February 1987 and June 1993. After this interval, however, Kaczynski resumed his bombing campaign and wrote letters to the *New York Times* declaring that his organization, the Freedom Club, was accountable for the attacks. In 1995, Kaczynski contacted several media organizations demanding the publication of his lengthy essay, "Industrial Society and Its Future" (the Unabomber Manifesto), promising to cease his attacks in return. On September 19, 1995, the *Washington Post* and *New York Times* ran the piece, which called for a revolution against industrial society and technology.

The distinctive style and content of this essay convinced David Kaczynski that his estranged brother was the author. David contacted the FBI with older letters Ted had written to newspapers, a search warrant was issued, and agents arrested Kaczynski on April 3, 1996. His lawyers sought an insanity defense plea, but Kaczynski refused this. On January 7, 1998, Kaczynski tried to hang himself, and later that month he was sentenced to life in prison without parole. Since then, Kaczynski has remained a productive writer and a collection of his essays, titled *Technological Slavery*, was published in 2010.

Daniel C. Dillard
Florida State University

See Also: 2001 to 2012 Primary Documents; Anarchists; Insanity Defense; McVeigh, Timothy; Montana; Terrorism; Violent Crimes.

Further Readings
Chase, Alston. *A Mind for Murder: The Education of the Unabomber and the Origins of Modern Terrorism*. New York: W. W. Norton, 2004.

Kaczynski, Theodore. *Technological Slavery: The Collected Writings*. Port Townsend, WA: Feral House, 2010.
Kaczynski, Theodore. *The Unabomber Manifesto: Industrial Society and Its Future*. Berkeley, CA: Jolly Roger Press, 1995.
Waits, Chris and Dave Shors. *Unabomber: The Secret Life of Ted Kaczynski*. Helena, MT: Independent Record, 1999.

Kansas

The history of crime and punishment in Kansas began with the birth of the state itself. With the Kansas-Nebraska Act of 1854, the people of the Kansas Territory were given the right, under popular sovereignty, to decide whether the territory would enter the United States as a free state or as a slave state. This decision effectively legalized armed conflict between the two sides, which continued until 1859 and resulted in the deaths of 56 people and in the territory remaining a territory. Shortly after the beginning of the American Civil War in 1861, Kansas gained entry as a free state, effectively legitimizing the abolitionist side of what many still viewed as an ongoing issue in Kansas. Those who sided with the Confederacy, such as Quantrill's Raiders, became outlaws and were subject to punishment by law.

Evolution of Law Enforcement
The distinction between lawman and outlaw in frontier Kansas often rested on who possessed the most firepower in a particular area. Many of the most infamous gunfighters spent time in Kansas in some of the most lawless towns known in the American Wild West. People such as Wyatt and Virgil Earp, Wild Bill Hickok, Belle Starr, Billy the Kid, Sam Bass, William Cody, Pat Garrett, Doc Holliday, Bat Masterson, and John Wesley Hardin all played a part in the foundation of the Kansas legal system. Two towns in particular, Abilene and Dodge City, played instrumental roles in the struggle to control crime within the new state. Abilene, an early stagecoach stop, grew into a major cattle town as the railroads pushed west across the plains. The Chisholm Trail ended

in Abilene, bringing thousands of cowboys and trail hands into the small town, quickly garnering it the reputation as one of the wildest towns in the west. "Wild" Bill Hickok served as the marshal in Abilene for a short time but ran afoul of the townsfolk when he accidentally shot his own deputy during a gunfight. Vigilante justice was common, and dueling (gun fighting) was a common form of punishment meted out not just by the marshal and his deputies but also by the average citizen on a number of occasions.

Dodge City, famous today for its setting as the location for the long-lasting television western *Gunsmoke*, was founded in 1872 near the Santa Fe Trail, the Great Western Cattle Trail, and the Arkansas River. With the arrival of the railroad, Dodge City became a major shipping point for the cattle trade—the "Queen of the Cow Towns" had a well-earned reputation for lawlessness. The Earp brothers and Bat Masterson began their law enforcement careers in Dodge City, yet it was not until the Kansas state legislature banned longhorn cattle from the state, thus effectively ending the influx of cowboys and trail hands working on cattle drives, that the rampant crime in Dodge City came to an end.

As the "Brass Buckle of the Bible Belt," Kansas approaches crime and punishment from a conservative viewpoint. The first "blue sky" laws were enacted in 1911 to protect investors against securities frauds and the "blue laws," designed to enforce religious standards such as Sunday as a day of worship and the restriction of alcohol sales, are still applicable within the state (although each county does have the right to amend the constraints of the laws). Kansas also preceded the federal constraints on the morality of motion pictures by enacting a strict censorship of motion pictures that remained in effect from 1915 to 1966.

Violence was not confined to the frontier settlement towns. Starting in the early 20th century, the DiGiovanni Sicilian mob family brought organized crime to Kansas City. During Prohibition, the family ran the bootlegging operations in town, gaining a reputation and engaging in illegal activities that soon required federal intervention. As with many of the early organized crime figures, federal tax evasion provided the readily available means of punishment for their crimes. Even with federal law enforcement working to bring down

Transient cowboys and trail hands affected the rate of crime in 19th-century Kansas. Above, a man dressed as a cowboy aims a pistol at a photographer in Newton, Kansas, in 1908.

the organization, DiGiovanni family members still managed to gain influence at the state level when their hand-picked candidate, Forrest Smith, was elected governor in 1948.

Statewide statistics on crime in Kansas, available starting in 1960, document the growth of criminal activity throughout the state, even though the population has remained relatively stable. In 2009, Kansas ranked 29th among states for the highest crime levels, down from 17th in 2007.

Controlling the criminal element in Kansas has not come easily or quickly; the enforcement of laws and the sentencing of criminals remained a strictly local affair until the formation of the Kansas Bureau of Investigation (KBI) in 1939. With the origin of a crime-fighting unit with legal jurisdiction throughout the state, the opportunity for criminals to simply move operations to another location decreased significantly, and enforcement became more uniform under the statutes found in Chapter 21 of the Kansas State Legal Code.

Capital Punishment

The controversy surrounding the death penalty remains a major issue in Kansas. As a territory, Kansas passed its first death penalty law in 1859. This law remained intact through the transition to statehood. However, Kansas law forbid public executions, and the hanging of William Dickson in 1870 resulted in a debate over the form of execution that lasted for 35 years, during which time no executions took place; the death penalty was ultimately repealed in 1907. Following the Great Depression and an increase in violent crime in Kansas City, the Kansas legislature reinstated legal executions in 1935.

Two of the most famous criminals executed in Kansas were Perry Smith and Richard Hickock. In 1959, Smith and Hickock, parolees from the Kansas State Penitentiary, killed a family of four in Holcomb, Kansas. The killings provided the story for Truman Capote's best-selling book *In Cold Blood*. The two men were sentenced to death and were hanged on April 14, 1965. George Ronald York and James Douglas Latham, who were both executed on June 22, 1965, were the most recent individuals to be executed in Kansas.

In 1972, the U.S. Supreme Court ruled that current capital punishment laws were unconstitutional under the Eighth and Fourteenth amendments. This ruling effectively halted all executions within the United States. A number of states revised their capital punishment laws to satisfy the high court's guidelines, and executions resumed. Kansas fulfilled these requirements and reinstated execution as a punishment in 1994, with lethal injection replacing hanging as the means of execution.

Robin Annette Hanson
St. Louis University

See Also: Capital Punishment; Kansas City, Missouri; *National Police Gazette*; Serial and Mass Killers.

Further Readings

Athearn, Robert G. *The Mythic West in Twentieth-Century America*. Lawrence: University Press of Kansas, 1988.

Capote, Truman. *In Cold Blood*. New York: Random House, 2002.

Kansas Bureau of Investigation. "2010 Kansas Crime Index." http://www.accesskansas.org/kbi/stats/docs/pdf/Crime%20Index%202010.pdf (Accessed September 2011).

Kansas City, Missouri

Missouri became a territory in 1812 and a state in 1820. After removal of the Osage Indians to west of the state line, Jackson County was organized and Independence was designated as its county seat. Kansas City evolved in 1889 from a tract of land located along the Missouri River. The area expanded throughout the 19th century, first in response to the great westward trails prior to the Civil War and then because of its strategic positioning as a hub of railroad transportation. Kansas City was overwhelmingly populated by descendants of European old stock.

At mid-century came waves of Irish, German, and Scandinavian immigrants, followed by a wide variety of "new immigrants" and Hispanics after 1900. After Europeans, the next-largest group of Kansas Citians were African Americans. Blacks first came to the area as slaves; then, in the years just after Reconstruction, thousands of "Exodusters" fled the south. Though they came with hope, they found themselves mired in prejudice and poverty, living in squalid housing, and enduring high crime rates and police contempt.

Court System

The first county court in 1827 predates both the city and the police department. The first court of common pleas was founded in Kansas City in 1855 with concurrent original and appellate jurisdiction; in 1871, the common pleas court was replaced by a criminal court with jurisdiction over the county, along with separate probate, law and equity, and circuit courts. The number of circuit judges for Jackson County increased to four in 1889, with three located in Kansas City, showing how the legal and population center of the county was shifting from Independence to Kansas City. Moreover, the U.S. Circuit and District Courts of the Western Division of the Western District of Missouri were ordered to conduct their sessions in Kansas City.

The greatest fear of progressive reformers was that jailing youthful offenders with adult criminals would turn them into career criminals. To break this cycle, a juvenile court was created in 1903, complete with facilities for youthful offenders. This attempt to save juvenile delinquents was less than successful. Statistics gathered by the deputy sheriff recorded that 50 percent of those incarcerated at the county jail were males under 23 years old. Judge E. Porterfield, writing on juvenile crime in 1931, cited many causes of juvenile delinquency: the boys were considered physically and mentally subnormal, they suffered from parental neglect, rejected paid labor, and mixed with vagrants and petty thieves. The judge wrung his hands at the sort of influences on youth that people of that era feared. These included smoking, movies, vicious magazines—and the desire to attract young girls with cars and money, both of which they stole to meet those needs.

Police Development

The first Kansas City Police Department (KCPD) was formed in 1874 under the Missouri State Metropolitan Police Law, giving control over the department to the state. Initially, there were 25 officers, and the department was located downtown in the city hall. Mounted patrols were introduced in the 1880s and stayed in existence for five decades. Frontier justice jeopardized the law when a vigilante committee was organized in the 1880s and threatened to hang criminals they captured; the chief responded by purchasing a Gatling gun for riot control. Housing arrested criminals presented another problem. An early log cabin jail could be taken apart by simply removing a log and releasing an inmate. Another jail, made of frame, was dragged down to the river and dumped in.

In 1908, Kansas City was one of the first departments to experiment with motorcycles and automobiles for patrol. That same year, a new charter created municipal courts. In 1911, the city jail closed and a municipal farm opened where prisoners could do agricultural work and/or quarry stone. By 1920, the department occupied 20 stations, mostly up to date with modern construction and cells for both men and women. Early in the 20th century, three officers lost their lives in the line of duty, and a statue honoring fallen police was erected in front of the department. It has been moved many times but today stands in front of the present police headquarters.

As the century passed, the department continued to acquire modern technology and innovations such as police radios, submachine guns, lie detector machines, radar, a punch-card records system, a new outdoor firearms training center, helicopters, in-car computer terminals, bullet-resistant vests, a new van where prisoners could be separated by gender or age, crime scene investigators, and an ordnance disposal robot. In 1973, women were recruited for the first time and were assigned to patrol duty. In May 2000, the department launched its first Website, and a Professional Standards and Fairness Committee was formed to guard against racial profiling.

This statue stands in front of the Kansas City Police Department above an inscription listing the names of the city's 119 fallen police. The city's police force consisted of 1,400 officers in 2012.

Crime

The darkest mark on the crime scene of Kansas City came with the connections between the infamous Pendergast machine and the presence of the mafia. Brothers Jim and Tom Pendergast started in immigrant neighborhoods of the inner city at the end of the 19th century. Here, they promoted and protected criminal activities that earned Kansas City the reputation for being "wide open" when it came to gambling, prostitution, drinking, and racketeering. Marginal characters were drawn to Kansas City because it was the only area in the vicinity on either side of the state line where liquor could be legally obtained. Moreover, the Pendergast machine demonstrated all the earmarks of urban bossism in America. Not only did the Pendergasts buy the votes of immigrants for the Democrat political machine, they dispensed patronage to family and friends, many of whom were Irish immigrants appointed to the KCPD, an estimated two-thirds of the force by World War I. In return, the police assured a "safe space" for vice activities and customers, while the police themselves were sometimes charged with assaulting prisoners and being intoxicated while on duty. Tom Pendergast's machine began to unravel when the KCPD went under state control again and he was imprisoned for income tax evasion.

Reliable crime statistics by the KCPD are not available prior to 1910, but between 1910 and 1930, crimes increased by 30 percent. Yet Kansas City's high crime rate in 1930 dropped by the next year to the lowest of 37 other American cities, illustrating the fluctuating nature of urban crime. Criminal statistics also varied according to the category of crime. By the early 1990s, methamphetamine had taken hold of the Kansas City suburb of Independence and infected the Kansas City area. The Drug Enforcement Administration (DEA) shut down more meth labs in Missouri than in California by the mid-1990s. The 21st century began with the lowest homicide rate since the 1970s and with declining violent and property crimes throughout Kansas City neighborhoods. By 2009, however, ministers in Kansas City were calling for a rally against gangs, drug dealers, and murderers, all criminals who also contribute to property crimes.

Donna Cooper Graves
University of Tennessee Martin

See Also: 1961 to 1980 Primary Documents; Court of Common Pleas; Missouri; Organized Crime, History of; Truman, Harry S. (Administration of).

Further Readings

Hayde, Frank R. *The Mafia & the Machine: The Story of the Kansas City Mob*. Fort Lee, NJ: Barricade Books, 2008.

Kansas City Police Department. *Kansas City Police Department*. Paducah, KY: Turner Publishing, 2001.

Missouri Valley Collection. Vertical File (Crime & Criminals Folder). Kansas City, MO: Kansas City Public Library.

Schirmer, Sherry Lamb and Richard D. McKenzie. *At the River's Bend: An Illustrated History of Kansas City, Independence and Jackson County*. Woodland Hills, CA: Windsor Publications, 1982.

Whitney, Carrie Westlake. *Kansas City, Missouri, Its History and Its People, 1808–1908, Illustrated*. Vol. I. Chicago: S. J. Clarke, 1908.

Katz v. United States

Katz v. United States serves as the foundation for Supreme Court decisions involving the Fourth Amendment to the Constitution. Decided in 1967, the case involved police recording the defendant's conversations as he transmitted wagering information over the telephone. The court held that the Fourth Amendment protects people who have a reasonable expectation of privacy, without regard to whether law enforcement made a physical intrusion into a protected area. Though the court divided on its rationale, *Katz*'s legacy has informed Fourth Amendment jurisprudence for 40 years and is the starting point for applying the Fourth Amendment to new technologies.

The government's case against Charles Katz developed amid the government's crusade to stop organized crime. Increased dramatically during President John Kennedy's administration, the efforts continued into the Lyndon Johnson administration. One important target was the proliferation of interstate gambling. Law enforcement officers learned that Katz was involved in the interstate communication of wagering information, specifically, point spreads on college football games. They followed him as he repeatedly used one of three telephone booths to transmit the information. After repeatedly observing this activity, the agents placed a microphone and recording equipment on top of one of the phone booths. When Katz made a call, they recorded it and, in the process, obtained the necessary evidence for conviction. Following his conviction, he appealed and the Ninth Circuit Court of Appeals ruled that the surveillance did not implicate the Fourth Amendment because the officers did not intrude upon the phone booth.

The Supreme Court considered the case in fall 1967. The case came during the Warren Court's efforts to reform criminal procedure. Earlier decisions had focused on the right to counsel and the application of the exclusionary rule to the states. Later cases would focus on prosecutorial disclosure of exculpatory information and the right to counsel during police interrogation. The court had attempted, in earlier cases, to reinterpret the Fourth Amendment but could not achieve a majority. By 1967, the majority was in place.

The government argued, based on the decision in *Olmstead v. United States*, that the recording was not covered by the Fourth Amendment. Katz had framed the issue for the court as one where the court had to decide whether or not the telephone booth was a constitutionally protected area. Justice Potter Stewart, writing for the court, reframed the issue, stating that the Fourth Amendment does not consider the place searched but focuses on the individual's expectation of privacy.

Therefore, Stewart decided that Katz had an expectation of privacy when he closed the door to the phone booth. Katz did not expect his conversations to be heard by anyone else, so the search and seizure of the conversations violated the Fourth Amendment. Stewart concluded his opinion by examining whether the search was reasonable. Despite the precautions taken by the government to minimize the intrusions, Stewart said that the agents had the option of obtaining a warrant. The judicial review was essential to ensure law enforcement acted reasonably.

Justice Stewart's opinion was not the only one, however, as four other justices filed opinions. Justice Byron White concurred in the judgment but wrote that, in these circumstances, the government needed a search warrant, but he did not see the need to rewrite the Fourth Amendment. He also noted that national security electronic surveillance was exempt from the search warrant requirement. Justice William Douglas also concurred in the judgment but wrote to distinguish his views from White's. Douglas did not think national security searches should be exempt. Justice John Marshall Harlan also concurred but decided the case based on the questions framed by Katz. He, too, did not think that the Fourth Amendment should be revised. Finally, Justice Hugo Black dissented, ruling that Chief Justice William Taft's reasoning in *United States v. Olmstead* should remain the law.

Despite the diverging opinions, *Katz* has remained the foundation for current Fourth Amendment interpretation. Its underlying principle that the amendment protects people and not places has been instrumental in the application of the Fourth Amendment to modern technologies. Current debates about thermal imaging, electronic surveillance, and global positioning systems rest upon the rationale adopted by the court in *Katz*.

Scott Ingram
High Point University

See Also: Bill of Rights; Electronic Surveillance; Gambling; *Olmstead v. United States*; Organized Crime, History of; Warren, Earl.

Further Readings
Katz v. United States, 369 F.2d 130 (1966).
Katz v. United States, 389 U.S. 347 (1967).
Kerr, Orin S. "The Fourth Amendment and New Technologies: Constitutional Myths and the Case for Caution." *Michigan Law Review*, v.102 (2004).
Kitch, Edmund W. "*Katz v. United States*: The Limits of the Fourth Amendment." *Supreme Court Review*, v.133 (1968).
Powe, Lucas A., Jr. *The Warren Court and American Politics*. Cambridge, MA: Belknap Press of Harvard University Press, 2000.

Katzenbach v. McClung

In *Katzenbach v. McClung*, the U.S. Supreme Court upheld Title II of the Civil Rights Act of 1964—which prohibits discrimination based on race, color, religion or national origin in any place of public accommodation—to a family-owned restaurant in Birmingham, Alabama. *McClung* was decided the same day as *Heart of Atlanta Motel v. U.S.*; together, these cases affirmed a broad federal power to regulate local businesses under the interstate commerce clause (Article I, Section 8, Clause 3).

Ollie's Barbecue, established in 1927 by Ollie McClung, Sr., had a 220-seat dining room for whites only as well as a carry-out window that served African Americans. The restaurant was located in a largely African American neighborhood on State Highway 149, 11 blocks from the nearest interstate highway and even farther from the nearest air, bus, or train terminal. During the previous year, McClung purchased about $70,000 in meat from a local wholesaler that imported it from Hormel, an out-of-state supplier.

After the Civil Rights Act took effect in July 1964, McClung continued refusing to serve African Americans in the dining room. He challenged the law, and an Alabama federal district court found in his favor. It ruled that the Civil Rights Act could not be enforced against Ollie's Barbecue because no customers were from out-of-state and the amount of food purchased by the restaurant did not substantially affect interstate commerce. (In contrast, Heart of Atlanta Motel advertised nationally, was located near two interstate highways, and interstate travelers constituted 75 percent of its guests.) When the U.S. Supreme Court decided to hear the appeal in *Heart of Atlanta Motel*, it took the government's appeal in *McClung* on expedited review from the district court.

On December 14, 1964—just six months after Congress passed the Civil Rights Act—the U.S. Supreme Court unanimously upheld its application to Heart of Atlanta Motel and to Ollie's Barbecue. (Justice John M. Harlan drafted a dissent in *McClung* on federalism grounds, but eventually joined the majority opinion.) The majority opinion of Justice Tom Clark upheld the law as an exercise of Congress's power to regulate interstate commerce under the "substantial effects" doc-

The photograph shows a sign for a hotel serving black travelers on a street of pawn shops in Memphis, Tennessee, around 1939. In Katzenbach v. McClung, *the majority opinion of the Supreme Court found that segregation of local businesses obstructed travel.*

trine. The amount of meat purchased by McClung was "insignificant" to the national market, he conceded. Citing *Wickard v. Filburn* (1942), *Gibbons v. Ogden* (1824), and congressional testimony, Clark demonstrated that if other local restaurants "similarly situated" to Ollie's Barbecue engaged in racial discrimination, national burdens to commerce and travel would result. "This obviously discourages travel and obstructs interstate commerce," Clark wrote, "for one can hardly travel without eating." Title II of the Civil Rights Act, he found, is "plainly appropriate in the resolution of what Congress found to be a national commercial problem of the first magnitude."

Three justices appended concurring opinions in *Heart of Atlanta Motel* to *McClung*, and each addressed Congress's power to enforce the Fourteenth Amendment's equal protection clause. Justice Hugo Black, from Alabama, wrote that the public accommodations provision is "wholly valid under the Commerce Clause and the Necessary and Proper Clause." He found "no need" to consider the Fourteenth Amendment. Justice Arthur Goldberg affirmed federal authority under the commerce clause, yet noted that "the primary purpose" of the Civil Rights Act "is the vindication of human dignity, and not mere economics." Goldberg found congressional authority under both the Fourteenth Amendment and the commerce clause. In his concurrence, Justice William O. Douglas said "I am somewhat reluctant here … to rest solely on the Commerce Clause." To Douglas, the guarantees secured by the Civil Rights Act "are clearly within the purview of our decisions under the Equal Protection Clause." Resting on the Fourteenth Amendment rather than the commerce clause

> … would have a more settling effect … thereby putting an end to all obstructionist strategies and allowing every person—whatever his race, creed or color—to patronize all places of public accommodation without discrimination whether he travels interstate or intrastate.

Clear reliance on equal protection would, Douglas said, "finally close one door on a bitter chapter in American history."

Ollie McClung, Sr., was "shocked" at the decision. But unlike Atlanta restaurant owner Lester Maddox, McClung—a Presbyterian preacher—stated "as law-abiding Americans, we must bow down to this edict." Later that week, Ollie's Barbecue began serving African Americans in the dining room without incident. The restaurant moved in 1968 and again in 1999 to a location in Hoover, Alabama, closer to interstate highways. Ollie's Barbecue closed in 2001, but bottles of Ollie's World's Best Bar-B-Q sauce remain on supermarket shelves throughout the south.

Frank J. Colucci
Purdue University Calumet

See Also: Alabama; Civil Rights Laws; Equality, Concept of; Georgia; Segregation Laws.

Further Readings
Cortner, Richard C. *Civil Rights and Public Accommodations: The* Heart of Atlanta Motel *and* McClung *Cases*. Lawrence: University Press of Kansas, 2001.
Durham, Michael. "Ollie McClung's Big Decision." *Life* (October 9, 1964).
Heart of Atlanta Motel v. U.S., 379 U.S. 241 (1964).
Katzenbach v. McClung, 379 U.S. 294 (1964)
Landsberg, Brian K. *Enforcing Civil Rights: Race Discrimination and the U.S. Department of Justice*. Lawrence: University Press of Kansas, 1997.
"The Supreme Court—Beyond a Doubt." *Time* (December 25, 1964).

Kennedy, John F. (Administration of)

Despite serving less than three years as the 35th president of the United States of America, John Fitzgerald Kennedy (1917–63) is one of the most popular and controversial presidents in the country's history. Kennedy succeeded Dwight D. Eisenhower, becoming president on January 20, 1961. Despite Kennedy's civil rights legacy, famous speeches, and high-stakes confrontations with the Soviet Union, he is perhaps best known for the controversy surrounding his own death.

Kennedy was assassinated on November 22, 1963, in Dallas, Texas. Although the official ruling is that Kennedy was shot by Lee Harvey Oswald, which is supported by the findings of the Warren Commission, a number of conspiracy theories have persisted. The assassination itself is one of most iconic crimes of the 20th century. Kennedy's brother Robert served as his attorney general under him and was famously responsible for a war on organized crime. Additionally, the Juvenile Delinquency and Youth Offenses Control Act was also passed in this period, and the infamous Boston Strangler was active during Kennedy's presidency.

The Kennedy family formed a political dynasty, and much of John Kennedy's political motivation emanated from his father, who had served as ambassador to the United Kingdom. Kennedy is connected with a number of leading universities, including Harvard, Princeton, the London School of Economics, and Stanford. He also had a military career prior to entering politics, serving in the U.S. Navy during World War II. Kennedy served as president during a number of crises at the height of the cold war. The Bay of Pigs Invasion during 1961 is a notable example and is largely seen as a disaster for Kennedy. Another defining episode was the Cuban Missile Crisis in 1962, which ensued as Soviet missile silos were installed in Cuba. The world held its breath, and historians of the period noted that the world was on the brink of all-out nuclear war during the crisis. Eventually, Soviet premier Nikita Khrushchev agreed to remove the missiles in exchange for a guarantee that America would not invade Cuba.

Robert Kennedy's tenure as attorney general is remembered for his associated crusade against organized crime. Until this time, the issue of organized crime had largely been neglected. For example, Federal Bureau of Investigation (FBI) director J. Edgar Hoover had failed to go after the organized crime syndicates and is accused by some of having links to the mob. Despite concerns about his lack of experience, Robert Kennedy was successful in reforming the Justice Department and setting up new organized crime investigations. Subsequently, a marked rise in convictions connected to organized crime activities was witnessed. The events of this period and earlier high-profile Mafia cases helped to create the Mafia's image for the public. Robert Goldfarb, who formed part of Kennedy's team, offers an insider view of the attorney general in his book *Perfect Villains, Imperfect Heroes: Robert Kennedy's War Against Organized Crime*. We can judge the impact of the Kennedy administration's war on organized crime by the extent to which it was hated by such groups.

Kennedy made a number of famous speeches as president, including on his inauguration on January 20, 1961, when he asserted: "And so, my fellow Americans: Ask not what your country can do for you—ask what you can do for your country." These words are woven into the fabric of history and are synonymous with the Kennedy legacy. As a contemporary and supporter of Martin Luther King, Jr., Kennedy's involvement with civil rights is well documented despite the political pressures he faced. In 1963, his civil rights bill was put before Congress, laying the foundations that his successor, Lyndon B. Johnson, built on. Indeed, many of Kennedy's positions on issues such as civil rights and immigration were later implemented by others. Kennedy paved the way for the crucial Civil Rights Act of 1964, while his brothers Edward and Robert were instrumental in the passing of the Immigration and Nationality Act of 1965. During Kennedy's presidency, the events of the civil rights movement brought a number of challenges and notable events related to riots and opposition to racial integration.

After less than three years as president, Kennedy's period in office was cut short in one of the defining moments of the 20th century. On November 22, 1963, Kennedy was shot by Lee Harvey Oswald as he was traveling in his motorcade through Dallas, Texas, while on the campaign trail. Oswald was himself killed on November 24, 1963, while being transferred to prison, having been arrested for shooting a police officer and subsequently linked to the Kennedy assassination. The Warren Commission under Lyndon B. Johnson concluded that Oswald was responsible for the assassination and that he was the sole perpetrator, rejecting various conspiracy theories. Yet discrepancies exist concerning the number of shots fired and from where the shots were fired. The Congressional House Select Committee on Assassinations in the late 1970s contradicted the findings of the Warren Commission, noting that the assassination was linked to a conspiracy.

Tony Murphy
University of Westminster

See Also: 1961 to 1980 Primary Documents; Civil Rights Laws; Johnson, Lyndon B. (Administration of); Kennedy, Robert F.; King, Martin Luther, Jr.; Organized Crime, History of; Oswald, Lee Harvey.

Further Readings
Giglio, James. *The Presidency of John F. Kennedy*, 2nd ed. Lawrence: University Press of Kansas, 2006.
Goldfarb, Ronald L. *Perfect Villains, Imperfect Heroes: Robert Kennedy's War Against Organized Crime*. New York: Random House, 1995.
"John F. Kennedy." BBC. http://www.bbc.co.uk/dna/h2g2/C54911 (Accessed January 2011).

Kennedy, Robert F.

Born into a wealthy and large family, Robert Kennedy was both a liberal reformer and an advocate of law-and-order policies. As a U.S. senator and as the U.S. attorney general, Kennedy was deeply interested in issues relating to crime and punishment. His belief in appropriate penalties for wrongdoers was sometimes controversial, and his positions on enforcing civil rights laws, aggressively prosecuting corrupt union officials, and confronting organized crime made him many enemies. Many of Kennedy's beliefs were shaped by his early experiences. Born into a family that emphasized public service and the importance of helping the downtrodden, Kennedy served as an icon for many who sought to use the government to effect change. Although his political career lasted little more than a decade, Kennedy played a significant role in shaping policy related to civil rights and corruption.

Early Life

Robert Francis Kennedy (RFK) was born November 20, 1928, in Brookline, Massachusetts. The seventh child of Joseph Kennedy and his wife Rose, he was born to a family of tremendous wealth and influence. Joseph Kennedy had wide and varied business concerns, including ownership of the Merchandise Mart in Chicago and interests in several Hollywood motion picture studios. The Kennedy family also was very active politically, with Joseph Kennedy serving as U.S. ambassador to the United Kingdom and as first chairman of the Securities and Exchange Commission, and Rose Kennedy's father having served as mayor of Boston. RFK was educated in public schools from kindergarten through the fifth grade and in private schools thereafter. During World War II, RFK joined the U.S. Navy, serving from 1944 through 1946. After the war ended, he entered Harvard University as a junior, graduating in 1948. After receiving his B.A. in government, he served briefly as a correspondent for the *Boston Post*, writing stories about the division of Palestine and the founding of Israel. In the fall of 1948, RFK entered the University of Virginia Law School, from which he graduated in 1951.

After graduating from the University of Virginia, RFK briefly returned to reporting for the *Boston Post* and then embarked on a seven-week tour of Asia with his brother, John F. Kennedy (JFK). In 1951, RFK took a position with the Criminal Division of the U.S. Justice Department. RFK resigned this position the following year to assist JFK in his campaign to be elected to the U.S. Senate seat from Massachusetts. In 1953, RFK was appointed by Wisconsin Republican Senator Joseph McCarthy to serve as an assistant counsel to the Senate Permanent Subcommittee on Investigations. After resigning a year later to assist his father on the Hoover Commission, which made recommendations to President Harry Truman with regard to administrative changes in the federal government. RFK became chief counsel to the Democratic minority in the U.S. Senate, becoming chief counsel to the majority when they regained control in 1955. Serving as chief counsel to the

Attorney General Robert F. Kennedy testifying at a Senate subcommittee hearing on crime in September 1963. Kennedy had an influential 44-month tenure as attorney general.

U.S. Senate Select Committee on Improper Activities in Labor and Management (the McClellan Committee) from 1957 until 1959, RFK gained national recognition in its investigation of International Brotherhood of Teamsters (IBT) executives David Beck and James Hoffa. Specifically, RFK assisted the McClellan Committee's investigation of alleged conspiracy between Hoffa and figures from organized crime to create as many as 15 "paper" local chapters of the IBT, that is, union chapters that existed only on paper. It was during this time that RFK's interest in criminal activity took root and his concerns about union intimidation were initiated.

Attorney General and Later Career
In 1959, RFK again resigned from government service to assist JFK's political ambitions, this time in a run for president of the United States. After JFK was elected president, he nominated RFK to serve as the U.S. attorney general. Although RFK's nomination was criticized because of his age (35) and inexperience, he performed well at his confirmation hearing and was confirmed by the U.S. Senate in January 1961. RFK presided over the Department of Justice for 44 months and was tremendously influential during that time. In addition to being U.S. attorney general, RFK served as an adviser to his brother, giving him a level of influence seldom known to prior holders of that cabinet position. As attorney general, RFK left a lasting legacy with regard to crime and punishment, especially with regard to civil rights enforcement and assaults on corruption and organized crime.

RFK's experiences in and out of the government built his commitment as a civil rights advocate. RFK embraced liberal causes such as civil rights that infuriated many other segments of the United States, including other supporters of JFK. RFK's passion for civil rights and human equality, coupled with his disdain for racial stereotypes common at the time, earned him great respect and support from the African American community and those whites who supported such policies. RFK was not afraid to use the Department of Justice to support the quest for equality. For example, he sent 400 U.S. marshals to protect Martin Luther King, Jr., after a series of death threats were made against King and his family, a move that outraged many southern whites. Similarly, RFK sent U.S. marshals to Oxford, Mississippi, to enforce a federal court order that James Meredith be admitted to the University of Mississippi. RFK also collaborated with JFK, and after his assassination, President Johnson, to ensure the passage of the Civil Rights Act of 1964, which outlawed the Jim Crow laws then common in the south.

As U.S. attorney general, RFK also maintained the crusade against organized crime and corruption that he had begun as chief counsel to the McClellan Committee. Although disagreements with J. Edgar Hoover, director of the Federal Bureau of Investigation (FBI), prevented a coherent strategy on how to proceed, prosecutions of the Mafia and union leaders increased by 800 percent during RFK's tenure as attorney general. RFK was especially relentless in pursuing his nemesis, James Hoffa. Specifically, RFK ordered investigations into Hoffa's financial dealings with the Mafia and electoral irregularities of IBT elections. Great personal animosity existed between the two men, and RFK and Hoffa frequently traded barbs in the press. This personal enmity culminated in nationally televised hearings during which RFK questioned Hoffa, ultimately leading to Hoffa's conviction on charges of jury tampering.

As attorney general, RFK was also responsible for carrying out the last federal execution in 1963 before the *Furman v. Georgia* case was decided by the U.S. Supreme Court in 1972. Although as a U.S. senator, RFK expressed willingness to support a bill that would abolish the death penalty, as attorney general he felt it was his obligation to support Victor Feguer's execution, despite pleas for clemency. Some have expressed the opinion that this decision reflected RFK's willingness to place political goals over personal beliefs.

After JFK's assassination in November 1963, RFK continued briefly as President Johnson's attorney general, resigning in 1964 to mount a campaign for the U.S. Senate seat for New York, which he ultimately won. Although Johnson and RFK disagreed frequently, both politically and personally, Johnson provided RFK with strong support during the election. Johnson's strong majority assisted RFK in defeating his Republican opponent. As a U.S. senator, RFK was keenly interested in legislation that furthered the civil rights struggle, especially that which called for integration of all public facilities and antipoverty initiatives that provided better housing, education, and medical care for those Americans traditionally excluded from the political process. RFK also was a strong supporter of the Voting Rights Act of 1965, which established extensive federal oversight of elections in those states that had traditionally excluded African American voters from the election process. RFK remained a severe critic of organized crime and corruption.

RFK's continued attacks on James Hoffa and the Mafia have led some to allege a conspiracy that resulted in his brother's and his own assassinations. While campaigning for president, on June 4, 1968, RFK was shot in a kitchen area in the Ambassador Hotel in Los Angeles while celebrating his win in the California Democratic presidential primary election. Although Sirhan Sirhan was later convicted of the crime, rumors persist that the Mafia was somehow involved. RFK's passion for civil rights and speedy punishment for criminals, especially those who betray the public trust, however, remain his most lasting legacies.

Stephen T. Schroth
Jason A. Helfer
Celestina D. Akyekum
Knox College

See Also: 1961 to 1980 Primary Documents; Civil Rights Laws; History of Crime and Punishment in America: 1950–1970; Johnson, Lyndon B. (Administration of); Justice, Department of; Kennedy, John F. (Administration of); Sirhan Sirhan.

Further Readings
Landsberg, B. K. *Enforcing Civil Rights: Race Discrimination and the Department of Justice.* Lawrence: University Press of Kansas, 1997.
Schlesinger, A. M., Jr. *Robert Kennedy and His Times.* Boston: Houghton Mifflin, 1978.
Thomas, E. *Robert Kennedy: His Life.* New York: Simon & Schuster, 2002.

Kent State Massacre

The Kent State Massacre occurred on May 4, 1970, when members of the Ohio National Guard opened fire on unarmed students who had gathered at Kent State University (KSU) in Kent, Ohio, to protest the recent American invasion of Cambodia. During the shootings, four students were killed and nine were wounded. The shootings led to a significant national response, which resulted in the only nationwide student strike in U.S. history. During that time, approximately four million students protested and 900 university campuses were closed throughout the country.

President Richard Nixon, elected in 1968, had promised to end the Vietnam War. However, specific actions, such as the reinstatement of the draft lottery on December 1, 1969, and the invasion of Cambodia on April 30, 1970, seemed to contradict this promise and thus exacerbated an already growing public anger. Additionally, the reinstatement of the draft created a fear among many academics and students that they would be forced to partake in a war that they did not condone. As a result, there was increasing public opposition to the Vietnam War.

In the three days prior to the Kent State Massacre, various protests occurred, some that resulted in vandalism and violence. On May 1, 1970, the Mayor of Kent, Leroy Satrom, declared a state of emergency. On May 2, 1970, Mayor Satrom made a request to Ohio Governor James Rhodes, asking that the Ohio National Guard be brought in for fear that local authorities could not contain the demonstrators. That night, the KSU Reserve Officer Training Corps (ROTC) building was burned, as more than 1,000 protesters surrounded the building and celebrated its burning. The following day, May 3, Governor Rhodes made a passionate speech, accusing the current demonstrators of being among the strongest, most militant, revolutionary group that had ever existed in America.

On May 4, a protest of approximately 2,000 students started in the KSU Commons. At this point, three unsuccessful attempts were made by the National Guard and campus patrolmen to disperse the crowd. When it became evident that the group was not going to leave, 77 National Guard troops with rifles fixed with bayonets were brought in and advanced on the protesters. The protesters decided to retreat to different areas of the campus, which were still in sight of the National Guard. Even though a number of students had left the area, many stayed and angrily

The Kent State Massacre, which led to an unprecedented nationwide strike by 4 million students, brought about an increased focus on the use of nonlethal weapons that continues today in the U.S. National Guard, police forces, and military. These U.S. Marines were undergoing training in nonlethal riot control techniques, including the use of pepper spray, in 2006.

confronted the guardsmen by throwing rocks and tear gas canisters. At 12:24 P.M., a sergeant fired on the students with his pistol, which prompted the guardsmen nearest the students to fire their rifles at the students. In total, 29 of 77 guardsmen were said to have fired 67 rounds of ammunition in a 13-second period. Four people were killed in the shooting and nine others were wounded. Two of the students killed were shot while simply walking to class.

In 2010, an audio recording of the incident that had been found in 2007 was analyzed by forensic audio experts, who concluded that the National Guard had been given an order to fire. The validity of this finding has been heavily debated, with some members of the National Guard explaining that the language found on the tapes is not language used in the National Guard.

Aftermath

There was an instant national response following the shooting, with millions of students protesting across the nation. This was followed by the closing of hundreds of college campuses. Included in this national response were lengthy discussions as to the constitutionality of banning the protests and as to whether the shooting of American citizens had been justified. Various media sources began referring to the shootings as a massacre, which served to further public discussion.

Following the shootings and the surge of university protests, President Nixon established the President's Commission on Campus Unrest, also known as the Scranton Commission. Their mission was to scrutinize the dissent and civil unrest occurring on college campuses throughout the country. In September 1970, the Scranton Commission published a report concluding that the Ohio National Guard shooting could not be justified and declaring that the incident must be the last time loaded rifles are used by guardsmen to confront student demonstrators. The Kent State Massacre, coupled with the Scranton Commission's report, forced the National Guard to revise its techniques of crowd control. Afterward, the U.S. Army reformed its crowd control tactics, focusing on avoiding casualties among protestors by developing less lethal weapons (such as pepper spray and rubber bullets). These types of crowd control tactics are still used today by police forces.

Eight of the 29 guardsmen who had claimed to have fired their weapons were indicted by a grand jury. In their defense, the guardsmen claimed to have been using self-defense in shooting at the crowds. Those in the criminal justice system generally accepted this rationale, and in 1974, U.S. district judge Frank Barristi dismissed all charges against the eight guardsmen, citing a lack of evidence by the prosecution.

A federal court civil action for wrongful death and injury was brought by the victims and their families against Governor Rhodes, the president of Kent State, and the national guardsmen. The case ended in unanimous verdicts for all defendants on all claims. However, this ruling was reversed by the Court of Appeals for the Sixth Circuit, which cited a mishandling of an out-of-court threat to a juror as the reason. The civil case was eventually settled through payment of $675,000 to each plaintiff and agreement that all defendants would publicly state their regret as to the incidents that occurred that day.

Andrew Ninnemann
JoAnna Elmquist
Butler Hospital and Brown University
Gregory L. Stuart
University of Tennessee, Knoxville

See Also: Civil Disobedience; News Media, Police in; Nixon, Richard (Administration of); Police Abuse; Political Crimes, Contemporary; Riots; Strikes.

Further Readings
Bills, Scott. *Kent State/May 4: Echoes Through a Decade*. Kent, OH: Kent State University Press, 1988.

The Report of the President's Commission on Campus Unrest; Including Special Reports: The Killings at Jackson State, the Kent State Tragedy. Washington, DC: U.S. Government Printing Office, 1970.

Kentucky

Kentucky is the 37thlargest state in terms of total area, and ranks 26th in terms of total population. In 2010, the state's population was 4,339,367, a 7.4 percent increase from 2000. The majority of the population is white (87.8 percent), with African Americans and Hispanics (7.8 percent and 3.1 percent, respectively) represented in smaller measure. Kentucky was originally part of Virginia before becoming the 15th state in the Union in 1792. Kentucky is well known for horse racing and the bourbon industry, as well as for having a dedicated following of college basketball.

Police
The Kentucky State Police (KSP) was formed in 1948, under the State Police Act, making Kentucky the 38th state to create a police force with statewide jurisdiction. The agency grew from its predecessor, the Kentucky Highway Patrol. The KSP began with only 40 sworn officers; today, there are more than 1,000 sworn officers. Their primary function is to reduce the number of traffic accidents on highways. The distinctive gray uniform first worn in the 1940s is still in use today. The Kentucky State Police formed its first drug enforcement unit in the 1970s. Kentucky's number one cash crop is marijuana; as such, Kentucky has created the Governor's Marijuana Strike Force, under the Cannabis Suppression Branch of the Kentucky State Police, which is dedicated to the eradication and suppression of marijuana-related activities.

Kentucky police were involved in a Supreme Court decision in May 2011 (*Kentucky v. King*). This case involved undercover police purchasing narcotics from a drug dealer, then attempting to make the arrest at the dealer's apartment. However, police went to the wrong apartment, smelled marijuana, and knocked on the door. They then heard sounds inside the apartment. Fearing destruction of evidence, the police kicked down the door and entered the home, where they found and arrested Hollis D. King, who was in possession of marijuana and cocaine.

The issue was related to warrantless searches conducted in exigent circumstances, and whether said searches violated the suspect's Fourth Amendment rights against unreasonable search and seizure. In an 8–1 ruling, the U.S. Supreme Court found that the police did not create the exigency by violating or threatening to violate the suspect's Fourth Amendment rights. In sum, if the police did not threaten or actually engage in an act that would violate the Fourth Amendment, then the exigent circumstances rule would still be applicable.

In the majority opinion written by Justice Samuel Alito, the court indicated that occupants of a home have other protections against warrantless searches. For instance, the occupants can simply tell the police that they cannot enter the home. If said occupants fail to take advantage of those protections, it is not the fault of the police. Justice Ruth Bader Ginsburg, the sole dissenting justice, stated that the emergency situation in question (i.e., a fear that the occupant would destroy the drug evidence if the police waited to get a warrant) was, in fact, not an actual emergency. Rather, there would be no reason for the occupants to destroy the drugs, unless they had reason to believe the police were coming (to which they were alerted by the police knocking).

Kentucky's first prison was the Kentucky State Penitentiary, otherwise known as the "Castle on the Cumberland." The prison is located in Eddyville, Kentucky, and is the state's only maximum-security male facility. It was completed in 1886. Death row inmates are housed in this facility, and Kentucky State Penitentiary is also where state executions are carried out. The facility has a maximum population of 856 inmates, who are classified based on offense. In the Kentucky State Penitentiary, white inmates constitute 65 percent of the prison population, with African American inmates and other inmates accounting for 34 percent and 1 percent, respectively.

Prison reform in Kentucky happened slowly. Early prisons were known for corruption among the guards and administration, while prisoners were treated poorly and lived in squalor. In 1875, 20 percent of inmates had pneumonia. In 1921, Frankfort prison reported that 41 percent of its prisoners had syphilis, which was attributed to poor sanitation at the facility. Governor Luke Blackburn campaigned on prison reform, and was known as the "Father of Prison Reforms in Kentucky." He granted pardons in an attempt to relieve prison overcrowding, overhauled the contract system by which prisons were built, and ultimately oversaw the development of a parole process.

From 1997 to 2009, the state's prison population expanded by 80 percent. From 1980 to 2010, the corrections budget increased from $30 million to $470 million. With an eye toward reform, lawmakers overhauled the state's drug laws, as well as its sentencing, probation, and parole system. This reform is expected to lower prison populations and expand drug treatment. In addition, this legislation is expected to save the state more than $422 million over the next decade. These savings will be applied to the existing correctional system in the state, with half required to be reinvested in the corrections budget, while the other half will be put toward assisting county jail costs. Governor Steve Beshear signed House Bill 463 into law on March 3, 2011.

Kentucky has a storied history with moonshine. In 1791, a federal excise tax led to an increase in home distilling, specifically of corn whiskey. Even after this tax was repealed in 1802, home distilling of whiskey continued because of the taxes that legitimate distillers had to pay. One reason given for the proliferation of moonshine distillers was the close proximity of legitimate distilleries. Such proliferation led to difficulties in enforcing the laws; when state officials would shut down one home operation, many more were ready to take its place. Moonshine is still made in Kentucky, though not nearly to the extent it once was.

Current Crime Statistics

In 2010, 121,289 serious crimes were committed in Kentucky. Violent crimes were recorded as: murder (180), rape (1,545), robbery (3,732), and aggravated assault (5,691). Property crimes were recorded as: burglary (29,170), larceny/theft (74,185), auto theft (6,075), and arson (711). Rape, aggravated assault, and arson all decreased from the previous year, while murder, burglary, larceny/theft, and auto theft increased.

In 2010, there was a murder every 48 hours, 40 minutes. The murder rate increased by 1.69 percent, and 64 percent of all murders in the state involved the use of a firearm. Rape, which decreased 1.4 percent, occurred every 5 hours, 40 minutes. Robbery, which saw the largest increase rate at 5.75 percent, was committed every 2 hours, 20 minutes. Overall, a serious crime (Part I offenses) occurred every 4 minutes, 20 seconds. The clearance rate for all violent crimes was 50.4 percent, compared to 21.5 percent of property crimes. In 2010, property crimes outnumbered violent crimes 9.9 to 1. There were 351,976 arrests in the state in 2010; 29,917 were for DUI, while 61,413 were for drug violations. Police officers were also victims, with 1,757 sworn officers assaulted during the year. Overall, the crime rate for Part I offenses in 2010 in Kentucky increased 1.26 percent from the previous year.

Robert A. Sarver, III
University of South Carolina, Upstate

See Also: Drug Abuse and Addiction, Contemporary; Penitentiaries; Supreme Court, U.S.

Further Readings
Kentucky State Police. "2010: Crime in Kentucky Report." http://kentuckystatepolice.org/pdf/cik_2010.pdf (Accessed September 2011).
Kentucky v. King No. 09-1272 302 S. W. 3d 649. http://www.law.cornell.edu/supct/html/09-1272.ZS.html. (Accessed August 2011).

Kevorkian, Jack

Murad "Jack" Kevorkian (1928–2011) was the second of three children, and the only boy born to Levon and Satenig Kevorkian of Pontiac, Michigan. Although the Kevorkian family was very religious and went to church on a regular basis, Jack was unable to blindly follow the doctrine of faith that he believed Christianity required. He constantly questioned his teachers, and by the age of 12, he had given up on attending church entirely. However, where Kevorkian failed as an obedient Christian, he more than succeeded as an academic. The same critical mind that would not allow him to accept things on faith continued to aid him in school, to the point where he was considered by his peers to be more intelligent than many of his professors. By age 17, he had graduated with honors from Pontiac High School and been admitted to the University of Michigan.

Although Kevorkian originally intended to become a civil engineer, he found the topic too "boring" and soon had his sights set on medical school. He graduated with his medical degree in 1952, and, after a 15-month detour as an army medic in Korea, became a specialist in pathology. It was during his residency at the University of Michigan Hospital in the 1950s that he originally became fascinated by death and dying, taking photographs of patients' eyes as they died. This soon led him to advocate experimentation on death row inmates while they were still alive. Kevorkian argued that in a method called "terminal human experimentation," condemned convicts could volunteer for "painless" medical procedures that would commence while they were still alive and

Jack Kevorkian speaking at the University of California, Los Angeles, in January 2011. He served over eight years of a 25-year prison sentence for an assisted suicide.

result in fatality. This suggestion earned Kevorkian the nickname "Dr. Death."

Because of several such radical ideas, Kevorkian became ostracized first by his peers, and then by the medical community at large. Even though he officially became a specialist in 1960, he was unsuccessful at running his own practice and was soon living out of his car and off the government. In 1986, Kevorkian first discovered research from the Netherlands on doctors who helped people to die using lethal injection. Shortly thereafter, he began writing new articles on the benefits of euthanasia. At the same time, he developed a suicide machine he christened the Thanatron. The machine consisted of three bottles that delivered successive doses of fluids: first a saline solution, then a painkiller, and finally, a fatal dose of the poison potassium chloride. It was not until 1990, however, that Kevorkian became truly infamous. That year, he assisted in the suicide of Janet Adkins, a 45-year-old Alzheimer's patient from Michigan. Kevorkian was immediately charged with murder, but the case was dismissed because of Michigan's indecisive stance on assisted suicide.

By 1991, Kevorkian was banned by court order from using his suicide machine, and his medical license was suspended. Unable to purchase the necessary medical fluids to work his machine, he simply created a gas mask that used carbon monoxide to painlessly assist suicides. Finally, Michigan passed a law outlawing assisted suicide, and Kevorkian was prosecuted for it four times. However, he was able to escape his charges unscathed, and it was not until the 1998 case of Thomas Youk that he was ever convicted. That year, Kevorkian allowed *60 Minutes* to air a video he had made of the lethal injection of Youk, who suffered from Lou Gehrig's disease. The difference this time was, instead of the patient being able to administer his own fatal dosage, Kevorkian had to do so instead. Additionally, in the following interview, he brashly challenged the courts to pursue him legally.

Kevorkian was charged with second-degree murder and this time chose to represent himself. On March 26, 1999, a jury in Oakland County convicted Jack Kevorkian of second-degree murder and the illegal delivery of a controlled substance. That April, he was sentenced to 25 years in prison, with a possibility of parole. Although he appealed several times, he was unsuccessful in those attempts. On June 1, 2007, after serving a little more than eight years of his sentence, Kevorkian was released from prison on good behavior. He also promised not to assist in any more suicides, although he continued to tour the lecture circuit speaking out for assisted suicide until his death on June 3, 2011.

Brandy B. Henderson
University of South Florida

See Also: Executions; Famous Trials; Michigan; Serial and Mass Killers.

Further Readings
"Jack Kevorkian Biography." Biography. http://www.biography.com/articles/Jack-Kevorkian-9364141?part=3 (Accessed December 2010).
Kevorkian, Jack. *Prescription: The Goodness of Planned Dying.* Amherst, NY: Prometheus Books, 1991.
Nicol, N., H. Wylie and J. Kevorkian. *Between the Dying and the Dead: Dr. Jack Kevorkian's Life and the Battle to Legalize Euthanasia.* Grand Terrace, CA: Terrace Books, 2006.

Kidnapping

Kidnapping, the illegal and/or forcible removal of someone against their will, has a long history in the North American colonies and in the United States. It was an integral part of the institution of slavery from its establishment in British colonial North America in 1619 through its dismantling in 1863–65. The kidnapping of white Anglo women by Native Americans was a stock theme in captivity narratives from the Puritan settlements through to the antebellum years. Kidnapping was frequently associated with lynching in the late 19th and 20th centuries, was a lucrative source of income for criminal bandit gangs in the early 1930s, and most recently was associated with post-9/11 rendition and secret detention programs.

Slavery
The human trafficking of Africans from the continent's Slave Coast and of persons of African

descent from the Caribbean to North American port cities was outlawed in 1808, but continued as part of a revitalized domestic slave trade anchored in the southern United States. At the same time, northern states such as Pennsylvania passed gradual emancipation laws in the years after the American Revolution, but their growing free black communities remained vulnerable to kidnapping. Free black adults and children were lucrative targets for criminal gangs determined to profit from their illegal sale into slavery as new cotton areas were developing in southern states such as Mississippi and Texas. Early abolitionist and antislavery societies successfully lobbied for antikidnapping statutes in several states, including New York, but local police were often reluctant to ensure effective enforcement, so African American community leaders and white allies organized vigilante societies and sometimes used force to rescue kidnapping victims. In other cases, they relied on the courts.

During the antebellum years, kidnapping of free and fugitive black Americans was reported regularly in the abolitionist press. One of the more famous cases was that of Solomon Northup, who was seized in Washington, D.C., in 1841 and sold in New Orleans, and eventually rescued in 1853, as recounted in Northup's *Twelve Years A Slave* (1853). However, some kidnap cases were more complex than simply white-on-black abductions. For example, in December 1837, John and Sophia Robinson, a free black couple from Boston, were convicted of kidnapping 5-year-old Elizabeth Bright from outside her home in Cambridge, Massachusetts, where she lived with her white guardian, Henry Bright. Formerly a slaveholder from Alabama, Bright had recently emancipated his slaves and moved to his home state of Massachusetts, along with his wife and the orphaned Elizabeth. Doubt over the sincerity of Bright's promise to raise Elizabeth as a free person seems to have motivated the Robinsons (who were linked to the black Garrisonian section of the abolitionist movement in 1830s Boston).

Carol Wilson identified around 100 kidnappings of free blacks between 1830 and 1861. Although the number of cases declined in the 1840s, the Fugitive Slave Act (1850) offered kidnappers some legal protections as state legislatures were obliged to ensure the return of escaped slaves to their masters, but those who assisted runaway slaves were subject to criminal sanctions. Free black communities in the border states of Maryland and Delaware remained particularly vulnerable.

In the years after the Civil War and Confederate defeat, kidnapping as a prelude to a severe beating or murder was utilized by the Ku Klux Klan against many African Americans and some whites in its attempts to restore the southern political order based on white supremacy and black subordination through terror and intimidation. The Klan retreated in the wake of the Enforcement Act (1871), but terror tactics continued to be a staple of racial, antilabor, and antiradical violence in the south and other parts of the United States. At least 3,500 African Americans were lynched in the southern states between the 1880s and the 1950s, and at least 1,300 persons were lynched mainly in the frontier west in the same period. Many victims were forcibly abducted from homes, workplaces, and jails. Luring and kidnapping were methods of procurement associated with the contract labor systems of lumber and turpentine operators, and with prostitution, for example, with the illegal importation of Chinese women into western states such as California in the late 19th century.

Ransom

The most useful and comprehensive legal and social history of ransom kidnapping in the United States remains Ernest Kahlar Alix's 1978 study. Using the *New York Times* archive as his main source, Alix identified 1,703 cases of kidnapping between 1874 and 1974. He identified 15 types of kidnapping altogether, including "white slavery," or snatching of mainly female victims for commercial prostitution; domestic relations kidnapping, usually of children, by divorced or separated parents or other family members; and abductions for the purposes of murder, sexual assault, robbery, or extortion. In 1874, the abduction of 4-year-old Charley Ross in Germantown, Philadelphia, resulted in the first ransom kidnapping in the United States.

Alix termed 236 of his identified cases as "classic kidnapping for ransom." The typical victim for the 100-year period was an adult white upper- or middle-class male, although child victims were a feature of the majority of cases prior to 1920.

In part, this was because of a series of notorious extortion kidnappings of working-class immigrant children by Italian American criminal gangs in early-20th-century cities such as New York and Chicago. Ransom kidnapping of children in the late 19th and early 20th centuries was framed by fears of urbanization and the dangers of the industrial city, and concerns drew on the context of social purity, educational and moralistic child protection concerns, as well as notions of common community obligations to child welfare.

Several kidnapping studies have focused on specific cases, or as in Paula Fass's study, have adopted a case-study approach focusing on one or two highly publicized kidnapping cases in a particular decade. Fass's examination of various forms of child abduction stretches from the Ross case, through the sensational 1932 Charles Lindbergh, Jr., cases; to the snatching of babies from nurseries by desperate infertile women, and rising 1950s concerns over sexually motivated abductions; to the rise in parental abductions in the later 20th century and the growing missing children's movement. It underlines the extent to which the social context and cultural meanings of kidnapping changed markedly since 1874. Changes in family, marital or divorce, and child custody laws from the 19th century have shaped the rising incidence of parental kidnapping, while 20th-century communication and transportation developments have also dramatically transformed kidnapping, from the ways in which victims are taken to the methods of negotiation between kidnapper, police, and family members. The increasingly aggressive and often salacious journalistic exploitation of violence against children that has come to define the reporting of many child abduction cases is another key theme in Fass's account.

Inevitably, several high-profile kidnapping-murders have received more scholarly attention than others, including the May 1924 Chicago kidnapping-murder of 14-year-old Bobbie Franks by wealthy, elite university-educated teenagers Richard Loeb and Nathan Leopold. Despite a ransom note being sent for Franks' safe return, even though he was already dead, there was no clear economic motive behind Loeb and Leopold's actions. Their families engaged famous criminal lawyer Clarence Darrow to defend their sons, but in a surprise legal maneuver, Darrow had Leopold and Loeb plead

Charles A. Lindbergh (center) after testifying about a $50,000 ransom payment. The year after the Lindbergh kidnapping, 27 other kidnappings involved ransoms from $40,000 to $100,000.

guilty to first-degree murder and kidnapping for ransom. Darrow elected to argue his case for mitigation, for death sentences not to be imposed on his clients, before a judge rather than a jury, which Darrow believed would be irretrievably hostile to his clients. During the three-month hearing, Darrow sought to persuade Judge John R. Caverly that sentences of life imprisonment were appropriate. An array of psychiatric experts testified on behalf of the defendants, that they were not insane but circumstances in their childhood and social development rendered them strange, different, and immature. Two weeks later, Leopold and Loeb each received life sentences plus 99 years. Caverly based his decision on the age of the defendants rather than the weight of the psychiatric evidence.

Lindbergh Case
The most famous kidnapping in the United States took place on March 1, 1932. The 20-month-old son of aviator Charles A. Lindbergh and Anne Morrow Lindbergh, daughter of a wealthy and socially and politically prominent New Jersey family, was taken from his bedroom in the family home located near Hopewell, New Jersey. Within days, a $100,000 ransom was demanded, and money was paid, but the child was not returned. Charles, Jr.'s body was discovered only miles from the house on May 12, 1932.

The case provoked an enormous outpouring of public sympathy, anguish, and curiosity within the context of acute economic anxieties in the wake of the Great Depression, weariness with Prohibition-related racketeering and violence, and amid rising fears over bandits and bank robbers. As Claire Bond Potter observes, newspapers consumed kidnapping stories and they became "a form of mass entertainment that compelled a moral reading." They also incited the public to action, for example, in offering their services as amateur detectives in the Lindbergh investigation or in support for increased state and federal law enforcement powers.

In June 1932, Congress passed the Lindbergh Law, which made kidnapping across state lines a federal felony. Many states passed tougher kidnapping statutes, and in many cases this became a capital crime. On July 29, 1933, the creation of a new Division of Investigation (from the bureaus of investigation, identification, and prohibition) within the Justice Department was announced, and from August 10, J. Edgar Hoover became its chief. It was tasked with waging war on racketeers, kidnappers, and other major criminals. It was to fight against the political and law enforcement corruption of the Prohibition years, restore law and order, and return America to the control of the respectable law-abiding American family.

In September 1934, Bruno Richard Hauptmann was arrested for spending a gold certificate marked as Lindbergh ransom money. Several thousand dollars of the ransom money were found in Hauptmann's garage, and rungs of the ladder used to climb to the child's bedroom window were tied forensically to wood in Hauptmann's attic. In one of the most eagerly awaited trials of the century that was reported in intense detail, he was convicted of first-degree murder and sentenced to death in early 1935. Hauptmann was executed at the New Jersey state prison on April 3, 1936, professing his innocence of the Lindbergh baby kidnapping and murder to the end. Over the decades, questions about Hauptmann's innocence or guilt, possible accomplices among the Lindbergh's domestic staff, and other collaborators continued to preoccupy several commentators and historians.

Other Kidnappings
The early 1930s were the high point of ransom kidnappings in the United States. In the early Depression years, particularly 1932–34, kidnapping was a lucrative source of income for bandit and criminal gangs that usually targeted middle-class and wealthy adult citizens. For example, in 1933, there were 27 major kidnappings, and ransoms of $40,000 to $100,000 were demanded and usually paid. These included the June 15 abduction of wealthy brewer William Hamm, Jr., in St. Paul, Minnesota, by the Karpis-Barker gang, and the July 22 abduction of millionaire oilman Charles F. Urschel of Oklahoma City by George "Machine Gun" Kelly and Harvey Bailey. An omnibus crime bill passed Congress in May and June 1934, which dramatically expanded the number of federal offenses. It increased federal crime control powers over interstate kidnapping, and included a 1934 capital amendment to the Lindbergh Law. Kidnappers who survived the Federal Bureau of Investigation (FBI) war and avoided the death penalty were often sent to the new federal prison at Alcatraz to serve out their prison sentences.

There were brief upsurges in ransom kidnappings in the 1950s and in the late 1960s and early 1970s. One of the more famous events was the February 1974 kidnapping of heiress Patricia Campbell Hearst from her home in Berkeley, California, by members of the Symbionese Liberation Army (SLA), a secretive anticapitalist and anti-police group advocating armed retaliation against financial and political elites. Hearst's subsequent transformation into an SLA soldier and participation as

"Tania" in a bank robbery with her captors led to debates over Stockholm Syndrome, the psychological effects of abduction, and the nature of female criminality, as well as FBI tactics. In the late 20th and early 21st centuries, parental or domestic relations kidnapping, kidnapping for sexual purposes often by offenders described as sexual predators, and international terrorism-related kidnappings have tended to attract greater scholarly and journalistic attention.

Vivien Miller
University of Nottingham

See Also: 1600 to 1776 Primary Documents; 1851 to 1900 Primary Documents; 1941 to 1960 Primary Documents; 1961 to 1980 Primary Documents; Famous Trials; Federal Bureau of Investigation; Fugitive Slave Act of 1850; Hauptmann, Bruno; Leopold and Loeb; Lindbergh Law; Slavery.

Further Readings
Alix, Ernest Kahlar. *Ransom Kidnapping in America, 1874–1974: The Creation of a Capital Crime.* Carbondale: Southern Illinois University Press, 1978.
Fass, Paula S. *Kidnapped: Child Abduction in America.* New York: Oxford University Press, 1997.
Gardner, Lloyd C. *The Case That Never Dies: The Lindbergh Kidnapping.* New Brunswick, NJ: Rutgers University Press, 2004.
Potter, Claire Bond. *War On Crime: Bandits, G-Men, and the Politics of Mass Culture.* New Brunswick, NJ: Rutgers University Press, 1998.
Reardon, Anne Marie. "The Peculiar Kidnapping Case of Elizabeth Bright," *Massachusetts Historical Review,* v.8 (2006).
Shaw, Robert L. *Child Abduction: Prevention, Investigation, and Recovery.* Westport, CT: Praeger, 2008.
Strunk, Mary E. *Wanted Women: An American Obsession in the Reign of J. Edgar Hoover.* Lawrence: University Press of Kansas, 2010.
Wilson, Carol. *Freedom At Risk: The Kidnapping of Free Blacks in America, 1780–1865.* Lexington: University Press of Kentucky, 1994.
Zierold, Norman. *Little Charley Ross: America's First Kidnapping for Ransom.* Boston: Little, Brown, 1967.

King, Martin Luther, Jr.

Reverend Dr. Martin Luther King, Jr., leader of the largest civil rights movement in the United States, was born in Atlanta, Georgia, to the Reverend Martin Luther King, Sr., and Alberta Williams King on January 15, 1929. His grandfather, the Reverend Adam Daniel Williams, was the first of three men in the King family to serve as pastor of Ebenezer Baptist Church in Atlanta. His grandfather served from 1914–31, followed by his father from 1931–60. Reverend Dr. Martin Luther King, Jr., joined his father as co-pastor of the church from 1960 until his death in 1968. The product of a segregated public school system in Georgia, Rev. Dr. Martin Luther King, Jr., started college early, having skipped the ninth and twelfth grades because of his excellent schoolwork. He entered Morehouse College at the age of 15 and obtained a B.A. degree in sociology in 1948. That same year, he was ordained into the Christian ministry by Ebenezer Baptist Church at the age of 19, and thereafter became an assistant pastor at Ebenezer Baptist Church in Atlanta.

Dr. King went on to earn a Bachelor of Divinity degree from Crozer Theological Seminary in Chester, Pennsylvania, where numerous honors were bestowed upon him, including an outstanding student award and a graduate fellowship that paid for the graduate university education of his choice. He also delivered the valedictory address at commencement and, although the vast majority of the members of his class were white, he was elected president of the senior class. In 1951, Dr. King entered Boston University and completed his dissertation titled "A Comparison of the Conceptions of God in the Thinking of Paul Tillich and Henry Nelson Weiman" and was awarded the doctoral degree in 1955.

During his early career, Dr. King grappled with the problems of segregation during the Jim Crow era, that is, the time period after the Civil War when blacks were living free from slavery but suffering harsh treatment under Jim Crow laws that made it difficult for blacks to move around as citizens in their own country. As a member of the executive committee of the National Association for the Advancement of Colored People (NAACP) and as the newly ordained pastor of Dexter Avenue Baptist Church in Montgomery, Alabama, Dr.

King began to mobilize blacks into a movement for change. In 1955, Dr. King assumed leadership of the Montgomery Improvement Association, the organization responsible for the Montgomery Bus Boycotts.

Civil Rights and the Courts

Burdened by the realization that race continued to be a barrier to the social, cultural, political, and economic development of the south, Dr. King forwarded a new social vision for America that placed morality and religion at the center of the struggle for inclusion. He believed that the court system was the perfect place to effect social change, since courts are charged with the responsibility of interpreting the laws of the nation. Therefore, Dr. King believed that the issue of racial equality could be litigated and properly examined within the boundaries of the nation's laws. Dr. King believed that the statement according inalienable rights to humans in the U.S. Constitution already included blacks as humans, but that the particular problem that was preventing blacks from enjoying those rights was the failure of white society to define blacks as having "personhood." The tactic of nonviolence in demonstrations and protests throughout the south, then, was used to force whites to confront the humanity or "personhood" of black citizens.

The *Dred Scott* decision of 1857, whereby the U.S. Supreme Court officially proclaimed that, though free, blacks were still subject to the dictates of their owners, and the *Plessy v. Ferguson* decision of 1896, whereby the U.S. Supreme Court declared that public accommodations could be "separate but equal," became the focus of Dr. King's equality doctrine and the test cases for nonviolence. Drawing on the teachings of Mohandas Ghandi, specifically, the concept of *Satyagraha*, or "firmness in the truth," Dr. King encouraged protesters during the fight for public accommodations to use nonviolent tactics like negotiation against their opponents. In so doing, Dr. King maintained the moral advantage over civil rights deniers who sought to bully, beat, and terrorize protesters into submitting to unjust laws. Nonviolence or passive resistance to violent action undertaken by those in power to subdue the subjugated served to expose the violent perpetrators' immorality in the face of human interaction. Instead of using violence to force change, Dr. King chose to utilize the court system to obtain access to an integrated public life that was protected by the Constitution.

Martin Luther King, Jr., stands at a set of microphones on December 3, 1963, a day during which he met with President Lyndon B. Johnson at the White House to discuss civil rights.

Nonviolent Tactics

The nonviolent tactics used in the civil rights movement led by Dr. King throughout the 1950s and 1960s relied heavily upon the legal concept of stare decisis, which requires courts to act with consistency in interpreting the laws of the land. The principle of stare decisis was used to usher in a new era of equality beginning with the *Brown v. Board of Education* decision in 1954 that eliminated the separate but equal criteria engendered by the previous *Plessy* decision.

During the most tumultuous years of the civil rights movement and while serving as the president of the Southern Christian Leadership Conference, Dr. King was arrested more than 20 times.

In a letter written during one of these detainments in response to fellow clergy who questioned the tactics that he used to bring about change in the south, Dr. King created a kind of manifesto for the civil rights movement identifying the goals and means by which to obtain equality. In the letter, famously titled *Letter From a Birmingham Jail*, Dr. King explained his belief in the law and the reasons why he was compelled to act upon some of the injustices that he witnessed taking place in the south.

Also during these years, Dr. King managed to publish several books that explained his philosophy about nonviolence and his vision for a more unified America. *Stride Toward Freedom* (1958), *The Measure of a Man* (1959), *Why We Can't Wait* (1963), *Strength to Love* (1963), *Where Do We Go From Here: Chaos or Community?* (1967), and *The Trumpet of Conscience* (1968), are some of his best-known works. Dr. King received numerous awards for his civil rights work, including a Nobel Peace Prize in 1964, the Spingarn Medal from the NAACP in 1957, Man of the Year by *Time Magazine* in 1963, the John Dewey Award from the United Federation of Teachers in 1964, and several honorary degrees from prestigious institutions such as Morehouse College, Howard University, Wesleyan College, and Yale University.

On April 4, 1968, Reverend Dr. Martin Luther King, Jr., was assassinated on the balcony of the Lorraine Motel in Memphis, Tennessee. He had traveled to Memphis to help organize a protest of the sanitation workers there who were protesting low wages and poor working conditions. Later, his body was entombed at the Freedom Plaza of the Martin Luther King Jr. Historic Site, officially deemed a national historic landmark in Atlanta, Georgia, in 1977.

Allison M. Cotton
Metropolitan State College of Denver

See Also: African Americans; Birmingham, Alabama; *Brown v. Board of Education*; Civil Disobedience; Civil Rights Laws; Justice, Department of; Kennedy, John F. (Administration of); Kunstler, William; Memphis, Tennessee; National Association for the Advancement of Colored People; *Plessy v. Ferguson*; Ray, James Earl; Riots; Segregation Laws.

Further Readings
Baldwin, Lewis V., et al. *The Legacy of Martin Luther King Jr.: The Boundaries of Law, Politics, and Religion*. Notre Dame, IN: University of Notre Dame Press, 2002.
Branch, Taylor. *Pillar of Fire: America in the King Years 1963–1965*. New York: Simon & Schuster Paperbacks, 1998.
Zepp, Ira G. *The Social Vision of Martin Luther King Jr*. Brooklyn, NY: Carlson Publishing, 1971.

King, Rodney

Rodney King (1965–2012) was an African American man residing in southern California who was the victim of an infamous videotaped assault by four officers (Sergeant Stacey Koon and Officers Theodore Briseno, Laurence Powell, and Timothy Wind) from the Los Angeles Police Department (LAPD) in March 1991. The beating was filmed by a resident (George Holiday) who observed King being beaten. The video of the beating was broadcast nationwide, fueling public outrage and exacerbating conflicts between members of minority communities and the police. In April 1992, the officers who beat King were acquitted of state charges, which served as the precipitating event for civil unrest throughout the United States, particularly within southern California.

The events on the tape were set in motion when a California Highway Patrol unit attempted to stop King for speeding. King did not stop and continued driving at a high rate of speed, eventually exiting the freeway, where the LAPD joined the pursuit. King eventually ended the pursuit by pulling to the side of the road and stopping. Police ordered King and his passengers out of the vehicle, at which time officers reported that King became uncooperative.

Officer Powell stated in his official report that he was almost knocked off his feet while attempting to force King to comply with commands to lie on the ground. Sergeant Koon (the LAPD supervisor on the scene) stated that King appeared to be under the influence of phencyclidine (PCP, a drug known to make people impervious to pain and difficult to control). Officers Powell, Wind, and

Briseno began striking King with their department-issued side-handle batons after Sergeant Koon attempted to use a Taser multiple times with no effect. Holiday's video shows the barrage of baton strikes from the officers, show Powell striking King in the head, knocking King to the ground. The video shows officers kicking King five or six times and striking him with a baton 56 times prior to being arrested. King was taken to the hospital; he was treated for multiple broken bones and received 20 stitches. Blood samples taken from King revealed the presence of alcohol and trace amounts of marijuana but no PCP.

Public Outcry and Response
The Rodney King incident was brought to the attention of police administrators when the tape produced by Holiday was aired on local television. The savage treatment of Rodney King prompted outrage from local residents, who demanded both answers and changes from the police department. In the wake of the attack, criminal charges were filed in state court against the three officers and one sergeant actively participating in the beating of King—those depicted on the Holiday tape.

The officers were acquitted on all charges, which resulted in riots that in Los Angeles alone killed 53 people and caused $1 billion in property damage. All four officers were eventually retried in federal court on civil charges; only Koon and Powell were convicted (each received a 30-month prison sentence). Officers Briseno and Wind were both fired from the LAPD after the incident despite being acquitted of criminal wrongdoing. In addition to the federal charges against two officers and the dismissal of the other officers involved, the city of Los Angeles settled a civil suit with King for $3.8 million.

In response to the public outcry surrounding the King incident, the city of Los Angeles appointed the Christopher Commission to investigate allegations of systemic institutionalized racial bias and mistreatment of African American citizens by police department personnel. The commission's report sustained many of these allegations of racial bias and brutal treatment by a select group of officers; several recommendations were made to correct the deficiencies noted. One of the many recommendations was to change the system for receiving citizen complaints, which was unnecessarily cumbersome and skewed in favor of the department. This is exemplified by the fact the both King's brother and Holiday attempted, with no avail, to report the King incident to the department in the days following the beating. The commission also recommended several other fundamental changes to correct the deficiencies noted within the organization; most of these changes have now been implemented after delays resulting from political turmoil.

The events captured on video in the early morning hours of March 3, 1991, were horrific. However, despite the deplorable treatment of Rodney King, the event served as the impetus for massive and sweeping positive changes within the LAPD, including the use of video cameras to record officer behavior, and updated policies and procedures for dealing with citizens on the street and complaints made by the citizens. Although many of these changes have taken time to implement, in the end they have benefited all citizens of and visitors to Los Angeles. Additionally, the changes have served as the impetus for drastically improving police community relations throughout the city and improving the reputation of the organization among policing professionals nationwide.

Jon Maskaly
University of South Florida

See Also: African Americans; Compton, California; Famous Trials; History of Crime and Punishment in America: 1970–Present; Los Angeles, California; Police, Contemporary; Police Abuse; Riots.

Further Readings
Loftus, Elizabeth and Laure Rosenwald. "The Rodney King Videotape: Why the Case Was Not Black And White." *University of Southern California Law Review*, v.66 (1996).
Schoch, Deborah and Rong-Gong Lin II. "15 Years After L.A. Riots, Tension Still High." *Los Angeles Times*. http://articles.latimes.com/2007/apr/29/local/me-riots29 (Accessed September 2011).
Warren, Christopher, et al. *Report of the Independent Commission on the Los Angeles Police Department*. Los Angeles, CA: Independent Commission on the Los Angeles Police Department, 1991.

Klebold, Dylan, and Eric Harris

Dylan Klebold and Eric Harris were the two high school teenagers who perpetrated the largest mass murder by students at an American school when they shot and killed 12 of their fellow students and one teacher and injured 24 others on April 20, 1999. The attack at Columbine High School in Littleton, Colorado, shocked the nation, and the event was covered live by major national news broadcasts. Both Harris and Klebold shot and killed themselves in the school following the attack. The attack at Columbine followed several other highly publicized shootings at schools in smaller rural or suburban towns in the United States during the mid- to late 1990s. But Columbine was particularly notable, due to the number of victims killed or injured, and the diligent and long-term planning of the two high school attackers. Even more stunning were the later revelations found by the police investigation of Harris and Klebold's actual plans, which were to kill hundreds of students in a devastating attack involving explosives in the school cafeteria.

Klebold and Harris were high school seniors, ages 17 and 18, respectively. Both were from white, middle-class families from the suburbs of Littleton, Colorado. Both youths had relatively uneventful childhoods until their high school years. They became friends and later became involved in one known criminal incident. They were arrested for burglarizing a van and placed into a juvenile diversion program, which both successfully completed. After the shootings, it was revealed that police had other information prior to the attack about the pair, including complaints from parents of one student about threats of violence made by Harris toward their son. This opened up the police to criticism for not being proactive in dealing with Harris, as a diligent investigation might have turned up the weapons and explosives he was stockpiling in his bedroom.

In the late morning of April 20, 1999, Klebold and Harris entered Columbine High with duffel bags filled with propane tanks rigged to explode. They set these duffel bags filled with these explosives strategically in the school's cafeteria, to fulfill their initial plan that the bombs would go off, collapsing the ceiling and creating mayhem, all occurring while the cafeteria was full of students and staff. Klebold and Harris's initial plan is that they would position themselves strategically outside to shoot students and staff fleeing from the events in the cafeteria. They also rigged their automobiles to explode sometime after the event was over, hoping to kill rescue workers, reporters, police, and others who were gathered outside in the aftermath of the attack. Neither of their car bombs went off.

When the explosives they set in the cafeteria did not detonate, Klebold and Harris held high-powered rifles, homemade explosives such as pipe bombs, and other weapons and began making their way back toward the school. En route into the school they shot at several students, killing or injuring several in the process. Within the school, a teacher named Dave Sanders began to evacuate students, leading some to safety before being shot by the attackers. An armed police officer assigned to the school traded gunfire with the assailants, but did not pursue the gunmen. He did radio dispatchers for additional police assistance, which arrived within several minutes.

Approximately 15 minutes into the attack, Klebold and Harris went to the school library, where some students and staff had taken cover under desks. This is where most of the murders occurred. Gunshot evidence and reports from survivors indicate that Klebold and Harris systematically shot at students hiding under desks in the library. About 45 minutes after beginning the attack, the two gunmen committed suicide in the library.

Aftermath

There was considerable speculation after the Columbine attacks about why Klebold and Harris did it. Many of the early reports about possible factors leading to the killings were erroneous. For example, although early reports indicated that the duo were victimized by bullying, leading to considerable attention to bullying efforts on the part of the U.S. government, later evidence indicates that Klebold and Harris bullied younger students and made fun of others often and were rarely victimized.

Later works also highlight the "perfect storm" of personalities that brought the duo together. Harris has been described by some as a classic sociopath and the architect of the attack. Klebold the school while the shooters were killing unarmed students in the library. Today, many departments have changed their active shooting policy, forgoing setting up a perimeter to immediately enter, pursue, and neutralize any active shooters.

Similarly, because police and medical personnel were not aware that both active shooters were dead, it took several hours to retrieve the wounded. In the interim, despite efforts by students to summon medical care, wounded teacher Dave Sanders bled to death before help arrived, leading to further criticism of the way emergency responders handled the event. Police were also criticized for the way they handled the investigation and report. Victims' families filed lawsuits, charging that information was continuously withheld or misrepresented.

Anthony Petrosino
WestEd

See Also: Child Murderers, History of; School Shootings; Serial and Mass Killers; Terrorism.

Further Readings
Columbine Review Commission. "Report of Governor Bill Owens' Columbine Review Commission." Denver: State of Colorado, 2001.
Cullen, Dave. *Columbine*. New York: Twelve, 2009.

A visitor reads about a 16-year-old victim of the Columbine High School shooting at a permanent memorial near the school soon after it was dedicated in September 2007.

was, according to some authors, depressed and suicidal, filled with anger and rage, who became a willing accomplice. One of the key questions after the killings was the culpability of the parents of Klebold and Harris, and how they could not know that their children were gathering weapons and explosives and planning the attack for about one year. Families of those slain or injured in the attack filed lawsuits against the Klebold and Harris parents, which were eventually settled out of court for $1.6 million in 2001.

The attack led to key changes in how police handle "active shooter" calls such as that at Columbine. Standard practice before Columbine was for police to respond to the scene, set up a perimeter, tend to the injured, and prepare for the inevitable hostage negotiations. This strategy led to great criticism by the victims' families, who could not understand how armed police could be waiting outside

Knapp Commission

The problem of police corruption came into the public spotlight when Frank Serpico, a New York City police officer, was shot in 1971 after attempting to report police corruption. The Knapp Commission was the most famous attempt to address police corruption in America. It was formed in 1970 in New York City to investigate the New York Police Department.

Frank Serpico became a New York City police officer in 1959. He worked as a patrol officer and then an identification officer before being assigned to work plainclothes. While working as a plainclothes police officer, Serpico became aware of widespread corruption in the New York Police Department, which included graft, bribery, extortion, and malfeasance. Serpico attempted to report the corruption through the police chain of command, but he had no success and was harassed because of his efforts. Eventually, Serpico and a fellow police officer, Sergeant David Durk, went to the *New York Times*, which began to report on the problem. Because of the public disclosure, the mayor of New York, John Lindsay, formed the Knapp Commission in 1970 to investigate the situation independently from the police department. He appointed John Knapp to head the commission.

Serpico's Harassment

It eventually became known in the New York Police Department that Serpico was the person who caused the investigation, and he began to experience serious harassment and abuse. On February 3, 1971, Serpico and three other police officers went on a drug investigation. During the course of the investigation, Serpico entered the apartment of the drug dealer, but his fellow officers did not come to his aid. Serpico was shot. His fellow officers failed to place an "officer shot" call for help, and a neighbor called for emergency services. In October 1971, the Knapp Commission began to hold public hearings on the problem of corruption in the New York Police Department. Serpico testified at the hearings and earned lasting fame for his bravery and for his comment that police corruption will never stop until the good police officers no longer fear the evil police officers and will be able to report corruption without fear of reprisal or retaliation.

Knapp Commission's Findings

The Knapp Commission made numerous findings, including the fact that vice officers systematically took bribes to not enforce gambling or narcotic drug laws and overlook gambling activities and narcotic drug trafficking. Further, the commission found that the police regularly overlooked prostitution and failed to enforce laws prohibiting it. Drug dealers and pimps, if they paid for protection, were simply left alone. The commission also found that the police were paid to "protect" grocery stores, construction sites, and bars; and that the police regularly extorted from motorists, tow truck operators, and unlicensed bars. These enforced payments were called "shakedowns."

The commission also found that police supervisors were given shares of the illegally obtained payments. The payments to police officers were usually referred to as the "pad." Further, the commission found that internal corruption was rampant, as police officers could pay for lucrative assignments within the department or for being given medical retirements. Police supervisors were also given a share of any profits from arrests that yielded a large amount of seized money. Further, and most disheartening, the Knapp Commission found that perjury on the New York Police Department was widespread and that fixing cases in court was a frequent practice if the suspect had the proper connections or could pay the expected bribe. The Knapp Commission found that there was no direct evidence linking higher levels of the police command structure in the corruption, but the commission indicated there was circumstantial evidence that commanding officers were involved in the corruption and knew about the problem.

The most famous finding by the Knapp Commission was its distinction between the types of corrupt police officer. Corrupt police officers were labeled either "meat eaters" or "grass eaters." Meat eaters were those who actively pursued opportunities for extortion and graft. They would take active steps to obtain money from people. Grass eaters, on the other hand, were those who simply accepted whatever money came their way. Grass eaters would not directly confront people and demand money, but they would accept the money that was offered from people or other officers to turn the other way or to forget something happened. Although meat eaters were considered more corrupt, the Knapp Commission did not absolve grass eaters from responsibility for their actions.

Methods to Reduce Corruption

The Knapp Commission issued its preliminary report on August 15, 1972, and its final report on December 27, 1972. Its recommendations included reducing the opportunities for police corruption (i.e., changing vice laws), reducing the temptation and increasing the risks of police corruption (i.e., prosecuting those who gave bribes and investigating police corruption), increasing the responsibility of supervisors for enforcement against corruption (i.e., reporting certain activities and enforcing disciplinary actions against corrupt police officers), changing the procedures that encourage corruption (i.e., changing arrest quotas, use of informants, and gratuities), changing management procedures (i.e., using reports of activity and name tags), reducing susceptibility to corruption (i.e., running background investigations and giving lateral promotions), and enlisting public support in the fight against corruption.

The Knapp Commission Report shocked the public. Many law-abiding citizens had no idea that corruption in the New York Police Department was so widespread. The public was incensed, and there were numerous calls for reform. The New York Police Department instituted a number of reforms. Many New York police officers were indicted, arrested, and convicted for their corrupt activities. It is questionable whether the reforms were sufficient or adequately executed. Just 20 years later, another commission was formed in New York City to investigate police corruption: the Mollen Commission. Ironically, in the Knapp Commission Report, the commissioners asked whether history would repeat itself and if the situation would arise again in 20 years.

Wm. C. Plouffe, Jr.
Independent Scholar

See Also: Code of Silence; Mollen Commission; New York City; Police, History of.

Further Readings
Chin, Gabriel, ed. *New York City Police Corruption Investigation Commissions 1894–1994*. Buffalo, NY: William S. Hein, 1997.
Kleinig, John. *The Ethics of Policing*. Cambridge: Cambridge University Press, 1996.
Mass, P. *Serpico*. New York: Harper Paperbacks, 2005.

Korematsu v. United States

The 1930s and the 1940s saw one of the most destructive wars in human history. World War II involved most of the nations of the world and the loss of millions of lives. During World War II, Germany and Japan engaged in numerous acts that constituted war crimes, for which a number of German and Japanese leaders were tried and imprisoned or executed. Some of these war crimes by Germany and Japan involved the imprisonment of both civilians and prisoners of war in concentration camps. In these concentration camps, inmates were subjected to slave labor, starvation, torture, medical experiments, and genocide.

The war with Japan started after the Japanese sneak attack on Pearl Harbor on December 7, 1941. Initially, there was little anti-Japanese animus after the attack. Some newspapers published statements that thousands of Japanese were, in fact, good hardworking Americans. However, approximately six weeks after the attack, the public attitude changed. A number of civilian and military authorities became fearful of the large numbers of Japanese residing on the west coast of the United States. As a result, on February 19, 1942, President Franklin D. Roosevelt signed Executive Order 9066, which authorized the secretary of war to designate military zones within which a curfew could be declared and from which any or all people may be excluded. By the end of 1942, without any criminal charges being brought or military hearings being held, more than 110,000 Japanese Americans had been forcibly placed into internment camps away from the West Coast.

A few of the Japanese Americans who were subject to the exclusion order tried to fight it. One was Gordon Hirayabashi. Hirayabashi became a conscientious objector and refused to comply with the curfew and when the time came for his transportation to an internment camp, he refused to go and turned himself in to the Federal Bureau of Investigation (FBI). He was convicted of violating the curfew and the exclusion order and sentenced to jail. He then appealed to the U.S. Supreme Court. The Supreme Court, in 1943, affirmed Hirayabashi's conviction for breaking curfew but avoided ruling on the evacuation order, justifying it on the assumptions that Japanese Americans had not become an integral part of the white population and were attached to Japan and its institutions. It was not until many years later that it was discovered that the U.S. government had suppressed an official Office of Naval Intelligence report that found that the vast majority of Japanese Americans were not a threat.

Evacuees of Japanese ancestry line up for lunch at the Santa Anita Assembly center in Arcadia, California, where more than 2,000 meals were served per hour. The Santa Anita Racetrack was requisitioned and the former racetrack grounds and horse stalls were converted to temporary barrack apartments for interned Japanese Americans. Evacuees lived at this center before being transferred to distant inland internment camps. Of the thousands that were forcibly relocated, only a few tried to fight the orders.

Another Japanese American, Fred Korematsu, also opposed his placement in an internment camp. Korematsu did not directly refuse to go but took other steps to avoid placement in the internment camps. He changed his name and underwent plastic surgery. He was eventually caught in 1942. He was convicted and also appealed to the U.S. Supreme Court. At the Supreme Court, Korematsu pressed the issue of the constitutionality of the evacuations, which had been ignored in the Hirayabashi case, and argued that by the time of Korematsu's arrest, any danger of invasion of the west coast by Japan was gone. The court rejected his arguments, relying on its previous decision in the *Hirayabashi* case, finding that Korematsu's exclusion was due to military necessity as a result of war with the Japanese empire and not because of his race.

The *Korematsu* decision has been subsequently and widely criticized as one of the worst decisions in the history of the U.S. Supreme Court. The internment camps have been compared to the concentration camps employed by Nazi Germany during World War II. Even though the medical experiments, torture, and genocide present in the German concentration camps did not exist in the Japanese American internment camps, the conditions were, nonetheless, harsh, with inadequate food, inadequate medical care, and inadequate facilities for housing and hygiene. Moreover, numerous Japanese Americans who had been forcibly placed into these internment camps lost not only their freedom but also much of their property.

It was not until the 1980s that some justice for Fred Korematsu and the other Japanese Americans who had been forcibly placed into the internment camps was done. Korematsu filed a petition with the U.S. District Court asking for relief. The federal court found that the U.S. government had deliberately omitted relevant information and provided misleading information to the Supreme Court in Korematsu's original case. In 1988, Congress enacted a bill that provided $20,000 for each victim of the Japanese American internment camps. Unfortunately, 60,000 of them had already died. In the history of American criminal justice, *Korematsu* stands for the practical principle that the Constitution and the Bill of Rights can and will be ignored by the courts when the government claims exigent circumstances, such as war, even when there is no reasonable threat.

Wm. C. Plouffe, Jr.
Independent Scholar

See Also: Internment; Japanese Americans; Race, Class, and Criminal Law; Racism; Supreme Court, U.S.; Xenophobia.

Further Readings
Irons, Peter. *The Courage of Their Convictions.* New York: Penguin, 1988.
Irons, Peter. *A People's History of the United States Supreme Court.* New York: Penguin, 2000.

Ku Klux Klan

The Ku Klux Klan (KKK, or Klan) is an organization that has at times been highly influential in U.S. politics. The group's name is derived from *kyklos* (Greek: circle), and it was originally founded in the aftermath of the American Civil War; since then, the KKK has had three discrete periods of existence. The influence that the Klan held changed over time. In the aftermath of the Civil War, the Klan operated as a secret society of vigilantes. From 1865 until the passage of the Force Acts, the Klan was involved in a number of violent episodes generally aimed at political opponents of the southern Democratic Party. The most powerful and centralized incarnation was the second, which existed from 1915 until the early 1940s. This Klan was heavily involved in white supremacist rhetoric and eventually evolved to rail against Catholics, Communists, and Jews as well as their traditional targets of violence. The contemporary incarnation of the Klan is only loosely connected and coincided with the civil rights movement beginning in the 1950s.

First Incarnation
Pulaski, Tennessee, was the seat of the first Ku Klux Klan organization. A small group of disgruntled Confederate veterans gathered in 1866 and discussed the creation of a secret group. A number of smaller towns in the south had drastically decreased in both population and economy. Pulaski was one such town. Prior to the outbreak of war, the town had some 3,000 inhabitants. After the war, those who returned found that most of the economic opportunities in either agriculture or business had dried up, and that there was very little work to be done. Frustrated and bored, this group of veterans decided to create the organization as a way to amuse themselves with costumes and night rides on horseback. Old pictures show the first KKK in a variety of uniforms. The white with conical cap and the burning cross is more associated with the second KKK. The night rides were the time for violent attacks, generally against African American residents. Klansmen stated that they were only vigilantes acting in the public interest, although this claim does not hold up to scrutiny. The order's insistence on mythical office names was present from its inception: the Grand Cyclops was the president, the Grand Magi the vice president, on down to Lictors, who were simply doormen at the meeting place.

A desire for entertainment gave way to political coercion. The group increased in size and eventually had members throughout the United States, and a national framework was created in 1867. Nathan Bedford Forrest served as the first Grand Wizard (national president) of the Klan, although he was not affiliated with the group before 1867. Forest officially "dissolved" the group in 1869, but it continued in a loosely organized system.

Although there was a national headquarters, headed by the Grand Wizard, there was little in the way of actual cooperation with local chapters continuing to operate independently. Around this time, the "prescript" was created by George Gordon, a former Confederate brigadier general. This functioned as a belief structure for the organization and reinforced white supremacy. During this period, there were two focuses to Klan violence: Republican politicians, whom the Klan perceived as northerners attempting to remake the south, and African Americans, who, the Klan wanted to terrify into political and social exile. In reaction to repeated coercion and political violence, William Holden, governor of North Carolina, called the state militia to break up a rally in 1870; shortly thereafter, the Force Act (1870) and Ku Klux Klan Act (1871) allowed Klansmen accused of vigilante violence to be tried in federal court. The Klan faded from the spotlight in the early 1870s, replaced by a variety of other vigilante groups.

Second Incarnation

The second Klan began life in 1915. A number of factors, including the release of D. W. Griffith's *The Birth of a Nation* and the sensational trial of Leo Frank, a Jewish American factory owner who allegedly raped a young girl in his employ, led to the foundation of the second Klan. William J. Simmons, who lived in Atlanta at the time, brought together a handful of interested individuals, including a few members of the Reconstruction-era Klan, and proclaimed the Klan's resurrection on top of Stone Mountain on Thanksgiving night, 1915. This Klan was far more organized than its predecessor—the foundation was that of a formal fraternal order. Kleagles (organizers or recruiters) would

Thousands of Ku Klux Klan members, including women (at right) marching within sight of the U.S. Capitol building in Washington, D.C., on August 8, 1925. Klan membership peaked at over 4 million in 1924 but declined rapidly only two years later. Current membership across all chapters is estimated to be between 5,000 and 8,000.

appear in a town, give speeches, and induct new members, who paid membership dues and bought their costumes. The Kleagle kept half of the money and sent the rest on to national headquarters.

While the original Klan resisted Republicans, the second incarnation opposed Jews, Catholics, immigrants, and Communists, and most infamously, African Americans, who they thought represented a danger to their perception of "proper" values and morality. The Klan chiefly spread in urban centers, especially those in places where large numbers of African Americans or immigrants had moved in recent years. The Klan thrived in locales as disparate as Indiana, Michigan, and Texas, although its national headquarters was established in Dallas, where the Women of the Ku Klux Klan existed as a temperance movement for some time. The membership of the Klan at its greatest extent in 1924 has been estimated at more than 4 million individuals.

The coercion tactics used by the second Klan were more public and flashy than those of the first Klan. The infamous burning cross was first used at this time, along with a continuance of night terror activities, lynching, and intimidation at polling places. The second Klan's greatest accomplishment was the election of Edward Jackson, a prominent member of the Indiana branch of the Klan, to the governor's chair. Shortly after this, Grand Dragon (state leader) of Indiana D. C. Stephenson was convicted on a rape-murder charge, and the Indiana Klan quickly lost members and power. After 1926, the influence of the second Klan plummeted. Although active into the 1940s, membership was minuscule in comparison to its 1924 heyday. In 1944, after a series of financial problems, a lien against the Klan for $685,000 was filed by the IRS, and the group dissolved at the national level.

Third Incarnation
From 1944 forward, "Ku Klux Klan" was a name taken by a number of local groups who fought against the civil rights movement. These groups were responsible for a number of deaths, many by bombing or burning, of civil rights activists, including Willie Edwards, Jr., Medgar Evers, and National Association for the Advancement of Colored People (NAACP) leader Vernon Dahmer. These acts of violence continued throughout the 1970s and into the 1980s, but the political focus of the various Klan groups tended to be on the busing of schoolchildren, the integration of schools and workplaces, and perceived injustices. Large-scale attention to the group is restricted to particular individuals such as former Grand Wizard David Duke, who regularly posts propaganda videos and solicits support on the Internet. Current membership across all chapters is estimated at between 5,000 and 8,000.

Robert W. Watkins
Florida State University

See Also: 1851 to 1900 Primary Documents; African Americans; *Brandenburg v. Ohio*; Civil Rights Act of 1866; Civil Rights Laws; Enforcement Acts of 1870–71; Lynchings; National Association for the Advancement of Colored People; Race-Based Crimes; Racism; Xenophobia.

Further Readings
Chalmers, David. *Hooded Americanism: The History of the Ku Klux Klan,* 3rd ed. Durham, NC: Duke University Press, 1987.
McLean, Nancy. *Behind the Mask of Chivalry: The Making of the Second Ku Klux Klan.* New York: Oxford University Press, 1995.
McVeigh, Rory. *The Rise of the Ku Klux Klan: Right-Wing Movements and National Politics.* Minneapolis: University of Minnesota Press, 2009.

Kunstler, William

William Kunstler (1919–95) was a polarizing figure in American legal circles. Kunstler symbolized the archetypal "radical lawyer," representing clients charged with criminal offenses or fighting for the civil rights of those whom many of his colleagues declined to serve. Although he was popular with those who possessed liberal viewpoints, many conservatives vilified Kunstler throughout his career. Kunstler's clients included the famous and infamous, including individuals such as Dennis Banks, Lenny Bruce, Stokely Carmichael, Angela Davis, Martin Luther King, Jr., Russell Means, Adam Clayton Powell, Jr., Jack Ruby, and Assata Shakur. Kunstler also represented the Chicago Seven and was a guiding force in both the American Civil Liberties Union (ACLU) and the National Lawyers Guild. A prolific author, Kunstler helped to shape public perceptions of criminal defense attorneys, to mold the techniques of many practitioners, and to influence the expectations of many criminal defendants.

Kunstler was born on July 7, 1919, in New York City. He graduated from DeWitt Clinton High School and then attended Yale College, graduating Phi Beta Kappa. Serving as a member of the U.S. Army during World War II, he attained the rank of major while deployed in the Pacific. Following his graduation from the Columbia University Law School, Kunstler was admitted to the New York state bar in 1948. Initially practicing business and family law during the 1950s, Kunstler became increasingly interested in criminal and civil rights law, in part because of his involvement with a series of radio programs broadcast on WNEW. In 1957, Kunstler began representing William Worthy, a reporter for the *Baltimore Afro-American*, who was one of 42 American citizens whose passports were seized by the U.S. Department of State after violating a travel ban involving China. Although the State Department offered to settle the case if Worthy would agree to make no further visits to communist nations, Kunstler attracted widespread media attention by refusing.

Freedom Riders

Kunstler, a member of the ACLU, soon became involved in many legal battles involving efforts to desegregate the American south. Kunstler represented members of the Freedom Riders, activists who traveled to the south to challenge segregated restaurants, lunch counters, bus terminals, and other historically separate facilities maintained for African American citizens engaged in interstate travel. Although the U.S. Supreme Court had ruled in *Boynton v. Virginia*, 364 U. S. 454 (1960), that such segregated facilities were a violation of the Interstate Commerce Act and therefore illegal, many Freedom Riders were arrested for challenging what local law enforcement authorities saw as important local laws. Kunstler worked to free those charged with violating segregation laws, building a reputation as a tireless advocate for controversial clients. Kunstler worked to remove many pending cases from local and state courts to U.S. District Courts, where he perceived his clients would have a better chance at a fair trial. Kunstler was the first attorney to use the removal process delineated under Title IX of the Civil Rights Act of 1964, allowing protesters at the 1964 World's Fair in New York City to be tried in federal, rather than state, court.

Defense of Criminals

Entering into a partnership with Arthur Kinoy in 1964, Kunstler began taking on more criminal defense work. His high-profile clients included filing a successful appeal that resulted in a new trial for Jack Ruby, the killer of Lee Harvey Oswald; and he defended Thomas Ruppert, a 17-year-old arsonist who burned down a New York Jewish community center, killing nine children and three adults. While his representation of such notorious clients gained Kunstler a great deal of enmity, it also made him increasingly famous. As a result, Kunstler was engaged to defend the Chicago Seven.

The Chicago Seven were charged with conspiring to incite a riot during the 1968 National Democratic Convention in Chicago. During the trial,

William Kunstler with defendant Gregory Lee Johnson, then part of the Revolutionary Communist Youth Brigade. Kunstler lectured about Texas v. Johnson *in 1989, which fought the right under the First Amendment to burn an American flag.*

Kunstler engaged in aggressive cross-examination of witnesses, causing a key police witness to contradict earlier testimony. Kunstler also battled with U.S. District Judge Julius Hoffman, and he was ultimately cited for contempt—this was overturned by the U.S. Court of Appeal for the Seventh Circuit. Kunstler's tactics ultimately proved effective, as two of the defendants were acquitted of all charges, and the remaining five were convicted of crossing state lines with the intent of inciting a riot. These convictions, and concurrent contempt citations, were reversed after Kunstler convinced the Seventh Circuit Court of Appeals that Judge Hoffman had erred in refusing to allow defense attorneys to screen potential jurors for cultural and racial biases. Although a new trial had been ordered, the Department of Justice decided not to retry the case.

Wounded Knee
Kunstler next represented Russell Means and Dennis Banks, leaders of the American Indian Movement (AIM) who were involved in the Wounded Knee incident in South Dakota. Members of AIM had held the town of Wounded Knee, South Dakota, for 71 days while engaged in a standoff with special agents of the Federal Bureau of Investigation (FBI) and U.S. marshals. Kunstler was successful in having the trial moved to Minnesota, alleging prejudice were the trial held in South Dakota, and many defendants were acquitted. Kunstler later represented AIM members involved in the slaying of two FBI special agents.

During the 1970s, Kunstler also was involved in defending a prisoner charged with killing a guard during the Attica prison riots. Although Kunstler's client, John Hill, was convicted of murder, he was granted executive clemency by New York Governor Hugh Carey in 1976. Beginning in 1983, Kunstler entered into a partnership with Ronald Kuby and continued to represent high-profile clients, such as Omar Abel-Rahman, charged with masterminding the 1993 World Trade Center bombing in New York City; members of the Gambino crime family; and Qubilah Shabazz, Malcolm X's daughter, alleged to have plotted the death of Nation of Islam leader Louis Farrakhan. Kunstler died of heart failure on September 4, 1995.

Stephen T. Schroth
Jason A. Helfer
Evan M. Massey
Knox College

See Also: American Civil Liberties Union; Chicago Seven/Democratic National Convention of 1968; Famous Trials; Indian Civil Rights Act; Lawyers Guild; National Association for the Advancement of Colored People; Oswald, Lee Harvey.

Further Readings
Kunstler, W. M. *Politics on Trial: Five Famous Trials of the 20th Century*. New York: Ocean Press, 2002.
Langum, W. J. *William M. Kunstler: The Most Hated Lawyer in America*. New York: New York University Press, 1999.